Risk Management

& Derivatives

René M. Stulz

SOUTH-WESTERN
CENGAGE Learning

Australia • Brazil • Japan • Korea • Mexico • Singapore • Spain • United Kingdom • United States

SOUTH-WESTERN
CENGAGE Learning

Risk Management & Derivatives
René M. Stulz

Editor-in-Chief: Jack Calhoun

Team Director: Michael P. Roche

Executive Editor: Michael R. Reynolds

Developmental Editor: Andrew McGuire

Marketing Manager: Charlie Stutesman

Production Editor: Margaret M. Bril

Manufacturing Coordinator:
Sandee Milewski

Compositor: Cover to Cover Publishing, Inc.

Internal and Cover Designer: Bethany Casey

Cover Photographer/Illustrator: PhotoDisc,
Inc.

For product information and technology assistance, contact us at
Cengage Learning Customer & Sales Support, 1-800-354-9706

For permission to use material from this text or product,
submit all requests online at **www.cengage.com/permissions**
Further permissions questions can be emailed to
permissionrequest@cengage.com

Library of Congress Control Number: 2002109008

ISBN-13: 978-0-538-86101-4

ISBN-10: 0-538-86101-0

South-Western
5191 Natorp Boulevard
Mason, OH 45040
USA

Cengage Learning is a leading provider of customized learning solutions with office locations around the globe, including Singapore, the United Kingdom, Australia, Mexico, Brazil, and Japan. Locate your local office at **www.cengage.com/global**

Cengage Learning products are represented in Canada by Nelson Education, Ltd.

To learn more about South-Western, visit
www.cengage.com/southwestern

Purchase any of our products at your local college store or at our preferred online store **www.ichapters.com**

Printed in the United States of America
1 2 3 4 5   15 14 13 12 11
FD039

To Pat, Phoebe, Jack, and Truffles

Brief Contents

Contents

Part 3 *Beyond Plain Vanilla Risk Management*   467

Preface

This book shows how to quantify financial risks and manage them. For a firm, the ability to manage risk is a source of competitive advantage. In particular, firms that manage risks well are better able to take advantage of growth opportunities. Derivatives are the instrument of choice to manage financial risks, and it is therefore critical for managers to understand how derivatives can be used to manage risks.

I started writing this book motivated by the difficulties that Procter & Gamble and others have had with derivatives. I finished it after the bankruptcy of Enron. The firms that have had difficulties with derivatives typically did so because their managers understood poorly how to use derivatives and not because they failed to understand the pricing of derivatives. However, existing textbooks do not train students to become users of derivatives. They train students to become traders. Few students in business schools become active traders of derivatives, whereas many become users of derivatives; even more would benefit from knowing when and how to manage risks with derivatives. Though the press likes to focus on the problems associated with derivatives, it never explains how distressed firms that were not using derivatives could have avoided their difficulties by using derivatives. To be a user of derivatives, one has to understand how risk management creates value and how derivatives can be used to manage risks. This book provides this understanding.

New derivatives are introduced all the time. Throughout their life, managers are constantly exposed to new financial products. The training of students has to ensure that they will be able to evaluate correctly the risks and suitability of these new financial products. Poor decisions on their part could result in large losses, while good decisions could significantly improve the performance of the firms for which they work. It makes little sense for these students to spend time understanding hand signals on the futures exchanges, but it is crucial for them to know why they have to worry about different pitfalls when they buy an exotic derivative over the counter than when they take a position in a derivative traded on an organized exchange. This book therefore spends time building skills for using derivatives in risk management rather than in providing minute details about organized derivatives markets and contracts.

End-Users Perspective

In sharp contrast to existing derivatives books that satisfy the needs of future traders, this book is designed to prepare students to become end-users. This book starts with an analysis of how risk management creates value for non-financial and financial corporations and how to measure risk. These chapters have a modern corporate finance foundation. The analysis considers risk measures such as value at risk and cash flow at risk. It shows how risk measures should be used within corporations to evaluate projects. The book then moves on to show how firms can manage risks with derivatives. After presenting forwards and futures and their pricing in one chapter, two chapters show how to use these contracts for hedging known exposures. The next chapter focuses on foreign exchange exposures (presenting techniques that can be used more generally whenever exposures depend on risk factors) followed by a chapter on interest rate risks. These two chapters not only consider the hedging of these risks with forwards and futures, but also investigate the nature of these risks and how to measure them. The book moves on to five chapters on options. The first chapter is mostly about why and how one would want to use options to hedge. The next two chapters are pricing chapters, one on the binomial model and one on the Black-Scholes model. The fourth chapter on options is focused on measuring risk in the presence of options and on more advanced option hedging strategies. The fifth chapter discusses options on bonds and interest rates, starting with an analysis of hedging with caps and floors. The book then leaves plain vanilla derivatives that are highly standardized to turn to more customized derivatives. This part of the book starts with a chapter that investigates the issues that arise when one uses such derivatives. It investigates microstructure issues, counterparty risk, pricing issues, and so on. This chapter is followed by chapters on swaps and exotics. These chapters are designed to be helpful to end-users rather than encyclopedic. They address pricing issues and hedging issues. The book then turns to a chapter on credit risks that looks at pricing and hedging of individual credits as well as portfolios of credits (reviewing CreditMetrics™ and CreditRisk+). Credit derivatives are considered as hedging tools. The last chapter discusses recent risk management developments and empirical evidence on current practice. It has an extensive discussion of the LTCM experience and the changes it has brought to risk management, as well as a review of the empirical evidence on how corporations use derivatives.

In contrast to existing derivatives books, this book looks at derivatives and risk management from the perspectives of managers rather than traders. It therefore uses corporate experience with derivatives and risk management to make important points. Examples are drawn from the experiences of Chase, Goldman Sachs, Enron, Bankers Trust, Ford Motor Company, Merck, Homestake, American Barrick, Metallgesellschaft, Procter & Gamble, Gibson Greetings, Barings, Granite Partners, Natwest, Bank One, Orange County, Daiwa, Berkshire Hathaway, IBM, the World Bank, Bank of America, Hasbro, Microsoft, Dell, LTCM, Salomon Smith Barney, and so on. Although most of the applications deal with corporations, some address problems of individuals (like wealth preservation and tax optimization). The book also has an international perspective.

In keeping with its focus on the needs of managers who are end-users of derivatives, this book makes an extremely limited use of mathematics. Except for some footnotes and boxes marked as technical, the book does not require knowledge of calculus and the materials marked as technical can be omitted without loss of continuity. The book does not use the techniques of continuous-time finance. It does not require extensive finance training. It is accessible to students who have gone through courses that present the principles of investments and corporate finance.

Text Features

Risk Management and Derivatives offers a number of text features designed to capture interest and aid in student learning.

Boxed Material. The book has two types of boxes. Some boxes present mini-cases. Other boxes, called Technical Boxes, present materials that require a stronger command of mathematics than the main text of the book. These Technical Boxes can be omitted without loss of continuity by students.

Chapter Summaries. Each chapter of the text contains a summary that allows students to reflect on what they've learned and also connect the content to material throughout the rest of the text.

Key Concepts. Key concepts are listed at the end of each chapter in order to focus students' studying on the most important material in the chapters.

Review Questions. Review questions test the students' knowledge and comprehension of the material within each chapter.

Questions and Exercises. The questions and exercises allow students to apply what they have learned, both conceptually and quantitatively.

Literature Note. The literature note at the end of each chapter allows students to conduct further research in a particular area of interest that has been discussed within the chapter.

Epilogue. An epilogue has been included after chapter nineteen in order to reinforce the big picture. While many textbooks leave students with bits and pieces of fragmented information, the epilogue of *Risk Management and Derivatives* ties the concepts of the text together into a unified whole in order to enhance understanding and application.

Supplements

A number of excellent supplements have been developed to accompany *Risk Management and Derivatives.*

Instructor's Manual with Solutions. The instructor's manual (ISBN 0-324-00386-2) contains answers to all questions and exercises included in the text. It also presents teaching tips on how to present the material in each chapter.

Spreadsheet Software. Easily downloadable from the web, these Excel templates illustrate the models used in the text including equity, foreign currency, interest rate derivatives, and exotic options.

Support Site. The support site for *Risk Management and Derivatives* can be accessed at http://stulz.swcollege.com. This site contains useful resources including access to Excel templates, "Newswire" current articles, and an Investment Analysis Calculator.

Acknowledgements

In the process of writing this book, I have received help from a large number of students and colleagues. The book was available on the web as I revised it and I received many unsolicited comments from colleagues throughout the world. At this point, so many individuals gave me comments that I cannot thank all of them by name. The book has been used in MBA classes at Ohio State as well as in executive programs in which I have taught. The students in these courses helped me improve the text and correct errors. The book has also been used at several other universities in manuscript form by MBA classes and advanced elective undergraduate classes. The undergraduate students of James Ang at Florida State were especially useful in the last revision with their written comments on individual chapters. Many research assistants worked on this book at various stages of its development. Craig Doidge, Ed Glidewell, Kuan-Hui Lee, Sergei Tischenko, Laura Tuttle, and Boyce Watkins worked on various chapters. Dong Lee and Rodolfo Martell did a great job in getting the book in its final shape, in checking the numbers of the final version, and in proofing the typeset version of the manuscript. My assistant, Robyn Scholl, coordinated all this effort with great skill. James Ang, Soehnke Bartram, Bernadette Minton, Patricia Reagan, Peter Tufano, Walter Wasserfallen, and Rohan Williamson gave me valuable comments throughout the writing process. I also received valuable help from Andy McGuire, Tom Sigel, and Chris Will at South-Western. Pat Peat did a marvelous job in improving the exposition. Marge Bril and Janet Sprowls graciously produced the typeset version of the book. Writing this book turned out to be more of an undertaking than I expected. My family had to cope with me writing this book, and Pat, Phoebe, and Jack deserve the greatest thanks for having had to put up with me bringing this project to completion.

I'd also like to thank the following reviewers, who looked at the chapters in various stages:

Yacine Ait-Sahalia, Princeton University; Stan Atkinson, Central Florida University; Robert Brooks, University of Alabama; David Chapman, University of Texas–Austin; Yea-Mow Chen, San Francisco State University; Roger Collier, Central Oklahoma University; Frank Fehle, University of South Carolina; J. Howard Finch, Florida Gulf Coast University; Wafica Ghoul, Davenport University; Jason Greene, Georgia State University; Kathleen Hagerty, Northwestern University; John Hand, Auburn University; Robert Hanson, Eastern Michigan University; John Harris, Clemson University; Mike Hemler, University of Notre Dame; Eric Higgins, Drexel University; Carl Hudson, Auburn University; George Jabbour, George Washington University; Rajiv Kalra, Moorhead State University; Daniel Kent, Northwestern University; Raman Kumar, Yale University; George Kutner, Marquette University; Malek Lashgari, Hartford University; David Loy, Illinois State University; Steven Mann, Texas Christian University; Cheryl McGaughy, Angelo State University; Tom Sanders, Miami University; Lawrence Schrenk, University of Baltimore; Adam Schwartz, University of Mississipi; Mark Shrader, Gonzaga University; Chris Stivers, University of Georgia; James Tipton, Baylor University; Marilyn Wiley, Florida Atlantic University

René M. Stulz is the Everett D. Reese Chair of Banking and Monetary Economics and the Director of the Dice Center for Research in Financial Economics at the Ohio State University. He previously taught at the University of Rochester and held visiting appointments at the Massachusetts Institute of Technology and the University of Chicago. Professor Stulz was a Marvin Bower Fellow at the Harvard Business School for the 1996–1997 academic year. He received his Ph.D. from the Massachusetts Institute of Technology. He holds an honorary doctorate from the University of Neuchâtel in Switzerland, is a Fellow of the Financial Management Association, and is president-elect of the American Finance Association.

Professor Stulz was editor of the *Journal of Finance* for twelve years and a co-editor of the *Journal of Financial Economics* for five years. He edits the corporate finance and banking abstracts for the Social Sciences Research Network and is also on the editorial board of several academic and practitioner journals. Further, he is a research associate of the National Bureau of Economic Research. Professor Stulz has published more than sixty papers in finance and economics journals, including the *American Economic Review*, the *Journal of Political Economy*, the *Quarterly Journal of Economics*, the *Journal of Financial Economics*, the *Journal of Finance*, and the *Review of Financial Studies*. His research addresses issues in corporate finance, banking, international finance, risk management, and investments. Currently, he is conducting research on the relationship between share-holder wealth and firm-wide risk, the impact of risk management on firm value, divestitures, banking crises, emerging market crises, contagion, and international equity flows.

Professor Stulz teaches in executive development programs in the U.S. and in Europe. He has consulted for major corporations, the New York Stock Exchange, and the World Bank. As a litigation consultant and expert witness, he has been involved in valuation, corporate finance, banking, derivatives, compensation, and international finance cases. He is a trustee of the Global Association of Risk Professionals, a director of Weggelin Fund Management, a director of Community First Financial Group, Inc., and the president of the Gamma Foundation.

Part 1

Why Risk Management?

Throughout history, the weather has determined the prospects of nations, businesses, and individuals. Nations have gone to war to take over land with a better climate. Businesses have faltered because the goods they produced were not in demand as a result of unexpected weather developments. People have starved when their crops failed because of poor weather.

Avoiding losses due to weather has been the dream of visionaries and the stuff of science fiction novels—until it became the work of financial engineers, who devise new financial instruments and strategies to enable firms and individuals to pursue their financial goals. Businesses and individuals can now use financial products to protect themselves against the financial consequences of bad weather. Financial instruments that help us deal with weather risks are just one example of the remarkable role of derivatives in managing risks.

In chemistry, a derivative is a "substance related structurally to another substance and theoretically derivable from it . . . a substance that can be made from another substance." Derivatives in finance work on the same principle. They are financial instruments whose promised payoffs are derived from the value of something else, generally called the underlying. The underlying is often a financial asset, but it does not have to be. In a weather derivative, the underlying can be the temperature at a specific location, such as Kennedy Airport in New York. More precisely, a derivative is a financial instrument with promised payoffs derived from the value of one or several contractually specified underlyings.

A **call option** on IBM gives the right to buy a fixed number of shares of IBM at a contractually specified price, the **exercise price**. A call option on IBM is a derivative with IBM common stock as its underlying. The payoff of the call is the difference between the value of the shares received and the payment made. This payoff has to be positive since the option holder does not have to buy the shares if it is not advantageous for him or her to do so.

The underlyings that determine the promised payoffs of a derivative can be anything that the contracting parties find useful. They might include stock prices, bond prices, interest rates, gold prices, egg prices, exchange rates, number of houses destroyed by hurricanes, and the number of personal bankruptcies within a calendar year in the United States. A derivative can have a payoff that depends on many underlyings. For example, Microsoft uses derivatives that have payoffs derived from the price of several foreign currencies.

Management can create value for shareholders by using derivatives to manage risk. Consider Garman Inc., which exports software to Europe. Its only foreign currency payment in the fiscal year is a payment of €100 million in six months. A euro is expected to be worth $1 in six months. Suppose that when the receivable is paid, one euro is worth only $0.90. If Garman has done nothing to manage its foreign exchange risk, it has an unexpected cash flow shortfall of $10 million. This loss forces it to cut its R&D budget, which damages its competitive position.

Garman Inc. can eliminate the risk of a large cash flow shortfall by buying a **put option** on the euro. A put option gives its holder the right to sell a fixed quantity of the underlying at the contractually agreed upon price, the exercise price. If Garman Inc. buys a put option on €100 million with a maturity of six months and an exercise price of $1 per euro, it can sell its euros for $1 per euro if the euro is less than $1 when it receives its payment. It has to pay a premium for this insurance, but with this insurance it will not have to cut its R&D program if the euro depreciates sharply. If Garman does not use derivatives to limit the risk of a cash flow shortfall, its equity value is reduced because investors impound in the stock price the possibility that the company will have to cut back its R&D following a depreciation of the euro.

Countless firms use derivatives to reduce risks associated with foreign currency transactions. Though researchers have only recently started to investigate the impact of the use of derivatives on firms' equity, one recent study shows that multinational firms that use currency derivatives have a higher value than multinational firms that do not. The research show that, for the same assets, the total value of the debt and of the equity of large multinational firms that use foreign currency derivatives is 3.6 to 5.3 percent higher than for comparable firms that do not use them.

Derivatives are useful not only to manage risks that corporations have already taken, but they also enable firms to change what they do, to think of new profitable strategies. For example, a new type of weather derivative enabled Bombardier of Canada, a manufacturer of snowmobiles, to adopt a marketing strategy that would have been too risky otherwise. In the winter of 1998, Bombardier offered buyers of snowmobiles in the U.S. Midwest a rebate of $1,000 if snowfall did not exceed a pre-set amount. It eliminated the risk of the rebate using a weather derivative based on a snowfall index. The derivative paid an amount based on the total number of millimeters of snow below an agreed upon amount. Bombardier estimates that the program generated an increase in sales of 38 percent, which is more than it paid for the derivative.

Though derivatives can be used to increase shareholder wealth substantially, they can seriously damage a firm when used without appropriate training and care. The fall of Barings in 1995 following losses in excess of $1 billion from derivatives trades showed that a long and distinguished history provides no insurance against a derivatives disaster. Barings was London's oldest merchant bank, had negotiated the purchase of Louisiana by the United States from Napoleon in 1803, and counted the Queen of England among its clients. Firms from Procter & Gamble to Metallgesellschaft have incurred large losses, received bad publicity, and fired executives because of derivatives trades. Orange County filed for bankruptcy because of losses in a county fund partly caused by derivatives. The manager of the fund was quoted after the debacle saying "I wish I had known more about these complex instruments."

If a firm uses derivatives when its managers are not equipped to do so, shareholders suffer. Derivatives are like jets. They make it possible to reach a destination faster, but untrained or poorly trained users can crash. There are books that teach how to build jets and books that teach how to fly jets. This book is about flying, not building. It is about using derivatives, not about the technical issues surrounding the pricing of derivatives. This book teaches how to successfully manage risks with derivatives.

Managing risk with derivatives often involves using derivatives to hedge. A **hedge** is a financial position put on to reduce the impact of a risk one is exposed to; to hedge means putting on a hedge. However, as we will see, sometimes it makes sense for a firm to choose derivatives positions that increase risks the firm is exposed to.

The remainder of this chapter explains first what is behind the growth of derivatives instruments that made this book possible. We then describe some basic ideas concerning derivatives as risk management tools and discuss how to use derivatives correctly. To illustrate some of the risk management issues managers face, we provide examples from Merck and Microsoft. Finally, we outline the book.

1.1. The growth of derivatives markets

Some of the earliest derivatives markets are the market for tulip options in 17th century Holland and the futures market for rice in Japan in the same century. Derivatives have been traded for centuries, but until recently derivatives markets were small and of limited economic importance. In the 1970s, changes in economic conditions and crucial developments in the theory of the pricing of derivatives created the conditions for the spectacular growth in derivatives markets we have experienced since then. According to the publication *The Economist*, use of derivatives increased by a factor of twelve in the 1990s alone.[1]

In developed economies, interest rate volatility increased sharply in the 1970s, making it imperative for firms and investors to find ways to hedge interest rate risks. Until the early 1970s, most currencies had fixed exchange rates. As fixed exchange rate arrangements collapsed, the volatility of exchange rates became an important source of risk for corporations. Figure 1.1 shows these changes in the

---

1 See "School Brief: Future Perfect," *The Economist*, November 27, 1999.

Figure 1.1   DM exchange rate and T-bill yield from January 1960 to December 1998

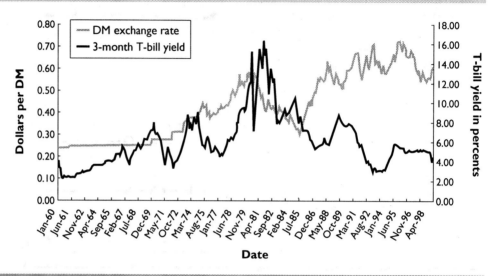

Source: Datastream.

behavior of exchange rates and interest rates for the dollar price of the German mark and for the 3-month T-bill yield. Other changes in the economic environment, such as the deregulation of several industries, the spectacular growth in international trade, and the globalization of financial markets, increased the demand for financial products to manage risk further.

Development of a formula by two financial economists in Boston in the early 1970s revolutionized the field of options and changed markets for derivatives forever. One of these financial economists, Fischer Black, was a consultant. The other, Myron Scholes, was an assistant professor at the Massachusetts Institute of Technology who had just earned a Ph.D. in finance from the University of Chicago. At that time, available options were almost exclusively stock options. The two men realized that by investing in a portfolio of stocks and bonds and actively managing that portfolio, one could obtain the same outcome as if one had invested in stock options. With this insight and the critical help of another assistant professor at the Massachusetts Institute of Technology, Robert Merton, they derived a formula that became instantly famous: the Black-Scholes formula for the pricing of options.

Almost immediately, the approach used by Black and Scholes to price options was found useful not only to price stock options, but also to price, evaluate the risk of, and hedge derivatives that have little resemblance to traditional options. Financial engineers could invent new instruments and find their value with the pricing method of the Black-Scholes formula.

In a risky world, there are many opportunities for trades whereby one party shifts risks to another party through derivatives. These trades must be mutually beneficial or they would not take place. Until the 1970s, the trading of risks mostly took the form of option and forward transactions. In a **forward contract**, one party agrees to buy the underlying from another party at maturity of the contract and pay for it then a price agreed upon when the contract is originated. In our example of Garman, Garman can buy a put to sell euros at a fixed price by paying a premium, but it can also enter a forward contract without paying anything now to sell €100 million at an agreed upon price, say $1 per euro, in six months. With the forward contract, Garman has to deliver €100 million to its counterparty in six months and receives $100 million for doing so regardless of the price of the euro.

Eventually, financial futures contracts were introduced, which are contracts akin to forward contracts but traded on exchanges. Then, the swaps market took off. **Swaps** are exchanges of cash flows derived from underlyings. In the simplest swap, one party promises to pay cash flows corresponding to the interest payments of fixed rate debt on a given amount to a party that promises to pay cash flows corresponding to the payments of floating-rate debt on the same principal amount. The **notional amount** of a derivative is the quantity of the underlying used to determine the payoff of the derivative. The amount on which the interest is computed in an interest-rate swap, the notional amount of the swap, is not exchanged.

The best indicator of the growth and significance of the derivatives industry is that observers debate whether derivatives markets are larger and more influential than the markets for stocks and bonds. The Bank for International Settlements (BIS) measures the size of the markets using the notional amount of derivatives. This measure is interesting because it proxies for the value of the underlyings against which claims are traded in the derivatives markets. According to the BIS as of the end of December 2001, the total notional amount of derivatives was $111 trillion. At that time, world GDP was $31.3 trillion and the capitalization of the stock markets of the industrialized countries was $21.2 trillion.

Another approach could be used to compute the size of the derivatives market. Instead of using notional amounts, we could measure the value of the derivatives outstanding. In the Garman example, the notional amount of the put is €100 million, but the value of the put is the price that it would fetch if sold. If the price of the euro is much higher than $1, the right to sell €100 million for $100 million would have little value. The BIS estimate of the total value of derivatives for the end of December 2001 is $3.8 trillion. The daily turnover of exchange rate and interest rate derivatives trading over the counter in April 2001 was estimated by the BIS at a total notional amount of $575 billion, while the daily turnover of exchange-traded exchange rate and interest rate derivatives measured using the notional amount was $2.2 trillion.

In today's derivatives markets, any type of financial payoff one can think of can be obtained at a price. If a corporation would benefit receiving a large payment in the unlikely event that Citibank and Chase default in the same month, it can go to an investment bank and arrange to enter the appropriate derivatives contract. If another corporation wants to receive a payment that is a function of the square of the yen/dollar exchange rate if the volatility of the S&P 500 exceeds 35 percent during a month, it can do so.

When anything is possible, but one does not have the required knowledge or experience, it is easy to make mistakes. It is of crucial importance to know how to use derivatives the right way to manage risk. This requires an understanding of how risk affects shareholder wealth, an understanding that was not available in 1970. The developments in finance that offer a framework for understanding how to use derivatives to maximize shareholder wealth date from the 1980s and the 1990s.

1.2. Some basic ideas concerning derivatives as risk management tools

Options and forward contracts are often called **plain vanilla derivatives** because they are the simplest derivatives. They differ in two critical ways. First, a call option contract gives a right to buy (or sell if it is a put option contract) the underlying at a fixed price whereas a forward contract gives an obligation to buy the underlying at a fixed price for the buyer and to sell at a fixed price for the seller. Second, an exchange of money takes place when one enters an option contract but no money changes hands when a forward contract is originated. These differences between options and forwards have important implications for how corporations and investors should use derivatives.

1.2.1. Options

The best-known options are on common stock. Whoever sells an option at inception of the contract is called the **option writer**. The call option writer promises to deliver shares for the exercise price, and the put option writer promises to pay the exercise price for shares. An option has value for its holder since the holder can never lose money by exercising the option but can make large gains. Consequently, an option writer is only willing to write an option if he is adequately compensated. The price at which an option can be bought is called the **option premium**.

Option contracts are for 100 shares but they are quoted per share. Consider a call option on Risky Upside Inc. The stock price is $50, and the price of a call option that gives the right to buy the stock at $50 per share, the exercise price, is $10. This call option gives the right to its holder to buy 100 shares of Risky Upside Inc. stock at $50 per share. The option premium per share is $10.

Options differ as to when the right they represent can be exercised. For **European options**, the right can be exercised only at maturity. For **American options**, the right can be exercised at maturity and before. Suppose investor Rubinstein believes that Risky Upside Inc. is likely to improve on its price of $50 per share over the next ten months. Rubinstein could buy 100 shares of Risky Upside Inc. for $5,000, but if the price drops sharply over the next ten months, she would lose much of her investment. If she wants to benefit from increases in the price of Risky Upside Inc. but limit her potential loss, she can buy a call option on Risky Upside Inc. stock for $1,000 (100 times $10 per share). The greatest loss she would then incur over the holding period is the price paid to acquire the option.

Figure 1.2 compares the gain of holding 100 Risky Upside Inc. shares for ten months and of buying a European call option on 100 shares with ten months to maturity. If after ten months the share price falls to $20, the investor who bought 100 shares loses $3,000, but the investor who bought the call option loses only the $1,000 premium paid for the call. If the share price increases to $110, the in-

Gains and losses from buying shares and a call option on Risky Upside Inc.

Figure 1.2

Panel A. Gain from buying shares of Risky Upside Inc. at $50 per share.

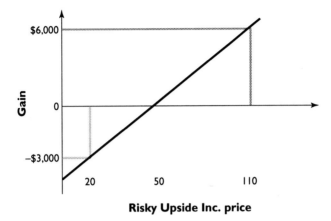

Risky Upside Inc. price

Panel B. Gain from buying a call option on shares of Risky Upside Inc. with exercise price of $50 for a premium of $10 per share.

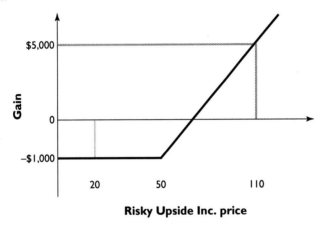

Risky Upside Inc. price

vestor who bought shares gains $6,000, but the investor who bought the option gains only $5,000—the gain of $6,000 from exercising the option minus the $1,000 premium paid.

In Figure 1.2, it would cost $1,000 to buy a call on 100 shares, but $5,000 to buy 100 shares. Options enable their holders to lever their resources. The same is true for many derivatives strategies. This implicit leverage can make the value of derivatives positions extremely volatile. By investing $1,000 of her own money to buy the call option, Rubinstein receives $100 more for each dollar the stock price exceeds the exercise price when she receives the payoff from the option. Consequently, Rubinstein gains from stock price increases as if she had invested in 100 shares even though she invests an amount of money only equal to the value of 20 shares. Without call options and only $1,000 to invest, Rubinstein would have to borrow $4,000 to be able to buy 100 shares if she wants to earn

$100 more per dollar the stock price exceeds the exercise price. The gain made upon exercising the option is therefore similar to the gain from a levered position in the underlying—a position consisting of purchasing shares with one's own money and some borrowed money.

By buying the call, Rubinstein earns much more if the stock price exceeds $50 at maturity and loses much more if it is below $50 than if she invests $1,000 in shares and does not borrow. If the stock price is at $110 when the option pays off, Rubinstein earns a return of 500 percent on her investment in the call. With an investment of $1,000 in shares, Rubinstein's return would be only 120 percent. In contrast, if the share price is $40, Rubinstein loses 100 percent of her investment if she buys the call, but only 20 percent of her investment if she buys shares. This example makes it clear that some derivatives can dramatically magnify price changes in the underlying. For each dramatic gain with a derivative, there is a counterparty that makes an equally dramatic loss.

Our example shows that the payoff of an option is nonlinear. This nonlinearity is typical of many derivatives. It complicates analysis of both the pricing and the risk of these financial instruments. Many derivatives debacles have come from the fact that firms and investors forgot that derivatives can be equivalent to leveraged positions in the underlying and that they have nonlinear payoffs.

1.2.2. Forward contracts

Because unexpected losses due to a depreciation of the euro force Garman to reduce its R&D investment, Garman's shareholders benefit if Garman succeeds in reducing its exposure to unexpected decreases in the value of the euro. If Garman buys a put option with an exercise price of $1 per euro, it can sell its euros for a least $100 million. To obtain this insurance, Garman pays the option premium. A forward contract enables Garman to eliminate its exposure to the euro completely without having to pay an option premium. The price specified in a forward contract is called the forward price. If the forward contract obligates Garman to sell €100 million at a price of $1 per dollar, it receives $100 million at maturity regardless of the price of the euro at that time. If it buys the put, Garman benefits from increases in the price of the euro. In contrast, with the forward contract, Garman's cash flow is the same irrespective of how much the euro appreciates or depreciates.

Garman's unhedged cash flow depends on the price of the euro in six months. Whenever a firm's cash flow depends on a variable, price, or quantity that can change unexpectedly for reasons beyond one's control, the variable is called a **risk factor**. The cash flow's **exposure** to a risk factor is the sensitivity of cash flow to unexpected changes in a risk factor. For a given exposure, a change in the risk factor increases cash flow approximately by the change in the risk factor times the exposure. Identifying the important risk factors for a firm and estimating the exposure of the firm's cash flow or of the firm's value to these risk factors is critical to the success of a risk management program. This task is often made difficult by the fact that exposures change as risk factors change unexpectedly. For example, a firm may export more as the dollar depreciates, so that its exposure to foreign currencies increases as the dollar depreciates. In the case of Garman, there is no uncertainty about the exposure. Garman has a fixed exposure of €100 million that ceases to exist after six months, so that the exposure has a maturity of six months.

Panel A of Figure 1.3 (on pages 12–13) shows the cash flow of Garman in six months if it does nothing to reduce its €100 million exposure. The market for a currency for immediate delivery is called the spot market or the cash market. Garman is **long** in euros, meaning that it benefits from an increase in the price of the euro. If Garman does nothing, its cash flow in six months is 100 million times the price of the euro on the cash market at that time.

Panel B of Figure 1.3 shows the payoff of a **short** forward position, which is a position to sell euros forward, at maturity of the contract in six months. The forward price is assumed to be $1. With the short forward position, Garman receives the forward price per euro delivered. The gain or payoff from the short forward position per unit is therefore the forward price minus the cash market price of the euro in six months. Garman's gain from the short forward position increases as the dollar price of the euro falls. If the euro is at $1.10 at maturity, Garman agreed to deliver euros worth $1.10 per unit at the price of $1, so that it loses $0.10 per unit or $10 million on the forward contract. In contrast, if the euro is at $0.90 at maturity, Garman receives $1 per unit for something worth $0.90 per unit, thereby gaining $10 million on the forward contract.

Panel C of Figure 1.3 shows Garman's cash flow in six months if it sells the euros forward. In six months, Garman sells the euros for $100 million. This cash flow can be decomposed into two pieces: what Garman would have received had it not sold the euros forward and the gain from the forward contract. The gain from the forward contract exactly offsets the shortfall Garman would have made relative to $100 million if it had sold the euros on the cash market.

A financial position that reduces the risk resulting from exposure to a risk factor is called a financial hedge. Here the financial hedge is the forward contract. A **perfect hedge** eliminates all the risk so that the hedged position, defined as the cash position plus the hedge (the euros plus the forward contract), has no exposure to the risk factor. In this example, the hedge is perfect.

Panel D of Figure 1.3 shows the cash flow of Garman if it buys a put instead of selling the euros forward. If Garman buys a put with exercise price equal to the forward price, its cash flow if the euro cash market price in six months is $0.90 will be $100 million minus the cost of the premium. This is because Garman exercises the put option to receive $100 million for its euros, but it had to pay a premium. Consequently, if Garman buys a put with an exercise price equal to the forward price, Garman's cash flow is less than with the forward contract unless the euro appreciates sufficiently so that the put is not exercised and the proceeds from selling the euro exceed the proceeds from selling the euros forward plus the cost of the option premium.

Whether Garman should reduce its exposure to the euro by selling euros forward or by buying a put depends on the specifics of the firm's situation. With buying the put, Garman earns less if the euro is lower than the forward price than if it sells euros forward. If these lower proceeds force Garman to cut back R&D, it should sell the euros forward. Suppose, however, that Garman would want to invest more in R&D if the euro appreciates because in that case it will export more to Europe. With this scenario, buying a put could be a better solution than selling euros forward because Garman would have a larger cash flow if the euro appreciates and hence would be better able to finance higher R&D expenditures.

Figure 1.3   Hedging with forward contract

Garman's income is in dollars and the exchange rate is the dollar price of one euro.

Panel A. Income to Garman if it does not hedge. Garman receives €100 million in six months, so that the dollar income is the dollar price of the euro times one million if the exporter does not hedge.

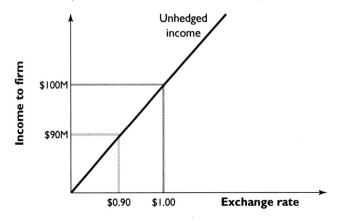

Panel B. Forward contract payoff. The forward price for the euro is $1. If the spot exchange rate is $0.90, the gain from the forward contract is the gain from selling €100 million at $1 rather than $0.90, which is $10 million.

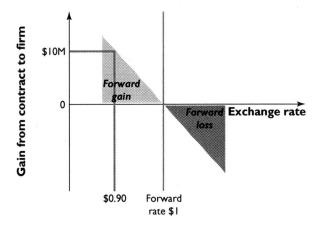

This example demonstrates four important lessons. First, through a financial transaction, Garman can eliminate all its risk without spending any cash to do so. This makes forward contracts extremely useful. The real world is more complicated than this, however. Finding the best hedge can be difficult and often the best hedge is not a perfect hedge.

Second, the firm cannot consider the gains and losses of derivatives positions independently from the rest of the firm. When firms use derivatives to hedge, only firm value matters. To eliminate the risk of the hedged position, Garman has to be willing to make losses on derivatives positions. When it takes a forward position, its hedged cash flow entails no uncertainty—it is fixed. When the euro turns out to be worth more than the forward price, Garman loses on the forward

Panel C. Hedged firm income. The firm sells its euro income forward at a price of $1 per euro. It therefore gets a dollar income of $100 million for sure, which is equal to the unhedged firm income plus the forward contract payoff.

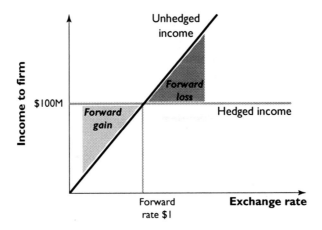

Panel D. Comparison of income with put contract and income with forward contract. Garman receives $100 million if it sells €100 million forward. With the put contract, Garman has to pay the premium, so that it receives less than $100 million if it exercises the put and gets to sell the euros at $1 per euro. If it does not exercise the put, it receives less than if it had not hedged, but more than with the forward hedge when the spot price of the euro exceeds the exercise price plus the option premium per euro.

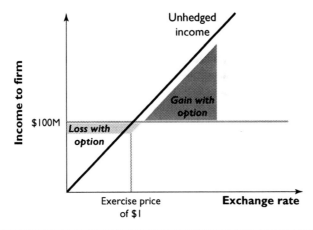

contract. This is the case when the price of the euro is $1.10. The loss on the forward contract exactly offsets the gain made on the value of the euros received at maturity.

Third, the forward price must be such that the forward contract has no value at *origination.* That is, when Garman enters the forward contract, it agrees to sell euros at the forward price. The counterparty in the forward contract must agree to buy euros at the forward price. No money changes hands except for the agreed-upon exchange of euros for dollars at maturity of the contract. If the forward contract were to have value at origination of the contract for the exporter, it would have to have negative value for someone on the opposite side, and there would be no one to be found to enter the contract. In this case, the counterparty would be better off not to enter the contract.

Fourth, Garman can decrease its euro exposure using different financial instruments. In this section, we saw that it could do so by selling euros forward or buying a put. We will see later that a firm in Garman's situation can use other financial instruments to decrease its exposure. The decision of which financial instrument to use to reduce an exposure depends on many considerations that we will explain in this book.

1.3. Using derivatives the right way for risk management

Rockfeller had it right when he said that one cannot get rich by saving. If we are to become rich, we have to take risks to exploit valuable opportunities where we have a comparative advantage. Firms and individuals must therefore avoid risks that are not profitable so that they can take on more risks that are advantageous. Derivatives enable them to shed risks and to take on risks cheaply.

To shed risks that are not profitable and take on the ones that are, it is crucial to understand the risks one is exposed to and to evaluate their costs and benefits. Individuals are not very good at thinking about risks without quantitative tools. We will overstate the importance of some risks and understate the importance of others. Most of us, for example, put too much weight on recent past experience. If a stock has been doing well, we will think that it will do unusually well in the future, so it has little risk. Most of us are reluctant to realize losses even though quantitative analysis shows that the tax code makes it advantageous for us to do so. People dealing with risk often take actions that cannot be justified on quantitative grounds. These tendencies are the subject of behavioral finance, which attempts to identify how the biases of individuals influence their portfolio decisions and asset returns.

To figure out which risks to bear and which risks to shed, one must have models to quantify the economic value of taking risks and shedding risks. Hence, to use derivatives the right way, one has to be able to make simple statements like: If I keep the exposure to weather risk, the value of the firm is X; if I shed the exposure to weather risk, the value of the firm after purchasing the appropriate financial instruments is Y; if Y is greater than X, I shed the weather risk. For individuals, it has to be that the measure of their welfare they focus on is affected by a risk, and they can establish whether shedding the risk makes them better off than bearing it.

To evaluate the economic value of taking risks and shedding risks, one has to be able to quantify risks. This requires statistics. One has to be able to trace the impact of risks on firm value or individual welfare. This requires economic analysis.

Finally, managers must know how a derivatives position will affect the risks the firm is exposed to. This requires understanding the instruments and how they are priced. A derivative might eliminate all of a risk, but it may also be priced so that one is worse off without the risk than with it. A derivatives salesperson could argue that a derivative is the right one to eliminate a risk we are concerned about, but a more thorough analysis might reveal that the derivative actually increases our exposure to other risks so that we would be worse off purchasing it.

To use derivatives the right way for risk management, one has to define an objective function. For a firm, the objective function is generally to maximize shareholder wealth. Objective functions are of little use unless we can measure the impact of choices on the objective. We therefore have to be able to quantify how various risks affect our objective function. Doing so, we will find some risks that make us worse off and, perhaps, others that make us better off. Having figured out which risks are costly, we need to investigate whether there are derivatives strategies that can be used to improve our situation. This requires us to be able to figure out the impact of these strategies on our objective function. The world is not static. Exposures to risks change all the time. Consequently, derivatives positions that were appropriate yesterday may not be so today. This means that we must have systems in place that make it possible to monitor our risk exposures.

Using derivatives the right way means that we look ahead and determine which risks we should bear and how. Once we have decided which risks we should bear, nature has to run its course. If a derivative is bought to insure against losses, it is reasonable to think that about half the time, the losses one insures against will not take place, and the derivative will therefore not produce a gain to offset losses. The outcome of a derivatives transaction does not tell us whether we were right or wrong in entering the transaction any more than whether our house burns down or not tells us whether we were right or wrong to buy fire insurance. Houses almost never burn down; we almost always incur a loss on fire insurance. We buy the insurance because we know *ex ante* that we are better off shedding the risk of having to pay to replace the house.

In the Garman example, if Garman entered a forward contract, the euro ended up either above or below the forward price of $1. If it ended up above, Garman lost money on the contract. The temptation is to say that the firm made a poor use of derivatives because it lost money on the derivative. This is not the way to think about derivatives, however.

When the decision was made to use the derivative, Garman determined that it was better off hedging the currency risk. It had no information that allowed it to expect the euro to appreciate and hence could not act on such information; that's not Garman's business. When it entered into the forward contract, it concluded that the cost of cutting investment in response to a loss on the euro absent hedging was high enough to justify locking in the dollar value of its foreign currency receivable at the forward price. Nothing happened subsequently that changed the validity of Garman's rationale to hedge.

Garman could have been tempted to base its hedging decision on its view of how the exchange rate was going to evolve over the next six months. When basing hedges on forecasts, a firm has to remember that for every firm thinking that a currency is overvalued, there is another one thinking with the same amount of conviction that the currency is undervalued. A firm might be unusually good at forecasting exchange rates, but to beat the market, one has to be better than the investors who have the best information. This disqualifies most of us. If mutual fund managers whose job it is to beat the market do not do so on average, why should a firm's employee or an individual investor think that he or she has a good enough chance of doing so that this should direct their choice of derivatives positions? Sometimes, we know something that has value and should trade on it. More often, though, we do not.

As it is easy and cheap to take positions in derivatives, a firm's position can change in an instant because of the actions of some individual who has authority to trade derivatives for the firm. This individual might even think that he is so good at forecasting future changes in exchange rates and interest rates that he should take financial positions to make profits for the firm. With no appropriate risk measures, such an individual can quickly take positions that could destroy the firm if things go wrong. It is therefore imperative for a firm that uses derivatives to monitor its derivative positions and to measure its risks accurately.

1.4. What does it take to use derivatives the right way for risk management?

Examples of the use of derivatives at two major companies demonstrate some of the issues that arise in managing risks. This preview of risk management in action shows the skills and tools a manager must master to manage risk and the issues he or she has to deal with.

1.4.1. Designing a foreign exchange hedging program at Merck

Merck is a multinational pharmaceutical company doing business in more than 100 countries. More than half of its sales are made abroad. Foreign sales are billed in local currencies. That is, a subsidiary selling in the United Kingdom would post UK prices and would bill its customers in pounds. Like all pharmaceutical companies, Merck has an extremely large R&D budget. A major concern of management is, as with Garman, that unexpected foreign exchange losses could force the company to retrench and to reduce its R&D expenditures, thereby becoming less competitive. Merck uses risk management to reduce the probability of such an outcome. Lewent and Kearney (1999) explain that when its risk management program was put in place, Merck addressed the issues in five steps:

> **Step 1. Understand the distribution of exchange rates.** Exchange rates are risk factors. Merck is primarily interested in the likelihood of adverse exchange rate movements. It has to quantify the probability of such adverse exchange rate movements.
>
> **Step 2. Estimate the impact of adverse exchange rate movements on the strategic plan.** Cash flows are exposed to foreign exchange movements. An adverse exchange rate movement decreases cash flows and hence limits the resources the company can use to fund R&D or to pay out as dividends.
>
> **Step 3. Decide whether to hedge, depending on external considerations and internal considerations.** The main external consideration is Merck's ability to keep dividends growing. A strong dollar appreciation would reduce dollar income from foreign subsidiaries and possibly endanger dividend growth. The main internal consideration is Merck's ability

to finance R&D expenditures that are essential to the future of the corporation.

Step 4. Choose the appropriate financial instruments. Firms can use many different financial instruments to hedge a foreign exchange exposure. Managers must be able to evaluate how the various instruments can help them achieve their specific goals. Merck decided to use plain vanilla options in its hedging program. Its rationale was that options enabled it to benefit from a weak dollar, while complete hedging did not. To hedge revenue, Merck uses put options on local currencies. At the end of 1999, a 10 percent weakening of the dollar would have reduced the value of its portfolio of options used for hedging revenue by $86.7 million.

Step 5. Determine how much to hedge. Merck decided (1) to hedge on a multi-year basis, (2) to avoid options that had little chance to pay off at maturity, and (3) to hedge only partially. Consequently, with this hedging program, Merck kept some exposure to exchange rate changes.

1.4.2. Measuring risks at Microsoft

In 20 years, Microsoft went from an idea of a Harvard dropout to a company that had at times the largest market capitalization in the United States, worth at its 1999 peak more than half a trillion dollars. At that time, it had accumulated a portfolio of fixed-income securities managed by its own portfolio management group (PMG), strategic equity positions, and foreign exchange holdings in excess of $35 billion. It had $18 billion of net revenues to deal with. It had no debt. Yet, because of the nature of its business, a technological innovation conceived in a garage or a backroom somewhere could wipe out billions of equity value overnight. It was therefore essential for the firm to have resources to cope with unexpected challenges and to be able to measure financial risks and manage them.

How can financial risk for such a company be measured? Microsoft built a financial risk reporting structure that looks like a tree. This tree is shown in Figure 1.4. The goal in building the tree was that at each node management and treasury would be able to identify, quantify, and manage financial risks.

To achieve its goal, Microsoft had to choose a risk measure. It chose to measure risk by the loss that, over a period of 20 days, would not be exceeded with a probability of 97.5 percent. An estimate of a loss for a portfolio over a period of time that is not exceeded at some probability level is called the value at risk, or VaR, of the portfolio. Historically, Microsoft had focused its risk management program on a number of different risks. It had an important options program for employees that created risks it was trying to manage. The company had huge foreign sales, with attendant foreign exchange exposures. It had a large investment portfolio. These various risks were managed separately. When it introduced VaR as a risk measure, Microsoft was able to start looking at risk in a holistic way; all risks were measured in the same way and could be evaluated at the company level, taking into account the interactions among and between the various risks the company was exposed to.

Microsoft installed systems that would enable it to compute estimates of VaR at all the nodes of the tree in Figure 1.4. Managers started the Gibraltar project

Figure 1.4   Microsoft's corporate tree

Each node will report market value, VaR, % VaR, (VaR/Market value), and previous % VaR. VaR numbers reported will be 20-day, 97.5% confidence.

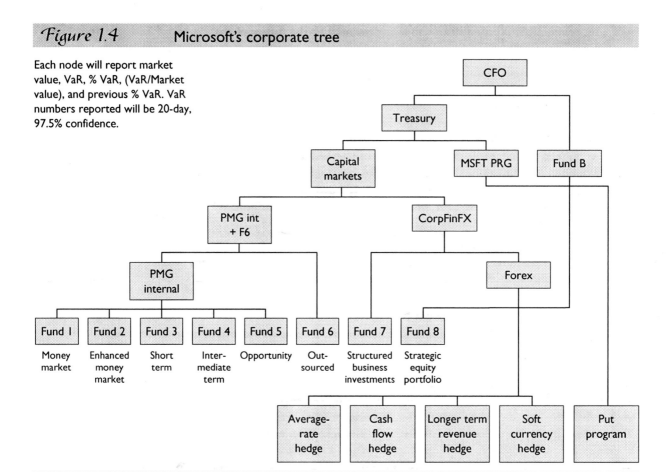

to establish an integrated system to capture data and provide statistics that could be used to evaluate it. The end product was a web-based system that enables executives to view the risk of the nodes of the tree online.

With this system, Microsoft knows what its financial risks are. Managers can continually monitor these risks and can decide what to do about them. To implement hedges, they use analytical options software that gives them the capability to design hedges using a variety of instruments. Microsoft typically uses forward contracts to hedge short-run exposures and options to hedge longer-run exposures. When it uses options to hedge revenues, it mostly uses average-rate options, a type of exotic option. The payoff of an average-rate call option per unit is the average exchange rate over a period of time minus the exercise price.

Microsoft's approach is to use only derivatives that it can price and understand. In its systems, Microsoft must be able to price the options it uses, monitor their risk, and design hedges using such options.

1.5. Learning to manage risks with derivatives the right way

This book has 19 chapters. Each chapter will help you to acquire the tools and skills you need to understand and implement risk management solutions such as those chosen by Merck and Microsoft. In Chapters 2 through 4, we investigate how to measure risk and how risk affects firm value. A crucial issue in risk measurement is that bad outcomes that are unlikely to happen affect firm value and individual welfare in ways that are quite different from other outcomes. Small cash flow fluctuations generally have little impact on firms. A large cash flow shortfall can mean default and bankruptcy. It is therefore essential to have quantitative measures of these unlikely outcomes. We introduce such measures in Chapter 4, which focuses mainly on the value at risk measure that Microsoft and countless other firms use.

Chapters 5 through 14 consider plain vanilla derivatives—forwards, futures, and options—that trade in highly liquid markets. Chapter 5 shows how to price forward and futures contracts. Chapters 6 and 7 provide extensive discussion of how to use forward and futures contracts to manage risk. We explain how to build hedges with forwards and futures contracts. Chapter 8 shows how to estimate and hedge foreign exchange exposures. The issues examined in Chapter 8 are similar to the issues Merck faced in setting up its risk management program. Chapter 9 focuses on interest rate risks.

Both Merck and Microsoft manage risks using options. Chapter 10 explains why options play an essential role in risk management. Chapters 11 and 12 show how to price options. Chapter 12 is completely dedicated to the Black-Scholes formula. Options complicate risk measurement, but we cannot pretend that they do not exist to avoid the risk measurement problem. Chapter 13 introduces techniques to measure risk in the presence of options and complex derivatives and presents further uses of options in risk management. Chapter 14 covers fixed-income options.

Chapters 15 through 18 show the benefits from using derivatives that trade over the counter in typically less liquid markets. Many of these derivatives are exotic derivatives. Taking positions in derivatives traded over-the-counter involves important issues we examine in Chapter 15. Among the derivatives uses we review, the losses of Gibson Greetings stand out; the firm lost roughly one year's earnings on derivatives positions. The derivatives salesman from Bankers Trust who dealt with Gibson Greetings was heard on trading room tapes saying: "These guys have done some pretty wild stuff. And you know, they probably do not understand it quite as well as they should. . . . And that's like perfect for us." Chapter 15 makes sure that no derivatives salesperson will say this about you.

Chapter 16 shows how to price and use swaps. Some swaps trade in highly liquid markets, but others do not. We saw that Microsoft uses exotic options called average-rate options. The use of exotic options in risk management is examined in Chapter 17. Chapter 18 shows how to measure credit risks and how to eliminate them with credit derivatives. Credit risks are important by themselves because they are a critical source of risk for firms. At the same time, one of the most recent growth areas in derivative markets involves credit derivatives, namely derivatives that can be used to lay off credit risks. Chapter 19 reviews recent developments and innovations in risk management and in the use of derivatives in risk management.

Derivatives are like finely tuned racing cars. We wouldn't let an amateur driver enter the Indianapolis 500 at the wheel of a race car. Neither would the weekend driver at the wheel of a Ford Escort have any chance of winning. The same is true with derivatives. Untutored users can crash and burn. Nonusers cannot win the race. This book will help you know how you can increase shareholder wealth by managing risks with derivatives.

Key Concepts

American options, 8	notional amount, 7
call option, 3	option premium, 8
European options, 8	option writer, 8
exercise price, 3	perfect hedge, 11
exposure, 10	put option, 4
forward contract, 6	risk factor, 10
hedge, 5	short, 11
long, 11	swaps, 7

Literature Note

The definition of derivative comes from the online version of the *Merriam-Webster Collegiate Dictionary*. See http://www.britannica.com. The evidence that firms using foreign exchange derivatives are worth more is presented by Allayannis and Weston (2001). "Come rain, come shine" by Gautam Jain and David Foster, Weather Risk Special Report, *Risk*, August 2000, pp. 16–17, discusses uses of weather derivatives. Bernstein (1992) provides an historical account of the interaction between research and practice in the history of derivatives markets. The spectacular growth in financial innovation is discussed in Miller (1992). Finnerty (1992) provides a list of new financial instruments developed since the discovery of the Black-Scholes formula. Black (1989) provides an account of the discovery of the Black-Scholes formula. Allen and Gale (1991), Merton (1992), and Ross (1989) provide analyses of the determinants of financial innovation. Brown and Chew (1999) have an extensive collection of readings on risk management. In that book, Callinicos (1999) reviews risk management at Microsoft and Lewent and Kearney (1999) review risk management at Merck. For the Bank for International Settlements surveys on derivatives use, see http://www.bis.org/.

Chapter 2

Investors and Risk Management

Chapter **2** Objectives

At the end of this chapter, you will:

1. Understand expected return and volatility for a security and a portfolio.

2. Know how to use the normal distribution to obtain the probability of ranges of returns for securities.

3. Be able to evaluate the risk of a security in a portfolio.

4. Know how the capital asset pricing model is used to obtain the expected return of a security and to compute the present value of cash flows.

5. Know how hedging affects firm value in perfect financial markets.

6. Understand how investors evaluate risk management policies of firms in perfect financial markets.

How do investors evaluate the risk management policies of firms in which they invest? More specifically, when do investors want a firm in which they hold shares to spend money to reduce the volatility of its stock price?

First, we have to know how investors decide to invest their money, and how the risk management policies of firms affect the riskiness of their investments. To do this, we describe some of the tools used to evaluate the distribution of the returns of securities and portfolios. Ignoring derivatives for the time being, investors have two powerful risk management tools that enable them to invest their wealth with a level of risk that is optimal for them. The first tool is **asset allocation**, which specifies how wealth is allocated across types of securities or asset classes. The second tool is **diversification**. A portfolio's degree of diversification is the extent to which the funds invested are distributed across securities to lessen the dependence of the portfolio's return on the return of individual securities.

This chapter shows that with these risk management tools investors do not need a firm to manage risk to help them achieve their optimal risk-return trade-off. Consequently, they benefit from a firm's risk management policy only if that policy increases the present value of the cash flows the firm expects to generate. The next chapter will show how a firm can use risk management to increase that present value.

2.1. Evaluating the risk and the return of individual securities and portfolios

Suppose an investor named John Smith has wealth of $100,000 that he wants to invest in equities for one year. His broker recommends two companies, IBM and XYZ. John knows about IBM, but has never heard of XYZ. He decides that first he wants to understand what his wealth would amount to after putting all his wealth in IBM shares for one year.

The return of a stock per dollar invested over a period of time is the total gain from holding the stock divided by the stock price at the beginning of the period. If the stock price is $100 at the beginning of the year, the dividend payments are $5, and the stock price appreciates by $20 during the year, the return per dollar invested or decimal return is (20 + 5)/100, or 0.25. Alternatively, we can express the return in percentage, so that a decimal return of 0.25 is a return of 25 percent. Unless we mention otherwise, returns are decimal returns.

For each dollar invested in the stock, John has one dollar plus the return of the stock at the end of the year. Since he puts all his wealth in IBM, his wealth at the end of the year is his initial wealth times one plus the return of IBM, or (Initial wealth)(1 + Return of IBM). In this example, John's wealth at the end of the year is $100,000(1 + 0.25), or $125,000. We first discuss how to figure out how likely various return outcomes are for a stock, and then do the same for a portfolio. Most readers may be familiar with these materials, but we include them because the concepts are basic to an understanding of derivatives and risk management.

Throughout the analysis in this chapter, we assume that the frictions that affect financial markets are unimportant. More specifically, we assume that there are no taxes, no transaction costs, no costs to writing and enforcing contracts, no restrictions on investments in securities, no differences in information across investors, and that investors take prices as given because they are too small to affect prices. Financial economists call markets that satisfy these assumptions **perfect financial markets**. Real-world financial markets are not perfect financial markets, but we make this assumption because it allows us to avoid distractions in discussing important concepts and to clarify the conditions under which financial risk management can increase firm value. Later on, we take into account financial markets imperfections and build on our understanding of perfect financial markets.

2.1.1. The distribution of the return of IBM
We first describe the concepts of return distribution, expected return, and return variance. We then show how to use the distribution of the return to infer the probability of various return outcomes for a stock. Finally, we address the implications of past returns for future returns.

2.1.1.A. Return distribution, expected return, and return variance
Because stock returns are uncertain, John has to figure out which outcomes are likely to occur and which are not. To do this, he uses basic statistical tools. The return of IBM is a random variable—we do not know what its value will be until that value is realized. A probability distribution provides a quantitative measure of the likelihood of the possible outcomes or realizations of a random variable by assigning probabilities to these outcomes. The statistical tool used to measure the likelihood of various returns for a stock is called the stock's **return probability distribution**. The most common probability distribution is the **normal distribution**. There is substantial empirical evidence that, for many purposes, the normal distribution provides a good but not perfect approximation of the true, unknown, distribution of stock returns.

With the normal distribution, all there is to know about the distribution of a stock's return is given by the expected return of the stock and by its variance. The **expected value** of a random variable is a probability-weighted average of all the possible distinct outcomes of that variable. Each distinct outcome has a probability, and all probabilities add up to one. For example, if the probability distribution of a stock specifies that it can have only one of two returns, 0.1 with probability 0.4 and 0.15 with probability 0.6, its expected return is $0.4 \times 0.1 + 0.6 \times 0.15$, or 0.13 in decimal form. IBM's **expected return** is the average return John would earn if next year were repeated over and over, each time yielding a different return drawn from the return distribution of IBM. Everything else equal, the higher the expected return, the better off the investor. If y is a random variable, we denote its expected value by $E(y)$.

The **variance** of a random variable is a quantitative measure of how the realizations of the random variable are distributed around their expected value; it provides a measure of risk. More precisely, it is the expected value of the square of the difference between the realizations of a random variable and its expected value, $E[y - E(y)]^2$. Using our example of a return of 0.10 with probability 0.4 and a return of 0.15 with probability 0.6, the decimal variance of the return is $0.4(0.10 - 0.13)^2 + 0.6(0.15 - 0.13)^2$ or 0.0006. For returns, the units of the variance are returns squared. The square root of the variance, however, is in the same units as the returns and is called the **standard deviation**. In finance, the standard deviation of returns is generally called the **volatility** of returns. We write Var(*y*) and Vol(*y*), respectively, for the variance and the volatility of random variable *y*. In our example, the square root of 0.0006 is 0.0245. Since the volatility is in the same units as the returns, we can use a volatility expressed as 2.45 percent. As returns are spread farther from the expected return, volatility increases. For example, if instead of having returns of 0.10 and 0.15 we have returns of 0.025 and 0.20, the expected return is unaffected but the volatility becomes 8.57 percent instead of 2.45 percent. Similarly, if IBM's return volatility is low, its return is likely to be close to its expected value, so that a return substantially greater or less than the expected return would be surprising. As IBM's volatility increases, a return close to the expected return becomes less likely.

Since investors prefer more to less, an increase in their expected wealth and hence in the expected return of their investments is good for them. However, investors are typically risk-averse, so, keeping the expected return on their wealth constant, they would prefer the volatility of the return on their wealth to be lower.

2.1.1.B. Using the return distribution to infer the likelihood of various return outcomes

The **cumulative distribution function** of a random variable *y* specifies, for any number *Y*, the probability that the realization of the random variable will be no greater than *Y*. We denote the probability that the random variable *y* has a realization no greater than *Y* as prob($y \leq Y$). For IBM, a reasonable estimate of the stock return volatility is 30 percent. With an expected return of 13 percent and a volatility of 30 percent, we can draw the cumulative distribution function for the return of IBM as plotted in Figure 2.1. For a given return, the function specifies the probability that the return of IBM will not exceed that return.

To use the cumulative distribution function, we choose a value on the horizontal axis, say 0 percent. The corresponding value on the vertical axis tells us the probability that IBM will earn less than 0 percent is 0.33. In other words, there is a 33 percent chance that over one year, IBM will have a negative return.

The easiest way to compute a probability is to use a spreadsheet program such as Excel. Box 2.1, Computing a probability using Excel, shows how to do this. Suppose John is worried about making losses. Using the normal distribution, we can tell him that there is a 33 percent chance he will lose money. This probabili-

Box 2.1	**Computing a probability using Excel**

The NORMDIST function of Excel is used to obtain probabilities for a normal distribution. Suppose we want to know how likely it is that IBM will earn less than 10 percent over one year. To get the probability that the return will be less than 10 percent, we choose *x* = 0.10. The mean is 0.13 and the standard deviation is 0.30. We finally write TRUE in the last line to obtain the cumulative distribution function. The result is 0.46. This number means that there is a 46 percent chance that the return of IBM will be less than 10 percent over a year.

Cumulative probability function for IBM and for a stock with same return and twice the volatility

Figure 2.1

The expected return of IBM is 13 percent and its volatility is 30 percent. The horizontal line corresponds to a probability of 0.05. The cumulative probability function of IBM crosses that line at a return almost twice as high as the cumulative probability function of the riskier stock. There is a 5 percent chance that IBM will have a lower return than the one corresponding to the intersection of the IBM cumulative distribution function and the horizontal line, which is a return of −36 percent. There is a 5 percent chance that the stock with twice the volatility of IBM will have a return lower than −0.66 percent.

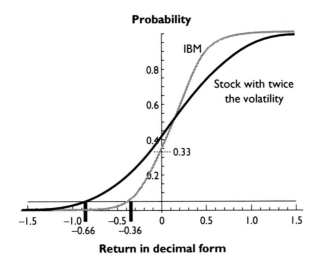

ty depends on the expected return. As the expected return of IBM increases, the probability of making a loss falls.

One concern John could have is that his wealth might not be sufficient to pay for living expenses. Suppose he needs to have $50,000 to live on at the end of the year. By putting all his wealth in a stock, he knows that he takes the risk that he will have less than that amount at the end of the year, but he wants the probability of that outcome to be less than 0.05. With the cumulative normal distribution with an expected return of 13 percent and a volatility of 30 percent, the probability of a 50 percent loss is 0.018. John can therefore invest in IBM given his objective of making sure that there is a 95 percent chance that he will have at least $50,000 at the end of the year.

Suppose John wants to understand how likely it is that his portfolio will have a value between $50,000 and $100,000 at the end of the year. We know that the probability that the portfolio will be worth less than $50,000 is 0.018 and the probability that the portfolio will be worth less than $100,000 is 0.33. The probability that the portfolio will be worth less than $100,000 is the sum of two probabilities: the probability that the portfolio is worth less than $50,000 and the probability that the portfolio is worth more than $50,000 but less than $100,000. The sum of these two probabilities is 0.33. Subtracting from 0.33 the probability that the portfolio will be worth less than $50,000, we get the probability that the portfolio will be worth more than $50,000 but less than $100,000:

0.33 – 0.018, or 0.312. The probability of 0.312 is the sum of the probability of all the possible values the portfolio could take between $50,000 and $100,000.

The **probability density function** tells us what the probabilities of these various portfolio values are. If a random variable takes discrete values, the probability density function tells us the probability of each of the values that the random variable can take. With the normal distribution, the random variable is continuous—there are many possible values over any range of numbers. In this case, the probability density function tells us the probability that the random variable will take a value within an infinitesimally small range of its possible values—it gives us the increase in prob($x \leq X$) as X increases by an infinitesimal amount.

In the case of IBM, we see that the cumulative distribution function first increases slowly, then more sharply, and finally again slowly. This explains why the probability density function of IBM shown in Figure 2.2 first has a value close to zero, increases to reach a peak, and then falls again. This bell-shaped probability density function is characteristic of the normal distribution. Note that this bell-shaped function is symmetric around the expected value of the distribution. For comparison, the figure also shows the distribution of the return of a security that has twice the volatility of IBM but the same expected return. The distribution of the more volatile security has more weight in the tails and less around the mean than IBM, implying that outcomes substantially away from the mean are more likely.

The distribution of the more volatile security shows a limitation of the normal distribution for simple returns: It has returns worse than –100 percent. Because

---

Figure 2.2   Normal density function for IBM assuming an expected return of 13 percent and a volatility of 30 percent and of a stock with the same expected return but twice the volatility

This figure shows the probability density function of the one-year return of IBM assuming an expected return of 13 percent and a volatility of 30 percent. It also shows the probability density function of the one-year return of a stock that has the same expected return but twice the volatility of return of IBM.

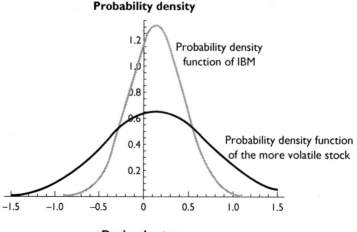

stocks have limited liability, the most one can lose owning a stock is what one paid for it, corresponding to a simple return of −100 percent. In general, this limitation is not important in that the probability of such a return is very small.

2.1.2. The distribution of the return of a portfolio

To be thorough, John wants to consider XYZ. He first wants to know if he would be better off investing $100,000 in XYZ rather than in IBM. He finds out that the expected return of XYZ is 26 percent and the return volatility is 60 percent, so that XYZ has twice the expected return and twice the volatility of IBM. Using volatility as a summary risk measure, XYZ is riskier than IBM. The probability that the price of XYZ will fall by 50 percent is 0.102. Consequently, John cannot invest all his wealth in XYZ if he wants his probability of losing $50,000 to be at most 0.05.

Since XYZ has a high expected return compared to IBM, though, John wants to consider investing something in XYZ, forming a portfolio of the two stocks. Section 2.1.2.A presents the computation of the return and the expected return of the portfolio, while section 2.1.2.B shows how to compute and use the return volatility of the portfolio.

2.1.2.A. The return and expected return of a portfolio The return of a portfolio is the weighted average of the return of the securities in the portfolio, where the weight for a security is the fraction of the portfolio invested in that security. The fraction of the portfolio invested in a security is called the **portfolio share** (or portfolio weight) of that security. Suppose John puts $75,000 in IBM and $25,000 in XYZ. The portfolio share of IBM is $75,000/$100,000, or 0.75. Portfolio shares sum to one since the entire portfolio must be invested. A negative portfolio share corresponds to a short sale. With a **short sale**, an investor borrows shares from a third party and sells them. With our assumption of perfect financial markets, the investor can then use the proceeds from the sale fully. To close the short-sale position, the investor must buy shares and deliver them to the lender. If the share price increases, the investor loses because he has to pay more for the shares he delivers than he received for the shares he sold.

Using w_i for the portfolio share of security i in a portfolio with N securities and R_i for the return on security i, the portfolio return is:

$$\sum_{i=1}^{N} w_i R_i = \text{Portfolio return} \qquad (2.1)$$

If the realized return on IBM is 20 percent and the realized return on XYZ is −10 percent, applying formula (2.1) the decimal return of the investor's portfolio is:

$$0.75(0.20) + 0.25(-0.10) = 0.125 \qquad (2.2)$$

With this return, the wealth of the investor at the end of the year is $100,000 \times (1 + 0.125)$, or $112,500.

At the start of the year, John wants to compute the expected return of the portfolio and the return volatility of the portfolio for different choices of portfolio shares to help allocate his wealth between IBM and XYZ shares. The portfolio weights are taken as given and therefore are treated as constants. The expected return of a portfolio is therefore the portfolio share weighted average of the expected return of the securities in the portfolio:[1]

$$\sum_{i=1}^{N} w_i E(R_i) = E(R_P) = \text{Portfolio expected return} \qquad (2.3)$$

Applying this formula using an expected return for IBM of 13 percent and an expected return for XYZ of 26 percent, the expected decimal return of the portfolio with a portfolio share of 0.75 in IBM and 0.25 in XYZ is:

$$0.75 \times 0.13 + 0.25 \times 0.26 = 0.1625 \qquad (2.4)$$

The expected wealth of the investor at the end of the year is E [(Initial wealth) × (1 + Portfolio return)]. Since (see footnote 1) the expectation of the product of a constant with a random variable is equal to the constant times the expectation of the random variable, the expectation of the investor's wealth at the end of the year is Initial wealth × [1 + E(Portfolio return)]. John therefore expects his wealth to be 100,000 × (1 + 0.1625), or \$116,250, at the end of the year.

2.1.2.B. The volatility of the return of a portfolio

An investor naturally wants to be able to compare the volatility of the stock portfolio to the volatility the portfolio would have if the entire amount were invested in one stock. To compute the volatility of a portfolio, it is best to compute the variance of the portfolio return first and then take its square root to get the volatility to avoid cumbersome square roots. To compute the variance of the portfolio return, we first need to review two properties of the variance.

The first property is that the variance of a constant times a random variable is the constant squared times the variance of the random variable. This implies that $\text{Var}(w_i R_i) = w_i^2 \text{Var}(R_i)$. The portfolio return is a weighted sum of returns. Consequently, to compute the variance of the portfolio return, we have to compute the variance of a sum. If a and b are random variables, to obtain the variance of $a + b$ we have to compute $E[a + b - E(a + b)]^2$. Remember that the square of a sum of two terms is the sum of each term squared plus two times the cross-product of the two numbers (the square of 5 + 4 is $5^2 + 4^2 + 2 \times 5 \times 4$, or 81). Consequently:

$$\begin{aligned}
\text{Var}(a + b) &= E[a + b - E(a + b)]^2 \\
&= E[a - E(a) + b - E(b)]^2 \\
&= E[a - E(a)]^2 + E[b - E(b)]^2 + \mathbf{2E[a - E(a)][b - E(b)]} \\
&= \text{Var}(a) + \text{Var}(b) + 2\text{Cov}(a, b) \qquad (2.5)
\end{aligned}$$

The bold term is the covariance between a and b, denoted by $\text{Cov}(a, b)$, which measures how a and b move together. The **covariance** is the expected value of the

---

1   To compute the portfolio's expected return, we use two properties of expectations. First, the expected value of the product of a random variable and a constant is equal to the constant times the expected value of the random variable. If $E(w_i R_i)$ is the expected return on security i times its portfolio share, this property of expectations implies that $E(w_i R_i) = w_i E(R_i)$. Second, the expected value of a sum of random variables is simply the sum of the expected values of the random variables. This second property implies that if the portfolio has only securities 1 and 2, $E(w_1 R_1 + w_2 R_2) = E(w_1 R_1) + E(w_2 R_2)$, which is equal to $w_1 E(R_1) + w_2 E(R_2)$ because of the first property.

product of the deviations of two random variables from their mean: $E[a - E(a)]$ $[b - E(b)]$. The covariance can take negative as well as positive values. Its value increases as a and b are more likely to exceed their expected values together. If the covariance is zero, the fact that a exceeds its expected value provides no information about whether b exceeds its expected value also. Equation (2.5) shows the second important property of variances for the case of two random variables: The variance of a sum of random variables is the sum of the variances of the random variables plus twice the covariance of each pair of random variables.

The covariance is closely related to the correlation coefficient. The correlation coefficient takes values between -1 and $+1$. If a and b have a correlation coefficient of 1, they move in lockstep in the same direction. If the correlation coefficient is -1, they move in lockstep in the opposite direction. Finally, if the correlation coefficient is zero, a and b are independent if they are normally distributed. Denote by $Corr(a, b)$ the correlation between a and b. If one knows the correlation coefficient, one can obtain the covariance by using the formula:

$$\textbf{Cov}(a, b) = \textbf{Corr}(a, b) \times \textbf{Vol}(a) \times \textbf{Vol}(b) \qquad (2.6)$$

The variance of $a + b$ increases with the covariance of a and b since an increase in the covariance makes it less likely that an unexpectedly low value of a is offset by an unexpectedly high value of b. In the special case where a and b have the same volatility, $a + b$ has no risk if the correlation coefficient is -1 because a high realization of one of the random variables is always exactly offset by a low realization of the other. Note that if a and b are the same random variables, they have a correlation coefficient of $+1$, so that $Cov(a, b)$ is $Cov(a, a) = 1 \times Vol(a) \times Vol(a)$, which is $Var(a)$ since the square of the volatility of a is its variance, so that the covariance of a random variable with itself is its variance.

From what we have just seen, John does not have enough information to compute the variance of the portfolio if he knows just the variance and the portfolio weights of the securities in the portfolio. He must also know how the securities in the portfolio covary. More generally, therefore, the formula for the variance of the return of a portfolio is:[2]

$$\sum_{i=1}^{N} w_i^2 \textbf{Var}(R_i) \; + \; \sum_{i=1}^{N} \sum_{j \neq i}^{N} w_i w_j \textbf{Cov}\left(R_i, R_j\right)$$

$$= \textbf{ Variance of portfolio return} \qquad (2.7)$$

Applying equation (2.7) to the portfolio of IBM and XYZ, we need to know the covariance between the returns of the two securities. If the correlation coefficient between the two securities is 0.5, the covariance is 0.5(0.30)(0.60), or 0.09, and the variance is:

$$0.75^2(0.3^2) + 0.25^2(0.6^2) + 2(0.25)(0.75)(0.5)(0.3)(0.6) = 0.11 \qquad (2.8)$$

---

2   This formula is obtained in the following way in the case of a portfolio with two assets, assets 1 and 2. Using the formula for the variance of a sum, the variance of the portfolio, $Var(w_1 R_1 + w_2 R_2)$, is equal to $Var(w_1 R_1) + Var(w_2 R_2) + 2Cov(w_1 R_1, w_2 R_2)$. Since we saw that if k is a constant and a a random variable, the variance of ka is $k^2 Var(a)$, $Var(w_1 R_1) + Var(w_2 R_2) + 2Cov(w_1 R_1, w_2 R_2) = w_1^2 Var(R_1) + w_2^2 Var(R_2) + 2w_1 w_2 Cov(R_1, R_2)$.

The volatility of the portfolio is the square root of 0.11, which is 0.3317. By investing less in IBM and more in a stock that has twice the volatility of IBM, John can increase his expected return from 13 to 16.25 percent, but in doing so he increases the volatility of his portfolio from 30 to 33.17 percent. Since the portfolio has a higher expected return than IBM but also a higher volatility, we cannot determine a priori which of the three possible investments the investor prefers (investing in IBM, XYZ, or the portfolio). We know that John would prefer the portfolio if it had a higher expected return than IBM and less volatility, but this is not the case. An investor who is risk-averse is willing to give up some expected return in exchange for less risk. If John dislikes risk sufficiently, he prefers IBM to the portfolio because IBM has less risk even though it has less expected return. By altering portfolio shares, the investor can create many different portfolios that differ in their risk and expected return.

2.2. Diversification, asset allocation, and expected returns

In section 2.2.1, we determine how diversification affects the distribution of the return of a portfolio. In section 2.2.2, we examine asset allocation when there is a risk-free asset. In section 2.2.3, we show how investors measure risk when they hold a diversified portfolio. Finally, in section 2.2.4, we explain how required expected returns are determined when investors care only about the expected return and the volatility of their portfolio. Once again, the reader may be familiar with the materials presented in this section, but a review is necessary to understand when risk management creates value.

2.2.1. Diversification and the return of a portfolio

The impact on the volatility of the investor's portfolio return of investing in XYZ depends on the correlation coefficient between XYZ and IBM. Figure 2.3 shows that the volatility of the portfolio with portfolio share of 0.25 in XYZ and 0.75 in IBM increases directly with the correlation coefficient between XYZ and IBM. Equation (2.1), however, shows that the expected return of a portfolio does not depend on the covariances and variances of the securities that constitute the portfolio. Consequently, it follows from Figure 2.3 that if the return correlation coefficient is zero, the volatility of the investor's portfolio falls from 30 to 26 percent without a change in expected return as she invests 25 percent of her wealth in XYZ instead of all of it in IBM, making her unambiguously better off.

That John should want to invest in XYZ despite its high volatility is made clear in Figure 2.4. The graph represents all the combinations of expected return and volatility that can be obtained by investing in IBM and XYZ when the correlation is zero. Such a graph drawn for any correlation coefficient between IBM and XYZ would have a similar shape. The upward-sloping part of the curve drawn in Figure 2.4 is called the **efficient frontier**. The investor wants to choose portfolios on the efficient frontier because, for each volatility, there is a portfolio on the efficient frontier that has a higher expected return than any other portfolio with the same volatility.

By choosing portfolios on the efficient frontier instead of holding only shares of IBM, the investor benefits from diversification. Diversification is such a good risk management tool that sometimes it can eliminate risk completely. To see this,

Portfolio volatility and correlation

Figure 2.3

This figure shows the volatility of a portfolio with a portfolio share of 0.75 in IBM and 0.25 in XYZ when IBM has a volatility of 30 percent and XYZ has a volatility of 60 percent as a function of the correlation coefficient between IBM and XYZ.

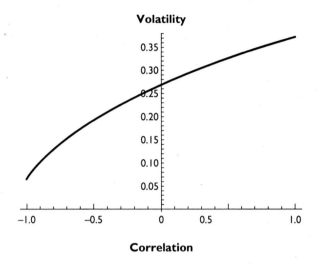

Efficient frontier without a riskless asset

Figure 2.4

The function represented in the figure gives all the combinations of expected return and volatility that can be obtained with investments in IBM and XYZ. The point where the volatility is the smallest has an expected return of 15.6 percent and a standard deviation of 26.83 percent. The upward-sloping part of the curve is the efficient frontier. The portfolio on the efficient frontier that has the same volatility as a portfolio wholly invested in IBM has an expected return of 18.2 percent.

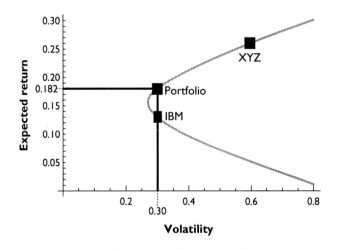

suppose that an investor can choose to invest among many uncorrelated securities that all have the same volatility and the same expected return as IBM: a volatility of 30 percent and an expected return of 13 percent. Dividing one's wealth among all these uncorrelated securities has no impact on the expected return, because all the securities have the same expected return. Using the formula for the variance of a portfolio, equation (2.7), however, we find that the volatility of the portfolio is:

$$\textbf{Volatility of portfolio} = \left[\sum_{i=1}^{N} (1/N)^2 (0.3)^2 \right]^{0.5} = \frac{0.3}{\sqrt{N}} \qquad \textbf{(2.9)}$$

Applying this result, we find that for $N = 10$, the volatility is 9 percent; for $N = 100$ it is 3 percent; and for $N = 1000$ it is less than 1 percent. As N is increased further, the volatility becomes infinitesimal.

In other words, by holding uncorrelated securities, one can eliminate portfolio volatility if one holds sufficiently many of these securities. Risk that disappears in a well-diversified portfolio is called **diversifiable risk**. In our example, all of the risk of each security becomes diversifiable as N increases.

In the real world, securities tend to be positively correlated because changes in aggregate economic activity affect most firms. News of the onset of a recession, for instance, is generally bad news for almost all firms. As a result, we cannot eliminate risk through diversification but we can reduce it. The risk that cannot be eliminated through diversification, the risk that remains, is often called **systematic risk**.

2.2.2. Asset allocation when there is a risk-free asset

So far, we have assumed that the investor forms the portfolio holding shares of two companies, IBM and XYZ. We now consider portfolio choice when there is also an asset that has no risk over the investment horizon of the investor. An example of such an asset is a Treasury bill (T-bill). T-bills are **zero-coupon bonds**. For zero-coupon bonds, the interest payment comes in the form of capital appreciation of the bond. Since T-bills have no default risk, they have a sure return if held to maturity. Box 2.2, Treasury bills, shows how they are quoted and how one can use a quote to obtain a yield.

John can decrease the volatility of year-end wealth by investing some fraction in risk-free bonds, perhaps half in risk-free bonds and the other half in the portfolio of risky assets with the lowest volatility. Assume that the bonds earn 5 percent over the year. This minimum-volatility portfolio of risky assets has an expected return of 15.6 percent and a standard deviation of 26.83 percent. With this asset allocation, John's portfolio would have a volatility of 13.42 percent and an expected return of 10.3 percent.

The efficient frontier in Figure 2.4 that was formed using only risky stocks is called the efficient frontier of risky assets. All combinations of the minimum-volatility portfolio and the risk-free asset lie on a straight line that intersects this efficient frontier of risky assets at the minimum-volatility portfolio. Figure 2.5 shows this straight line. Portfolios on the straight line to the left of the minimum-volatility portfolio have positive investments in the risk-free asset. In contrast,

Treasury bills   *Box* 2.2

T-bills are securities issued by the U.S. government that mature in one year or less. They pay no coupon, so that the investor's dollar return is the difference between the price paid on sale or at maturity and the price paid on purchase. Suppose that T-bills maturing in one year sell for $95 per $100 of face value. This means that the holding period return computed annually is 5.26 percent ($100 \times 5/95$) because each investment of $95 returns $5 of interest after one year.

T-bills are quoted on a bank discount basis. The price of a T-bill is quoted as a discount:

$$D_t(t + n/365) = (360/n)[100 - P_t(t + n/365)]$$

where $D_t(t + n/365)$ is the discount for a T-bill that matures in n days and $P_t(t + n/365)$ is the price of the same T-bill. The bank discount method uses 360 days for the year. Suppose that the price of a 90-day T-bill, $P_t(t + 90/365)$, is $98.5. In this case, the T-bill would be quoted at a discount of 6.00. From the discount rate, one can recover the price using the formula:

$$P_t(t + n/365) = 100 - (n/360)D_t(t + 365/n)$$

For our example, we have $100 - (90/360)6.00 = 98.5$.

Efficient frontier with a risk-free asset   *Figure* 2.5

The function giving the expected returns and volatilities of all combinations of holdings in IBM and XYZ is reproduced here. The risk-free asset has a return of 5 percent. By combining the risk-free asset and a portfolio on the frontier, the investor can obtain all the expected return and volatility combinations on the straight line that meets the frontier at the portfolio of risky assets chosen to form these combinations. The figure shows two such lines. The line with the steeper slope is tangent to the efficient frontier at portfolio m. The investor cannot form combinations of the risk-free asset and a risky portfolio that dominate combinations formed from the risk-free asset and portfolio m.

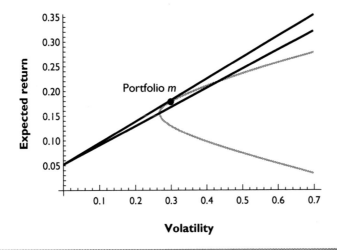

portfolios to the right of the minimum-volatility portfolio require borrowing in the risk-free asset. Figure 2.5 suggests that the investor could do better by combining the risk-free asset with a portfolio more to the right on the efficient frontier of risky assets than the minimum-volatility portfolio because all possible combinations would have a higher return. There is no way that the investor can do better than combining the risk-free asset with portfolio *m*, however, because in that case the straight line is tangent to the efficient frontier of risky assets at *m*. The portfolio *m* is therefore called the **tangency portfolio**. There is no straight line starting at the risk-free rate that touches the efficient frontier of risky assets at least at one point and that has a steeper slope than the line tangent to *m*.

Whenever investors face the same universe of securities and agree on the expected returns, volatilities, and covariances of securities, they end up looking at the same efficient frontier of risky assets and they all want to invest in portfolio *m*. This can be possible only if portfolio *m* is the market portfolio.

The **market portfolio** is the portfolio of all securities available. Security *i*'s portfolio share in the market portfolio is the ratio (market value of the outstanding supply of security *i*)/ (market value of the outstanding supply of all securities). The value of securities held by all investors together must be the market value of the outstanding supply of all securities. If a security's portfolio share in portfolio *m* were greater than that security's portfolio share in the market portfolio, investors would want to hold more of that security than its outstanding supply. This cannot be an equilibrium. As investors want to hold too much of a security, its expected return has to fall so that investors want to hold less of it. In equilibrium, the expected return of each security must be such that its outstanding supply and no more than its outstanding supply is held by investors.

If all investors have the same views on expected returns, volatilities, and covariances of securities, all of them hold the same portfolio of risky securities, portfolio *m*, the market portfolio. To achieve the right volatility for their invested wealth, they allocate their wealth to the market portfolio and to the risk-free asset. Investors who have little aversion to risk borrow to invest more than their wealth in the market portfolio. The most risk-averse investors put most or all of their wealth in the risk-free asset.

2.2.3. The risk of a security in a diversified portfolio

The extra expected return of a security (or of a portfolio) over the risk-free rate is called the **risk premium** of the security (or portfolio). The risk premium is the reward the investor expects to receive for bearing the risk associated with that security or portfolio. If R_m is the return of portfolio *m*, and R_F is the risk-free rate, $E(R_m) - R_F$ is the risk premium on the market portfolio.

For John to hold the market portfolio, the risk premium on any security has to be just sufficient. Any change in the portfolio's expected return resulting from a very small increase in the investor's holdings of the security must just compensate for the change in the portfolio's risk. If this is not the case, the investor will want to hold a different portfolio, and will no longer hold the market portfolio.

The variance of the return of the market portfolio is the return covariance of the market portfolio with itself. Denote by w_i^m the portfolio share or weight of security *i* in the market portfolio. Since the covariance of a sum of random variables with R_m is equal to the sum of the covariances of the random variables with R_m, it follows that $\text{Var}(R_m)$ is equal to a portfolio share weighted sum of the return covariances of the securities with the market portfolio return:

$$\text{Var}\!\left(R_m\right) = \text{Cov}\!\left(R_m, R_m\right) = \text{Cov}\!\left(\sum_{i=1}^{N} w_i^m R_i, R_m\right)$$

$$= \sum_{i=1}^{N} w_i^m \text{Cov}\!\left(R_i, R_m\right) \tag{2.10}$$

Equation (2.10) shows that a portfolio is risky to the extent that the returns of its securities covary with the return of the market portfolio. The part of the return of a security that covaries with the market portfolio is systematic risk that cannot be eliminated through diversification, since it is part of the risk of the market portfolio and the market portfolio has to be held. The part of the return of security i that does not covary with the market portfolio is diversified away when the investor holds the market portfolio—it is diversifiable risk that the investor does not know is there because it does not affect the volatility of the portfolio.

2.2.4. The capital asset pricing model

With our assumptions, investors care only about the systematic risk of securities and not about their diversifiable risk because the risk of the market portfolio depends only on the systematic risk of securities. Consequently, investors will require a risk premium to bear systematic risk but will not be compensated for bearing diversifiable risk because any investor can get rid of such risk costlessly. A security's systematic risk is proportional to the covariance of its return with the return of the market portfolio. In equation (2.10), if the return of security k has twice the covariance with the return of the market portfolio than the return of security q, it contributes twice to the variance of the market return as security q. Investors should therefore receive twice the reward for holding security k than for holding security q. Otherwise, they would not hold the market portfolio. To see this, suppose that q and k have the same risk premium. An investor could create a portfolio with the same return variance as the market portfolio but with a greater expected return by holding more of security q and less of security k than in the market portfolio.

The result that the risk premium on a security is proportional to its systematic risk is the key insight of the **capital asset pricing model (CAPM)**. The CAPM equation is:

$$E(R_i) - R_F = \beta_i\!\left[E(R_m) - R_F\right]$$

$$\beta_i = \frac{\text{Cov}\!\left(R_i, R_m\right)}{\text{Var}\!\left(R_m\right)} \tag{2.11}$$

The CAPM tells us that the expected excess return of a risky security is equal to the systematic risk of that security measured by its beta times the market's risk premium. A security's beta (β) is the covariance of the return of the security with the return of the market portfolio divided by the variance of the return of the market portfolio. With the CAPM, if the return of security k has a covariance with the market return that is twice the covariance with the market return of security q, it has twice the **beta** of security q and twice the risk premium. In equation (2.11), the covariance of the return of a security with the market return is divided by the variance of the market return so that a security that has the same systematic risk as the market earns the same risk premium as the market. The covariance of the return of that security with the return of the market is equal to the variance of the market, so that it has a beta of one.

The relation between expected return and beta that results from the CAPM is shown in Figure 2.6. The relation is called the **security market line**. Any portfolio for which the CAPM does not hold is one that investors will want to go long or short in. Consequently, the CAPM must apply to any portfolio. The beta of a portfolio is the portfolio share weighted average of the betas of the securities in the portfolio.

We can apply the CAPM to IBM. Suppose that the risk-free rate is 5 percent, the market risk premium is 6 percent, and the beta of IBM is 1.33. In this case, IBM's expected return is:

Expected return of IBM = 5% + 1.33[6%] = 13%

This is the expected return we used earlier for IBM. Box 2.3, The CAPM in practice, shows how we produce these numbers.

2.3. Diversification and risk management

Once we understand how an investor values a firm using the CAPM, we can find out when risk management increases firm value. For simplicity, let's start with a gold mining firm, Pure Gold Inc. Financial markets are assumed to be perfect as

---

Figure 2.6   The CAPM

The straight line titled the security market line gives the expected return of a security for a given beta. This line intersects the vertical axis at the risk-free rate and has a value equal to the expected return on the market portfolio for a beta of one.

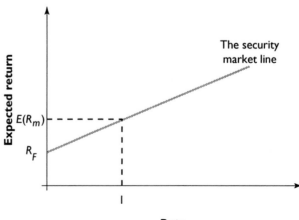

The CAPM in practice

Box 2.3

The CAPM provides a formula for the expected return on a security required by capital markets in equilibrium. To implement the CAPM to obtain the expected return on a security, we need to:

Step 1. Identify a proxy for the market portfolio.

Step 2. Identify the appropriate risk-free rate.

Step 3. Estimate the risk premium on the market portfolio.

Step 4. Estimate the beta of the security.

If we are trying to find the expected return of a security over the next month, the next year, or further in the future, all steps involve forecasts except for the first two steps. Using zero-coupon bonds of the appropriate maturity, we can always find the risk-free rate of return for the next month, the next year, or longer in the future, but we always have to forecast the risk premium on the market portfolio and the beta of the security.

What is the appropriate proxy for the market portfolio? Remember that the market portfolio represents how the wealth of investors is invested when the assumptions of the CAPM hold. We cannot observe the market portfolio directly, so we have to use a proxy for it. Most applications of the CAPM in the United States involve the use of some broad U. S. index, such as the S&P 500, as a proxy for the market portfolio. Estimates of the risk premium have decreased substantially over recent years. Some academics and practitioners argue that it should be 4 percent or even less. Using historical data, the estimate is much higher. We compromise with an estimate of 6 percent.

How do we get beta? Consider a security that has traded for a number of years. Suppose that the relation between the return of that security, $R_c(t)$, and the return of the proxy for the market portfolio, $R_m(t)$, is expected to be the same in the future as it was in the past. In this case, one can estimate beta over the past and apply it to the future. To estimate beta, we use linear regression and define a sample period. Five or six years of monthly returns are typical. Having defined the sample period, one estimates an equation over the sample period using regression analysis:

$$R_c(t) = c + bR_m(t) + e(t)$$

In this equation, $e(t)$ is residual risk. It has zero mean and is uncorrelated with the return on the market portfolio. Hence, it corresponds to unsystematic risk. The estimate for b will then be used as the beta of the stock.

Let's look at an example using data for IBM. We have monthly data from January 1992 through the end of September 1997, 69 observations in total. We use as the market portfolio the S&P 500 index. Using Excel, we can get the beta estimate for IBM using the regression program in data analysis under tools. We use the return of IBM in decimal form as the dependent or Y variable and the return on the S&P 500 as the independent or X variable. We

(continued)

Box 2.3 (continued)

use a constant in the regression. The Excel output is reproduced below. The estimates are:

Return on IBM = –0.00123 + 1.371152 (Return on S&P 500)

The standard error associated with the beta estimate is 0.333592. The difference between the beta estimate and the unknown true beta is a normally distributed random variable with zero mean. Using our knowledge about probabilities and the normal distribution, we can find that there is a 95 percent chance that the true beta of IBM is between 0.7053 and 2.037004.

The t-statistic is the ratio of the estimate to its standard error. It provides a test here of the hypothesis that the beta of IBM is different from zero. A t-statistic greater than 1.65 means that we can reject this hypothesis in that there is only a 10 percent chance or less that zero is in the confidence interval constructed around the estimate of beta. Here, the t-statistic is 4.110271. This means that zero is 4.110271 standard errors from 1.371152. The probability that the true beta would be that many standard errors below the mean is the p-value 0.00011.

As the standard error falls, the confidence interval around the coefficient estimates narrows. Consequently, we can make stronger statements about the true beta. The R-square coefficient of 0.201376 means that the return of the S&P 500 explains a fraction 0.201376 of the volatility of the IBM return. As this R-square increases, the independent variable explains more of the variation in the dependent variable.

As one adds independent variables in a regression, the R-square increases. The adjusted R-square takes this effect into account and hence is a more useful guide of the explanatory power of the independent variables when comparing regressions that have different numbers of independent variables.

Summary Output

Regression Statistics

Multiple R	0.44875
R Square	0.201376
Adjusted R-square	0.189457
Standard Error	0.076619
Observations	69

	Coefficients	Standard Error	t-Stat	P-value
Intercept	–0.00123	0.010118	–0.12157	0.903604
X Variable	1.371152	0.333592	4.110271	0.00011

before. The firm will produce one million ounces of gold this year, but after that it will no longer produce gold and it liquidates. For simplicity, the firm has no costs. At the end of the year, the firm has a cash flow of C corresponding to the market value of one million ounces of gold. The firm then pays that cash flow to equity as a liquidating dividend.

Viewed from today, the cash flow is random. The value of the firm today is the present value of receiving the cash flow in one year. We denote this value by V. If the firm is riskless, its value V is its cash flow discounted at the risk-free rate, $C/(1 + R_F)$. If the gold price is fixed at \$350 an ounce and the risk-free rate is 5 percent, the value of the firm is \$350 million/(1 + 0.05), or \$333.33 million.

Now suppose the cash flow is random because the gold price is random. In this case, the random liquidating cash flow C is the market value of the firm at the end of the year. The gain on holding the shares of the firm is therefore $C - V$, where V is the value of the firm at the beginning of the year. The return on shares is therefore $(C - V)/V$. Since C is equal to a quantity of gold times the gold price, the return is perfectly correlated with the gold price, so the firm must have the same beta as gold. Shareholders receive the cash flow in one year for an investment today equal to the value of the firm. This means that the cash flow is equal to the value of the firm times one plus the rate of return of the firm. We know that the expected return of the firm has to be given by the CAPM. Consequently, firm value must be such that:

$$E(C) = V\left(1 + R_F + \beta\left[E(R_m) - R_F\right]\right) \qquad (2.12)$$

If we know the distribution of the cash flow C, the risk-free rate R_F, the β of the firm's shares, and the risk premium on the market $E(R_m) - R_F$, we can compute V because it is the only variable in the equation that we do not know. Solving for V, we get:

$$\frac{E(C)}{1 + R_F + \beta\left[E(R_m) - R_F\right]} = V \qquad (2.13)$$

The value of the firm is therefore the expected cash flow discounted at the appropriate discount rate from the CAPM. Using this formula, we can value Pure Gold. Let's say that the expected gold price is \$350. In this case, the expected payoff to shareholders is \$350 million, which is one million ounces times the expected price of one ounce. As before, we use a risk-free rate of 5 percent and a risk premium on the market portfolio of 6 percent. We assume a beta of 0.5. Consequently:

$$\frac{E(C)}{1 + R_F + \beta\left[E(R_m) - R_F\right]} = \frac{\$350 \text{ million}}{1 + 0.05 + 0.5(0.06)} = \$324.074 \text{ million}$$
$$(2.14)$$

We can extend this approach to firms expected to remain in existence more than one year. The value is again the present value of the cash flows to shareholders. Nothing else affects the value of the firm for its shareholders—they care only about the present value of cash the firm generates over time for them. We can therefore value a firm's equity in general by computing the sum of the present values of all future cash flows to shareholders using the same approach we used to value one year's future cash flow. For a levered firm, we often consider the value of the firm to be the sum of debt and equity: the present value of the cash flows to the debt and equity holders.

Cash flow to shareholders is computed as net income plus depreciation and other noncash charges minus investment. To get cash flow to the debt and equity holders, one adds to cash flow to equity the payments made to debt holders. The cash flow to shareholders does not necessarily correspond each year to the payouts to equity because firms smooth dividends. A firm may have a positive cash flow to equity holders in excess of its planned dividend; it keeps the excess cash flow in liquid assets and pays it to shareholders later. All cash generated by the firm after debt payments belongs to the shareholders, however, and hence contributes to firm value whether it is paid out in a year or not.

2.3.1. Risk management and shareholder wealth

Would shareholders want a firm to spend cash to reduce the volatility of its cash flow when the only benefit of risk management is to decrease share return volatility? To answer this question, let's assume that the shareholders of the firm are investors who care only about the expected return and the volatility of their wealth invested in securities. These investors hold a diversified portfolio of risky assets, the market portfolio or a portfolio not too different from it, and choose the risk of their end-of-period wealth by allocating their wealth between the risk-free asset and their diversified portfolio of risky assets.

To reduce its volatility, a firm must reduce either its diversifiable risk or its systematic risk. We consider these two approaches to reducing volatility in turn. The firm can reduce risk either through financial transactions or through changes in its operations.

2.3.1.A. Financial risk management policy to reduce the firm's diversifiable risk Assume Markowitz Inc. has a market value of $1 billion and that its management can transfer the diversifiable risk of the firm's shares to an investment bank by paying $50 million. We can think of such a transaction as a hedge offered by the investment bank that exactly offsets the firm's diversifiable risk. Would shareholders ever want the firm to make such a payment when the only benefit to them is to eliminate the diversifiable risk of their shares? We already know that firm value does not depend on diversifiable risk when expected cash flow is given.

Consider then a risk management policy eliminating diversifiable risk that reduces expected cash flow by its cost, but has no other impact on expected cash flow. Since the value of the firm is the expected cash flow discounted at the rate determined by the systematic risk of the firm, this risk management policy does not affect the rate at which cash flow is discounted. In terms of our valuation equation, this policy reduces the numerator of the valuation equation without a change in the denominator, so that firm value is reduced.

Shareholders are diversified; they have no reason to care about diversifiable risks. Therefore, they are not willing to discount expected cash flow at a lower rate if the firm makes cash flow less risky by eliminating diversifiable risk. This means that if shareholders could vote on a proposal to implement risk management to decrease the firm's diversifiable risk at a cost, they would vote no and refuse to incur the cost as long as the only effect of risk management on expected cash flow is to reduce expected cash flow by the cost of risk management.

Managers, therefore, will never be rewarded by shareholders for decreasing the firm's diversifiable risk at a cost because shareholders can eliminate the firm's diversifiable risk through their own diversification at zero cost. For shareholders to value a reduction in diversifiable risk, it has to increase their wealth and hence the share price.

2.3.1.B. Financial risk management policy to reduce the firm's systematic risk

Is it worthwhile for management to incur costs to reduce the firm's systematic risk through financial transactions? Suppose IBM decides to reduce its beta because it believes this will make its shares more attractive to investors. It can easily do this by taking a short position in the market, since such a position has a negative beta. The proceeds of the short position can be invested in the risk-free asset.

In our discussion of IBM, we saw that the beta of IBM is 1.33. This means that a dollar invested in IBM has the same systematic risk as $1.33 invested in the market portfolio. Consequently, if IBM were an all-equity firm, the management of IBM could make IBM a zero-beta firm by selling short $1.33 of the market portfolio per dollar of shareholder equity and investing the proceeds in the risk-free asset.

Would investors be willing to pay for IBM management to do this? The answer is no because this action creates no value for the shareholders. In perfect financial markets, shareholders could eliminate the systematic risk of their IBM shares on their own by following the strategy we used when we showed why the CAPM must hold. They would not be willing to pay for the management of IBM to do something that they could do at zero cost on their own if they want to.

The reduction in systematic risk, however, decreases the denominator of the present value formula for shares, since it decreases the discount rate. Why is it that this does not increase the value of the shares? The reason is that reducing systematic risk has a cost, in that it reduces expected cash flow. To get rid of its systematic risk, IBM has to sell the market short. Selling the market short earns a negative risk premium since holding the market long has a positive risk premium. Hence, the expected cash flow of IBM has to fall by the risk premium of the short sale.

The impact of the short sale on firm value is therefore the sum of two effects. The first effect is the reduction in expected cash flow and the second is the drop in the discount rate. The two effects cancel out. Going short in the market is equivalent to getting perfect insurance against market fluctuations. In perfect markets, insurance is priced at its fair value. This means that the risk premium IBM would earn by not changing its systematic risk has to be paid to an entity that will now bear this systematic risk.

Hence, financial risk management in this case simply determines who bears the systematic risk—but IBM's shareholders charge the same price for market risk as anybody else, since that price is determined by the CAPM. Consequently, IBM management cannot create value by selling market risk to other investors at the price that shareholders would require to bear that risk.

2.3.1.C. Does using operations to reduce risk make a difference? What if the firm changes its systematic or its unsystematic risk by changing its operations? The same reasoning applies in this case also, but with a twist. Let's first look at unsystematic risk. Reducing unsystematic risk does not make shareholders better off if the only benefit of doing so is to reduce share return volatility. It does not matter, therefore, whether the decrease in share volatility is due to financial transactions or to operating changes. If the firm can change its operations costlessly to reduce its beta without changing its expected cash flow, however, firm value increases because expected cash flow is discounted at a lower rate. Hence, decreasing cash flow beta through operating changes is worth it if firm value increases as a result.

In financial markets, every investor charges the same for systematic risk. This means that nobody can make money from selling systematic risk to one group of investors instead of another. The ability to change an investment's beta through operating changes depends on technology and strategy. A firm can become more flexible so that it has lower fixed costs in cyclical downturns. This greater flexibility translates into a lower beta. If flexibility has low cost but a great impact on beta, the firm's shareholders are better off if the firm improves its flexibility. If greater flexibility has a high cost, though, shareholders will not want it because this will decrease share value.

2.3.2. Risk management and shareholder clienteles

One gold firm, Homestake, had for a long time a policy of not hedging at all. Homestake justified this policy in its 1990 annual report (p. 12):

> So that its shareholders might capture the full benefit of increases in the price of gold, Homestake does not hedge its gold production. As a result of this policy, Homestake's earnings are more volatile than those of many other gold producers. The Company believes that its shareholders will achieve maximum benefit from such a policy over the long-term.

The rationale for this policy is that some investors want to benefit from gold price movements, and that giving them this benefit increases firm value because they are willing to pay for it. These investors form a clientele the firm caters to. Our analysis so far has not accounted for the possible existence of clienteles such as investors wanting to bear gold price risks. In the world of the CAPM, investors care only about their portfolio's expected return and volatility, not about its sensitivity to other variables, such as gold prices.

The CAPM has limitations in explaining the returns of securities. Small firms, for instance, earn more on average than predicted by the CAPM. It is also possible that investors require a risk premium to bear some risks other than the CAPM's systematic risk; they might, for instance, want a risk premium to bear inflation risk. The presence of such risk premiums could explain why small firms earn more on average than the CAPM predicts.

It could be the case, then, that investors value gold price risk. To see the impact of additional risk premiums besides the market risk premium on our reasoning about the benefits of hedging, let's suppose that Homestake is right, and see what this implies for our analysis of the implications of hedging for the value of Pure Gold Inc., the gold mining firm we valued earlier.

Suppose first that Pure Gold Inc. hedges its gold price risk with a forward contract on gold. It produces one million ounces, so that it wants to sell one million ounces of gold forward. There is no uncertainty about Pure Gold's production, so that we can focus on its value per ounce of gold produced. The price of gold in one year is S and the current forward price is F.

Let's start by assuming there is no clientele effect to establish a benchmark. In this case, the CAPM applies. Empirically, gold has a beta close to zero, and we assume that the gold beta is actually zero. In this case, all the risk of Pure Gold is diversifiable. Let's verify that hedging does not affect firm value in this case. Pure Gold eliminates gold price risk by selling gold forward. The cash flow per ounce of gold to shareholders when the gold is sold forward is F, which is known today. Firm value today per ounce of gold produced is F discounted at the risk-free rate. If the firm does not hedge, the expected cash flow to shareholders per ounce is $E(S)$, which is known today also. In this case, firm value per ounce is obtained by discounting $E(S)$ at the risk-free rate since there is no systematic risk.

The difference between the hedged value of the firm and its unhedged value per ounce is $[F - E(S)]/(1 + R_F)$. The hedged firm is worth more than the unhedged firm if the forward price exceeds the expected spot price, which is true if $F - E(S)$ is positive. Remember that with a short forward position the firm receives F for delivering gold worth S per ounce. $F - E(S)$ is therefore equal to the expected payoff from selling one ounce of gold forward at the price F.

If this expected payoff is positive, an investor can expect to make a profit from entering a short forward position without using any of his resources, since no cash changes hands when a forward position is entered. In equilibrium, the only way the investor can expect to make money without investing any money is if the expected payoff is a reward for bearing risk. Yet we have assumed that the risk associated with the gold price is diversifiable, so that $F - S$ represents diversifiable risk. The expected value of $F - S$ has to be zero, since diversifiable risk does not earn a risk premium. Consequently, $F = E(S)$, and hedging does not affect the firm's value.

Suppose now the case where gold has a positive beta. By taking a long forward position in gold that pays $S - F$, an investor takes on systematic risk. The only way investors would enter such a position is if they are rewarded with a risk premium, which means that they expect to make money on the long forward position. Hence, if gold has systematic risk, it must be that $E(S) > F$, so that the expected payoff to shareholders is lower if the firm hedges than if it does not. However, since a forward contract must have zero value for both parties to be willing to enter the contract, the present value of receiving S in one year and paying F must be zero.

If the firm is hedged, the cash flow has no systematic risk, and the expected cash flow is discounted at the risk-free rate. If the firm is not hedged, the cash flow has systematic risk, so that the higher expected cash flow of the unhedged firm is discounted at a higher discount rate than the lower expected cash flow of the hedged firm. The lower discount rate used for the hedged firm just offsets the decrease in expected cash flow resulting from hedging, so that the present value of expected cash flow is the same whether the firm hedges or not.

We can extend this argument to the case where some investors value exposure to gold for its own sake—perhaps because they feel that it is a hedge against systemic threats. These investors are willing to pay for gold exposure, and as a result the risk premium attached to gold price risk is lower than predicted by the CAPM. Consequently, the forward price has to be higher than otherwise because investors require less compensation to bear gold price risk. If the firm does not hedge, its share price reflects the benefit from exposure to gold that the market values because its discount rate is lower. If the firm hedges, its shareholders are no longer exposed to gold. To hedge, however, the firm sells gold at a higher forward price than if no investors value exposure to gold for its own sake, so in this case the firm's expected cash flow is higher.

Shareholders can earn the premium for gold exposure either because the unhedged firm has a lower discount rate—because of its exposure to gold—or because the hedged firm sells gold forward at a higher price—it has a greater cash flow. The firm has a natural exposure to gold; it is just a matter of which investors bear it. By our reasoning, it does not matter whether the firm's shareholders themselves value gold exposure or not. If the firm's shareholders value gold exposure, they will get it one way or another, but gold exposure will always be priced so that the expected return of investors is not affected by where they get that exposure. If the firm gets rid of its gold exposure, the firm's shareholders can buy it on their own. If the firm's shareholders do not want the gold exposure, they can sell it on their own. No matter how investors who value gold exposure get this exposure, they will have to pay the same price for it, or otherwise the same good—gold exposure—would have different prices on the capital markets, making it possible for investors to profit from these price differences.

An important lesson of this analysis is that the value of the firm is the same whether the firm hedges or not, and however the forward price is determined. If hedging were to create value, there must be opportunities for riskless profits, called **arbitrage profits**, with our assumptions. Suppose that the value of the gold-producing firm is higher if it is hedged than if it is not. Let's assume that each share of the unhedged gold-producing firm pays the value of one ounce of gold. In this case, an investor can create a share of a hedged gold-producing firm on his own by buying a share of the unhedged firm and selling one ounce of gold forward at the price F to hedge. The investor's cash cost today is the price of a share since the forward position has no cash cost today. Having created a share of the hedged firm through **homemade hedging**, the investor can then sell the share hedged through homemade hedging at the price of the share of the hedged firm. There is no difference between the two shares, and hence they should sell for the same price. Through this transaction, the investor makes a profit equal to the difference between the share price of the hedged firm and the share price of the unhedged firm. This profit has no risk attached to it. Consequently, firm value must be the same whether the firm hedges or not with our assumptions.

Let's apply what we have learned to Homestake's clientele argument for not hedging. With perfect financial markets, anybody can get exposure to gold without Homestake's help by taking a long forward position. Whenever investors can do what the firm does on their own and at the same cost—in other words, whenever homemade hedging is possible—the firm cannot possibly create value through hedging. In 2001, Homestake was acquired by American Barrick. American Barrick historically had a policy of protecting itself fully against price declines that could affect its revenue from its anticipated production over the next three years. From American Barrick's perspective, this policy created value for its shareholders—but for reasons we will discuss in the next chapter.

We have shown that Homestake's hedging policy cannot benefit its shareholders even if there is a clientele of investors who value exposure to gold, but we did not address the plausibility of Homestake's claim that investors who value exposure to gold would want to obtain this exposure by buying Homestake shares. That claim has to be questioned. Suppose you are an investor who wants to benefit from increases in the gold price over the coming year. You face the following choice: You can obtain gold exposure by buying Homestake shares and holding them for one year or you can buy a financial security, a gold-indexed zero-coupon bond, that pays you the dollar value of 100 ounces of gold in one year. The gold-indexed zero-coupon bond would be a much better way to obtain gold exposure than Homestake shares. The reason is that the price of Homestake shares might fall over the year even though the gold price increased—a mine could flood, for instance. Hence, using Homestake shares to bet on an increase in the gold price might fail. Provided that the default risk of the gold-indexed zero-coupon bond is trivial, betting on the gold price increase by buying the gold-indexed zero-coupon bond would always be successful if the gold price increases. Gold-indexed bonds can be purchased and there are other securities you could buy that have a payoff indexed to the gold price.

2.3.3. The risk management irrelevance proposition

The major lesson is that a firm cannot create value by hedging risks when it costs the same for the firm to bear these risks directly than to pay the capital markets to bear them. For our purposes in this chapter, the only cost of bearing risks within the firm is the risk premium the capital markets attach to these risks when they value the firm. The same risk premium is required by the capital markets for bearing these risks outside the firm. Consequently, shareholders can alter the firm's risk on their own through homemade hedging at the same terms as the firm, and the firm has nothing to contribute to the shareholders' welfare through risk management. Let's confirm that this is the case by looking at the types of risk the firm faces:

1. **Diversifiable risk.** Diversifiable risk does not affect the share price, and investors do not care about it because it gets diversified within their own portfolios. Hence, eliminating it does not affect firm value.

2. **Systematic risk.** Shareholders require the same risk premium for systematic risk as all investors. Hence, eliminating it for the shareholder just means that the investors who take it on bear it at the same cost. Again, this cannot create value.

3. **Risks valued by investors differently from what the CAPM would predict.** Again, shareholders and other investors charge the same price for bearing such risks.

The bottom line can be summarized in the **hedging irrelevance proposition**: Hedging a risk does not increase firm value when the cost of bearing the risk is the same whether the risk is borne within the firm or outside the firm by the capital markets.

2.4. Summary

In this chapter, we first examined how investors evaluate the risk of securities. We saw how we can use a distribution function to evaluate the probability of various outcomes for the return of a security. The ability to specify the probability that a security will experience a return lower than some pre-specified benchmark will be of crucial importance throughout this book. We then saw how investors can diversify, and that the ability to diversify affects how an investor evaluates the riskiness of a security. A security's contribution to the risk of the market portfolio is its systematic risk; its diversifiable risk does not affect the riskiness of the portfolio. This fundamental result allowed us to present the capital asset pricing model, which states that a security's risk premium is given by its beta times the risk premium on the market portfolio. The CAPM allows us to compute the value of future cash flows. We saw that only the systematic risk of cash flows affects the rate at which investors discount expected future cash flows.

We then showed that, in perfect financial markets, hedging does not affect firm value, whether hedging systematic or unsystematic risks through financial instruments. Further, we demonstrated that even if investors have preferences for some types of risks, like gold price risks, hedging is still irrelevant in perfect financial markets. If it costs the same for a firm to bear a risk as it does for the firm to pay somebody else to bear it, hedging cannot increase firm value.

Key Concepts

arbitrage profits, 44

asset allocation, 32

beta, 36

capital asset pricing model (CAPM), 35

covariance, 28

cumulative distribution function, 24

diversifiable risk, 32

diversification, 22

efficient frontier, 30

expected return, 23

expected value, 23

hedging irrelevance proposition, 45

homemade hedging, 44

market portfolio, 34

normal distribution, 23

perfect financial markets, 23

portfolio share, 27

probability density function, 26

return probability distribution, 23

risk premium, 34

security market line, 36

short sale, 27

standard deviation, 23

systematic risk, 32

tangency portfolio, 34

variance, 23

volatility, 24

zero-coupon bonds, 32

Review Questions

1. Assume a stock return follows the normal distribution. What do you need to know to compute the probability that the stock's return will be less than 10 percent during the coming year?

2. What does the variance of the return of a portfolio depend on?

3. What does diversification of a portfolio do to the distribution of the portfolio's return?

4. What is beta?

5. When does beta measure risk?

6. For a given expected cash flow, how does the beta of the cash flow affect its current value?

7. How does hedging affect firm value if financial markets are perfect?

8. Why can hedging affect a firm's expected cash flow when it does not affect its value?

9. Why does the fact that some investors have a preference for gold exposure have no bearing on whether firms should hedge gold exposure?

10. What is the risk management irrelevance proposition?

Questions and Exercises

1. The typical level of the monthly volatility of the S&P 500 index is about 4 percent. Using a risk premium of 6 percent and a risk-free rate of 5 percent per year, what is the probability that a portfolio of $100,000 invested in the S&P 500 will lose $5,000 or more during the next month? How would your answer change if you used current interest rates from T-bills?

2. During 1997, the monthly volatility on the S&P 500 increased to about 4.5 percent from its typical value of 4.0 percent. Using the current risk-free rate, construct a portfolio worth $100,000 invested in the S&P 500 and the risk-free asset that has the same probability of losing $5,000 or more in a month when the S&P 500 volatility is 4.5 percent as a portfolio of $100,000 invested in the S&P 500 when its volatility is 4 percent.

3. Compute the expected return and the volatility of return of a portfolio that has a portfolio share of 0.9 in the S&P 500 and 0.1 in an emerging market index. The S&P 500 has a volatility of return of 15 percent and an expected return of 12 percent. The emerging market has a return volatility of 30 percent and an expected return of 10 percent. The correlation between the emerging market index return and the S&P 500 is 0.1.

4. If the S&P 500 is a good proxy for the market portfolio in the CAPM, and the CAPM applies to the emerging market index, use the information in question 3 to compute the beta and risk premium for the emerging market index.

5. Compute the beta of the portfolio described in question 4 with respect to the S&P 500.

6. A firm has an expected cash flow of $500 million in one year. The beta of the common stock of the firm is 0.8 and this cash flow has the same risk as the firm as a whole. Using a risk-free rate of 5 percent and a risk premium on the market portfolio of 6 percent, what is the present value of the cash

flow? If the beta of the firm doubles, what happens to the present value of the cash flow?

7. Using the data in the previous question, consider the impact on the firm of hedging the cash flow against systematic risk. If management wants to eliminate the systematic risk of the cash flow completely, how could it do so? How much would the firm have to pay investors to bear the systematic risk of the cash flow?

8. Consider the situation you analyzed in question 6. To hedge the firm's systematic risk, management has to pay investors to bear this risk. Why is it that the value of the firm for shareholders does not fall when the firm pays other investors to bear the cash flow's systematic risk?

9. The management of a gold-producing firm agrees with the hedging irrelevance result and has concluded that it applies to the firm. However, the CEO wants to hedge because the price of gold has fallen over the last month. He asks for your advice. What do you tell him?

10. Consider again an investment in the emerging market portfolio of question 3. You consider investing $100,000 in that portfolio because you think it is a good investment. You decide that you are going to ignore the benefits from diversification, in that all your wealth will be invested in that portfolio. Your broker nevertheless presents you with an investment in a default-free bond in the currency of the emerging country, which matures in one year. The expected return on the foreign currency bond is 5 percent in dollars, its volatility is 10 percent, and the correlation of its return with the dollar return of the emerging market portfolio is 1. Compute the expected return of a portfolio with $100,000 in the emerging market portfolio, −$50,000 in the foreign currency bond, and $50,000 in the domestic risk-free asset that earns 5 percent per year. How does this portfolio differ from the portfolio that has only an investment in the emerging market portfolio? Which one would you choose and why? Could you create a portfolio with investments in the emerging market portfolio, in the emerging market currency risk-free bond, and in the risk-free asset that has the same mean return but a lower volatility?

Literature Note

Much research examines the appropriateness of the assumption of the normal distribution for security returns. Fama (1965) argues that monthly stock returns are well-described by the normal distribution and that these returns are independent across time. We will see later that, while the normal distribution is a good starting point, it is sometimes necessary to make different distributional assumptions.

The fundamental research on diversification and the CAPM is mainly the work, respectively, of Markowitz (1952) and Sharpe (1964), who were awarded a share of the Nobel Memorial Prize in Economics in 1990. Textbooks on investments cover this material in much greater detail. Elton, Gruber, Brown, and Goetzmann (2002) provide an extensive presentation of portfolio theory. Valuation theory using the CAPM is discussed in corporate finance textbooks or in textbooks specialized in valuation. For corporate finance textbooks, see Brealey and Myers (2002) or Jordan, Ross, and Westerfield (2002). A book devoted to valuation is Copeland, Koller, and Murrin (1996).

The hedging irrelevance result is discussed in Smith and Stulz (1985). This result is a natural extension of the leverage irrelevance result of Modigliani and Miller (1958). Modigliani and Miller (1958) argue that in perfect markets leverage cannot increase firm value. Their result led to the award of a Nobel Memorial Prize in Economics in 1990 for Miller. Modigliani received such a Prize earlier for a different contribution.

Chapter 3
Creating Value with Risk Management

Chapter **3** Objectives

At the end of this chapter, you will:

1. Understand when risk management creates value for firms.

2. Know which types of risks a corporation should hedge to create value.

3. Be able to evaluate how much value risk management can create in a corporation.

Mr. Smith is the CFO of Software Inc. He has worked hard to keep up with new developments in finance. He recently attended an advanced executive development program where much time was spent discussing the Modigliani and Miller propositions. Understanding that shareholders can hedge on their own account, he has paid scant attention to risk management. However, looking at his firm's situation, he discovers that it will not be able to make use of a valuable tax shield arising from past losses because exchange rate losses have unexpectedly reduced his firm's net income. The tax shield will be gone forever after this year. Yet, had the firm been profitable this year, the tax shield would have allowed the corporation to reduce its tax bill by $50 million. He realizes that if he had been able to hedge his income against exchange rate fluctuations, Software Inc. would have been richer by $50 million. Instead, because he had not hedged, $50 million of shareholder wealth walked out the door. In this chapter, we show that there are many reasons to hedge.

A risk management program cannot increase firm value when it costs the same to bear a risk within the firm or outside the firm. We established this result, called *the risk management irrelevance proposition*, in Chapter 2. The irrelevance proposition holds when financial markets are perfect. If the proposition holds, any risk management program that a firm puts in place can be replicated by any investor through "homemade" risk management. The risk management irrelevance proposition is useful because it allows us to find out when homemade risk management is not equivalent to risk management by the firm. This is the case whenever risk management by a firm affects firm value in a way that investors cannot mimic. In this chapter, we identify situations where there is a wedge between the cost of bearing a risk within the firm and the cost of bearing it outside the firm. Such a wedge requires the presence of financial markets imperfections (perfect markets have no frictions—no transactions costs, no taxes, perfect competition, no costs of writing contracts).

Chapter 2 uses the example of a gold-producing firm. We continue that example here. Pure Gold Inc. is exposed to gold price risk. It can bear that risk within the firm. This means the firm has lower income if the price of gold is unexpectedly low and higher income if it is unexpectedly high. If the irrelevance proposition holds, the only cost of bearing this risk within the firm is that shares are worth less if gold price risk is systematic risk, because in this case shareholders require a risk premium to compensate them for gold price risk. Similarly, the only cost to the firm of having gold price risk borne outside the firm is that the firm has to pay a risk premium to induce the capital markets to take that risk. The risk premium the capital markets require is the same the shareholders require. Consequently, it makes no difference for firm value whether the gold price risk is borne by shareholders or by the capital markets, which is what the risk management irrelevance proposition states.

For risk management to increase firm value, it must be more expensive to take a risk within the firm than to pay the capital markets to take it. For Pure Gold, risk management creates value if an unexpectedly low gold price entails costs for the firm that it would not have for the capital markets. Suppose that with an unexpectedly low gold price, the firm does not have funds to invest, and hence has to give up valuable projects because it would be expensive for the current shareholders to raise funds in the capital markets with such a low gold price. Thus, shareholders not only lose income now with unexpected low gold prices, but they also lose future income because the firm cannot take advantage of investment opportunities. Pure Gold bears an extra, indirect, cost or burden from the low gold prices. Indirect costs resulting from financial losses are called **deadweight costs**.

To understand deadweight costs, suppose you asked yourself how Pure Gold could be put back in the situation it would have been in had gold prices not been low. If all it takes is to make up the loss Pure Gold experienced on its sales of gold, then there are no deadweight costs—no additional losses caused by the low gold prices. However, if, in addition, Pure Gold has to be compensated for profits it did not earn because of investments it could not make, there are deadweight costs.

The reason risk management creates value for Pure Gold if there are deadweight costs associated with gold price risk is that risk management reduces or eliminates deadweight costs. If the gold price risk is borne by the capital markets, Pure Gold does not incur additional costs resulting from low gold prices since it makes no losses from low gold prices. In this case, the cost of putting the gold price risk off on the capital markets is less than the cost the firm will pay if it bears the risk within the firm and sacrifices future opportunities by not being able to invest when the gold price is low.

In this chapter, we investigate how a firm can use risk management to increase firm value. We discuss the reasons why a firm might find it more expensive to bear a risk within the firm than pay the capital markets to bear that risk. We thus show the sources of the benefits of risk management.

In the previous chapter, we gave the example of Homestake as a gold mining firm that had a policy of not hedging its gold price exposure. As you saw, management based its policy on the belief that Homestake's shareholders value gold price exposure. We showed that this belief is wrong because investors can get gold price exposure without Homestake on terms at least as good as those that Homestake offers, and most likely better. So, is Hometake's value lower than it would have been with hedging? Throughout this chapter, for each source of value of hedging we document, we investigate whether this source of value applies to Homestake.

In the next chapter, we integrate these various sources of gain from risk management to build an integrated risk management strategy.

3.1. Bankruptcy costs and costs of financial distress

In our analysis of the value of risk management in Chapter 2, we take the distribution of Pure Gold's cash flow before hedging (the cash flow from operations) as a given. We assume that it sells one million ounces of gold at the end of the year and then liquidates. Pure Gold has no debt. The gold price is assumed to be normally distributed with a mean of $350 per ounce. There are no operating costs for simplicity. All the cash flow accrues to the firm's shareholders. This situation is represented by the straight line in Figure 3.1, where cash flow to

Figure 3.1   Cash flow to shareholders and operating cash flow

The firm sells one million ounces of gold at the end of the year and liquidates. There are no costs. The expected gold price is $350.

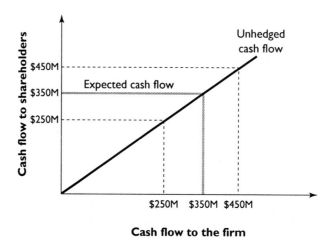

Pure Gold is on the horizontal axis and cash flow to the holders of financial claims against it is on the vertical axis. In this case, the only claimholders are the shareholders. In perfect financial markets, all cash flows to the firm accrue to the firm's claimholders, so there is no gain from risk management.

At the end of the year, Pure Gold distributes the cash flow to its owners, the shareholders, and liquidates. If the firm hedges by selling its production at the forward price, the shareholders get the proceeds from selling the firm's gold production at the forward price. Suppose the forward price is $350. If the gold price turns out to be $450, for example, the hedged firm receives $350 per ounce by delivering on the forward contract, while the unhedged firm would receive $450 per ounce.

The shareholders, however, can obtain for themselves the payoff of the unhedged firm when the firm is hedged and vice versa. This is shown in Figure 3.2. An investor who owns the hedged firm and takes a long forward position on personal account receives $350 per ounce of gold from the hedged firm plus ($450 − $350) per ounce from the forward contract, for a total payoff of $450 per ounce, which is the payoff per ounce for the unhedged firm. Hence, even though the firm is hedged, investors can create for themselves the payoff of the unhedged firm.

Now, suppose Pure Gold has some debt. We still assume that markets are perfect, that the distribution of the cash flow from operations is given, and that there are no taxes. At the end of the year, the cash flow to the firm is used first to pay off the debtholders, and then shareholders receive what is left over. The firm's claimholders still receive all of the firm's cash flow, and the firm's cash flow is not changed by leverage, but there are now two groups of claimholders, debtholders

Creating the unhedged firm out of the hedged firm   *Figure 3.2*

The firm produces one million ounces of gold. It can hedge by selling one million ounces of gold forward. The expected gold price and the forward price are $350 per ounce. If the firm hedges and shareholders do not want the firm to hedge, they can recreate the unhedged firm by taking a long position forward in one million ounces of gold.

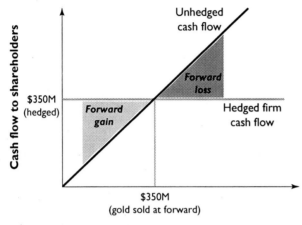

and shareholders. Leverage does not affect firm value. It simply specifies how the pie—the firm's operating cash flow—is divided among its claimants—the debtholders and the shareholders. Since the cash flow to claimholders is the firm's entire cash flow, risk management does not affect firm value.

In the real world, it is costly for firms to file for bankruptcy and renegotiate debt. Firms have to hire lawyers, incur court costs, and need to pay for all sorts of financial advice. Costs incurred as a result of a bankruptcy filing are called **bankruptcy costs**. The present value of future bankruptcy costs reduces the value of a firm that has debt relative to one that does not. While there are benefits to leverage, for the time being we ignore them. As shown in Figure 3.3, these bankruptcy costs create a "wedge" between cash flow to the firm and cash flow to the firm's claimholders. This wedge corresponds to the bankruptcy costs incurred by the owners.

The extent to which bankruptcy costs affect firm value depends on their extent and on the probability that the firm will have to file for bankruptcy. The probability that a firm will be bankrupt is the probability that it will not have enough cash flow to repay the debt. We know how to compute this probability for a normally distributed cash flow. Figure 3.4 shows how the distribution of cash flow from operations affects the probability of bankruptcy. If Pure Gold hedges its risk completely, it reduces its cash flow volatility to zero because the claimholders receive the present value of gold sold at the forward price. In this case, the probability of bankruptcy is zero and the present value of bankruptcy costs is also zero. As cash flow volatility increases, the present value of bankruptcy costs increases because bankruptcy becomes more likely. This means that the present value of cash flow to Pure Gold's claimholders falls as cash flow volatility increases.

Figure 3.3   Cash flow to claimholders and bankruptcy costs

The firm sells one million ounces of gold at the end of the year and liquidates. There are no transactions costs. The expected gold price is $350. Bankruptcy costs are $20 million if cash flow to the firm is $250 million. Suppose that the firm can have a cash flow of $250 million with probability p or a cash flow of $450 million with probability $1 - p$. Expected cash flow of the unhedged firm is given by the equation $p \times \$230M + (1 - p) \times \$450M$ and is plotted by the dotted line. The case where the forward price of gold is $350 and equal to expected gold price corresponds to $p = 0.5$. With this case, expected cash flow of the hedged firm is $350 million and expected cash flow of the unhedged firm is $340 million.

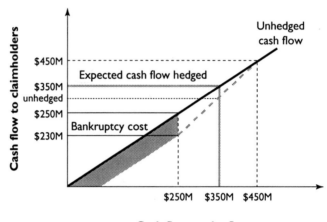

Therefore, by hedging, Pure Gold increases its value; that is, it does not have to pay bankruptcy costs, and hence its claimholders get all of the firm's cash flow. In this case, homemade risk management by the firm's claimholders is not a substitute for the firm's risk management. If the firm does not reduce its risk, its value

Figure 3.4   Expected bankruptcy costs as a function of volatility

The firm produces one million ounces of gold and then liquidates. It is bankrupt if the price of gold is below $250 per ounce. The bankruptcy costs are $20 per ounce. The gold price is distributed normally with expected value of $350. The volatility is in dollars per ounce.

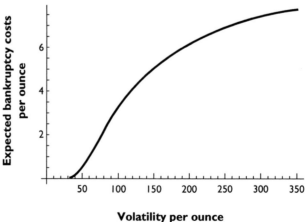

is lower by the present value of bankruptcy costs. Homemade risk management can do nothing about this deadweight cost of low gold prices.

3.1.1. Bankruptcy costs and firm value

We can use the present value equation to show that risk management increases firm value when the only financial market imperfection is the presence of bankruptcy costs that affect firm value. We therefore assume that markets are perfect for hedging instruments traded in capital markets, so that hedging involves no transaction costs. Remember that in the absence of bankruptcy costs, the firm's claimholders receive the cash flow at the end of the year when the firm is liquidated. Under our new assumptions, the claimholders receive the cash flow only if the firm is not bankrupt. Denote this cash flow by C. If the firm is bankrupt, the claimholders receive C minus the bankruptcy costs. Consequently, the value of the firm is now:

Value of firm = PV(C – Bankruptcy costs)

We know from Chapter 2 that the present value of a sum of cash flows is the sum of the present values of the cash flows. Consequently, the value of the firm is equal to:

Value of firm   =   PV(C)   –   PV (Bankruptcy costs)

= Value of firm without bankruptcy costs

– Present value of bankruptcy costs

Let's now consider the impact of risk management on firm value. If the hedge eliminates all risk, then the firm does not incur the bankruptcy costs. Hence, the cash flow to the firm's owner is what the cash flow would be in the absence of bankruptcy costs, which is C. This means that with such a hedge the claimholders get the present value of C rather than the present value of C minus the present value of bankruptcy costs. Assuming that no market imperfections affect the cost of hedging instruments, the gain from risk management is:

Gain from risk management   =   Value of firm hedged

– Value of firm unhedged

= PV (Bankruptcy costs)

A simple example of the benefit of hedging is as follows. We assume that the interest rate is 5 percent and that gold price risk is unsystematic risk. The forward price is $350. Because gold price risk is unsystematic risk, the forward price is equal to the expected gold price (from the analysis in Chapter 2). As before, Pure Gold produces one million ounces of gold. Consequently, $PV(C)$ is equal to $350M/1.05, or $333.33 million. The present value of the hedged firm is the same (this is because expected cash flow, $E(C)$, is equal to one million times the expected gold price, which is the forward price).

To get the present value of the bankruptcy costs, we must specify the debt payment and the distribution of the cash flow. Let's say that the bankruptcy costs are $20 million, the face value of debt is $250 million, the gold price is normally distributed, and its volatility is 20 percent. The firm is bankrupt if the gold price falls below $250. The probability that the gold price will fall below $250 is 0.077 using the approach developed in Chapter 2. Consequently, the expected bankruptcy costs are $0.077 \times \$20M$, or $1.54 million. By the use of risk management, Pure Gold ensures that it is never bankrupt, thus increasing its value by the present value of $1.54M. Since gold price risk is assumed to be unsystematic risk, we discount the expected bankruptcy costs at the risk-free rate of 5 percent to get a present value of bankruptcy costs of $1.47 million ($1.54M/1.05).

In the presence of bankruptcy costs, the risk management irrelevance theorem no longer holds. The cost to Pure Gold of bearing gold price risk is $1.47 million. Because we assume that gold price risk is diversifiable, the cost of having the capital markets bear this risk is zero. The capital markets therefore have a comparative advantage over the firm in bearing gold price risk.

Note that if gold price risk is systematic risk, capital markets will charge a risk premium for bearing the gold price risk—the same risk premium that shareholders charge in the absence of bankruptcy costs. Hence, the capital markets still have a comparative advantage for bearing risk; it is measured by the bankruptcy costs saved by having the capital markets bear the risk. There is nothing that shareholders can do on their own to avoid the impact of bankruptcy costs on Pure Gold's value, so homemade risk management cannot eliminate these costs.

3.1.2. Bankruptcy costs, financial distress costs, and the costs of risk management programs

A study of bankruptcy for 31 firms over the period from 1980 to 1986 by Weiss (1990) finds an average ratio of direct bankruptcy costs to total assets of 2.8 percent, with a high of 7 percent. Other researchers find similar estimates. Bankruptcy also entails large indirect costs. Managers spend much of their time dealing with the firm's bankruptcy proceedings instead of managing operations. Managers of a firm in bankruptcy lose control of some decisions. They might not be allowed to undertake costly new projects, for example.

Many of these indirect costs start accruing as soon as a firm's financial situation becomes unhealthy. The costs firms incur because of a poor financial situation are called **costs of financial distress**. Costs of financial distress can occur even if the firm never files for bankruptcy or never defaults. Managers have to think about finding ways to conserve cash to pay off debtholders. They might cut investment, which means the loss of future profits. Potential customers may become reluctant to deal with the firm, leading to losses in sales.

Our analysis of the benefits of risk management in reducing bankruptcy costs holds for all costs of financial distress also. Any time costs of financial distress divert cash flow away from the firm's claimholders, they reduce firm value. Reducing firm risk by minimizing the present value of costs of financial distress naturally increases firm value.

Reducing the costs of financial distress is one of the most important benefits of risk management. Consequently, we study in more detail how risk management can be used to reduce specific costs of financial distress in later sections in this chapter.

In the example, Pure Gold eliminates all of its bankruptcy costs through risk management. If managers identify other costs of financial distress that occur when the firm's cash flow is low, they could eliminate them as well through risk management. Some risks, however, are too expensive to reduce through risk management. In the absence of risk management costs, though, we would always eliminate all bankruptcy and financial distress risks.

There are transaction costs of taking positions in forward contracts. The transaction costs of risk management increase the cost of paying the capital markets to take the risk. As transaction costs increase, risk management becomes less attractive. If the firm bears a risk internally, it does not pay these transaction costs.

3.1.3. Bankruptcy costs, Homestake, and Enron

At the end of the 1990 fiscal year, Homestake had cash balances of more than $300 million. Its long-term debt was $72 million, and it had unused credit lines amounting to $245 million. Homestake could have repaid all its long-term debt and still have had large cash balances. Bankruptcy was not likely. Suppose it had more long-term debt, though. Would bankruptcy and financial distress costs then be a serious issue?

Homestake's assets are its mines and its mining equipment. These assets do not lose value if Homestake defaults on its debt. If it makes sense to operate the mines, the mines will be operated, whoever owns them. Neither bankruptcy costs nor financial distress costs in this case provide an important reason for Homestake to practice risk management. Homestake is an example of a firm for which the reduction of financial distress costs is not an important benefit of risk management.

For many financial institutions, the mere appearance of some possibility of financial distress is enough to threaten the firm. In a bank, concerns of financial distress could prompt a run on the bank.

An example of how financial distress can lead to disaster is that of Enron. Enron was the seventh largest firm in the United States. It had a large and profitable online trading business—it traded energy, broadband, credit risks, and other goods. When its management lost credibility and its debt was downgraded from investment grade in November 2001, this started a sequence of events that led Enron to file for bankruptcy within weeks because financial distress removed the underpinnings of its trading business. Who wants to trade with an entity that has a significant probability of default?

3.2. Taxes and risk management

Risk management creates value when it is more expensive to take a risk within the firm than to pay the capital markets to bear that risk. Corporate taxes are a good example. These taxes can increase the cost of taking risks within the firm.

We all accept that if a dollar of taxes has to be paid, paying it later is better than paying it sooner. While derivatives are sometimes used to create strategies that move income to later years, for now we focus on how managing risk, as opposed to timing income, can reduce the present value of taxes.

To understand the argument, it is useful to think about one important tax planning practice. If you know that in some future year your tax rate will be lower, you should try to recognize income in that year rather than today or in years your tax rate is higher. Pension plans are the prime example. If you can defer taxation on current income through a pension plan, you do so assuming that your retirement years' tax rate will be lower than the tax rate in your high-earning years.

Risk management, rather than altering in which tax year income is recognized, aims to alter the risks one takes to decrease expected tax payments in a given year. Suppose there are some outcomes—often called states of the world in finance—where this year's income is high and taxed at a high rate, and other outcomes where it is low and taxed at a low rate. For instance, if gold prices are high, gold companies have high income and a high tax rate. If we can rearrange the risks we take so that we have less income when the tax rate is high and more income when the tax rate is low, the present value of taxes paid is reduced.

Let's consider Pure Gold again. A firm generally pays taxes only if its revenue exceeds some level. Let's assume that Pure Gold pays taxes at the rate of 50 percent on the cash flow in excess of $300 million and does not pay taxes if its cash flow is below $300 million. For simplicity, we assume in this section that it is an all-equity firm, so there are no bankruptcy costs.

Figure 3.5 graphs Pure Gold's after-tax cash flow as a function of the pretax cash flow. We see a difference between the firm's operating cash flow and what its shareholders receive, and this is due to taxes. Now, assume further that there is a 50 percent chance the gold price will be $250 per ounce and a 50 percent chance it will be $450, so the expected gold price is $350. Assuming that gold price risk is unsystematic risk, the forward price for gold is the expected gold price of $350. As before, the interest rate is 5 percent.

In the absence of taxes, the value of Pure Gold is the present value of the expected cash flow, $350 million discounted at 5 percent, or $333.33 million.

Figure 3.5   Taxes and cash flow to shareholders

The firm pays taxes at the rate of 50 percent on cash flow in excess of $300 per ounce. For simplicity, the price of gold is either $250 or $450 with equal probability. The forward price is $350.

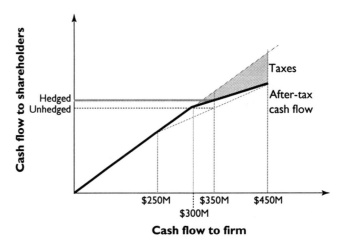

With taxes, the present value of the firm for its shareholders is reduced, because the firm pays taxes when the gold price is $450. In this case, the firm pays taxes of 0.5($450 − $300)1M, or $75 million. With taxes, the value of the firm's equity is:

Value of firm with taxes = *PV* (Gold sales − Taxes)

= *PV* (Gold sales) − *PV* (Taxes)

= *PV* (Firm without taxes) − *PV* (Taxes)

= $333.33M − 0.5 × $75M/1.05

= $333.33M − $35.71M

= $297.62M

Let's figure what it costs shareholders to have the firm bear gold price risk compared to having the firm lay off the gold price risk by selling gold forward. To do this, we have to compare firm value if gold is sold on the spot market after it is produced with firm value if gold is sold at the forward price. Remember that the gold price can be either $250 or $450. If the gold price is $250, the shareholders get $250 per ounce. If the gold price is $450, they get $375 per ounce ($450 minus taxes at the rate of 50 percent on $150). The expected cash flow to the shareholders is therefore (0.5 × $250) + (0.5 × $375), or $312.5 per ounce. Since the expected cash flow would be $350 absent taxes, expected taxes are $37.5 per ounce. If the gold price is fixed at the forward price instead, so that cash flow is not volatile, shareholders receive $325 per ounce once they pay taxes at the rate of 50 percent on $50. In this case, expected taxes are $25 per ounce. Taking present values, the equity value is $309.52 per ounce if gold is sold at the forward price and $297.62 if gold is sold at the spot market price. Hence, it costs the shareholders $11.90 per ounce for having the firm bear the gold price risk, or $11.90 million for the firm as a whole.

The reason the firm saves taxes through risk management is straightforward. If the firm's income is low, the firm pays no taxes. If the firm's income is high, it pays taxes. If Pure Gold shifts a dollar from when income is high to when income is low, it saves the taxes it would pay on that dollar when the income is high. In our example, shifting income of a dollar from when income is high to when income is low saves $0.50 with probability 0.5.

Homemade risk management cannot work in this case. If the firm does not use risk management to eliminate its cash flow volatility, its expected taxes are higher by $12.5 million. This is money that leaves the firm and does not accrue to shareholders. Through homemade risk management, shareholders can eliminate the volatility in the share price resulting from gold price volatility, but they cannot affect the taxes the firm pays, so that the tax saving from risk management at the firm level cannot be obtained by shareholders through homemade risk management.

Let's figure out how shareholders would practice homemade risk management. Shareholders receive $375 per share or $250 per share from the firm with equal probability. To eliminate the gold price risk resulting from holding a share of Pure Gold, a shareholder can take a forward position so that the hedged payoff is the same whatever the gold price. Let h be the short forward position per ounce. Remember that the forward price is assumed to be $350 per ounce. Therefore, a short forward position of one unit pays $350 – $250 if the gold price is $250 and $350 – $450 if the gold price is $450. To eliminate the impact of gold price risk, the shareholder must choose h so that the income is the same whatever the gold price:

$$\$250 + h(\$350 - \$250) = \$375 + h(\$350 - \$450)$$

Solving for h, we get 0.625. By selling short 0.625 ounces forward, the shareholder guarantees a payoff of $312.5 per ounce at the end of the year. If the gold price is $250 per ounce, the shareholder receives $250 per share from the firm and $0.625 \times (\$350 - \$250)$, or $62.50, from the forward position. This amounts to $312.50. The shareholder is clearly better off if the firm hedges directly, since in that case she gets $325, or $12.50 more than if the firm does not hedge and she practices homemade risk management.

3.2.1. The tax argument for risk management

The tax argument for risk management is straightforward: If it moves a dollar away from a possible outcome in which the taxpayer is subject to a high tax rate and shifts it to a possible outcome where the taxpayer incurs a low tax rate, a firm or an investor reduces the present value of taxes to be paid. The tax rationale for risk management applies whenever income is taxed differently at different levels. The tax code introduces complications in the analysis. Some of these complications decrease the value of hedging, whereas others increase it. Some of these complications are discussed next.

1. **Carrybacks and carryforwards.** A firm that has negative taxable income can offset future or past taxable income with a loss in this tax year, subject to limitations. One limitation is that losses can be carried back or carried forward only for a limited number of years. In addition, no allowance is made for the time value of money. To see the importance of the time value of money, suppose a firm makes a gain of $100,000 this year and then a loss of $100,000 in three years. It has no other income. The tax rate is 30 percent. Three years from now, the firm can offset the $100,000 gain of this year with its loss. But it must pay $30,000 in taxes this year, and it gets back only $30,000 in three years, so it loses the use of the money for three years.

2. **Tax shields.** There is a wide variety of tax shields. One is the tax shield on interest paid. Another is the tax shield on depreciation. Firms also have tax credits. All these complications mean that a firm's marginal tax rate can be quite variable. Further, tax laws change, so at various times firms and investors know that taxes will rise or fall. In such cases, the optimal risk management program is one that increases cash flows when taxes are low and reduces them when they are high.

3. **Personal taxes.** Our discussion ignored taxes paid by investors. Suppose that taxes paid by investors decreased the forward price. In this case, hedging would be less advantageous at the firm level because the forward price would be less attractive. There is no reason to suspect that taxes

create biases in the prices of forward contracts—or other derivative contracts—that make hedging at the firm level unattractive.

It is difficult to capture all real-life complications in an analytical model to evaluate the importance of the tax benefits of risk management. To cope with this problem, Graham and Smith (1999) use a simulation approach instead. They do not take into account personal taxes, but otherwise they incorporate all the relevant features of the tax code. They simulate a firm's income, and then evaluate the tax benefit of hedging. For about half the firms, there is a tax benefit from hedging. The typical benefit is that a 1 percent reduction in the volatility of taxable income for a given year reduces the present value of taxes by 1 percent.

3.2.2. The tax benefits of risk management and Homestake

In 1990, Homestake paid taxes of $5.827 million. It made a loss on continuing operations because it wrote down its investment in North American Metals Corporation. Taxation in extraction industries like minerals and oil and gas companies is notoriously complicated. However, the annual report shows why Homestake's tax rate differs from the statutory tax rate of 34 percent as follows (in thousands of dollars):

Homestake loss: $13,500 at 34% would yield taxes of	$ (4,600)
Depletion allowance	(8,398)
State income taxes, net of federal benefit	(224)
Nondeductible foreign losses	18,191
Other, net	858
Total	$ 5,827

Homestake paid taxes even though it lost money. The exact details of the nondeductible foreign losses are not available from the annual report. Therefore, we cannot say for sure that risk management could have decreased taxes paid by Homestake. However, risk management enables a firm to shift income from states of the world with high tax rates to states of the world with low tax rates. Perhaps risk management could have enabled Homestake to avoid paying taxes while it was making a loss.

Decreases in the price of gold could easily lead to a situation where Homestake would make losses. Avoiding these losses would smooth out taxes over time and hence would increase firm value. Based on the information in the annual report, we cannot quantify this benefit. Petersen and Thiagarajan (2000) compare American Barrick and Homestake in great detail. They find that Homestake has a tendency to time the recognition of expenses when gold prices are high to smooth income. Obviously, in the year discussed here, smoothing income that way did not prevent Homestake from having to pay taxes while it was making a loss.

3.3. Optimal capital structure and risk management

Generally, interest paid is deductible from income. A levered firm that pays interest on debt therefore pays less in taxes than one without interest payments for the same operating cash flow. Debt has a tax benefit, which increases the value of the levered firm relative to the value of the unlevered firm. In the presence of costs of financial distress, an increase in the firm's debt has an offsetting cost resulting from the increased likelihood of financial distress. Risk management enables the firm to have a higher debt level, and hence a greater tax shield from debt, for any likelihood of financial distress.

3.3.1. The tax shield of debt, costs of financial distress, and risk management

Let's see how risk management enables a firm to increase its tax benefits from debt without increasing its probability of financial distress. Suppose that the costs of financial distress are so high for Pure Gold that it is never worthwhile for Pure Gold to issue an amount of debt so that it defaults when it sells gold for $250. Absent risk management, Pure Gold can issue risk-free debt so that its debt payments at maturity are $250 million. It can use the proceeds of the debt issue to pay a dividend to shareholders. With that debt level, the interest rate on debt is the risk-free rate of 5 percent, so that Pure Gold pays interest of $11.90 million and borrows $239.10 million. The firm's value for its shareholders is the present value of $0.5 \times \$250M + 0.5 \times [\$450M - 0.5 \times (\$450M - \$300M - \$11.90M)]$, or $315.475 million.

Using risk management, Pure Gold can issue more risk-free debt and therefore reduce the present value of its tax payments. With risk management, it can lock in pre-tax income of $350 million and therefore can commit to pay $350 million in the form of debt principal, debt interest, and tax payments.

Since the tax shield increases with the debt principal outstanding, Pure Gold wants to issue as much debt as it can without incurring costs of financial distress. Since Pure Gold does not need the cash raised through debt for investment, it pays it out to the shareholders as a dividend. Figure 3.6 plots firm value imposing the constraint that total debt and tax payments cannot exceed $350 million. In this case, Pure Gold can always make its debt payments, so that we assume that there are no costs of financial distress. If the firm sells more debt, it is bankrupt. Consequently, if F is the principal amount of the debt issued, it must be that:

$$\text{Debt principal } + \text{ Debt interest } + \text{ Taxes } = \$350M$$

$$F + 0.05F + 0.5 \times (\$350M - \$300M - 0.05F) = \$350M$$

Solving for F, we get $317.073 million. To see that this works, note that the firm has to pay taxes on income of $350M - \$300M - 0.05 \times \$317.073M$, corresponding to $17.073 million. The debt payments are $317.073M + 0.05 \times \$317.073$, or $332.927 million. The sum of debt payments and taxes is therefore exactly $350 million.

By issuing more debt than F, Pure Gold would always be bankrupt as we have seen already. If it issued less debt instead, it could increase debt and make the shareholders better off. To see this, suppose the firm had $1 million less of debt. Its dividend to shareholders would fall by $1 million and it would have $1.05 million less of debt payments at the end of the year. The decrease in debt payments would reduce the tax shield of debt by $0.25 million, so that the shareholders would receive $1.025 million at the end of the year instead of $1 million

Firm after-tax cash flow and debt issue   *Figure 3.6*

The firm has an expected pre-tax cash flow of $350 million. The tax rate is 0.5 and the risk-free rate is 5 percent. The figure shows the impact on after-tax cash flow of issuing more debt, assuming that the IRS disallows a deduction for interest of debt when the firm is highly likely to default.

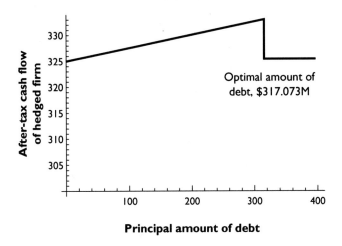

today if the firm issued debt instead. The present value of $1.025 million is less than $1 million, so that shareholders are worse off.

In general, firms cannot eliminate all risk, so that debt is risky. By having more debt, firms increase their **tax shield from debt** but increase the present value of costs of financial distress. The **optimal capital structure** of a firm balances the tax benefits of debt against the costs of financial distress. A firm can reduce the present value of the costs of financial distress through risk management by making financial distress less likely. As a result, it can take on more debt. This is the case even if the firm cannot eliminate all risk as in the case of Pure Gold.

One complication we have ignored is that investors pay taxes too. Miller (1978) has emphasized that this complication can change the analysis. Suppose investors pay taxes on bond income but not on capital gains. In this case, they will want a higher return on debt than on equity to offset the high taxes. A higher yield would reduce the tax benefit of debt to the firm. The consensus among financial economists is that personal taxes may limit the corporate benefits from debt but not eliminate them. Whether there are personal taxes or not, the corporation will want to maximize the value of its tax shields.

3.3.2. Does Homestake have too little debt?

Homestake pays taxes every year. Most years, its tax rate is close to the statutory rate of 34 percent. In 1990, as we saw, Homestake paid taxes at a rate that exceeded the statutory rate. It has almost no debt, and its long-term debt is dwarfed by its cash balances. It surely has too little debt.

By increasing its debt, Homestake takes advantage of the tax shield of debt and reduces its taxes. An increase in debt similarly amplifies the importance of risk management.

3.4. Should the firm hedge to reduce the risk of large undiversified shareholders?

Investors who own well-diversified portfolios are relatively unaffected by firm-specific events. On average, their risks balance out, except for the systematic risks of the economy as a whole, which can be controlled by investors through their asset allocation. For other investors who have a large position in a firm, these risks do not balance out. Managers, for example, may have a large stake in the firm for control reasons or because of a compensation plan. Other large investors might value a control position. Investors who cannot diversify firm-specific risk care about the risks that the firm bears. They might want the firm to reduce risk, unless they can reduce it more cheaply through homemade risk management.

Suppose Pure Gold has only one large shareholder who holds 10 percent of the shares and nothing else. This undiversified shareholder cares about the diversifiable risk of the gold mining firm. She wants to reduce the risk of her investment. To do this, she could sell her stake and invest in a diversified portfolio and the risk-free asset. Second, she could keep her stake but use homemade hedging. Third, she could try to convince the firm to hedge.

The firm may have a comparative advantage in hedging and homemade hedging may not be possible for this large investor. Why should the firm expend resources to hedge to please that large investor? If the only benefit of hedging is that this large investor does not have to hedge on her own, the firm uses resources to hedge without increasing firm value. If the firm gains from having the large shareholder, however, then it can make sense to hedge to make it possible for the large shareholder to keep her investment in the firm.

3.4.1. Large undiversified shareholders can increase firm value

Large shareholders can increase firm value. Smaller and highly diversified shareholders have little reason to pay much attention to what a particular firm is doing. Their smaller stakes give them little benefit from evaluating carefully the actions of managers. A shareholder with a large undiversified stake in a firm will follow the actions of management carefully with an interest in increasing the value of the firm. Evaluating managers and trying to improve what they do is called monitoring management. Larger shareholders get greater financial benefits from monitoring management than smaller ones.

There are two reasons why shareholder monitoring can increase firm value. First, an investor might become a large shareholder because he has some ability in evaluating the actions of management in a particular firm. Such an investor has knowledge and skills that are valuable to the firm. If management chooses to maximize firm value, management welcomes such an investor and listens to him carefully.

Second, managers do not necessarily maximize firm value; they maximize their welfare like all economic agents. Doing so sometimes involves maximizing firm value. What a manager does depends on the incentives. If an action increases firm value but is very risky, a manager on a fixed salary may decide against it because a firm that is bankrupt cannot pay her salary. Monitoring can make it more likely that managers maximize firm value.

A large shareholder who finds that management failed to take an action that maximizes firm value might draw the attention of other shareholders to this fact. In some cases, a large shareholder may even convince another firm to attempt a takeover to remove management and take actions that maximize firm value.

A firm's risk generally makes it unattractive for a shareholder to have a stake large enough to make monitoring worthwhile. If it hedges, a firm may make ownership more attractive to a shareholder who has some advantage in monitoring management. As the large shareholder takes such a larger stake, all other shareholders benefit from the monitoring.

3.4.2. Risk and the incentives of managers

One way shareholders can ensure that managers are motivated to maximize the value of the company's shares is through a managerial compensation contract that gives managers a stake in how well the firm does. If managers earn more when the firm does better, this induces them to work harder. Managerial compensation related to the stock price also can have adverse implications for managers. In fact, making managerial compensation depend strongly on any part of the stock return that is not under control of management could be counterproductive. Suppose a firm has large stocks of raw materials that are required for production. In the absence of a risk management program, the value of these raw materials fluctuates over time. Random changes in the value of raw materials may be the main contributors to the volatility of a firm's stock price, yet managers have no control over the price of raw materials. Making managerial compensation depend strongly on the stock price in this case forces management to bear risks, but provides no incentive effects and does not align management's incentives with those of shareholders.

In general, it makes sense to tie managerial compensation to some measure of value created without trying to figure out what is and is not under management's control. If the firm can reduce its risk through hedging, firm value depends on variables that management controls; in this case, relating compensation to firm value does not force managers to bear too much risk and does not induce them to make decisions that are not in the interest of shareholders to eliminate this risk. When managers work hard to increase their compensation, they also work hard to increase shareholder wealth.

Ownership of shares in the firm ties managers' welfare more closely to shareholders' welfare. If they own shares, managers bear risk. Since managers are not diversified shareholders, they care about the firm's total risk. This may lead them to be conservative in their actions. To the degree risk is reduced through risk management, the total risk of the firm falls, and managers become more willing to take risks. Firmwide hedging thereby makes managerial stock ownership a more effective device to induce managers to maximize firm value.

A risk management program eliminates sources of fluctuation in market value due to forces that are not under management's control. This reduces the risk attached to management's human capital and makes it less likely that managers will undertake risk-reducing activities that diminish firm value. If the risk attached to management's human capital is lower, there may be a willingness to accept a lower compensation. Saving compensation enhances firm value.

Not every form of compensation that depends on firm value motivates management to reduce firm risk. Managerial compensation contracts that include call options on the firm's stock create incentives to take risks. To see how options might induce management not to hedge when hedging would maximize firm value, suppose Pure Gold's management owns a call option on 1,000 shares with exercise price of $350 per share. For simplicity, we assume that management received these options in the past and that exercise of the options does not affect firm value. Assuming a tax advantage to hedging, as we have discussed, firm value is maximized if the firm hedges. Hedging locks in a firm value before managerial compensation of $309.52. Management's options are worthless in this case. If the firm does not hedge, there is a 50 percent chance that the shares will be worth $375, which represents a 50 percent chance that the options will pay off. In this case, management chooses not to hedge even though shareholders would be better off otherwise.

3.4.3. Large shareholders, managerial incentives, and Homestake

The Homestake proxy statement for 1990 shows that the directors own 1.1 percent of the shares. Homestake's CEO, Harry Conger, owns 137,004 shares directly and has the right to acquire 243,542 shares through an option plan. The shares in the option plan have an average exercise price of $14.43, but the share price in 1990 never dropped below $15.30. Managers and directors hold few shares directly and less than is typical for a firm of that size; most of managers' ownership is in the form of options. There is not much incentive for management to protect its stake in the firm through hedging.

A large shareholder who monitors management might be able to increase firm value. To attract such a shareholder, the firm might have to commit to a risk management program. Yet it does not seem that management would want such an outcome. Homestake has one large shareholder, Case, Pomeroy and Co. This company owns 8.2 percent of the shares. Two executives of that company are on the board of directors. Case has been decreasing its stake in Homestake and has a standstill agreement with Homestake that prevents it from buying more shares and gives Homestake rights of first refusal when Case sells shares.

3.5. Stakeholders

Besides large undiversified shareholders, there are individuals and companies whose welfare depends on how well a firm is doing but who cannot diversify the impact of firm risks on their welfare. They can be workers, suppliers, or customers. Such individuals and firms are often called **stakeholders**. Does it make sense to reduce firmwide risk to reduce the risk borne by these individuals and companies?

3.5.1. When should firms care about stakeholders?

It is not unusual to hear that a firm should be managed for its stakeholders. In general, though, owners of the firm want the firm to be managed to make them better off, so that maximizing the welfare of stakeholders cannot be a legitimate corporate goal. Yet it is sometimes advantageous for shareholders to reduce the risks that stakeholders bear. Shareholders may want stakeholders to make long-term firm-specific investments. The firm, for instance, might want workers to learn skills that would have minimal value outside the firm. Or it might want a supplier to devote R&D to design parts that only the firm will use. In another case, the value of a product customers buy depends on the firm's implicit warranty. In all these cases, the stakeholders will be reluctant to make firm-specific investments if they question the firm's financial health. If the firm gets in financial trouble, it may not be able to live up to its part of the bargain—that the stakeholders are investing in exchange for benefits from the firm over the long term.

Hedging makes it easier for the firm to honor its bargain with stakeholders. It can hedge at lower cost than the monetary compensation it would have to give to stakeholders to offset the impact on their welfare of the firm's risk. Without reducing risk, a firm may be able to get the stakeholders to make the requisite investments only by "bribing" them to do so. This means paying workers more so that they will learn the requisite skills, paying the suppliers directly to invest in R&D, and selling products more cheaply to compensate for the risks associated with the warranty. Such economic incentives are more expensive than hedging. Managing risk can therefore help the firm in getting others to make firm-specific investments and lower its costs of doing so.

3.5.2. Stakeholders and Homestake

Are stakeholders important for Homestake? Most likely, no. There is no reason to suspect that workers or suppliers have to make important firm-specific investments whose value would be seriously damaged if Homestake had financial difficulties. The welfare of Homestake's workers and suppliers depends on whether it makes sense to exploit Homestake's mines, not on whether Homestake is financially healthy. Should Homestake fail financially and file for bankruptcy, the new owners of the mine would still want to take advantage of the firm-specific investments made by workers and suppliers if it makes sense to extract gold from Homestake's mines.

A risk management program cannot make it profitable for Homestake to extract gold from its mines when otherwise it would not be. To understand this, suppose the price of gold falls to $150 per ounce, Homestake's extraction cost is $300, and Homestake hedged so that it sold gold forward for $350 per ounce. Rather than extract gold, Homestake is better off buying gold on the spot market to deliver on its forward contracts. It makes a profit of $200 per ounce this way. Producing gold, it only makes a profit of $50 per ounce.

Buyers of gold do not care about its provenance, so Homestake does not have to worry about relationships with customers.

3.6. Risk management, financial distress, and investment

So far, we have paid little attention to the fact that firms are ongoing entities that have opportunities to invest in valuable projects. Suppose Pure Gold has the opportunity to open a profitable new mine a year from now. A large investment must be made first. Without sufficient internal resources, the firm has to borrow or sell equity to finance the opening of the mine. If the costs of external financing are too high, Pure Gold might not be able to open the mine, and shareholders would lose the expected profits.

We investigate the main reasons why firms might not be able to invest in profitable projects because the cost of external financing is too high, and show how risk management can help avoid such situations.

3.6.1. Debt overhang

Too much debt induces shareholders to take on negative net present value projects and to avoid investing in valuable projects because they require issuing equity that dilutes their stake in the firm. When a firm has so much debt that it leads it to make investment decisions that benefit shareholders but affect its total value adversely, the firm has a **debt overhang**. As long as a firm has debt and risk, there is some possibility it may end up with a debt overhang. The probability that the firm might experience a debt overhang in the future reduces its value today. Consequently, risk management that reduces this probability increases firm value today.

A debt overhang can make shareholders take actions that reduce firm value but increase the value of the firm's equity. To see this, consider a firm, Highly Levered Gold (HLG). HLG never intended to have high leverage, but after successive mining disasters, it became highly levered because losses ate away at its equity. Suppose that the financial situation of HLG is such that if firm value does not increase sharply before the maturity of its debt, shareholders will receive nothing and the creditors will own the firm. Suppose further that if shareholders do nothing, HLG's value cannot increase sufficiently to enable it to repay its creditors. To make it more likely that firm value will increase sufficiently to make their shares valuable, shareholders can increase HLG's risk. If they take projects that have some chance of a large payoff but otherwise lose money, shareholders make money if the projects do well but do not lose money if the projects do poorly since they would have received nothing anyway. In fact, shareholders will be willing to take these long-shot projects even if they have a negative net present value.

When a firm has a large debt overhang, its shareholders may decide against raising funds to finance valuable new projects. Suppose that HLG has a valuable investment opportunity: By investing $10 million, the firm acquires a project that has a positive net present value of $5 million. The project is small enough that it will not enable HLG to repay its debt. The firm has no cash. The only way it can invest is by raising funds.

Borrowing is not an option. Consequently, HLG would have to sell equity to raise funds. Consider the impact of having an investor invest one dollar in new equity. The investor will only invest the dollar if she can expect to earn an appropriate return given the risk she takes. If an investor invests one dollar in a new share, that money most likely will end up in the pockets of the creditors since the most likely outcome is that the firm will not have money left after paying the creditors. This extra dollar will be a windfall for the creditors. Since the creditors will receive that dollar without having to pay for it, the old shareholders will have to pay for it through a reduction in the value of their stake brought about by the fact that they have to share the equity payoffs with the new investor. Hence, even though the project would increase firm value, the current shareholders will not want the firm to take it because it will not benefit them. The only way the firm would take the project is for shareholders to renegotiate with creditors so that they get more of the payoff of the project. Such a renegotiation is difficult and costly, and sometimes, no such renegotiation succeeds.

To understand why the debt overhang leads to underinvestment, let's look at a simple example. Suppose HLG can sell one million ounces of gold at either $450 or $250 at the end of the year. Each outcome has a probability of 0.5. Gold price risk is not systematic risk. HLG has debt payments of $400 million. The value of the debt is therefore [(0.5 × $250M) + (0.5 × $400M)]/1.05, or $309.524 million. The value of equity is 0.5 × $50M/1.05, or $23.8095 million. Now, HLG receives an investment opportunity that pays $10 million for sure but costs $5 million. It has to raise $5 million to finance the investment opportunity.

Firm value without the investment opportunity is $350M/1.05, or $333.33 million. With the investment opportunity, it is $360M/1.05, or $342.857 million. Taking the investment opportunity increases firm value, but who benefits from the investment opportunity? If the gold price is $250, the bondholders get all the benefit of the funds raised—they get $10 million more. If the gold price is $450, the shareholders get all the benefit of the funds raised. The value of equity therefore increases by 0.5 × 10M/1.05, or $4.7619 million. The shareholders raise $5 million, but equity increases by less. Since the new shareholders must receive $5 million worth of claims against the firm, the value of the claims of the old shareholders must fall from $23.8095 million to $23.5714 million. The share price must fall as the firm takes advantage of the new investment opportunity even though firm value increases. The old shareholders therefore prefer that the firm does not raise funds and does not invest in the investment opportunity. The firm therefore underinvests—it does not invest in a project that is a positive net present value project for the firm.

The value of a firm in the capital markets is lower when there is a probability that it may not enter into valuable projects because its financial health might be poor. Reducing this probability through risk management increases firm value as long as risk management is cheap enough.

3.6.2. Information asymmetries and agency costs of managerial discretion

The key problem management faces in raising funds is that managers know more about the firm's projects than the outsiders they are dealing with. When one party to a deal knows more than the other, we call this an **information asymmetry**. Suppose that the firm's equity with its current projects is $100 million. Managers believe that by raising $100 million of new equity and investing the proceeds, they can invest in a project with a net present value of $50 million. If they ask you to invest, you have to figure out the return on your investment based on the information provided to you by management.

Generally, managers benefit from firm growth, so that they have much to gain by undertaking new projects, which can lead to biases. They may tend to minimize problems. Even if they are completely unbiased and reveal all the information they have to potential investors, you as an investor cannot easily tell that. Often, management has enough to gain from undertaking a project that it might want to invest even if the chance of success is low enough that the project is a negative net present value project.

The costs associated with management's opportunity to undertake projects that have a negative net present value when it is advantageous for them to do so are called **agency costs of managerial discretion**. When managers have discretion to take actions, they can pursue their own objectives, which creates agency costs. That is, the agent's interests, or management's interests, are not aligned with the interests of the principals who hire management, namely, the shareholders.

Agency costs of managerial discretion make it harder for a firm to raise funds and increase the cost of funds. If outsiders are not sure that the project is as likely to pay off as management claims, they want more compensation for providing the funds. Even if the project is as described, having to pay a higher expected compensation reduces the profits from the project. The project may not be profitable because the cost of capital for the firm is too high.

There is more than one way to reduce the costs of managerial discretion and hence reduce the costs of the funds raised. A firm could entice a large shareholder to come on board. This shareholder would see the company from the inside, and would be better able to assess whether the project is valuable. Or a risk management strategy might preserve ongoing firm value and hence might enable the firm to take the project. A firm whose value is not in doubt may be able to borrow against assets rather than try to borrow against the future project.

A risk management strategy that preserves firm value might help the firm to finance the project for another reason. Investors who look at a firm's history have to figure out what a loss in firm value implies. In general, it will be difficult for outsiders to see exactly what is going on. They will therefore always worry that the true explanation for the losses is incompetent management. There could be many explanations for a loss in firm value. Firm value could fall because a stock of raw materials fell in value, because the economy is in a recession, because a plant burned down, or because management is incompetent. Outsiders cannot be sure. If it reduces risk through risk management, the firm makes it easier for investors to assess the ability of management since it eliminates some sources of unexpected losses.

3.6.3. The cost of external funding and Homestake

Is it really the case that external funding can be more expensive than internal funding? The answer is yes. There is much empirical evidence that shows that firms with poor cash flow have to cut back investment. The problem with that evidence is that poor cash flow might signal bad investment opportunities, in which case it would not be surprising to see that firms with poor cash flow cut investment. However, this is not the whole story. Lamont (1997) shows that drops in oil prices led oil companies to cut back investment in their non-oil activities. An oil company that sees its cash flow drop has no reason to reduce investment in the department stores it owns unless external financing is more costly than internal financing, so that when the firm has to switch from internal financing to outside financing, the cost of capital increases and some investments are no longer worthwhile.

Box 3.1, Warren Buffett and Catastrophe Insurance, provides an example where an insurance product is priced in a way that can be explained only by the existence of steep costs of external finance because of agency costs. The example also shows that the agency costs and information asymmetries discussed in this section can make risk management products more expensive.

Warren Buffett and Catastrophe Insurance   *Box 3.1*

Insurance companies hedge some of their exposure to catastrophes such as earthquakes, hurricanes, or tornadoes by insuring themselves with reinsurers. A typical reinsurance contract promises to reimburse an insurance company for claims due to a catastrophe within some range. For example, an insurance company could be reimbursed for up to $1 billion of California earthquake claims in excess of $2 billion. Catastrophe insurance risks are diversifiable risks, so bearing these risks should not earn a risk premium. This means that the price of the insurance should be the expected losses discounted at the risk-free rate. Yet, in practice, the pricing of reinsurance does not work this way.

Let's look at an example. In the fall of 1996, Berkshire Hathaway, Warren Buffett's company, sold reinsurance to the California Earthquake Authority in the amount of $1.05 billion insured for four years. The annual premium was 10.75 percent of the annual limit, or $113 million. The probability that the reinsurance would be triggered was estimated at 1.7 percent at inception by EQE International, a catastrophe risk modeling firm. Ignoring discounting, the annual premium was therefore 530 percent of the expected loss (0.1075 is 530 percent of 0.017). If the capital asset pricing model had been used to price the reinsurance contract, the premium would have been $17.85 million in the absence of discounting and somewhat less with discounting.

How can we make sense of this huge difference between the actual premium and the premium predicted by the capital asset pricing model? A reinsurance contract is useless if there is credit risk; that is, the reinsurer has to have liquid assets that enable it to pay the claims. The problem is that holding liquid assets creates managerial discretion agency costs. It is difficult to ensure that a reinsurer will indeed have the money when needed. Once the catastrophe has occurred, the underinvestment problem would prevent the reinsurer from raising the funds because the benefit from raising the funds would accrue to the policyholders rather than to the investors. The reinsurer therefore has to raise funds when the policy is agreed upon. Hence, in the case of this example, the reinsurer would need, if it did not have the capital, to raise $1.05 billion minus the premium.

The investors have to be convinced that the reinsurer will not take the money and run or take the money and invest it in risky securities. Yet the reinsurer has strong incentives to take risks unless its reputational capital is extremely valuable. In the absence of valuable reputational capital, the reinsurer can gamble with the investors' money. If the reinsurer wins, it makes an additional profit. If it loses, the investors or the insurer's clients lose.

Another problem with reinsurance is due to information asymmetries and agency costs in the investment industry. The reinsurer has to raise money from investors, but the funds provided would be lost if a catastrophe occurs. Most investment takes place through money managers who act as agents for individual investors. In the case of funds raised by reinsurance companies, the money manager is in a difficult position. Suppose that he decides that investing with a reinsurance firm is a superb investment. How can the individual

(continued)

investors who hire the money manager know that he has acted in their interest if a catastrophe occurs? They will have a difficult time deciding whether the money manager was right and they were unlucky or the money manager was wrong. This problem leads the money manager to require ample compensation for investing with the reinsurance firm.

Berkshire Hathaway has reputational capital that makes it unprofitable to gamble with investors' money. Consequently, it does not have to write a complicated contract to ensure that there will not be credit risk. Since it has already large reserves, it does not have to deal with the problems of raising large amounts of funds for reinsurance purpose. Could these advantages be worth as much as it seems in the great difference between the California premium and the theoretical price? There is no evidence that there were credible reinsurers willing to enter cheaper contracts. With perfect markets, such reinsurers would have been too numerous to count.

Source: Kenneth Froot, "The limited financing of catastrophe risk: An overview," *The Financing of Property Casualty Risks,* University of Chicago Press, 1997.

Homestake could repay all its debt with its cash reserves, so that debt overhang is not an immediate issue. The firm also has enough cash that it could finance large investments out of internal resources. Yet if gold prices fell, Homestake's resources would shrink over time. At some point, its ability to undertake new projects might be compromised. When gold prices are low, Homestake might have few good investment opportunities. However, if it expects to have more valuable investment opportunities if gold prices fall, it might want to put in place a risk management program that insures that it will have appropriate financial resources to finance these investment opportunities.

3.7. Summary

In this chapter, we have investigated ways that firms without risk management can leave money on the table. They can:

1. Bear more bankruptcy costs and financial distress costs than they should.

2. Pay more taxes than they should.

3. Have less leverage than they should.

4. Have managers provided with poor incentives.

5. Fail to retain valuable large shareholders.

6. Fail to get stakeholders to make firm-specific investments.

7. Find it unprofitable to invest in positive net present value projects.

8. Find it profitable to take bad projects.

We have identified benefits from risk management that can increase firm value. In the next chapter, we move on to the question of whether and how such benefits can provide the basis for the design of a risk management program.

Key Concepts

agency costs of managerial discretion, 71
bankruptcy costs, 55
costs of financial distress, 58
deadweight costs, 53

debt overhang, 70
information asymmetry, 71
optimal capital structure, 65
stakeholders, 68
tax shield from debt, 65

Review Questions

1. How does risk management affect the present value of bankruptcy costs?

2. Why do the tax benefits of risk management depend on the firm having a tax rate that depends on cash flow?

3. How do carrybacks and carryforwards affect the tax benefits of risk management?

4. How does risk management affect the tax shield of debt?

5. Does risk management affect the optimal capital structure of a firm? Why?

6. Does it pay to reduce firm risk because a large shareholder wants the firm to do so?

7. How does the impact of risk management on managerial incentives depend on the nature of management's compensation contract?

8. Is risk management profitable for the shareholders of a firm that has a debt overhang?

9. How do costs of external funding affect the benefits of risk management?

Literature Note

Smith and Stulz (1985) provide an analysis of the determinants of hedging policies that covers the issues of bankruptcy costs, costs of financial distress, stakeholders, and managerial compensation. Diamond (1981) shows how hedging makes it possible for investors to evaluate managerial performance more effectively. DeMarzo and Duffie (1991) and Breeden and Viswanathan (1998) show that hedging is valuable because of information asymmetries between managers and investors. Froot, Scharfstein, and Stein (1993) derive explicit hedging policies when firms would have to invest suboptimally in the absence of hedging because of difficulties in securing funds to finance investment. Stulz (1990, 1996) discusses how hedging can enable firms to have higher leverage. Stulz (1990) focuses on the agency costs of managerial discretion. Hedging makes it less likely that the firm will not be able to invest in valuable projects, so it can support higher leverage. One reason debt is valuable is because it prevents managers from making bad investments. Tufano (1998) makes the point that reducing the need to go to the external capital markets also enables managers to avoid the scrutiny of the market. This will be the case if greater hedging is not accompanied by greater leverage. Myers (1977) was the first one to provide an analysis of debt overhang, showing how it can lead shareholders to be unwilling to raise funds for valuable new projects. The empirical evidence on the positive relation between investment and cash flow is discussed in Hubbard (1998). Bessembinder (1991) and Mayers and Smith (1987) analyze how hedging can reduce the underinvestment problem. Leland (1998) provides a model where hedging increases firm value because (1) it increases the tax benefits from debt and (2) it reduces the probability of default and the probability of incurring distress costs. Ross (1997) also models the tax benefits of hedging. Petersen and Thiagarajan (1998) provide a detailed comparison of how hedging theories apply to Homestake and American Barrick.

Chapter 4

A Firm-Wide Approach to Risk Management

Chapter **4** Objectives

At the end of this chapter, you will:

1. Understand how to choose a risk measure.

2. Know how to measure value at risk (VaR) and cash flow at risk (CaR).

3. Be able to use VaR and CaR to make investment decisions.

4. Know how to manage risk when risk is measured by VaR or CaR.

Early in the 1990s, the CEO of JP Morgan, Dennis Weatherstone, wanted to know the bank's risk at the end of the trading day. He asked his staff to devise a risk measure that would yield one number that could be communicated to him at 4:15 PM each trading day and would give him an accurate view of the bank's risk. He wanted to have a sense of the risk of bad outcomes that would create problems for the bank. In Chapter 2, we considered three risk measures: volatility, systematic risk, and unsystematic risk. None of these measures provides a direct answer to the question Weatherstone wanted answered because none of them specifically measures downside risk. The risk measure that Weatherstone eventually received from his staff was an estimate of the bank's trading portfolio **value at risk (VaR)**, defined as the loss in value of the portfolio that has a 5 percent probability of being exceeded the next day.

Chapter 3 showed that there are five major reasons why risk management can increase shareholder wealth. These reasons are:

1. Risk management can reduce the present value of bankruptcy and financial distress costs.

2. It can make it more likely that the firm will be able to take advantage of valuable investment opportunities.

3. It can reduce the present value of taxes paid by the corporation.

4. It can increase the firm's debt capacity.

5. It reduces the cost to stakeholders, large shareholders, and managers of bearing firm-specific risk.

In general, these benefits from risk management come from the fact that bad outcomes for firms have knock-on effects or deadweight costs. A gold mining firm faced with lower gold prices can lose more than just the loss in immediate sales revenue. As a result of low gold prices, it may not be able to invest in profitable projects. It is therefore important to be able to quantify downside risk—the risk of bad outcomes. VaR is such a measure of downside risk.

Chapter 3 provides us with a catalog of benefits from risk management. Though such a catalog is an important starting point in understanding risk management, it is only the first step. For risk management to be used to maximize firm value, one must concretely define how risk is measured and how it is managed. A bad outcome for an individual investment might be offset by a good outcome for another investment and therefore have no deadweight costs, while a bad outcome for the firm as a whole will have deadweight costs. Consequently, the risk that has to be measured and managed is firm-wide risk. This chapter presents a framework that makes it possible to do that.

In the first part of the chapter, we show how the benefits of risk management presented in Chapter 3 lead to the choice of a risk measure. For some firms, that risk measure is VaR. The choice of a risk measure depends on the characteristics of the firm. Armed with a risk measure, a firm can evaluate the impact of new projects on its risk and assess the profitability of existing and new activities. Having specified the choice of a risk measure, we then discuss the tools available for risk management. Firms can manage their cost of total risk through equity, through their choice of projects, or through transactions in financial markets. Different tools have different costs and benefits. Derivatives are generally the most cost effective tool to manage firm risk.

4.1. Measuring risk for corporations

To understand the considerations that affect a firm's choice of a risk measure, we look at two concrete examples that demonstrate the trade-offs involved in choosing risk measures: first, financial firms, and second, nonfinancial corporations.

4.1.1. Measuring value at risk in a financial firm

A financial firm's ability to conduct business depends on its creditworthiness. Financial firms generally have customers who are also creditors. A depositor in effect lends his money to a bank. A firm that enters into a derivatives contract with an investment bank is a creditor if it expects to receive a payment from the bank at maturity. The buyer of a life insurance policy is a creditor of the insurance company. Customers of any financial firm are extremely sensitive to its credit risk because they cannot diversify this risk and often cannot hedge it.

Customers of financial firms have a dramatically different attitude toward credit risk from investors in capital markets. Even if you are willing to hold risky bonds as part of a diversified portfolio, you generally want your checking account to have no risk. A check is a substitute for cash. If your checking account is subject to significant credit risk, a check for $100 could be worth less than $100. Each transaction made using a check drawn on the checking account would require a negotiation to determine the appropriate compensation for credit risk paid to the seller.

Similarly, a firm that enters a forward contract with a financial firm wants the forward contract to serve as an effective hedge. If the financial firm has substantial credit risk, it might not deliver on the forward contract. This possibility makes the forward contract less useful as a hedging device. Finally, no policyholder would be willing to pay half as much for a life insurance contract that has a 0.5 probability of paying off because of credit risk.

An increase in the probability of default risk can have a dramatic impact on a financial firm's business. As default risk becomes significant, customers withdraw their money, the derivatives business dries up, and the life insurance business disappears. Shareholder wealth in a financial firm is fragile, probably more so than at any other type of corporation.

Because customers are creditors in financial firms, financial firms are highly leveraged. The more business a financial firm has for a given amount of capital, the greater its leverage. An adverse shock to a financial firm can cause its equity to disappear quickly as customers react to the shock by withdrawing their business. Costs of financial distress are significant for financial firms because often the mere hint of financial distress can create a run on the firm that eliminates its value as an ongoing business.

A financial firm must control its risks with extreme care. It must make sure there is little probability that it will lose customers because of credit risk. Its risk management effort must focus on computing, monitoring, and managing a measure of risk that corresponds to the probability that it will lose customers because of credit risk.

What type of event would make a bank risky for its customers? Its assets are loans and securities; its liabilities are deposits and debt. Some assets, securities, are often marked to market; other assets and liabilities are typically kept at book value. Marked to market means that values on the balance sheet are market values. Changes in the value of assets marked to market represent a gain or loss for the bank that impacts earnings, the value of equity, and regulatory capital. If the net value of the securities held by the bank falls sharply, the bank may have difficulties meeting its obligations. Banks also typically have derivatives positions that could require them to make large payments in the future. We can think of all positions in traded securities and derivatives as the bank's portfolio of traded financial instruments.

As long as the bank has risky traded financial instruments and is leveraged, it cannot be completely safe. Any event that exposes the bank to losses in its portfolio above a critical size is dangerous. The bank must keep the probability of losses above a critical size from traded financial instruments low. To manage its risk, the bank has to specify both this critical loss size and the acceptable probability that this loss size will be exceeded.

Let's consider Trading Bank Inc., or TB. Say TB decides that it wants the probability of a loss exceeding 10 percent of the value of its traded financial instruments over one day to be lower than 5 percent. That is, 95 percent of the time, the return of the portfolio must be higher than –10 percent. To compute this probability, TB has to know the distribution of the gains and the losses of the portfolio.

Let's assume that the return of the portfolio is normally distributed. The expected return is 10 percent and the volatility is 20 percent. We can use the analysis in Chapter 2 to find the probability that the portfolio will incur a loss exceeding 10 percent over one day. The probability that the return will be lower than some number x over a day, Prob[Return < x], is given by the cumulative normal distribution function evaluated at x.

Figure 4.1 shows how we can use the cumulative normal distribution to find the probability that the portfolio will incur a loss of at least 10 percent over one day. We pick the return of –10 percent on the horizontal axis and read the probability on the vertical axis corresponding to the level of the cumulative normal probability distribution, which is 16 percent. Or, by looking at the probability equal to 5 percent on the vertical axis, we can get on the horizontal axis that the firm has a 5 percent probability of losing at least 23 percent. If the return on TB's portfolio of traded financial instruments is distributed normally, once we know the volatility of the return and the expected return, we have all the information we need to compute any statistic for the distribution of gains and losses.

Suppose that TB follows this approach. It has a portfolio of traded financial instruments worth $2 billion, so a 10 percent loss is equal to $200 million. TB does the numbers, and finds that it has a 5 percent probability of incurring a loss of at least 23 percent, or $460 million. If TB had decided that it could only afford to

Using the cumulative distribution function   *Figure 4.1*

The figure graphs the cumulative distribution function of a normally distributed return with expected value of 10 percent and volatility of 20 percent. From this graph, the probability of a loss of 23 percent or greater is 0.05.

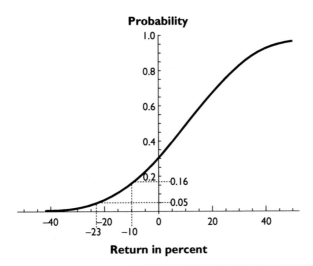

Return in percent

have a loss of $200 million or more with a probability of 5 percent, it has too much risk. What can TB do to reduce its risk? It can sell risky financial instruments and put the proceeds in risk-free assets. Or it can hedge more, if appropriate hedging instruments are available. The risk measure lets TB decide how to manage the risk of its portfolio of traded financial instruments, so that its customers do not worry about being exposed to significant credit risk.

The dollar loss that will be exceeded with a given probability over some given measurement period is called *value at risk* or *VaR*. VaR can be computed for a firm, a portfolio, or a trading position. The zth quantile of a distribution is a number such that there is a probability of z percent that the random variable is below that number and $(100 - z)$ percent that it is above. The VaR at the probability level of z percent is the loss corresponding to the zth quantile of the cumulative probability distribution of the value change at the end of the measurement period. VaR at the probability level of z percent is the dollar loss that has a probability z percent of being exceeded over the measurement period. Formally, VaR is the number such that Prob[Loss > VaR] = z percent.

Note that this definition makes no assumption about the distribution function of the loss. Throughout the book, we will use z percent as 5 percent unless we specify otherwise. If VaR is a loss that is exceeded with probability of z percent, there is a $(100 - z)$ percent probability that the loss will not be exceeded. We can therefore consider an interval from minus VaR to plus infinity such that the probability of the firm's gain belonging to that interval is $(100 - z)$ percent. In statistics, an interval constructed this way is called a one-sided confidence interval. One can also think of VaR as the maximum loss in the $(100 - z)$ percent confidence interval, or in short, the maximum loss at the $(100 - z)$ percent confidence level. If we compute the VaR at the 5 percent probability level, it is therefore also the maximum loss at the 95 percent confidence level. We are 95 percent sure that the firm's gain will be in the interval from minus VaR to plus infinity.

In Chapter 2, we considered three risk measures. These measures were volatility, systematic risk, and nonsystematic risk. None of these measures provides a measure of the risk of bad outcomes, and so none of these measures would have provided the information about the riskiness of JP Morgan that Dennis Weatherstone wanted each day at 4:15 PM. In general, there is no direct relation between VaR and these three risk measures. (You will see in this chapter that the normal distribution is an exception to this statement.)

With many types of securities, it is possible for volatility to increase and VaR to fall at the same time, which may seem a paradox. The following is an example for why volatility can increase and the corporation can be better off, so that volatility is an inappropriate risk measure. Suppose a corporation has the opportunity to receive a free lottery ticket that pays off in one year. This ticket has a small chance of an extremely large payoff. Otherwise, it pays nothing. If the firm accepts the free lottery ticket, its one-year volatility will be higher, because the value of the firm now has a positive probability of an extremely large payoff that it did not have before. A firm that focuses on volatility as its risk measure would therefore conclude that taking the lottery ticket makes it worse off if the volatility increase is high enough. Yet there is no sense in which the firm can be made worse off by receiving something for free that can have only positive value. Shareholders would always want management to take the lottery ticket, so under some circumstances they will want management to increase firm volatility. The firm's VaR would not be increased if the firm accepts the free lottery ticket.

Figure 4.2 shows an illustration of how return volatility can fail to convey the information that Dennis Weatherstone wanted. We show the return frequency distribution for two different portfolios. These two portfolios are constructed to have the same return volatility of 30 percent. One portfolio holds $100 million of a common stock and has normally distributed returns. The other portfolio holds $76.89 million in the risk-free asset and call options on 1.57 million shares of the same common stock as the first portfolio with exercise price per share equal to the current stock price and maturity in one year. The portfolio with options does not have normally distributed returns. While the two portfolios have the same return volatility, the portfolio with options has a very different VaR from the portfolio without options. The stock portfolio has a one-year 5 percent VaR of $41.93 million, while the portfolio holding the risk-free asset and options has a one-year 5 percent VaR of $15 million (we cover calculation of the VaR of portfolios with options in Chapter 13).

The reason volatility is not useful to evaluate the risk of bad outcomes is because the portfolios have very different worst-case returns. The worst returns of the portfolio with options are much less negative than the worst returns of the stock portfolio because the portfolio with options has no stock exposure when the stock has poor returns. Bad returns for the stock portfolio might bankrupt the bank, but bad returns for the portfolio with options might not. Beta and unsystematic risk cannot help us understand the distribution of bad outcomes either. Since both the risk-free asset and a volatile stock can have a beta of zero, beta is not helpful in understanding downside risk. If the stock in the two portfolios we just considered has a beta of zero, the volatility of the return of the portfolios is

Frequency distribution of two portfolios over a one-year horizon   *Figure 4.2*

The stock portfolio is invested in a stock that has an expected return of 15 percent and a volatility of return of 30 percent over the measurement period. The other portfolio has calls on 1.57 million shares of the stock with exercise price of $100 per share that cost $23.11 million and the rest invested in the risk-free asset earning 6 percent.

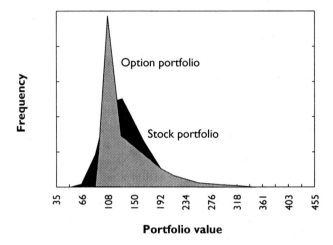

unsystematic risk, but in this case the portfolio with the greater unsystematic risk has less downside risk. Hence, unsystematic risk is not useful to measure downside risk. Had JP Morgan's staff provided Dennis Weatherstone with the systematic risk of the bank or its unsystematic risk, he would not have received an appropriate answer to his question.

The plots in Figure 4.2 indicate we need to understand the distribution of the returns of the bank's positions to compute its VaR. To answer Dennis Weatherstone's question, his staff had to know the value of all the marked-to-market positions of the bank at the end of the trading day and had to have a forecast of the joint distribution of the returns of the various securities held by the bank. As we will see in later chapters, forecasting the distribution of returns and computing VaR can be challenging when securities are complex.

Computing the VaR is straightforward, though, when the returns are normally distributed. A random variable follows the standard normal distribution when it is normally distributed, has an expected value of zero, and a volatility equal to one. The probability that a random variable following the standard normal distribution takes a value lower than −1.65 is 5 percent. The fifth quantile of the standard normal distribution is therefore −1.65. Any normally distributed random variable can be transformed into a random variable that follows the standard normal distribution by subtracting the mean from the random variable and dividing the resulting variable by the volatility of the random variable. If z is a normally distributed random variable, $u = [z - E(z)]/[\text{Vol}(z)]$ follows the standard normal distribution because it has mean zero and volatility equal to one. Consequently, the fifth quantile of the distribution of z can be obtained from the fifth quantile of u since -1.65 = Fifth quantile of $[z - E(z)]/[\text{Vol}(z)]$. Using this result, we have a formula for the fifth quantile of z:

Fifth quantile of $z = -1.65 \times \text{Vol}(z) + E(z)$

Hence, if the return of a portfolio is distributed normally, the fifth quantile of the return distribution is the expected return minus 1.65 times the return volatility. For changes computed over one day, this number is generally negative. VaR is the loss corresponding to the fifth quantile. It is therefore the absolute value of this negative change, or 1.65 times the volatility of the return minus the expected return.

Suppose a bank has a portfolio of traded assets with an expected return of 0.1 percent and a volatility of 5 percent. The fifth quantile of the return distribution is 0.1 percent $- 1.65 \times 5$ percent, or -8.15 percent. For VaR, we take the absolute value of the fifth quantile, or 8.15 percent. Note that the VaR is then simply 1.65 times the volatility minus the expected return. Hence, if the bank's value is $100 million, the VaR is 8.15 percent of $100 million, or $8.15 million.

In general, the expected return over one day is small compared to the volatility. This means that ignoring the expected return has a trivial impact on an estimate of the VaR for one day. In practice, therefore, the expected return is ignored. With normally distributed returns and zero expected change, the formula for VaR is:

Formula for VaR when returns are distributed normally and expected return can be ignored

If the portfolio return is normally distributed, has zero mean, and has volatility σ over the measurement period, the 5 percent VaR of the portfolio is:

VaR = $1.65 \times \sigma \times$ Portfolio value

The VaR in the example would then be $1.65 \times 5\% \times \$100M$, or $8.25 million.

In this case, there is a direct relation between volatility and VaR; VaR increases directly with volatility. In general, however, as shown in Figure 4.2, portfolios with the same return volatilities can have different VaRs, and portfolios with the same VaRs can have different volatilities.

An important issue is the time period over which the VaR should be computed. Remember that a financial firm wants to monitor and manage the size of potential losses so that the probability of financial distress is not too large. If a bank can measure its risk and change it once a day, the one-day VaR is useful to control risk over time. At the end of a day, managers decide whether the VaR for the next day is acceptable. If it is not, they take actions to change that risk. If it is acceptable, they do nothing. At the end of the next day, they go through the process again. However, if the bank is stuck with its portfolio for a number of days because the markets for the securities it holds are illiquid, then the one-day VaR is not relevant because it does not measure a risk the bank can manage. In this case, the bank would have to measure VaR over a period over which it could change its portfolio.

The bank will care about its risk over longer horizons. For example, it will worry about the impact of adverse earnings on its regulatory capital. Controlling the one-day VaR throughout the year will help in averting earnings shortfalls. However, the bank will also have to measure risk at longer horizons. It is not clear how one would compute a one-year VaR for a trading portfolio and what it would mean for a bank. The bank could compute a one-year VaR, assuming that the VaR over the next day will be maintained for a year, but the number would be meaningless. The bank's risk changes on a daily basis as trades are made. Further, if the financial firm incurs large losses or if its risk increases too much, it will immediately take steps to reduce its risk. When computing its risk over one year, the bank will have to take into account the policies it implements to manage risk.

Credit risks are generally a substantial source of risk for banks because of their loan portfolio. However, banks do not have the information to compute changes in the riskiness of their loan portfolio on a daily basis. Loans are not marked to market every day and firms release accounting data that might be useful at most on a quarterly basis. This means that a bank typically estimates credit risks over a different period of time than it measures risks associated with the market value of securities it holds (market risks). As we will see in Chapter 18, however, VaR can be used to measure the risk of a portfolio of loans.

VaR plays an important role in financial firms not only as a risk management tool, but also as a regulatory device. Box 4.1, VaR, banks, and regulators, shows that large banks can use VaR to compute their regulatory capital.

VaR, banks, and regulators   *Box 4.1*

The U.S. regulatory agencies adopted the market risk amendment to the 1988 Basle Capital Accord, which regulates capital requirements for banks to cover credit risk, in August 1996. This amendment became effective in January 1998. It requires banks with significant trading activities to set aside capital to cover market risk exposure in their trading accounts.

The central component of the regulation is a VaR calculation. The VaR is computed at the 1 percent level for a ten-day (two-week) holding period using the bank's own model. The capital the firm must set aside depends on this VaR in the following way. Let $VaR_t(1\%,10)$ be the VaR of the trading accounts computed at the 1 percent level for a ten-day trading period at date t. The amount of capital the bank has to hold for the market risk of its trading accounts is given by:

Required capital for day $t + 1$ =

$$\text{Max}\left[VaR_t(1\%,10); S_t \times \frac{1}{60} \sum_{i=1}^{59} VaR_{t-i}(1\%,10)\right] + SR_t$$

where S_t is a multiplier and SR_t is an additional charge for idiosyncratic risk. The terms in square brackets are the current VaR estimate and an average of

(continued)

Box 4.1   (continued)

the VaR estimate over the last 60 days. The multiplier S_t depends on the accuracy of the bank's VaR model. The multiplier is determined by back testing the bank's VaR for a one-day period at the 1 percent level over the last 250 days. If the bank exceeds its daily VaR four times or less, it is in the green zone and the multiplier is set at 3. If the bank exceeds its daily VaR five to nine times, it is in the yellow zone and the multiplier increases with the number of cases where it exceeds the VaR. If the bank exceeds its daily VaR ten times or more, its VaR model is deemed inaccurate and the multiplier takes a value of 4. Hence, by having a better VaR model, the bank saves on regulatory capital.

Banks routinely provide information on their VaR in their annual reports. The accompanying illustration shows the daily trading revenue and the daily VaR of Credit Suisse First Boston in 2000. As we can see, this illustration shows that the VaR was never exceeded during that year. The VaR is computed on a ten-day horizon at the 99 percent confidence level using two years of historical data. The illustration scales down the ten-day VaR to a one-day VaR. It is surprising that in this firm the VaR estimates are so much lower than the worst trading outcomes. Research by Berkovitz and O'Brien (2001) shows that the models that banks use for regulatory reporting tend to be extremely conservative.

Illustration   **The trading revenue of Credit Suisse First Boston in 2000**

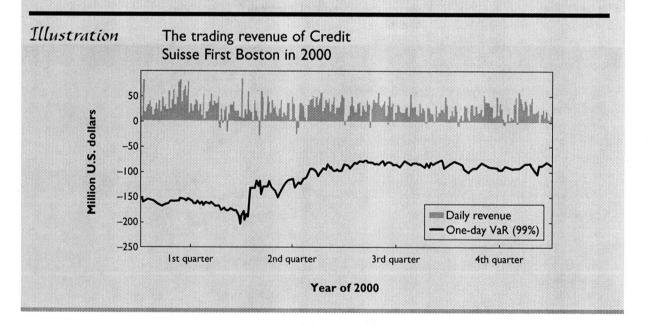

Financial firms have other risks besides market and credit risks. Someone might make a mistake in a specific transaction. A standardized contract might include a clause that turns out to be invalid and its discovery could create large losses. A trader might find a chink in the accounting software of the bank that allows him to hide losses in a trading position. Top management might make a bad strategic decision. These are operational risks. Risk managers are only starting to find useful ways to quantify such risks.

4.1.2. Implementing VaR

How did the staff of JP Morgan come up with a VaR estimate? The details of the procedure used within the bank are not available. However, JP Morgan made publicly available in 1994 a method to estimate VaR that is closely related to the method used internally. The approach is called RiskMetrics™. Eventually, JP Morgan formed a company called RiskMetrics that provides risk management consulting based on the approach developed within the bank.

To estimate VaR, one has to forecast the fifth percentile of the distribution of the return of the portfolio of traded assets. As we will see later, there are a number of ways to do this. The RiskMetrics™ approach assumes that the continuously compounded return (log return) of the portfolio of traded assets over the next day is normally distributed. If an asset has price S_t at t, the log return from t to T is $\ln(S_T/S_t)$. If the log of a random variable is normally distributed, the random variable follows a **lognormal distribution**. When an asset price has a log return normally distributed, the price itself has a lognormal distribution. A normally distributed random variable can take values from minus infinity to plus infinity, while a lognormal random variable can take only positive values. This makes the lognormal distribution attractive for prices of financial assets. Figure 4.3 compares the normal and lognormal distributions.

We have seen that when a portfolio has a normally distributed return the 5 percent VaR can be obtained by multiplying the forecast of the volatility of the return of the portfolio by 1.65 (when the expected return can be ignored). Consequently, to obtain an estimate of the VaR, the RiskMetrics™ approach has to come up with an estimate of the volatility of the return of the portfolio. We remember from Chapter 2 that to obtain the volatility of the return of a portfolio, we require knowledge of portfolio weights, of the return volatility of the assets that compose the portfolio, and of the return correlations among these assets. This presents three problems. First, we must have a complete inventory of the asset holdings. Second, a bank like JP Morgan would have tens of thousands of different assets in its portfolio. (As another example, the hedge fund LTCM had 60,000 different positions at the time of its collapse.) Some way to simplify the computations has to be found since otherwise millions of correlations would have to be estimated (if the bank has 100,000 assets, one would have to estimate the correlation of each asset return with the other 99,999 assets). Third, an approach to forecast volatilities and correlations has to be devised.

The inventory problem would seem to be straightforward since presumably a bank knows which assets it has at a point in time. However, a moment's reflection suggests that it is more complicated than that. JP Morgan, for example, was making markets from 20 different locations and had more than 100 trading units. All the information has to be available at one point in time so that the appropriate computations can be performed. A bank may have this information at one point in time, but perhaps not in a usable form—some of it might be in written form, some might be on one computer system, and some might be on another computer system. Also, to compute the volatility of a portfolio, portfolio weights have to be available, which requires knowledge of prices. All the prices used have to be accurate, which again may be a problem. What if an asset has not traded for the last month? A process has to be devised that makes it possible to have price estimates for all the assets included in the VaR computation.

Figure 4.3	Normal and lognormal density and cumulative distribution functions

The random variable has mean of 1.1 and volatility of 0.25. With the normal distribution, negative values are possible. The normal density function is symmetric, but the lognormal is not. The lognormal distribution has positive skewness because a lognormal variable can take large positive values, but can never take negative values.

Panel A. Density distribution functions

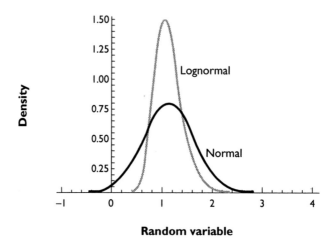

Panel B. Cumulative distribution functions

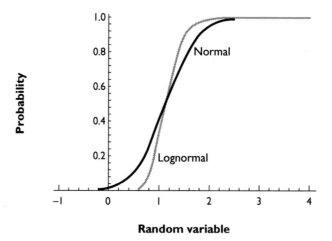

Since it is not practical to compute millions of correlations, RiskMetrics™ uses a mapping procedure. Rather than focusing on the volatilities and correlations of thousands of assets, RiskMetrics maps the bank's portfolio into broad asset classes, the RiskMetrics™ assets, for which it forecasts volatilities and correlations. For example, RiskMetrics™ does not use volatilities of individual stocks, but rather treats a portfolio of stocks in one country as an investment in that country's market portfolio. Similarly, it does not compute the volatility for each T-bill, T-note, and T-bond, but treats each government security as a portfolio of zero-coupon bonds and provides volatilities and correlations for a number of different zero-coupon bonds. At the end of 2001, RiskMetrics™ provided daily volatilities and correlations for assets in 33 countries. Its daily dataset had 387 volatilities and 74,691 correlations. To obtain a VaR estimate using the Risk-Metrics™ approach, we must therefore map the portfolio we have into a portfolio of RiskMetrics™ assets.

Finally, RiskMetrics™ requires the use of forecasts of volatilities and correlations. Volatilities and correlations change over time, sometimes sharply. There are periods when volatilities tend to be high because there is a great deal of uncertainty about the future. For example, stock and bond volatilities across the world were extremely high in the fall of 1998. Tremendous effort has been expanded to devise models for forecasting volatility. The main lesson from all this effort is that volatility is predictable at short horizons. If volatility was high over the last week for a financial asset, then it can be expected to be high tomorrow. However, the fact that volatility was high over the last week does not mean it will be high in six months. The persistence of volatility is short-term. Since, with daily VaR, we are attempting to estimate volatility over the next day, the persistence of volatility has to be taken into account.

The way RiskMetrics™ takes into account the fact that volatility is predictable is by giving more weight to recent observations in computing volatility forecasts. Suppose you want to estimate daily volatility for the S&P 500. You could obtain such an estimate the way you would typically estimate the volatility of a random variable: by taking the square root of the average of past squared returns. However, if you were to weight every squared return equally, you would ignore the fact that high recent volatility means that volatility tomorrow is going to be high. You can remedy this by putting more weight on recent observations. RiskMetrics™ uses declining weights in weighting past observations, so that the most recent returns affect the estimate of volatility more than returns six months ago.

With this approach, RiskMetrics™ assumes that the distribution of returns changes over time. Consequently, it cannot be that returns are drawn from a normal distribution with unchanging mean and volatility. Instead, the conditional distribution of returns is normal—meaning that conditional on the information available today, the distribution of tomorrow's return is normal, but the normal distribution from which the return is drawn for the next day will change as new information becomes available.

When JP Morgan first made RiskMetrics™ available, it made it possible for everybody to download the forecasts of the volatilities and correlations freely from the Internet. Further, it made available all the technical details of how to implement the RiskMetrics™ approach. RiskMetrics continues to make these datasets available, but now the forecasts for the next day are no longer freely available—they are free with a six-month lag.

4.1.3. Measuring cash flow at risk in a nonfinancial firm

Let's now consider a manufacturing firm that exports a product, Export Inc. The firm has foreign currency receivables and, consequently, has exposure to foreign exchange rate risks. Let's say it does not currently hedge, does not have derivatives or financial assets, and cannot raise outside funds. This firm views its main risk as the risk that it will have a cash flow shortfall relative to expected cash flow that is large enough to endanger the firm's ability to remain in business and finance the investments it wants to undertake.

A bad cash flow for a week or a month is not a problem for such a firm. Cash flows are random and seasonal; some weeks or some months will have lower cash flows. Export Inc. has a problem if bad cash flows cumulate, so it is concerned about cash flows over a longer period of time, such as a year or more.

The risk that concerns the firm is the likelihood that it will have a cash shortfall over the coming fiscal year. Low cash flow by the end of that year will force it to change its plans. It has the funds available to carry on with its investment plans for this year, and it has enough reserves that it can ride out the year.

To evaluate the risk that cash flow will be low enough to create problems, Export Inc. has to forecast the distribution of its cash flow. It has two choices. If a specific cash flow level is the lowest the firm can have without incurring costs of financial distress, it can use the cumulative distribution of cash flow to determine the probability of a cash flow lower than this threshold. Alternatively, the firm can decide it will not allow the probability of serious problems to exceed some level. In this case, it evaluates the cash flow shortfall corresponding to that probability level. If the cash flow shortfall at that probability level is too great, the firm has to take actions to reduce the risk of its cash flow.

This last approach is equivalent to the VaR approach, except that it is applied to cash flow. The cash flow shortfall corresponding to the probability level chosen by the firm is thus called **cash flow at risk**, or **CaR**, at that probability level. A CaR of $100 million at the 5 percent level means that there is a probability of 5 percent that the firm's cash flow will be lower than its expected value by at least $100 million. We can therefore define cash flow at risk as follows:

Cash flow at risk

Cash flow at risk (CaR) at p percent is the cash flow shortfall (defined as expected cash flow minus realized cash flow) such that there is a probability p percent that the firm will have a larger cash flow shortfall. If realized cash flow is C and expected cash flow is E(C), we have:

$$\textbf{Prob[E(C) – C > CaR]} = \textbf{\textit{p}\,\%}$$

Let's look at an example of these computations. Suppose Export forecasts its cash flow for the coming year to be $80 million. The forecasted volatility is $50 million. The firm believes that the normal distribution is a good approximation of the true distribution of cash flow. It wants to make sure that there is no more than a 5 percent probability of having to cut investment and/or face financial distress. It knows it will be in this situation if its cash flow falls below $20 million. Hence, the firm wants to limit the probability that its cash flow shortfall exceeds $60 million (expected cash flow of $80 million minus cash flow of $20 million) to be at most 5 percent.

Remember that if z is a random variable that follows the normal distribution, then $u = [z - \mathrm{E}(z)]/[\mathrm{Vol}(z)]$ follows the standard normal distribution. If z is cash flow, then the absolute value of $z - \mathrm{E}(z)$ is the shortfall of cash flow when z is lower than $E(z)$. Consequently, the cash flow shortfall at the 5 percent probability level is given by $-1.65 = -[\text{Cash flow shortfall}]/[\text{Volatility of cash flow}]$, or $1.65 \times [\text{Volatility of cash flow}]$ is the cash flow shortfall or CaR at the 5 percent probability level. It follows that for our example the CaR is equal to 1.65 times volatility, or $1.65 \times \$50$ million, which corresponds to a cash flow shortfall of $82.5 million. This means there is a 5 percent probability that the cash flow shortfall will be at least $82.5 million or, alternatively, that cash flow will be lower than $-\$2.5$ million ($80 million minus $82.5 million). Since the CaR exceeds the firm's target, the cash flow is too risky for the firm to achieve its goal. It must therefore take actions that reduce the risk of cash flow and ensure that 95 percent of the time it will earn at least $20 million.

How would Export estimate CaR? It would have to forecast cash flow and its distribution. To do that, it would have to figure out the risk factors that affect its cash flow and estimate their distribution. Conceptually, this would be similar to forecasting the risk factors for VaR. In practice, there are some differences. First, with CaR, we have to forecast the distribution of risk factors for one year instead of perhaps one day for VaR. Second, the impact of risk factors on cash flow is often complicated because cash flow can be a nonlinear function of a risk factor. For example, if a firm sells computers in France, the number of computers sold as well as their price in France may depend on the dollar price of the euro. We examine this issue in Chapter 8.

4.1.4. VaR or CaR?

Should a corporation measure and control firm value at risk, cash flow at risk, or both? A firm that depends solely on its cash flow to take advantage of its growth opportunities has to manage the risk of cash flow for the coming year. Otherwise, the firm can incur costs of financial distress and may have to cut investment if its cash flow is unexpectedly low. CaR is a measure of the risk that cash flow will fall below some critical value. It is therefore an appropriate risk measure for such a firm. A risk measure that focuses on the risk of the total market value of the firm would not be appropriate because controlling that risk measure would not enable the firm to implement its investment program: Firm value could be high even though cash flow for the year is low.

The reasoning changes if the firm has other resources to finance investment. This will be the case if the firm has assets (including financial assets) that it can sell to finance investment or it has access to capital markets to raise funds. A firm can choose to liquidate assets, especially financial assets, if its cash flow is low. It may have to reduce investment if it simultaneously has low cash flow from operations and the assets that can be liquidated to finance capital expenditures have low value. The CaR measure can be extended in a straightforward way in this case. Instead of focusing solely on cash flow from operations, the firm adds to cash flow from operations the change in the value of the assets that can be sold to finance investment. It then computes the CaR on this measure of cash available for investment.

A firm that has access to capital markets has resources to finance next year's investments in addition to this year's cash flow. If its credit is good, it will be able to raise funds at low cost. If its credit deteriorates, the firm may find it too expensive to access capital markets. To the extent that the firm's credit does not depend only on the coming year's cash flow, it is not enough for the firm to measure the risk of this year's cash flow.

Generally, firm value is an important determinant of a firm's ability to raise funds. If the firm can freely use the capital markets to make up for cash flow shortfalls as long as its value is sufficiently high, then the relevant risk measure is firm value risk. A firm's value is the present value of its cash flows. This means that firm value risk depends on the risk of all future cash flows. The appropriate measure of firm value risk is firm VaR.

Most firms are somewhere between free access to capital markets and dependent only on the cash flow of this year to finance next year's investment. Not surprisingly, investment banks pay a lot of attention to VaR. For example, in November 2000, Goldman Sachs had a firm-wide one-day VaR for its trading instruments of $22 million. The firm-wide VaR was computed assuming normally distributed returns and a 5 percent probability level. At the same time, however, Goldman Sachs had many assets that were nontraded assets. It computed a measure similar to CaR by estimating the impact on its net revenue from changes in the fair value of its nontraded assets of a 10 percent drop in the S&P 500. It assessed the loss in net revenue to be $240 million. Many nonfinancial firms estimate a VaR for the derivative products they hold. Dell Computers computes a VaR for its foreign exchange derivative instruments and reported a one-day 5 percent VaR of $21.4 million on February 2, 2001.

In measuring cash flow at risk, nonfinancial firms have focused on measuring the risk resulting from specific market risks, such as currency risks, or from most market risks they face. For example, at the end of 2000, Ford estimated that it had a 1 percent probability of a cash flow shortfall in excess of $300 million over the next 18 months because of exchange rate fluctuations. Another firm, BHP, an Australian conglomerate, estimated its CaR taking into account all market risks to be A$1.6 billion. Cash flow is not affected by market risks only. For example, a firm's cash flow could fall dramatically because of a new competitor. However, firms have so far done little to integrate such risks in their cash flow at risk measures.

4.2. VaR, CaR, and firm value

Firms measure risk because risk impacts shareholder wealth. To maximize shareholder wealth, firms have to control their risk so that they have the optimal amount of risk. Therefore, if the firm cares about risk measured by VaR or CaR, it has to evaluate all its actions in light of their impact on its risk measure. If increases in a firm's risk are costly, the firm will reject some projects because of their impact on its risk, or it might choose to undertake projects because they reduce its risk—for example, it might take positions in derivatives to hedge. This means that computing the NPV of a project as a stand-alone project and taking all positive NPV projects is not the right solution for a firm that is concerned about VaR or CaR.

We consider how firms choose projects when VaR or CaR is costly, and show how they should evaluate the profitability of their activities.

4.2.1. The impact of projects on VaR

The **VaR impact of a project** is the change in VaR brought about by the project. For the purpose of concreteness, think of a project as a trade that involves investing in a new security and financing the investment with the sale of a security in the portfolio. This trade affects both the expected return of the portfolio and its volatility. Assume the securities have normally distributed returns. Suppose that the portfolio is held for a long enough period that the expected return has to be taken into account when computing VaR. The VaR for the return is 1.65 times the volatility of the portfolio minus the portfolio's expected return.

In Chapter 2, we showed how to compute the expected return and the volatility of a portfolio. We saw that the change in the expected return of the portfolio resulting from buying security i and selling security j in the same amounts is equal to the expected return of security i minus the expected return of security j times the size of the trade expressed as a portfolio share Δw, $[E(R_i) - E(R_j)]\Delta w$. We also discussed in Chapter 2 how a small change in the portfolio share of a security affects the volatility of the portfolio. We saw that the impact of the small change on the volatility depends on the covariance of the return of the security with the return of the portfolio. We demonstrated there that a trade that increases the portfolio share of a security that has a positive return covariance with the portfolio and decreases the portfolio share of a security that has a negative return covariance with the portfolio increases the volatility of the portfolio. Hence, such a trade has a positive volatility impact.

Denote the portfolio we are considering now by the subscript p, remembering that this is an arbitrary portfolio. The volatility impact of a small trade that increases the portfolio share of security i in the portfolio by Δw and decreases the portfolio share of security j by the same amount has an impact on the volatility of the portfolio as follows:

$$\textbf{Volatility impact of trade} = \left(\beta_{ip} - \beta_{jp}\right) \times \Delta w \times \text{Vol}\left(R_p\right) \qquad \textbf{(4.1)}$$

(Technical Box 4.2, Impact of trade on volatility, gives the exact derivation of the formula.) β_{ip} is the covariance of the return of security i with the return of portfolio p divided by the variance of the return of portfolio p. If the firm's portfolio, portfolio p, is the market portfolio, β_{ip} is the CAPM beta, but otherwise β_{ip} differs from the CAPM beta. If the expected return of the portfolio is assumed to be zero, the VaR impact of the trade is 1.65 times the volatility impact of the trade times the value of the portfolio. If the trade increases the expected return of the portfolio, this increase decreases the VaR relative to what it would be with a lower expected return because all possible portfolio returns are increased by the increase in expected return. Let W be the initial value of the portfolio. The VaR impact of the trade is therefore:

VaR impact of trade

$$= -\left(E\left(R_i\right) - E\left(R_j\right)\right) \times \Delta w \times W$$

$$+ \left(\beta_{ip} - \beta_{jp}\right) \times 1.65 \times \text{Vol}\left(R_p\right) \times \Delta w \times W \qquad \textbf{(4.2)}$$

Technical Box 4.2 Impact of trade on volatility

Remember the definition of the variance of the portfolio return given in equation (2.3):

$$\text{Var}\left(R_p\right) = \sum_{i=1}^{N} w_i^2 \, \text{Var}(R_i) + \sum_{i=1}^{N} \sum_{j \neq i}^{N} w_i w_j \text{Cov}\left(R_i, R_j\right)$$

Taking the derivative of the formula for the variance with respect to w_i, the impact of an increase in the portfolio share of security i of Δw on the variance is:

Impact of trade Δw on $\text{Var}\left(R_p\right)$

$$= 2w_i \text{Var}(R_i) \Delta w + 2 \sum_{j \neq i}^{N} w_j \text{Cov}\left(R_i, R_j\right) \Delta w$$

The volatility is the square root of the variance. Consequently, taking the derivative of volatility with respect to the variance, a change in the variance of $\Delta \text{Var}(R_p)$ changes the volatility by $0.5\Delta\text{Var}(R_p)[\text{Var}(R_p)]^{-0.5} = 0.5\Delta\text{Var}(R_p)/\text{Vol}(R_p)$. We substitute in this expression the change in the variance brought about by the increase in the holding of security i to get the impact on portfolio return volatility:

$$0.5\left[2w_i \text{Var}(R_i)\Delta w + 2\sum_{j \neq i}^{N} w_j \text{Cov}\left(R_i, R_j\right)\Delta w \right] / \text{Vol}\left(R_p\right)$$

$$= \left[w_i \text{Var}(R_i)\Delta w + \sum_{j \neq i}^{N} w_j \text{Cov}\left(R_i, R_j\right)\Delta w \right] / \text{Vol}\left(R_p\right)$$

$$= \text{Cov}\left(R_i, R_p\right)\Delta w / \text{Vol}\left(R_p\right)$$

$$= \beta_{ip} \text{Vol}\left(R_p\right)\Delta w$$

Equation (4.1) follows from computing the impact of increasing the portfolio share of security i by Δw and decreasing the portfolio share of security j by the same amount.

In other words, a trade increases the VaR of a portfolio if the asset bought has a higher beta coefficient with respect to the portfolio than the asset sold, or if it has a lower expected return. The role of beta is not surprising since we know that an asset with a higher beta contributes more to the risk of the portfolio.

The firm has to decide whether the expected return impact of the trade is high enough to justify its VaR impact. To make this decision, the firm has to know the cost attached to an increase in VaR. We assume that the increase in the total cost of VaR can be approximated for small changes by a constant incremental cost of VaR, which we call the marginal cost of VaR per unit. A firm that knows how much it costs to increase VaR can then make the decision by comparing the expected gain of the trade and the increase in the total cost of VaR resulting from the trade:

Expected gain of trade net of increase in total cost of VaR

= Expected return impact of trade $\times$ Portfolio value

– Marginal cost of VaR per unit $\times$ VaR impact of trade   (4.3)

The marginal cost of VaR per unit captures all the costs the firm incurs by increasing VaR by a dollar. These costs might be the greater costs of financial distress or might be the costs of the actions the firm takes to avoid having an increase in the probability of financial distress. We consider these actions below.

Let's consider an example. Ibank Inc. has a portfolio of $100 million consisting of equal investments in three securities. Security 1 has an expected return of 10 percent and a volatility of 10 percent. Security 2 has an expected return of 20 percent and a volatility of 40 percent. Finally, security 3 has an expected return of 15 percent and a volatility of 60 percent. Security 1 is uncorrelated with the other securities. The correlation coefficient between securities 2 and 3 is –0.4. Using the formula for the expected return of a portfolio, we have:

$$(1/3) \times 0.1 + (1/3) \times 0.2 + (1/3) \times 0.15 = 0.1500$$

The formula for the volatility of a portfolio gives us:

$$[(1/3)^2 \times 0.1^2 + (1/3)^2 \times 0.4^2 + (1/3)^2$$
$$\times 0.6^2 - 2 \times (1/3) \times (1/3) \times 0.4 \times 0.4 \times 0.6]^{0.5} = 0.1938$$

Ibank's VaR is $16.977 million, or 16.977 percent of the value of the portfolio, because the return corresponding to the fifth quantile of the distribution of returns is 0.1500 – 1.65(0.1938), or –16.977 percent. Let's assume that this VaR is such that Ibank would not experience financial distress should its portfolio fall by 16.977 percent but would face difficulties for a larger loss.

Suppose Ibank sells security 3 and buys security 1 in an amount corresponding to 1 percent of the portfolio value, or $1 million. The expected return impact of the trade is:

$$(0.1 - 0.15) \times 0.01 = -0.0005$$

This means that the trade reduces the expected return of the portfolio by 0.05 percent.

To compute the VaR impact, we have to compute the beta of each security with respect to the portfolio. This requires us to know the covariance of each security with the portfolio. The covariances of the securities with the portfolio are

$Cov(R_1, R_p) = 0.0033$ and $Cov(R_3, R_p) = 0.088$.[1] To compute the VaR impact, we can obtain the beta of assets 1 and 3. The beta of asset 1 is $Cov(R_1, R_p)/Var(R_p)$, or $0.0033/0.1938^2$, which is 0.088. The beta of asset 3 is $0.088/0.1938^2$, or 2.343. The VaR impact before taking into account the expected revenue of the trade obtained using equation (4.2) is therefore:

$$-(0.10 - 0.15) \times 0.01 \times \$100M +$$
$$(0.088 - 2.343) \times 1.65 \times 0.1938 \times 0.01 \times \$100M = -\$671{,}081$$

Selling security 3 and buying security 1 reduces Ibank's VaR by $671,081 and the expected return of the portfolio (before taking into account the cost of VaR) by $50,000.

Now that we know the VaR impact of the trade, we need to figure out the marginal cost of VaR. For a given capital structure, an increase in VaR increases Ibank's probability of distress. One way for Ibank to avoid an increase in the probability of distress when VaR increases is to reduce its leverage. This has a cost, which is a measure of the cost of VaR as long as the cheapest way for Ibank to offset the impact of VaR on the probability of distress is through a decrease in leverage.

To estimate the cost of VaR for Ibank, suppose Ibank's capital structure is optimal before the trade. After the trade it has less risk, so it can increase its leverage, which reduces its overall cost of capital—perhaps because it lowers agency costs or because it increases the firm's tax shield of debt. After the trade the probability of a loss of $16.977 million, the pre-trade VaR, is less than 5 percent, so that the probability of financial distress falls. Ibank can substitute debt for equity after the trade to bring its probability of distress back to 5 percent. Since a loss of $16.977 million did not put Ibank in distress before the trade, Ibank could reduce its equity so that the VaR after the trade plus its reduction in equity are equal to $16.977 million without affecting its probability of financial distress. Ibank's VaR falls by $671,081, so that it can reduce its equity by that amount if substituting debt for equity does not affect firm value. In this case, the increase in leverage has all the benefits of an increase in leverage without the main cost of an increase in leverage; namely, it does not increase the firm's probability of distress relative to its target probability of distress. We would therefore expect the increase in leverage to increase firm value. An increase in firm value for a given face value of outstanding debt decreases the probability of distress. Suppose that Ibank investigates the benefit to it from substituting debt for equity, keeping the present value of the costs of financial distress constant, and finds that firm value increases by 10 percent of the decrease in the amount of equity. The reduction in equity required to keep the probability of distress constant has to be such that the

---

1   The covariance is computed as follows:

$$Cov(R_1, R_m) = Cov(R_1, (1/3)R_1 + (1/3)R_2 + (1/3)R_3)$$
$$= (1/3)(Var(R_1) + Cov(R_1, R_2) + Cov(R_1, R_3))$$
$$= (1/3)(0.01 + 0 + 0)$$
$$= 0.0033$$

VaR after the trade plus the reduction in equity has to be equal to the VaR before the trade. In this case, a decrease in VaR of $1 allows the firm to reduce equity by $1.11. This is because a reduction in equity of $1 increases VaR by only $0.90 since it increases the firm's expected profit by $0.10, so that equity has to increase by $1/0.9, or $1.11, to reduce VaR by $1. The net impact of the trade on the firm's profits taking into account the benefit from the reduction in VaR would be −$50,000 + 0.10 × 1.11 × $671,081 = $24,490. Based on this calculation, Ibank would make the trade even though it makes a loss when it is evaluated ignoring its impact on the firm's VaR.

The impact of a trade on VaR we computed is an approximation of the true impact that is correct when the trade is infinitesimally small. For larger trades, the formula for the impact of a trade on VaR we derived is not appropriate. VaR depends on variances, covariances, and portfolio weights. Adding a small amount of an uncorrelated security in a portfolio reduces risk because of greater diversification, but as that amount is increased, eventually the portfolio becomes less diversified and its risk increases. Consequently, VaR is not linear with portfolio weights—firm value does not keep increasing as trade size is increased. The VaR of a portfolio is not the sum of the VaRs of the investments of the portfolio in individual securities or, equivalently, the VaR of a firm is not the sum of the VaRs of its divisions. Therefore, one cannot simply add and subtract the VARs of the positions bought and sold when trades are large. Instead, one has to compare the VaR with the trade and the VaR without the trade to evaluate the impact of large trades on VaR.

The formula for the VaR impact of a trade uses the covariances of security returns with the portfolio return. A large trade changes these covariances, which makes the use of the formula inappropriate. Figure 4.4 plots the firm's VaR as a function of the trade size. This plot shows that if the firm wants to minimize its VaR, a trade much larger than the one contemplated would be required.

4.2.2. Evaluating the impact of a large project on CaR

The **CaR impact of a project** is the change in CaR brought about by the project. Suppose a firm using CaR considers a new project that is significant given the firm's size. If the project were small, we could use the project's marginal impact on CaR (it would be the same formula as for VaR except with return replaced by cash flow and VaR replaced by CaR). Since the project is not a marginal project, we evaluate the impact of a new project on CaR by comparing the CaR with the project to the CaR without the project.

Let C_E be the cash flow from all the current projects and C_N be the cash flow from the new project considered. Assuming that cash flow is normally distributed, the 5 percent CaR without the project is given by:

$$1.65\text{Vol}(C_E) \tag{4.4}$$

The CaR after the project is taken becomes:

$$1.65\text{Vol}\left(C_E + C_N\right)$$

$$= 1.65\left[\text{Var}\left(C_E\right) + \text{Var}\left(C_N\right) + 2\text{Cov}\left(C_E, C_N\right)\right]^{0.5} \tag{4.5}$$

Figure 4.4 VaR as a function of trade size

The trade size is expressed as a fraction of portfolio value.

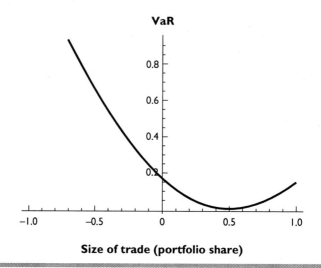

Size of trade (portfolio share)

The impact of taking the project on CaR depends on its variance and on its covariance with the current projects. A project with a higher variance of cash flow increases CaR more because such a project is more likely to have large losses. However, these large losses affect CaR more adversely if they tend to occur when the firm is doing poorly, so that a project whose cash flow covaries more with a firm's existing cash flow increases that firm's CaR more.

If CaR has a cost, we can treat that cost as another cost of the project. Hence, the NPV of the project is decreased by the impact of the project on the cost of CaR. The cost of CaR is the cost as of the beginning of the year resulting from the probability of having a low cash flow that prevents the firm from taking advantage of valuable investment opportunities. The present value of this cost should be deducted from the NPV of the project computed using the CAPM. Consequently, the firm takes all projects whose NPV using the CAPM exceeds their impact on the cost of CaR.

Let's consider an example, assuming again that cash flow is normally distributed. Suppose a firm has expected cash flow of $80 million with volatility of $50 million. It now considers a project that requires an investment of $50 million with volatility of $50 million. The project has a correlation coefficient of 0.5 with current ongoing projects. It has a beta computed with respect to the market portfolio of 0.25. The project has only one payoff in its lifetime, and that occurs at the end of the year. The expected payoff of the project before taking into account the CAPM cost of capital for the initial investment is $58 million. We assume a risk-free rate of 4.5 percent and a market risk premium of 6 percent. Consequently, the cost of capital of the project using the CAPM is 4.5 percent plus 0.25 × 6 percent. With this, the NPV of the project using the CAPM is $58M/1.06 – $50M, or $4.72 million.

A firm that does not care about total risk takes this project. But the volatility of the firm's cash flow in million dollars with the project is:

$$\left(50^2 + 50^2 + 2 \times 0.5 \times 50 \times 50\right)^{0.5} = 86.6025$$

Hence, taking the project increases the volatility of the firm's cash flow by $36.6025 million. The CaR before the project is 1.65($50M), or $82.5 million. The CaR after the project becomes 1.65($86.6025M), or $142.894 million. A firm for which the cost of CaR is $0.10 per dollar of CaR would reject the project because the project has a negative NPV adjusted for the cost of CaR: $4.72M – 0.10($60.394M), or –$1.32 million.

For a project with cash flows over many years, it is not enough for the firm to subtract the cost of CaR associated with the first year of the project. To the extent that the cost of CaR impact of the project in future years can be assessed, it has to be taken into account in computing the value of the project. Each year's project cash flow must be decreased by the impact of the project that year on the firm's cost of CaR. If the impact of the project on the cost of CaR is evaluated at the beginning of each year and takes place with certainty, the project's contribution to the firm's cost of CaR is discounted to today at the risk-free rate.

4.2.3. Allocating the cost of CaR or VaR to existing activities

If CaR is costly for a firm, an activity's contribution to CaR is an economic cost that must be taken into account when evaluating the profitability of the activity. An activity might require little funding, yet it might make a large contribution to the firm's CaR or VaR. Suppose that Conglo Inc. has a division that takes positions in futures contracts in commodities, the WeTrade division. The division has assets worth $1 million. WeTrade uses the firm's liquid assets as collateral for its trades. It has large futures positions. At the end of the year, WeTrade makes a profit of $10 million. The CFO of Conglo Inc. understands that to measure the economic profit of a division, he has to take into account the opportunity cost of the capital used by WeTrade. Since WeTrade has assets of $1 million, he assesses a capital charge of $0.16 million, multiplying the assets of the division by the firm's cost of capital, 16 percent. Viewed this way, WeTrade is spectacularly successful, since it has a return on capital of almost 1,000 percent. The CFO of the company is therefore tempted to recommend that the CEO sell the firm's other divisions.

The CFO's estimate of the economic profits of WeTrade misses a critical cost of this division. The futures contracts the division has could make large losses. Conglo Inc. with the WeTrade division has more risk than without it. Suppose that Conglo Inc. has no risk without the WeTrade division. Measuring the CaR of the WeTrade division, the CFO finds that the division has a 5 percent chance of losing $100 million over the fiscal year. If Conglo Inc. loses that amount or higher, it is in default; if it loses less, it is not in default. For Conglo Inc. to have the same risk of default with the WeTrade division as without it, it therefore needs to have $100 million of additional equity. With this additional capital, Conglo Inc. has a buffer enabling it to lose $100 million and then be in the same situation it would have been in without the WeTrade division. The CFO evaluates the net cost of this additional equity and finds that it will amount to $10 million over the fiscal year. His computation is based on the cost to the firm of substituting equity for debt. After taking into account the cost the WeTrade division imposes on Conglo Inc. because it increases CaR, the WeTrade division makes a slight economic loss—$0.16 million (trading profit of $10 million minus $10 million net cost of capital to bear the risk of the WeTrade division and minus the cost of the funding capital of 16 percent of $1 million).

As long as the WeTrade division is not held accountable for its contribution to the risk of the firm, its managers have incentives to take on more risk. Further, because Conglo Inc. thinks that the WeTrade division makes economic profits when it does not, managers will direct more resources towards that division and will compensate its managers better. In the process, Conglo Inc. becomes increasingly risky, so that the other divisions might be unable to undertake projects that would be truly economically profitable because of the deadweight costs imposed by the WeTrade division. For example, as the WeTrade division grows, the debt rating of Conglo Inc. falls, making it harder for the manufacturing divisions to sell their products because of concerns about warranties.

If a firm can access capital markets, one can think of the cost of CaR or VaR for an activity as the net cost of the capital required to offset the impact of the activity on the firm's CaR or VaR. This capital is often called the risk capital. If the firm increases its risk capital by substituting equity for debt, the net cost of the capital is the total cost of the new equity minus the total cost of debt saved, taking into account all the costs—transaction costs, tax shields lost, impact on agency costs, and so on. When we evaluate the profitability of an activity, we have to take into account not only the capital used to fund the activity but also the capital required to support the risk of the activity. In the case of the WeTrade division, this additional capital is $100 million and dwarfs the funding capital of $1 million.

Suppose that now the CFO of Conglo Inc. understands that CaR is costly. He knows the cost of CaR for the firm as a whole and has to decide how to charge the firm's divisions (or projects) for the cost of CaR. Let's assume that Conglo Inc. has N divisions. Allocating proportional amounts of CaR to each division would make no sense because some divisions may be riskless and others may have considerable risk. The firm therefore has to find a way to allocate CaR to each division that takes into account the risk of the division and how it contributes to firm risk.

We know that the contribution of a security to the risk of a portfolio is measured by the covariance of its return with the return of the portfolio or by the beta of that security with the portfolio. Using this insight of modern portfolio theory, we can measure the contribution of the risk of a division to Conglo's CaR by the **cash flow beta** of the division. A division's cash flow beta is the covariance of the cash flow of the division with the cash flow of the firm divided by the variance of the cash flow of the firm.

Let's see how using cash flow betas allows Conglo's CFO to allocate CaR to the various divisions. The cash flow of division i is C_i. Conglo's total cash flow is the sum of the cash flows of the activities, which we write C. We assume that the cash flows are normally distributed. Consequently, the CaR of this firm is 1.65Vol(C).

Remember that the variance of a random variable is the covariance of the random variable with itself, so that $Var(C_i)$ is equal to $Cov(C_i, C_i)$. Further, covariances of cash flows of the various activities with the cash flow of division i can be added up so that the sum of the covariances is equal to the covariance of the cash flow of division i with the firm's cash flow, $Cov(C_i, C)$.

The variance of the firm cash flow is therefore the sum of the covariances of the cash flow of the divisions with the cash flow of the firm:

Firms cash flow variance

$$= Var(C)$$

$$= \sum_{i=1}^{N} \sum_{j=1}^{N} Cov(C_i, C_j)$$

$$= \sum_{i=1}^{N} Cov\left(C_i, \sum_{j=1}^{N} C_j\right)$$

$$= \sum_{i=1}^{N} Cov(C_i, \text{Firm cash flow } C) \qquad (4.6)$$

Equation (4.6) shows that increasing the covariance of the cash flow of a division with the firm's cash flow increases the variance of the firm's cash flow. If we divide $Cov(C_i, C)$ by $Var(C)$, we have the cash flow beta of activity i with respect to firm cash flow, β_i. The cash flow betas of the firm's divisions sum to one:

$$\sum_{i=1}^{N} \beta_i$$

$$= \sum_{i=1}^{N} Cov(C_i, C) / Var(C)$$

$$= Var(C) / Var(C)$$

$$= 1 \qquad (4.7)$$

A division with a greater cash flow beta therefore contributes more to the firm's CaR. Since the cash flows beta sum to one, the cash flow beta of a division is the proportional contribution of the division to the firm's CaR:

Contribution of division to CaR

The fraction of CaR that is due to division i is equal to the beta of division i with respect to firm cash flow, $\beta_i = Cov(C_i, C)/Var(C)$

Consequently, the contribution of division i to the cost of CaR is equal to the cash flow beta of the division times the firm's cost of CaR.

A firm that uses VaR must also be able to evaluate whether its activities are profitable. Consider a bank that has a number of traders. It must be able to allocate VaR across these traders so that it can evaluate the profitability of traders net of the cost of their contribution to the firm's VaR. Remember that with VaR, we use the distribution of the change in the value of the portfolio or firm instead of the distribution of cash flow. If changes in value are normally distributed, the analysis we performed for CaR applies to VaR. The change in portfolio value is the sum of the changes in value of the traders' positions. The variance of the change in portfolio value is equal to the sum of the covariances of the changes in the value of the positions with the change in value of the portfolio. Consequently, we can compute the beta of a trader's position with respect to the portfolio, namely, the covariance of the change in position value with the change in portfolio value divided by the variance of the change in portfolio value. This position beta measures the proportional contribution of the position to the VaR.

Let's see how we can decompose VaR among N traders. The book of trader i is the portfolio share of the net value of his book times the value of the portfolio, $w_i W$. The return of the trader is R_i. Consequently, the change in firm portfolio value due to trader i is $w_i R_i W$. Let R_P be the return of the firm's portfolio. In this case, the VaR of the portfolio value is:

VaR of portfolio

$$= 1.65 \text{Vol}(R_P) W$$

$$= 1.65 \text{Var}(R_P) W / \text{Vol}(R_P)$$

$$= \sum_{i=1}^{N} w_i \text{Cov}(R_i, R_P) \left[\frac{1.65 \text{Vol}(R_P) W}{\text{Var}(R_P)} \right]$$

$$= \sum_{i=1}^{N} w_i \left[\frac{\text{Cov}(R_i, R_P)}{\text{Var}(R_P)} \right] \text{VaR(Portfolio)}$$

$$= \sum_{i=1}^{N} w_i \beta_{iP} \text{VaR(Portfolio)} \tag{4.8}$$

Consequently, using the same reasoning as with CaR, the proportional contribution of a trader's book is:

Contribution of trader to VaR

The fraction of VaR that is due to trader i is the portfolio share of his book times the beta of his return with respect to the portfolio return

Suppose Joe Smith, a trader, had $50 million at the start of the year and $75 million at the end of the year, so that his profit and loss statement shows a gain of $25 million. To find out whether the trading was profitable, we have to take into account the opportunity cost of the $50 million. Say that Joe's firm has a cost of capital of 15 percent and that this is a reasonable measure of the opportunity cost of $50 million. After this capital allocation, Joe has a profit of only $17.5 million, or $25 million minus 15 percent of $50 million. This capital allocation, however, does not take into account the impact of the trader's activity on the VaR of the firm and its cost. Suppose that the VaR of the firm is $200 million and that the beta of the return of the trader with the return of the firm is 4. The firm's value at the beginning of the year is $1 billion. The portfolio share of the trader is therefore $50M/$1B, or 0.05. Joe also contributes 20 percent of VaR. Let's now assume that the cost of VaR is $20 million. In this case, Joe contributes $4 million of the cost of VaR. His contribution to the economic profits of the firm is therefore $17.5 million minus $4 million, or $13.5 million.

Firms that evaluate economic profits taking into account the contribution of activities to the risk of the firm do so in a number of different ways and give different names to the procedure. One approach that is often used, however, is called RAROC by financial firms, which stands for *risk-adjusted return on capital.* Box 4.3, RAROC at Bank of America, discusses the application of this approach at one financial firm.

4.3. Managing firm risk measured by VaR or CaR

When firm risk, whether measured by VaR or CaR, is costly, a firm can increase its value if it can reduce its cost of risk for given expected profits. There are two ways to do this. First, the firm can reduce the cost of risk for a given level of VaR or CaR. Second, the firm can reduce risk itself.

4.3.1. Reducing the cost of risk for a given level of VaR or CaR

A financial firm is concerned that a drop in value will increase its credit risk and lead to an exodus of its customers. The firm's credit risk is inversely related to its equity capital since equity capital provides funds that can be used to compensate customers in the event that the firm's traded assets lose value. The same reasoning applies to a nonfinancial firm that focuses on CaR. The firm is concerned about its CaR because a bad cash flow outcome means that the firm cannot invest as much as would be profitable. If the firm raises more capital, it can use it to create a cash reserve or to decrease debt. In either case, the firm's ability to pursue its investment plan increases with its equity capital. By increasing its equity capital, a firm reduces the cost of VaR or CaR because equity capital acts as a buffer that diminishes the deadweight costs of adverse outcomes.

If equity capital has no opportunity cost, there is no reason for a firm to be concerned about its VaR or CaR risk. The firm can simply increase its capital up to the point where a bad outcome in cash flow or in the value of its securities has no impact on credit risk. Let's make sure that we understand how increasing the firm's equity impacts CaR and its cost (the reasoning is the same for VaR). Remember that CaR measures a dollar shortfall. If the firm raises equity and uses it to just expand the scale of its activities, CaR actually increases because the cash flow of the firm after the equity issue is just a multiple of the firm's cash flow before the equity issue.

To issue equity in a way that reduces the firm's risk, the proceeds of the equity issue have to be invested so that CaR does not increase. CaR is costly because a bad cash flow outcome makes the firm more financially constrained; the more

---

Box 4.3   RAROC at Bank of America

In November 1993, a Risk and Capital Analysis Department was formed at Bank of America and charged with developing a framework for risk-adjusted profitability measurement. The requirement was that the system would be operational within four months. The bank decided to measure risk over a one-year horizon. Four risks were identified: credit risk, country risk, market risk, and business risk. Credit risk is the risk of borrower default. Country risk is the risk of loss in foreign exposures arising from government actions. Market risk is the risk associated with changes in market prices of traded assets. Business risk corresponds to operational risk associated with business units as ongoing concerns after excluding the other three risks. For each of these risks, the bank is concerned about unexpected risk and how it will affect its own credit rating. For example, it regularly makes provisions for credit losses. Consequently, normal credit losses do not affect earnings but unexpected credit losses do.

Bank of America decided to have an amount of capital such that the risk of default is 0.03 percent per year, which guarantees an AA rating. It concluded that to ensure a probability of default no greater than 0.03 percent across its various businesses, it had to allocate capital of 3.4 standard deviations to market risks and 6 standard deviations to credit risks. The reason it allocates different amounts of capital to different risks is that it views market risks as being normally distributed whereas credit risks are not. All capital allocated is charged the same hurdle rate, which is the corporate-wide cost of equity capital. A project is evaluated based on its economic profit, calculated as earnings net of taxes, interest payments, and expected credit losses. The capital required for the project is then determined based on the credit risk, market risk, country risk, and business risk of the project. The risk-adjusted expected economic profit is then the expected economic profit minus the hurdle rate times the allocated capital.

Bank of America applies the above approach to evaluate its business units. For each business unit, it computes its RAROC as follows:

RAROC of business unit =

$$\frac{\textbf{Economic profit of unit} - \textbf{Capital allocated} \times \textbf{Hurdle rate}}{\textbf{Capital allocated}}$$

Source: Christopher James, RAROC based capital budgeting and performance evaluation: A case study of bank capital allocation, working paper 96-40, Wharton Financial Firms Center, The Wharton School, Philadelphia, PA.

financial slack the firm has, the less likely it is to become financially constrained. Financial slack includes the firm's unused borrowing capacity. A firm can expand its financial slack by having less debt and more liquid assets. Investing the proceeds of the equity issue in risk-free investments or using them to pay back debt does not change the firm's CaR, but it reduces the cost of CaR. As the firm builds up slack, a bad cash flow outcome has less of an impact on investment because the firm can use its slack to offset the cash flow shortfall.

You might argue that the firm does not have to raise equity now to cope with a cash flow shortfall that might occur some time in the future. It can raise the equity when the shortfall occurs. This would be correct if the firm faced the same cost of raising equity after the cash flow shortfall as before. In general, this is not the case. After a cash flow shortfall, outsiders often can't tell whether it occurred because of bad luck, because of managerial incompetence, or because managers are pursuing objectives other than the maximization of shareholder wealth. As a result, equity capital will tend to be most expensive (or even impossible to get) precisely when obtaining it has most value for the firm.

There are a variety of problems with increasing capital. As a firm raises equity to reduce its cost of CaR, it must keep its operations unchanged and use the proceeds to pay back debt, which reduces debt costs, or to invest in risk-free assets. Suppose the firm issues equity to buy back debt. The equity holders expect a return on their equity commensurate with its risk. By issuing equity to buy back debt, the firm makes the remaining debt less risky, which is a benefit to the remaining debtholders. Hence, shareholders do not capture the whole benefit of increasing the firm's equity capital; some of it goes to the debtholders. Further, shareholders lose the tax shield on the debt bought back and replaced by equity. Issuing equity to reduce the cost of CaR thus has costs for the shareholders. The costs are increased further by the fact that management can do anything with this new money that it wants unless the firm becomes bankrupt or is taken over. Hence, management must convince equity holders that it will invest the new money profitably. Doing so is difficult because of information asymmetries and because of agency costs. Managers generally benefit from having more resources under their control. With more assets, the firm is less likely to become bankrupt, and managers have more perks and are paid more. The problem is that since management benefits from having more resources, it may want to raise equity even when it does not have good uses for the new funds.

Having enough equity to make risk management irrelevant is generally not an option because new equity is expensive. An estimate is that if a firm with $1 billion worth of equity sells $100 million of new equity, its net resources increase by only about $70 million. The increase in net resources associated with an equity issue is therefore only a fraction of the equity raised because of the costs of raising equity capital. First, there is a transaction cost. Investment bankers have to be paid. This cost can be of the order of 5 percent of the value of the new equity— or more for smaller issues or issues by smaller firms. Second, there is a stock price impact. When a firm announces an equity issue, the value of its existing equity falls on average by about 2.5 percent. There is some debate as to whether some or all of this fall in the equity price represents a cost of issuing equity or is simply the result that the market learns about the true value of the firm when it issues equity, information that the market would have learned anyway.

The evidence on costs is only for firms that issue equity. It does not include firms that give up profitable projects instead of issuing equity. We know that firms give up valuable projects instead of issuing equity because of the research that shows the impact of firm liquidity on investment. This literature shows that firms with fewer liquid assets typically invest less, controlling for the value of the investment opportunities. In other words, if two firms have equally valuable investment opportunities, the one with fewer liquid assets invests less.

4.3.2. Reducing risk through project choice

When firm risk is costly, the firm can choose projects so that its risk is low. This means that the firm may give up projects with high profits if these projects increase firm risk substantially and may choose unprofitable projects because they might reduce firm risk. Should a firm avoid investing in projects that might have high payoffs simply because they would increase firm risk significantly? Should it invest in activities not because they are the most profitable but because they have a favorable impact on firm risk?

Traditionally, firms have viewed diversification across operations as a way to manage their risk. When they invest in a project whose return is imperfectly correlated with existing projects instead of a project whose return is perfectly correlated with them, the firm increases risk less. Reducing risk through diversification is cheap when it involves buying financial assets. It is more expensive when it involves managing unrelated activities. A firm that has firm-specific capital that gives it a comparative advantage to develop some types of projects does not have the same comparative advantage for projects that are diversifying activities. Nonfinancial diversification can require another layer of management.

Empirical evidence demonstrates that the costs of diversification within firms are typically significant. The simplest way to evaluate these costs is to compare a diversified firm to a portfolio of specialized firms whose assets match the assets of the diversified firm. Research documents a "diversification discount," in that a diversified firm is worth less than the matching portfolio of specialized firms. The exact extent of the discount is a matter of debate.

4.3.3. Using derivatives and other financial instruments to reduce risk

We have said that firms can reduce their cost of risk by increasing their equity capital or by choosing to invest in projects that reduce risk. Both of these approaches to managing firm risk involve substantial costs. The third alternative is to reduce risk through the use of financial instruments. This costs less. The reason is that transaction costs associated with trades in financial instruments are generally low. They are measured in basis points. In the most liquid markets, such as the spot foreign exchange market, they are even lower. When it uses financial instruments to manage risk, the firm achieves two outcomes. First, it reduces its risk, which means that it increases its value. Second, it can structure a possible new project so as to minimize its hedged risk. This means that the relevant measure of the project's contribution to firm-wide risk is its contribution net of hedging activities. It is possible for an unhedged project to contribute too much to the risk of the firm to be worthwhile, but once the project is hedged, it becomes a worthwhile project that the firm can take profitably. Using financial instruments to reduce risk can allow a firm to grow more and to be worth more. The firm can use financial instruments already available in financial markets or create new ones.

Firms cannot eliminate all risks through financial instruments. Information asymmetries we have discussed between the firm and investors come into play.

Suppose Export Inc. takes a short forward position in the euro. Its counterparty has to be confident that the firm will pay at maturity if it incurred a loss on the contract. If there is no doubt that Export Inc. hedged, it will have the euros at maturity. But what if the firm is in trouble at maturity, so that senior bondholders have a claim on the euros? Or what if the firm just said it wanted to hedge, but in fact is speculating? Export Inc.'s counterparty may require collateral, but Export Inc. may not have suitable collateral. Alternatively, Export Inc.'s counterparty may make the terms of the contract less attractive to Export Inc. so that it receives some compensation for taking on some credit risks.

Another reason a firm cannot eliminate all risks through financial transactions is the existence of moral hazard. **Moral hazard** is the risk resulting from the ability of one party to a contract to take unobserved actions that adversely affect the value of the contract for the other party. Absent moral hazard, a firm could buy a contract that compensates it for a cash flow shortfall that exceeds a threshold. Firms would like to obtain such insurance, but generally it is not feasible. The insurance company knows that the firm can make its cash flow worse. In fact, managers could go on vacation, the firm could collect the insurance, and shareholders would be as well off as if management had worked very hard! When moral hazard is important, the cost of insuring a risk can become as large as the maximum loss one can incur. When that happens, it makes no sense to buy insurance since it would be less costly to bear the risk in the first place.

Finally, the use of derivatives can be limited by the costs of acquiring the derivatives. Trading in standardized derivatives is often extremely cheap. However, not all of the firm's hedging needs can be satisfied with standardized derivatives. The firm may require complicated financial instruments. Such instruments are more expensive to trade. In some cases, they have to be designed explicitly for the firm, which can increase their cost sharply. When CaR is costly, though, it makes sense to use derivatives to reduce CaR only to the extent that doing so provides a net saving for the firm. If taking a position in a derivative to reduce CaR costs more than the saving in the cost of CaR brought about by the reduction in CaR, it does not make sense to take that position.

4.4. Summary

In Chapter 3, we showed how firms can benefit from risk management. In this chapter, we showed how the analysis of Chapter 3 implies that firms will want to manage specific risk measures. We therefore introduced VaR and CaR. Estimating a firm's risk is the starting point of using risk management to increase firm value. Once a firm estimates its risk, it has to figure out the cost of bearing this risk and whether there is an amount of risk that leads to higher shareholder wealth. We argued that when evaluating new projects, firms have to evaluate the cost of bearing their risk. We then showed that a firm has a number of tools available to manage firm risk. Firms can increase their equity capital, take projects that decrease firm-wide risk, or use financial instruments to hedge risks. Derivatives often provide the most efficient tools to manage firm risk. The reason for this is that this tool is often cheap and flexible. Derivatives can be designed to create a wide range of cash flows and their transaction costs are generally extremely low compared to the costs of using other risk management tools.

Key Concepts

Review Questions

1. Why do firms require a risk measure?

2. What is VaR?

3. How does VaR differ from variance?

4. How is the VaR of a portfolio computed if returns on assets are normally distributed?

5. Why is VaR an appropriate risk measure for financial firms?

6. What is CaR?

7. When would a firm use CaR?

8. How do you choose a project if VaR is costly?

9. How do you choose a project if CaR is costly?

10. How do you measure a division's contribution to the firm's CaR?

11. Should the contribution of a division to the firm's CaR affect the firm's estimate of its profitability?

12. Why and how should you use VaR to evaluate the profitability of a trader?

13. How can the firm reduce CaR or VaR?

14. How can the firm reduce its cost of CaR or VaR for given levels of CaR or VaR?

15. How does moral hazard limit the ability of a firm to manage its risk?

Questions and Exercises

1. Consider a firm with a trading book valued at $100 million. The return of these assets is distributed normally with a yearly standard deviation of 25 percent. The firm can liquidate all of the assets immediately in liquid markets. How much capital should the firm have so that 99 days out of 100, the firm's return on assets is high enough that, after liquidating its portfolio, it would have capital left?

2. Consider the firm in question 1. Now the firm is in a situation where it cannot liquidate its portfolio for five days. How much capital does it need to have so that 95 five-day periods out of 100, it ends the period with positive capital if it has to liquidate its portfolio?

3. How does your answer to question 2 change if the firm's trading book has an annual expected return of 10 percent?

4. A firm has a trading book composed of two assets with normally distributed returns. The first asset has an annual expected return of 10 percent and an annual volatility of 25 percent. The firm has a position of $100 million in that asset. The second asset has an annual expected return of 20 percent and an annual volatility of 20 percent as well. The firm has a position of $50 million in that asset. The correlation coefficient between the returns of these two assets is 0.2. Compute the 5 percent annual VaR for that firm's trading book.

5. Consider a trade for the firm in question 4 where it sells $10 million of the first asset and buys $10 million of the second asset. By how much does the 5 percent VaR change?

6. Consider a firm with a portfolio of traded assets worth $100 million with a VaR of $20 million. This firm considers selling a position worth $1 million to purchase a position with the same value in a different asset. The covariance of the return of the position to be sold with the return of the portfolio is 0.05. The asset it acquires is uncorrelated with the portfolio. By how much does the VaR change with this trade?

7. Growth Inc. has a yearly cash flow at risk of $200 million. An increase in the equity Growth Inc. has to serve as a cushion against losses has a net cost for the firm of 12 percent per year. Growth Inc. can expand the scale of its activities by 10 percent. The firm wants to increase its equity capital so that it could absorb a cash flow shortfall equal to its CaR after expanding its activities so that its probability of default after experiencing such a shortfall would be the same as if it had not expanded its activities. How much equity capital does it have to raise? How much must the project earn before taking into account the capital required to protect it against losses to be profitable?

8. Consider the choice of two mutually exclusive projects by Innovate Inc. The first project is a scale expanding project. By investing $100 million, Innovate Inc. expects to earn $20 million a year net of funding costs. The project is infinitely lived, so that there is no depreciation. This project also increases cash flow at risk by $50 million. The second project requires no initial investment and is expected to earn $25 million. This project increases the cash flow at risk by $200 million. Under which conditions will the first project be more advantageous than the second project assuming that neither project has systematic risk?

9. The treasurer of a firm tells you that he just computed a one-year VaR and a one-year CaR for his firm. He is puzzled because both numbers are the same. How could that be the case?

10. A division in a firm where CaR is costly has just found a way to hedge its cash flow costlessly. What is the impact of this discovery on the division's economic profits calculated ignoring the cost of CaR? What is the impact of this discovery on the division's economic profits taking into account the cost of CaR?

Literature Note

For an analysis of risk management in financial firms and the role of risk capital, see Merton (1993) and Merton and Perold (1993). VaR is presented in the RiskMetrics™ technical manual and in Jorion (1997). For a discussion of RAROC, see Zaik, Walter, Kelling, and James (1996). Litterman (1997) discusses the marginal VaR and plots VaR as a function of trade size. Matten (1996) provides a book-length treatment of the issues related to capital allocation. Saita (1999) discusses a number of organizational issues related to capital allocation. Froot and Stein (1998) provide a theoretical model where they derive optimal hedges and capital budgeting rules. Stoughton and Zechner (1998) extend such an approach to take into account information asymmetries. The internal models approach for regulatory capital is presented in Hendricks and Hirtle (1997). Santomero (1995) provides an analysis of the risk management process in commercial banks. The computation of CaR at BHP is discussed in Bainbridge and Kennedy (2001).

Smith (1986) reviews the literature on the stock price impact of selling securities. Myers and Majluf (1984) discuss the case where a firm does not issue equity because doing so is too expensive. Stulz (1990) examines the implications of the agency costs of managerial discretion on the firm's cost of external finance. Fazzari, Hubbard, and Petersen (1988) provide a seminal analysis of how investment is related to liquidity. Opler, Pinkowitz, Stulz, and Williamson (1999) show how investment is related to slack. Lang and Stulz (1994) and Berger and Ofek (1995) discuss the costs of diversification.

The positions of LTCM at the time of its collapse are described in "Risk managers of the year: LTCM oversight committee," *Risk Magazine*, January 2000, 32–33. The history of RiskMetrics is discussed in "The Story of RiskMetrics" in the same issue of *Risk Magazine*.

Part 2

Hedging with Forwards, Futures, and Options Contracts

Chapter 5

Forward and Futures Contracts

Chapter 5 Objectives

At the end of this chapter, you will:

1. Know how forward contracts are priced.

2. Understand how futures contracts differ from forward contracts.

3. Know the determinants of the price of futures contracts.

We have established that risk management can be used to increase firm value and enhance the welfare of investors. In the remainder of the book, we show how to do it. Most of our focus is on how to use the derivatives available in the marketplace and create new ones to increase firm value through risk management. However, we also discuss how derivatives can be used by individuals to improve their welfare, for instance in portfolio strategies. There are too many types of derivatives for us to provide a complete catalogue of their specific properties and uses. Instead, we describe how to understand and use derivatives in general, starting in this chapter with the simplest derivatives, forward and futures contracts.

Mr. Hedge's firm has a large foreign exchange exposure. In one year, it will receive 2 billion euros, so that its cash flow at that time, absent hedging, will depend on the dollar price of the euro. He assesses that the risk associated with that exposure adversely affects the value of the firm's equity by $15 million. By eliminating this exposure, Mr. Hedge could increase the wealth of the firm's shareholders by $15 million. To offset the exposure, he decides to take a short position in a euro forward contract for €2 billion. This means that, at maturity of the contract, the firm will have to deliver the €2 billion it receives then and will be paid the forward price in dollars for the euros delivered. With the forward contract, the firm's cash flow in one year no longer depends on the price of the euro: It is fixed at €2 billion times the forward price of the euro. Mr. Hedge calls up a bank to receive a quote for a forward contract on the euro maturing in one year. The bank offers to buy the euros in one year at a price of $0.90 per euro. Therefore, the forward price is $0.90.

Mr. Hedge accepts the forward contract offered by the bank, presuming that the price offered is competitive. It turns out that the bank did not really want that contract on its books, so it offered an extremely low price. The forward price consistent with forward pricing theory on that day would have been $0.91 and not $0.90. This means that in one year, the firm receives $1.80 billion instead of the $1.82 billion it would have received had it entered a fairly priced forward contract. Discounted at the continuously compounded rate of 5 percent, the loss to the firm from entering the forward contract with the low forward price is $19.02 million. By entering the mispriced forward contract, Mr. Hedge caused shareholders to lose more money than he would have caused them to gain by eliminating risk—on net, the shareholders lost $4.02 million.

To use derivatives to increase shareholder wealth, one has to know how they are priced so that one can identify whether a price is acceptable given existing market conditions. In this chapter, we show how Mr. Hedge could have assessed the price offered to him by the bank using the pricing theory for forward contracts. We also explain how to price futures contracts and discuss a number of features of forward and futures contracts that have to be taken into account by users of these contracts. In the four chapters that follow, we examine the uses of forward and futures contracts in risk management.

To price forward and futures contracts, we apply the fundamental method used to price derivatives in general. This method is called **pricing by arbitrage**. Let's see how this method works in principle for a derivative security that is purchased now, has no cash flows until maturity, and makes a payoff at maturity. For this derivative, the method of pricing by arbitrage requires us to find a portfolio, whose investments can be changed over time, that does not use the derivative, but also that has no cash flows until maturity and has the same payoff as the derivative. Such a portfolio is called a **replicating portfolio**. Ignoring transaction costs and other market imperfections, a replicating portfolio must have the same current value as the derivative. Otherwise, the replicating portfolio and the derivative yield the same payoffs for different prices. That is, if the same payoffs can be obtained for different prices, there is an arbitrage opportunity: one can simultaneously buy the payoff at the low price and sell it at the high price, making money for sure—an unlikely and ephemeral event because traders actively seek out such opportunities and in the process make them disappear. Consequently, the value of the replicating portfolio is the price of the derivative in the absence of arbitrage opportunities.

In forward and futures markets, transaction costs are generally so low as to be inconsequential. Therefore, we use the convenient and simplifying assumption of perfect financial markets (except at the end of the chapter). For the analysis, this means there are no transactions costs, no taxes, no difference between borrowing and lending rates, and no restrictions on short sales. We start with the simplest case: forward contracts on T-bills.

In section 5.2 we extend the analysis to forward contracts on commodities, stocks, and currencies. In section 5.3 we introduce futures contracts, and explain how and why they differ from forward contracts. We give a detailed example of how a futures position evolves through time. In section 5.4 we discuss how forward and futures prices relate to each other and to future spot prices.

5.1. Pricing forward contracts on T-bills

We introduced forward contracts in Chapter 1 and have been using them ever since. Remember that a forward contract is a purchase contract with delivery and payment taking place at maturity of the contract, on terms agreed upon when the parties enter into the contract. We now want to understand how the forward price is determined at the origination of the contract. For that purpose, we study a forward contract on T-bills. We assume that financial markets are perfect, so that there are no transaction costs or taxes.

Suppose Mr. Smith considers on March 1 a forward contract to buy on June 1 T-bills maturing on August 30 at the price of 97 cents per dollar of face value for a total face value of $1 million. A timeline of the transaction is given in Figure 5.1. Money changes hands only at maturity of the contract. The forward price per dollar of face value is $0.97, that is, the price agreed upon on March 1 for delivery on June 1 of bills that mature on August 30. In this case, the forward contract specifies:

1. **The goods to be exchanged for cash:** $1 million of face value of T-bills maturing on August 30.

2. **The date when the exchange is to take place:** June 1.

3. **The price to be paid:** $0.97 per dollar of face value.

5.1.1. Valuing a forward position using the method of pricing by arbitrage

Mr. Smith would like to know whether $0.97 is an advantageous forward price for him. Denote the June 1 cash market price of the T-bills delivered on the

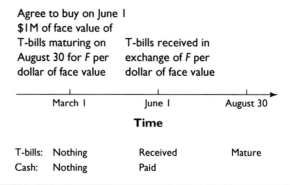

Figure 5.1   Time line for long forward contract position

forward contract by $P_{\text{June 1}}$(August 30) per dollar of face value. The payoff of the long forward position on June 1, ($P_{\text{June 1}}$(August 30) − $0.97)1M, is the payoff of receiving bills for $1 million of face value, worth $P_{\text{June 1}}$(August 30)1M, and paying a fixed amount for them, $0.97 million.

Mr. Smith does not have to enter a forward contract to buy 90-day T-bills on June 1 to have 90-day T-bills in his possession on June 1 and pay the forward price for them at that date. On March 1, he can buy T-bills maturing on August 30 and borrow the present value of $0.97 million to be repaid on June 1. This portfolio, which consists of a long position in the T-bills maturing August 30 financed by a 3-month loan that matures on June 1, has the same payoff as the forward contract since Mr. Smith pays $0.97 million on June 1 and has at that time T-bills maturing on August 30. This portfolio therefore constitutes a replicating portfolio for the forward contract. A negative value of the replicating portfolio means that somebody taking a long position in the portfolio receives a cash inflow when taking the position—literally, the portfolio has a negative value, so that we receive money back when investing in the portfolio.

Buying the T-bills with the forward contract costs nothing to Mr. Smith on March 1; he will pay $0.97 million on June 1. Since he has to pay $0.97 million with the replicating portfolio on June 1 also, if the replicating portfolio costs money on March 1, then Mr. Smith prefers the forward contract to the replicating portfolio. The forward contract is advantageous to Mr. Smith only as long as he does not make money by taking a position in the replicating portfolio on March 1. To determine whether the forward contract is advantageous to Mr. Smith, we have to value the replicating portfolio.

We know from Chapter 2 that the value of a portfolio is the sum of the value of its component securities. To value the replicating portfolio, we can value separately the long position in T-bills maturing on August 30 and the position corresponding to borrowing the present value of the forward price.

1. The value on March 1 of a payoff equal to −$0.97 million on June 1. A negative payoff, like −$0.97 million, means a cash outflow. You are paying a fixed amount on June 1. To create a negative payoff at a future date, you borrow an amount such that the repayment of principal and interest at maturity matches the required cash outflow. To repay $0.97 million, we borrow today the present value of $0.97 million, which is $P_{\text{March 1}}(\text{June 1})0.97\text{M}$. A simple way to borrow is to sell T-bills short. Selling a T-bill short means borrowing the T-bill and selling it. When the short sale is reversed, we buy the T-bill and deliver it to the investor who lent us the T-bill initially. The gain from the short sale is the negative of the change in the price of the T-bill. If the T-bill increases in value, we lose money with the short sale, since we have to buy the T-bill back at a higher price than we sold it. Box 5.1, Repos and borrowing using Treasury

---

Repos and borrowing using Treasury securities as collateral   *Box 5.1*

Typically, borrowing for those who hold inventories of Treasury securities is done in the repo market. A **repo** is a transaction that involves a spot market sale of a security and the promise to repurchase the security at a later day at a given price. One can view a repo as a spot market sale of a security with the simultaneous purchase of the security through a forward contract. A repo where the repurchase takes place the next day is called an overnight repo. All repos with a maturity date of more than one day are called term repos. A repo amounts to borrowing using the Treasury securities as collateral. For this reason, rather than stating the price at which the underlying security is bought back at a later day, the contract states a rate that is applied to the spot price at origination to yield the repurchase price. For instance, consider a situation where dealer Black has $100 million of Treasury securities that he has to finance overnight. He can do so using a repo as follows. He can turn to another dealer, dealer White, who will quote a repo rate, say 5 percent, and a haircut. The haircut means that, though White receives $100 million of Treasury securities, he provides cash for only a fraction of that amount. The haircut protects White against credit risk. The credit risk arises because the price of the securities could fall. In this case, Black would have to pay more for the securities than they are worth. If he could walk away from the deal, he would make a profit. However, since he has to pay for only a fraction of the securities to get all of them back if there is a haircut, he will pay as long as the price is below the promised payment by an amount smaller than the haircut. For example, if the haircut is 1 percent, Black receives $100 \times (1/1.01) = \$99.0099$ million in cash. The next day, he has to repay $100 \times (1/1.01) \times (1 + 0.05/360) = \$99.024$ million. Hence, if the securities had fallen in value to $99.05 million, Black would still buy them back. With this transaction, Black has funds for one day. Because this transaction is a forward purchase, Black benefits if the price of the securities that are purchased at maturity have an unexpectedly high value. With Treasury securities, therefore, the borrower benefits if interest rates fall. Viewed from White's perspective, the dealer who receives the securities, the transaction is called a **reverse repo**. A reverse repo can be used to sell Treasury securities short in the following way. After receiving the securities, the dealer can sell them. He then has to buy them back to deliver them at maturity of the reverse repo. He therefore loses if the price of the securities increases because he has to pay more for them than he receives when he delivers them at maturity.

securities as collateral, discusses how short sales of Treasury securities work. Assuming $P_{March\ 1}$(June 1) = \$0.969388, we receive \$0.969388 × 0.97 × 1M on March 1, which is \$0.940306 million. The value of our short position on March 1 is –\$0.940306 million.

2. The value of a payoff equal to $P_{June\ 1}$(August 30)1M on June 1. T-bills are zero-coupon bonds, so that they have no cash flows until maturity. A bill maturing on August 30 is worth P_{June1}(August 30) on June 1, and can be delivered on the forward contract at that date. Let's assume that $P_{March\ 1}$(August 30) is equal to \$0.95, so that we pay \$0.95 × 1M, or \$0.95 million to buy the bills.

We have now valued the replicating portfolio for the forward contract. The portfolio has a long position in T-bills that mature on August 30, which costs \$0.95 million, and a short position worth –\$0.940306 million, for a total value of \$0.95M – \$0.940306M, or \$0.009694 million. Holding the portfolio until June 1, we then have $P_{June\ 1}$(August 30)1M – \$0.97M, which is exactly the payoff of the long forward position.

We find that the replicating portfolio is worth \$0.009694 million. By taking a long position in the forward contract, Mr. Smith pays nothing today to receive at maturity something that is worth today \$0.009694 million. The forward contract is a good deal for Mr. Smith. To take advantage of this good deal, he can take a long forward position. However, a long forward position involves a risk since at maturity he has to buy T-bills at the forward price and the T-bills might be worth less than what he has to pay for them. Since the replicating portfolio pays the same as a long forward position, Mr. Smith can hedge this risk by going short the replicating portfolio. By doing this, Mr. Smith creates a portfolio that pays \$0.009694 million now, has no other cash flows, and requires no investment of his own. An opportunity to make money for sure without any investment of one's own is called an arbitrage opportunity.

To exploit the arbitrage opportunity, Mr. Smith sells the replicating portfolio short and takes an offsetting long position in the forward contract. He receives a cash inflow of \$0.009694 million on March 1 and has no other cash flows, so that the cash inflow on March 1 is his riskless profit. Selling the replicating portfolio short involves selling short T-bills maturing on August 30 for \$1 million face value and buying T-bills maturing on June 1 for \$0.97 million face value. Denote by F the forward price set on March 1. The net proceeds from the short sale of the replicating portfolio are:

Cash flow on March 1 from establishing a short position in the replicating portfolio

$$= [P_{March\ 1}(August\ 30) - P_{March\ 1}(June\ 1)F] \times 1M$$

$$= \$0.95M - \$0.969388 \times 0.97 \times 1M$$

$$= \$0.95M - \$0.940306M$$

$$= \$0.009694M$$

On June 1, Mr. Smith pays for the T-bills bought forward with the proceeds of the T-bills maturing that day and uses the T-bills maturing on August 30 he receives from the forward position to close his short T-bills position. Therefore, Mr. Smith has neither a cash inflow nor a cash outflow on June 1:

Payoff of short position in the replicating portfolio on June 1 + Payoff of long forward position on June 1

$$= [F - P_{\text{June 1}}(\text{August 30})]1M + [P_{\text{June 1}}(\text{August 30}) - F]1M$$

$$= 0$$

This confirms that there is an arbitrage opportunity for Mr. Smith at the forward price of $0.97. As long as the replicating portfolio has a value different from zero, money can be made without risk. Infinite profits are for the taking if the forward price and the T-bill prices do not change.

If the forward contract is priced so that the replicating portfolio has negative value, Mr. Smith can obtain the payoff of the forward contract by taking a long position in the replicating portfolio and he receives money as he takes this position. Mr. Smith could make arbitrage profits in this case by taking a long position in the arbitrage portfolio and a short position in the forward contract. Table 5.1 shows that if the forward price is $0.99, Mr. Smith receives a positive cash flow today of $9,694.12 without owing money later.

The only time Mr. Smith cannot make riskless profits is when the forward price is such that the replicating portfolio has zero value. The price of the replicating portfolio is the present value of the payoff obtained through the forward contract—that is, the value of the forward contract for Mr. Smith. If a forward contract does not have zero value at inception, it means that one of the parties is losing money by taking a position in the contract and that the other party can make money through an arbitrage transaction—that party, Mr. Smith here, receives a gift from the counterparty in the forward transaction. In real-world markets, gifts get snapped up by traders who live for such opportunities and such

Arbitrage trade when F = $0.99 per dollar of face value	*Table 5.1*

In this case, the replicating portfolio for a long forward position is worth $0.95 − $0.969388 × 0.99 = −$0.009694. To exploit this, we short the contract and go long the replicating portfolio for a long forward position.

Positions on March 1		Cash flow on March 1	Cash flow on June 1
Short forward position		0	$0.99 − $P_{\text{June 1}}(\text{August 30})$
Replicating portfolio for long position	Long bill maturing on August 30	−$0.95	$P_{\text{June 1}}(\text{August 30})$
	Borrow present value of F	$0.969388 × 0.99 = $0.959694	−$0.99
Net cash flow		$0.009694	0

gifts disappear quickly. The replicating portfolio has a price of zero if the forward price satisfies the equation:

$$[P_{\text{March 1}}(\text{August 30}) - P_{\text{March 1}}(\text{June 1})F]1M = 0$$

Solving this equation for F:

$$F = \frac{P_{\text{March 1}}(\text{August 30})}{P_{\text{March 1}}(\text{June 1})}$$

With the numbers that Mr. Smith faces:

$$[\$0.95 - \$0.969388 \times F]1M = 0$$

Solving for the unknown forward price, we get F = \$0.98. At this forward price, the replicating portfolio for the long position has no value and there is no arbitrage opportunity.

5.1.2. A general pricing formula

We have shown that the forward price and the T-bill prices on March 1 must be such that $[P_{\text{March 1}}(\text{August 30}) - P_{\text{March 1}}(\text{June 1})F]1M = 0$, which implies that F $= P_{\text{March 1}}(\text{August 30})/P_{\text{March1}}(\text{June 1})$. Our analysis holds equally well if the forward contract has a different maturity or requires delivery of a bill with a different maturity. Consequently, we have a general formula for the pricing of forward contracts on T-bills.

Formula for the pricing of forward contracts on T-bills

The forward price per dollar of face value, F, of a contract entered into at date t for delivery of bills at date $t + i$ that mature at $t + j$ must be such that the replicating portfolio for a forward position has no value at inception:

Price at time *t* of deliverable T-bill with maturity at time *t + j*
– Present value of forward price to be paid at time *t + i* = 0

$$P_t(t + j) - P_t(t + i)F = 0 \qquad (5.1)$$

The replicating portfolio has zero value only when:

$$F = \frac{P_t(t + j)}{P_t(t + i)} \qquad (5.2)$$

In the example, $P_t(t + j) = P_{\text{March 1}}(\text{August 30}) = \$0.95$ and $P_t(t + i) = P_{\text{March 1}}$ (June 1) = \$0.969388, so that F = \$0.98.

5.1.3. Pricing the contract after inception

In real-world markets, the forward price of \$0.97 that Mr. Smith contemplated on March 1 would not last. If Mr. Smith did not snap up the contract, somebody else would have. Suppose that Mr. Smith was quick enough to take advantage of his good fortune and was able to enter the forward contract. Time has now elapsed, so that it is now April 15. Mr. Smith would like to know the value of his forward position.

On April 15, the replicating portfolio for the long position in the forward contract has an investment for $1 million face value in T-bills maturing on August 30 and a short position for $0.97 million face value in T-bills maturing on June 1. Since interest rates change over time, the value of the replicating portfolio changes also. To price the forward contract, we have to price the portfolio on April 15:

Value of replicating portfolio on April 15

$$= [P_{\text{April 15}}(\text{August 30}) - P_{\text{April 15}}(\text{June 1})0.97]1M$$

This portfolio replicates the payoff of the forward contract since on June 1 it is worth $P_{\text{June 1}}(\text{August 30})1M - \$0.97M$.

Let's see how this works with an example. Suppose that on April 15, $P_{\text{April 15}}$ (June 1) = $0.96 and $P_{\text{April 15}}$(August 30) = $0.93605. In this case, we have:

Value of replicating portfolio on April 15

$$= [P_{\text{April 15}}(\text{August 30}) - P_{\text{April 15}}(\text{June 1})\$0.97]1M$$

$$= \$0.93605M - \$0.96 \times 0.97M$$

$$= \$0.00485M$$

Since the forward contract was worth $0.009694 million on March 1, it lost value from March 1 to April 15.

There is another way to value the forward contract on April 15. Suppose Mr. Smith wants to find out how much he would receive or pay to get out of the forward contract. One way to get out of a forward contract is to enter a new forward position of opposite sign: The long enters a short forward position for the same maturity date and with the same T-bills to be delivered. Using our formula, the forward price on a contract originated on April 15 for delivery on June 1 of T-bills maturing on August 30 should be $0.97505. Mr. Smith could therefore cancel his position on April 15 by taking a short forward position to sell on June 1 T-bills maturing on August 30 for $0.97505 per dollar of face value. On June 1, he would receive $0.97505 million and pay $0.97 million, using the bills received for delivery on the short contract. Consequently, he would make a net gain of $0.00505 million irrespective of interest rates on June 1.

Since Mr. Smith would receive $0.00505 million on June 1 if he cancels his position by entering an offsetting contract, it must be that the value of the forward contract on April 15 is the present value of $0.00505 million. This means that the value of the position per dollar of face value on April 15 is the present value of the difference between the forward price of the contract entered into on March 1 and the forward price of a contract entered into on April 15, where the discounting takes place from the maturity date of the contract to April 15. This value is $0.00485 million. Not surprisingly, this is exactly the value of the replicating portfolio per dollar of face value.

Our analysis shows the formula for the value of a forward position.

Formula for the value of a forward position

Define $P_t(t + i)$ as the value of a zero-coupon bond at date t that pays $1 at date $t + i$. The value at date t of a long forward position entered into at forward price F per dollar of face value maturing at date $t + i$ requiring delivery of a T-bill maturing at date $t + j$ is the value of the replicating portfolio for a long forward position at t:

$$P_t(t + j) - P_t(t + i)\,F \tag{5.3}$$

The value of a short forward position per dollar of face value is the value of the replicating portfolio for such a position at that date:

$$P_t(t + i)F - P_t(t + j) \tag{5.4}$$

5.2. Generalizing our results

The key to pricing a forward contract on a T-bill lies in our ability to construct a replicating portfolio. Pricing by arbitrage states that the value of the forward position must be equal to the value of its replicating portfolio. The replicating portfolio consists of a long position in the deliverable asset of the forward contract financed by borrowing.

Consider now a forward contract that matures on June 1 entered into on March 1 on a stock that pays no dividends. Let $S_{\text{March 1}}$ be the stock price on March 1, $S_{\text{June 1}}$ be the stock price at maturity of the contract, and F be the forward price per share. The payoff of a long forward position is $S_{\text{June 1}} - F$. We already know that we replicate $-F$ by borrowing the present value of F so that we have to repay F on June 1. We have to figure out how to create a portfolio today that pays $S_{\text{June 1}}$ on June 1. Because the stock pays no dividends, the current value of the stock to be delivered at maturity of the forward contract is the stock price today. By buying the stock on March 1 and holding it until June 1, we own the deliverable asset for the forward contract at maturity.

Consequently, the replicating portfolio works as follows. Buy one share of the stock today and sell short T-bills maturing on June 1 for face value equal to the forward price. With this portfolio, we spend $S_{\text{March 1}}$ to purchase the stock and sell T-bills short for face value equal to F. On June 1, we have to pay F to settle the short sale of T-bills. After doing so, we own the stock and have no short T-bill position. The forward price must be the price at which the replicating portfolio has zero value, therefore $S_{\text{March 1}} - P_{\text{March 1}}(\text{June 1})F$ must be equal to zero. Solving for the forward price, we have that F is equal to $S_{\text{March 1}}/P_{\text{March 1}}(\text{June 1})$. If the forward price differs from the value given by this formula, there exists an arbitrage opportunity.

We can now price a forward contract on a stock. We also can do much more. With the forward contract on a stock and the forward contract on T-bills, the current value of the asset delivered at maturity of the contract is the current spot price of the asset and this value must be equal to the present value of the forward price. As long as the deliverable asset's current value is its spot price, the forward contract can be priced that way regardless of the underlying asset.

Formula for the forward price F of an asset with current price S_t and no payouts before maturity of the contract at $t + i$

Let $P_t(t + i)$ be the price at t of a zero-coupon bond that pays \$1 at $t + i$ and r be the continuously compounded interest rate for that zero-coupon bond. The replicating portfolio for the contract must have zero value, which implies that:

$$S_t - P_t(t + i)F = S_t - Fe^{-r \times i} = 0 \qquad (5.5)$$

Solving this expression for F yields and using r as the continuously compounded interest rate:

$$F = \frac{S_t}{P_t(t + i)} = S_t e^{r \times i} \qquad (5.6)$$

The assumption of no cash flows for the deliverable asset before maturity of the contract is extremely important here. Let's find out what happens when this assumption does not hold. Suppose we construct a replicating portfolio on March 1 for a forward contract maturing on June 1 on a stock that pays a dividend $D_{April\ 15}$ on April 15. For simplicity we assume that the dividend is already known. In this case, the forward contract requires delivery of the stock ex-dividend, but the price of the stock on March 1 includes the right to the dividend payment. The stock on March 1 is not the deliverable asset for the forward contract. The deliverable asset is the stock without the dividend to be paid before maturity of the contract. Consequently, the cost on March 1 of buying the deliverable asset is no longer $S_{March\ 1}$, but instead is $S_{March\ 1}$ minus the present value of the dividend, $S_{March\ 1} - P_{March\ 1}(April\ 15)D_{April\ 15}$, where $P_{March\ 1}(April\ 15)$ is the price on March 1 of a zero-coupon bond that pays \$1 on April 15.

We can generalize this to the case of multiple payouts and arbitrary dates.

Forward price for a contract on an asset with multiple payouts before maturity

The forward price at t, F, for delivery at date $t + i$ of an asset with price S_t that has N intermediate payouts of $D_{t + \Delta h}$, $h = 1,...,N$, is given by:

$$F = \frac{S_t - \sum_{h = 1}^{h = N} P_t(t + \Delta h)D_{t + \Delta h}}{P_t(t + i)} \qquad (5.7)$$

Let's look at an example. Consider a forward contract entered into at date t with delivery in one year of a share of common stock that pays dividends quarterly. The current price of the stock is \$100. The dividends are each \$2 and paid at the end of each quarterly period starting now. To compute the present value of the dividends to be paid, we need the prices of zero-coupon bonds that mature when dividends are paid. The zero-coupon bond prices are \$0.98 for the zero-coupon bond maturing in three months, \$0.96 for the bond maturing in six months, \$0.93 for the bond maturing in nine months, and \$0.90 for the bond maturing in one year. Consequently, we have $S_t = 100$, $P_t(t + 1) = 0.90$, $P_t(t + 0.75) = 0.93$, $P_t(t + 0.5) = 0.96$, $P_t(t + 0.25) = 0.98$, and $D_{t+1} = D_{t+0.75} = D_{t+0.5} = D_{t+0.25} = 2$. Using the formula, we have:

$$F = \frac{100 - 0.98 \times 2 - 0.96 \times 2 - 0.93 \times 2 - 0.90 \times 2}{0.90} = 102.73$$

If we had ignored the dividends, we would have obtained a forward price of $111.11. The forward price is higher when dividends are ignored because they reduce the cost of the replicating portfolio—they are like a rebate on buying the replicating portfolio.

The analysis extends naturally to a forward contract on a portfolio. The deliverable asset could be a portfolio including investments in different stocks in specified quantities. The quantities could be those that correspond to a stock index like the S&P 500. In this case, we would have a forward contract on the S&P 500. The S&P 500 index is equivalent to the value of a portfolio invested in 500 stocks where the investment weight of each stock is its market value divided by the market value of all the stocks in the index. Therefore, one can construct a portfolio of stocks whose return exactly tracks the S&P 500.

5.2.1. Foreign currency forward contracts

Consider a forward contract where you agree on March 1 to purchase 100,000 Swiss francs on June 1 at a price of F. The price of the deliverable asset for spot delivery, the Swiss franc, is $S_{\text{June 1}}$ at maturity of the contract. The payoff of the contract at maturity is $100,000(S_{\text{June 1}} - F)$. To create a replicating portfolio for the forward contract, you have to purchase an asset on March 1 that pays 100,000 Swiss francs on June 1. You can purchase today an amount of Swiss francs such that on June 1 you have 100,000 Swiss francs by buying Swiss franc T-bills for a face value of 100,000 Swiss francs maturing on June 1.[1] Define r^{SFR} to be the appropriate continuously compounded interest rate for Swiss T-bills maturing on June 1 and r to be the interest rate for U.S. T-bills maturing at the same date. To buy Swiss T-bills on March 1 maturing on June 1 with face value of 100,000 Swiss francs, you have to pay $100,000 S_{\text{March 1}} e^{-r^{\text{SFR}} \times 0.25}$ on March 1. The present value of the forward price times 100,000 is $100,000 F e^{-r \times 0.25}$. These two amounts must have equal value, so that the forward price F is $S_{\text{March 1}} e^{(r - r^{\text{SFR}}) \times 0.25}$.

Generalizing the formula for the forward price to a contract maturing at date i, we obtain the following result.

Pricing formula for a foreign exchange forward contract

Let S_t be the spot price of the foreign currency at date t, r^{FX} the continuously compounded interest rate on a foreign currency T-bill maturing at date $t + i$, and r the continuously compounded interest rate on a U.S. T-bill maturing at the

---

1 A technical issue should be mentioned here. Not all countries have T-bills, but many countries have the equivalent of T-bills, namely a default-free asset that pays one unit of local currency at maturity. Whenever we talk about a T-bill for a foreign country, we therefore mean an instrument that is equivalent to a U.S. T-bill.

same date. A forward contract on the foreign currency maturing at date i originated today must have a forward price F per unit of foreign currency such that the replicating portfolio has zero value at origination:

$$S_t e^{-r^{FX} \times i} - F e^{-r \times i} = 0 \qquad (5.8)$$

This formula implies that the forward price must be:

$$F = S_t e^{(r - r^{FX})i} \qquad (5.9)$$

Let's suppose a contract is entered into at t that matures one year later. Suppose the Swiss franc, S_t, is worth 70 cents, $r^{FX} = 0.04$, $r = 0.20$. Using our formula, we have that $F = \$0.7 e^{(0.20 - 0.04) \times 0.25} = \$0.728568$. In this case, the forward price of the Swiss franc is higher than its current spot price. For foreign currencies, the current spot price is the spot exchange rate, and the forward price is called the forward exchange rate. If the forward exchange rate is above the spot exchange rate, the currency has a forward premium. The forward exchange rate pricing formula is often expressed using interest rates. Box 5.2, Interest rate parity, shows that we can use the interest rate formulation profitably to understand how interest rates across countries are related.

5.2.2. Commodity forward contracts

There are also forward contracts on commodities, like gold or sugar. Suppose that on March 1 you know you will want 1,000 ounces of gold on June 1. You can buy the gold forward, or you can buy it today and finance the purchase until June 1. There is a difference between holding the gold now and having a long forward position in gold: holding gold has a **convenience yield**. The convenience yield is the benefit one derives from holding the commodity physically. In the case of gold, the benefit of having the commodity is that one could melt it to create a gold chain that one can wear. Hence, if the cash buyer has no use for gold, she could lend it, and whoever borrows it would pay the convenience yield to the lender. The rate at which the payment is determined is called the gold lease rate.

As before, let's denote the cash market or spot price of the deliverable on March 1 by $S_{\text{March 1}}$. In this case, $S_{\text{March 1}}$ is the gold price on March 1. Further, let's assume that the convenience yield accrues continuously at a rate of c percent per year. To create a replicating portfolio for a long position in the forward contract, one does not have to buy 1,000 ounces of gold on March 1 because the gold one buys has a convenience yield—we can rent the gold until June 1 to somebody who will pay us the lease rate and we can use the rent to buy additional gold. Therefore, we only have to buy $1,000 e^{-c \times i}$ ounces of gold for the replicating portfolio, where i is the fraction of a year corresponding to the time to maturity of the contract. In our example, i is equal to 0.25, so that the replicating portfolio has a long position of $1,000 e^{-0.25c}$ ounces of gold and a short position in T-bills maturing on June 1 for face value F. To create a replicating portfolio for a short position in the forward contract, one has to sell the commodity short, which involves compensating the counterparty for the loss of the convenience yield. To sell gold short, one therefore has to pay the lease rate.

Though the lease rate for gold is relatively constant, the convenience yield of other commodities can vary dramatically as holders may gain a large benefit from

Box 5.2   Interest rate parity

Suppose that a U.S. investor faces (continuously compounded) annual interest rates of 5 percent in the United States and 1 percent in Switzerland for 90 days. He would like to know whether it is more advantageous to invest in the United States or in Switzerland. The investment in Swiss francs might change value because of changes in the exchange rate. For instance, if the investor invests $1 million in Switzerland at the exchange rate of $0.7 per Swiss franc, he might earn 1 percent per annum on this investment but exchange the Swiss francs into dollars in 90 days at an exchange rate of $0.8 per Swiss franc. In this case, he would gain 14.57 percent of his investment for an annualized rate of return of 54.41 percent! This is because he gets 1/0.7 Swiss francs or 1.4286 Swiss francs initially that he invests at 1 percent, thereby having 1.4321 Swiss francs at maturity ($e^{0.01(90/360)}/0.7$). He then converts his Swiss francs at $0.8, thereby obtaining $1.1457 in 90 days. Hence, despite earning a lower interest rate in Switzerland than in the United States, the investor gains by investing in Switzerland. The exchange rate gain is an exchange rate return of 53.41 percent ($\ln[0.8/0.7] \times 360/90$) measured at an annual continuously compounded rate. The total return is the sum of the exchange rate return plus the interest earned, or 53.41% + 1% = 54.41%.

We know, however, that the investor could sell the proceeds of his Swiss franc investment forward at an exchange rate known today. Doing this, the investor is completely hedged against exchange rate risk. He gets $Fe^{0.01(90/360)}/0.7$ in 90 days, where F is the forward exchange rate, irrespective of the spot exchange rate at that date. Consequently, F has to be such that investing at the risk-free rate in the United States would yield the same amount as investing in Swiss francs and selling the proceeds forward to obtain dollars. Let's define the annualized exchange rate return from buying Swiss francs and selling them forward as the forward premium and use the notation f for this exchange rate return. We use continuous compounding, so that for our example, the forward premium solves the equation $F = \$0.7e^{f(90/360)}$, so that we have $f = \ln[F/0.7] \times 360/90$. It must be the case, since a hedged investment in Swiss francs is risk free, that the return of this investment is equal to 5 percent per annum. The return of investing in Swiss francs is 1 percent + f. Hence, it must be that f = 4 percent computed annually. We can then solve for the forward exchange rate such that $0.04 = \ln[F/0.7] \times 360/90$. This gives us F = $0.7070. The result that the foreign interest rate plus the forward premium must equal the domestic interest rate to avoid arbitrage opportunities is called the interest rate parity theorem:

Interest rate parity theorem

When the domestic risk-free rate, the forward premium, and the foreign risk-free rate are for the same maturity and continuous compounding is used, it must be true that:

Domestic risk-free rate
= Forward premium + Foreign risk-free rate   (IRPT)

The interest rate parity theorem states that, after hedging against foreign exchange risk, the risk-free asset earns the same in each country. There is a considerable amount of empirical evidence on this result. This evidence shows that most observed forward prices satisfy the interest rate parity theorem if there are no foreign exchange controls and if transaction costs are taken into account. We discuss the impact of transaction costs in the last section of this chapter.

The interest rate parity theorem as well as the result for the pricing of foreign exchange forward contracts have a powerful implication. If one knows interest rates at home and in the foreign country, we can compute the forward exchange rate. Alternatively, if one knows the forward premium and the interest rates in one country, we can compute interest rates in the other country. Illustration 1 shows graphically how one can do this. (Note that the result in equation (IRPT) holds only approximately when one does not use continuously compounded returns.)

Illustration 1   **Term structures in the home and foreign country used to obtain the term structure of forward premiums**

The interest rate parity result states that the continuously compounded yield difference is equal to the forward premium. Consequently, we can obtain the forward premium that holds in the absence of arbitrage opportunities, whether a contract exists or not, if we know the yield difference.

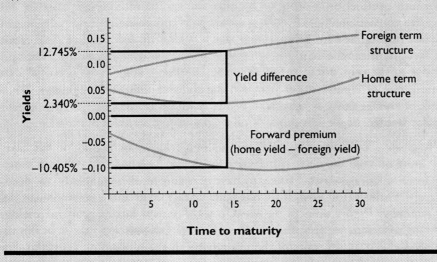

holding the commodity—chainsaws are very valuable the day following a hurricane, but this is not so for chainsaws bought forward with delivery a month after the hurricane.

This approach gives us a formula for the forward price for a commodity.

Forward price formula on a commodity with a convenience yield

Let r be the continuously compounded interest rate at t on a T-bill maturing at $t + 1$. The forward price at date t, F, for delivery of one unit of a commodity at date i that has a price today of S_t and has a convenience yield of c percent per unit of time is priced so that the replicating portfolio has zero value:

$$\mathbf{S_t e^{-c \times i} - F \times e^{-r \times i} = 0} \qquad (5.10)$$

Consequently, the forward price must satisfy:

$$\mathbf{F = S_t e^{(r-c)i}} \qquad (5.11)$$

Let's look at an example of a contract entered into at t that matures 90 days later. Suppose that the price of gold today is $40 per ounce, the convenience yield is 2 percent annually continuously compounded, and the price for a 90-day zero-coupon bond is $0.98 per dollar of face value. We have S_t = $40, c = 0.02, i = 0.25, and r = 0.0808 percent. Consequently:

$$\mathbf{F = \$40 e^{(0.0808 - 0.02) \times 0.25} = \$40.6126}$$

Without the convenience yield, the replicating portfolio would be more expensive, and as a result the forward price would be higher. The forward price without the convenience yield is $40.8162.

Often, it is costly to store the deliverable commodity. For instance, replicating a forward contract on heating oil requires storing the oil. Storage costs are like a negative convenience yield: they make the forward contract more advantageous because buying forward saves storage costs. While the convenience yield reduces the forward price relative to the spot price, storage costs increase the forward price relative to the spot price. To see this, let's suppose storage costs occur at a continuous rate of v percent per year and the contract matures in 90 days. We can think of storage costs as a fraction of the holdings of oil that we have to sell to pay for storage, or we can think of oil evaporating because it is stored.

To create a replicating portfolio for the long position in heating oil, we have to buy more oil than we need at maturity for delivery because we will lose some in the form of storage costs. Hence, to have one unit of oil at maturity, we need to buy $e^{0.25v}$ units of oil now. If oil has both storage costs and a convenience yield, we require $e^{0.25(v-c)}$ units of oil now. To get a general formula for the pricing of forward contracts, we also want to allow for cash payouts at a rate d. In this case, we need $e^{0.25(v-c-d)}$ units of the underlying in the replicating portfolio. For a contract entered into at t and maturing at $t + i$, this reasoning leads to the general formula for the forward price.

General formula for the forward price

Let r be the continuously compounded interest rate at t on a T-bill maturing at $t + i$. At date t, a forward contract for delivery of a good at date $t + i$ available at t for price S_t, with a continuously computed payout rate of d percent per year, a convenience yield of c percent, and storage costs of v percent, must have a forward price F such that the replicating portfolio has zero value:[2]

$$S_t e^{(v-c-d)i} - Fe^{-r \times i} = 0 \qquad (5.12)$$

The forward price must be:

$$S_t e^{(r+v-c-d)i} = F \qquad (5.13)$$

Let's look at an example. Consider a ton of copper which costs \$2,000. Suppose that the interest rate is 10 percent, storage costs are charged at the rate of 6 percent, and there is a convenience yield of 4 percent. The forward contract is for 90 days. Using our formula, we have that \$2,000 $e^{(0.10 + 0.06 - 0.04) \times (90/360)}$ = \$2,060.91. This means that the forward price exceeds the spot price of the commodity.

Assuming that r, v, c, and d do not depend on S_t, equation (5.13) shows that the forward price has certain properties as follows:

1. The forward price is higher if the current price of the good to be delivered at maturity of the contract is higher at inception of the contract. With no arbitrage opportunities, we are indifferent between buying the good forward or buying it today and borrowing until maturity of the forward contract. However, an increase in the price of the good increases the cost of buying it today, so that borrowing the present value of the forward price before the increase in the price of the good is no longer enough to finance the purchase of the good. The forward price therefore has to increase to keep us indifferent between buying the good forward and buying the good today and financing the purchase through borrowing.

2. The forward price is higher when the interest rate is higher at inception of the contract. Suppose the interest rate is r. The forward price has to be such that we can buy the good and finance it at the rate r until the delivery date of the forward contract by borrowing the present value of the forward price. If the interest rate is r' instead, so that $r' > r$, we cannot finance the purchase of the good by borrowing the present value of the forward price. Consequently, the forward price has to be higher when the interest rate is higher.

3. The forward price is higher if storage costs are higher at inception of the forward contract. Higher storage costs make it more expensive to buy the good today and finance it through borrowing for a given forward price. Consequently, to make the replicating portfolio costless, the forward price has to increase with storage costs so that the proceeds from borrowing the

---

2 Note that this general formula can be extended to allow time variation in r, v, c, and d. Further, discrete payouts or storage costs can be accommodated by discounting these costs on the left-hand side using the appropriate discount rate. Viewed this way, the current value of the good delivered at date $t + i$ is its current price plus the present value of storage costs minus the present value of holding the good (payouts and convenience yield).

present value of the forward price cover the costs of buying and storing the good.

4. The forward price is lower if the convenience yield and the payout rate are higher. A higher convenience yield and payout rate decrease the cost of buying the good and holding it, so that the forward price must be lower for the replicating portfolio to have zero value.

The sum $(r + v - c - d)$ is generally called the **cost of carry**, in that it is the cost of financing a position in the underlying good until maturity of the contract. For gold, c is small (lease rates are typically of the order of 2 percent) and v is trivial. For oil, c can be extremely large relative to v. Hence, typically the present value of the forward price of gold exceeds the spot price, while the present value of the forward price for oil is lower than the spot price. It is common to describe the price for future delivery as in **contango** when it exceeds the spot price and in **backwardation** otherwise.

The arbitrage approach cannot always be used to price forward contracts. In particular, it may not be possible to establish a short position. If selling the commodity short is not possible, then the forward price can be lower than given by equation (5.13). This is because the only riskless way to take advantage of a forward price that is lower than predicted by equation (5.13) is to buy forward and sell the commodity short to hedge the forward position. If it is difficult to sell short though, this means that one has to make an extremely large payment to the counterparty in the short sale. Consequently, use of the commodity is extremely valuable, and the convenience yield is high. This means that there is a convenience yield for which the formula holds. When the arbitrage approach cannot be used, one has to price the forward contract so that a position in the contract earns just enough to compensate the long for the risk she is taking. For instance, if the capital asset pricing model applies, the expected profit the long requires increases with the beta of the underlying asset, so that the forward price increases relative to the expected spot price with beta.

A bigger difficulty is that for perishable commodities the replicating portfolio approach becomes meaningless because holding the portfolio becomes more expensive than the spot price of the commodity. Think of replicating a long position in a one-year forward contract on roses. In this case, the forward contract has to be priced using a model that specifies the risk premium that investors require to take a long position in the forward contract (e.g., the CAPM) rather than by using the arbitrage approach.

5.2.3. Counterparty risk in forward contracts

Forward contracts are generally traded over the counter (OTC). Therefore, any contract that two traders can agree on can be made. No exchange rules have to be satisfied. For example, foreign currency forward contracts are traded on a worldwide market of traders linked to each other through phones and screens.

Suppose that you have a long position to buy gold forward. The forward position makes money if the gold price at the end of the year exceeds the forward price, but only if the forward seller honors the terms of the contract at maturity. If the forward seller cannot deliver at maturity because of a lack of financial resources or other reasons, the forward contract is useless, and the gain the firm expected to make does not materialize. The risk that one side in a derivatives contract will fail to honor the contract is called **counterparty risk**. When a firm enters a contract, it has to take this risk into account. If the risk of counterparty default is too great, the forward contract is useless or worse. Note that if the firm has a long position, the short makes a profit by delivering gold if the gold price has fallen and therefore will do so. Hence, for the long, counterparty risk means that she is more likely to take delivery when she made a loss and is less likely to take delivery when she made a gain. To adjust for the impact of default risk, the long wants a lower forward price and the price may be so low that no trade takes place.

The problem with default risk for the long in our example is that it requires careful examination of the short's business. This raises the costs of forward contracting. One way to eliminate this difficulty is for the long to enter a contract only if the counterparty has a high debt rating indicating a low probability of default. Another way is to require the short to post a bond that guarantees performance on the contract. This can work as follows.

When entering a contract, the short sets aside an amount of money with a third party, possibly in the form of securities, that is forfeited if he does not deliver on the forward contract. If the value of the assets deposited as collateral is large enough, default becomes unlikely. The difficulty is that such an arrangement has to be negotiated and the party who holds the collateral has to be designated and compensated. Further, if the losses that can occur over the life of the contract are large, then the collateral will have to be large as well. We saw in Chapter 3 that firms often hedge to avoid situations when they might lack funds to invest and face difficulties in raising funds in the capital markets. Forcing a firm to post a large amount of collateral is therefore likely to prevent it from hedging; the firm would have to set aside funds that have a high opportunity cost or funds that it does not have. Requiring a large amount of collateral makes it less likely that firms and individuals will want to enter a contract.

Rather than posting a large amount of collateral to cover possible losses for the life of the contract, it could be more efficient to require less collateral that covers potential losses over a short period of time, but then to transfer the gains and losses as they accrue. In this case, whenever the collateral becomes insufficient to cover potential losses over a short period of time it would be replenished; if the counterparty fails to do this, the contract is closed, but without creating a loss for one of the parties to the contract.

In this way of dealing with default risk, the short receives gains as they accrue, and if he starts making losses, he pays them as they accrue. This arrangement could be renewed every period, so that over every period the short has no incentive to default because the posted collateral is sufficient to cover the potential losses during the period. We have focused on a situation where the long is concerned about the default risk of the short. If the short is concerned about default of the long, a similar arrangement can be made by the long.

5.3. Futures contracts

The best way to view futures contracts is to think of them as forward contracts with added features designed to make counterparty risk economically trivial.

Futures contracts are contracts for deferred delivery like forward contracts, but they have four important features that forward contracts do not have. First and most importantly, futures contracts are standardized contracts that trade on organized exchanges. Second, gains and losses are paid by the parties every day as they accrue. This procedure, called **marking the contract to market**, is equivalent to closing the contract at the end of each day, settling gains and losses, and opening a new contract at a price such that the new contract has no value. Third, collateral is posted to ensure performance on the contract. Fourth, the counterparty in a long futures contract position is not the short, but an institution set up by the exchange called the **clearinghouse** that has enough capital to make default extremely unlikely.

To open a futures contract in the United States, one has to have a commodity trading account with a futures commission merchant regulated by the Commodity Futures Trading Commission (CFTC), and have enough money in it to cover the required initial collateral, called the contract's **initial margin**. The initial margin is set by the broker, but has to satisfy an exchange minimum. Like forward contracts, futures contracts have no value when entered into. Since the long does not make a payment to the short when a futures contract is opened, the futures contract would have negative value for the short at origination if it had positive value for the long. In this case, therefore, the short would not enter the contract. The same reasoning explains why the contract cannot have positive value for the short at origination. The long makes a gain if the price increases after opening the contract, and the short loses.

If we make a loss on a day, our account is debited by the loss. The amount that an account changes in value on a given day is called that day's **settlement variation**. After having paid or received the day's settlement variation, our futures position has no value since gains and losses are paid up. After opening the futures position, the balance in our account has to be at least equal to the **maintenance margin** before the start of trading each day. The maintenance margin is lower than the initial margin. Following losses, we receive a **margin call** if the account balance falls below the maintenance margin. In this case, we have to replenish the account to bring its balance to the initial margin. If we make gains, we can withdraw the amount by which the margin account exceeds the initial margin.

Futures contracts are traded on futures markets that have well-defined rules. The trading takes place in a designated location and the contracts have standardized maturities and sizes. Because the contracts are traded daily, a futures position can always be closed immediately. All one has to do is enter the opposite futures position to cancel out the initial position. If we close the contract this way in the middle of the day, we are still responsible for the change in the value of the contract from the beginning of the trading day to the middle of the trading day.

As a first approximation, on a given date, the futures price on a contract is equal to the forward price on a forward contract opened on that date with the same maturity as the futures contract. So, if a futures contract on gold matures in June, the futures price on March 5 is the forward price for a forward contract entered into on March 5 maturing when the June gold futures contract matures. The futures price changes all the time when markets are open. Since the forward price depends on the price of gold through the formula given in equation (5.13), any change in the price of gold changes the futures price.

Immediately before maturity, buying a good through a futures contract is almost like buying it in the cash market. In both cases, one receives delivery almost at the same time for the same good. For example, the futures contract on a foreign currency has delivery two days after it stops trading. Consequently, if one buys euros on the futures market immediately before a contract's maturity, one gets euros two days later. Had one bought euros on the cash market, one would also get euros two days later. This means that at maturity, the futures price and the cash market price must be the same. Before maturity, the futures price never wanders far from the cash market price. The similarity of futures contracts and forward contracts helps understand why this is the case. With the forward contract pricing formula, the forward price is tied to the cash market price and we saw that the forward price gets closer to the cash price as time to maturity shortens. The convergence of the futures price towards the cash market price is shown in Figure 5.2. for the Swiss franc contract maturing in June 1999.

5.3.1. Counterparty risk with futures contracts

If A enters a long futures position in a Swiss franc futures contract and B takes the offsetting short position, A is not the counterparty to B. This is because, immediately after A and B have agreed to the futures trade, the clearinghouse steps in. The clearinghouse will take a short position with A, so that it is responsible for selling the Swiss francs to A, and it will take a long position with B, so that it is responsible for buying the Swiss francs from B. The clearinghouse therefore has no net futures position—it has offsetting long and short positions. The long and the short in a futures contract make payments to or receive payments from the exchange's clearinghouse. This means that if one takes a position in a futures contract, the only default risk one has to worry about is the default risk of the clearinghouse.

Futures positions are traded on the exchange by members of the exchange. Therefore, to have a futures position, the order has to pass through a member.

Swiss franc spot exchange rate and futures price of the contract maturing in June 1999 from the start of trading of the contract   *Figure 5.2*

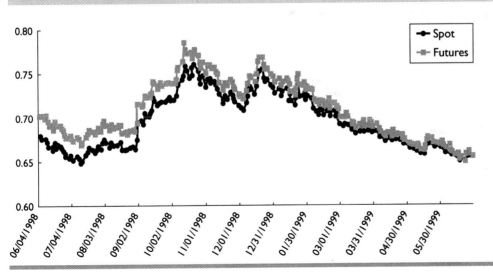

Members have accounts with the clearinghouse where they deposit margin corresponding to their net positions (the position left after the short positions are offset against the long positions to the extent possible). In addition to the margin accounts, clearinghouses have capital provided by members and their resources are well known. Consequently, default risk in futures contracts is almost nil, at least for well-known exchanges.

Clearinghouses in the United States have demonstrated they can successfully withstand dramatic shocks to the financial system. For example, more than $2 billion dollars changed hands in the clearinghouse of the Chicago Mercantile Exchange during the night following the crash of October 19, 1987. Yet the futures markets were able to open the next morning because all payments to the clearinghouse had been made. The fact that the final payments were made on Tuesday morning with a few minutes to spare and that the CEO of a major bank was awakened in the middle of the night to get a transfer done shows how close the markets came to not opening on October 20, however.

Another dramatic example shows the central role of the clearinghouse. Nick Leeson had apparently been a successful futures and options trader for Barings Securities since arriving in Singapore in the spring of 1992. By the beginning of 1995, he had accumulated extremely large positions that were designed to make a profit as long as the Nikkei index in Japan stayed relatively stable in the 19,000–21,000 range. Things started poorly for Leeson that year, but on January 17 they got much worse as an earthquake devastated the industrial heartland of Japan around Kobe. On the day of the quake, the Nikkei was at 19,350. Two weeks later it was at 17,785. Leeson's positions had large losses.

To recover, he took a large long position in the Nikkei futures contract traded in Singapore. It is not clear why he did so. He may have believed that the Nikkei had fallen so much that it would rebound, or even that he himself could push the index up through his purchases. In the span of four weeks, his position had reached 55,399 contracts. As these contracts made losses, margin calls were made, and Barings had to come up with additional money. By Friday, February 25, Barings had losses of 384 million pounds on these contracts that exceeded the capital of the Barings Group, the parent company. Barings was effectively bankrupt and unable to meet margin calls.

For each long position of Leeson, there was an offsetting short position held by somebody else. Had Leeson's contracts been forward contracts without collateral, the forward sellers would have lost the gains they expected to make from the fall in the Nikkei index since Barings, now bankrupt, could not honor the contracts. But the contracts were futures contracts, so that standing between the short and long positions there was the clearinghouse of the Singapore futures exchange. No short lost money. The clearinghouse lost instead.

5.3.2. A brief history of financial futures

Futures markets operate in many different countries and have quite a long history. For a long time, these markets traded mostly futures contracts on commodities. In the early 1970s, exchange rates became more volatile, and many investors wanted to take positions to exploit this volatility. The interbank market did not welcome individuals who wanted to speculate on currencies. With the support of Milton Friedman, an economist at the University of Chicago, the

Chicago Mercantile Exchange started trading foreign currency futures contracts. These contracts were followed by contracts on T-bills, T-bonds, and T-notes. In the beginning of the 1980s, the Kansas City Board of Trade started trading a futures contract on a stock index. Since indices are copyrighted, trading a futures contract on an index requires approval of the holder of the copyright. The Kansas City Board of Trade entered into an agreement with Value Line to use its index, a geometric average of stock prices that does not correspond directly to a basket of stocks.[3] There is no way to "deliver" the Value Line index. Consequently, a futures contract on the Value Line index must be settled in cash. If investors hold a long position in the contract at maturity, they receive the difference between the value of the index and the futures price in cash if it is positive and pay it otherwise. Subsequently, the Chicago Mercantile Exchange started trading a contract on the S&P 500 index. Though one can replicate the performance of the S&P 500 exactly by holding a portfolio that has the same composition as the index, the exchange chose delivery in cash because such a delivery simplifies the procedure considerably. Since then, many more cash-settled financial futures contracts have started trading all over the world.

The real-world development of stock index futures shows that our arbitrage approach is far from academic. Many financial firms opened arbitrage departments whose role was to exploit discrepancies between the S&P 500 futures price and its theoretical price. They took advantage of automated trading mechanisms whereby they could sell or buy a large portfolio whose return carefully tracked the return of the S&P 500 with one computer instruction. For a number of years, these arbitrage transactions were profitable for the firms with the lowest transaction costs that quickly managed to take advantage of discrepancies. A researcher evaluating the profitability of arbitrage strategies during the 1980s on a futures contract on an index similar to the Dow Jones index found that only firms that had low transaction costs and traded within a few minutes of observing the discrepancy could make money [Chung (1991)].

In the late 1980s, index arbitrage was often seen as the source of artificial volatility in stock prices, but there was little discussion about stock index arbitrage in the 1990s. Arbitrage opportunities seem much less frequent.

5.3.3. Cash versus physical delivery

Participants in futures markets typically do not take delivery. They generally close out their position before maturity. The ability to close a position before maturity is especially valuable for the contracts that do not have cash delivery—otherwise, the long in pork bellies contracts would have to cope with truckloads of pork bellies. Contracts in which delivery of physicals takes place at maturity—that is, pork bellies for the pork bellies contract or T-bonds for the T-bond contract—have some additional risks over the contracts with cash delivery.

Consider a futures contract on a specific variety of grain. A speculator with enough resources could be tempted to buy this variety of grain both on the futures market and on the cash market. At maturity, she might then be in a position where the sellers on the futures market have to buy grain from her to

---

3 Let a, b, and c be three stock prices. A geometric average of these prices is $(a \times b \times c)^{1/3}$. A basket of stocks with one share each of stocks a, b, and c would have a value given by $a + b + c$.

deliver on the futures market. She could ask for a very high price on the grain. Such a strategy is called a corner. When delivery takes place in cash instead, the futures sellers would not need to have the grain on hand at maturity. They simply have to write a check for the change in the futures price over the last day of the contract.

A corner is most likely to be successful if the product is defined so narrowly that its supply is quite limited. As the supply of the deliverable commodity increases, a corner requires too much capital to be implemented. If a variety of grain is in short supply, the solution is to allow the short to deliver other varieties that are close substitutes, possibly with a price adjustment. This way, the deliverable supply is extended, and the risk of a corner becomes less.

Financial futures contracts that require physical delivery also generally allow the short to choose among various possible deliverable instruments with price adjustments. Obviously, there is no risk that a long could effect a corner on the euro. For T-bonds and T-notes, however, there would be such a risk if only one issue is deliverable. Box 5.3, The cheapest to deliver bond and the case of Fenwick Capital Management, shows how this issue is handled for the T-bond and T-note contracts and provides an example of a successful corner in the T-note futures contract.

Box 5.3   The cheapest to deliver bond and the case of Fenwick Capital Management

The Chicago Board of Trade (CBOT) started trading the T-bond futures contract in August 1977. The contract requires delivery of T-bonds with a face value at maturity of $100,000. To limit the possibility of a successful corner, the contract defines the deliverable T-bonds broadly as long-term U.S. Treasury bonds that, if callable, are not callable for at least 15 years or, if not callable, have a maturity of at least 15 years. The problem with such a broad definition is that the short always wants to deliver the bonds that are cheapest to deliver. This means that the short will find those bonds with $100,000 face value that cost the least to acquire on the cash market. In the absence of price adjustments, the bond with the longest maturity would generally be the cheapest bond to deliver if interest rates have increased. This is because this bond will have a low coupon for a long time to maturity, so it will sell at a low price compared to par. If the supply of that bond is small, there could be a successful short squeeze for that bond. Such a squeeze might force the short to deliver different bonds.

The CBOT allows a great number of bonds to be deliverable, but makes these bonds comparable through price adjustments. When a short delivers bonds, the amount of money the short receives is called the invoice price. This invoice price is computed as follows. First, the settlement futures price is determined. Second, this futures price is multiplied by a conversion factor. The conversion factor is the price the delivered bond would have per dollar of face value if it were priced to yield 8 percent compounded semiannually. Finally, the accrued interest to the delivery date is added to this amount.

The conversion factor is an attempt to make all deliverable bonds similar. This works only imperfectly. The ideal method is one that would make the product of the futures price and the conversion factor equal to the cash price of all deliverable bonds. This does not happen with the method chosen by the exchange. At any time, there are bonds whose cash market price is higher than their invoice price. Which bond is the cheapest to deliver depends on interest rates. Typically, if interest rates are low, the cheapest to deliver bond will be a bond with a short maturity or early first call date because this bond will have the smallest premium over par. In contrast, if interest rates are high, the cheapest bond to deliver will be a bond with a long maturity or first call date.

The pricing is a bit more complicated when interest rates are highly volatile. As a first step in pricing the T-bond contract, one can use as the deliverable instrument the T-bond that is currently cheapest to deliver. More precise pricing requires taking into account that the cheapest bond to deliver could change over the life of the contract.

The T-note market works the same way. Regardless of these regulations, one cannot completely dismiss the risk of manipulation in these markets. In July 1996, the Commodity Futures Trading Commission fined Fenwick Capital Management for having cornered the market of the cheapest to deliver note on the June 1993 contract. The cheapest to deliver note was the February 2000 note with a coupon of 8.5 percent. Although the supply of that note was initially $10.7 billion, there had been a lot of stripping—in other words, the notes had been converted to portfolios of zero-coupon bonds corresponding to coupon and principal payments. Fenwick bought $1.4 billion of that issue and had a long position in the T-note contract of 12,700 contracts of $1.27 billion notional of notes. In June 1993, it was very difficult to find the February 2000 note. Consequently, most shorts had to deliver the next cheapest note, an 8.875 percent May 2000 note. That note cost them an extra $156.25 a contract. Fenwick got that note delivered on 4,800 of its contracts. This yielded a profit of $750,000.*

* See Floyd Norris, "The S.E.C. says it happened: A corner in the Treasury market," *The New York Times,* July 11, 1996, page C6.

5.3.4. Futures positions in practice

To see better the workings of futures contracts, let's look at a specific case where you take a long position in a Swiss franc futures contract on March 1, 1999, and hold this position during the entire month. On March 1, we must establish an account with a certified futures commission merchant, a broker for simplicity, if we do not have one. When the position is opened, the broker determines the initial margin that we must deposit and the maintenance margin. The initial and maintenance margins cannot be less than those set by the exchange, but they can be more. Whenever we incur a loss, the amount is withdrawn from our account.

The change in price that determines whether we made a gain or incurred a loss over a particular day is determined by the change in the settlement price. The settlement price is fixed by the exchange according to prices at the end of the trading day. An increase in the settlement price means that we gain with a long position. This gain is added to the margin account. A decrease in the settlement price means that we committed to buy Swiss francs at a higher price than the one we could obtain now, so we incurred a loss.

On March 1, 1999, the settlement price on the June contract is $0.6908. The contract is for 125,000 Swiss francs. This means that the value of 125,000 Swiss francs using the futures price of the June contract on March 1 is $86,350. Many futures price contracts have **price limits**. In the case of the Swiss franc contract in 1999, the limit is effectively a change of $0.04 from a reference price determined during the first fifteen minutes of trading. If the limit is hit, trading stops for five minutes. After the five minutes, the limit is expanded, and trading resumes as long as the new limit is not hit immediately. Price limits change over time. In 2001, for example, the Swiss franc contract had no price limits.

There is some debate as to the exact role of price limits. Some argue that they make it possible for providers of liquidity to come to the markets and smooth price fluctuations; others say that they are another tool the exchange uses to limit default risk.

Figure 5.3 shows how the June 1999 Swiss francs futures contract price evolves during March 1999. The contract price at the end of the month is lower than at the beginning, so holding a long position in the contract during that month is not profitable. The last price in March is $0.6792; the dollar value of the Swiss francs of the contract is then $84,900. The net sum of the payments made by the long during the month of March is equal to the difference between $86,350 and $84,900, namely $1,450, and represents the loss of the long position.

Figure 5.3   Daily gains and losses from a long position in the Swiss franc June futures contract during March 1999

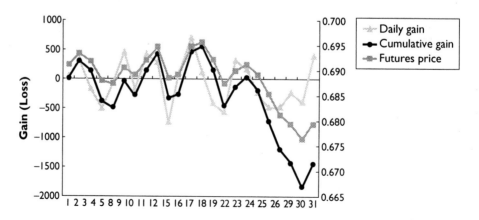

Figure 5.4 provides the evolution of the margin account assuming there are no withdrawals and the margin account earns no interest. We assume that the appropriate initial and maintenance margins are respectively $2,500 and $2,000. Two additional margin payments are required when the account falls below the maintenance margin of $2,000. These margin payments are $712.5 on March 25 and $725 on March 29. The data used for the two figures are reproduced in Table 5.2.

5.4. How to lose money on futures and forward contracts

There is much more to understand about futures and forwards, including whether the pricing of futures differs from the pricing of forwards. We will also evaluate whether a difference between the futures price and the expected price of the deliverable asset or commodity represents a real arbitrage opportunity. Finally, we will discuss the impact of financial market imperfections on the pricing of forwards and futures.

5.4.1. Pricing futures contracts

If marking to market does not matter, there is no difference between a futures contract and a forward contract in perfect markets as long as the margin consists of marketable securities. This is because an investor can always deposit the margin in the form of marketable securities so that there is no opportunity cost of making the margin deposit. The typical approach is to treat futures like forwards, and use the forward pricing results for futures. This provides a good first approximation for pricing, but the approximation has its pitfalls.

If you treat futures like forwards, you might be tempted to think that any difference between the forward price and the futures price represents an arbitrage opportunity. In any comparison of forward and futures prices, you will have to examine the reasons prices differ carefully.

Margin account balance and margin deposits from a long position in the Swiss franc June futures contract during March 1999   *Figure 5.4*

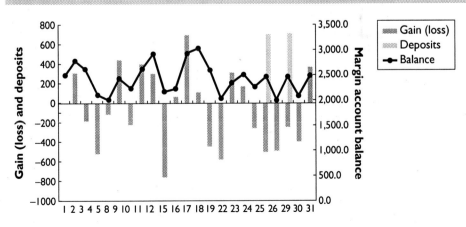

Date

Table 5.2 Long Swiss franc futures position during March 1999 in the June 1999 contract

Date	Futures price (F)	F*contract size (SFR125,000)	Gain (Loss)	Margin account (before add. deposit)	add. deposit	Margin account (after add. deposit)
3/1/99	0.6908	86,350.0	0	2,500.0	0	2,500.0
3/2/99	0.6932	86,650.0	300.0	2,800.0	0	2,800.0
3/3/99	0.6918	86,475.0	(175.0)	2,625.0	0	2,625.0
3/4/99	0.6877	85,962.5	(512.5)	2,112.5	0	2,112.5
3/5/99	0.6869	85,862.5	(100.0)	2,012.5	0	2,012.5
3/8/99	0.6904	86,300.0	437.5	2,450.0	0	2,450.0
3/9/99	0.6887	86,087.5	(212.5)	2,237.5	0	2,237.5
3/10/99	0.6919	86,487.5	400.0	2,637.5	0	2,637.5
3/11/99	0.6943	86,787.5	300.0	2,937.5	0	2,937.5
3/12/99	0.6883	86,037.5	(750.0)	2,187.5	0	2,187.5
3/15/99	0.6888	86,100.0	62.5	2,250.0	0	2,250.0
3/16/99	0.6944	86,800.0	700.0	2,950.0	0	2,950.0
3/17/99	0.6953	86,912.5	112.5	3,062.5	0	3,062.5
3/18/99	0.6918	86,475.0	(437.5)	2,625.0	0	2,625.0
3/19/99	0.6872	85,900.0	(575.0)	2,050.0	0	2,050.0
3/22/99	0.6897	86,212.5	312.5	2,362.5	0	2,362.5
3/23/99	0.6911	86,387.5	175.0	2,537.5	0	2,537.5
3/24/99	0.6891	86,137.5	(250.0)	2,287.5	0	2,287.5
3/25/99	0.6851	85,637.5	(500.0)	1,787.5	712.5	2,500.0
3/26/99	0.6812	85,150.0	(487.5)	2,012.5	0	2,012.5
3/29/99	0.6793	84,912.5	(237.5)	1,775.0	725.0	2,500.0
3/30/99	0.6762	84,525.0	(387.5)	2,112.5	0	2,112.5
3/31/99	0.6792	84,900.0	375.0	2,487.5	0	2,487.5

Source: *The Wall Street Journal*, various issues (3/2/99 – 4/1/99).

There are both forward contracts and futures contracts on the major foreign currencies. At times these contracts have identical maturities. Suppose a trader learns on March 1 that the futures price for a Swiss franc contract maturing in June, $G_{March\ 1}(June)$, is higher than the forward price for a contract initiated that day maturing on the same date, $F_{March\ 1}(June)$, with identical delivery conditions. The trader might be tempted to short the futures contract and take a long position in the forward contract.

There is a problem with this attempt to arbitrage the difference between the forward price and the futures price. With the forward contract, all the gain or loss is paid at maturity. With the futures contract, the gains and losses are paid as they accrue.

Suppose then that the Swiss franc appreciates from March 1 through the maturity of the June contract. The trader will have to make settlement variation payments as his losses on the futures contract are marked to market. We know that immediately before the futures contract expires, the futures price is equal to the spot price, S_{June}. The short in a futures contract who holds the position to maturity receives settlement variation equal to the differences between the futures price when he entered the position and the spot price at maturity. In this case, the short has to pay $S_{June} - G_{March\ 1}(June)$ over time since the spot price at maturity exceeds the futures price when he entered the futures position. We know that the payoff from a long forward position is equal to the difference between the spot price at maturity and the forward price, $S_{June} - F_{March\ 1}(June)$. Consequently, the trader would seem justified to think that the payoffs of the futures contract exactly offset the payoffs of the forward contract except for his profit corresponding to the difference between the forward price and the futures price when he enters the contract, since in June he gets:

$$S_{June} - F_{March\ 1}(June) - [S_{June} - G_{March\ 1}(June)]$$

$$= G_{March\ 1}(June) - F_{March\ 1}(June)$$

Yet the payoffs accrue differently over time. In this example, the trader must pay the settlement variation on the futures position before he receives the payoff of the forward contract. Suppose the trader borrows to pay for the settlement variation and plans to repay at maturity. The total amount borrowed before interest will be $S_{June} - G_{March\ 1}(June)$. At maturity, the payoff from the forward contract will be enough to repay this amount, but the trader has to pay interest also. The money he can use to pay interest is the difference between the futures price when he started his strategy and the forward price, or what he believes will be his arbitrage profit, $G_{March\ 1}(June) - F_{March\ 1}(June)$. If the difference between the futures price and the forward price is smaller than the interest owed, the trader will have to use other funds to pay for it. If he has no other funds or if his other funds are sufficiently limited that he cannot pay all the interest due, his attempt at arbitraging the difference between the forward and the futures price bankrupts him.

A futures contract can be made into a contract with payoff only at maturity through reinvestment and borrowing. That is, as we make a gain, we invest the gain in the risk-free asset until maturity. At maturity, we receive the gain plus an interest payment. As we incur a loss, we borrow to pay the loss, and again at maturity we have to pay for the loss and for the cost of borrowing. Just this way, the daily settlement feature of futures contracts affects the payoff at maturity; it magnifies both gains and losses through the interest payments.

Possible mark-to-market gains and losses do not affect the futures price as long as interest rates are constant and are the same for our lending and our borrowing. This is because, when we enter the contract, there is no reason to think that we will benefit from the marking to market—expected gains are matched by expected losses, and interest received on investing expected gains matches interest paid on money borrowed to pay for these losses. Things get more complicated if interest rates change over time. If interest rates are high when we make gains and low when we have to borrow because we incur losses, we are of course better off because the expected interest gain on investing profits exceeds the expected interest loss in borrowing to cover losses.

Because gains and losses on a forward contract are not paid when they accrue, we receive or make no interest payments over the life of the contract. If the reinvestment feature is advantageous to us, the futures price must then exceed the forward price to offset the benefit of the reinvestment to make the investor indifferent between a forward contract and a futures contract. The opposite occurs if the interest rate is higher when we have to borrow than when we get to lend. Basically, the futures price may exceed the forward price simply because interest rates are higher when the long in the futures contract makes gains. If this is the case, taking a long position in the forward contract and a short position in the futures contract does not make profits. It is a zero net present value transaction, but not an arbitrage opportunity since the payoff of that strategy depends on how the futures price evolves over the life of the contract. In our example of the trader brought to bankruptcy by such a trade, the futures price was assumed to increase over the life of the contract. Had the futures price been assumed to fall, the trader would have made money because he would have had the use of the cash generated by the settlement variation of the contract until maturity.

The daily settlement feature of futures contracts has an important impact on futures prices. Let's look at a simple example that is shown in Figure 5.5. Suppose that we have three dates, 1, 2, and 3. The futures price at date 1 is $2. At date 2, it can be $1 or $3 with equal probability. At date 3, the futures price for immediate delivery is equal to the spot price at that time and delivery takes place. Suppose first that the interest rate is a constant 10 percent, so that a one-period zero-coupon bond costs $0.909. In this simple example, reinvestment of the proceeds takes place only once, at date 2. At date 2, if the price is $1, the futures

---

Figure 5.5   **Marking to market and hedging**

To make a futures contract have payoffs only at maturity, one borrows marked-to-market losses and invests marked-to-market gains. In this example, the futures price and the forward price are equal at $2 at date 1. The futures price then falls to $1 at date 2 and stays there. Consequently, at date 3, the spot price is $1. The payoff of the forward contract at date 3 is –$1 for a long position. The payoff for the futures contract is –$1 at date 2. To make the futures contract have a payoff at date 3 only, like the forward contract, one can borrow $1 at date 2 that one repays at date 3. Hence, if the interest rate is 10 percent for each period, one loses $1.1 with the futures contract at date 3 in this example.

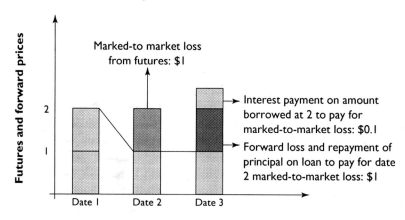

buyer has to borrow that amount and pay it. In this case, the futures buyer has to repay $1/0.909 = 1.1$ at date 3. Or, if the price is $3, the futures buyer receives $1. Investing $1 for one period yields $1.1 at date 3. Since the futures buyer has a probability of 0.5 of gaining $0.1 through reinvestment and the same probability of losing that amount, there is no expected benefit from reinvestment.

Suppose next that the price of a one-period bond at date 2 is $0.893 if the futures price is $3 and $0.926 if the price is $1. The futures buyer now gains $0.12 from investing the gain $(1/0.893 -1)$ and loses $0.08 from paying interest on borrowing when the price is $1. In this case, because the interest rate is higher when the futures buyer gains than when he loses, there is an expected gain from reinvestment of $0.02 $(0.5 \times 0.12 - 0.5 \times 0.08)$. The futures price has to be higher than the forward price to ensure that holding the futures contract does not have a positive net present value.

Finally, if the price of the one-period zero-coupon bond is $0.926 when the futures buyer makes a profit and $0.893 when he incurs a loss, the futures buyer loses from reinvestment since he receives 0.08 with probability 0.5 and has to pay 0.12 with the same probability. Therefore, the futures price has to be lower than the forward price.

Keeping the futures price constant, the expected profits of the holder of a long futures position increase when the correlation between interest rates and the futures price increases. Consequently, for futures sellers to be willing to enter contracts where the futures price is positively correlated with interest rates, the futures price of such contracts must be higher. Therefore, an increase in the correlation between interest rates and futures prices results in an increase in the futures price relative to the forward price. With this reasoning, one expects the futures price to exceed the forward price when interest rates are positively correlated with the futures price. When interest rates are negatively correlated with the futures price, the reverse should happen: the forward price should exceed the futures price.

A number of researchers examine the relation between forward and futures prices. Some of them focus on currencies and generally find only trivial differences between the two prices. Researchers who investigate the difference between forward and futures prices on fixed income instruments, like T-bills, find greater differences. This is not surprising because there is a high negative correlation between interest rates and the price of T-bills. However, this correlation cannot explain all of the difference between futures and forward prices, leaving a role for taxes and liquidity, among other factors.

5.4.2. The role of the expected future spot price

Suppose an investor expects the spot exchange rate for the Swiss franc 90 days from now to be at 74 cents and observes a forward contract price for delivery in 90 days of 70 cents. If the investor is right, 90 days from now she can buy Swiss francs at 70 cents and expect to resell them on the spot market at 74 cents. Let's consider how we can understand this expected profit and whether markets could be efficient with such an expected profit.

Of course, it could simply be that the investor is misinformed. In other words, the market could be right and she could be wrong. In this case, the strategy would not produce an expected gain if the investor only knew what the market knows. Second, it could be that the market expects the spot rate to be 70 cents and the investor is right. In this case, in expected value, the strategy would make a profit. Remember, however, that there is substantial volatility to exchange rates, so that even though the true expected spot rate is 74 cents, 90 days from now the actual exchange rate could turn out to be 60 cents, and the transaction would result in a loss.

Is it possible that the investor is right in her expectation of a spot exchange rate of 74 cents and that the forward contract is correctly priced at 70 cents per Swiss franc? Taking a long forward position because one believes that the forward price is lower than what the spot price will be when the contract matures is not an arbitrage position. That is, this position can incur losses. It can also make greater gains than expected.

Risk is the key. You know from Chapter 2 that investors are rewarded by the market for taking some risks. In particular, if the capital asset pricing model (CAPM) holds, investors are rewarded for taking systematic risks. Suppose that a foreign currency has a beta of one. In this case, bearing currency risk is like bearing market risk. The investor expects to be rewarded for bearing this type of risk. An investor who has a long forward position is rewarded for bearing risk by a lower forward price. This increases the expected profit, given the investor's expectation of the future spot price.

Hence, in the example, if the investor expects the spot price to be at 74 cents but the forward price is at 70 cents, she makes an expected profit of four cents per Swiss franc when she enters a forward contract she expects to hold to maturity. This expected profit is compensation for bearing systematic risk. If a long forward position has a negative beta, then the forward price exceeds the expected spot price because the short position has a positive beta and must be compensated for bearing systematic risk.

Before the logic of the CAPM became dominant in the pricing of contracts, it was often argued that markets for future delivery should be in backwardation when hedgers are short in the markets for future delivery. In such a situation, speculators have to be long and have to be compensated for the risk they take. Therefore, the price for future delivery has to be lower than the expected cash price so that the speculators can expect to make a profit. With the CAPM, speculators will only be compensated for taking on systematic risk. Otherwise, speculators will flock to the market for future delivery until prices are set so that speculators are only compensated for taking on systematic risk.

Much of the research on the relationships among forward prices, futures prices, and expected spot prices focuses on the foreign exchange market. The bottom line is that if we average contracts over very long periods of time, the forward prices of these contracts on average equal the spot prices at maturity. Hence, on average, the forward price is the expected spot price. At the same time, it has been shown that forward contracts on a currency for which interest rates are high are on average profitable.

The two findings are not contradictory: Countries will sometimes have high interest rates and other times low interest rates. This means that at any particular time the forward price is unlikely to be equal to the expected spot price. There is some evidence that shows that the current spot price is a better forecast of the future spot price for major currencies than the forward exchange change rate.

5.4.3. The impact of financial market imperfections

Throughout this chapter, we have made the assumption that markets are perfect. In this case, if the forward price differs from its theoretical value, there is an arbitrage opportunity. For instance, if the forward price is higher than its theoretical value, it pays to sell forward and hedge the transaction by buying the deliverable asset and financing the purchase with a loan that matures with the contract. Suppose now that there are some transaction costs. In this case, the actual forward price may not be equal to the theoretical forward price.

Say that k_F is the proportional transaction cost for the forward contract (for instance, a commission that has to be paid to the broker), k_A the proportional transaction cost on purchasing the deliverable asset, and k_B the proportional transaction cost on borrowing. In this case, taking advantage of a forward price that is too high compared to its theoretical value in perfect markets requires paying transaction costs of $k_F F_t$ on the forward position, $k_A S_t$ on purchasing the deliverable asset, and $k_B S_t$ on borrowing. The total transaction costs for the long to hedge his position are therefore $k_F F_t + k_A S_t + k_B S_t$. Hence, if the difference between the forward price and its theoretical value is positive, there is an arbitrage opportunity only if that difference exceeds the transaction costs of going long the contract and hedging the position. Similarly, if the difference between the forward price and its theoretical value is negative, that difference has to exceed the transaction cost of shorting the contract and hedging the short position for there to be an arbitrage opportunity.

According to this reasoning, we can construct an expanded formula for the forward price. Let Ω^L be the sum of the transaction costs that have to be paid in taking advantage of an arbitrage opportunity when the forward contract price is too low. Remember that in this case one exploits the arbitrage opportunity with a long forward position and a short position in the replicating portfolio. Let Ω^S be the sum of the transaction costs that have to be paid to exploit an arbitrage opportunity arising because the forward contract price is too high. In this case, one has to go short the forward contract and long the replicating portfolio. When there are transaction costs, there is no arbitrage opportunity as long as the difference between the forward price and the replicating portfolio is not sufficient to cover the transaction costs one would incur to take advantage of this difference. Consequently, letting r be the continuously compounded interest rate at t for a T-bill maturing at $t + i$, we must have:

Forward price in the presence of transaction costs

$$\mathbf{S}_t - \Omega^L \leq \mathbf{F}e^{-r \times i} \leq \mathbf{S}_t + \Omega^S \qquad \text{(5.14)}$$

To check the formula, note that it can be rewritten as:

$$-\Omega^S \leq \mathbf{S}_t - \mathbf{F}e^{-r \times i} \leq \Omega^L$$

If the forward price is lower than its theoretical value in perfect markets, the term in the middle is positive. Since transaction costs are positive, this means that the left-hand side inequality is satisfied. If the right-hand side inequality is not satisfied, then the costs of forming an arbitrage portfolio are less than the profit from forming the arbitrage portfolio before transaction costs. If the forward price is too high, the middle term is negative and one would like to short the forward contract, using a long position in the replicating portfolio to hedge. To avoid arbitrage opportunities, the gain from doing this has to be lower than the transaction costs.

It is real-world frictions that make the forward price (and the futures price by extension) different from the theoretical price assumed to hold if markets are perfect. In some cases, the costs of taking advantage of arbitrage opportunities are minuscule, so that we would expect the discrepancies to be extremely small. This would be so if you try to arbitrage forward price discrepancies for contracts with short-term standard maturities on foreign exchange for major currencies, which would be maturities of 30, 90, and 180 days. The transaction costs for arbitraging a 10-year foreign exchange forward contract would be more significant.

Whether the costs in taking advantage of an arbitrage opportunity are important or not depends on the liquidity of the deliverable asset, on the trading expertise of the arbitrageur, and on the credit risk of the arbitrageur. A major money center bank faces much lower arbitrage costs than a weakly capitalized occasional participant in the foreign exchange market.

5.5. Summary

The key to pricing forward contracts is that they can be replicated by buying the underlying asset and financing the purchase until maturity of the contract. This allows us to price the contracts by arbitrage. This means that we can price a forward contract without having a clue as to the expected value of the underlying asset at maturity. To price a forward contract on a currency, we therefore do not need to know anything about the determinants of changes in exchange rates. The forward price depends on: the interest rate that has to be paid to finance the purchase of the underlying asset, the cost to store it, and the benefit from holding it. As financing and storage become more expensive, the forward price increases compared to the current price of the underlying asset. As the benefit of holding the underlying asset increases, the forward price falls compared to the price of the underlying asset. Forward contracts can have substantial default risk. Futures contracts, however, have a built-in mechanism that reduces and almost eliminates default risk. This mechanism is the clearinghouse, daily settlement, and the posting of a margin. The daily settlement feature allows participants in futures markets to reinvest their gains. The futures price exceeds the forward price when this feature is advantageous to the long, which is the case when unexpected increases in futures prices are positively correlated with interest rate changes. We then discussed that forward and futures contracts may have systematic risk. Systematic risk reduces the forward and futures prices to compensate the long for bearing the risk. Finally, transaction costs and other market imperfections are responsible for small deviations of forward prices from theoretical prices. The next step is to learn how to use forward and futures contracts for risk management.

Key Concepts

backwardation, 130
clearinghouse, 132
contango, 130
convenience yield, 125
cost of carry, 130
counterparty risk, 131
initial margin, 132
maintenance margin, 132

margin call, 132
marking the contract to market, 132
price limits, 138
pricing by arbitrage, 114
replicating portfolio, 115
repo, 117
reverse repo, 117
settlement variation, 132

Review Questions

1. What is a forward contract?

2. What is the spot price?

3. What is a replicating portfolio for a forward contract?

4. What is required for the price of a forward contract to be such that there is an arbitrage opportunity?

5. What is the impact of dividends on the forward price in a contract to buy a stock forward?

6. What is the convenience yield?

7. Why do storage costs matter in pricing forward contracts?

8. How do futures contracts differ from forward contracts?

9. What is the maintenance margin in a futures contract?

10. What is the difference between cash and physical delivery for a futures contract?

11. What happens if a price limit is hit?

12. Why would the futures price differ from the forward price when both contracts have the same underlying and the same maturity?

13. Does the futures price equal the expected spot price at maturity of the futures contract?

14. Why would an arbitrage opportunity in perfect financial markets not be an arbitrage opportunity in the presence of financial market imperfections?

Questions and Exercises

1. Suppose that on January 10, a one-year default-free zero-coupon bond is available for $0.918329 per dollar of face value and a two-year default-free zero-coupon bond costs $0.836859 per dollar of face value. Assuming that financial markets are perfect, suppose you want to own $1.5 million face value of one-year zero-coupon bonds in one year and you want to pay for them in one year at a price you know today. Design a portfolio strategy that achieves your objective without using a forward contract.

2. Using the data in question 1, suppose that you learn that the forward price of one-year zero-coupon bonds to be delivered in one year is $0.912 per dollar of face value. What is the price today of a portfolio that replicates a long position in the forward contract?

3. Using the replicating portfolio constructed in question 2, construct a strategy that creates arbitrage profits given the forward price of $0.912. What should the forward price be so that you would not be able to make arbitrage profits?

4. Suppose that you enter a long position in the forward contract at a price of $0.911285 per dollar of face value for a total amount of face value of $1.5 million. One month later, you find that the 11-month zero-coupon bond sells for $0.917757 and that the 23-month zero-coupon bond sells for $0.829574. Compute the value of your forward position at that point.

5. Given the prices of zero-coupon bonds given in question 4, how did the price of a one-year zero-coupon bond for delivery on January 10 the following year change over the last month? Did you make money having a long forward position?

6. Consider a Treasury bond that pays a coupon every six months of $6.50 per $100 of face value. The bond matures in 10 years. Its current price is $95 per $100 of face value. You want to enter a forward contract to sell that bond in two years. The last coupon was paid three months ago. The zero-coupon bond prices for the next two years are $P_t(t + 0.25) = 0.977508$, $P_t(t + 0.5) = 0.955048$, $P_t(t + 0.75)$ 0.932647, $P_t(t + 1) = 0.910328$, $P_t(t + 1.25) = 0.888117$, $P_t(t + 1.5) = 0.866034$, $P_t(t + 1.75) = 0.844102$, $P_t(t + 2) = 0.822341$. Using these zero-coupon bond prices, find the forward price per dollar of face value for a contract for the purchase of $100 million of face value of the 10-year bond such that the value of the replicating portfolio is zero.

7. Using the zero-coupon bond prices in question 6, price a forward contract on oil. The current price per barrel is $18. The contract has maturity in one year. The inventory cost is 3 percent at a continuously compounded rate. The convenience yield associated with having oil in inventory is 5 percent per year. Given this, what is the forward price per barrel?

8. Consider the contract priced in question 7. Suppose that immediately after having entered the contract, the convenience yield falls to 2 percent. How is the forward price affected assuming that nothing else changes?

9. You are short the Swiss franc futures contract for five days. Assume that the initial margin is $2,000 and the maintenance margin is $1,500. The contract is for 100,000 Swiss francs. The futures price at which you enter the contract at noon on Monday is $0.55. The Monday settlement price is $0.56. The settlement prices for the next four days are $0.57, $0.60, $0.59, and $0.63. You close your position on Friday at the settlement price. Compute the settlement variation payment for each day of the week. Show how your margin account evolves through the week. Will you have any margin calls? If yes, for how much?

10. Suppose that on Monday at noon you see that the forward price for the Swiss franc for the same maturity as the maturity of the futures contract is $0.57 and that you believe that the exchange rate is not correlated with interest rate changes. Does this mean that there is an arbitrage opportunity? If not, why not? Does it mean that there is a strategy that is expected to earn a risk-adjusted profit but has risk?

Literature Note

The topics discussed in this chapter have generated an extremely large literature. Specialized textbooks on futures, such as Duffie (1989) or Siegel and Siegel (1990) develop this material further. Brennan (1986) and Kane (1980) provide interesting theoretical studies of the mechanisms used in futures markets to reduce counterparty risk. Melamed (1996) provides a good history of financial futures and a wealth of stories. The comparison of futures and forward contracts is analyzed theoretically in Cox, Ingersoll, and Ross (1981) and Jarrow and Oldfield (1981). Richard and Sundaresan (1981) provide a general equilibrium model of pricing of futures and forwards. Routledge, Seppi, and Spatt (2000) derive forward prices when the constraint that inventories cannot be negative is binding, and show that this constraint plays an important role. When the constraint is binding, the case position has value that the forward position does not have. Cornell and Reinganum (1981), French (1983), Grinblatt and Jegadeesh (1996), and Meulbroek (1992) compare forwards and futures for currencies, copper, and Euro deposits.

Theoretical and empirical studies that compare the future expected spot exchange rate and the forward exchange rate are numerous. Hodrick (1987) reviews some of these studies, and Froot and Thaler (1990) provide an analysis of this literature, arguing that departures of the forward exchange rate from the future expected spot exchange rate are too great to be consistent with efficient markets. For a study of interest rate parity in the presence of transaction costs, see Rhee and Chang (1992). The Barings debacle is chronicled in Rawnsley (1995).

Chapter 6

Hedging Exposures with Forward and Futures Contracts

Chapter 6 Objectives

At the end of this chapter, you will:

1. Know how to measure the risk of specific exposures to risk factors.

2. Understand risk-minimizing hedges with forward and futures contracts when a perfect hedge is possible.

3. Understand how to compute risk-minimizing hedges with futures contracts when there is basis risk.

4. Be able to implement risk-minimizing hedging strategies.

In this chapter, we investigate how we can use forward and futures contracts to minimize risk. Export Inc. expects to receive one million Swiss francs in three months for computers it sold to a Swiss firm. Because of this receivable, Export's cash flow in three months is risky. The source of the risk is the Swiss franc exchange rate. No other risk affects Export's cash flow. We saw in the introduction that an identifiable source of risk is called a risk factor, and a cash flow's sensitivity to a risk factor is called its exposure to that risk factor. Here, an increase in the dollar price of the Swiss franc of one penny in three months increases the firm's cash flow by one million times $0.01 or $0.01 million. Consequently, the firm's exposure to the dollar price of the Swiss franc, the change in the firm's cash flow per unit change in the exchange rate, is the exposure of having one million Swiss francs.

To determine whether and how to hedge this cash flow, Export first has to measure the cash flow's risk and then figure out how much of that risk it wants to bear. In Chapter 4, we introduced value at risk (VaR) and cash flow at risk (CaR) as risk measures for firms. In this chapter, we first show how to obtain volatility, CaR, and VaR measures for an exposure such as Export's Swiss franc exposure. We consider risk-minimizing hedges of a foreign currency position when risk is measured by volatility, CaR, and VaR. We first assume Export can eliminate all risk resulting from its Swiss franc exposure and wishes to do so. In this case, the risk-minimizing hedge is the hedge that eliminates all risk when such a hedge is both feasible and costless.

Hedging decisions when no hedge eliminates all the risk are more complicated, however. In this case, the firm has to find out which hedge minimizes risk. We show how to find and implement this hedge.

6.1. Measuring risk: Volatility, CaR, and VaR

Suppose Export Inc. on March 1, 1999, expects to receive one million Swiss francs on June 1 of the same year. We assume for simplicity that there is no default risk on the part of the firm's customer, so there is no uncertainty as to whether the Swiss francs will be paid. Further, interest rates are assumed to be constant. The only uncertainty has to do with the dollar value of the Swiss francs when they are received.

The one million Swiss francs are Export's only cash flow between March 1 and June 1. Suppose that the firm incurs distress costs if this cash flow is low. We saw in Chapter 4 that an appropriate risk measure in this case is cash flow at risk. The CaR at the 5 percent level is the cash flow shortfall relative to expected cash flow that has a 5 percent probability of being exceeded. To compute the CaR for Export, we need the probability distribution of the cash flow in three months.

Let's assume that the changes of the exchange rate are identically independently distributed and that their distribution is normal. We use the abbreviation **i.i.d.**, to denote random variables that are identically independently distributed. If changes are i.i.d., past changes provide no information about future changes. This means that a large increase in the exchange rate during one month tells us nothing about the exchange rate change for the next month. Such an assumption provides a reasonable starting point since, otherwise, investors would have incentives to trade so that it would become reasonable—a large increase that predicts a further large increase would lead investors to buy Swiss francs, which would increase the price of the Swiss franc and hence reduce the expected increase. With the assumption that changes are i.i.d., we can estimate the mean and the variance of the changes using the tools provided in Technical Box 6.1, Estimating mean and volatility. Using monthly data for the dollar price of the Swiss franc from March 1988 through February 1999, we obtain a mean monthly change of –$0.000115 and a variance of 0.000631. Figure 6.1 shows a plot of the dollar price of the Swiss franc over the period used to estimate the mean and variance of the exchange rate change.

With our assumptions, the variance for each period is the same, and the changes are uncorrelated. To see what this implies for the variance over multiple future periods, let's look at the variance of the exchange rate as of May 1 viewed from March 1. We use this two-month interval to make things easier to follow. Remember that we denote a spot price by S. The spot price of the Swiss franc, its exchange rate on May 1, is $S_{\text{March 1}}$ plus the change in March, ΔS_{March},

---

Estimating mean and volatility   *Technical Box 6.1*

Suppose that we have T different observations of past changes and want to forecast the change and its volatility for $T+1$. Let's use the notation $\Delta S_i = S_i - S_{i-1}$. With this notation, the expected change is simply the average of the changes over the estimation period:

$$E(\Delta S_{T+1}) = \overline{\Delta S} = (1/T) \sum_{i=1}^{T} \Delta S_i$$

Suppose we use as our estimation monthly quotes of the dollar price of the Swiss franc from March 1988 through February 1999. The mean of the monthly change in the exchange rate over the estimation period is –0.000115. Over the estimation period, the Swiss franc depreciated against the dollar. The expected variance of the change for $T+1$ is:

$$\text{Var}(\Delta S_{T+1}) = \frac{1}{T-1} \sum_{i=1}^{i=T} (\Delta S_i - \overline{\Delta S})^2$$

Note that the estimate of the variance differs from the average of the squared deviations of the changes from their mean. Since we have T squared deviations, the average would divide the sum of the squared deviations by T. Instead, we divide the sum by $T-1$ to avoid a bias in the estimate of the variance. As the number of observations becomes large, it makes little difference whether we divide by T or $T-1$. In the case of the Swiss franc, we have 131 observations, so the adjustment is $131/(131-1)$. The historical variance is 0.000626 and the variance after the adjustment is 0.000631.

Figure 6.1   Plot of the Swiss franc exchange rate

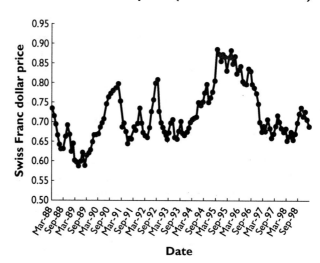

Swiss Franc dollar price (Mar. 1988–Feb. 1999)

and the change in April, ΔS_{April}. The variance of $S_{May\ 1}$ is therefore obtained as follows:

$$
\begin{aligned}
\mathbf{Var(S_{May})} &= \mathbf{Var(S_{March\ 1} + \Delta S_{March} + \Delta S_{April})} \\
&= \mathbf{Var(\Delta S_{March}) + Var(\Delta S_{April}) + 2Cov(\Delta S_{March},\ \Delta S_{April})} \\
&= \mathbf{Var(\Delta S_{March}) + Var(\Delta S_{April})} \\
&= \mathbf{2Var(\Delta S_{March})}
\end{aligned}
$$

$Var(S_{March\ 1})$ is equal to zero since we know the exchange rate on that day. The i.i.d. assumption implies that $Cov(\Delta S_{March},\ \Delta S_{April}) = 0$ and that $Var(\Delta S_{March}) = Var(\Delta S_{April})$. The variance of the change in the exchange rate over two periods is therefore twice the variance of the change over one period. The same reasoning leads to the result that the variance of the exchange rate in N periods is N times the variance of a one-period change to the exchange rate. Since the volatility is the square root of the variance, it follows that the volatility of the exchange rate over N periods is $\sqrt{N}$ times the volatility per period. This rule is called the **square root rule for volatility**.

Square root rule for volatility

If a random variable is identically independently distributed with volatility per period σ, the volatility of that random variable over N periods is $\sigma \times \sqrt{N}$.

This rule does not work if changes are correlated because, in that case, the variance of the sum of the changes depends on the covariance between the changes.

Let's now look at an horizon of three months. The monthly volatility is the square root of 0.000631, which is 0.0251197. To get the three-month volatility, we multiply the one-month volatility by the square root of three, $0.0251197 $\times$ \sqrt{3}$, which is 0.0435086. The volatility of the payoff to the firm, the dollar payment in three months, is therefore $0.0435086 $\times$ 1M$, or $43,508.60. The expected change of the exchange rate over three months is three times the expected change over one month, which is $3(-\$0.000115) = -\$0.000345$.

Because the monthly exchange rate change is normally distributed, the sum of three monthly changes also is normally distributed. We know that with the normal distribution, there is a probability of 0.05 that a random variable distributed normally will have a value lower than its mean by 1.65 times its standard deviation. Using this result, there is a 0.05 probability that the exchange rate will be lower than its expected value by at least $0.0717892 ($1.65 $\times$ 0.0435086) per Swiss franc. For Export, there is a 0.05 probability that it will receive an amount that is at least $71,789.20 ($0.0717892 $\times$ 1,000,000$) below the expected amount. Suppose that the current exchange rate is $0.75 and we use the distribution of the exchange rate we have just estimated. In this case, the expected exchange rate is $0.75–$0.000345, or $0.7496550. The expected cash flow is 1 million $\times$ $0.749655, or $749,655. If there is a 5 percent probability that the firm's cash flow shortfall relative to its expected value will exceed $71,789.20, this means there is a 5 percent chance the cash flow will be lower than $749,655 – $71,789.20, or $677,865.80. The CaR is therefore $71,789.20. If Export wants its cash flow to exceed $710,000 95 percent of the time, it now has taken too much risk because its target CaR is $39,655 ($749,655 – $710,000.)

The calculations are similar for value at risk. Suppose that Export computes the value of its long Swiss franc position and is concerned about its change over the next day. In that case, value at risk is an appropriate risk measure. To compute VaR, we require the market value of the long Swiss franc position. The price of a three-month zero-coupon bond in Swiss francs is 0.96 Swiss francs. Since an increase in the price of the Swiss franc tomorrow by one cent increases the present value tomorrow of the Swiss francs Export Inc. will receive on June 1 by 960,000 $\times$ $0.01, or $9,600, Export has an exposure of 960,000 Swiss francs over the next day. The price of one Swiss franc on March 1 is $0.75, so the dollar value of the Swiss franc payoff on that day is $0.75 $\times$ 0.96 $\times$ 1M = $720,000. Over the next day, the expected change in the exchange rate is trivial and can be ignored. Further, we assume that interest rate uncertainty can be ignored. To find the volatility of the exchange rate change over one day, we use the square root rule. Let's use 21 trading days per month. This means that the volatility over one day is the square root of 1/21 times the monthly volatility. We therefore have a daily exchange rate volatility given by $\sqrt{(1/21)}$ $\times$ $0.0251107, which is $0.0054796. The volatility over the next day of the present value of the Swiss franc payment Export will receive on March 1 is therefore 960,000 $\times$ $0.0054816, or $5,260.41. Let's assume that the daily change in the dollar price of the Swiss franc is normally distributed. There is a 5 percent chance that the position will lose at least 1.65 $\times$ $5,260.41 or $8,679.69, over the next day.

Remember that a long forward position of one Swiss franc maturing on June 1 is equivalent to a portfolio of a long position in a Swiss T-bill with face value of one Swiss franc maturing on June 1 and a short position in a dollar T-bill maturing on June 1 with face value equal to the forward price.

If interest rate changes can be neglected, the risk of a long forward position in Swiss francs is therefore the risk of a long position in a Swiss T-bill with face value equal to the number of Swiss francs purchased forward, because under our assumptions the short position in dollar T-bills has no risk. When we compute Export's three-month CaR, we therefore also compute the CaR of a three-month forward contract. When we compute Export's one-day VaR, we also compute the one-day VaR of a three-month forward contract.

6.2. Hedging when there is no basis risk

Export has taken on too much risk. It has to figure out how to reduce its risk. We explore how Export can eliminate risk using the forward market, the money market, and the futures market:

1. The forward contract and money market solutions. Export Inc. can use a forward contract to hedge. A hedge is a position in a hedging instrument put on to reduce the risk resulting from the exposure to a risk factor. Suppose Export sells its exposure to the risk factor forward. The hedge is a short position of 1 million Swiss francs in a forward contract maturing on June 1. Denote the forward price today on a forward contract that matures in three months agreed upon on March 1 by $F_{\text{March 1}}$. Export receives $1M \times F_{\text{March 1}}$ for its Swiss francs, realizing a gain from having put on the forward position of $F_{\text{March 1}} - S_{\text{June 1}}$ per Swiss franc sold forward. Therefore, Export has on June 1:

Cash position + Gain from forward position =

$$S_{\text{June 1}} \times 1M + [F_{\text{March 1}} \times 1M - S_{\text{June 1}} \times 1M] = F_{\text{March 1}} \times 1M$$

We can also compute the hedge for a one-unit exposure to a risk factor. Generally, for a long exposure to a risk factor, a hedge typically involves a short position in the financial instrument and the size of the hedge is defined as the size of that short position. The **hedge ratio** is the size of the hedge for a one-unit exposure to a risk factor. In this example, the hedge ratio is one because the firm goes short one Swiss franc forward for each Swiss franc of exposure.

Consider now the impact of a forward hedge on our risk measures. Since the forward price is known today, there is no risk to the hedged position as long as there is no counterparty risk with the forward contract. This makes the volatility of the hedged payoff equal to zero. Since the CaR is 1.65 times the volatility of the hedged payoff, the hedged payoff has a CaR of zero.

Define $P_{\text{March 1}}(\text{June 1})$ to be the price on March 1 of a T-bill with a face value of \$1 maturing on June 1. Assuming no counterparty risk, the dollar present value of the hedged Swiss francs on March 1 is $P_{\text{March 1}}(\text{June 1}) \times F_{\text{March 1}} \times 1M$. Define $P_{\text{March 2}}(\text{June 1})$ to be the price on March 2 of a T-bill with one dollar face value maturing on June 1. Since the value of the position is the present value of the hedged payoff, this hedge makes the one-day VaR of the hedged position equal to zero as long as there is no uncertainty about the T-bill price on March 2.

One-day VaR of hedged position

= 1.65 × Vol(Change in present value of hedged position over one day)

= 1.65 × Vol[$P_{\text{March 1}}$(June 1)$F_{\text{March 1}}$ −$P_{\text{March 2}}$(June 1)$F_{\text{March 1}}$]

= 0

For Export, therefore, the same hedge makes the volatility, the CaR, and the VaR all equal to zero (as long as interest rates are deterministic or interest rate risk is sufficiently small that it can be safely ignored). This is because all three risk measures are linear functions of the volatility of the risk factor when exposure is a constant and the risk factor is distributed normally. In this chapter, we focus on this case, so that by obtaining volatility-minimizing hedges we also obtain CaR-minimizing hedges and VaR-minimizing hedges.

Since you know from Chapter 5 that a long forward position in a foreign currency can be replicated by a long position in the foreign currency T-bill with the same maturity as the forward contract and a short position in the domestic currency T-bill, Export could hedge using money market instruments and achieve the same result as when it hedges with the forward contract.

2. The futures solution. Export can use a futures contract to hedge. Suppose that there is a futures contract with a maturity such that the Swiss francs are delivered on June 1. The delivery date of this contract exactly matches the maturity of Export's exposure. While going short the exposure eliminates all risk with the forward contract, this is not the case with the futures contract. Futures contracts have daily settlement, so the firm receives gains and losses throughout the life of the contract. In Chapter 5, we saw that we can transform a futures contract into the equivalent of a forward contract by reinvesting the gains at the risk-free rate whenever they occur, and borrowing the losses at the risk-free rate as well. The appropriate risk-free rate is the rate paid on a zero-coupon bond from the time the gain or loss takes place to the maturity of the contract. Since a gain or loss made today is magnified by the interest earned, we need to adjust our position for this magnification effect.

Let's assume for simplicity that interest rates are constant. A gain incurred over the first day of the futures position can be invested on March 2 until June 1 if one wants to use it on June 1 to offset a loss on the cash position at that date. The converse is so for a loss; we borrow and the repayment offsets any gain. This means that over the next day the firm has to make only the present value of the gain or loss that it requires on June 1 to be perfectly hedged. Therefore, the futures position on March 1 has to be a short position in Swiss francs, 1M × $P_{\text{March 2}}$(June 1). $P_{\text{March 2}}$(June 1) is not known on March 1. So, the firm must use its forecast of the T-bill price on March 2. We take this price to be the T-bill price on March 1—a more precise approximation would use the yield of the T-bill on March 1, but discount one dollar to be paid on June 1 back to March 2 at that yield.

Remember that one dollar invested in the T-bill on March 1 becomes $1/P_{\text{March 1}}$(June 1) dollars on June 1. Any dollar gained on March 1 can be invested until June 1 when the gain made the first day plus the interest income on that gain will correspond to what the gain would have been on a futures position of one million Swiss francs.

Gain on June 1 from change in value of futures position on March 1

= **Change in value of futures position on March 1/$P_{March\ 1}$(June 1)**

= **$P_{March\ 1}$(June 1) $\times$ 1M $\times$ Change in futures price of 1 Swiss franc on March 1/$P_{March\ 1}$(June 1)**

= **Change in futures price of 1 Swiss franc on March 1 $\times$ 1M**

This change in the hedge to account for the marking to market of futures contracts is called **tailing the hedge.** Remember that the forward hedge is a short position equal in the size to the exposure to the risk factor. To obtain the futures hedge, we take into account the marking to market of futures contracts by tailing the hedge. To tail the hedge, we multiply the forward hedge on each hedging day by the present value on the next day (when settlement takes place) of a dollar to be paid at maturity of the hedge. The tailed hedge ratio for a futures contract is less than one when the hedge ratio for a forward contract is one. The March 1 price of a dollar to be paid on June 1 is $0.969388. Therefore, the tailed hedge consists of selling short 969,388 Swiss francs for June 1, even though the exposure to the Swiss franc on June 1 is one million Swiss francs. Note now that on the next day, March 2, the gain on the futures position can be invested only from March 3 onward. Hence, tailing the hedge on March 2 involves multiplying the exposure by the present value on March 3 of a dollar to be paid on June 1. This means that the tailed hedge changes over time. For constant interest rates, the tailed hedge rises over time to reach the exposure at maturity of the hedge.

When we use this procedure, the sum of the gains and losses brought forward to the maturity of the hedge is equal to the change in the futures price between the time one enters the hedge and the maturity of the hedge. Technical Box 6.2, Proof by example that tailing works, provides an example showing that this is indeed the case.

If we tail the hedge, we can use a futures contract to create a perfect hedge. Tailing is often neglected in practice, but ignoring tailing can lead to a large hedging error. For a hedge with a short maturity, the present value of a dollar to be paid at maturity of the hedge is close to $1, so tailing does not affect the hedge much and is not an important issue. An exposure that has a long maturity is a different matter. Suppose a firm wants to hedge a cash flow that it receives in 10 years. In this case, the present value of a dollar to be paid at maturity of the hedge might be 50 cents on the dollar, so that the volatility-minimizing hedge would be half the hedge one would use without tailing. With a hedge ratio of one, the firm would effectively be hedging more exposure than it has. This is called overhedging.

Let's consider an example where overhedging occurs. Suppose that Export receives the one million Swiss francs in 10 years and does not tail the hedge. Let's assume that the futures price is the same as the 10-year forward price on March 1, which we take to be $0.75 for the sake of comparison, and that the present value of $1 to be received in 10 years is $0.50. Now suppose the Swiss franc

Proof by example that tailing works

Let's make sure that tailing works to create a perfect hedge when the futures contract matures at the same time as the exposure by using the three-period example of section 5.4.1. We have three dates: 1, 2, and 3. The futures contract matures at date 3. At that date the futures price equals the spot market price since it is the price determined at date 3 to buy the foreign currency at that date. The futures price is $2 at date 1. It goes to either $3 or $1 at date 2 and stays there at date 3. For simplicity, the spot price and the futures price are assumed to be the same. The interest rate is 10 percent per period, so that a zero-coupon bond that pays $1 in one period costs $0.909. We are trying to hedge an exposure of 100 units.

A. Futures hedge without tailing

We go short 100 units at date 1 on the futures market. There are two possible outcomes with equal probability: (1) the futures price falls to $1 at date 2, and (2) the futures price increases to $3 at date 2. Suppose first the futures price falls to $1 at date 2. We make a profit of $100 on the futures market that we get to invest at the risk-free rate. We earn $10 of interest, so that at date 3 the futures profit is $110. At date 3, the spot price is $1. We lost $100 on the cash market since our position was worth $200 at date 1 but is worth only $100 at date 3. Our hedged position at date 3 is worth $100 plus $110, or $210. Suppose that instead the futures price goes to $3 at date 2. We lose $100 on the futures contract. To bring all the cash flows to date 3 to compute the value of the hedged position at that date, we have to borrow $100 at date 2. At date 3, we have to repay $110, but we made a profit of $100 on the cash market. As a result, our hedged position at date 3 is worth $300 − $110, or $190. The variance of our hedged position is $0.5 \times (190 - 200)^2 + 0.5 \times (210 - 200)^2$, or 100.

B. Futures hedge with tailing

The tailing factor is 0.909. We therefore sell short 90.9 units at date 1. At date 2, if the futures price is $1, we gain $90.9, which we invest for one period to get $100 at date 3. At date 3, the value of our hedged position is the sum of our $100 cash market position and our $100 futures gain, for a total of $200. At date 2, the tailing factor is 1, since we will not be able to invest profits we make on our futures position at date 3 because it is the end of the hedging period. Therefore, at date 2, we increase our short position to 100 contracts. If the futures price is $3 at date 2, we lose $90.9. We borrow that amount at date 2 and have to repay $100 at date 3. Therefore, at date 3, our hedged position is worth a $300 cash market position and a $100 futures loss, for a total of $200. Since our hedged position always has the same value at date 3, it has no variance.

In this example, the hedged position with a hedge that is not tailed is risky, while the hedged position with a tailed hedge has no risk. The risk of the position that is not tailed comes from the fact that at date 1 we do not know whether we will make a gain at date 2 and hence have interest income at date 3, or if we will incur a loss at date 2 and hence have to pay interest at date 3.

futures price increases tomorrow by 10 cents and stays there for the next 10 years. Without tailing the hedge, Export goes short one million Swiss francs on the futures market. In 10 years, Export will receive $850,000 by selling one million Swiss francs on the cash market, but it will have incurred a loss of 10 cents per Swiss franc on its short futures position of one million Swiss francs after one day. If Export borrows to pay for the loss, in 10 years it has to pay $0.10 \times 1M \times (1/0.50)$, or $200,000. Hence, by selling short one million Swiss francs, Export will receive from its hedged position $850,000 minus $200,000, or $650,000, in comparison to a forward hedge where it would receive $750,000 in 10 years for sure. This is because its futures hedge is too large. The tailed hedge of $0.5 \times 1M$ Swiss francs would have been just right. With that hedge, Export would receive $750,000 in 10 years corresponding to $850,000 on the cash position minus a loss of $100,000 on the futures position (an immediate loss of $50,000, which amounts to a loss of $100,000 in 10 years).

The higher the exchange rate at maturity, the greater Export's loss if it goes short and fails to tail its hedge. Hence, the position in futures that exceeds the tailed hedge Export should have taken represents a speculative position. Overhedging when one is long in the cash market amounts to taking a short speculative position.

Note that the marking-to-market feature of the futures contract creates cash flow requirements during the life of the hedge. With a forward hedge, no money changes hands until maturity of the hedge. This is not so with the futures hedge; money changes hands whenever the futures price changes. One must therefore be prepared to make payments when required to do so. We talk more about this issue in the next chapter.

6.3. Hedging when the basis is not zero

We have been assuming there is a Swiss franc futures contract maturing when Export Inc. receives the Swiss franc cash payment. If so, the futures price equals the spot price on that date. This is not true if the futures contract does not mature on June 1. Suppose there is no contract maturing on June 1 available to Export, so it uses a futures contract maturing in August instead. With this contract, Export would have a Swiss franc futures position after June 1 that would not be hedging a cash flow exposure. After June 1, therefore, the futures position would create a currency risk for Export and would no longer be a hedge. Consequently, Export would have to close its futures position on June 1. Since Export receives the cash payment it hedges on June 1, the adjustment factor for tailing the hedge is the price of a zero-coupon bond that pays $1 on June 1, the maturity date of the hedge, and not the price of a zero-coupon bond that matures when the futures contract matures. In this case, assuming a tailed hedge, the payoff of the hedged position on June 1 is:

Payoff of cash position + Payoff of hedge

$$= 1M \times S_{June\ 1} - 1M \times (G_{June\ 1} - G_{March\ 1})$$

$$= 1M \times G_{March\ 1} + 1M \times (S_{June\ 1} - G_{June\ 1})$$

where $G_{\text{March } 1}$ is the futures price when the position is opened on March 1. The term in parentheses in the second line is the basis on June 1. The **basis** is usually defined as the difference between the spot price and the futures price on a given date.[1]

There is **basis risk** if the relation between the futures price and the spot price is not deterministic. With our example, there would be no basis risk if the futures contract were to mature when Export receives the 1 million Swiss francs since, in that case, the term in parentheses is identically equal to zero and the value of the cash position is the futures prices times 1 million.

Basis risk exists whenever the hedging instrument has a payoff that is not perfectly correlated with the payoff being hedged. For instance, airlines started to hedge the price of jet fuel actively following the Gulf War. Their hedging can make a large difference in their cash flow. When fuel prices increased sharply in 2000, Delta gained $684 million on its hedges. There is no futures contract for jet fuel. There are futures contracts for crude oil of various grades and locations and futures contracts for heating oil. The difference between crude oil prices, heating oil prices, and the price of jet fuel changes randomly. Delta uses only heating oil contracts to hedge. The relevant basis for Delta is therefore the difference between the price of jet fuel and the oil futures price. Since the price of heating oil does not change one for one with the price of jet fuel, Delta bears basis risk when it hedges.

6.3.1. The volatility-minimizing hedge when there is a deterministic relation between the futures price and the spot price

When the spot price is a constant plus a fixed multiple of the futures price, we can create a perfect hedge. In this case, the relation between the futures price and the spot price is deterministic, so that the basis is known if the futures price is known. The method used to find the hedge when the spot price is a linear function of the futures price will also be useful when there is basis risk. Let's assume that the futures price and the spot exchange rate are tied together so that for any change in the futures price of Δ, the spot exchange rate changes exactly by 0.9Δ. This means that if we know the change in the futures price from March 1 to June 1, we also know the change in the spot exchange rate and the change in the basis (it is -0.1Δ, since the change in the basis is the change in the spot exchange rate minus the change in the futures price).

With our example, we can plot past changes in the spot exchange rate against past changes in the futures price. For simplicity, we assume that the changes have an expected value of zero, so that they are also unexpected changes. If there is an exact linear relation between these changes, the plot would look like Figure 6.2. Because the change in the spot exchange rate is always 0.9 times the change in the futures price, all the points representing past observations of these changes plot on a straight line. We use simulated data that satisfy the conditions of the example.

Export wants a hedge to protect itself against exchange rate surprises. It wants the unexpected change in the value of its futures position to exactly offset the

---

1 This is more precisely called the spot-futures basis. Authors sometimes call the basis the difference between the futures price and the spot price, which is called the futures-spot basis.

Figure 6.2   Relation between cash position and futures price when there is a deterministic relation between the futures price and the spot price

In this example, the change in the cash price is 0.9 times the change in the futures price. We have 100 observations. These observations are generated assuming that the change in the futures price has an expected value of zero and a standard deviation of one.

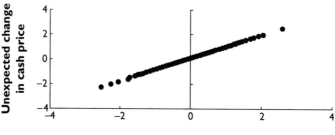

Unexpected change in futures price

unexpected change in the value of its cash market position. The value of Export's cash market position on June 1 is $1M \times S_{June\ 1}$. Using our assumption about the relation between the futures price and the spot exchange rate, an unexpected change of the futures price of Δ units is associated with a change in the value of the cash position of $1M \times 0.9 \times \Delta$. The exposure of the cash position to the futures price is therefore $1M \times 0.9$ Swiss francs futures, or 900,000 Swiss francs futures, since a unit change in the futures price changes the value of the cash position by 900,000 times the change in the futures price. Another way to put this is that the change in value of the cash position is exactly equivalent to the change in value of a futures position of 900,000 Swiss francs.

Suppose that Export goes short h Swiss francs on the futures market. In that case, the impact of an unexpected change in the futures price of Δ changes the value of Export's futures position by $-h \times \Delta$. Because of the linear relation between the futures price and the spot exchange rate, a change in the futures price of Δ corresponds to a change in the spot exchange rate of $0.9 \times \Delta$. Therefore, when the futures price changes by Δ, the value of Export's cash position changes by $0.9 \times 1M \times \Delta$. The change of the value of the hedged position is the change in value of the cash position plus the change in value of the hedge:

Change in value of the hedged position = $0.9 \times 1M \times \Delta - h \times \Delta$

Figure 6.3 plots the value of the hedged position as a function of the change in the exchange rate and of h. Panel A shows when the hedged position makes a gain because of changes in the exchange rate, while Panel B shows when it incurs a loss. Suppose h is 500,000. In this case, the net impact of a one cent increase in the futures price is to increase the value of the cash position by $0.9 \times 0.01 \times 1M$, or by $9,000, and to decrease the value of the futures position by $-500,000 \times 0.01$, or $5,000, for a net gain of the hedged position of $4,000. With h equal to 500,000, a decrease in the exchange rate of one cent decreases the value of the cash position by $9,000, and increases the value of the futures position by

Change in value of the hedged position as a function of the exchange rate change and the size of the hedge h   *Figure 6.3*

Panel A. Exchange rate changes and hedge sizes for which Export makes a gain.

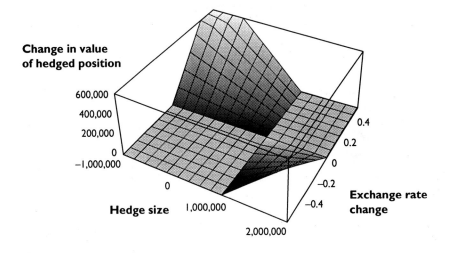

Panel B. Exchange rate changes and hedge sizes for which Export Inc. incurs a loss.

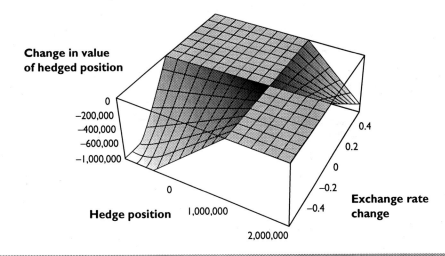

$5,000, so that a decrease in the exchange rate of one cent incurs a loss for Export. Panel A shows that the hedged position makes a gain when h is below 900,000, and the exchange rate appreciates, and incurs a loss when h is above 900,000 and the exchange rate depreciates. The only value of h where the hedged position never makes a gain is 900,000. Panel B shows that the position incurs a loss when h is below 900,000 and the exchange rate depreciates. It makes a gain when h is above 900,000 and the exchange rate appreciates. The only value of h where the hedged position never makes a loss is 900,000. Consequently, the only way Export does not lose as the exchange rate changes is if it sells Swiss franc futures for 900,000 Swiss francs. In this case, a change in the exchange rate always has offsetting effects on the value of the cash position and the value of the futures position. This value of h is the solution obtained by requiring that the change in the value of the hedged position is equal to zero regardless of the change in the exchange rate:

$$0.9 \times 1M \times \Delta - h \times \Delta = 0$$

With $h = 900,000$, the volatility of the payoff of the hedged position is zero, so a short futures position equal to the exposure of the cash position to the futures price is the volatility-minimizing hedge. Since the exposure of Export to the futures price is 900,000, Export goes short 900,000 Swiss franc futures. We saw that Export has an exposure of 1,000,000 to the Swiss franc on June 1. If Export went short Swiss franc futures for an amount equal to its exposure to the spot exchange rate instead of its exposure to the futures price, an increase in the futures price of one cent would increase the value of the cash market position by $0.9 \times 1M \times \$0.01$, or \$9,000, and would decrease the value of the futures position by $1M \times \$0.01$, or \$10,000, so that the value of the hedged position would fall by $-0.1 \times 1M \times \$0.01$, or \$1,000. That is, if the firm goes short its exposure to the spot exchange rate on the futures market, the value of its hedged position would depend on the futures price and would be risky. This is because in this example the spot exchange rate does not move one for one with the futures price. The hedged position has no risk, however, if the firm goes short its exposure to the futures price.

In our example, the hedged position has no risk because Export has no exposure to the spot price if it has no exposure to the futures price. The reason why Export can eliminate its exposure to the spot price by eliminating its exposure to the futures price is that the futures price and the spot price are perfectly correlated in our example, so that eliminating one exposure takes care of the other one. This perfect correlation results from the fact that for each change in the futures price, there is a known and certain change in the spot price. When a firm has no exposure with a risk factor, its hedged position is uncorrelated with that risk factor. Here, when the hedged position is uncorrelated with the futures price, it is also uncorrelated with the spot price.

The hedge ratio is the short futures position per unit of exposure to the risk factor. The hedge ratio for Export is 0.9. Writing the volatility-minimizing hedge as a function of the hedge ratio, we have:

**Volatility-minimizing hedge
= Volatility-minimizing hedge ratio × Exposure to the risk factor**

$$900,000 = 0.9 \times 1M$$

The hedge ratio depends only on the exposure to the futures price of one unit of the Swiss franc. Therefore, the hedge ratio would be the same for any firm hedging a Swiss franc exposure in the same circumstances as Export regardless of the size of its exposure. In other words, if there was another firm with an exposure of 100 million Swiss francs, that firm could use the same hedge ratio as Export, but its hedge would be a short Swiss franc futures position of $0.9 \times 100M$.

6.3.2. Hedging when the basis is random

When there is basis risk, hedging is more complicated since the change in the futures price is randomly related to the change in the spot exchange rate. Let's assume again that the distribution of changes in the spot exchange rate and the futures price is the same in the past as it will be over the hedging period. We assume that the futures contract is the only hedging instrument available. Now, when we plot past futures price changes against spot price changes, they do not plot on a straight line as in Figure 6.2, but rather randomly around a line with a slope of 0.9 as shown in Figure 6.4 (using simulated data). We assume instead that for each realization of the change in the futures price, the change in the spot exchange rate is 0.9 times that realization plus a random error that is not correlated with the futures price. This random error corresponds to the basis risk and is the only source of uncertainty in the relation between the spot exchange rate and the futures price.[2]

This means we can no longer know for sure what the spot price will be, given the futures price. The best we can do is to forecast the spot price given the futures price. Since the spot price is 0.9 times the futures price plus noise that cannot be forecasted, our best forecast of the spot price is 0.9 times the futures price. The forecasted exposure of Export to the futures price is therefore $0.9 \times 1M$, or 0.9 per unit of exposure to the risk factor. Export's volatility-minimizing hedge is to go short the forecasted exposure to the hedging instrument. With this hedge, the unexpected change in the cash position is expected to be equal to the unexpected

---

Relation between cash position and futures price changes when the futures price changes are imperfectly correlated with the cash position changes   *Figure 6.4*

In this example, the change in the cash price is 0.9 times the change in the futures price plus a normally distributed random error with expected value of zero and standard deviation of 0.5. We have 100 observations. These observations are generated assuming that the change in the futures price has an expected value of zero and a standard deviation of one.

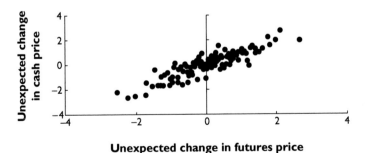

Unexpected change in futures price

---

2   We are assuming a linear relationship between changes in the spot exchange rate and the futures price, but the relation does not have to be linear. For instance, the basis could be smaller on average when the futures price is high. We will see later how the analysis is affected when the relationship is not linear.

change in the futures position plus a random error that cannot be predicted and hence cannot affect the hedge.

Why, in the presence of basis risk, can't we find a hedge that reduces the volatility of the hedged cash flow more than a hedge equal to the forecasted exposure of the cash position to the futures price? The value of the hedged cash flow is equal to the value of the cash position plus the payoff from the futures hedge. We therefore want to find a hedge that reduces the volatility of the hedged cash flow more than the hedge consisting of going short the forecasted exposure of the cash flow to the futures price. If we do not succeed, then we cannot improve on a hedge that goes short the forecasted exposure. Let ΔS be the change in the spot exchange rate and ΔG be the change in the futures price over the hedging period. The hedged cash flow per Swiss franc is therefore:

Hedged cash flow

$$= \text{Cash market position on March 1} + \text{Change in value of cash position} + \text{Hedge position payoff}$$

$$= S_{\text{March 1}} + (S_{\text{June 1}} - S_{\text{March 1}}) - h \times (G_{\text{June 1}} - G_{\text{March 1}})$$

$$= S_{\text{March 1}} + \Delta S - h \times \Delta G$$

We know that the change in the cash market position per Swiss franc is forecasted to be 0.9 times the change in the futures price. Using this relation, we get an expression for the hedged cash flow per unit of exposure to the Swiss franc:

Hedged cash flow when forecasted exposure of the Swiss franc to futures price is 0.9

$$= S_{\text{March 1}} + 0.9\Delta G + \text{Random error} - h \times \Delta G$$

$$= S_{\text{March 1}} + (0.9 - h)\Delta G + \text{Random error}$$

Consequently, the hedged cash flow is risky for two reasons when the forecasted exposure of the cash position to the futures price is known. First, as seen from the first term in the last line of the equation, any difference between the hedge and the forecasted exposure of 0.9 makes the hedged cash flow depend on the change in the futures price, ΔG, so that its value can be predicted given the change in the futures price. If the hedge ratio is less than 0.9, the hedged cash flow increases with the futures price, otherwise it falls with it. It is only when the hedge ratio is the forecasted exposure that the hedged cash flow does not depend on the change in the futures price. Second, the hedged cash flow is risky because of basis risk. Basis risk means that the change in the spot price given the change in futures price is not what we expected. In other words, it could be that the change in the spot price from March 1 to June 1 is 1.1 times the change in the futures price. Since we hedged based on a forecasted exposure of 0.9, our hedge ratio was too low because the spot exchange rate changed more than we expected and therefore we went short too few Swiss francs.

We saw in Chapter 2 that to find the volatility of a sum of random variables we take the square root of the variance of the sum of the variables. The volatility of the hedged cash flow per unit exposure to the Swiss franc is therefore:

Volatility of hedged cash flow per unit exposure to the Swiss franc

$$= [(0.9 - h)^2 \times \text{Var}(\Delta G) + \text{Var}(\text{Random error})]^{0.5}$$

Remember that the volatility of k times a random variable is k times the volatility of the random variable. Consequently, the volatility of Export's hedged cash flow is simply one million times the volatility of the hedged cash flow per unit of Swiss franc exposure. Remember that by assumption the random error is uncorrelated with the futures price. Setting the hedge equal to the expected exposure to the futures price of $0.9 \times 1M$, we eliminate the impact of the volatility of the futures price on the volatility of the hedged cash flow. There is nothing we can do about the random error with our assumptions, so the volatility of the hedged cash flow is equal to the volatility of the random error. Hence, going short the forecasted exposure to the hedging instrument is the volatility-minimizing hedge ratio.

It is more realistic to acknowledge that Export does not know the forecasted exposure of the risk factor to the hedging instrument. All Export knows is that the distribution of past changes in the spot exchange rate and the futures price is the same as the distribution of these changes over the hedging period. Therefore, Export uses the past observations in Figure 6.4 to find the risk-minimizing hedge.

To minimize risk, Export has to offset the impact of unexpected changes in the value of its cash position. Export wants to find a position in futures so that the unexpected change in the value of that position matches the unexpected change in the value of its cash position as closely as possible. This turns out to be a type of forecasting problem. Instead of forecasting both the change in the futures price and the change in the value of the cash position between March 1 and June 1, Export instead forecasts the change in the value of the cash position between March 1 and June 1, given the change in the futures price in that period. Per unit of exposure to the risk factor, this amounts to finding what value times the unexpected change in the futures price from March 1 to June 1 is the best forecast of the unexpected change in the value of the spot exchange rate for the period in the sense that the forecasting error has the smallest volatility. The volatility-minimizing hedge is then to go short h per unit of exposure to the risk factor. If the change in the futures price is useless to forecast the change in value of the risk factor, then h is equal to zero and the futures contract cannot be used to hedge the risk factor. This is equivalent to saying that for the futures contract to be useful to hedge the risk factor, changes in the futures price have to be correlated with changes in the risk factor.

We already know how to obtain the best forecast of a random variable, given the realization of another random variable. We faced such a problem in Chapter 2 when we wanted to know how the return of IBM is related to the return of the stock market. Using the S&P 500 as a proxy for the stock market, we found that the return of IBM can be expected to be IBM's beta times the return of the market plus a random error due to IBM's idiosyncratic risk. Beta is the forecast of the exposure of the return of IBM to the return of the market. If past returns are distributed like future returns, IBM's beta is the regression coefficient in a regression of the return of IBM on the return of the market. To obtain beta using an ordinary least squares regression (OLS), we had to assume that the returns of IBM and the returns of the S&P500 were i.i.d.

If the past changes in the spot exchange rate and the futures price have the same distribution as the changes over the hedging period, the regression coefficient of the change in the spot price on a constant and the change in the futures price over past periods is our best estimate of the exposure and is the volatility-minimizing hedge ratio. Export can therefore obtain the hedge ratio by estimating a regression. Figure 6.5 shows the regression line Export obtains using the 100 observations of Figure 6.4. If we denote the change in the spot exchange rate corresponding to the i-th observation by ΔS_i and the change in the futures price by ΔG_i, Export Inc. estimates the regression:

$$\Delta S_i = \text{Constant} + h \times \Delta G_i + \epsilon_i \tag{6.1}$$

where ϵ_i is the regression error or residual associated with the i-th observation. A negative value of the residual means that if the futures price has fallen, the exchange rate has fallen by more than predicted by the regression. Consequently, if we are short the futures contract and the futures price falls, the gain we make on the futures contract is insufficient to offset the loss we incur on our cash position. The slope of this regression line gives Export's estimate of the exposure to the futures price per Swiss franc, and hence its hedge ratio. If the expected changes are different from zero, this affects only the estimate of the constant in the regression. The estimate of the constant will be different from zero if the expected value of the dependent variable is not equal to the coefficient estimate times the expected value of the independent variable. Consequently, the analysis holds just as well if the expected change is different from zero, but in that case the regression is misspecified without a constant term. From now on, therefore, we do not restrict expected changes to be zero.

The volatility-minimizing hedge for one unit of exposure is the regression coefficient in a regression of changes in the spot exchange rate on a constant and on changes in the futures price. The formula for the volatility-minimizing hedge for one unit of exposure is therefore:

Figure 6.5   Regression line obtained using data from Figure 6.4

The regression in this figure is estimated using the data from Figure 6.4. The changes in cash price are regressed on a constant and the change of the futures price.

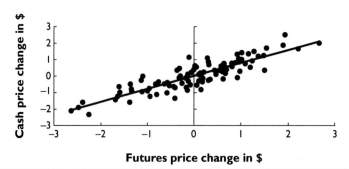

Volatility-minimizing hedge for one unit of exposure to the risk factor

$$h = \frac{\text{Cov}(\Delta S, \Delta G)}{\text{Var}(\Delta G)} \qquad (6.2)$$

If the exposure to the risk factor is 1 million, we can obtain the volatility-minimizing hedge by multiplying the volatility-minimizing hedge per unit of exposure to the risk factor by 1 million. Alternatively, we can regress changes in the value of the firm's cash position on the futures price changes. The numerator of the hedge formula is $\text{Cov}(1M \times \Delta S, \Delta G)$ or $1M \times \text{Cov}(\Delta S, \Delta G)$, which is the covariance of an exposure of 1 million to the risk factor with the futures price, and the denominator is unchanged. Hence, in this case, we would get a hedge equal to 1 million times the hedge per unit exposure.

The formula for the volatility-minimizing hedge ratio holds even if we cannot estimate a regression and there is no linear relation between the change in the futures price and the change in the spot exchange rate. This is because the volatility-minimizing hedge has to be such that the hedged cash flow is uncorrelated with the change in the futures price over the hedging period. To see this, suppose that Export picks a hedge ratio of 0.8 instead of 0.9. In this case, the hedge position is too small. If the Swiss franc futures price falls by Δ, Export loses 0.9Δ on its cash position but gains only 0.8Δ on its futures position per Swiss franc of cash position. Hence, Export loses money when the futures price falls and makes money when the futures price increases. To reduce the volatility of its hedged cash flow, Export would therefore want to increase its hedge ratio. If it increases its hedge ratio so that it exceeds 0.9, however, the opposite happens. In this case, it expects to lose money when the futures price increases and to make money when the futures price falls. The only case where Export does not expect to either make a gain or incur a loss when the futures price unexpectedly increases is when it chooses the hedge ratio given by h in equation (6.2). For all other hedge ratios, the hedged cash flow is more volatile and is correlated with the futures price.

Let's see what a choice of h that makes the hedged cash flow uncorrelated with the change in the futures price implies. To do this, we compute the covariance of the hedged cash flow per unit of cash position with the futures price and set it equal to zero.

Cov[Hedged cash flow per unit of cash position, ΔG]

$$= \text{Cov}[S_{\text{March 1}} + \Delta S - h\Delta G]$$

$$= \text{Cov}[\Delta S, \Delta G] - h\text{Var}[\Delta G]$$

Setting the covariance equal to zero yields the same relationship as the hedge ratio in equation (6.2), but we did not use a regression to obtain the hedge ratio this way. This volatility-minimizing hedge ratio is the covariance of the change in the spot exchange rate with the change in the futures price divided by the variance of the change in the futures price. As long as we know the distribution of the change of the spot exchange rate and the change of the futures price over the hedging period, we can compute the volatility-minimizing hedge ratio because we can compute the covariance and the variance from the distribution of the changes.

We can extend this result beyond exchange rates. To see this, note that we can write the hedged cash flow as:

General formula for hedged cash flow

Hedged cash flow =

Cash position at maturity of hedge −

$h \times$ [Futures price at maturity of hedge −Futures price at origination of hedge]   (6.3)

The covariance of the hedged cash flow with the futures price has to be zero. A nonzero covariance creates risk because it implies that when the futures price changes unexpectedly, there is some probability that the hedged cash flow does too. We can reduce this risk by changing the futures position to eliminate the covariance. We can ignore the futures price at origination of the hedge since it is a constant that does not affect the covariance. Consequently, we require that:

Cov(Cash position at maturity of hedge −
$h \times G_{\text{Maturity of hedge}}, G_{\text{Maturity of hedge}}$)

= Cov(Cash position at maturity of hedge,
$G_{\text{Maturity of hedge}}$) − $h \times$ Var($G_{\text{Maturity of hedge}}$)

= 0

where $G_{\text{Maturity of hedge}}$ denotes the futures price of the contract used for hedging at the maturity of the hedge. Solving for the volatility-minimizing hedge, we get:

General formula for volatility-minimizing hedge of arbitrary cash position

$$h = \frac{\textbf{Cov(Cash position at maturity of hedge, Futures price at maturity of hedge)}}{\textbf{Var(Futures price at maturity of hedge)}}$$ (6.4)

This is the classic formula for the volatility-minimizing hedge. To hedge an arbitrary cash position, we go short h units of the hedging instrument. The hedge obtained in equation (6.2) is a special case of the hedge obtained in equation (6.4). If the cash flow in equation (6.4) is a one unit exposure to the Swiss franc, we get the hedge in equation (6.2). Note that we make no assumption about exposure being constant to obtain (6.4). As a result, this formula holds for any random cash flow we wish to hedge. Nor does equation (6.4) assume that there is a linear relation between the change in value of the cash position and the change in the futures price. The linearity assumption is needed only if one wants to obtain the hedge from a regression of changes in the cash position on changes in the futures price. This means that the formula for the hedge obtained in equation (6.4) is extremely general. Generality in a hedging formula is less important than the ability to implement the formula, however. In the rest of this chapter, we focus on the implementation of the hedge ratio when it is obtained from a regression. Technical Box 6.3, Deriving the minimum-volatility hedge, provides a mathematical derivation of the volatility-minimizing hedge.

Deriving the minimum-volatility hedge

The minimum-variance futures hedge given by equation (6.4) can be obtained directly by minimizing the variance of the hedged payoff at maturity. Consider hedging an exposure with a futures contract. We know that the payoff of the hedged position is equal to the value of the cash position at maturity plus the payoff of the hedge. With a futures contract, the payoff of the hedge is given by minus one times the product of the size of the short futures position, h, and of the difference between the futures price at maturity of the hedge and the futures price at origination of the hedge. Since the futures price at initiation of the hedge is given, the variance of the hedged cash position depending only on the hedged cash position (denoted "cash") at maturity of the hedge using a hedge h is:

Variance of payoff of hedged position = Var(Cash – hG)

= Var(Cash) + h^2Var(G) –2 hCov(Cash, G)

We can compute how a change in h affects the variance of the hedged position by taking the derivative of the function with respect to h:

$$\frac{d\text{[Variance of hedged position]}}{dh} = 2h\text{Var(G)} - 2\text{Cov(Cash, G)}$$

By setting this derivative equal to zero, we obtain the hedge ratio that minimizes the variance of the hedged position:

$$h = \frac{\text{Cov(Cash, G)}}{\text{Var(G)}}$$

Remember that h is the volatility-minimizing hedge ratio before tailing, so that the number of units we need to short on the futures market is h times the current value of a zero-coupon bond that pays \$1 at maturity of the hedge.

6.3.3. The volatility-minimizing hedge and regression analysis

Does the length of the period over which we hedge matters? Suppose that Export B Inc. receives one million, but at some other time than Export. If Export hedges over three months and Export B hedges over some other period, can the two firms estimate their hedge ratios using the same regression and use the same hedge ratio before tailing? The answer is yes as long as an unexpected futures price change of Δ has the same impact on the forecast of the cash position change whatever the time interval over which the unexpected futures price change takes place and whatever the sign or magnitude of Δ. This will be the case if the cash position change per unit is expected to be 0.9 times the futures price change for any time interval over which the futures price change takes place—in other words, whether this time interval is one minute, two days, five weeks, or two months—and whether the futures price change is \$1 or –\$10. We call this the assumption of a **constant linear relation** between futures price and cash position changes.

To ensure that we can apply linear regression analysis without additional qualifications, we assume that over any time interval of identical length, the futures price changes are independently identically normally distributed, that the cash position changes are independently identically normally distributed, and that there is a constant linear relation between the futures price changes and the cash position changes. We call this assumption the **multivariate normal changes model**. Technical Box 6.4, The statistical foundations of the linear regression approach to obtaining the minimum-variance hedge ratio, discusses conditions that lead to this assumption and what the assumption implies.

Technical Box 6.4 **The statistical foundations of the linear regression approach to obtaining the minimum-variance hedge ratio**

We first need to find a period in the past when the joint distribution of the changes in the cash price and in the futures price is the same as the joint distribution we expect to apply in the hedging period. This period does not have to be the immediate past. It might be that the immediate past is unusual, perhaps a period of unusual turbulence that is not expected to repeat itself soon. In this case, one would not use data from this immediate past period.

We then require that the joint distribution of changes in the cash price and changes in the futures price is such that we can estimate their relation using linear regression. It is a property of jointly normally distributed variables that their changes are linearly related.[*] A linear relation between changes holds under more general conditions.

To be able to use our hedge using ordinary least squares (OLS), the distribution of the changes over time must satisfy some important conditions. ΔS_i is the cash price change over the i-th period, and ΔG_i is the futures price change over the i-th period. We assume that ΔS_i and ΔG_i are jointly normal for any i. To use ordinary least squares, we require that:

A1. The distribution of the cash price change is i.i.d.

A2. The distribution of the futures price change is i.i.d.

A3. $Cov(\Delta S_i, \Delta G_i)$ = Constant, for all i's.

A4. $Cov(\Delta S_i, \Delta G_j)$ = 0, where j denotes the j-th period, for all $i \neq j$.

These assumptions require that the cash price change for a given period be uncorrelated with the cash price change and the futures price change for any other period. When two or more random variables each are normal i.i.d., and in addition satisfy assumptions A3 and A4, the multivariate normal changes model applies to them.

---

[*] Any statistics textbook that discusses the multivariate normal distribution generally has this result. See, for instance, Mood, Graybill, and Boes (1974).

We can use regression analysis to find the relationship between the cash price changes and the futures price changes. We would like to know, however, how the hedge ratio depends on the length of the period of time over which the hedge is maintained and on the interval over which changes are measured.

We assume that the multivariate normal changes model holds using daily changes. We want to see whether it also holds from the perspective of Export Inc., which hedges over three months. The change in a cash price over any period longer than one day is just the sum of the daily changes, and the same is true for the change in the futures price. We know that the sum of normally distributed random variables follows a normal distribution. Consequently, if the cash price changes follow a normal distribution over days, the change in the cash price over any period of time is the sum of these changes and hence is also normally distributed. The same applies to futures price changes.

Let's look more closely at the implications of these assumptions for the distributions over a period of time. If the expected cash price change is the same over any day, the expected cash price change over N days is simply N times the daily expected cash price change. Let $\text{Var}(\Delta S_{\text{One day}})$ and $\text{Var}(\Delta G_{\text{One day}})$ be the variance of the one-day change of the cash price and the variance of the one-day change of the futures price. The change of the cash price over N trading days is then distributed normally with a variance equal to N times the variance of the one-day cash price change, or $N \times \text{Var}(\Delta S_{\text{One day}})$. The same applies for the variance of the change in the futures price. The square root rule can be used to get the volatilities over N days since the changes are independent.

Let's now look at the covariance between the changes of the cash price and the futures price over N days. Define ΔS_i to be the change over day i and $\Delta S_{N\text{ days}}$ the change over N days. The covariance over the N trading days is:

$$\text{Cov}[\Delta S_{N\text{ days}}, \Delta G_{N\text{ days}}]$$

$$= \text{Cov}\left[\sum_{i=1}^{N} \Delta S_i, \sum_{i=1}^{N} \Delta G_i\right]$$

Note now that $\text{Cov}(\Delta S_i, \Delta G_j)$ is equal to zero because changes are independent over non-overlapping periods. Further, since the changes are i.i.d., their distribution is the same for each day.

$$\text{Cov}\left(\sum_{i=1}^{N} \Delta S_i, \sum_{i=1}^{N} \Delta G_i\right)$$

$$= \sum_{i=1}^{N} \text{Cov}(\Delta S_i, \Delta G_i)$$

$$= N \times \text{Cov}(\Delta S_i, \Delta G_i)$$

(continued)

Technical Box 6.4 (continued)

We already know that the variance computed over N daily changes is N times the variance over one daily change. Consequently, the hedge ratio over N days is:

$$\text{Hedge ratio} = \frac{N \times \text{Cov}[\Delta S_i, \Delta G_i]}{N \times \text{Var}[\Delta G_i]}$$

$$= \frac{\text{Cov}[\Delta S_i, \Delta G_i]}{\text{Var}[\Delta G_i]}$$

It follows from this that the hedge ratio is the same over any hedging period as long as our assumptions are satisfied. This is a far-reaching result, because it tells us that the estimate of the hedge ratio is not affected by the measurement interval or by the length of the hedging period when the multivariate normal changes model applies. If our assumptions hold, therefore, how we estimate the hedge ratio is not dictated by the length of the hedging period. We should not expect to find a different estimate for the hedge ratio if we use daily or weekly data.

Hence, Export Inc. and firms with different hedging periods can estimate the hedge ratio using the same regression and can use the same hedge ratio. We can estimate the hedge ratio with greater precision as we have more observations, but the regression approach yields an unbiased estimate of the hedge ratio, whatever the measurement interval.

We implement the regression analysis to find the volatility-minimizing hedge ratio for hedging a Swiss franc cash position with a futures Swiss franc contract, assuming that the constant linear relation assumption holds. To estimate the relation between futures price changes and cash price changes, we can therefore use weekly changes over a period of time, the sample period. Let's assume that we use the shortest–maturity contract to hedge. We denote by ΔS_i the change in the exchange rate for period i and by ΔG_i the change in the futures price for the same period. Using periods of one week, we regress the change in the spot exchange rate on the change in the Swiss franc futures contract of shortest maturity for the period from September 1, 1997 to February 22, 1999, and obtain (t-statistics in parentheses):

$$\Delta S_i = \text{Constant} + h \times \Delta G_i + \epsilon_i \tag{6.5}$$

$$0.00 \qquad\qquad 0.94$$

$$(0.03) \qquad\qquad (32.91)$$

ϵ_i is the change in the exchange rate during the i-th week that is not explained by the regression model. With equation (6.5), if the Swiss franc futures price unexpectedly increases by one cent in one week, the Swiss franc spot exchange rate is expected to increase 0.94 cents. However, because the model does not explain all the changes in the spot exchange rate, it could turn out that the Swiss franc spot exchange rate increases by 0.96 cents. In that week, ϵ_i would be 2 cents.

The regression coefficient for the futures price change is estimated with great precision. The regression suggests that the futures price and the spot price move very closely together. To hedge one unit of spot Swiss franc, one should short 0.94 Swiss francs on the futures market. With an exposure to the risk factor of one million Swiss francs, Export Inc. should therefore short 940,000 Swiss francs on the futures market.[3]

Note that the dependent and independent variables in the regression equation are changes. While it might seem more direct to use the spot exchange rate and the futures price instead, this could yield highly misleading results. The reason is that a random variable with i.i.d. changes follows a random walk. While the changes have a well-defined mean, the random variable itself does not. Neither the exchange rate level nor the futures price have a constant mean. The expected value of a random variable with i.i.d. changes increases over time if the change has a positive expected value. Since the random variable trends up, the longer the period over which we compute the average, the higher the average. We might think that two random variables that follow random walks are positively correlated because they happen to trend up over a period of time and hence move together, even though their changes are uncorrelated. You might find, for example, that the average height of U.S. residents and the U.S. national income per capita are correlated over long periods of time, because both have positive time trends. Yet the unexpected change in the national income per capita for one year is uncorrelated with the unexpected change in height for that year.

To the extent that the relationship between unexpected changes in the Swiss franc spot exchange rate and unexpected changes in the Swiss franc futures price is constant and changes are i.i.d., whatever the measurement interval, we could use any measurement interval we want. Since more observations allow us to estimate the relation between the two random variables more precisely, we might want to use shorter measurement intervals—days or even minutes. There is a problem with using shorter intervals, however; price changes are not always measured accurately.

Price data are noisy for a number of reasons. Market imperfections such as transaction costs are one reason. If changes in price are small compared to the noise in the data, we end up getting poor measures of the real relation. This means that using very short measurement intervals might give poor results. At the same time, though, using a long measurement interval means that we have few data points and imprecise estimates.

In highly liquid markets with small bid-ask spreads, it is reasonable to use daily data. In less liquid markets, weekly or monthly data are generally more appropriate. Although we use weekly data for the example in equation (6.5), we would get almost the same estimate using daily data (0.91), but the estimate would have been more precise—the t-statistic using daily data is 52.48.

---

3 You may remember from Chapter 5 that the size of the Swiss franc contract is 125,000 Swiss francs. Please note that for the moment we abstract from the details of the contract and assume that we can short 940,000 Swiss francs.

6.3.4. The effectiveness of the hedge

Since the volatility-minimizing hedge is the slope coefficient in a linear regression, we can use the output of the regression program to evaluate the effectiveness of the hedge. The R^2 of a regression tells us the fraction of the variance of the dependent variable that is explained by the independent variable over the estimation period. The R^2 of our IBM regression measures how much of IBM's return is explained by the return of the market over the estimation period. If IBM's return is perfectly correlated with the return of the market, the R^2 is one. If the return of IBM is uncorrelated with the return of the market, however, the R^2 is zero.

To obtain the volatility-minimizing hedge per unit of exposure to the Swiss franc, we regress the changes of the spot exchange rate on the changes of the futures price:

$$\Delta S_i = a + h \times \Delta G_i + \epsilon_i$$

ϵ_i corresponds to the basis risk that cannot be hedged. With the i.i.d. assumption, the distribution of the changes does not depend on the period, so that we can write ΔS for the exchange rate change, ΔG for the futures price change, and ϵ for the basis risk that cannot be hedged. Taking the variance of the exchange rate changes, we have:

$$\text{Var}(\Delta S) = h^2 \text{Var}(\Delta G) + \text{Var}(\epsilon)$$

Since h is the hedge ratio, this equation states that the variance of the cash position is equal to the variance of the hedge position plus the variance of the risk left over after going short futures using the hedge ratio h. Hence, rearranging the equation, the variance of the hedged position over the estimation period when the volatility-minimizing hedge ratio is used is equal to the variance of the regression residual in the regression of the spot exchange rate on the futures price:

$$\text{Var}(\Delta S) - h^2 \text{Var}(\Delta G) = (1 - R^2)\text{Var}(\Delta S) = \text{Var}(\epsilon)$$

This equation shows again that minimizing the variance of the forecasting error of the spot exchange rate conditional on the futures price minimizes the variance of the hedged cash flow. The ratio $h^2 \text{Var}[\Delta G]/\text{Var}[\Delta S]$ equals R^2. If the regression has an R^2 of one, which would be the case of no basis risk, the hedged position has no variance. If the R^2 is equal to zero, though, the variance of the hedged position equals the variance of the unhedged position.

In a regression with a single independent variable, the R^2 equals the square of the correlation coefficient between the dependent variable and the independent variable. Consequently, the effectiveness of the hedge is directly related to the coefficient of correlation between the cash position and the futures contract used to hedge. A hedging instrument must have changes correlated with the changes in the value of the cash position, or it is useless. Since the volatility is the square root of the variance, the square root of R^2 tells us the fraction of the volatility of the cash price explained by the hedging instrument.

The R^2 measures the fraction of the variance of the cash position we could eliminate if we use the volatility-minimizing hedge during the estimation period. In the regression for the Swiss franc, equation (6.5), the R^2 is equal to 0.934. This means that using the volatility-minimizing hedge eliminates 93.4 percent of the variance of the cash position, whatever the size of the exposure to the risk factor. Export Inc. would have been able to eliminate 93.4 percent of the variance of its cash position if it had used the volatility-minimizing hedge during the estimation period.[4]

Note that the ratio of the variance of the hedged position and the variance of the unhedged position is equal to $1 - R^2$. Taking the square root of the ratio gives us the ratio of the volatility of the hedged position and the volatility of the unhedged position. Consequently, the volatility of the hedged position as a fraction of the volatility of the unhedged position is the square root of $1 - R^2$. Since R^2 is 0.934, the square root of $1 - R^2$ is the square root of $1 - 0.934$, or 0.26. Consequently, the volatility of the hedged position is 26 percent of the volatility of the unhedged position. Through hedging, we therefore eliminated 74 percent of the volatility of the unhedged position.

Remember that we have assumed that the joint distribution of the cash position changes and the futures price changes does not change over time. The performance of the hedge during the estimation period is thus a good predictor of the performance of the hedge over the hedging period. In the case of the Swiss franc example, the volatility-minimizing hedge ratio turns out to be about the same for the hedging and the estimation periods. If we estimate our regression over the hedging period using weekly changes, the regression coefficient also is 0.94, and the R^2 is 0.983. Using the hedge ratio of 0.94, we end up with a volatility of the hedged payoff of 0.00289 compared to a volatility of the unhedged payoff of 0.02099. The hedge eliminates 87 percent of the volatility of the unhedged payoff, or more than 98.3 percent of the variance. Consequently, the hedge performs well during the hedging period.

It is important to understand that to hedge in the presence of basis risk, we exploit a statistical relation between futures price changes and cash position changes. Consequently, the performance of the hedge depends on the random error associated with this statistical relation. When R^2 is high, the volatility of the random error is low, so the cash position change must typically be close to its predicted value conditional on the futures price change. As R^2 declines, the volatility of the random error proportionately increases, and large differences between the cash position change and its predicted value are more likely. It may even become possible for hedging to do more harm than good ex post. This is because when the volatility of the random error becomes large, even though we forecast a positive relation between futures price changes and spot exchange rate changes, ex post the futures price might have risen and the spot exchange rate might have fallen. If this event occurs, Export incurs losses both on its cash position and its futures position. Absent hedging, Export would have incured losses only on its cash position.

---

4 To check this, let $Var(\Delta S)$ be the variance for one unit of cash position. The hedged variance is $(1 - R^2)Var(\Delta S)$, so that the ratio of hedged variance to unhedged variance is $1 - R^2$. Suppose now that the exposure is n units instead of one unit. This means that we have n identical cash positions and n identical hedged positions. The variance of n times a random variable is n^2 times the variance of the random variable. Therefore, the variance of the cash position is $n^2 Var(\Delta S)$ and the hedged variance for n units hedged is $n^2(1 - R^2)Var(\Delta S)$. The ratio of the hedged variance to the unhedged variance is therefore $1 - R^2$ for an exposure to the risk factor of n irrespective of the size of n.

There are two different key reasons a hedge may perform poorly. One reason is that the futures price explains little of the variation of the cash market price. This is the case with a low R^2. We could know the true exposure of the cash price to the futures price, yet have a low R^2. With a low R^2, it is important to check whether other futures contracts would not be more helpful in hedging. In Export's case, it is hedging a Swiss franc exposure with a Swiss franc contract. The R^2 is very high because the underlying of the futures contract is the same as the exposure, so that basis risk arises only because the maturity of the futures contract does not match the maturity of the exposure. Think back, however, to the airline industry example. An airline has jet fuel exposure and is trying to hedge with crude oil or heating oil contracts. If the R^2 is low using one of these contracts, it might be higher using the others. However, there is nothing in our derivation of the volatility-minimizing hedge that precludes a firm from using several different contracts to hedge. Often it will have to. Some airlines use both heating oil contracts and crude oil contracts to hedge jet fuel. We will see more on this in the next chapter.

The other reason is that we estimate the hedge imprecisely, so the hedge is a short position equal to the true exposure to the futures price plus an error. The precision of the estimate is given by the t-statistic and the standard error of the estimate. In our example, the t-statistic is quite high, so the standard error is very small. Since the t-statistic is the estimated coefficient divided by the standard error, the standard error is 0.94 divided by 32.91, or 0.03 for the regression with weekly data. There is a 5 percent chance that the true hedge ratio exceeds 0.94 by 0.03×1.65, or 0.0495, and there is a 5 percent chance that it is below 0.94 by more than 0.0495. Alternatively, there is a 90 percent confidence interval for the true hedge ratio of $(0.94 - 0.0495, 0.94 + 0.0495)$. When a hedge ratio is estimated this precisely, the probability of going short when we would go long if we knew the true hedge ratio is less than one in a trillion.

The probability of making the wrong choice rises as the precision of the estimate falls. A low t-statistic (less than 2 by a rule of thumb) with a low R^2 (less than 0.25 by a rule of thumb) means that hedging is unlikely to be productive. To see this, note that if we are not hedged, the CaR and VaR measures are the exposure times 1.65 the volatility of the changes in the exchange rate. However, if we are hedged and there is some chance we have the wrong hedge ratio, then one has to take into account the fact that with a hedge ratio of the wrong sign we make a bigger loss if the exchange rate falls since we also lose on our hedge. This means that if the hedge ratio is wrong, we have a bigger loss, which translates into a larger CaR and VaR when we take into account the risk of having the wrong hedge.

A hedge could fail for a more fundamental reason. If the multivariate normal changes model does not hold for the changes of the cash price and the futures price, we could have precise estimates of the statistical model over a period of time by chance—but by the wrong statistical model. That is, the relation between changes of the cash price and of the futures price may be completely different during the hedging period. One possibility could be the situation we will consider in section 6.5: returns are i.i.d. while changes are not. Another possibility could be that the relation between the changes in the cash price and changes in the futures price has changed over time. It is therefore always important to check whether the relation we estimate holds throughout the estimation period. A good way is to divide the estimation period into two subperiods and estimate the relation for each subperiod. A relation that holds for only one subperiod is suspect.

We can check that the relation between the Swiss franc spot exchange rate and the Swiss franc futures price is stable over the sample period. We estimated the relation from September 1997 to February 1999 using weekly data. Our estimate of the regression coefficient for that period is 0.94. If we divide the period into two subperiods of nine months, we get a coefficient of 0.96 with a t-statistic of 22.81 for the first subperiod, and 0.93 with a t-statistic of 23.09 for the second subperiod. Therefore, we have no reason to be concerned that the relation is unstable or changes over time.

6.4. Putting it all together in an example

Consider now Export's situation on March 1, 1999. Table 6.1 shows market data for that day for the three types of hedging instruments we have discussed. It includes interest rate data, currency market data, and futures data. Our exporter will receive the one million Swiss francs on June 1. Foreign exchange contracts have a two-day settlement period. This means that our exporter must enter contracts that mature two days before June 1 so that it then delivers the Swiss francs on that day for these contracts. Let's look at the various possible hedges:

1. Forward market hedge. The 3-month forward price is at $0.6902. Selling the Swiss francs forward would therefore yield at maturity $690,200.

2. Money market hedge. Using eurodollar rates, the exporter could borrow for three months the present value of one million Swiss francs at the annual rate of 1 3/8 percent and invest these proceeds in dollars at the rate of 4 15/16 percent. Euro-rates are add-on rates, so the amount borrowed is one million Swiss francs minus the interest to be paid, which is 1 3/8 percent × 1/4 × amount borrowed. So, we have:

**Amount borrowed = 1M Swiss francs –
[(1 3/8 × 1/4)/100] × Amount borrowed**

Solving for the amount borrowed yields 996,574.3 Swiss francs. This amount in dollars is 0.6839 × 996,574.3, or $681,557.20. Investing this at the rate of 4 15/16 percent yields interest of $8,413. Consequently, Export ends up with $681,557.20 + $8,413 = $689,970.20. This is slightly worse than the $690,200 Export would get using the forward market.

This is unlikely to offer an arbitrage opportunity or even a profit opportunity, however. The eurodollar rates are London rates and the foreign currency data are U.S. afternoon data. This mismatch can be sufficient to create what might look like arbitrage opportunities. Another issue is that only one foreign currency price is quoted for each maturity, which ignores the bid-ask spread on foreign exchange.

3. Futures hedge. There are several different Swiss franc contracts traded at the Chicago Mercantile Exchange. These contracts are all for 125,000 Swiss francs, but they have different maturities. The available maturities are for the

Table 6.1   Market data for March 1, 1999

This is a summary of the market data Export would have considered to decide how to hedge. The data is obtained from the *Wall Street Journal* and the *Financial Times*.

Panel A. Spot and forward exchange rates for SFR

Maturity	Price	
Spot	0.6839	
1-m forward	0.6862	
3-m forward	0.6902	

Panel B. Futures contracts

Maturity	Open	High	Low	Settlement
March	0.6907	0.6923	0.6840	0.6845
June	0.6973	0.6974	0.6902	0.6908
September	0.6995	0.6995	0.6980	0.6974

Panel C. Treasury bill data

Maturity	Days to Maturity	Bid	Ask	Ask Yield
4-Mar-99	2	4.50	4.42	4.48
11-Mar-99	9	4.52	4.44	4.51
1-Apr-99	30	4.51	4.47	4.55
8-Apr-99	37	4.49	4.45	4.53
3-Jun-99	93	4.59	4.57	4.69
10-Jun-99	100	4.56	4.54	4.66

Panel D. Euro-rates

Maturity	US$ Bid	US$ Ask	SFR Bid	SFR Ask
Overnight	4 15/16	5 1/32	1 1/8	1 5/8
7 days	4 27/32	4 31/32	1 3/16	1 9/32
1 month	4 27/32	4 31/32	1 5/32	1 5/16
3 months	4 15/16	5 1/16	1 7/32	1 3/8

months of March, June, September, and December. The maturing contract stops trading two business days before the third Wednesday of the contract month, so that the June contract does not require delivery of Swiss francs on the day that Export gets its Swiss franc payment. To hedge its exposure, Export could take a long position in the June contract and close it when the exposure matures. The volatility-minimizing hedge is to go short 0.94 contracts before tailing. This means going short 940,000 Swiss francs, which corresponds to 7.52 contracts. The June T-bill price is $98.8194, so the tailing factor is slightly more than 0.9881. The volatility-minimizing tailed hedge involves 7.44 contracts. Since Export must short a round number of contracts, it chooses to go short 7 contracts.

Suppose Export could enter futures positions at the daily settlement price so that we can use the daily settlement quotes for our example. The June futures price is 0.6908 on March 1, 1999. On May 27, 1999, the June contract settled at 0.6572. This means that the total settlement variation is $29,400 on Export's futures position [−(0.6572 − 0.6908) × 7 × 125,000]. On Thursday, May 27, 1999, the spot rate for the Swiss franc is 0.6559.[5] Hence, the cash position is equal to $655,900. Ignoring the interest earned on the settlement variation, the value of the hedged position is $655,900 + $29,400, or $685,300.

When the firm takes the futures position, it has to make margin deposits. In March 1999, the initial margin required by the exchange was $2,160 for each contract. The broker Export would have dealt with could have required a higher initial margin, but not a lower one. Consequently, Export would need to make a deposit of at least roughly $15,120 to open the futures position. Since the futures price drops over time, the firm would benefit from daily marking to market.

How would Export decide which instrument to use? In a world of perfect financial markets, Export would go for the highest value of the hedged position, which in this case is the forward contract. However, the fact that the three solutions yield slightly different values for the hedged cash flow can be the case only if markets are not perfect. Those market imperfections that are material will critically affect Export's decision. We will discuss market imperfections more in the next chapter. However, three issues that we have already discussed must be considered by Export:

- **Credit risk.** Suppose Export has significant credit risk. This will most likely make the forward market hedge and the money market hedge impractical, since counterparties will be concerned about Export Inc.'s credit risk.

- **Demand for flexibility.** Remember that futures contracts are traded on exchanges, so Export can get out of a futures position easily. If a firm foresees reasons it might want to change the hedge, this will make the forward market hedge and the money market hedge impractical as well.

- **Cost of risk.** Futures hedges have basis risk. When risk is expensive, perfect hedges obtainable with forward contracts are more advantageous than futures hedges.

The exposure of Export was constant. However, suppose that a firm, say Trading Inc., had an exposure that could change in a couple of days, so that it focuses on hedging exposures over the short run and has to be prepared to change its hedges quickly as exposures change. Would the trade-off between futures and forward contracts differ for that firm? Trading Inc. would be more concerned about its ability to trade out of derivatives positions. As we saw, it is easier to get out of a futures position than to get out of a forward position. Trading Inc. would have to be concerned about the liquidity of the contracts in which it takes positions. Even though it is easy to take futures positions, taking such positions in illiquid

---

5 We are using Thursday instead of Friday because the Monday following is a U.S. holiday.

markets can be expensive because one has to offer price concessions. Hence, Trading Inc. might focus on using short maturity contracts because they tend to be more liquid than other contracts.

6.5. Hedging when returns rather than level changes are i.i.d.

So far, the analysis has assumed that the changes of the cash position and the changes of the futures price have the same joint distribution over time and are serially uncorrelated. In the case of increments to exchange rates, this made sense. There is little reason to believe that the expected change in the exchange rate and the volatility of the exchange rate change systematically with the level of the exchange rate. In the case of changes in present values, as argued in Chapter 4, it is often more appropriate to assume that returns rather than value changes are i.i.d. For example, with the CAPM, the expected return is constant as long as beta, the risk-free rate, and the market risk premium do not change. Hence, the expected dollar change on a common stock increases as the price of a stock increases, so that stock price changes are not i.i.d., but returns are, when the CAPM holds.

One simple way to check whether the assumption of i.i.d. level changes is appropriate is through a simple experiment. Since, the distribution of changes is always the same, with i.i.d. changes, we can put changes in two bins: the changes that take place when the price or present value is above the sample median and the other changes. The mean and volatility of changes in the two bins should be the same if the i.i.d. changes model holds.

When the distribution of the returns and not the distribution of level changes is i.i.d., the regression of the dollar changes of the cash position on the dollar increments of the hedging instrument is misspecified. Remember that the regression coefficient in such a regression is the covariance of the dollar increments of the cash position with the dollar increments of the hedging instrument divided by the variance of the dollar increments of the hedging instrument. If returns and not dollar changes are i.i.d., the covariance term in the regression coefficient depends on the value of the cash position and on the price of the hedging instrument. Therefore, it is not constant. The correct regression is to regress the returns of the cash position on the returns of the hedging instrument because, if returns are i.i.d., the covariance between the returns of the cash position and the returns of the hedging instrument is constant. A regression of the returns of the cash position on the returns of the hedging instrument gives us the volatility-minimizing hedge ratio for a dollar of exposure.

Suppose we want to hedge $1 million of IBM stock against market risk. The regression of IBM returns on market returns gives us IBM's CAPM beta, which is 1.1. IBM's beta is also the hedge ratio per dollar of investment in IBM. This coefficient means that we need to be short the market for $1.1 for each $1 we are long in IBM. This means that we must short the market for $1.1 million. The amount we have to go short the market is the product of the regression coefficient and the value of the cash position we are hedging.

The general result for the hedge ratio when returns are i.i.d. is:

Volatility-minimizing hedge when returns are i.i.d.

Define r(cash) to be the return on the cash position, and r(hedge) the rate of change of the price of the hedging instrument. The volatility-minimizing hedge is:

$$\begin{array}{l} \textbf{Volatility-minimizing} \\ \textbf{hedge of cash position} \end{array} = \frac{\textbf{Cov}[r(\textbf{cash}), r(\textbf{hedge})]}{\textbf{Var}[r(\textbf{hedge})]} \times \textbf{Cash position} \qquad \textbf{(6.6)}$$

Equation (6.6) makes clear that the risk-minimizing hedge in this case depends on the size of the cash position. As the cash position increases, the volatility-minimizing hedge involves a larger dollar amount short in the hedge instrument.

We already saw that when returns are i.i.d., the regression approach gives us a volatility-minimizing hedge for a cash position of one dollar. We have not addressed the issue of the measurement interval of returns. Nothing is changed in the analysis if continuously compounded returns are i.i.d. Using log changes in the regression analysis gives us the volatility-minimizing hedge per dollar of cash position. The one question that arises is whether using log changes instead of simple returns makes an important difference in the computation of the volatility-minimizing hedge. The answer is that generally it does not.

Consider the following example. Mr. Big has a portfolio of $100 million invested in the world market portfolio of the Datastream Global Index on September 1, 1999. The index is 1,071.53 at that date. He is pessimistic about the return of his portfolio over the next month, but does not want to sell because of tax consequences. To protect himself, he wants to hedge and has settled on a futures hedge. Since the United States is the largest component of the world market portfolio, he decides to use the S&P 500 futures contracts traded at the Chicago Mercantile Exchange.

To find out the volatility-minimizing futures position, Mr. Big has to specify a regression. Since he has a portfolio of securities, it makes sense to assume that returns are i.i.d. rather than value changes. He therefore assumes that the log changes of the world market portfolio and the log changes of the futures prices are i.i.d. Regressing the monthly log changes of the world market portfolio on a constant and the log changes of the futures contract from January 1, 1991 to September 1, 1999, Mr. Big finds that:

$$\Delta \textbf{Log(World index)} = c \quad + \quad \beta \Delta \textbf{Log(S\&P 500 futures)} + \epsilon$$

$$-0.00235 \quad + \quad 0.86057$$

$$(-1.05) \qquad (14.10)$$

The t-statistics are below the coefficients. The coefficients show that the world index is positively related to the S&P 500 futures. The coefficient on the S&P 500 is estimated precisely. The R^2 of the regression is 0.6554. This means that if the hedging period is like the estimation period, Mr. Big can eliminate 41.30 percent of the volatility of the return of the world market portfolio through his hedge. Consider now implementing this hedge. Tailing is trivial in this case and can be ignored. The S&P futures contract is for 500 times the S&P 500. On

September 1, 1999, the S&P 500 is at 1,331.06, so the contract is for a position in the S&P 500 of $665,530. The regression coefficient for the S&P 500 is 0.86057. This means that one would like a position in the S&P 500 futures of $86,057,000 (i.e., 0.86057 × $100M). The expected increase in the value of the portfolio if the S&P 500 increases by 1 percent is 0.86057 × $100M, or $860,570.

To get the number of S&P 500 futures contracts, we divide $86,057,000 by 665,530. The result is 129.306, which we round to 129 contracts. On October 1, the hedged portfolio is worth:

Initial cash portfolio	$100,000,000
Change in value of cash portfolio	−$1,132,026
($100M × (1,059.4 − 1,071.53)/1,071.53)	
Change in value of S&P 500 futures	
(−129 × 500 × (1,282.81 − 1,331.06))	$3,112,125
New portfolio value	$101,980,099

Note that, in this case, in the absence of hedging Mr. Big would have lost more than $1 million. Because of the hedge, he ends up earning almost $2 million. One might argue that this shows how valuable hedging is since he can earn almost $2 million instead of losing more than $1 million. However, while hedging helps Mr. Big avoid a loss, the fact that he earns that much on the hedged portfolio is actually evidence of an imperfect hedge. Remember that if he hedges a portfolio of stocks completely, the hedged portfolio is a risk-free asset that earns the risk-free rate. On September 1, 1999, the risk-free rate would have been less than 0.5 percent a month, so that the risk-free return on the hedged portfolio would have been less than $500,000. He therefore earned on the hedged portfolio close to a million dollars because the hedged portfolio was not risk-free.

Consider now the situation of Mr. Big on October 1, 1999. If he wants to keep hedging, then he has to reexamine his futures positions at that time. This is because his hedge was based on the value of his investment—the hedge ratios were per dollar invested—so that when the value of his investment changes, he has to change his hedges. He now has $101,980,099 invested in the world market portfolio, assuming that he reinvests all the futures gains in the world market portfolio. To hedge, assuming that the regression coefficients are still valid, he needs a position in the S&P 500 of 0.86057 × $101,980,099, or $87,761,014. At that date, the S&P 500 is at 1,282.81, so the number of contracts we would like is 87,761,014/(1,282.81 × 500) = 136.82, which we round to 137 contracts. Hence, the S&P 500 position increases by eight contracts.

This example calls for readjusting the hedge every month. If the cash position and the futures prices are highly volatile, one should adjust the hedge when significant changes occur.

6.6. Summary

In this chapter, we learned how to hedge with forward and futures contracts. We started with a computation of the risk of an exposure to a risk factor using three risk measures, volatility, CaR, and VaR. We showed that going short the exposure to a risk factor sets the volatility, the CaR, and the VaR associated with an exposure equal to zero when a perfect hedge is feasible.

The difference between the cash market price and the futures price is called the basis. A perfect hedge is possible if there is no uncertainty about the basis. However, to implement that perfect hedge with futures contracts, one has to take into account the daily settlement feature of futures contracts, which requires the hedge to be tailed. With tailing, the futures position is smaller in absolute value than what it would be if the futures contract were exactly like a forward contract by an interest rate factor corresponding to the price of a discount bond that matures when the hedge matures.

In general, the basis is random because of market imperfections and because typically there is no futures contract that matures exactly when the cash market exposure matures and where the deliverable good is exactly the cash market good. When a perfect hedge is not feasible because of basis risk and when the costs of hedging can be neglected, the risk-minimizing hedge is to go short the exposure of the cash position to the futures price if transactions costs are not significant. This risk-minimizing hedge is the minimum-volatility hedge. The exposure generally has to be estimated. When the joint distribution of changes in the cash price and changes in the futures price is i.i.d., the estimate of the exposure of the cash position to the futures price is the slope of a regression of the changes of the cash price on the changes of the futures price. We examined the issues that arise in implementing the minimum-volatility hedge in the context of an example involving hedging a Swiss franc cash position.

For financial assets, the joint distribution of cash price changes and futures price changes is usually not i.i.d., but the joint distribution of returns is. In this case, the minimum-volatility hedge is obtained by multiplying the slope in a regression of cash returns on the rate of change of the futures price by the size of the cash position. We saw how to implement such a hedge in an example involving hedging the world market portfolio with an S&P 500 futures contract.

Key Concepts

basis, 161
basis risk, 161
constant linear relation, 171
hedge ratio, 156
i.i.d., 152

multivariate normal changes model, 172
square root rule for volatility, 154
tailing the hedge, 158

Review Questions

1. How do you compute the volatility of the exchange rate change over three months when you know the volatility of the change over one month and the exchange rate changes are i.i.d.?

2. How do you compute the volatility of a foreign exchange exposure?

3. How do you compute the VaR of a foreign exchange exposure?

4. How do you compute the CaR of a foreign exchange exposure?

5. What is the impact of a perfect forward hedge on the CaR of a foreign exchange exposure?

6. When does tailing improve a futures hedge significantly?

7. What is the risk-minimizing hedge in the absence of basis risk?

8. What is the risk-minimizing hedge in the presence of basis risk?

9. How do you forecast exposure in the presence of basis risk?

10. What are the two key reasons why a hedge based on forecasted exposure might perform poorly?

11. How do you estimate the effectiveness of a hedging strategy with past data?

12. How do you decide the number of contracts in your hedge when divisibility is an issue?

13. What are the advantages of a futures hedge over a forward hedge?

14. When is a forward hedge strategy preferable?

Questions and Exercises

1. Consider a firm that expects to sell 10 million barrels of oil at the cash market price in one year. It wants its one-year 5 percent CaR to be at most $5 million. The price of a barrel is currently $15 with a one-year standard deviation of $2. What is the CaR of the firm in the absence of hedging assuming that the price change is distributed normally?

2. Consider now the situation where there is a forward contract that the firm can use to sell oil forward. The forward price is $16 per barrel. How many barrels must the firm sell forward to reduce its CaR to $5 million?

3. Suppose now that there is a futures contract that matures exactly in one year that requires delivery of the type of oil that the firm produces. The contract is assumed to be perfectly divisible for simplicity. The interest rate for a one-year zero-coupon bond is 10 percent. Interest rates are assumed to be constant. How many barrels must the firm sell today on the futures market to minimize its CaR?

4. Using the data in question 3, assume now that the firm sells 10 million barrels on the futures market with delivery in one year and does not change its position over the year. How does the interest rate affect the firm's CaR?

5. Suppose now that the futures contract requires delivery of a different grade of oil than the one the firm produces, but maturity of the contract is in one year. What information would you need to compute the volatility-minimizing hedge for the firm?

6. You are told by a consultant that the slope of a regression of the change in the price of the oil the firm produced on the change in the price of the oil that is delivered with the futures contract is 0.9 with a t-statistic in excess of 10. What would be your minimum-volatility hedge before tailing? How would tailing affect that hedge?

7. The R^2 in the regression discussed in question 6 is 0.85. What can you learn from this number?

8. Suppose that there is no futures contract that matures in exactly one year. There is, however, a futures contract that matures in 18 months. A regression of changes in the cash market price of the oil the firm produces on the changes in the futures price of the contract that matures in 18 months using past history yields a slope of 0.8 with an R^2 of 0.6. How many barrels should the firm sell on the futures market if it wants to minimize its CaR?

9. Does your answer to the previous question change if you are told that the deliverable grade of oil for the contract that matures in 18 months is not the grade of oil that the firm produces?

10. How would the risk-minimizing hedge derived in question 8 change over time?

11. What could go wrong with the risk-minimizing hedge derived in question 8?

Literature Note

The method of using regression ratios to hedge was first proposed by Johnson (1960) and Stein (1961). Much recent work has addressed the issue of how to estimate the minimum-volatility hedge when the i.i.d. assumption does not hold. See Cechetti, Cumby, and Figlewski (1988) and Baillie and Myers (1991) for approaches that use econometric techniques that take into account changes in the joint distribution of the cash market price and the hedging instrument. See Kawaller (1997) for a discussion of tailing. The airline example comes from "Delta wins on fuel," by Alexandra Ness, *Risk*, June 2001, p. 8.

Chapter 7

Optimal Hedges for the Real World

Chapter **7** Objectives

At the end of this chapter, you will:

1. Understand how market imperfections affect hedging policies.

2. Be able to incorporate hedging costs in the hedging decision.

3. Know how one can reduce hedging costs by taking advantage of diversification.

4. Understand why a widely publicized hedging strategy failed.

In Chapter 6, we learned how to hedge with forwards and futures. However, we ignored many real-world complications. We assumed that financial markets are perfect. Suppose that Mr. Hedge considers eliminating an exposure of 100 million euros in five years. He will be confronted with many problems that would not arise in a world of perfect financial markets. In such a world, contracts would be perfectly divisible, have the same maturity as the exposure, and liquidity would never be a problem. The real world does not work like this. Mr. Hedge might not be able to trade a futures contract that matures more than a few years in the future. If he attempts to trade that contract, he will be concerned about the impact of his trade on prices because of a lack of liquidity. In this chapter, we learn how to cope with such issues. They make the real world challenging.

One key assumption when we assume that financial markets are perfect is that there are no transactions costs. Suppose Mr. Hedge finds that to hedge his euro exposure he has to incur transaction costs of $1 million. How would Mr. Hedge know if shareholders are better off if he hedges? He would have to trade off the cost of laying off the exposure against the benefit of reducing risk. We extend the analysis to consider **hedging costs** and how they affect the hedging decision.

The cost of putting on a hedge is the adverse impact on firm value or cash flow of putting on the hedge before taking into account the benefit of the hedge. Examples of hedging costs are the transactions costs, monitoring costs, and design costs that are incurred when putting on a hedge. Firms almost always are exposed to multiple risk factors. Firms with multiple risk factors can reduce hedging costs by treating their exposures as a portfolio. The portfolio approach takes advantage of the principle of diversification, which means that multiple exposures are offsetting to some degree, and the firm can put on a smaller hedge than if it hedges each exposure separately.

To consider portfolios of exposures, we first assume all exposures have the same maturity. We show how to adapt the approach of the previous chapter to construct a minimum-volatility hedge for the portfolio of exposures. In the next case, a firm has multiple cash flows accruing at one point in time and cash flows accruing at different times. In this case, diversification can take place across exposures at one point in time and across exposures with different maturities. We show how the firm should measure the risk and hedge portfolios of exposures with different maturities.

To illustrate the practical difficulties of hedging in the real world, we conclude the chapter with a famous real-world story, the Metallgesellschaft story. Metallgesellschaft had large short oil positions with maturities stretching out to ten years. It could not find futures contracts on oil that it could trade in the quantities it needed to hedge with maturities beyond one year. Metallgesellschaft therefore had to use short maturity futures to hedge long maturity exposures. To construct a hedging strategy, Metallgesellschaft used some of the tools presented in Chapter 6 and in this chapter. However, it also ignored some important ideas we addressed—for instance, the result presented in Chapter 6 that futures hedges have to be tailed and the result discussed in this chapter that basis risk decreases the optimal volatility-minimizing hedge. Partly as a result of not taking into account these ideas, Metallgesellschaft lost hundreds of millions of dollars through its hedging strategy.

7.1. Implementing the minimum-variance hedge in the real world

Many implementation details arise when one wants to hedge an exposure with a futures contract. The issues we discuss arise because financial markets are imperfect. With perfect financial markets, creating new futures contracts would be costless and the demand for a contract would be perfectly elastic, so that any exposure could be hedged without having the trade affect the futures price. A market where one can trade without any price impact regardless of the size of the trade is highly liquid. Many markets are not this way. Markets are made liquid by liquidity providers—market markers. The number and resources of liquidity providers are limited. As a result, they focus on the markets where their resources are most valuable. When liquidity falls, the buyer or the seller must sweeten the deal to make it worthwhile for a trader to be the counterparty. This makes it expensive to trade in markets with poor liquidity. As a result, liquidity begets liquidity—people want to trade in liquid markets and flee illiquid markets. It therefore will not be possible to trade futures contracts for some maturities and for some deliverable goods because these contracts will have no liquidity and therefore will not be offered by the exchanges. At any time, there will be only a limited number of liquid contracts. This means that firms and investors may not be able to trade a contract with a maturity or a deliverable good that matches their exposure exactly.

Let's go back to Mr. Hedge. He has a five-year euro exposure. Turning to the Chicago Mercantile Exchange for a futures contract in August 2001, he finds that the contract with price information with the longest maturity is December 2002. Hence, Mr. Hedge has no choice but to use contracts that mature before his exposure in order to hedge with futures contracts.

7.1.1. Hedging, contract maturity, and basis risk

Export Inc. expects to receive one million Swiss francs on June 1. We have seen that the Swiss franc contracts traded at the Chicago Mercantile Exchange are for 125,000 Swiss francs. The available maturities are for the months of March, June, September, and December. In Chapter 6, we assumed that Export would use the June contract. It could, however, take a position in the March contract, close that position near the maturity of the contract, and then open a position in the June contract, or it could take a position in the September contract. If there are no financial market imperfections except for the absence of a contract maturing on June 1 and if there is no basis risk, Export can use any futures contract to hedge as long as it adjusts the hedge in the way we now demonstrate.

We write $G_t(T)$ as the price at t for a futures contract that matures at T. If domestic and foreign interest rates are constant so that there is no basis risk, we know that futures and forward prices are the same. From Chapter 5, we know that in this example the futures price on June 1 for a contract that matures at date T is:

$$G_{June\ 1}(T) = [P^{SFR}_{June\ 1}(T)/P_{June\ 1}(T)]S_{June\ 1} \qquad (7.1)$$

where $P^{SFR}_{June\ 1}(T)$ is the Swiss franc price on June 1 of a zero-coupon bond that pays one Swiss franc at date T, $S_{June\ 1}$ is the dollar price of a Swiss franc on June 1, and $P_{June\ 1}(T)$ is the dollar price on June 1 of a zero-coupon bond that pays $1 at date T.

Using equation (7.1), a change in the exchange rate over the hedging period equal to ΔS has an impact on the futures price as follows:

$$\Delta G = [P^{SFR}_{June\ 1}(T)/P_{June\ 1}(T)]\Delta S \qquad (7.2)$$

Export wants a hedge ratio h so that $\Delta S - h\Delta G = 0$. A position of $P_{June\ 1}(T)/P^{SFR}_{June\ 1}(T)$ in the futures contract moves one for one with the spot exchange rate, so that going short that position in the futures market hedges one Swiss franc. Consequently, if Export uses a hedge ratio of $P_{June\ 1}(T)/P^{SFR}_{June\ 1}(T)$ before tailing, it has a perfect hedge. For one Swiss franc of exposure, the payoff of the hedged position is:

$$
\begin{aligned}
\Delta S - h\Delta G &= \Delta S - \left[P_{June\ 1}(T)/P^{SFR}_{June\ 1}(T)\right]\Delta G \\
&= \Delta S - \left[P_{June\ 1}(T)/P^{SFR}_{June\ 1}(T)\right]\left[P^{SFR}_{June\ 1}(T)/P_{June\ 1}(T)\right]\Delta S \\
&= \Delta S - \Delta S = 0 \qquad (7.3)
\end{aligned}
$$

This hedge ensures that the hedged cash position is worth $[P_{June\ 1}(T)/P^{SFR}_{June\ 1}(T)]S_{March\ 1}$ per Swiss franc paid on June 1. The payoff of the hedged position does not depend on the exchange rate at maturity of the hedge and is therefore riskless.

This analysis lets us express a general formula for the hedge ratio in the absence of basis risk. Suppose that we are at date t and hedge a payoff occurring at date $t + i$ with a futures contract that matures at date T, where T is later than $t + i$. Using the formulation for the futures price with a convenience yield developed in Chapter 5, we have that the futures price at date $t + i$ is:

$$G_{t+i}(T) = e^{[r_{t+i}(T) - c_{t+i}(T)](T - (t+i))}S_{t+i} \qquad (7.4)$$

where the futures contract is on an underlying asset with price S_{t+i} at t and expires at T, $r_{t+i}(T)$ is the continuously compounded yield from $t + i$ on a zero-coupon bond maturing at T, and $c_{t+i}(T)$ is the continuously compounded convenience yield over the interval of time from $t + i$ to T. With this formula, a change of ΔS in the spot price increases the futures price by $\Delta G = e^{[r_{t+i}(T) - c_{t+i}(T)](T - (t+i))}\Delta S$. Hence, to balance the change of ΔS in the cash position, we need a hedge ratio $h = e^{-[r_{t+i}(T) - c_{t+i}(T)](T - (t+i))}$ so that $\Delta S = h\Delta G$.

In the absence of basis risk, we can create a perfect hedge by rolling over positions in contracts that have a shorter maturity than the cash market exposure. To see this, suppose that we use the March contract, and immediately before maturity of that contract on March 21 we switch to the June contract. We assume that interest rates do not change unexpectedly since otherwise the basis would be random. For each dollar of cash position, we go short a tailed hedge of $[P_{March\ 1}$ $(March\ 21)/P^{SFR}_{March\ 1}(March\ 21)]$ March contracts on March 1 at the price of $G_{March\ 1}(March\ 21) = P^{SFR}_{March\ 1}(March\ 21)/P_{March\ 1}(March\ 21)]S_{March\ 1}$. Remember, though, that we are hedging an exposure that matures on June 1. Hence, any cash flow from the futures position is carried forward to June 1, so that the tailing factor must be a zero-coupon bond paying \$1 on June 1.

Suppose that we get out of this position on March 19, which is shortly before maturity of the March contract. At that date, we will have gained $P_{\text{March 19}}$ (June 1)$[S_{\text{March 1}} - S_{\text{March 19}}]$ from the short position, but this gain becomes $S_{\text{March 1}} - S_{\text{March 19}}$ on June 1. We then go short on March 19 a tailed hedge of $P_{\text{March 19}}(\text{June 1})/P^{\text{SFR}}_{\text{March 19}}(\text{June 1})$ of the June contract. The tailing factor is again a zero-coupon bond that pays \$1 on June 1. On June 1, we exit our short futures position after having gained $S_{\text{March 19}} - S_{\text{June 1}}$. Adding up the gains from the futures position, we have $S_{\text{March 1}} - S_{\text{June 1}}$, which exactly offsets the losses from the cash position. Hence, in the absence of basis risk, we can create a perfect hedge by rolling contracts over.

7.1.2. Basis risk, the hedge ratio, and contract maturity

In perfect markets, basis risk occurs in futures because of interest rate, convenience yield, payout, and storage cost uncertainty. In imperfect markets, our pricing formulas do not hold exactly, which adds additional basis risk. Let's consider how basis risk affects the hedge ratio and the volatility of the hedged position, so that we understand better which contract to use.

Let $B_{\text{June 1}}(T)$ be the basis of the Swiss franc futures contract that matures at T on June 1 and $G_{\text{June 1}}(T)$ the futures price on June 1 for a contract that matures at T. Remember that we define the basis as the difference between the cash market price and the futures price. Consequently, the futures price on June 1, $G_{\text{June 1}}(T)$, is equal to $S_{\text{June 1}} - B_{\text{June 1}}(T)$. The optimal hedge ratio is still the one we obtained earlier, but now we replace the futures price by the spot price minus the basis to see directly the impact of basis risk on the hedge ratio:

$$
\begin{aligned}
h &= \frac{\text{Cov}\left[S_{\text{June 1}}, G_{\text{June 1}}(T)\right]}{\text{Var}\left[G_{\text{June 1}}(T)\right]} \\[2mm]
&= \frac{\text{Cov}\left[S_{\text{June 1}}, S_{\text{June 1}} - B_{\text{June 1}}(T)\right]}{\text{Var}\left[S_{\text{June 1}} - B_{\text{June 1}}(T)\right]} \\[2mm]
&= \frac{\text{Var}(S_{\text{June 1}}) - \text{Cov}\left[S_{\text{June 1}}, B_{\text{June 1}}(T)\right]}{\text{Var}(S_{\text{June 1}}) + \text{Var}\left[B_{\text{June 1}}(T)\right] - 2\text{Cov}\left[S_{\text{June 1}}, B_{\text{June 1}}(T)\right]}
\end{aligned} \tag{7.5}
$$

If the basis is uncorrelated with the spot exchange rate, the numerator is simply the variance of the spot exchange rate. In this case, the optimal hedge ratio is the variance of the spot exchange rate divided by the sum of the variance of the spot exchange rate and of the basis. Since variances are always positive, the greater the variance of the basis the lower the optimal hedge ratio.

To understand why basis risk reduces the optimal hedge ratio when the basis is uncorrelated with the spot price, it is useful to consider the payoff of the hedged position per Swiss franc:

$$
\begin{aligned}
& S_{\text{June 1}} - h \times \left[G_{\text{June 1}}(T) - G_{\text{March 1}}(T)\right] \\[2mm]
={} & S_{\text{June 1}} - h \times \left[S_{\text{June 1}} - B_{\text{June 1}}(T) - G_{\text{March 1}}(T)\right] \\[2mm]
={} & (1 - h)S_{\text{June 1}} + h \times B_{\text{June 1}}(T) + h \times G_{\text{March 1}}(T)
\end{aligned} \tag{7.6}
$$

Suppose that we choose $h = 1$. In this case, the payoff of the hedged position does not depend on the exchange rate at maturity, $S_{June\ 1}$. Yet we do not have a perfect hedge because the payoff of the hedged position increases one for one with the basis at maturity, $B_{June\ 1}(T)$. The variance of the hedged position is:

**Variance of hedged position =
$(1 - h)^2$[Variance of spot exchange rate] + h^2[Variance of basis]   (7.7)**

Figure 7.1 shows how the variance of the hedged position changes as the hedge ratio h and the variance of basis risk change, keeping the variance of the spot exchange rate constant. As the hedge ratio increases from zero, the contribution of the variance of the spot exchange rate to the variance of the hedged position falls. At the same time, however, the contribution of the variance of the basis to the variance of the hedged position increases. Close to $h = 1$, the contribution of the variance of the cash position to the variance of the hedged position is quite small (because $(1 - h)^2$ is small) in comparison to the contribution of the variance of the basis (because h^2 is close to 1). Consequently, close to $h = 1$, one can decrease the variance of the hedged position by reducing the hedge ratio slightly.

Equation (7.5) implies that a basis that covaries positively with the cash price increases h. This is not surprising. A basis that is high when the cash price is high means that the futures price has less covariance with the cash price. A larger futures position is therefore needed to achieve the same covariance of the futures position with the cash position as in the case of no basis risk. The opposite takes place if the basis is low when the cash price is high.

Figure 7.1   Variance of hedged payoff as a function of hedge ratio and variance of basis risk

In this figure, basis risk is assumed to be uncorrelated with the futures price.

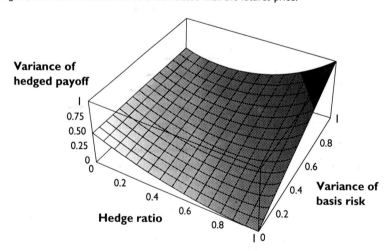

7.1.3. Cross-hedging

So far, we have paid a lot of attention to the example of hedging a Swiss franc exposure with a Swiss franc futures contract. Much of the hedging taking place is not as straightforward. There may be no futures contract on the cash position we want to hedge. Recall the example of the airlines that cannot use jet fuel contracts to hedge jet fuel because such contracts do not exist. We saw that Delta uses heating oil contracts to hedge jet fuel. When one uses a futures contract to hedge a cash position on a good that would not be deliverable with the futures contract, one uses a **cross-hedge**. Our approach to finding the optimal hedge ratio is not different in the case of a cross-hedge. We find that ratio by regressing the changes in the cash position on the changes in the futures price of the contract we plan to use assuming that the multivariate normal changes model holds. If we have a choice of contracts, we use the contract that provides the most effective hedge using our measure of hedging effectiveness. Often, one might choose to use several different futures. For example, while Delta uses only heating oil contracts to hedge jet fuel, many airlines use both heating oil and crude oil contracts.

7.1.4. Liquidity

In perfect markets, we would always hold the contract that matures when our exposure matures if such a contract is available. Otherwise, we would be taking on unnecessary basis risk. In the presence of transaction costs, however, this need not be the case. When we open a futures position, we have to pay a commission and deposit a margin. In addition, if our transactions are large, they may affect prices; we may have to offer more advantageous prices than current market prices so that somebody will be willing to take the opposite side of the transaction. This is called the **market impact** of our trade.

The extent of the market impact depends on the liquidity of the market. In highly liquid markets, most trades have no impact on prices. In futures markets, the shortest maturity contract has the greatest liquidity. Contracts that have the longest maturity are often extremely illiquid. This lack of liquidity means that when we try to trade, we end up getting very unfavorable prices because we have to offer substantial price concessions to get the trade done.

One measure of the liquidity of a futures market is the **open interest**. In the case of a futures contract with a given maturity, we add up all the long positions to get the open interest of the contract. Alternatively, we could add up the short positions and get the same number. Generally, the open interest falls as one moves from contracts with short maturities to contracts with long maturities.

Contracts with long maturities sometimes do not trade at all during a day. Consider the situation of Export Inc. Export will receive a payment of one million Swiss francs on June 1 and has to decide on March 1 how to hedge its exposure. In Chapter 6, we assumed that Export would use the June contract. Yet, on March 1, 1999, the open interest for the March Swiss franc contract was 56,411 contracts, but only 6,093 for the June contract and 322 for the September contract (as reported by the *Wall Street Journal*). **Rollover risk** is the risk that arises because the difference between the price of the contract we close and the price of the contract we open is random. Because contracts with long maturities are so illiquid, it might be worth it to take a position in the shortest maturity contract and then roll it over into the next contract as the shortest maturity contract matures. While it is true that proceeding this way presents rollover risk, the benefit of trading in more liquid markets might more than offset the cost of the rollover risk.

Suppose that Export hedges first with the March contract and then rolls over its position into the June contract. There is basis risk because Export does not know when it sets up the hedge what the basis will be for the June contract when it rolls over on March 19. With a tailed position hedging one Swiss franc to be received on June 1, the proceeds from the hedge on June 1 are $G_{\text{March 1}}(\text{March } 21) - S_{\text{March 19}}$ from the position in the March contract (assuming that the basis risk when that position is closed can be ignored since the position is closed almost when the contract matures) and $G_{\text{March 19}}(\text{June } 20) - G_{\text{June 1}}(\text{June } 20)$ from the position in the June contract, assuming the June contract matures on June 20. An unexpectedly high basis of the June contract on March 19 increases the payoff from the hedge; an unexpectedly low basis has the opposite effect. When there is basis risk at the rollover date, Export cannot create a riskless position through futures hedging. Since Export incurs basis risk by rolling over that it would not incur by using the contract maturing in June only, it would seem that it makes no sense to first take a position in the March contract and then a new position.

This argument would be reasonable in the case of Export, especially given the small size of the required futures position. If Export required a large futures position, it would have to think about the price impact of its trading. However, this argument would make no sense for Mr. Hedge. Whatever Mr. Hedge does, as long as he uses futures contracts, he will have to bear rollover risk since he cannot take a position in a five-year futures contract. As we saw, however, there is no volume in the longest maturity quoted contract, so that trading that contract would move prices and make hedging expensive. Mr. Hedge will be better off using short maturity contracts and rolling them over.

7.1.5. Imperfect divisibility

Throughout the discussion, we have assumed that futures contracts are perfectly divisible. They are not. For example, for the Swiss franc contract, we have to buy or sell Swiss franc futures in units of 125,000 Swiss francs, and our exposure is not always in units of 125,000 Swiss francs. The fact that we have to trade contracts of fixed size is one disadvantage of futures relative to forward contracts.

Let's see how we handle this problem in determining the optimal hedge. If the optimal hedge is not divisible into a round number of contracts, we have to round out the hedge. In some cases, however, rounding out means we might be better off not hedging at all. Suppose we have an exposure of 62,500 Swiss francs expiring in three months and there is a futures contract expiring in three months. In this case, the volatility of the hedged position when we go short one contract is the same as the volatility of the unhedged position:

$$\text{Volatility of unhedged position} = \text{Vol}\left(62{,}500 S_{t+0.25}\right)$$

$$\text{Volatility of hedged position}$$

$$= \text{Vol}\left[62{,}500 S_{t+0.25}\right] - 125{,}000\left[S_{t+0.25} - G_t(t+0.25)\right]$$

$$= \text{Vol}\left[-62{,}500 S_{t+0.25}\right] = \text{Vol}\left[62{,}500 S_{t+0.25}\right] \tag{7.8}$$

In this case, we are indifferent between hedging and not hedging if the exposure is 62,500 Swiss francs. This is because our exposure is exactly equal to half a contract. Suppose the exposure is 50,000 Swiss francs. In this case, the volatility of the unhedged position is $Vol[50,000S_{t+0.25}]$. The volatility of the hedged position, however, is $Vol[75,000S_{t+0.25}]$. Therefore, one is better off not hedging at all.

To minimize the risk of the hedged position, the solution is to take a position in the round number of contracts closest in absolute value to the volatility-minimizing hedge. We can use the example of Export Inc. to see that this intuitive solution is the right one. Using regression analysis, the minimum-volatility hedge using the June contract is to go short 940,000 Swiss francs, or 7.52 contracts. The price of a T-bill that matures when the exposure matures is $98.8194 on March 1, 1999, so the tailing factor is slightly more than 0.9881. The optimal tailed hedge involves 7.44 contracts. Export has to decide whether to go short 8 or 7 contracts. With our solution, we would use 7 contracts. Let's compare the variance of the hedged position with 7 contracts and with 8 contracts. Over the estimation period, the weekly standard deviation of the Swiss franc change is 0.01077, the weekly standard deviation of the futures price changes is 0.01107, and the weekly covariance between the two changes is 0.000115. Suppose Export evaluates the hedge position weekly. Remember that marking to market increases the payoffs of a futures contract by the inverse of the tailing factor. Export can take into account the marking to market by dividing the futures volatility by 0.9881 for the first week. For 7 contracts, the variance of the hedged position is:

Variance of hedged position for first week =

$$\textbf{position with 7 contracts } (1{,}000{,}000 \times 0.01077)^2$$
$$+\ (7 \times 125{,}000 \times 0.01107/0.9881)^2$$
$$-\ 2 \times 1{,}000{,}000 \times 7 \times 125{,}000 \times 0.000115/0.9881$$
$$=\ 8{,}416{,}120.70 \tag{7.9}$$

The variance of the hedged position using 8 contracts is 8,737,305.30. Given this, Export chooses to go short 7 contracts initially. Since the tailing factor gets closer to 1 over time, the optimal hedge increases, so that eventually—in this case the last week—the number of contracts increases to 8.

7.1.6. The multivariate normal changes model: Cash versus futures prices

Models are approximations, and the multivariate normal changes model is no different from any other model. There are many reasons why it might not hold exactly. One reason has to do with how futures contracts are priced. Recall from Chapter 5 that if the interest rate and the convenience yield are constant, the futures contract is priced like a forward contract. In this case, the futures price is equal to the price of the deliverable good times a factor that depends on the interest rate and time to maturity. If the futures price depends only on the price of the deliverable good, the interest rate, and the convenience yield, it must satisfy the formula:

$$\textbf{G}_{t+i}\textbf{(T)} = e^{(r-c)(T-(t+i))}\textbf{S}_{t+i} \tag{7.10}$$

where $G_{t+i}(T)$ is the futures price at $t + i$ for a contract maturing at T, r is the annual continuously compounded interest rate, c is the convenience yield, and S_{t+i} is the spot price of the deliverable good at $t + i$.[1]

The futures price change from $t + i$ to $t + i + k$, where k is a period of time such that $t + i + k < T$, is:

$$G_{t+i+k}(T) - G_{t+i}(T) =$$
$$e^{(r-c)(T-(t+i+k))} S_{t+i+k} - e^{(r-c)(T-(t+i))} S_{t+i} \qquad (7.11)$$

Since $e^{(r-c)(T-(t+i))}$ changes over time if $r - c$ is different from zero, futures price changes can be i.i.d. only if $r - c$ is equal to zero assuming that the change of the price of the deliverable good is i.i.d. Otherwise, if r is greater than c, $e^{(r-c)(T-(t+i))}$ is greater than one and drops over time to become closer to one as maturity approaches. Consequently, the futures price change for a given spot price change falls over time as a proportion of the change of the price of the deliverable good. The opposite occurs if r is smaller than c.

In our regression analysis, we effectively assume that basis risk due to the fact that we do not hold the futures contract to maturity is a first-order phenomenon, while the impact of predictable changes in the distribution of the futures price is not. If we hold a contract to maturity or if basis risk due to the fact that we do not hold it to maturity is unimportant, we may be better off to use cash price changes of the deliverable good rather than futures price changes in our regression. The reason is that the multivariate normal changes model is more likely to hold exactly for changes in the price of the deliverable good than for changes in the futures price.

Since the futures price is not the cash price, we then need to use the futures price formula to adjust the hedge if we do not hold the futures contract to maturity (similar to the analysis of section 7.1.1.). Hence, if the regression coefficient is β, we use as hedge ratio before tailing $\beta / e^{(r-c)(T-t^*)}$, where t^* is the maturity of the hedge. This is because a change of ΔS in the cash price changes the futures price by $\Delta S \times e^{(r-c)(T-t^*)}$, so that on average the futures price changes more than the cash price if r is greater than c. We take this into account when constructing our hedge.

Let's consider an example. Suppose we expect to hold a contract close enough to maturity that the contract's basis risk with respect to the deliverable good is trivial. The deliverable good is not the good we are trying to hedge, though. We are planning to get out of a wheat contract immediately before maturity, but the wheat grade we hedge is different from the wheat grade that is delivered on the contract. The hedge has basis risk, in that the prices of the two grades of wheat at maturity might be different from what we expect. In this case, what we care about at maturity of the hedge is not how the futures price differs from the cash price, but how the cash price we hedge differs from the cash price of the deliver-

---

1 We ignore payouts and storage costs for simplicity. Taking payouts and storage costs into account changes the formula as shown in Chapter 5 but has no impact on the rest of the analysis.

able good. Hence, to estimate that relation, we are better off to estimate a regression of changes in the cash price of our exposure on the cash price of the deliverable good if we believe that cash prices follow the multivariate normal changes model.

7.2. The costs of hedging

Risk is costly for Export. Consequently, if hedging has no cost, it chooses to minimize risk. We saw that Export can eliminate its Swiss franc risk completely in the absence of basis risk. Although it is possible for hedging to be costless, generally costs are involved. Sometimes these costs are small enough compared to the benefits that they can be ignored. In other cases, the costs cannot be ignored, and the firm must trade off the costs and benefits of hedging. We focus only on the marginal costs associated with a hedge in our analysis. For a firm, there are also costs involved in maintaining a risk management operation. These costs include salaries, databases, computer systems, and so on. These are sunk costs that do not affect the hedging decision.

When exposure is measured exactly, as it is with Export, hedging can affect expected payoffs for two reasons. First, ignoring transaction costs, the hedge can affect the expected payoff because the price for future delivery is different from the expected spot price for the date of future delivery. Second, putting on the hedge involves transaction costs.

If we know the beta of the Swiss franc, we can compute the market's expected spot exchange rate for the maturity of the forward contract when the CAPM holds. If the beta of the Swiss franc is zero, then the market's expected spot exchange rate is equal to the forward exchange rate. Let's suppose that this is the case. If Export has the same expectation for the spot exchange rate as the market, then there is no cost of hedging except for transaction costs. Suppose, however, that Export believes that the expected price for the Swiss franc at maturity of the exposure is higher than the forward exchange rate. In this case, Export believes that the forward exchange rate is too low. With our assumptions, this is not because of a risk premium but because the market is wrong from Export's perspective. By hedging, the firm reduces its expected dollar payoff by the exposure times $E(S_{June\ 1}) - F_{March\ 1}$, where $E(S_{June\ 1})$ is Export's expectation of the price of the Swiss franc on June 1, $S_{June\ 1}$, as of the time that it considers hedging, which is March 1, and $F_{March\ 1}$ is the forward price on March 1 for one Swiss franc delivered on June 1. This reduction in expected payoff is a cost of hedging. Hence, the firm must decide whether it is worth it to eliminate all risk. Box 7.1, The cost of hedging and Daimler-Benz's FX losses, shows how one company thought through this issue at a point in time.

The firm faces costs of hedging in the form of transaction costs. Export would have to consider the fact that the bid-ask spread is narrower on the spot market than on the forward market. This means that if there is no systematic risk, the expected spot exchange rate for a sale is higher than the forward exchange rate for a short position. The difference between these two values represents a transaction cost due to hedging. We can think of the transaction cost of hedging as captured by a higher forward price for a firm that wants to buy the foreign currency forward and as a lower forward price for a firm that wants to sell the

---

Box 7.1   **The costs of hedging and Daimler-Benz FX losses**

In the first half of 1995, Daimler-Benz had net losses of DM 1.56 billion. These losses, the largest in the group's 109-year history, were due to the fall of the dollar relative to the DM. Daimler-Benz Aerospace (DASA) has an order book of DM 20 billion, 80 percent of it denominated in dollars. Consequently, a fall in the dollar reduces the DM value of the payments Daimler-Benz will receive from fulfilling the contracts it has agreed to.

The company uses both options and forwards to hedge. On December 31, 1994, the Daimler-Benz group had DM 23 billion in outstanding currency instruments on its books and DM 15.7 billion of interest rate instruments. Despite these large outstanding positions, it had not hedged large portions of its order book. German accounting rules require the company to book all expected losses on outstanding orders, so that Daimler-Benz had to book losses due to the fall of the dollar. Had Daimler-Benz hedged, it would have shown no losses.

Why did Daimler-Benz not hedge? According to *Risk Magazine*, Daimler-Benz claimed its banks' "forecasts for the dollar/Deutschmark rate for 1995 were so diverse that it held off hedging large portions of its foreign exchange exposure. It claims 16 banks gave exchange rate forecasts ranging from DM 1.20 to DM 1.70 per dollar." Some analysts explained the lack of hedging by their understanding that Daimler-Benz had a view that the dollar would not fall below DM 1.55. With this view, hedging would have been expensive—it would have had to sell dollars at a cheaper price than it expected to get without hedging. Daimler-Benz's view turned out to be wrong since the dollar fell to DM 1.38. However, the company blamed its losses on its bankers.

If a company simply minimizes the volatility of its hedged cash flow, it should be completely indifferent to forecasts of the exchange rate. If it has a forecast of the exchange rate that differs from the forward exchange rate, however, it bears a cost for hedging if it sells the foreign currency forward at a price below what it expects the spot exchange rate to be. One would think that if forecasts differ too much across forecasters, this reveals by itself that there is a great deal of uncertainty about the future spot exchange rate. Therefore, the benefits of hedging should be greater. This was obviously not the reasoning of Daimler-Benz. It is unclear whether the company thought that it could hedge a forecasted depreciation or whether it was unable to pin down the costs of hedging and therefore did not want to hedge.

Source: Andrew Priest, "Daimler blames banks' forex forecasts for losses," *Risk Magazine 8*, No. 10 (October 1995), p. 11.

foreign currency forward. There may also be commissions and transaction taxes in addition to this spread.

When the manager of Export responsible for the hedging decision evaluates the costs and benefits of hedging, she has to compare the benefit from hedging, which is the reduction in the cost of cash flow at risk (CaR), with the cost of hedging. Remember that the cost of CaR, discussed in chapter 4, is the adverse impact on the firm of incurring the risk of the shortfall in cash flow measured by CaR. Suppose the manager assumes that one unit of CaR always costs $0.50 and that hedging is costly because the forward exchange rate is too low by two cents. She could conclude that the forward exchange rate is lower than the expected spot exchange rate by 2 cents either because of transaction costs or because the market has it wrong. The forward exchange rate quote in the *Wall Street Journal* for March 1, 1999, for delivery three months later is $0.6902. Hence, if the forward exchange rate is too low by 2 cents, Export expects the spot exchange rate to be $0.7102 on June 1. In this case, going short one million Swiss francs on the forward market saves the costs of CaR. In Chapter 6, CaR for Export was estimated to be $71,789.20. Consequently, hedging increases firm value by 0.5 × $71,789.20 = $35,894.60. At the same time, however, the manager of Export expects to get $20,000 more by not hedging than by using the forward hedge. In this case, the cost of CaR is so high that Export hedges even though the forward contract is mispriced. If the forward contract is mispriced by 4 cents instead, the firm loses $40,000 in expected payoff by hedging and gains only $35,894.60 through the elimination of the cost of CaR. It obviously does not pay for the firm to hedge in this case, even though risk reduces firm value.

Can the firm have valuable information that leads it to conclude that the market's expectation is wrong? If markets are efficient, such information is hard to come by, but this does not mean that it does not exist or that a firm cannot get it. The problem is that it is too easy to believe that one has such information. Some individuals and institutions have tremendous resources at their disposal and spend all their time searching for such mistakes. Individuals and institutions for whom watching the markets is at best a part-time activity are not likely to have information that is valuable. Having publicly available information, such as newspaper articles, analyst reports, or consensus economic forecasts, is not worth much. Since everybody can trade on that information, it is incorporated in prices quickly.

A test of whether information is valuable, at least from the perspective of Export's manager, is whether she is willing to trade on that information on her own account. If she is not, why should the shareholders take the risk? Remember that the risk involves a cost, namely the impact of the risk on CaR. The bet the manager wants to take has to be good enough to justify this cost.

Let's go back to the case where the forward exchange rate is mispriced by $0.04 when the cost of CaR is $0.50 per unit of CaR. In this case, it does not pay for Export to hedge. Suppose that Export does not hedge but rather takes on more foreign exchange risk by going long Swiss francs on the forward market to take advantage of the mispricing on the forward market. Each Swiss franc it purchases on the forward market has an expected profit of $0.04 and increases CaR by $0.0717892. Each dollar of CaR costs the firm $0.50. So, the net expected gain from purchasing a Swiss franc forward is $0.04 − 0.5 × $0.0717892, or $0.0041054. In this case, Export can keep increasing its risk by buying Swiss francs forward with no limits. In this example, therefore, the firm is almost risk-neutral. When a risk has enough of a reward, there is no limit to how much the firm takes of this risk. It therefore does not make sense to assume that the cost of CaR is fixed per unit of CaR whatever the amount of risk the firm has. Eventually, the cost of CaR has to increase, so that the firm does not take more risks.

The optimal hedge is the one that maximizes the firm's expected cash flow, taking into account the cost of CaR. Let Export go short h Swiss francs on the forward market. Suppose further that the cost associated with CaR is a constant, α, times the square of CaR, $\alpha(\text{CaR})^2$, so that the total cost of CaR is a quadratic function of CaR. Quadratic cost functions are commonly used in economics. With this cost formulation, the cost of CaR per unit of CaR, the marginal cost of CaR, increases with the level of CaR as shown in Figure 7.2. Figure 7.2 shows how the total cost of CaR and the marginal cost of CaR increase with CaR.

With a quadratic cost function for CaR, the expected payoff net of the cost of CaR for Export is:

Figure 7.2   Total and marginal cost of CaR when total cost is equal to αCaR^2

Panel A. Total cost of CaR.

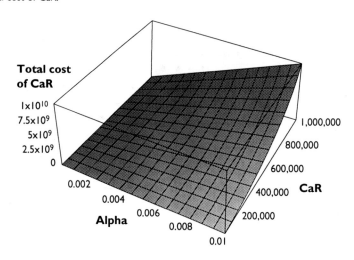

Panel B. Marginal cost of CaR.

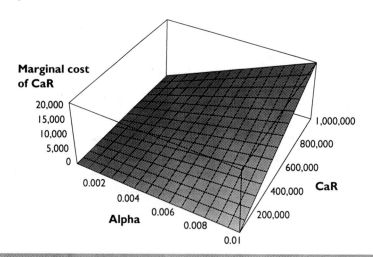

Expected cash flow net of the cost of CaR

= Expected cash flow −Cost of CaR

= Expected cash flow − α(CaR)^2

= 1M × E(S$_{June\ 1}$) − h × [E(S$_{June\ 1}$) −F $_{March\ 1}$]
  − α[(1M − h)1.65Vol(S$_{June\ 1}$)]^2　　　　　　　(7.12)

where h is the hedge, the number of Swiss francs sold short forward. The un-hedged position of Export is then one million Swiss francs minus h. Figure 7.3 shows the expected cash flow net of the cost of CaR as a function of h with our assumptions and shows that it is a concave function. Since the expected cash flow net of the cost of CaR first increases and then falls as α increases, there is a hedge ratio that maximizes this expected cash flow. Assuming an expected spot exchange rate of $0.7102, a forward exchange rate of $0.6902, and a volatility of the spot exchange rate of 0.0435086, we find that the optimal hedge is to go short 980,596 Swiss francs if α is $0.0001 per unit, and to go short 805,964 Swiss francs if α is $0.00001 per unit. Since hedging has a positive cost because the forward exchange rate is too low, the firm hedges less as the cost of CaR falls.

We can solve for the optimal hedge directly. At the margin, the cost of hedging has to be equal to the benefit of hedging. Consequently, we can find it by setting the cost of hedging slightly more (the marginal cost of hedging) equal to the benefit from doing so (the marginal benefit).

By hedging, one gives up the expected spot exchange rate to receive the forward exchange rate for each Swiss franc one hedges. Consequently, by hedging Δ

Expected cash flow net of CaR cost as a function of hedge　　　*Figure 7.3*

We use an expected Swiss franc spot exchange rate of $0.7102, a forward exchange rate of $0.6902, and a cost of CaR of 0.0001 and 0.00001. With this example, hedging involves going short the Swiss franc, which reduces the expected cash flow because the spot exchange rate exceeds the forward exchange rate. Consequently, if $\alpha = 0$, no hedging would take place and the firm would go long on the forward market. The fact that risk is costly makes the expected cash flow net of CaR a concave function of the hedge, so that there is an optimal hedge. As α falls, the optimal hedge falls also.

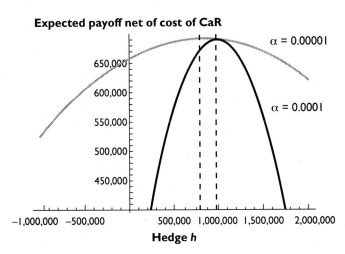

Expected payoff net of cost of CaR

$\alpha = 0.00001$

$\alpha = 0.0001$

Optimal hedge for $\alpha = 0.0001$,
short SFR980,596

Optimal hedge for $\alpha = 0.00001$,
short SFR805,964

650,000
600,000
550,000
500,000
450,000

−1,000,000　−500,000　　500,000　1,000,000　1,500,000　2,000,000

Hedge h

more units of the cash position, expected cash flow changes by $\Delta(F_{\text{March 1}} - E(S_{\text{June 1}}))$, where Δ represents a very slight increase in the size of the hedge. The marginal cost of hedging is therefore:

$$\text{Marginal cost of hedging} = -\Delta[F_{\text{March 1}} - E(S_{\text{June 1}})] \qquad (7.13)$$

For given Δ, the marginal cost of hedging does not depend on h. Further, the marginal cost of hedging depends only on the difference between the spot exchange rate the firm expects and the forward exchange rate as long as neither transaction costs nor the forward exchange rate depend on the size of the hedge.

The marginal benefit of hedging is the decrease in the cost of CaR resulting from hedging Δ more units of the cash position when Δ represents a very slight increase in the size of the hedge:[2]

Marginal benefit of hedging for firm with hedge h

$$= \text{cost of CaR for hedge } h - \text{cost of CaR for hedge } (h + \Delta)$$

$$= \alpha\left((1M - h)1.65\text{Vol}\left[S_{\text{June 1}}\right]\right)^2 - \alpha\left(1M - h - \Delta\right)1.65\text{Vol}\left[S_{\text{June 1}}\right]\right)^2$$

$$= 2\alpha\left(1M - h\right)\Delta\left(1.65\text{Vol}\left[S_{\text{June 1}}\right]\right)^2 - \alpha\Delta^2\left(1.65\text{Vol}\left[S_{\text{June 1}}\right]\right)^2$$

$$= 2\alpha\left(1M - h\right)\Delta\left(\text{CaR per unit of exposure}\right)^2 \qquad (7.14)$$

To go to the last line, we use the fact that as long as Δ is small enough, the square of Δ is so small that the second term in the next to last line can be ignored. Because the cost of risk for the firm is α times CaR squared, the marginal benefit of hedging turns out to have a simple form. The marginal benefit of hedging depends on α, the unhedged exposure (one million Swiss francs minus h), and the square of CaR per unit of exposure. The CaR per unit of exposure is fixed. Consequently, the marginal benefit of hedging falls as the unhedged exposure falls. In other words, the more hedging takes place, the less valuable the next unit of hedging. Since the firm's CaR falls as the firm hedges more, it follows that the lower the CaR, the lower the marginal benefit of hedging.

Figure 7.4 shows the marginal cost and the marginal benefit curves of hedging. The intersection of the two curves gives us the optimal hedge. Increasing the marginal cost of hedging moves the marginal cost of hedging curve up, and therefore reduces the extent to which the firm hedges. Increasing the cost of CaR for a given hedge h moves the marginal benefit curve of hedging up and leads to more hedging.

We can solve for the optimal hedge by equating the marginal cost and the marginal benefit of the hedge. When we do so, Δ drops out because it is on both sides of the equation. This gives us:

$$h = 1M - \frac{E(S_{\text{June 1}}) - F_{\text{March 1}}}{2\alpha\left(\text{CaR per unit of exposure}\right)^2} \qquad (7.15)$$

---

2 This marginal benefit can be obtained by taking the derivative of the cost of CaR with respect to the size of the hedge.

Marginal cost and marginal benefit from hedging   *Figure 7.4*

We use an expected spot exchange rate of $0.7102, a forward exchange rate of $0.6902, and a cost of CaR of 0.0001 and 0.00001. With this example, hedging reduces the expected cash flow because the expected spot exchange rate exceeds the forward exchange rate. Consequently, if $\alpha = 0$, no hedging would take place and the firm would go long on the forward market. The fact that risk is costly makes the expected cash flow net of CaR a concave function of the hedge, so that there is an optimal hedge. As α falls, the optimal hedge falls also.

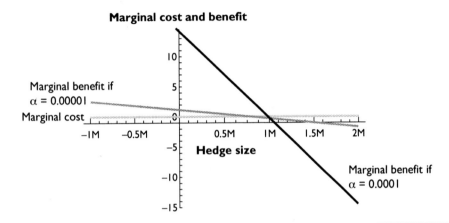

Suppose that the forward exchange rate is $0.6902, the expected spot exchange rate is 2 cents higher, α is equal to 0.0001, and the CaR per Swiss franc is $0.0717892. In this case, the optimal hedge applying our formula is to sell forward 980,596 Swiss francs. Not surprisingly, the optimal hedge is the same as when we looked at Figure 7.3. Figure 7.5 shows the optimal hedge for different values of the expected spot exchange rate at maturity of the exposure and different values of α. The hedge ratio becomes one as α becomes large. When α is not too large, the optimal hedge ratio is below one if the forward exchange rate is below the expected spot exchange rate and above one otherwise. As the expected spot exchange rate increases, the hedge falls and can become negative. As the forward exchange rate increases, the optimal hedge increases because it is profitable to sell the Swiss franc short when the forward exchange rate is high relative to the expected spot exchange rate.

This approach to hedging when CaR is costly gives a general formula for the optimal hedge:

Optimal hedge when CaR is costly

The optimal hedge (the size of a short position to hedge a long exposure) when the cost of CaR is $\alpha(\text{CaR})^2$ and when the cost of hedging does not depend on the size of the hedge, is given by the expression:

$$h = \text{Exposure} - \left(\frac{\text{Expected cash price per unit} - \text{Price for future delivery per unit}}{2\alpha\,(\text{CaR per unit of exposure})^2} \right) \qquad (7.16)$$

Figure 7.5	Optimal hedge as a function of the spot exchange rate and α when the cost of CaR is $\alpha(CaR)^2$

We use a forward exchange rate of $0.6902.

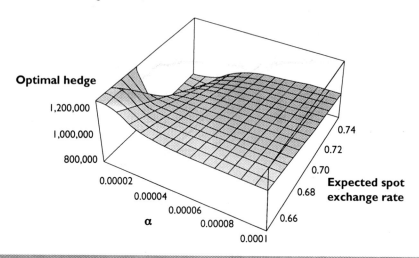

To understand this expression for the optimal hedge, suppose first that the cost of CaR is very high. In this case, α is very large, so the second term in the expression is trivial. This means that h is about equal to the total exposure and hence close to the hedge that we would take in the absence of hedging costs. (Remember from Chapter 6 that in the absence of basis risk, the minimum-volatility hedge is to go short the exposure, so that h is equal to the exposure.) As α falls, so that CaR becomes less expensive, it becomes possible for the firm to trade off the cost and benefit of hedging. The marginal cost of hedging is the price for future delivery minus the expected spot price. As the expected spot price increases, Export's expected hedged cash flow falls compared to its expected unhedged cash flow. As this marginal cost increases, the firm hedges less. The extent to which the firm hedges less depends on the benefit of hedging. As the benefit from hedging increases, the expression in parentheses becomes closer to zero in absolute value, so that the firm departs less from the minimum-volatility hedge. (The details of the derivation of this result are provided in Technical Box 7.2, Derivation of the optimal hedge when CaR is costly.)

Let's apply this analysis to Trading Inc. Trading Inc. has the same exposure as Export Inc., but this exposure comes from having a portfolio of Swiss francs T-bills with face value of one million Swiss francs maturing on June 1. Trading is concerned about its one-day VaR. We saw how to compute this one-day VaR for March 1, 1999, in Chapter 6. VaR is computed for portfolios of assets and liabilities marked to market. In this case, the relevant exposure for VaR is the one arising from the current value of the portfolio of Swiss francs T-bills. So far, we have computed the one-day VaR assuming that the expected change in value of the portfolio over one day is zero. In this case, it is optimal to reduce VaR to zero

Derivation of the optimal hedge when CaR is costly   *Technical Box 7.2*

To obtain equation (7.16), assume that the firm's cash flow consists of receiving n units of spot at some future date and selling h units of spot at the forward price of F per unit for delivery at the same date. (The analysis is the same for a futures price G for a tailed hedge assuming fixed interest rates.) With this notation, the expected cash flow net of the cost of CaR (computed for that expected cash flow) for an exposure of n and a hedge of h is:

Expected cash flow net of cost of CaR
= Expected income minus cost of CaR

$$= (n - h)\text{E(S)} + h\text{F} - \alpha\text{CaR}^2 \tag{1}$$

This equation follows because we sell $n - h$ units on the spot market and h units on the forward market. Remember that the CaR with a hedge h assuming that changes are normally distributed is $1.65\text{Vol}[(n - h)\text{S}]$ where S denotes the spot price at the delivery date. Substituting the definition of CaR in equation (1), we have:

Expected cash flow net of cost of CaR
$$= (n - h)\text{E(S)} + h\text{F} - \alpha(1.65\text{Vol}[(n - h)\text{S}])^2 \tag{2}$$

To maximize the expected cash flow net of the cost of CaR, we take the derivative with respect to h and set it equal to zero, remembering that $\text{Vol}[(n - h)\text{S}]$ is equal to $(n - h)\text{Vol(S)}$:

$$\text{-E(S)} + \text{F} + 2\alpha 1.65(n - h)\text{Vol(S)} \times 1.65\text{Vol(S)} = 0 \tag{3}$$

Solving for h and rearranging, we get the formula:

$$h = n - \frac{\text{E(S)} - \text{F}}{2\alpha 1.65^2 \text{Var(S)}} \tag{4}$$

Recall that 1.65Vol(S) is the CaR of one unit of unhedged exposure. Using the definition of CaR therefore yields equation (7.16) in the text.

if VaR is costly because there is no offsetting gain from taking on risk. If there is an offsetting gain that is economically important, then one must trade off the impact of hedging on the expected change in portfolio value with the benefit from reducing the VaR through hedging. This is the same trade-off as the one we just analyzed with Export. Hence, to find the optimal hedge when one is using VaR and when hedging is expensive, one has to equate the marginal impact of the hedge on the expected return with the marginal benefit of the hedge on the cost of VaR.

7.3. Multiple exposures with same maturity

Let's now see what happens when Export Inc. has two exposures that mature on June 1. One cash flow is the cash flow of one million Swiss francs. The other exposure is a cash flow of one million yen. Let's write $S_{\text{June 1}}^{\text{yen}}$ for the spot exchange rate of the yen on June 1 and $S_{\text{June 1}}^{\text{SFR}}$ for the spot exchange rate of the Swiss franc at the same date. The variance of the unhedged cash flow is now:

Variance of unhedged cash flow $= \text{Var}\left[1M \times S_{\text{June 1}}^{\text{yen}} + 1M \times S_{\text{June 1}}^{\text{SFR}}\right] =$

$$\text{Var}\left[1M \times S_{\text{June 1}}^{\text{yen}}\right] + \text{Var}\left[1M \times S_{\text{June 1}}^{\text{SFR}}\right] + 2\text{Cov}\left[1M \times S_{\text{June 1}}^{\text{SFR}}, 1M \times S_{\text{June 1}}^{\text{yen}}\right]$$

(7.17)

This formula is similar to the formula for the variance of the return of a portfolio with two stocks. Not surprisingly, the variance of the total cash flow depends on the covariance between the cash flows. Consequently, the general formula for the variance of unhedged cash flow when there are m cash flows accruing at date T is:

Variance of unhedged cash flow accruing at time T =

$$\sum_{i=1}^{i=m} \sum_{j=1}^{j=m} \text{Cov}\left[C_i(T), C_j(T)\right]$$

(7.18)

where $C_i(T)$ is the i-th cash flow accruing at time T. (Remember that the covariance of a random variable with itself is its variance.) When a firm has several distinct cash flows accruing at the same point, there is a diversification effect like that in investment portfolios. The diversification effect is due to the fact that the covariance of two random variables is less than the product of the standard deviations of the two random variables if the coefficient of correlation is less than one. The variance of total unhedged cash flow falls as the correlation coefficient between the two cash flows falls. If the correlation coefficient between the two cash flows is negative, the firm may have little aggregate risk. A firm can take advantage of this diversification effect to reduce the extent to which it has to hedge through financial instruments to reach a target CaR.

Let's look at an extreme example. Suppose that the yen and the Swiss francs cash flows have the same variance but are perfectly negatively correlated. In this case, the aggregate unhedged cash flow of the firm has no risk, and no hedging is required. Yet if the firm looked at these cash flows one at a time, it would conclude that it has two cash flows that need to be hedged. It would hedge each cash flow separately. If it used forward contracts for each, it could eliminate all risk. In fact, this is risk that the firm does not need to eliminate because in the aggregate it cancels out.

When hedging is costly, the diversification effect means a firm can reduce hedging costs by reducing the number and size of the hedges it puts on. To take this diversification effect into account, the firm should compute optimal hedges based on its aggregate cash flow, not its individual cash flows. Using our example, the aggregate unhedged cash flow is:

$$\textbf{Unhedged cash flow} \; = \; \text{1M} \times S^{yen}_{June\;1} \; + \; \text{1M} \times S^{SFR}_{June\;1} \qquad (7.19)$$

Suppose we can use both a Swiss franc futures contract and a yen futures contract that mature on June 1 or later. In this case, the hedged cash flow is:

$$\textbf{Hedged cash flow} \; = \; \textbf{Unhedged cash flow} \; -$$
$$h^{SFR}\Big[G^{SFR}_{June\;1} - G^{SFR}_{March\;1}\Big] - h^{yen}\Big[G^{yen}_{June\;1} - G^{yen}_{March\;1}\Big] \qquad (7.20)$$

where h^{SFR} is the number of units of the Swiss franc futures and h^{yen} is the number of units of the yen futures we short before tailing. The Swiss franc futures contract has price $G^{SFR}_{June\;1}$ on June 1, and the yen futures contract has price $G^{yen}_{June\;1}$. With tailing, $G^{SFR}_{June\;1} - G^{SFR}_{March\;1}$ is the gain from a long position in the Swiss franc futures contracts from March 1 to June 1 equal every day to the present value of a zero-coupon bond the next day that pays one Swiss franc on June 1.

Since we now have exposures in two currencies, we want to find a portfolio of futures positions so that changes in value of that portfolio offset as closely as possible unexpected changes in the value of the cash position. We can use a regression to find the futures portfolio that best predicts changes in the value of the cash position.

Let's assume that the exchange rate and futures price changes have the same joint distribution over time and that they satisfy the multivariate normal changes model presented in Chapter 6. This means we can use ordinary least squares regression to obtain the volatility-minimizing hedges. We know Export Inc.'s exposures, so we can compute what the value of the cash position would have been for past values of the exchange rates. Hence, we can regress changes in the value of the cash position using historical exchange rates on a constant and changes in the futures prices.

The regression coefficients provide us with optimal volatility-minimizing hedges because we assume that the distribution of past changes is the same as the distribution of future changes. The optimal hedges are given by the regression coefficients. Here, the dependent variable is the change in value of the cash position. Consequently, the coefficient for the change in the Swiss franc futures price is the number of Swiss francs for future delivery that one goes short, and the coefficient for the change in the yen futures price is the number of yen for future delivery that one goes short. The regression is therefore:

$$\Delta S^{SFR}_t \times \text{1M} + \Delta S^{yen}_t \times \text{1M} = \textbf{constant}$$
$$+ \, h^{SFR} \times \Delta G^{SFR}_t + h^{yen} \times \Delta G^{yen}_t + \epsilon_t \qquad (7.21)$$

where ΔS^{SFR}_t is the change in the Swiss franc spot exchange rate over a period starting at t (the period is a day if we use daily observations). ϵ_t is the random error of the regression. To hedge the cash flow, Export Inc. should go short h^{SFR} Swiss francs and h^{yen} yen for future delivery.

The number of Swiss francs for future delivery Export Inc. should go short differs from the hedge when Export Inc. has only a Swiss franc exposure. The hedge differs because the Swiss franc futures contract helps hedge the yen exposure and because the yen futures contract helps hedge the Swiss franc exposure. We discuss these two reasons for why the Swiss franc futures position differs in this chapter from what it was in the previous chapter in turn.

1. The Swiss franc futures contract helps hedge the yen exposure. Suppose that the slope in a regression of changes in the dollar value of the yen cash flow on changes in the Swiss franc futures price is not zero. In this case, Export could use the Swiss franc futures contract to reduce the risk of the yen exposure. If the covariance between changes in the yen spot exchange rate and changes in the Swiss franc futures price is positive, going short the Swiss franc futures contract helps hedge the yen exposure so that Export thus goes short the Swiss franc futures contract to a greater extent than if it had only the Swiss franc exposure. If the covariance is negative, Export has to buy Swiss francs for future delivery to hedge the yen exposure. Since it is optimal to sell Swiss francs for future delivery to hedge the Swiss franc exposure, this means that Export Inc. sells fewer Swiss francs for future delivery than it would if it had only a Swiss franc exposure.

2. The yen futures contract helps hedge the Swiss franc and yen exposures. The Swiss franc futures contract is at best an imperfect hedge for the yen exposure. Suppose that the yen futures contract is a perfect hedge for the yen exposure and the Swiss franc futures price is positively correlated with the yen spot exchange rate. If Export uses the yen contract also, it will be able to hedge the yen exposure perfectly with that contract and it can also take a smaller short position in the Swiss franc futures contract than it would if it used only the Swiss franc futures contract. It might even turn out that the yen futures contract is useful to hedge the Swiss franc exposure in conjunction with the Swiss franc futures contract—this would be the case if the yen futures price is correlated with the basis risk of the Swiss franc futures contract.

We can use the same regression approach to find the optimal hedge whatever the number of different futures contracts we use to hedge an aggregate cash flow. If Export Inc. has a cash flow at date T corresponding to fixed payments in x currencies, and there are m futures contracts to hedge the total cash flow, we could obtain positions in these m futures contracts by regressing the change in the total cash flow on the changes of the m futures contracts. Since the total cash flow is the sum of known payments in foreign currencies, the hedges can be obtained from a regression using historical data on exchange rates and futures prices assuming constant joint distributions of futures prices and exchange rates over time.

Firms have many different exposures to risk. Focusing on exposures of aggregate cash flows makes it possible to take advantage of diversification across cash flows in a very important way. There are not always good hedges for every exposure separately. Possible hedges may have too much basis risk. When a firm considers its aggregate cash flow, there may be some good hedges if the basis risks get diversified in the portfolio.

Though our discussion focused on cash flow exposures, the same conclusions apply when one hedges the value of a portfolio. Let's turn to an example to see this. We examine the optimal hedge of a portfolio in Chapter 6. Mr. Big has a portfolio of $100 million invested in the world market portfolio of the Datastream Global Index on September 1, 1999. He is pessimistic about the return of his portfolio over the next month, but does not want to sell because of tax consequences. To protect himself, he wants to hedge and has settled on a futures hedge. In Chapter 6, Mr. Big reasons that, since the United States is the biggest component of the world market portfolio, it makes sense for him to hedge with the S&P 500 futures contract traded at the Chicago Mercantile Exchange. This hedge allows him to eliminate 80.96 percent of the volatility of his portfolio.

By using a regression of the world market portfolio return on the S&P 500 futures return, Mr. Big already applies the portfolio method of this chapter. Mr. Big could have decided to consider each stock he owns separately. If he did this, he would find that his exposure estimates are poor for many stocks. This is because diversifiable risk accounts for most of the return volatility of individual stocks. At the portfolio level, however, systematic risk accounts for most of the return volatility because diversifiable risk is diversified away. If Mr. Big attempts to hedge individual stocks, he would conclude that hedging makes little sense for most of his stocks and therefore would be able to reduce the volatility of his portfolio very little. He could go a step further and decide to treat his U.S. stocks as a portfolio and attempt to hedge that portfolio. He would then be left with the risk of his non-U.S. stocks. By hedging the world market portfolio against its U.S. exposure, Mr. Big uses the S&P 500 futures contract to hedge the return of the securities from other countries. This is useful because the return of these securities is correlated with the U.S. market return.

The world market portfolio has exposures to other markets besides the U.S. market. We can investigate whether Mr. Big could improve his hedge by using a second futures contract. The second biggest component in the world market portfolio is Japan. Let's see how Mr. Big could improve his hedge by using the futures contract on the Nikkei traded on the Chicago Mercantile Exchange as well as the S&P 500 contract. The payoff of that contract is in dollars. Regressing the monthly (continuously compounded) return of the world market portfolio on a constant and the rates of change of the futures prices from January 1, 1991, to September 1, 1999 gives us:

$$\Delta \ln(\text{World index}) = c + \beta \Delta \ln(\text{S\&P 500}) + \gamma \Delta \ln(\text{Nikkei}) + \epsilon$$

$$0.0048 \quad\quad 0.6905 \quad\quad\quad 0.2161$$

$$(0.26) \quad (12.79) \quad\quad\quad (7.72) \quad\quad\quad\quad (7.22)$$

We provide the t-statistics below the coefficients. These coefficients show that the return of the world index is positively related to the return of the S&P 500 futures and of the Nikkei futures. The exposure of the world market to the S&P 500 futures is greater than its exposure to the Nikkei futures. Both exposure coefficients are estimated precisely. The standard error of the estimate of the S&P 500 futures coefficient is 0.054 and the standard error of the estimate of the Nikkei futures coefficient is 0.028.

Consider now the implementation of this hedge where the hedge is adjusted every month. Effectively, we hedge over a month, so that tailing is trivial and can be ignored. The Nikkei contract is for $5 times the Nikkei. Consequently, the contract is for a position in the Nikkei worth $89,012.40 on September 1, 1999, since on that day the Nikkei stands at 17,802.48. The S&P contract is for 500 times the S&P 500. The S&P 500 is at 1,331.06 on September 1, 1999, so that the contract corresponds to an investment of $1,331.06 \times 500$ in the S&P 500, namely $665,530. The regression coefficient for the S&P 500 is 0.6905. This means that one would like a position in the S&P 500 futures of $69,050,000 (i.e., $0.6905 \times \$100M$). A one percent increase in that position is $690,500. The expected increase in the value of the portfolio if the S&P 500 increases by one percent is $0.6905\% \times \$100M = \$690,500$ as well. To obtain the number of S&P 500 futures contracts, we divide 69,050,000 by 665,530. The result is 103.7, which we round out to 104 contracts. To get the number of Nikkei contracts, we would like a Nikkei position worth $21,010,000. The best we can do is 236 contracts since 21,010,000/89,012.40 = 236.03.

Using both the S&P 500 and the Nikkei futures contracts to hedge has two important implications for Mr. Big. First, adding the Nikkei futures contract to the hedging strategy improves the R^2 from 0.6554 to 0.7845. This R^2 means that we can expect to eliminate 88.57 percent of the volatility of the world market portfolio with the two futures contracts but 80.96 percent with only the S&P 500 contract.[3] Second, adding the Nikkei futures contract reduces the position in the S&P 500 contract. If Mr. Big uses only the S&P 500 contract, the regression coefficient on the S&P 500 is 0.86057, but if he uses the Nikkei as well it is 0.6905. The short position in the S&P 500 falls from 129 contracts to 104 contracts. The reason for this is that, absent the use of the Nikkei contract, the S&P 500 helps hedge the Japanese exposure because the S&P 500 return is correlated with the Nikkei return. When Mr. Big uses the Nikkei futures contract, the Nikkei futures is a better hedge for the Japanese exposure than the S&P 500 futures, so that the short position of the S&P 500 futures falls since the S&P 500 futures is no longer needed to hedge Japanese exposure.

7.4. Cash flows occurring at different dates

We have shown the benefit of using a total cash flow approach to obtaining the optimal hedge ratios. Even though a firm has large cash flows in a number of different currencies, it might need relatively little hedging. This is a simplified world, though. In the real world, payments typically accrue at different dates, thereby creating exposures that have different maturities.

When payments occur at different dates, how does a firm decide which cash flow volatility it should minimize? If it tries to minimize the cash flow volatility at each date, it ignores the diversification that takes place across payments at different dates. For example, suppose that Export Inc. receives a payment of one million Swiss francs on June 1 and must make a payment of one million Swiss francs ten days later. Hedging each cash flow separately ignores the fact that the exchange rate exposure of the payment Export will receive is already reduced to a great extent by the payment it will make.

---

3 Remember that R^2 is the fraction of the variance of the dependent variable explained by the independent variables. To obtain the fraction of the volatility, one has to take the square root of R^2.

The only way to take advantage of diversification across time is to bring all future payments to a common date to make them comparable. One solution is to use borrowing and lending to bring the cash flows to the end of the accounting period, and then consider the resulting cash flow at that time. A second solution is to bring all future payments back to the present date. This solution involves taking present values of future payments to be received and made. In this case, we should be concerned about the risk of the changes of the present value of the firm over the period.

One measure of such risk is VaR. If all cash flows to the firm are taken into account in this case, and the multivariate normal changes model holds for the cash flows, VaR is directly proportional to the volatility of firm value changes. Rather than minimizing the volatility of cash flow at one particular date, volatility minimization now requires that we minimize the volatility of the changes in the present value of the firm for the next period of time. The optimal hedges will change over time because payments are made and received, so that the present value of the payments exposed to exchange rate fluctuations changes over time.

To understand this, assume now that Export Inc. receives a payment of one million Swiss francs on June 1 and must make a payment of one million Swiss francs on a different date, date T. Suppose Export Inc. wants to hedge with a futures contract that matures after date T. The present value of the payments on March 1 is:

$$\textbf{Present value of the payments } =$$
$$\left(P_{\text{March 1}}^{\text{SFR}}(\textbf{June 1}) - P_{\text{March 1}}^{\text{SFR}}(\textbf{T}) \right) \times S_{\text{March 1}} \times \textbf{1M} \qquad (7.23)$$

where $P_{\text{March 1}}^{\text{SFR}}(T)$ is the price on March 1 of a zero-coupon bond paying one Swiss franc at T. The exposure is $1M\left(P_{\text{March 1}}^{\text{SFR}}(\text{June 1}) - P_{\text{March 1}}^{\text{SFR}}(T)\right)$ Swiss francs. Viewed from March 1, the firm has little exposure if T is close to June 1. This is because the two zero-coupon bonds have similar values, so that until June 1 the positive gain from an appreciation of the Swiss franc on the dollar value of the payment to be received offsets the loss from an appreciation of the Swiss franc on the dollar value of the payment to be made.

One way to see how having to make a Swiss franc payment at date T limits Export's Swiss franc exposure is to compute a one-day VaR. Suppose that T is September 1, $P_{\text{March 1}}^{\text{SFR}}(\text{June 1}) = 0.96$, and $P_{\text{March 1}}^{\text{SFR}}(\text{September 1}) = 0.92$. Using the data for the Swiss franc exchange rate from Chapter 6, we have:

$$\textbf{One-day VaR } = \textbf{1.65Vol}\left(\Delta S_{\text{March 1}}\right) \times$$
$$\textbf{1M}\left[P_{\text{March 1}}^{\text{SFR}}(\textbf{June 1}) - P_{\text{March 1}}^{\text{SFR}}(\textbf{September 1}) \right]$$
$$= \textbf{1.65} \times \textbf{0.0054816} \times \textbf{1M} \times |\textbf{0.96} - \textbf{0.92}|$$
$$= \$\textbf{361.8} \qquad (7.24)$$

where $| \, 0.96 - 0.92 \, |$ denotes the absolute value of $0.96 - 0.92$, and Vol $(\Delta S_{\text{March 1}})$ denotes the volatility of the one-day change of the Swiss franc spot exchange rate. The one-day VaR of \$361.80 is dramatically less than if Export

Inc. is to receive only the payment of one million Swiss francs on June 1, which is \$8,683, or $1.65 \times 0.0054816 \times 1M \times 0.96$. If Export Inc. makes the payment a long time in the future, its VaR becomes closer to what it would be absent that payment because the present value of the payment to be made is smaller, so that its current exposure is greater.

To find the hedge that minimizes the volatility of hedged firm value, Export needs to find a minimum-volatility hedge ratio for a one-day Swiss franc exposure and then multiply this hedge ratio by its exposure. We already know that the volatility-minimizing hedge ratio over one day can be obtained by regressing the daily change in the Swiss franc exchange rate on the daily change in the futures price. Letting ΔS_t be the change in the spot exchange rate and ΔG_t be the change in the futures price from date t to the next day, the regression coefficient is $\text{Cov}(\Delta S_t, \Delta G_t)/\text{Var}(\Delta G_t)$. This gives us the hedge ratio per unit of exposure. The exposure is $1M \left[P^{SFR}_{\text{March 1}}(\text{June 1}) - P^{SFR}_{\text{March 1}}(\text{September 1}) \right]$ Swiss francs. Consequently, multiplying the exposure with the hedge ratio, we have the optimal hedge h:

$$h = 1M\left[P^{SFR}_{\text{March 1}}(\text{June 1}) - P^{SFR}_{\text{March 1}}(\text{September 1}) \right]\left(\frac{\text{Cov}(\Delta S_t, \Delta G_t)}{\text{Var}(\Delta G_t)} \right) \quad (7.25)$$

Using a regression coefficient of 0.94, a maturity for the payment to be made of September 1, $P^{SFR}_{\text{March 1}}(\text{June 1}) = 0.96$ and $P^{SFR}_{\text{March 1}}(\text{September 1}) = 0.92$, the optimal hedge consists in going short 37,600 Swiss francs as opposed to going short 902,400 Swiss francs if there was no payment to be made. Over the next day, the two Swiss franc exposures almost offset each other so that the VaR is small and only a small hedge is required.

Exposures change over time. This is not an important issue when, as in our initial discussion of Export's hedging in Chapter 6, there is only one exposure that matures and disappears. With cash flows occurring at different dates, however, things are dramatically different. Here, as of June 1, the offsetting effect of the two exposures disappears. Consequently, on June 2, the exposure of Export Inc. is the exposure resulting from having to make a one million Swiss franc payment at date T. Hence, the exposure rises sharply on June 1, which makes the hedge change dramatically. Before the payment is received on June 1, Export Inc. goes short Swiss francs for future delivery by a small amount. After the payment is received, the only Swiss franc exposure of Export Inc. is the payment it has to make later. As of that time, an unhedged Export Inc. is short Swiss francs without the offset of receiving a Swiss franc payment. This means that after June 1, Export Inc. must change its hedge from being short Swiss francs for future delivery to being long Swiss francs for future delivery. Figure 7.6 shows how the hedge changes over time. The VaR also evolves over time, in that it is very low until June 1, when it increases dramatically.

Sometimes a firm cannot take advantage of diversification in cash flows across time. Consider a firm that plans on using this year's cash flow for next year's investment. The firm cannot go to the capital markets or to a bank to borrow. It has a payment that is to be made at the end of this year and will have to make a payment at the end of the following year. The payment to be made reduces its exposure. Yet this diversification effect may not help the firm. Suppose the exchange

Short position to hedge Export Inc.'s exposure	*Figure* 7.6

The hedging period starts on March 1. Export Inc. receives a payment of one million Swiss francs on June 1 and must make a payment of one million Swiss francs on September 1. The price on March 1 of a zero-coupon bond paying $1 on June 1 is $0.96 and the price on March 1 of a zero-coupon bond paying $1 on September 1 is $0.92. The optimal hedge ratio for an exposure of one Swiss franc is 0.94. March 1 is time 0 and September 1 is time 0.5.

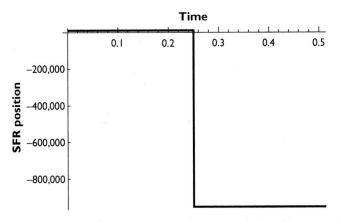

rate is unexpectedly low at the end of this year, so that the firm has a lower cash flow than expected and has to cut back investment. The fact that the lower exchange rate means that the present value of what the firm owes is also lower is irrelevant if the firm cannot use this gain to raise cash to finance investment. Hence, when a firm has limited or no access to external funds, it may have to ignore some of the time diversification of its exposures. Such a firm cannot use VaR—it is concerned about this year's cash flow risk, while VaR allows its exposures across years to partly offset each other. This firm would therefore compute CaR for this year, bring all cash flows that occur during the year to a common end-of-year date.

7.5. Metallgesellschaft

In December 1993, Metallgesellschaft AG headquartered in Frankfurt, Germany, faced a crisis. It had lost over $1 billion on oil futures contracts. Its chief executive was fired. A package of loans and debt restructuring was put together, and eventually large amounts of its assets were sold. The losses brought about a drastic reorganization of the firm.

Metallgesellschaft's losses are among the highest reported by firms in conjunction with the use of derivatives. Are derivatives to blame? The firm's board of directors thought so and changed the firm's strategy after becoming aware of the losses. Some prominent scholars thought the directors panicked when they had no reason, and gave up a sound business strategy.

Metallgesellschaft is a large German company with interests in metal, mining, and engineering businesses. In 1993, it had sales in excess of $16 billion, assets of about $10 billion, and 15 major subsidiaries. MG Corp, a U.S. subsidiary and trading operation of Metallgesellschaft, had equity capital of $50 million. It had an oil business organized in a subsidiary called MG Refining and Marketing

(MGRM). MGRM had a 49 percent stake in a refiner, Castle Energy. MGRM had contracted to buy from Castle its output of refined products, amounting to approximately 46 million barrels per year at guaranteed margins for up to 10 years. MGRM then turned around and offered retailers long-term contracts in refined products at fixed prices. It thought its expertise would enable it to make this strategy profitable.

MGRM offered three types of contracts. The first type required the buyer to take delivery of a fixed amount of refined product per month. These contracts, most of them with a maturity of 10 years, accounted for 102 million barrels of future deliveries. The second type of contract had fixed prices but gave considerable latitude to buyers concerning when they would take delivery. These contracts, again mostly running 10 years, accounted for 52 million barrels of future deliveries. Essentially, at the end of 1993, MGRM had guaranteed delivery at fixed prices of 154 million barrels of oil. A third type of contract had flexible prices.

To alleviate credit risk, MGRM allowed buyers to take fixed-price contracts for a fraction of their purchases of oil not exceeding 20 percent. It further included cash-out options. With the first type of contract, buyers could cash out and receive half the difference between the near-term futures price and the fixed price times the remaining deliveries. With the second type of contract, buyers would receive the full difference between the second-nearest futures contract price and the fixed price times the amount not yet delivered.

These contracts exposed MGRM to fluctuations in oil prices. Since it would pay spot prices to Castle and would receive fixed prices from retail customers, increases in oil prices could potentially bankrupt the company. MGRM therefore decided to hedge. To analyze the issues involved in MGRM's hedging, let's assume for simplicity that the fixed-price contracts have no credit risk, no flexible delivery dates, and no cash-out options. The contracts have a maturity of 10 years and MGRM would keep paying spot prices to Castle over the next 10 years. The simplest way for MGRM to eliminate all risks would be to buy a strip of forward contracts where each forward contract has the maturity of a delivery date and is for a quantity of oil corresponding to the quantity that has to be delivered on that date. If MGRM had done this, it would have been perfectly hedged. It would no longer have had an exposure to oil prices.

MGRM chose not to buy a strip of forward contracts for two reasons. First, buying a strip of forward contracts would have been expensive. It would have required using over-the-counter markets of limited liquidity. This made a strategy using short-term futures contracts more attractive. However, with this strategy, there was basis risk that would not have existed with forward contracts. This basis risk necessitated the computation of a minimum-volatility hedge using the approach we presented in Chapter 6.

Mello and Parsons (1995) later figured that the minimum-volatility hedge would have involved buying 86 million barrels in the short-maturity futures contract. Pirrong (1997) estimates the minimum-volatility hedge differently, and under most of his assumptions the minimum-volatility hedge is smaller than the one obtained by Mello and Parson. One can argue about some of the assumptions of these studies, but it is certainly the case the minimum volatility hedge involved a long position in the short maturity futures contract of much less than MGRM's 154 million barrels commitment.

This is the case for two important reasons. In Chapter 6, we talked about the necessity to tail the hedge and pointed out that tailing can have a dramatic impact when we are hedging exposures that mature a number of years in the future. Here, Metallgesellschaft is hedging some exposures that mature in 10 years. When hedging exposures like this, the tailing factor should be the present value of a zero-coupon bond paying $1 in 10 years. This sharply reduces the size of the hedge. In addition, remember from our analysis that basis risk reduces the size of the hedge relative to the cash position. In this case, rolling over short-term contracts exposes MGRM to substantial rollover risk that should reduce its position.

Despite these considerations, MGRM bought 154 million barrels in short-maturity contracts. Some of these contracts were futures contracts, but others were traded over the counter. Hence, in no sense did MGRM use a minimum-volatility hedge.

This brings us to the second reason why MGRM did not buy a strip of forward contracts. The minimum volatility hedge of 86 million barrels is computed ignoring expected returns altogether—it just minimizes the volatility of the hedged position. MGRM, however, thought that while it did not have good information about future spot prices it had good information on the basis. Its view was that prices for future delivery typically are lower than spot prices and that, consequently, there is money to be made by being long futures as the futures price must rise towards spot prices over the life of a contract. As we saw in Chapter 5, such a relationship between spot prices and futures prices is called backwardation. Many have argued that it arises because hedgers are naturally short, so that the speculators must be long and must be compensated for taking the risk of the contract by an expected profit. Such an argument is inconsistent with the logic of the CAPM where only systematic risk is priced; it makes sense only if one believes that the logic of the CAPM does not apply to futures contracts.

Since MGRM had an exposure to the price of oil, the positive expected return on futures increased its long position relative to the optimal hedge. MGRM ended up having a long position of 154 million barrels of oil. The argument that makes sense of such a position is that with this position MGRM was exposed to the basis but not to oil prices—eventually, it would take delivery on every one of the contracts as it rolled them over.

From the perspective of optimal hedging theory as we have developed it, the long position of 154 million barrels can be decomposed into a pure hedge position of 86 million barrels of oil and a speculative position of 68 million barrels of oil. MGRM was net long in oil prices. As prices fell dramatically in 1993, it lost on its futures positions. Each dollar fall in the price of oil required margin payments of $154 million. While the losses on the minimum-volatility position were exactly offset by gains on the fixed-price contracts, the losses on the speculative positions had no offset; they were losses in the market value of Metallgesellschaft. In other words, assuming that the computation of the minimum-volatility hedge is correct, the futures loss of $154 million for a dollar fall in the price of oil was offset by an increase in the value of the long-term contracts of $86 million. The net loss for Metallgesellschaft of a $1 fall in the price of oil was $68 million.

MGRM's speculative position was based on gains from backwardation. In 1993, the markets were not in backwardation, but in contango. Contango describes a situation where futures prices are above spot prices. Hence, the source of gains MGRM counted on turned out to be illusory that year. Instead of making rollover gains from closing contracts at a higher price than the contracts being opened, Metallgesellschaft made rollover losses on the order of $50 million every month.

The massive losses on futures contracts grew to more than $1 billion. Some of these losses were offset by gains on the fixed-price contracts, but the net loss to the corporation was large because of the speculative position. The losses on futures contracts were current cash drains on the corporation because the gains on the fixed-price contracts would not be recovered until later. A hedging program that generates a cash drain of about $1 billion on a corporation with assets of $10 billion creates serious problems, although Metallgesellschaft could have raised funds to offset this liquidity loss.

If Metallgesellschaft thought that MGRM's speculative position was sound at the inception of the hedge program, it should have still thought so after the losses, and hence should have kept taking that position in order to maximize shareholder wealth. Losses, though, make people look at their positions more critically. It became harder to believe that backwardation was a free lunch.

Was the MGRM debacle a hedge that failed, or did Metallgesellschaft shrink from its speculation? After all, if it really believed that backwardation made money, the losses of 1993 were irrelevant. The strategy had to be profitable in the long run, not necessarily on a month by month or year by year basis. Losses could lead Metallgesellschaft to give up on the strategy only if it changed its position as to the expected profits of the speculation or could not afford the liquidity costs of the speculation.

Since Metallgesellschaft had lines of credit that it did not use, the most likely explanation is that the company gave up on the strategy. As it changed direction, the board wanted the new management to start on a clean slate, and so it decided to take all its losses quickly. This practice of taking a bath around management changes is not unusual, as discussed in Weisbach (1995).

What do we learn from the Metallgesellschaft experience? Mostly that large losing futures positions create liquidity drains due to the requirement to maintain margins, and also that it pays to compute the correct minimum-volatility hedges. When a company implements a hedging program with futures contracts, it is crucial to plan ahead for meeting the liquidity needs resulting from losing futures positions. The VaR of the futures contract provides an effective way to understand the distribution of the liquidity needs. With VaR, we know that over the period for which the VaR is computed, we have a 5 percent chance of losing that amount. A hedge that develops losing futures positions is not a bad hedge. On the contrary, if the hedge is properly designed, losing futures positions accompany winning cash positions, so that on net the company receives or loses nothing in terms of present values. It is true that gains and losses of positions might have implications for a company's liquidity. For Metallgesellschaft, the gains from a fall in oil prices would have to be paid over time by the holders of long-term contracts, while the losses from futures prices had to be paid immediately.

A hedged position that has no economic risk can be risky from an accounting perspective. This issue played a role in the case of Metallgesellschaft. In principle, a hedge can be treated from an accounting perspective in two different ways. First, the cash position and the hedge can be treated as one item. In this case, the losses on the hedge are offset by gains in the cash position, so that losses on a hedge position that is a perfect hedge have no implications for the earnings of the firm. Alternatively, the hedge position and the cash position can be treated separately. If accounting rules prevent the gains in the cash position that offset the losses in the hedge position from being recognized simultaneously, a firm can make large accounting earnings losses on a hedged position because gains on the cash position are not recognized at the same time as the losses on the hedge.

In this case, there could be no economic losses because cash position gains and losses on the hedge would offset each other exactly, yet there could be large accounting losses followed by large accounting gains as hedging losses would be recognized first and cash position gains would be recognized later. In the case of Metallgesellschaft, such a situation arose because accounting statements did not mark the cash position to market as oil prices changed, but the hedge losses were accounting losses as they occurred.

An intriguing question with the Metallgesellschaft case is whether the firm would have done better had it not hedged than with the hedge it used. From a risk management perspective, the only way this question makes sense is to ask whether Metallgesellschaft had more risk with the wrong hedge than with no hedge at all. The answer to that question depends on the assumptions one makes. A least one study, the one by Pirrong (1997), reaches the conclusion that an un-hedged Metallgesellschaft would have been less risky than the Metallgesellschaft with the hedge it used. Irrespective of how this question is decided, however, the risk of Metallgesellschaft would have been substantially smaller had it used the appropriate volatility-minimizing hedge. However, if one believes that back-wardation is a source of profits, Metallgesellschaft with the volatility-minimizing hedge would have been less profitable *ex ante*.

7.6. Summary

In this chapter, we examined some issues that arise because financial markets are not perfect. Financial market imperfections create basis risk. In a world of perfect financial markets, it would be costless to create new futures contracts, liquidity would not be an issue, and there would be contracts for any exposure a hedger might be concerned about. In the real world, there are few futures contracts compared to the plethora of exposures firms and investors want to hedge and liquidity is often a first-order determinant of the optimal hedge. We saw that basis risk reduces the size of the hedge. Liquidity can make it optimal to use short maturity contracts. Using contracts that have a shorter maturity than the exposure exposes the hedger to rollover risk. Rollover risk is the risk that the contract one must open has a price that differs from the price of the contract one is getting out of.

Hedging can be expensive, but it need not be so. When one hedges with derivatives traded in highly liquid markets, hedging generally has a low cost. Nevertheless, it is important to be able to deal with situations where the costs of hedging are high. To do so, one has to have a clear understanding of the costs of the risks that one is trying to hedge. We saw how this understanding can be put in quantitative terms to derive an optimal hedge. We showed that firms with lower costs of hedging or greater costs of risk hedge more. We then showed that treating exposures as portfolios of exposures reduces the costs of hedging because doing so takes into account the diversification across risks. In general, when a firm has exposures maturing at different dates, one has to focus on their present value or their value at a terminal date.

We concluded the chapter with the Metallgesellschaft story. At the very least, this story shows that the practical issues that have to be resolved in implementing a hedging program matter a great deal. Metallgesellshaft used short maturity contracts to hedge a long maturity exposure. It had the wrong hedge ratio. It lost hundreds of millions of dollars because of risk it thought it did not have.

Key Concepts

cross-hedge, 195

hedging costs, 190

market impact, 195

open interest, 195

rollover risk, 195

Review Questions

1. Why could hedging be costly?

2. Why hedge at all if hedging is costly?

3. What is rollover risk?

4. What is the marginal cost of CaR?

5. What does the optimal hedge depend on if hedging is costly?

6. What is a cross-hedge?

7. Why does diversification across exposures reduce hedging costs?

8. How does diversification across exposure maturities reduce hedging costs?

9. How does the optimal hedge change through time if returns are i.i.d.?

10. What were the weaknesses of the hedge put on by Metallgesellschaft?

Questions and Exercises

1. Consider a firm that has a long exposure in the Swiss franc for which risk, measured by CaR, is costly. Management believes that the forward price of the Swiss franc is low relative to the expected spot exchange rate at maturity of the forward contract. Suppose that management is right. Does that necessarily mean that the firm's value will be higher if management hedges less than it would if it believed that the forward price of the Swiss franc is exactly equal to the expected spot exchange rate?

2. Suppose you hedge jet fuel using oil futures. A consultant tells you that the basis risk in this hedge (the cash price you are hedging minus the oil futures price) is positively correlated with the changes in the S&P futures price. How could you use this information to improve your hedge?

3. A firm will receive a payment in one year of 10,000 shares of company XYZ. A share of company XYZ costs $100. The beta of that company is 1.5 and the yearly volatility of the return of a share is 30 percent The one-year interest rate is 10 percent The firm has no other exposure. What is the one-year CaR of this company?

4. Suppose the volatility of the market return is 15 percent and XYZ hedges out the market risk. What is the CaR of XYZ after it hedges the market risk?

5. Suppose that the marginal cost of CaR is $0.001 \times$ CaR for XYZ and it costs 0.2 cents for each dollar of the market portfolio XYZ sells short. Assuming that XYZ hedges up to the point where the market cost of CaR equals the marginal cost of hedging, how much does XYZ sell short?

6. Suppose that in our example of hedging the world market portfolio, we had found that the t-statistic of the Nikkei is 1.1 instead. What would be your concerns in using the Nikkei contract in your hedging strategy? Would you still use the contract to hedge the world market portfolio?

7. Suppose that a firm will receive 1 billion yen in 10 years. It wants to hedge the present value of this payment using the shortest maturity yen futures contract and roll over into the contract maturing in the two days before maturity of the shortest maturity contract. Suppose that this strategy means that the firm rolls its position over every month. How should this firm estimate its hedge ratio?

8. In question 7, could the firm improve its hedge using an additional futures contract? If yes, which?

9. You hire a consultant who tells you that if your hedge ratio is wrong, you are better off if it is too low rather than too high. Is this correct?

10. Suppose that Metallgesellshaft had 10-year exposures and that the minimum-volatility hedge ratio before tailing is 0.7. Assume that the 10-year interest rate is 10 percent. What is the effective long position in oil of Metallgesellschaft per barrel if it uses a hedge ratio of 1 per barrel? Does Metallgesellshaft have a greater or lower exposure to oil prices in absolute value if it uses a hedge ratio of 1 or a hedge ratio of 0?

Literature Note

Portfolio approaches to hedging take into account the expected gain associated with futures contracts as well as the risk reduction resulting from hedging. A number of papers discuss such approaches, including Rutledge (1976), Peck (1975), Anderson and Danthine (1981, 1983), Makin (1978) and Benninga, Eldo, and Zilcha (1984). Stulz (1984) develops optimal hedges in the presence of transaction costs. The analysis of this chapter which uses CaR and Var is new, but given our assumptions it is directly related to the analysis of Stulz (1984). Witt, Schroeder, and Hayenga (1987) compare different regression approaches to obtaining hedge ratios. Bailey, Ng, and Stulz (1992) study how hedges depend on the estimation period when hedging an investment in the Nikkei 225 against exchange rate risk. Extending optimal hedging models to take into account the liquidity of the hedging firms turns out to be difficult as demonstrated by Mello and Parsons (2000). However, their work shows that firms with limited liquidity may not be able to hedge as much and that careful attention has to be paid to liquidity.

Culp and Miller (1994) present the view that the hedging strategy of Metallgesellschaft was sensible. Edwards and Canter (1995), Mello and Parsons (1995) and Pirrong (1997) provide estimates of the minimum-volatility hedge for Metallgesellschaft.

Chapter 8

Identifying and Managing Cash Flow Exposures

Chapter **8** *Objectives*

At the end of this chapter, you will:

1. Understand how to hedge when exposures are uncertain.

2. Be able to design hedges using pro forma statements.

3. Know how to use economic models in the construction of hedging strategies.

4. Be able to use Monte Carlo analysis and regression analysis to obtain hedge ratios.

In the previous two chapters, we learned how to evaluate and hedge risks when exposures are fixed. Firms often face exposures that vary with risk factors. An example is where Export Inc.'s Swiss franc exposure depends on how competitive the firm is in Switzerland and how its competitiveness is affected by exchange rate changes. Another example is a bank that has a portfolio of mortgages. Typical mortgages can be prepaid without penalty. As interest rates fall below the mortgage rate, mortgages get prepaid. This means that the interest rate exposure of the bank changes as interest rate decreases because its high interest rate mortgages get prepaid. A third example is an airline exposed to the price of jet fuel. If oil prices increase sharply, the economy slows down and so does air travel. Consequently, as oil prices increase, an airline's consumption of jet fuel falls and so does its exposure to jet fuel.

Our key example in the previous two chapters was Export Inc. with a fixed exposure of one million Swiss francs on June 1. A fixed currency exposure arises, when a firm has receivables and payables in foreign currencies. There are several kinds of currency exposures. A firm's **transaction exposure** to a currency is the exposure that results from having receivables and payables in that currency. Transaction exposure results from past business deals. If Export were a car manufacturer, its transaction exposure to the Swiss franc might correspond to cars already sold but not yet paid for. A firm's **contractual exposure** to a currency is its exposure to that currency resulting from contractual commitments, both booked (there is a receivable) and unbooked (there is no receivable at this point). The company could also have (implicit or explicit) contracts to sell cars in the future at a fixed Swiss franc price. There is no transaction at this point; the cars may not have been produced and they certainly have not been shipped. Nevertheless, the present value of these contracts depends on the Swiss franc exchange rate. In general, however, the amount of business a firm does in a foreign country is affected by foreign exchange rate changes. An appreciation of the Swiss franc could enable the company to decrease the Swiss franc price of a car without reducing its dollar income from selling the car. By reducing the Swiss franc price of the car, the firm would become more competitive in Switzerland and could sell more cars. Hence, the firm's exposure to the Swiss franc will depend on the Swiss franc exchange rate because it affects the number of cars and the price of cars it sells in Switzerland. As a result, rather than having a fixed exposure to the Swiss franc, the firm has an exposure that depends on the exchange rate. A firm's **competitive exposure** to a risk factor is the sensitivity of the firm's cash flow to a change in the risk factor resulting from changes in the firm's competitive position.

In this chapter, we focus on how to estimate and hedge exposures that depend on risk factors such as the foreign exchange rate. In particular, we want to understand how to identify and quantify competitive exposures so that we can hedge them.

When an exposure is not fixed, a firm has both price risk and quantity risk. **Price risk** is what we have focused on so far: the risk resulting from unexpected changes in prices. **Quantity risk** is the risk associated with the actual exposure being different from the expected exposure. The quintessential example is the case of a grower wanting to hedge a wheat crop against unexpected changes in the price of wheat. The grower could hedge by going short the expected exposure with futures. His problem when hedging is that he does not know how many bushels he will harvest. Because the crop is random, the grower does not know his actual exposure for sure. If he goes short his expected crop, he may be insufficiently hedged (underhedged) if the actual crop is greater than expected and excessively hedged (overhedged) if it is smaller. By being underhedged, the grower has sold too few bushels on the futures market, so that some of his crop is not hedged and his income is lower if the price of wheat is unexpectedly low. By being overhedged, the grower has sold too many bushels on the futures market, so that given the size of his crop, he ends up being net short wheat and his income is higher if the price of wheat is lower than expected.

We first discuss the problem of hedging when all we know is the correlation between quantity and price risks. We then turn to exposures that depend explicitly on hedgeable risk factors. We focus our discussion on foreign exchange exposures, but the techniques we develop can be used whenever exposures are uncertain.

We show how to use pro forma analysis to identify the determinants of a firm's exposures. We frequently have to model a firm's cash flow to quantify its exposures, and Monte Carlo simulations are an important tool for this type of analysis. We discuss how to use Monte Carlo simulations to evaluate exposures and construct hedges. We also see how the regression approach developed in Chapters 6 and 7 can be used to evaluate firm exposures.

8.1. Price and quantity risks

We consider the optimal hedge when both quantity and price are random. Let's go back to Export Inc. Export expects on March 1 to receive one million Swiss francs on June 1. How does the analysis change when this cash flow is risky in Swiss francs?

8.1.1. Risky foreign currency cash flows

A foreign currency cash flow can be risky for many reasons. Suppose Export plans to sell computers in Switzerland on June 1. The Swiss franc price of the computers is fixed over time, but Export does not know how many computers it will sell. The cash flow in Swiss francs on June 1 is simply the number of computers Export sells times the price of the computers. In this case, the Swiss franc cash flow is random, so that the exposure to the Swiss franc is itself random. Or Export has already sold the computers, but there is default risk. If the purchaser defaults, Export earns less than the promised payment. Again, the exposure in Swiss francs is random because Export does not know how many Swiss francs it will receive on June 1.

Hedging can make a firm with random exposures worse off than if it had not hedged. Suppose Export sells computers to Risque Cie. It expects to receive one million Swiss francs and sells these Swiss francs forward. We know that selling forward one million Swiss francs would be the volatility-minimizing hedge absent quantity risk and that this hedge would make the hedged position riskless.

If Risque Cie defaults on the payment, Export may receive some Swiss francs or, in the worst scenario, nothing. Figure 8.1 shows Export's cash flow if it sells one million Swiss francs forward at $0.70 per Swiss franc as a function of how

Figure 8.1

Dollar cash flow of Export Inc. as a function of the dollar price of the Swiss franc and the amount paid by Risque Cie when Export sells one million Swiss francs forward at 0.7 per Swiss franc

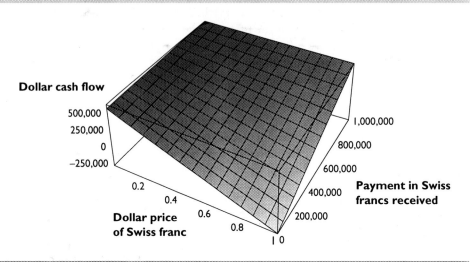

much it gets paid by Risque Cie and of the dollar price of the Swiss franc on June 1. If the price of the Swiss franc on June 1 is higher than the forward price and Export is paid only a fraction of the amount owed in Swiss francs, Export Inc. ends up having a negative cash flow even though it hedged its exchange rate exposure. This is because it does not have enough Swiss francs to deliver on its forward contract and has to buy Swiss francs on the spot market at a price higher than the forward exchange rate. Further, a firm that hedges can have a negative cash flow when a similar firm that does not hedge would never have a negative cash flow. Note that if Export does not hedge, its lowest cash flow is zero, but if it hedges, is not paid, and the Swiss franc is worth $0.80, Export has a negative cash flow of $100,000 when it sells Swiss francs forward at $0.90 per Swiss franc. In this scenario, Export would have a negative cash flow as long as it sold any Swiss francs forward to hedge.

How should Export hedge when its cash flow is random in foreign currency? Let c be the random Swiss franc cash flow and S be the exchange rate on June 1. In this case, Export's dollar cash flow on June 1 is cS. The expected cash flow is therefore $E(cS)$, and the variance of the dollar cash flow is $Var(cS)$. While we can decompose the variance of a sum of random variables into a sum of variances and covariances of the random variables, there is no such decomposition for products of random variables. The only way to compute $Var(cS)$ is to treat cS as a single random variable, and compute the variance that way. This single random variable, which we write C, is the dollar cash flow, so that $C = cS$.

We assume Export wants to take a futures position on March 1 that minimizes the volatility of the hedged cash flow on June 1. To start, we consider only hedges that involve a position in a single Swiss franc futures contract. Let $G_{June\ 1}$ be the price on June 1 of the Swiss franc futures contract Export uses. To avoid the issue of basis risk, we assume that the contract matures on June 1. We want to find h, which is the number of units of the futures contract Export should go short to hedge the dollar cash flow before tailing. If Export shorts h units of the futures contract, it makes a profit on the futures position of $-h(G_{\text{June 1}} - G_{\text{March 1}})$. Consequently, the hedged cash flow is the cash flow on June 1 plus the futures profit:

Hedged cash flow = C – h(G$_{\text{June 1}}$ – G$_{\text{March 1}}$)

We are back to the problem we solved in Chapter 6: trying to hedge a random payoff, C. Before, the random payoff was the random price, the exchange rate S, times a fixed quantity—one million Swiss francs in our example. Whether we call the random payoff S × 1M or C, the optimal hedge obeys the same formula. In Chapter 6, we wanted to find a futures position whose unexpected gain in value over the life of the hedge would best match an unexpected cash flow shortfall. The solution to that problem is to set h equal to the best predictor of the relation between cash flow and the change in the futures price. If the multivariate normal changes model holds for C (the random variable) and the futures price, the formula for this best predictor is given by the formula for the regression coefficient in a regression of cash flow changes on futures price changes.

Hence, the volatility-minimizing hedge for a random cash flow is:

$$h = \frac{\text{Cov(C, G)}}{\text{Var(G)}} \tag{8.1}$$

where G is the futures price at maturity of the hedge. This formula holds whenever we want to use a specific futures contract to hedge a random cash flow. The formula does not care about what C is. If we want to hedge rainfall with the Swiss franc futures contract, we would still use this formula, and we could still find the optimal hedge ratio using regression analysis if the proper conditions are met.

8.1.2. Optimal hedges with quantity risk

Quantity risk can dramatically alter the volatility-minimizing hedge as well as its effectiveness. Let's look at a simple quantitative example where quantity risk affects the exposure of Export Inc. Suppose the Swiss franc exchange rate in three months is either $0.50 or $1.50 with equal probability. The futures contract matures in three months, so the futures price in three months is the spot exchange rate, and the futures price today is $1. The firm's cash flow in foreign currency in three months is either 0.5 million Swiss francs or 1.5 million Swiss francs with equal probability, so its expected value is 1 million Swiss francs. Table 8.1 shows the possible combinations of the exchange rate and the Swiss franc cash flow for three assumptions about the correlation between the exchange rate and the Swiss franc cash flow: perfect positive correlation, no correlation, and perfect negative correlation.

To find out how to hedge Export's income, we need to know how cash flow covaries with the foreign exchange rate. Suppose first that the cash flow is perfectly positively correlated with the foreign exchange rate. In other words, the cash flow is 1.5 million Swiss francs when the foreign exchange rate is $1.50, and it is 0.5 million Swiss francs when the exchange rate is $0.50. The dollar cash flow is therefore either $2.25 million or $0.25 million with equal probability, so that

	Swiss franc cash flow and exchange rate outcomes for Export Inc. under various correlation assumptions		

Table 8.1 Swiss franc cash flow and exchange rate outcomes for Export Inc. under various correlation assumptions

	Cash flow in Swiss francs		
Dollar price of Swiss franc	Perfect positive correlation	No correlation	Perfect negative correlation
$1.5	1.5M	1.5M	0.5M
$1.5	1.5M	0.5M	0.5M
$0.5	0.5M	1.5M	1.5M
$0.5	0.5M	0.5M	1.5M

the expected cash flow is $1.25 million. This case is similar to the case where the grower has a large crop when the price of wheat is high: Quantity uncertainty increases cash flow volatility.

To compute the volatility-minimizing hedge using equation (8.1), we need to compute the covariance of the cash flow and the futures price and the variance of the futures price. The covariance between cash flow and the futures price and the variance of the futures price are, respectively:

$$0.5 \times (2.25M - 1.25M) \times (1.5 - 1) + 0.5 \times (0.25M - 1.25M) \times (0.5 - 1) = 0.5M \qquad \text{(Covariance)}$$

$$0.5 \times (1.5 - 1)^2 + 0.5 \times (0.5 - 1)^2 = 0.25 \qquad \text{(Variance)}$$

The optimal hedge is the ratio of the covariance and the variance, a short position equal to 0.5M/0.25 = 2 million Swiss francs.

In this example, the dollar cash flow depends only on the exchange rate because quantity and price risks are perfectly correlated. Remember that the formula does not care about what the random payoff in the covariance formula represents. As long as that random payoff is perfectly correlated with a futures price, the futures contract can be used to eliminate all risk. As a result, we can eliminate all risk because there is effectively only one source of risk, the exchange rate, and we can hedge that source of risk.

Let's now see what happens when quantity risk is uncorrelated with price risk. Suppose that the probability of the exchange rate taking the value $1.50 is 0.5. In this case, each state of the world is equally likely and has probability 0.25. We cannot construct a perfect cash flow hedge using only the currency futures contract. This is because the futures contract has the same payoff in these distinct states of the world. It pays the same when the exchange rate is $1.50, whether the Swiss franc cash flow is 1.5 million Swiss francs or 0.5 million Swiss francs. Consequently, the dollar cash flow is not perfectly correlated with the exchange rate. The volatility of the unhedged cash flow is $0.75 million.

One solution is to find additional hedging instruments whose payoff is correlated with the Swiss franc cash flow. In the absence of such instruments, the best we can do is to find the futures position that minimizes the volatility of the hedged position, knowing that we cannot make this volatility zero. This position is again given by the formula (8.1). The expected unhedged cash flow is $1 million.

Computing the covariance between the cash flow and the futures price, we have:

$$0.25 \times (2.25M - 1M) \times (1.5 - 1) + 0.25 \times (0.75M - 1M) \times (1.5 - 1) + 0.25 \times (0.75M - 1M) \times (0.5 - 1) + 0.25 \times (0.25M - 1M) \times (0.5 - 1) = 0.25M$$

Solving for the optimal hedge, we divide the covariance of 0.25 million by the variance of the futures price, which is 0.25 as before. We therefore find that the optimal hedge is to short one million Swiss francs, so that the firm goes short its expected exposure. The volatility of the hedged cash flow in this case is $559,017, so that by hedging, the best Export can do is to eliminate 25.46 percent of the volatility of unhedged cash flow.

Finally, suppose the futures price is perfectly negatively correlated with the Swiss franc cash flow. In this case, the exchange rate is $0.50 when the cash flow is 1.5 million Swiss francs and is $1.50 when the cash flow is 0.5 million Swiss francs. The firm receives $0.75 million when the exchange rate is low and the same amount when the exchange rate is high. No hedge is required to minimize the volatility of the dollar cash flow because the dollar cash flow in this case has no volatility.

The expected Swiss franc exposure is the same for each one of our examples, namely one million Swiss francs. Despite this, however, the optimal hedge is to go short two million Swiss francs when quantity risk and exchange rate risk are perfectly positively correlated, to go short one million Swiss francs when quantity risk and exchange rate risk are uncorrelated, and finally to take no futures position when quantity risk and exchange rate risk are perfectly negatively correlated. The effectiveness of the futures contract in hedging Export's cash flow depends on the correlation between Export's exposure and the price of the Swiss franc. In our example, the volatility of hedged cash flow is highest when exposure and exchange rate are uncorrelated.

8.2. The exposures of Motor Inc.

In general, quantities sold over time depend on many factors in addition to prices. For example, the sales of snowmobiles will depend on snowfall. Consequently, quantities sold depend on risk factors, so that uncertainty about cash flow arises because of uncertainty about prices as well as about quantities sold. We can use our understanding of how a firm makes money to assess both the quantity risks and the price risks it is exposed to. Often, consultants call the process of finding the risks a firm is exposed to a risk map for the firm. The best way to consider the various risks that can affect a firm and how to measure their impact on firm value is to look at an example. Let's suppose that Motor Inc. is a car producer in the United Kingdom that exports part of its production to the United States.

We would like to understand the distribution of future cash flows. This is a complicated undertaking because the cash flow for each year can be affected by a large number of variables. Some of these variables are directly under the control of Motor's management, such as plans the management has for the firm. For example, managers know they want to expand production by building a new factory that will start operations in three years. Other variables are not under the control of management. Some of these variables are specific to Motor's operations. For example, a factory could be destroyed by fire, or a strike that would stop production could take place. Such unique risks can be quantified, but no financial instruments are available to hedge these risks. Motor can reduce these risks in a variety of ways. It can install sprinklers and various alarm systems to minimize the danger of losing a plant to a fire. Once it has taken such protective measures, the only way that Motor can protect itself further against such risks is through insurance.

Motor faces risks that affect other firms as well. Business cycle risks affect all firms to some extent. Market risks—risk of changes in prices of financially traded instruments—matter for most if not all firms. A depreciation of the dollar, for example, means that, for a constant dollar price of its cars in the United States, Motor receives fewer pounds. An increase in the price of crude oil might mean that the demand for cars falls, and Motor's sales drop.

There is nothing Motor can do to affect the price of the dollar in pounds or the price of crude oil. For risk factors that affect many firms and are not under the control of individual firms, firms can often use financial instruments to hedge. An example of such a financial instrument is a futures contract on the dollar. The payoff of such a financial instrument does not depend at all on Motor's actions. However, Motor can sell dollars using this futures contract to reduce the dependence of its pound income on the dollar exchange rate. To do this, Motor has to figure out the size of the futures position that hedges its exchange rate risks. This position depends on how exchange rate changes affect Motor's future cash flows.

We measure the exposure of cash flow to a specific risk factor by the change in the value of a cash flow or the value of a financial asset for a unit change in that risk factor:

Exposure of cash flow to risk factor = Change in cash flow per unit change in risk factor   **(8.2)**

Let's consider a base case of constant exchange rates, no inflation, and no other source of uncertainty in Motor's cash flow. We assume that Motor will export 22,000 cars to the United States in 2002, sell each car for $20,000, and receive £0.50 per dollar. It will also sell 22,000 cars in the United Kingdom. In this case, Motor will receive $440 million from U.S. car sales. If the only effect of a change in the exchange rate for Motor is to change the pound value of the dollar sales, then Motor's exposure to the exchange rate is equal to $440M × Change in exchange rate = $440 million. Suppose that the dollar appreciates 10 percent, so that its price in pounds goes from £0.50 to £0.55. Multiplying the dollar exposure by the change in the pound price of the dollar, the cash flow impact of the appreciation is an increase in cash flow equal to $440M × £0.05, which is £22 million.

8.2.1. Cash flow exposure and time horizon

We can measure the exposure of firm value to the exchange rate by computing the exposure of discounted future cash flows to the exchange rate. The exposure changes as the cash flow measurement period is farther in the future. To see this, suppose first that we compute Motor's exposure to the dollar exchange rate for its next quarterly cash flow. Much of that exposure is fixed because it depends on transactions that have already been undertaken. For instance, the cars that will be sold in the United States during this quarter are already there; the prices have already been agreed upon with the dealers, and so on. In the short run, most cash flow exposure arises from booked transactions and pre-existing financial positions. For the time being, we ignore the exposures arising from financial positions and focus on the firm's other exposures.

Motor's exposure for the quarterly cash flow four quarters from now consists of two components. One component is the transaction exposure resulting from booked transactions. That is, Motor expects to receive or to make payments for dollar transactions that are already contracted for and booked today.

The other component is the contractual exposure not associated with booked transactions. Motor has contractual agreements, implicit or explicit, that affect its exposure in the future. It has made commitments to dealers about prices. Such commitments create contractual exposures that do not show up on the firm's balance sheet, yet any change in the exchange rate affects the value of the firm through its effect on the domestic currency value of these commitments.

Motor's promise to deliver a fixed number of cars to dealers in the United States at a fixed dollar price creates a contractual exposure. The pound value of the payments from the dealers is the dollar value of these payments translated at the exchange rate prevailing when the payments are made. For such an exposure, the relevant exchange rate is the nominal exchange rate at the time of these payments.

The exposures at longer horizons, however, are competitive exposures. Very little of the exposure of cash flow three years from now is contractual exposure. Recognize that, as the exchange rate changes, Motor can change its production, marketing, and sourcing strategies. If the exchange rate changes so that keeping U.S. sales constant is not profitable, Motor can change its sales. It can develop new markets or new products. The nature of the firm's competitive exposures thus depends on the markets in which the firm does business.

Competitive exposures are sometimes called operating exposures, or economic exposures. However, exposures associated with the firm's current operations do not capture the strategic implications of exchange rate changes that are part of the firm's competitive exposures—exchange rate changes affect not only the profitability of current operations but what the firm does and where it does it.

8.2.2. Competitive exposures

There is much literature on competitive exposures that emphasizes the importance of the type of competition the firm faces. To understand this, let's consider two cases for Motor's U.S. sales. At one extreme, Motor could have no competitors. In this case, the key determinant of Motor's exposure to the dollar exchange rate would be the price-sensitivity of the demand for its cars (i.e., the percentage change in demand for a percent change in the price).

Figure 8.2 shows what happens when the demand is not very price-sensitive. Panel A shows the demand curve in pounds, and Panel B shows it in dollars. Whatever the case considered, Motor sells cars up to the point where the

---

Figure 8.2   Impact of a depreciation of the dollar on Motor's exports when competition is limited

Panel A. Impact on the pound price of cars sold in the United States

Before the depreciation of the dollar, the pound price of cars sold in the United States is P and is given by the point on the demand curve DD corresponding to the quantity where the marginal revenue curve MR intersects the marginal cost curve MC. As the dollar depreciates, the demand shifts to DD' and the marginal revenue curve shifts to MR'. The price in pounds falls to P' and the quantity exported falls to Q'.

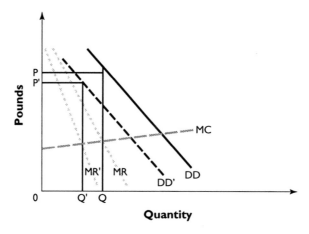

Panel B. Impact on the dollar price of cars sold in the United States

Before the depreciation of the dollar, the dollar price of cars sold in the United States is P and is given by the point on the demand curve DD corresponding to the quantity where the marginal revenue curve MR intersects the marginal cost curve MC. As the dollar depreciates, the marginal cost curve moves to MC'. The dollar price increases to P' and the quantity exported falls to Q'.

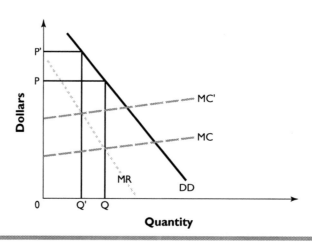

marginal revenue (the impact on total revenue of selling one more car) equals the marginal cost (the impact on total cost of selling one more car). As the dollar depreciates, there is no effect on the demand curve in dollars. For any quantity sold, however, the demand curve in pounds falls by the extent of the depreciation of the dollar. Hence, a depreciation of the dollar shifts the demand curve in pounds downward in Panel A but leaves the demand curve in dollars unchanged in Panel B.

If costs are denominated exclusively in pounds, the marginal cost curve in pounds is unaffected by the depreciation of the dollar. The net effect of the depreciation of the dollar is to reduce the quantity and increase the dollar price of the cars sold in the United States. The dollar price of cars sold does not, however, increase by the full amount of the depreciation. For Motor as a monopolist, the exchange rate exposure is roughly equal to the dollar revenue before the depreciation.

The opposite case is that Motor sells cars in a highly competitive market. In this case, as shown in Figure 8.3, the marginal revenue curve is equal to the demand curve. The demand for Motor's cars is highly price-sensitive. Suppose first that the competitors of Motor are American firms with dollar costs, so that nothing changes for Motor's competition as the dollar depreciates.

Looking at Panel A of Figure 8.3 (demand curve is in pounds), we see that a depreciation of the dollar moves the demand curve downward by the extent of the depreciation. Equivalently, when we look at Panel B, we see that the dollar marginal cost curve is shifted upward by the depreciation.

The depreciation actually pushes the pound demand curve completely below the pound marginal cost curve, so that it is no longer profitable for the firm to sell in the United States. In this case, Motor's exposure depends on its ability to shift sales away from the United States. If the firm can shift sales rapidly and at low cost, it may not have much exposure to the exchange rate.

What if Motor is a small automaker in a highly competitive U.S. market dominated by German car makers? Suppose that the demand for the market as a whole is not price-sensitive, but the demand for Motor's cars is extremely price-sensitive because German cars are good substitutes for Motor's cars. Motor thus has very little ability to set its prices. In this case, the key determinant of Motor's exposure to the dollar exchange rate is how the euro and the pound prices of the dollar move together. Suppose Motor expects the two exchange rates to move closely together, or that a depreciation of the dollar with respect to the pound also means a depreciation of the dollar with respect to the euro. Consequently, the German producers increase their dollar prices and Motor can do the same. Then the impact of the depreciation on cash flow should be fairly small.

But suppose that the pound price of the dollar and the euro price of the dollar move independently. Now an appreciation of the pound against the dollar without an appreciation of the euro against the dollar has an adverse effect on Motor's income from dollar sales and may force it to exit the U.S. market. An appreciation of the euro against the dollar that is not accompanied by an appreciation of the pound against the dollar is good news for Motor because its competitors in the United States raise their dollar prices. In this case, Motor has

| **Figure 8.3** | Impact of a depreciation of the dollar on Motor's exports when the market for its cars is very competitive |

Panel A. Impact on the pound price of cars sold in the United States

Before the depreciation of the dollar, the pound price of cars sold in the United States is P and is given by the point on the demand curve DD corresponding to the quantity where the marginal revenue curve MR intersects the marginal cost curve MC. As the dollar depreciates, the demand shifts to DD' and the marginal revenue curve shifts to MR'. Sales in the United States are no longer profitable.

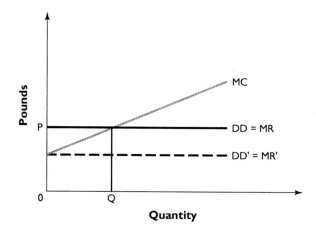

Panel B. Impact on the dollar price of cars sold in the United States

Before the depreciation of the dollar, the dollar price of cars sold in the United States is P and is given by the point on the demand curve DD corresponding to the quantity where the dollar marginal revenue curve MR intersects the marginal cost curve MC. As the dollar depreciates, the dollar marginal cost curve shifts upward to MC'. Sales in the United States are no longer profitable.

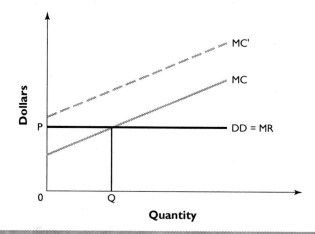

an exposure to the euro even though it does not export to Germany. The reason for this is that its competitors are German.

This is a highly simplified analysis, but it shows how one has to consider the firm's competitive position to evaluate its exchange rate exposure. We have assumed that the only source of Motor's exchange rate exposure is its revenue from the United States. In general, however, some of Motor's costs also depend on the exchange rate. For example, Motor could incur some costs in the United States to sell cars there. This complicates the analysis. In this case, the pound cost of Motor's cars sold in the United States falls as the pound appreciates since the dollar costs are now less in pounds. This shifts the marginal cost curve downward, and hence reduces Motor's loss from an appreciation of the pound.

8.3. Using the pro forma statement to evaluate exposures

Motor's cash flow statement for 2001 is given in Table 8.2. We can forecast Motor's cash flow statement for a particular year based on assumptions about the variables that affect cash flow. This is a pro forma statement. In preparing the pro forma statement, Motor must make assumptions about risk factors. The pro forma approach to evaluating cash flow exposures estimates the exposure of each item of the pro forma statement to a risk factor by how much the item would change if that risk factor changes by a given amount. Adding the exposures across all items of the cash flow statement tells us the exposure of cash flow for a given change in the risk factor.

Suppose that the only risk factor that affects Motor's cash flow is the dollar/pound exchange rate. Motor's cash flow exposure to the exchange rate is the sum of the exposures of the components of the cash flow statement. To see this, consider our simple cash flow statement:

Cash flow = Sales – Costs of goods sold – Investment – Taxes

The exposure of cash flow to the exchange rate as defined by equation (8.2) is the impact of a unit change in the exchange rate on cash flow. Consequently, the impact on cash flow of a £0.01 change in the pound price of the dollar is (cash flow exposure) × 0.01.

The base case for Motor's cash flow for 2002 assumes 10 percent growth in sales, costs, and investment from the cash flow statement for 2001, a tax rate of 25 percent, and an exchange rate of £0.50 per dollar:

Sales – Costs of goods sold – Taxes – Investment = Cash flow

£440M – £330M – 0.25 × £110M – £55M = £27.5M

Cash flow statement of Motor Inc. for 2001 (in million pounds)	*Table 8.2*

The exchange rate is £0.5 per dollar. The tax rate is assumed to be 25 percent.

Sales in United States 20,000 units at $20,000 each	200
Sales in United Kingdom 20,000 units at £10,000 each	200
Cost of sales	(300)
Taxes 0.25 × (£400 – £300)	(25)
Investment	(50)
Net cash flow	25

A change in the exchange rate can affect every component of cash flow, but suppose for now that it changes only the pound value of U.S. sales, keeping the dollar value of these sales unchanged. In this case, the exposure of cash flow is simply the amount of U.S. sales times one minus the tax rate of 25 percent. The tax rate is generally ignored in discussions of exposure, but it is important. Dollar depreciation reduces the firm's cash flow and its taxable income. Each pound lost because of the drop in the pound value of dollar sales means that taxes paid are reduced by a quarter of a pound. If the dollar price per car and the number of cars sold in the United States are constant, the dollar revenue is constant. The dollar exposure of Motor's cash flow is then simply its dollar revenue times one minus the tax rate. In this case:

Cash flow exposure of Motor Inc. to the dollar
= Dollar revenue of Motor Inc. × (1 − 0.25)

Using the pro forma cash flow statement, this corresponds to $440M × (1 − 0.25), or $330 million. The cash flow exposure can then be used to compute cash flow under different assumptions about exchange rate changes. If managers believe that the worst possible exchange rate move is a 10 percent depreciation, they can use the exposure measure to compute the resulting cash flow shortfall. A 10 percent depreciation means that cash flow has a shortfall of:

Cash flow exposure of Motor Inc. to the dollar
× Pound value of 10% depreciation of the dollar

Remember that we assume the dollar to be worth £0.50 in the base case. This means that a 10 percent depreciation of the dollar brings the dollar from £0.50 to £0.45. Under our assumptions, this shortfall is thus £16.5 million, or $330M × 0.05.

An alternative calculation uses the exposure to compute the volatility of cash flow. If the dollar exchange rate is the only risk affecting cash flow:

Volatility of cash flow in pounds = Exposure × Volatility of exchange rate

Suppose that the volatility of the exchange rate is 10 percent per year. In this case, the pound volatility of the 2002 cash flow viewed from the end of 2001 depends on the volatility of the exchange rate over a one-year period. This gives us a cash flow volatility of 10 percent of £0.50 × $330M, or £16.5 million. The volatility of cash flow allows us to compute cash flow at risk, CaR. Remember that if the cash flow is distributed normally, the fifth percentile of the distribution of cash flow is 1.65 times the volatility of cash flow. Consequently, £16.5M × 1.65 gives us £27.225 million. There is one chance in twenty that the cash flow shortfall will be at least £27.225 million below projections assuming no change in the exchange rate.

8.4. Modeling cash flow exposures

The analysis of Motor's exchange rate exposure becomes more complicated if either the dollar price of cars or the quantity of cars sold in the United States also changes with the dollar exchange rate. Ignoring taxes and investment for simplicity, the cash flow is the revenue from selling cars minus the cost of producing the cars sold. To compute the worst outcome for a dollar depreciation, we have to make assumptions about the demand curve and the marginal cost curve. We can use our understanding of the economics of the firm to do that.

A simple way for Motor to proceed with the pro forma approach is to estimate the number of cars sold and the price for a given change in the exchange rate. It can then compute the cash flow for a given exchange rate. To estimate its CaR, Motor would have to construct a schedule of possible exchange rate scenarios, assign a probability to each exchange rate, and estimate dollar sales for each exchange rate.

Table 8.3 shows an example of such a schedule. The schedule assumes that Motor's dollar sales increase as the dollar appreciates. Costs increase also since Motor is producing more cars. This would correspond to a situation where Motor can cut dollar prices as the dollar appreciates and increase its sales volume. Taxes are ignored for simplicity.

We can use the schedule to compute Motor's expected dollar exposure, which is $458 million. Note, however, that the actual exposure is different for each exchange rate since the dollar sales depend on the exchange rate, so that Export has quantity risk. The table has five equally likely outcomes. CaR is computed from the fifth percentile of the cash flow distribution, which corresponds to the worst outcome among the five possible outcomes. This means that the CaR of Motor when it is unhedged is the expected cash flow of £93.50M minus £52M, or £41.50M.

Motor could proceed more analytically and construct a model of dollar sales as a function of the exchange rate. Doing so would force Motor to be consistent across scenarios and would provide it with more precise estimates of its CaR and exposures (since this approach differs from the one used to obtain the estimates of Table 8.3, it leads to different estimates). We consider the case corresponding to Figure 8.3, where for simplicity we assume that Motor sells only in the United States and that there are no taxes. Let's further assume that Motor's marginal revenue of selling in the United States is fixed and does not depend on Motor's actions because it sells in a highly competitive market. In this case, the dollar marginal revenue is equal to the price of a car, which is assumed to be $20,000.

Cash flow scenarios for Motor for different exchange rates   *Table 8.3*

Sales in dollars	Exchange rate (pound price of dollar)	Pound sales income	Costs	Cash flow	Probability
$560M	0.60	£336M	£200M	£136M	0.2
$500M	0.55	£275M	£160M	£115M	0.2
$440M	0.50	£220M	£130M	£90M	0.2
$410M	0.45	£184.5M	£110M	£74.5M	0.2
$380M	0.40	£152M	£100M	£52M	0.2

Motor's marginal cost in pounds depends on its cost function. We assume that Motor's total cost is given by the following function:

Cost = 10M + 0.25 × (Quantity produced)²

Using our cost function, the marginal cost of a car is:

Marginal cost of a car = 0.5 × (Quantity produced)

Let S be the price of a dollar in pounds. Motor chooses its car production so that the marginal revenue from selling one more car equals the marginal cost of producing it. Marginal revenue is S × 20,000. Setting marginal revenue equal to marginal cost, we have:

Quantity produced = S × 40,000

The cash flow is:

Cash flow = Quantity produced × Car price – Cost of producing the cars

= (S × 40,000) × S × 20,000 – 10M – 0.25 (S × 40,000)²

= 400M × S² – 10M   (8.3)

Figure 8.4 shows the cash flow in pounds as a function of the pound price of the dollar. Cash flow depends on the square of the exchange rate. The reason is that as the dollar appreciates, so that S increases, both the pound cash flow from selling one car and the number of cars sold increase. Consequently, if the exchange rate is high, Motor receives more dollars and hence has a larger dollar exposure. The fact that cash flow is not a linear function of the exchange rate has extremely important implications for exposure calculations. It implies that the change in

---

Figure 8.4   Motor's cash flow as a function of the pound price of a dollar

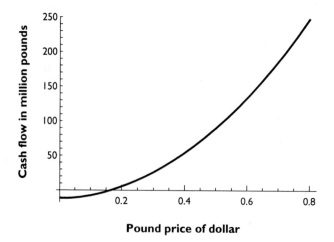

cash flow is not proportional to the size of the change in the exchange rate: the change in cash flow if the exchange rate increases by some amount is not twice the change in cash flow if the exchange rate increases half that amount. The exposure now depends on the exchange rate change and the level of the exchange rate.

To see this, suppose we start from an exchange rate of £0.50 and it falls to £0.45. In this case, the quantity of cars sold in the United States becomes 18,000 and cash flow falls to £71 million. Consequently, the change in cash flow per unit change in the exchange rate is £19M/0.05, or $380 million. However, if we consider a change in the dollar so that it depreciates by 50 percent, the profit falls by £75 million, so that the exposure per unit change is £75M/0.25, or $300 million. Had the initial exchange rate been £0.80 instead, a drop of £0.05 to £0.75 would have led to a loss of £31 million since income would have fallen from £246 million to £215 million. Consequently, at £0.80, the exposure of cash flow per unit change is $620 million. This means that to compute the loss resulting from a depreciation of the dollar we have to compute the cash flow for the exchange rate after the depreciation and compare it to the cash flow before the depreciation. Instead of having one exposure measure that applies irrespective of the magnitude of the exchange rate change, we now have an exposure measure for each exchange rate change.

What is the volatility-minimizing hedge for Motor? We already know that the volatility-minimizing hedge satisfies equation (8.1). We assume that there is no basis risk, so that the futures price at maturity of the hedge is equal to the spot price, S = G. Applying the equation, we have:

$$h = \frac{\text{Cov}\left[\text{Cash flow, S}\right]}{\text{Var(S)}}$$

$$= \frac{\text{Cov}\left[400M \times S^2 - 10M, S\right]}{\text{Var(S)}} \tag{8.4}$$

Calculation of the volatility-minimizing hedge is not straightforward since we need to know the covariance of the square of the exchange rate with the exchange rate. Motor can solve for h explicitly using the distribution of the exchange rate. This is possible as long as the distribution of the square of the exchange rate can be obtained from the distribution of the exchange rate. We assumed that the exchange rate is normally distributed with an expected value of £0.50 and a volatility of 0.1. With that assumption, the volatility-minimizing hedge is to short $400 million.

The hedge depends on the distribution assumed for the exchange rate. The normal distribution is a symmetric distribution, so that the expected value of the excess of the random variable over its mean if that excess is positive has the same absolute value as the excess of the random variable over its mean if that excess is negative. More generally, for any constant k and normally distributed random variable x, $E[x - E(x) \mid x > E(x)] = -E[x - E(x) \mid x < E(x)]$, where $E[x - E(x) \mid x > E(x)]$ means the expected value of $x - E(x)$ given that x is greater than its mean, $E(x)$. The lognormal distribution is a skewed distribution. With the lognormal distribution, the expected value of the excess of the random variable over its mean if that excess is positive is greater than the absolute value of the expected value of the excess of the random variable over its mean if that excess is negative. For any constant k and lognormally distributed random variable x, $E[x - E(x) \mid x > E(x)]$ $> - E[x - E(x) \mid x < E(x)]$. To understand why this is so, remember that we use the lognormal distribution for stock prices. With the lognormal distribution for stock prices, the stock price cannot be negative. However, it can take any value that is positive, no matter how great compared to the mean.

To see how the distribution of the exchange rate change affects the hedge, let's compare the volatility-minimizing hedge when the exchange rate is normally distributed to the case when it is lognormally distributed. If we assume that S is lognormally distributed with expected value of 0.5 and with volatility 0.1, the volatility-minimizing hedge requires selling $424.32 million on the futures market. Technical Box 8.1, Computing the hedge, provides the details of the calculation of the hedge when the exchange rate is normally distributed as well as when it is lognormally distributed.

As exchange rate volatility increases, the number of dollars sold forward increases if the exchange rate is lognormally distributed, which is shown in Figure 8.5, but does not change if the exchange rate is normally distributed. This is due to the skewness of the lognormal distribution, which increases the covariance of cash flow with the exchange rate and hence makes the hedge ratio larger. Since skewness increases with volatility for the lognormal distribution, greater volatility makes the hedge ratio larger.

In general, it is not possible to get a formula that gives us the hedge when the exposure is not linear. When such a formula cannot be obtained, two approaches make it possible to get the hedge. The first approach uses the delta exposure measure. The second approach uses simulations (discussed in section 8.6.).

Figure 8.5   **Volatility-minimizing hedge as a function of σ**

σ is the parameter in the lognormal distribution. Keeping the expected exchange rate constant, the size of the volatility-minimizing hedge increases with σ.

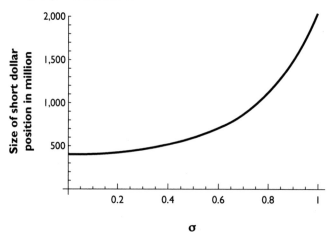

Computing the hedge   *Technical Box 8.1*

Note first that:

$$\frac{Cov\left(400S^2, S\right)}{Var(S)} = \frac{400E\left[\left(S^2 - E\left(S^2\right)\right)\left(S - E(S)\right)\right]}{E\left[\left(S - E(S)\right)^2\right]}$$

$$= \frac{400\left[E\left(S^3\right) - E(S)E\left(S^2\right)\right]}{E\left(S^2\right) - E\left(S^2\right)}$$

We can then get $E(S^2)$ and $E(S^3)$ using properties of the normal distribution if S is normally distributed. If x is normally distributed with mean a and standard deviation b:

$$E\left(x\right) = a$$

$$E\left(x^2\right) = a^2 + b^2$$

$$E\left(x^3\right) = a^3 + 3ab^2$$

In our example, a is 0.5 and b is 0.1. Consequently, $E(S^2)$ is 0.26, and $E(S^3)$ is 0.14. Plugging the numbers in the formula for the hedge gives us:

$$\frac{Cov\left(400S^2, S\right)}{Var(S)} = \frac{400E\left[\left(S^3\right) - E(S)E\left(S^2\right)\right]}{E\left(S^2\right) - E(S)^2}$$

$$= \frac{400\left[0.14 - 0.5 \times 0.26\right]}{0.26 - 0.5 \times 0.5}$$

$$= 400$$

Turning to the lognormal distribution, let x be distributed lognormally with mean and variance:

$$E\left(x\right) = Exp\left[\mu + 0.5\sigma^2\right]$$

$$Var\left(x\right) = Exp\left[2\mu + \sigma^2\right]\left[Exp\left(\sigma^2\right) - 1\right]$$

We then have:

$$E\left(x^2\right) = Exp\left[2\mu + 2\sigma^2\right]$$

$$E\left(x^3\right) = Exp\left[3\mu + 9\sigma^2/2\right]$$

For $E(S)$ to be 0.5 and $Var(S)$ to be 0.01, we need $\mu = -0.712758$ and $\sigma = 0.198042$. We can then get $E(S^2)$ to be equal to 0.26 and $E(S^3)$ to be equal to 0.140608. This gives us a hedge of $424.32 million.

For small changes in the exchange rate, the change in exposure associated with a change in the exchange rate is a second-order effect that can be ignored. Consequently, to hedge against small changes in a risk factor, we can go short the exposure to that risk factor at the current value of that risk factor. The delta measure of exposure is the exposure measure that is appropriate for a small change in the risk factor, so that the optimal hedge for a small change in the risk factor is to go short the delta exposure with respect to that risk factor. As long as large changes are a succession of small changes, we can simply adjust our hedge as the risk factor changes, so that hedging against small changes works out.

The delta measure of exposure with respect to a risk factor is given by:[1]

Delta exposure of cash flow to a risk factor

> = **Cash flow change per unit change in the risk factor evaluated for an infinitesimal change in the risk factor**   (8.5)

The delta exposure approach to computing exposures treats cash flow as if it were a linear function of the risk factor at the current level of the risk factor. This amounts to treating the exposure as a constant. For Motor, computing the delta exposure at the current exchange rate amounts to approximating exposure by the exposure the firm has at the current exchange rate for a small change in the exchange rate. The exposure is then given by the delta exposure of the cash flow to the exchange rate. Using the delta exposure, the impact of a change in the exchange rate on cash flow is then computed as the product of the delta exposure times the change in the exchange rate.

The slope of the cash flow function in Figure 8.6 measures the change in cash flow for an infinitesimal change in the exchange rate. Expressed in terms of a unit change in the exchange rate, the delta exposure is equal to $400 million for an exchange rate of £0.50, which corresponds to the U.S. sales revenue in dollars at that exchange rate. Using the delta exposure, we find that a £0.05 increase in the value of the dollar increases pound profits by £20 million, since we have £0.05 × $400M. Note now that this implies that we need a hedge where we gain £20 million if the pound price of the dollar decreases by £0.05. We therefore want to be short the delta exposure of $400 million, or $20M/0.05.

As the exchange rate changes, the delta exposure changes and the hedge has to be adjusted. In this case, an increase in the exchange rate increases the delta exposure, so that one has to sell more dollars short as the pound price of the dollar increases.

The delta exposure approach is an approximation, but it does well here. We already saw that Motor's net cash flow at an exchange rate of £0.50 is £90 million and that its net cash flow at an exchange rate of £0.45 is £71 million. Hence, computing the net cash flow change due to a depreciation of the dollar exchange rate of £0.05 yields a change of £19 million. With the delta approximation, we

---

1   If cash flow is a function that can be differentiated, the cash flow risk factor delta is technically the partial derivative of cash flow with respect to the risk factor.

Cash flow and exchange rate

Figure 8.6

This figure gives the cash flow for Motor Inc. as a function of the pound price of the dollar. Cash flow is a non-linear function of the exchange rate. The delta foreign exchange rate exposure measures the impact of a small increase in the exchange rate by using the slope of the cash flow function. This approach is accurate for small changes in the exchange rate, but here for larger increases it predicts a bigger fall in cash flow than actually occurs. If the exchange rate falls from £0.50 to £0.25, the loss predicted by the delta exposure of $400 million is £100 million, while the actual loss predicted by the cash flow function is £75 million.

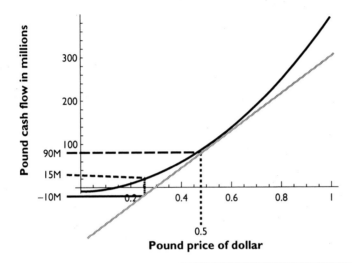

estimate this change to be £20 million, or £0.05 × 400M. The approximation is therefore fairly good in this case.

The delta approximation can be imprecise for larger changes in the risk factor and can even lead to absurd results. For example, suppose that the pound price of the dollar falls by £0.25 without Motor having a chance to adjust its hedge. In this case, the delta measure implies a loss of £0.25 × 400M, or £100 million. We have seen that the actual loss when we compute the profits explicitly at that new exchange rate is £75 million, or three-quarters of the predicted loss. The approximation does not work well for large changes because for large changes the firm adjusts production and sales, whereas the delta approximation assumes that everything stays unchanged.

If we use the delta measure, we are short $400 million, so that we gain £100 million as the pound price of the dollar falls by half. Yet, our cash flow falls by £75 million, so that we make an unexpected gain in our hedged position of £25 million. One might be tempted to say that there is no reason to complain since we make more money than expected. However, in terms of risk management, what matters is that we make an unexpected gain, so that our cash flow is volatile. What we want to do through hedging is minimize the volatility of hedged cash flow. Here we do not succeed because the cash flow is not a linear function of the exchange rate. As a result of this feature of cash flow, a static hedge (a hedge that is unchanged over the hedging period) cannot work equally well for all changes in the exchange rate. A hedge that works well for small changes may not work well for large changes.

The result that the exposure to a small exchange rate change is equal to sales in that currency at the current exchange rate is a result that holds well beyond our example. Marston (1996) argues that this result holds in a large number of cases. For instance, it holds both in the monopolistic case and the duopoly case where the firms take into account the impact of their actions on their competitor.

8.5. Using regression analysis to measure exposure

Measuring a firm's exposure can be quite complicated even in extremely simplified examples. If we are concerned about how exchange rate changes affect the value of a large firm with many different activities, an analytic approach similar to the one described earlier would seem difficult to implement. Even if we were able to implement such an approach, we would want to have some way to check whether its results are sensible. An important way to evaluate a firm's exposure is simply to look at the history of that firm. One may regress cash flow on risk factors if one believes that the joint distribution of cash flow and risk factors is relatively constant. Alternatively, one may regress the stock return (the rate of change of the present value of future cash flows) on rates of change of risk factors. Such an approach is quite valuable when one believes that the future will not be too different from the past.

A firm's exposure to a risk factor makes its equity value sensitive to this risk. We can evaluate this sensitivity using regression analysis. We decompose the random return of the firm into one part that depends on the risk factor and one part that does not. We would like to estimate the sensitivity of the firm's equity to some risk factor. We can obtain this sensitivity by regressing the return of the firm's equity on the percentage change or return of that factor:

$$R_{i,t} = \alpha_i + \beta_i R_{x,t} + \epsilon_{i,t} \qquad (8.6)$$

In this regression, $R_{i,t}$ is the firm's cash flow or return on its securities, α_i is the constant, β_i measures the exposure of the firm to the particular risk factor, $R_{x,t}$ is the return of the risk factor, and $\epsilon_{i,t}$ is the error term. The beta measure of the sensitivity of the value of the firm to the risk factor of interest is valid whether this factor is the interest rate, foreign exchange rate, commodity prices, and/or some macroeconomic variable of interest. We assumed that the i.i.d. returns model holds for all the variables in the regression.

There is an important difference between the analytical approach used in the previous section and the regression approach. All sources of correlation of firm value with the U.S. dollar/pound exchange rate affect the beta coefficient. One should be cautious using regressions and should evaluate the results using our understanding of the firm's economic situation. For example, suppose Motor sells to Canada instead of selling to the United States, but we do not know this. If we estimate a regression of Motor's equity return on the change in the U.S. dollar/pound exchange rate. Motor's sales to Canada would affect Motor's regression beta on the U.S. dollar/pound exchange rate because the Canadian dollar/pound exchange rate is correlated with the U.S. dollar/pound exchange rate. As a result, we might conclude that the firm is exposed to a U.S. dollar/pound exchange rate when it is not because it is exposed to a risk factor that is correlated with the currency used in the regression. If the correlation between the U.S. dollar and the Canadian dollar exchange rates is stable, then using the U.S. dollar to hedge works, but probably not as well as using the Canadian dollar. However, if the correlation is not stable, then changes in the correlation between the two currencies can create serious problems. In that case, using the U.S. dollar as a hedge for the true risk factor may no longer work if the correlation has changed, but since we don't know that the U.S. dollar proxies for the true risk factor, the Canadian dollar, we don't know that it no longer works! This means that we should always be cautious when using regressions and evaluate the results using our understanding of the firm's economic situation.

To estimate the sensitivity of the equity of Motor to the U.S. dollar/pound exchange rate only, we have to estimate the regression controlling for other sources of risk that affect the equity of Motor and are correlated with the U.S. dollar/pound exchange rate. This means that if there are two sources of risk for Motor's equity, like the U.S. dollar/pound exchange rate and the Canadian dollar/pound exchange rate, we would have to regress the return on Motor's equity on the two sources of risk. However, if we are interested in Motor's sensitivity with respect to exchange rates for the purpose of risk management, we would have to regress Motor's equity return only on the sources of risk for which hedging instruments are available and will be used. If the only hedging instrument we intend to use is a forward contract on the U.S. dollar, we can use this contract to partly hedge the firm's exposure to the Canadian dollar since that currency's changes are correlated with those of the U.S. dollar.

To estimate the exposure of the firm to several risk factors, we use a multiple regression. With such a regression, we regress the return on the firm's equity on all the sources of risk we are interested in. For example, if we are concerned about the firm's exposure to the stock market as well as to one other risk factor, we estimate the multiple regression:

$$R_{i,t} = \alpha_i + \beta_i R_{m,t} + \gamma_i R_{x,t} + \epsilon_{i,t} \tag{8.7}$$

where $R_{m,t}$ is the return on the market portfolio, β_i is the exposure of the firm to the stock market, $R_{x,t}$ is another risk factor, and γ_i is its exposure to the additional risk factor. In the case of exchange rates, Jorion (1990) uses the regression in equation (8.7) to evaluate the exposure of U.S. multinational firms to the dollar price of a trade-weighted basket of foreign currencies. He shows that the exposure to the price of a basket of foreign currencies systematically increases as a firm has more foreign operations.

A multiple regression analysis could be used to evaluate all of a firm's exposures to risk factors, but it is hard to estimate exposures to many risk factors precisely using the regression approach. A firm may be exposed to exchange rates from more than one country as well as to interest rates and to commodity prices it uses as inputs to production. The implementation of the multiple regression approach then uses many different risk factors as independent variables. The problem that arises with this approach, though, is that risk factors are correlated.

A good example is General Motors, a large automobile manufacturer with global sales and competition. Its Opel subsidiary is located in Europe and accounts for a large portion of the firm's international vehicle sales. A high percentage of these sales are made in the German market. General Motors faces major competition from Japanese firms in both the North American and the European markets. Finally, a high percentage of the firm's vehicle sales are financed, so we expect vehicle sales are exposed to the level of interest rates. We would expect that the firm is exposed to the value of the yen and euro against the dollar and to the level of U.S. interest rates. We will assume that the exposure of GM against the euro is well approximated by its exposure against the German mark (DM), so that we can use a long time-series of GM returns in our regression analysis.

If we first want to know the exposure of GM to the value of the German mark, while controlling for the general market factors, we consider the following regression:

$$R_{GM,t} = \alpha_{GM} + \beta_{GM} R_{m,t} + \gamma_{GM} R_{DM,t} + \epsilon_{GM,t} \tag{8.8}$$

where the dependent variable is the monthly return on GM, $R_{m,t}$ is the return on the market portfolio (here the S&P 500 index), $R_{DM,t}$ is the percentage change in the dollar price of the DM, and β_{GM} and γ_{GM} represent the exposures of GM to the market and the mark/dollar exchange rate, respectively. The resulting regression for monthly exchange rate and returns data from 1973–1995 is the following:

$$R_{Gm,t} = \underset{(0.368)}{0.001} + \underset{(11.157)}{0.924} R_{m,t} + \underset{(2.642)}{0.335} R_{DM,t} + \epsilon_{GM,t} \tag{8.9}$$

where the numbers in parentheses represent the t-statistics of the regression coefficient. A 10% appreciation of the DM leads to a 3.35 percent increase in the value of the firm's equity, keeping the level of the stock market constant. The positive coefficient on the percentage change in the dollar price of the DM reflects the increased value of the German operations as the DM appreciates.

To test the firm's exposure to the value of the yen because of competition from the Japanese firms in the North American market, we estimate a separate regression. An increase in sales of the Japanese firms should result in a decrease in sales for GM. We define $R_{¥}$ as the percentage change in the dollar price of the yen. We also use as an explanatory variable $R_{B,\,t}$, which is the percentage change in interest rates for corporate bonds of maturities from 3 to 10 years. To test the firm's exposure to these factors, we estimate the regression:

$$R_{Gm,t} = \alpha_{GM} + \beta_{GM} R_{m,t} + \gamma_{GM} R_{DM,t}$$
$$+ \delta_{GM} R_{¥,t} + \lambda_{GM} R_{B,t} + \epsilon_{GM,t} \tag{8.10}$$

where α_{GM} is a constant, β_{GM} is the firm's systematic risk, and γ_{GM}, δ_{GM}, and λ_{GM} are the sensitivities to the rates of change of the German mark, Japanese yen, and U.S. interest rates, respectively. The estimates (t-statistics in parentheses) are:

$$R_{Gm,t} = \underset{(0.181)}{0.007} + \underset{(11.300)}{0.965} R_{m,t} + \underset{(2.997)}{0.472} R_{DM,t}$$
$$- \underset{(-2.092)}{0.353} R_{¥,t} - \underset{(-1.902)}{0.198} R_{B,t} \tag{8.11}$$

GM has significant exposures to the mark, to the yen, and to the level of U.S. interest rates. A depreciation of the yen relative to the U.S. dollar reduces firm value. Also, an increase in U.S. interest rates reduces firm value. A 10 percent appreciation in the dollar relative to the yen and the DM along with a 10 percent increase in interest rates leads to a decrease of 3.53 and 1.98 percents from the yen and the interest rate, respectively, and an increase of 4.72 percent as a result of the DM increase. This results in a 0.79 percent reduction in the value of the firm's equity.

The example of General Motors shows how we can analyze the exposure of a firm to various financial prices by including these prices in a linear regression. We can include a firm's input prices or any other risk factors we feel may be important after evaluation of the firm and industry characteristics along with a pro forma analysis. Careful examination of the results of regressions like these help managers determine the proper risk management strategy for the firm.

There are at least three reasons for caution about the use of the regression approach. First, regression coefficients are based on past information and relationships may not hold for the firm in the future. Think about GM. The world automotive industry had experienced relatively little competition until the 1970s. More intense competition began in the early 1980s. GM would have estimated exposures for the 1980s poorly using data from the 1970s.

Second, the firm may be exposed to more market risks than those used in the regressions. To understand how much of the volatility in equity is explained by the market risks used in the regression, we already know that we can use the R^2 of the regression. The R^2 of the second regression is 35 percent. This shows that our risk factors explain slightly more than one-third of the variance of General Motors' stock. Further examination of the characteristics of the firm, including its financial position, sourcing, marketing, and the competitive nature of the industry would identify additional risk factors.

Finally, regressions assume a simple linear relation between the cash flows of the firm and the financial risk factors. This may not be appropriate. The relation could be nonlinear. For example, the interaction between two market risks can matter for firm value. We can incorporate nonlinear effects in a regression, but to know that they pertain, we already must have a good understanding of the firm's exposures.

The regression approach nevertheless is a way to check our understanding of a firm's exposures. If our analytical approach tells us that an increase in the price of the euro affects a firm adversely and the regression approach tells us the opposite, it is reasonable to ask some tough questions about the analytical approach. An advantage of the regression approach is that the firm can use the estimated exposures as hedge ratios for the present value of the cash flows.

8.6. Monte Carlo approaches

What if a firm's current situation is quite different from its recent history? The historical distribution of its cash flow is not a useful guide to the distribution of its cash flow in the future, so that its historical exposures estimated through a multiple regression do not correctly describe the exposures that will be relevant in the future. In such a situation, we might obtain the distribution of the firm's cash flow analytically and compute exposures from the analytical distribution of cash flow. However, this is often not possible because too many risk factors affect cash flow and they may do so nonlinearly, so that even if we know the distribution of the risk factors, we may not know the distribution of cash flow. When we cannot compute the distribution of cash flow analytically, we must simulate the firm's cash flow. We can then use the simulated cash flows to estimate the firm's CaR, to quantify its exposures, and to obtain the optimal hedge ratio.

Remember that when dollar sales depend on the exchange rate, the cash flow of Motor is a function of the square of the exchange rate:

Cash flow of Motor = 400M × S² – 10M

The simplest way to get CaR when cash flow is a nonlinear function of random variables is to perform a **Monte Carlo analysis**. Such an analysis generates realizations of a function of random variables from draws of these random variables from their joint distribution. If we know the distribution of the exchange rate, we can generate squared values of the exchange rate without difficulty even if the squared exchange rate does not have a statistical distribution to which we can give a name. Instead of having a historical sample, we have a simulated sample. These realizations can then be analyzed the same way that we would analyze an historical sample.

Cash flow depends on the exchange rate, S. Therefore, we first have to identify the distribution of S. We then use a random number generator to draw values of S from this distribution. For each drawing, we compute cash flow.

Suppose we repeat this process 10,000 times. We end up with 10,000 possible cash flows. We can treat these cash flows as realizations from the distribution of cash flow. This is like having a sample. If we repeat the process more often, we have a larger sample. We can then use the sample to estimate the mean, volatility, and the fifth percentile of cash flow. The larger the number of drawings, the better we can estimate the distribution of cash flow, but an increase in the number of drawings means that the computer has to work longer to create our sample. This may be an issue for more complicated cash flow functions.

Earlier, we assumed a normally distributed exchange rate with an expected value of £0.50 and a volatility of 0.1. Let's now see what the cash flow volatility is if sales change so that cash flow is given by equation (8.3) and is a function of the square of the exchange rate. We simulate $N(0.5, 0.01)$, where $N(0.5, 0.01)$ is a normally distributed variable with mean 0.5 and variance of 0.01.

According to a Monte Carlo simulation with 10,000 drawings, expected cash flow is £93.99 million, the volatility is £40.39 million, and the fifth percentile shortfall is £58.99 million (93.99M – 35.00M). The distribution of the cash flow is given in Figure 8.7, Panel A.

Note first that the expected cash flow is not £90 million, which is the cash flow if the exchange rate is at its expected value of £0.50. There are two reasons for the discrepancy. First, with the Monte Carlo simulation, we draw a sample. Different samples lead to different results. The results are expected to differ less for larger samples. Second, because the cash flow is a nonlinear function of the exchange

Distribution of Motor Inc.'s cash flow   *Figure 8.7*

The exchange rate is £0.50 for the dollar with a return volatility of 10 percent per year and an expected return of zero. Marginal revenue is $20,000 per car. The cash flows are obtained through a Monte Carlo simu-
lation with 10,000 draws using @Risk.

Panel A. Distribution of Motor Inc. cash flow for normally distributed exchange rate

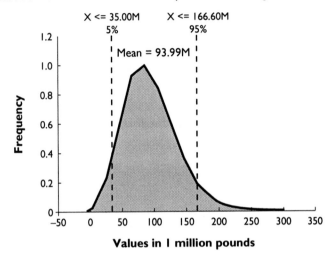

Panel B. Distribution of Motor Inc. cash flow for lognormally distributed exchange rate

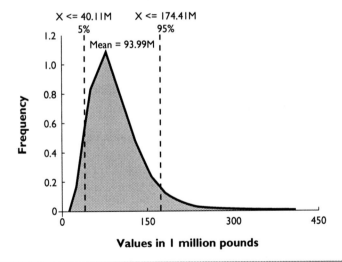

rate, its expectation is not equal to the cash flow evaluated at the expected exchange rate.

It is interesting to compare the results when the exchange rate is normally distributed to results when it is lognormally distributed. Because the lognormal
distribution is skewed to the right, it means that the expected value of cash flow
shortfalls is smaller than when the distribution of the exchange rate is symmetric.
When the exchange rate is lognormally distributed with expected value of 0.5 and
volatility of 0.1, the CaR is £53.88 million. The distribution of cash flow when
the exchange rate is lognormally distributed is given in Panel B of Figure 8.7.

Using the output of the Monte Carlo simulation, we can obtain the optimal hedge ratio. We can compute it explicitly using equation (8.1) or by regressing cash flow on the exchange rate. We find that the optimal hedge ratio involves going short $400 million with a normally distributed exchange rate and $424.256 million with a lognormally distributed exchange rate.

We can use the Monte Carlo method when there are multiple sources of risk as well. Technical Box 8.2, British Inc., describes a Monte Carlo analysis that involves exchange rates for a number of years in the future and cash flows that depend on past and current exchange rates as well as on whether a competitor enters the market.

After having computed cash flows for each year in each simulation trial of a Monte Carlo analysis, we have the distribution of the cash flows given the

---

Technical Box 8.2   **British Inc.**

British Inc. is a car producer in the United Kingdom. It has a vehicle in a market segment that it now dominates in the United Kingdom and wants to expand its success to the U.S. market. The firm is worried about the impact of changes in the exchange rate on the net present value of the project. An analyst is therefore asked to evaluate the exposure of the net present value of the project as well as the exposure of each annual cash flow to the dollar/pound exchange rate. To evaluate the exposures the analyst uses her knowledge of the costs of British Inc. and of its competitive position in the U.S. market.

The demand function for the cars in the U.S. is assumed to be:

Number of cars customers are willing to buy
= 40,000 – Dollar price of a car

The marginal cost of a car is £7,500 per unit and it is assumed to be constant over time. At an exchange rate of $2 per pound, it is optimal for the firm to sell 25,000 cars at $15,000. The analyst realizes that there is a strong possibility that a U.S. producer will enter the market segment with a comparable vehicle. This will have an effect on the pricing and thus the sales volume of British Inc. cars. The demand function with an entrant becomes:

Demand = 40,000 – 1.25 × Dollar price of a car

Consequently, the entrant makes the demand for British Inc. cars more sensitive to price. The analyst believes that the probability that British Inc. will face a competitor is 75 percent if the exchange rate exceeds $1.95 per pound and 25 percent otherwise. To sell in the United States, British Inc. has to spend £100 million in 2001. It can then sell in the United States starting in 2002. Depreciation is straight line starting in 2001 over five years. The tax rate on profits is 45 percent if profits are positive and zero otherwise. British Inc. fixes the dollar price of its cars at the end of a calendar year for all of the following calendar year. The sales proceeds in dollars are brought back to the United Kingdom at the end of each calendar year at the prevailing exchange rate.

(continued)   *Technical Box 8.2*

This example includes ten random variables: whether an entrant comes in or not, and the exchange rate for each calendar year from 2001 to 2009. Whether an entrant comes in or not is distributed binomially with a probability of 0.75 if the exchange rate in 2001 exceeds 1.95. The percentage change of the exchange rate from one year to the next is distributed normally with mean of 2.2 percent and standard deviation of 14.35 percent. These random variables do not influence the present value in a straightforward way. We argue in the text that the Monte Carlo analysis is particularly useful in the presence of path-dependencies. In this case, there are two important path dependencies: first, the cash flows depend on whether there is an entrant in 2001 which itself depends on the exchange rate; second, the cash flow for one year depends on that year's exchange rate as well as on the exchange rate the year before.

We performed a Monte Carlo analysis using 400 trials. The output of the Monte Carlo analysis (shown in Illustration 1) can be used to understand the exposure of British Inc. to the dollar/pound exchange rate in many different ways. Here, we show two of these ways. First, the figure shows the relation between the 2003 cash flow and the exchange rate in that year. At high exchange rates, it becomes likely that the cash flow will be negative and there is a decreasing nonlinear relation between pound cash flow and the dollar/pound ex-

Illustration 1 British Inc. Corporation

This Illustration shows the relation between the pound cash flow in 2003 and the dollar price of the pound in 2003 for the British Inc. simulation. We draw four hundred different exchange rate series from 2001 to 2009. For each of these exchange rate series, we use the binomial distribution to obtain the decision of whether a competitor enters the market or not. Based on the realization of the random variables, we compute the cash flows from 2001 to 2009. The 2003 cash flows and their associated 2003 exchange rates are then plotted on the illustration.

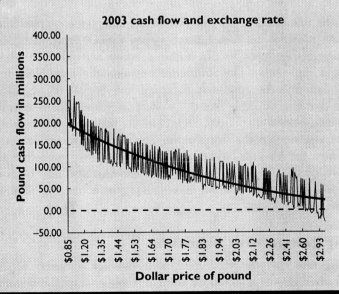

2003 cash flow and exchange rate

(continued)

Technical Box 8.2 *(continued)*

change rate. Because of the path dependencies we emphasized, the cash flow depends on the exchange rate in earlier years also.

An alternative way to use the output of the Monte Carlo analysis is to regress the pound net present value of the project (NPV) of selling in the United States on the future exchange rates. This shows the sensitivity of the net present value to future exchange rates. The NPV is measured in million pounds. We get:

$$NPV = \underset{(28.95)}{1285} - \underset{(-0.500)}{16.123}X_{2001} - \underset{(-4.382)}{144.980}X_{2002} - \underset{(-1.951)}{61.34}X_{2003}$$

$$- \underset{(-1.245)}{39.270}X_{2004} - \underset{(-3.225)}{109.892}X_{2005} - \underset{(-1.230)}{42.596}X_{2006}$$

$$- \underset{(-0.307)}{9.843}X_{2007} - \underset{(-2.509)}{82.941}X_{2008} - \underset{(-0.612)}{14.318}X_{2009}$$

where X_j is the exchange rate in year j and t-statistics are in parentheses below the regression coefficients. The R^2 of this regression is 78 percent. Whereas the NPV is negatively related to all exchange rates, not all future exchange rates are equally important determinants of the net present value. This is not surprising. First, the net present value calculation puts less weight on the cash flows that are received farther in the future. Second, our example has complicated path dependencies. Note, however, that some exchange rates have an extremely large effect on the NPV. For example, if the 2002 dollar price of the pound is unexpectedly higher by 10 cents, the NPV is lower by 14.5 million pounds. The NPV obtained by averaging across 400 trials is £345 million. A 10 cents deviation in the 2002 exchange rate (about 4 percent) corresponds to a change in the NPV of slightly more than 4 percent.

distribution of the risk factors. We can then relate cash flows to risk factors. In particular, we can measure the covariance between a given year's cash flows and the exchange rate in that year. We can obtain a hedge coefficient for that year's cash flow using a regression. The difference between the regression approach using historical data and the approach discussed here is that the regression approach assumes that the future is like the past. The Monte Carlo approach assumes that the distribution of the risk factors in the future is the same as in the past. It does not assume that the distribution of cash flows is the same as in the past. Consequently, the Monte Carlo approach could be used for a firm that has no history. However, since to do so, we have to model how cash flow or firm value depend on the risk factors, we take on model risk, that is, the risk that we have the wrong model.

8.7. Hedging competitive exposures

Foreign exchange rate changes affect firm value through a variety of different channels. Firms often choose to focus on some of these channels, but not others. A firm might be concerned about transaction exposure but not about competitive exposure. Focusing on the wrong exposure can have dramatic implications for a corporation.

A good example is a European airline concerned about the volatility of its cash flow. It therefore decides to hedge its transaction exposure. Its most important transaction is an order of planes from Boeing. The payment will be made in dollars. The company interprets this to mean that the firm is short dollars and hedges by buying dollars forward. During the period that the hedge is maintained, the dollar depreciates and the airline gets in financial trouble despite being hedged.

What went wrong? Focusing on transaction exposure, the airline neglected the exposure inherent to its operations. The prices the airline charges are fixed in dollars because of the structure of the airline market. Hence, if the dollar falls, the airline loses income in its home currency. Because of the airline's blindness to its competitive exposure, its risk management policy was inadequate. Had the firm taken into account its competitive exposure, it could have hedged its cash flow effectively. For that airline, hedging transaction exposure does not hedge cash flow. The airline cannot increase ticket prices denominated in dollars, so dollar depreciation means less income.

Suppose that the airline had hedged cash flow properly. It would make money as the dollar falls to offset the loss of its ticket sales net of the benefit it receives from having to pay Boeing less in its home currency. Having hedged properly, the airline would not be in financial distress. However, it does not follow that the airline's operations would be unaffected by the exchange rate change.

Hedging to keep operations unchanged as exchange rates change does not make sense. At the new exchange rate, the airline is not as profitable before the income from hedging. Some flights that were profitable before may no longer be so. Even with hedging, it does not make sense for an airline to continue flights that are no longer profitable. This is because each unprofitable flight makes a loss. If the airline stops these flights, it eliminates the losses. The airline should not waste money made on its hedges on unprofitable flights. The fact that the airline is hedged allows it to make operating decisions without being constrained by a lack of funds. For example, it could be that if it had not hedged, it would not have enough working capital and would be unable to fly profitable routes.

Despite the importance of competitive exposure for the future cash flows of firms, many firms are content to hedge only transaction and contractual exposures using financial instruments. When it comes to hedging competitive exposure, if they do it at all, they turn to "real" hedges. That is, they use the firm's operating strategy to reduce the impact of real exchange rate changes. For Motor, a real hedge would be to produce in the United States as well as in the United Kingdom. This way it would still be able to sell profitably in the U.S. market if the pound appreciates because it could sell cars produced in the United States. Such a strategy sometimes makes sense, but in general having production in different countries can be quite expensive. The transaction and management costs of hedging with financial instruments are fairly trivial by comparison.

8.8. Summary

Quantity and price risks have an impact on a firm's risk management policies. While quantity risks do not change the formula for the optimal hedge with futures and forwards, the size of the hedge differs when quantity is random and when it is not. Quantity risks make it harder to figure out a firm's exposure to a risk factor. Exchange rate changes, in particular, can have a complex impact on firm value because they change revenue per unit as well as the number of units sold.

There are three approaches that make it possible to figure out exposures when there are quantity risks. First, the pro forma approach works from the cash flow statement and identifies directly how changes in the exchange rate affect the components of cash flow. In its simplest form, the pro forma approach ignores how quantity is related to risk factors and simply estimates changes in cash flows for different assumptions about risk factors. A more sophisticated approach takes into account how quantities are related to risk factors. Generally, this is done using our knowledge of the economics of the firm. A model of cash flow has to be constructed. Sometimes, we can construct an analytical model where we can derive the distribution of cash flow and the relationship between the risk factors and cash flow. When it is too difficult to obtain the distribution of cash flow and cash flow exposures using an analytical model of the firm's cash flow, we can use multiple regressions or the Monte Carlo approach. Using stock returns, one can estimate how the present value of cash flows is related to risk factors. The Monte Carlo method allows us to estimate the impact of changes in risk factors and to compute CaR in complex situations. The Monte Carlo method is quite versatile and makes it possible to estimate exposures when alternative approaches do not work.

We concluded the chapter with an important point. The fact that a firm is hedged against unanticipated changes in a price—foreign exchange, interest rate, commodity price—is not an excuse for the firm to ignore the implications of the changes in that price on its operations. Consider an airline that is fully hedged against increases in the price of jet fuel and the price of jet fuel increases. If the value of the airline is higher by cancelling flights because of the high price of jet fuel, it should do so, regardless of whether it is hedged or not. Hedging should never dictate operating policies. The best operating policies as well as the best hedging policies are those that maximize shareholder wealth.

Key Concepts

competitive exposure, 224
contractual exposure, 224
delta exposure of cash flow to a
 risk factor, 242
exposure of cash flow to risk
 factor, 230

Monte Carlo analysis, 248
price risk, 224
quantity risk, 224
transaction exposure, 224

Review Questions

1. What is transaction exposure?
2. What is contractual exposure?

3. What is competitive exposure?

4. What is quantity risk?

5. Why does correlation between price risk and quantity risk matter for hedging?

6. What is delta exposure?

7. How does one use the pro forma statement to evaluate exposures?

8. Can you give an example where cash flow exposure changes with the level of the exchange rate?

9. What is the regression approach to estimating exposure?

10. Why use Monte Carlo analysis to determine exposure?

Questions and Exercises

1. An estimate by Goldman Sachs is that a 10 percent depreciation of the Japanese yen translates to a 2.5 percent decrease in the price of Chinese exports in Chinese currency. How could that be?

2. Suppose that McDonald's hedges its current purchases of potatoes against an unanicipated increase in the price of potatoes, so that if the price of potatoes increases, it receives a payment equal to the current purchases of potatoes times the change in the price of potatoes. How should an increase in the price of potatoes affect the price of fries at McDonald's?

3. Suppose that purchasing power parity holds exactly. What would a 10 percent depreciation of the Japanese yen imply for prices in Japan and China?

4. How could a U.S. car dealer in Iowa City that sells cars produced in the United States by a U.S. car manufacturer have a competitive exposure to the euro?

5. Consider a farmer who wants to hedge his crop. This farmer produces corn in Iowa. If his crop is smaller than expected, then so is the crop of most farmers in the United States. Should the farmer sell more or less than his expected crop on the futures market? Why?

6. A wine wholesaler buys wine in France. He proceeds as follows: He goes on a buying trip in France, buys the wines, and ships them to the United States. When the wines arrive, he calls retailers and offers the wine for sale. There is a shipping lag between the time the wine is bought in France and the time it arrives in the United States. The wholesaler is concerned about his foreign exchange exposure. His concern is that he has to pay for his purchases in French francs when the wine arrives in the United States. Between the time the wine is bought in France and the time it is sold in the United States, the French franc could appreciate, so that the wine becomes more costly in dollars. What are the determinants of the cash flow exposure of the wholesaler to the dollar price of the French franc?

7. Suppose you are a German manufacturer that competes with foreign firms. You find that your cash flow is normally distributed and that for each

decrease in the euro price of the dollar by 1/100th of a euro, your cash flow falls by one million euro. Yet, when the euro appreciates, you sell fewer cars. How do you hedge your cash flow? How does quantity risk affect your hedge?

8. Consider the analysis of Motor Inc. in section 8.2. Suppose that Motor Inc. exports instead 11,000 cars to the United States and 11,000 cars to Sweden. Let's assume that the price of a Swedish krona in pounds is the same as the price of a U.S. dollar and the price of a car sold in Sweden is Kr20,000. We assume now that the jointly normal increments model holds. The volatility of each currency is 0.10 pounds per year. The two prices have a correlation of zero. What is the CaR in this case?

9. Let's go back to the base case discussed in the text where Motor Inc. exports 22,000 cars to the United States. Let's assume that half the costs of producing a car are incurred in dollars six months before the sale and that all sales take place at the end of the calendar year. The U.S. interest rate is 10 percent per annum. What is Motor Inc.'s exposure to the dollar?

10. Assume that the volatility of the pound price of the dollar is 0.10 pound per year. What is the CaR corresponding to the situation of question 9?

Literature Note

The problem of hedging quantity and price risks is a long-standing problem in the hedging literature with futures. As a result, it is treated in detail in most books on futures. Equation (8.1) is derived and implemented in Rolfo (1980). The problem of hedging foreign currency cash flows is at the center of most books on international corporate finance. An early but convincing treatment of the issues as well as a collection of papers is found in Lessard (1979). Shapiro (1999) provides a state-of-the-art discussion, but international financial management books generally do not focus on the quantitative issues as much as we do in this chapter. Levi (1994) has the best textbook analysis in terms of demand and supply curves and is the inspiration for our discussion. Marston (1996) provides a careful analysis.

The discussion of exchange rate dynamics is basic material in international finance textbooks. A good treatment can be found in Krugman and Obstfeld (2000). The regression approach has led to a large literature. Adler and Dumas (1984) develop this approach as an exposure measurement tool. Jorion (1990) is a classic reference. For references to more recent work and new results, see Griffin and Stulz (2001). Williamson (2001) has a detailed analysis of exposures in the automotive industry. His work underlies our analysis of GM. The role of real hedges has led to a number of papers. Mello, Parsons, and Triantis (1995) have an interesting paper in which they analyze hedging in the presence of flexible production across countries. Logue (1995) questions hedging competitive exposures with financial instruments and Copeland and Joshi (1996) argue that firms often hedge too much against changes in foreign exchange rates because of the diversification effect discussed in Chapter 7. They also provide the airline example discussed in section 8.7. Stulz and Williamson (1997) provide more details on some of the issues examined in this chapter as well as more references.

Chapter 9

Measuring and Managing Interest Rate Risks

Chapter **9** Objectives

At the end of this chapter, you will:

1. Understand the trade-off between fixed and floating rate debt.

2. Be able to measure interest rate exposures.

3. Have tools to measure interest rate risks with VaR and CaR.

4. Understand how interest rate models can be used to measure and hedge interest rate risks.

In 1994, interest rate increases caused a loss of $1.6 billion for Orange County, California, ultimately leading the county to declare bankruptcy. If Orange County had measured risk properly, this loss would most likely never have happened. In this chapter, we introduce tools to measure and hedge interest rate risks. We show how Orange County could have used these tools. Much of our analysis deals with how interest rate changes affect the value of bond portfolios, but we also discuss how financial institutions as well as nonfinancial corporations can hedge interest rate risks associated with their funding. Firms can alter their interest rate risks by changing their mix of fixed and floating rate debt. We investigate the determinants of the optimal mix of floating and fixed rate debt and show how a firm can use a futures contract to switch from floating rate debt to fixed rate debt.

Financial institutions are naturally sensitive to interest rate risks. We therefore examine how financial institutions measure and manage their exposure to interest rate changes and explain why these institutions care about this exposure. Interest rate risks affect a firm's cash flow as well as its value. The techniques to measure and manage the cash flow impact and the value impact of interest rate changes differ and are generally used by different types of institutions.

Duration is a popular approach to measure interest rate risk. We show how duration is computed, how it is used, when it is appropriate, and how one can improve on duration. We also present approaches to measure interest rate risk that do not rely on duration. We explain how to estimate VaR for simple fixed-income securities with and without duration.

9.1. Debt service and interest rate risks

There is generally an optimal mix of floating rate and fixed rate debt for a firm at a particular time. A eurodollar futures contract is one instrument to hedge the interest rate risks of floating rate debt. An alternative financial instrument is a forward rate agreement.

9.1.1. Optimal floating and fixed rate debt mix

A firm's choice of funding is part of its risk management strategy. Noncallable fixed rate debt has a fixed coupon payment. The debt service does not make cash flows volatile because there is no uncertainty about payments that have to be made to service the debt. Floating rate debt has interest rate payments tied to an index, generally an interest rate—for example, the U.S. prime rate. The variability of the debt service may heighten or reduce the volatility of cash flows.

A firm whose business produces revenues that are higher when interest rates are high has more variable cash flow with fixed rate funding than with floating rate funding where the debt payments increase with interest rates. With this type of floating rate debt, the firm will have high interest rate payments when its revenues are high. A firm with the same floating rate debt whose revenues fall as interest rates increase may not be able to make interest payments when interest rates are high. Such a firm would be better off to seek funding with interest rate payments that are inversely related to the level of interest rates.

Debt maturities affect the interest rate sensitivity of a firm's cash flows. Fixed rate debt that matures in one year means that in one year the firm has to raise funds at the market rates prevailing at that time. Hence, its cash flows in the future will depend on the rates it has to pay on this new debt. Credit spreads that firms have to pay can change over time as well. A credit spread is the difference between the interest payment a firm has to promise and the payment it would have to make if its debt were risk-free. This means that short-term debt makes future cash flows more volatile because the firm does not know the credit spread it will have to pay in the future.

There is no reason for a firm's optimal financing mix to stay constant. If a firm suddenly has too much floating rate debt, it can proceed in one of two ways. First, it can buy back floating rate debt and issue fixed rate debt. Doing this involves flotation costs that can be substantial. Second, the firm can hedge the interest rate risks of the floating rate debt. This transforms the floating rate debt into fixed rate debt since the interest payments of the hedged debt do not fluctuate. Often, hedging the interest rate risks of floating rate debt is cheaper than buying back floating rate debt and issuing new fixed rate debt.

A firm might want to move from fixed rate debt to floating rate debt to make its debt payments positively correlated with its operating income. Rather than buy back fixed rate debt and issue floating rate debt, the firm might be better off using derivatives to change its debt service to make it more like floating rate debt.

In some cases, companies can issue debt offshore at lower rates. Longer-term borrowing offshore is generally available for fixed rate debt only. Firms that want floating rate financing but have the ability to borrow cheaply at fixed rates offshore will often sell fixed rate debt offshore and then transform the fixed rate debt into floating rate debt using derivatives.

9.1.2. Hedging debt service with the eurodollar futures contract

Let's now look at how a firm would change the interest rate risks of its debt service. Suppose Steady Inc. has $100 million of face value of floating rate debt. The interest rate is reset every three months at the London Interbank Offer Rate (LIBOR) prevailing on that date, called the reset date. Steady wants to hedge the interest rate risk associated with the coupon to be set in four months and to be paid three months later. **LIBOR** is the rate at which a London bank can borrow in dollars from another London bank. The loan would be made in dollars deposited outside the United States. Such dollars are usually called eurodollars to denote that they are dollars located offshore. They are not subject to strict U.S. banking regulations. Lending and borrowing in eurodollars is much less regulated. The eurodollar market offers more advantageous lending and borrowing rates than the domestic dollar market because the cost of doing business for London banks is lower than for U.S. domestic banks.

LIBOR is provided by the British Bankers Association through a designated information vendor. The designated information vendor polls at least eight banks from a list reviewed annually. Each bank "will contribute the rate at which it could borrow funds, were it to do so by asking for and then accepting interbank offers in reasonable market size just prior to 11.00 AM" for various maturities. The British Bankers Association averages the rates of the two middle quartiles of the reporting banks for each maturity. The arithmetic average becomes the LIBOR for that day published at noon, London time, on more than 300,000 screens globally.

LIBOR is an add-on rate paid on the principal at the end of the payment period. Suppose that today, date t, the interest rate has just been reset, so that the interest rate is known for the next three months. Three months from now, at date $t + 0.25$, a new interest rate will be set for the period from date $t + 0.25$ to date $t + 0.5$. The interest rate at date $t + 0.25$ is unknown today. The interest payment for the period from date $t + 0.25$ to date $t + 0.5$ is 0.25 times the three-month LIBOR determined on the reset date, date $t + 0.25$, and it is paid at the end of the payment period, date $t + 0.5$. If three-month LIBOR at the reset date is 6 percent, the payment at $t + 0.5$ is $0.25 \times 6\% \times \$100M$, which is \$1.5 million. The general formula for the LIBOR interest payment is (Fraction of year) $\times$ LIBOR $\times$ Principal.

LIBOR computations use a 360-day year day count. Typically, the payment period starts two business days after the reset date, so that the end of the payment period with quarterly interest payments is three months and two business days after the reset date. The interest rate payment for the period from $t + 0.25$ to $t + 0.5$ made at date $t + 0.5$ is equal to the principal amount, \$100 million, times 0.25 because it is a quarterly payment, times LIBOR at $t + 0.25$, which we write $RL_{t + 0.25}$. To obtain the value of that payment at the beginning of the payment period, we discount it at $RL_{t + 0.25}$ for three months:

$$\text{Value of interest payment at beginning of payment period} = \frac{\$100M \times 0.25RL_{t + 0.25}}{1 + 0.25RL_{t + 0.25}}$$

With LIBOR of 6 percent at $t + 0.25$, we have:

$$\frac{\$100M \times 0.25 \times 0.06}{1 + 0.25 \times 0.06} = \$1.478M$$

The appropriate futures contract to hedge the interest payment for the next payment period is the eurodollar contract. The eurodollar futures contract is the most liquid futures contract in the world when using open interest as a gauge of liquidity. The eurodollar futures contract is traded on the Chicago Mercantile Exchange. It is for a eurodollar deposit with three-month maturity and a \$1 million principal value. The futures price is the Exchange's index for three-month eurodollar time deposits. The index is 100 minus the futures yield on eurodollar time deposits. If futures were forwards, the futures yield would be the forward rate for eurodollar time deposits for delivery at maturity of the contract. Because of the daily settlement of futures, the futures yield is only approximately equal to the forward rate. At maturity, the index is 100 minus the yield on eurodollar deposits. Each basis point increase in the index results in a gain to the long in one futures contract worth \$25. Cash settlement is used. The yield used for the cash settlement is the offered yield obtained by the Exchange through a poll of banks.[1]

---

1   These banks are not the same as those the British Bankers Association uses to obtain LIBOR, so that the eurodollar yield used for settlement is not exactly LIBOR. In our discussion, though, we ignore this issue since it is of minor importance.

Table 9.1 shows the futures prices on a particular day from the freely available 10-minute lagged updates on the Chicago Mercantile Exchange web site. Eurodollar futures are traded to maturities of up to 10 years.

Eurodollar futures prices	*Table 9.1*

Eurodollar

Daily Prices (Wednesday, May 10, 2000)

Date		Open	High	Low	Last	Chge	Prev. Volume	Prev. Open_Int
5/10/00	May 00	932700	932850	932650	932775	125	1520	35446
5/10/00	Jun 00	931400	931650	931350	931500	50	50676	503450
5/10/00	Jul 00	930200	930300	930200	930250	100	451	7331
5/10/00	Aug 00	929350	929400	929100	929150	300	41	2540
5/10/00	Sep 00	928050	928500	928000	928100	150	82742	563283
5/10/00	Oct 00	926000	926400	926000	926400	500	0	35
5/10/00	Dec 00	925300	925950	925050	925450	350	74909	458937
5/10/00	Mar 01	924500	925200	924250	924750	450	60037	359860
5/10/00	Jun 01	923650	924400	923550	924000	500	34372	247951
5/10/00	Sep 01	923400	924100	923300	923750	500	21612	186444
5/10/00	Dec 01	922950	923700	922900	923300	450	10536	137124
5/10/00	Mar 02	923450	924000	923300	923800	500	10597	126764
5/10/00	Jun 02	923550	924000	923500	923900	550	5784	88815
5/10/00	Sep 02	923600	924000	923450	923900	550	4897	87919
5/10/00	Dec 02	923150	923550	922950	923450	550	4286	72646
5/10/00	Mar 03	923650	924050	923350	923950	550	4950	72575
5/10/00	Jun 03	923350	923750	922950	923700	600	2148	49702
5/10/00	Sep 03	923150	923550	922750	923500	600	4117	49648
5/10/00	Dec 03	922550	922950	922100	922900	600	1837	37798
5/10/00	Mar 04	922950	923350	922500	923300	600	2019	32982
5/10/00	Jun 04	922550	922950	922100	922900	600	1912	29965
5/10/00	Sep 04	922250	922650	921800	922600	600	2320	25471
5/10/00	Dec 04	921550	921950	921100	921900	600	2557	26416
5/10/00	Mar 05	921900	922300	921450	922250	600	2135	18824
5/10/00	Jun 05	921300	921900	921100	921900	600	288	11228
5/10/00	Sep 05	920950	921550	920750	921550	600	276	9930
5/10/00	Dec 05	920250	920800	920050	920800	550	201	7055
5/10/00	Mar 06	920500	921050	920300	921050	550	201	7478
5/10/00	Jun 06	920350	920700	919950	920700	550	170	6494
5/10/00	Sep 06	920000	920350	919600	920350	550	145	6108
5/10/00	Dec 06	919300	919650	918900	919600	500	145	6085
5/10/00	Mar 07	919650	919900	919150	919850	500	145	4740
5/10/00	Jun 07	919000	919550	918800	919500	500	97	3798
5/10/00	Sep 07	918700	919250	918500	919150	450	72	3647
5/10/00	Dec 07	918000	918550	917800	918400	400	72	5130
5/10/00	Mar 08	918250	918800	918050	918650	400	97	4289
5/10/00	Jun 08	917900	918450	917700	918300	400	243	4593
5/10/00	Sep 08	917550	918100	917350	917950	400	217	4152

(*continued*)

Table 9.1 (continued)

Date		Open	High	Low	Last	Chge	Prev. Volume	Prev. Open_Int
5/10/00	Dec 08	916850	917400	916650	917200	350	241	3180
5/10/00	Mar 09	917550	917650	916900	917450	350	240	2647
5/10/00	Jun 09	916550	917300	916550	917100	350	55	2554
5/10/00	Sep 09	916200	916950	916200	916750	350	55	2438
5/10/00	Dec 09	915500	916250	915500	916050	350	55	1724
5/10/00	Mar 10	916400	916500	915750	916300	350	55	692

Composite	Volume	Open_Int
5/9/00	389526	3319890

Remember that Steady wants to hedge the interest rate risk of the coupon to be set in four months. A short position in the futures contract expiring in four months quoted today at 95 allows Steady to lock in a rate of 5 percent for that coupon. Since Steady will have to pay a coupon on $100 million, let's look at a hedge consisting of a short futures position for $100 million. One hundred minus the index is called the implied futures yield. In this case, the implied futures yield is 5 percent (100 − 95). Four months pass, and now eurodollar deposits are offered at 6 percent. In this case, the index at maturity of the contract is at 94. Since Steady is short, it makes money as the index falls. The settlement variation (the cash flows from marking the contract to market) over the four months Steady held on to the position is 100 basis points annualized interest (6% − 5%) for three months applied to $100 million. Hence, Steady receives 0.25 × 0.01 × $100M, which amounts to $250,000. Steady has to pay interest on the $100 million at 6 percent for three months, 0.25 × 0.06 × $100M, or $1.5 million. The interest expense net of the gain from the futures position will be $1.5M − $0.25M, which is $1.25 million. This corresponds to an interest rate of 5 percent. As long as the daily settlement feature of futures can be neglected, Steady's hedge eliminates the interest rate risk associated with the coupon to be set in four months.

Because of daily settlement, the $100 million short futures position does not completely eliminate Steady's risk from the coupon payment to be set in four months. The interest has to be paid three months after the reset date, while the futures settlement variation accrues over time. To obtain a more exact hedge, the futures hedge should be tailed. The tailing factor discussed in Chapter 6 was a zero-coupon bond paying $1 at maturity of the futures contract. Here, however, because interest paid on the loan is paid three months after the maturity of the futures contract, Steady can invest the settlement variation of the futures contract for three more months. To account for this, the tailing factor should be the present value of a zero-coupon bond that matures three months after the maturity of the futures contract. Computation of the tailing factor is explained in Technical Box 9.1, The tailing factor with the eurodollar futures contract.

The tailing factor with the eurodollar futures contract   *Technical Box 9.1*

We are at date t and want to hedge an interest rate payment to be made at date $t + 0.5$ based on an interest rate determined at date $t + 0.25$, the reset date. We therefore want to use a eurodollar futures contract that matures at date $t + 0.25$. Let's define F to be the implied futures yield at date t for the contract that matures at $t + 0.25$. Settlement variation on the contract from t to $t + 0.25$ is $0.25(RL_{t + 0.25} - F_{t + 0.25})$ times the size of the short position. At $t + 0.25$, we get to invest the settlement variation for three months at the rate of $RL_{t + 0.25}$. This means that at $t + 0.5$ we have $(1 + 0.25 \times RL_{t + 0.25}) \times 0.25 (RL_{t + 0.25} - F_{t + 0.25})$ times the short position. We therefore want to choose a short position h such that at $t + 0.5$ we have no interest rate risk. The net cash flow at $t + 0.5$ is equal to minus the interest payment plus the proceeds of the short position:

$$-0.25 \times RL_{t + 0.25} \times \$100M +$$
$$h \times \left(1 + 0.25 \times RL_{t + 0.25}\right) \times 0.25 \times \left(RL_{t + 0.25} - F_{t + 0.25}\right)$$

If we choose h so that at $t + 0.25$ it is equal to $\$100M/(1 + 0.25 \times RL_{t + 0.25})$, we end up with:

$$-0.25 \times RL_{t + 0.25} \times \$100M +$$
$$\left(\begin{array}{c} \$100M/\left(1 + 0.25 \times RL_{t + 0.25}\right) \times \left(1 + 0.25 \times RL_{t + 0.25}\right) \\ \times 0.25 \times \left(RL_{t + 0.25} - F_{t + 0.25}\right) \end{array} \right)$$
$$= -0.25 \times F_{t + 0.25} \times \$100M$$

Consequently, if h is such that at date $t + 0.25$ its value is $\$100M/(1 + 0.25 \times F_{t + 0.25})$, we eliminate the interest rate risk and our net cash flow at date $t + 0.5$ is equal to an interest payment based on the futures yield known when we enter the futures contract.

To have a futures position of $100M/(1 + 0.25 \times F_{t + 0.25})$ at date $t + 0.25$, note that $1/(1 + 0.25 \times F_{t + 0.25})$ at date $t + 0.25$ is the present value of one dollar paid at $t + 0.5$ discounted at the implied futures yield. This must be equivalent to the value at t of a zero-coupon bond maturing at $t + 0.5$, which has a risk equivalent to LIBOR deposits. Therefore, if we use as the tailing factor such a zero-coupon bond that matures at $t + 0.5$, we will have the appropriate futures position at $t + 0.25$. At date t, we therefore take a short position equal to 100 million times the price of such a zero-coupon bond. At date t, the price of such a bond is the price of a dollar to be paid at $t + 0.5$ discounted at six-month LIBOR.

In our example, Steady could take a floating rate debt coupon and eliminate its interest rate risk through a hedge. It could do this for every coupon to be paid on the hedge, making the hedged floating rate debt equivalent to fixed rate debt. As long as there are no risks with the hedge, Steady does not care whether it issues fixed rate debt or it issues floating rate debt that it hedges completely against interest rate risks.

The eurodollar futures contract lets us take fixed rate debt and make it floating as well. A long position in the eurodollar futures contract calls for a payment corresponding to the increase in the implied futures yield over the life of the contract. Adding this payment to an interest payment on fixed rate debt makes the payment a floating rate payment whose value depends on the interest rate. With this contract, therefore, the interest rate risk of the firm's funding is no longer tied to the debt the firm issues. For given debt, the firm can obtain any interest rate risk exposure it thinks is optimal.

To understand how the futures contract is priced, suppose we borrow on the euromarket for six months, invest the proceeds on the euromarket for three months, and roll over at the end of three months into another three-month investment. The payoff from the strategy in six months increases with the interest rate in three months that is unknown today. If we hedge the interest rate risk with the eurodollar contract, our strategy has no risk (we ignore possible credit risk) and therefore its payoff should be zero since we invested no money of our own.

The futures contract is for $1 million, so we can eliminate the interest rate risk on an investment of $1 million in three months. The present value of $1 million available in three months is $1 million discounted at the three-month rate. Suppose that the three-month rate is 8 percent annually and the six-month rate is 10 percent annually. We can borrow for six months at 10 percent and invest the proceeds for three months at 8 percent. In three months, we can reinvest the principal and the interest for three months at the prevailing rate. At the 8 percent rate, the present value of $1 million available in three months is $980,392. We therefore borrow $980,392 for six months and invest that amount for three months. In six months, we have to repay $980,392 plus 5 percent or $1,029,412. To hedge, we short one eurodollar contract. In three months, we have $1 million that we invest for three months. Since we have to repay $1,029,412, our hedged investment must be worth the same in six months. If our investment is worth more (ignoring the daily settlement of futures) we make a sure profit since we bear no interest rate risk. If it is worth less we make a sure loss that we can transform into a sure profit by investing for six months and borrowing short term. The only way we end up with $1,029,412 is if the futures contract allows us to lock in an annual rate of 11.765 percent. With this calculation, the futures price should therefore be 100 − 11.765, or 88.235.

The price of the futures contract of 88.235 ignores that futures contracts have daily settlement, so that departures from that price do not represent pure arbitrage opportunities. The example shows, however, that the key determinant of the futures price has to be the three-month forward rate implied by the term structure of LIBOR rates.

Suppose that in three months the eurodollar rate is 15 percent. In that case, we lose 3.235/4 per $100, or $0.80875 per $100, on our futures position (15% − 11.765% for three months). We therefore invest in three months $1M − $8,087.5/1.0375 for three months at 15 percent yearly. We end up with proceeds of $1,029,412, which is what we would have gotten had interest rates not changed. Our hedge works out exactly as planned.

9.1.3. Forward rate agreements

A **forward rate agreement** (FRA) is another way to hedge interest rate risk. Forward rate agreements (FRAs) are traded over the counter. In an FRA, the buyer commits to pay the fixed contract rate on a given amount over a period of time, and the seller pays the reference rate (generally LIBOR) at maturity of the contract. The principal on which the interest payment is computed is used solely for computation—it is not exchanged at maturity—and is called the FRA's notional amount.

Steady Inc. can enter an FRA today to hedge the interest rate risk on its coupon to be set in four months. It wants to be the buyer paying the contract rate for three months starting in four months. The contract rate is 5 percent on a $100 million notional amount starting in four months for three months. With this contract, Steady Inc. locks in a 5 percent borrowing rate. This is because it will pay the 5 percent and the seller would pay the three-month LIBOR set in four months on $100 million. Steady can then take the payment it receives and use it to pay the debt service on its floating rate debt. It is then left with paying 5 percent on its debt. The payment from the FRA is computed so that Steady receives in four months the three-month LIBOR minus 5 percent discounted at LIBOR for three months. This ensures that the FRA is a perfect hedge.

In other words, if the LIBOR rate is 6 percent in four months, the payment Steady receives in four months is 6 percent annual for three months minus 5 percent annual for the same period discounted at 6 percent annual for that period. This amounts to $0.25 \times 0.01 \times \$100M/(1 + 0.25 \times 0.06)$, or $246,305. Steady has to make a floating rate payment of $1.5 million in seven months (which is $0.06 \times 0.25 \times \$100M$). Since Steady receives $246,305 that it can invest for three months at 6 percent to then have $250,000, its net payment in seven months is $1.25 million. This is the payment that Steady would have to make at a 5 percent rate.

We have used an FRA to hedge one future cash flow. However, Steady Inc. might have issued a bond with many coupon payments, so that Steady would have to hedge many future payments. It could do so by entering many FRA agreements. We will see in Chapter 16 that a firm can buy the equivalent of a package of FRA agreements to hedge cash flows such as those that Steady is seeking to hedge. Such packages are called interest-rate swaps. By entering a swap, Steady would agree to make fixed rate payments on a notional amount equal to the bond's principal amount and would receive floating rate payments on the same notional amount. For each coupon date, the payments would be equivalent to those of an FRA.

9.2. The interest rate exposure of cash flow and earnings for financial institutions

Financial institutions, such as banks and insurance companies, can measure and hedge the impact of interest rate changes on their cash flow, earnings, or their portfolio value. Any change in portfolio value is a change in shareholder wealth. Portfolio value is the present value of the future cash flows that accrue to the portfolio. However, cash flows and earnings measured over quarters or years can matter for shareholder wealth regardless of their impact on the value of the portfolio.

For example, regulatory capital is adversely affected by earnings losses. A large earnings loss that the bank expects to be offset later could put the bank out of business, force it to raise outside funds, or force it to restructure if its regulatory capital is not sufficient to meet existing regulatory capital requirements.

Financial institutions generally use marked-to-market accounting only for some accounts. For example, in a bank, trading books are marked to market because the securities are held for sale, but loans are not marked to market. When a trading book is marked to market, a reduction in the value of the securities in the book has an adverse effect on the bank's earnings. However, when interest rate increases reduce the market value of fixed rate loans, this reduction is not reflected in the bank's earnings. Consequently, a bank that is concerned about stabilizing earnings, perhaps because of regulatory capital concerns, might be concerned mostly about the impact of interest rate changes on interest payments it receives and has to make.

Most of a bank's liabilities are deposits from customers. Its assets are commercial and personal loans, construction loans, mortgages, and securities. A bank faces interest rate risks as well as other risks. If interest rate risks are uncorrelated with other risks, they can be analyzed separately from other risks. If they are correlated with other risks, the bank cannot separate interest rate risks from other risks when estimating its total risk. Even if the bank focuses mostly on its total risk, it is helpful for it to understand its interest rate risks. Doing so can help it hedge those risks and understand the implications of changes in interest rates.

Banks have generally used various exposure measures that tell them how their net interest income (NII) is affected by changes in interest rates. If Safebank Corp. keeps its holdings of assets and liabilities unchanged, a change in interest rates impacts NII only through changes in the interest payments of its existing assets and liabilities. As interest rates change, some assets and liabilities are affected during a period and others are not; those whose interest rates payments change this way are said to reprice during that period. For example, suppose that Safebank has adjustable rate mortgage loans where the mortgage rate adjusts every six months to reflect interest rate changes. The interest rate on these mortgages was adjusted yesterday. This means that over the next period of six months, these mortgages do not reprice—the monthly interest payment does not change to reflect a change in rates. However, when Safebank evaluates which assets reprice in a period of six months starting in three months, it includes these adjustable rate mortgages among the assets that reprice over that period.

Contractual terms determine which assets and liabilities reprice over a period. For example, interest payments on outstanding fixed rate mortgages never reprice, but interest payments on outstanding deposits with short maturities reprice quickly. The net result is that a bank with a large portfolio of fixed rate mortgages financed with short maturity deposits therefore experiences a drop in its interest income as interest rates increase.

A bank whose liabilities reprice faster than its assets is called **liability sensitive**. This is because the increase in interest rates increases the payments made to depositors more than it increases payments received. Or, if the bank's liabilities include a lot of time deposits for one year and more, and its floating-rate loans reprice monthly, an increase in interest rates would increase inflows more than outflows over the near-term and the bank would be **asset sensitive**.

Why would Safebank care about net interest income in this way? It may want its earnings to be unaffected by interest rate changes. If it is liability sensitive, it can change its exposure with financial instruments. First, it could rearrange its portfolio so that its assets are more interest rate sensitive. It could sell some of the fixed rate mortgages it holds and buy floating rate assets or short-term assets. Alternatively, it could take futures positions that benefit from interest rate increases. Since interest rate futures prices fall when interest rates increase, this would mean shorting interest rate futures contracts.

A number of approaches are used to measure the exposure of net interest income to interest rate changes. The simplest and best known is gap measurement. The **dollar maturity gap** over a repricing interval is the amount of assets that reprice over that interval minus the amount of liabilities that reprice over that interval. The first step in gap measurement is to choose a repricing interval of interest.

Suppose we want to find out how Safebank's income over the next three months is affected by a change in interest rates over that period. The only payments affected by the change in rates are the payments on assets and liabilities that reprice within the period. A deposit account whose interest rate is fixed for six months has the same interest payments over the next three months irrespective of how interest rates change over the next month. This means that to evaluate the interest rate sensitivity of the bank's interest income over the next three months, we have to know only about the assets and liabilities that reprice over the next three months.

Assume Safebank Corp. has $100 billion in assets, of which $5 billion assets reprice over the next year. It also has $10 billion of liabilities that reprice over that period. $5 billion is a measure of the bank's asset exposure to the change in rates and $10 billion is a measure of the bank's liability exposure to the change in rates. This bank has a one-year dollar maturity gap of –$5 billion. The gap can also be expressed as a percentage of assets. In this case, the bank has a **percentage maturity gap** of –5 percent.

Table 9.2 shows how Chase Manhattan reported gap information in its annual report for 1998. The first row of the table gives the gap measured directly from the bank's balance sheet. The gap for 1–3 months is $(37,879) million. The parentheses indicate a negative value and mean that between 1 and 3 months the bank's liabilities that reprice exceed the assets that reprice by $37,879 million. Derivatives contracts that are not on the balance sheet of the bank affect its interest rate exposure. Here, the derivatives add to the bank's interest rate gap over the next three months. As a result, the bank's gap including off-balance sheet derivatives for that period is $(42,801) million.

Though the balance sheet gap at a short maturity is negative, it becomes positive for longer maturities. The cumulative interest rate sensitivity gap for 7–12 months is $(37,506) million. This gap tells us that including all assets and liabilities that reprice within one year, the bank has an excess of liabilities over assets

Table 9.2   Interest rate sensitivity table for Chase Manhattan

Each row represents the difference in value between the assets and liabilities in the category described that reprice within a period.

At December 31, 1998 (in millions)	1–3 Months	4–6 Months	7–12 Months	1–5 Years	Over 5 Years
Balance Sheet	$(37,879)	$ 480	$ 6,800	$43,395	$(12,796)
Derivative Instruments Affecting Interest Rate Sensitivity*	(4,922)	803	(2,788)	2,542	4,365
Interest Rate Sensitivity Gap	(42,801)	1,283	4,012	45,937	(8,431)
Cumulative Interest Rate Sensitivity Gap	$(42,801)	$(41,518)	$(37,506)	$ 8,431	$ —
% of Total Assets	(12)%	(11)%	(10)%	2%	— %

* Represents net repricing effect of derivative position, which include interest rate swaps, futures, forward rate agreements, and options that are used as part of Chase's overall asset-liability management.

of $37,506 million. However, for 1–5 years, the cumulative gap is $8,431 million because there is a large positive gap of $45,937 million for the repricing period of 1–5 years.

A drawback of gap measures is that they are static measures. They take into account the assets and liabilities as they currently are and assume that they will not change. This can make these measures extremely misleading.

To see this, let's consider Safebank again. The bank has a –$5 billion one-year gap. On an annual basis, therefore, a 100 basis point decrease in rates would increase interest income by $50 million since the bank's income from assets would fall by $50 million, and its interest payments on deposits would decrease by $100 million. Suppose that $50 billion of the bank's assets are fixed rate mortgages. These mortgages do not reprice during the year, but as interest rates fall it becomes more advantageous for some of the holders of fixed rate mortgages to refinance their mortgages. Suppose that half of the mortgages are refinanced at the new lower rate, now 100 basis points lower than Safebank's outstanding mortgages. In this case, $25 billion of the mortgages are refinanced and hence repriced. As a result, $25 billion of assets are repriced in addition to the $5 billion used in the gap measure. Instead of having an exposure of –$5 billion, the bank has an exposure of $20 billion.

Using the gap measure blindly, Safebank would make a dramatic mistake in assessing its exposure to interest rates. If it hedged its –$5 billion gap, hedging would actually add interest rate risk.

To hedge the –$5 billion gap the bank would have to go short interest rate futures so that it benefits from an increase in rates. The true exposure is such that the bank makes a large loss when interest rates fall, so that it would have to be long in futures. By being short, the bank adds to the loss it makes when interest rates fall. The additional complication resulting from mortgages is, however, that the refinancing effect is asymmetric: the bank loses income if rates fall but does not gain income if the interest rates increase. These asymmetries have an impact on hedging.

A static measure like a gap measure is more appropriate for banks that have "sticky" portfolios. For instance, suppose that Safebank Corp. has a portfolio of 8 percent mortgages when market rates are at 12 percent. A 100 basis point decrease in interest rates will not affect refinancings. In this case, a static measure may be a good indicator of interest rate exposure. If instead market rates are 8.5 percent, a 100 basis point decrease may motivate refinancings.

Other assets and liabilities can also be affected. Suppose you hold a two-year CD. One month after buying the CD, interest rates increase sharply. Depending on the early withdrawal provisions of the CD, you might withdraw your money and incur the penalty to reinvest at the new rate. A static measure does not help the bank to measure its exposure in this case.

Another disadvantage of the gap measure is that it presumes that the change in interest rates is the same for all assets and liabilities that reprice within an interval. This need not be the case. There can be caps and floors on interest payments that limit the impact of interest rate changes. It can also be the case that some interest payments are more sensitive to rate changes than others. For example, the prime rate tends to be sticky and some floating rate payments can be based on sticky indexes or lagging indexes.

A lower interest payment on a loan reduces both earnings and cash flow. Therefore, there is a direct connection between a gap measure and a cash flow at risk or earnings at risk measure (the earnings shortfall at some probability level). Suppose that Safebank has a one-year gap of −$10 billion and that a useful rule of thumb for Safebank is that it can treat its cash flow as if half of the interest payment of the assets and liabilities that reprice is at the interest rate prevailing at the beginning of the year and half is at the interest rate prevailing at the end of the year. Suppose that the standard deviation of the interest rate is 50 basis points. If the rate is 5 percent now and its changes are normally distributed, there is a 5 percent chance that the rate in one year will be greater than 5 percent + 1.65 × 0.5%, or 5.825 percent. This means that there is a 0.05 probability of a shortfall in interest income of 0.825% × 0.5 × $10B for the year, or $41.25 million. We can therefore go in a straightforward way from a gap measure to a CaR based on gap that takes into account the distribution of the interest rate changes. This CaR makes all the same assumptions that gap does plus the assumption that interest rate changes are normally distributed. We know how to compute CaR for other distributions using the simulation method, so that we can compute the gap CaR for alternate distributions of interest rates changes.

Another approach is to look at the bank's balance sheet in a more disaggregated way and explicitly model the cash flows of the various assets and liabilities as a function of interest rates. In this way, we can take into account the dependence of the repayment of mortgages on interest rates as well as limits on interest payment changes embedded in many floating rate mortgage products. Rates for different assets and liabilities can be allowed to respond differently to interest rate shocks. Once we have modeled the assets and liabilities, we can figure out how the bank's NII changes with an interest rate shock. A standard approach is to use the model to simulate the impact on NII over a period of time of a given change in interest rates, say 100 basis points or 300 basis points.

Bank One provides a good example. At the end of 1999, Bank One reported that an immediate increase in rates of 100 basis points would reduce its pretax earnings by 3.4 percent and that an immediate drop in rates of 100 basis points would increase its earnings by 3.7 percent. Bank One is fairly explicit about how it measures the impact of interest rate changes on earnings. It examines the impact of a parallel shock of the term structure, so that all interest rates change by 100 basis points for a shock that increases interest rates. It then makes a number of assumptions about how changes in interest rates affect prepayments. It takes into account the limits on interest payments incorporated in adjustable rate products. As part of its evaluation of a change in interest rates on earnings, Bank One estimates the impact of changes in interest rates on fee income as well as on deposits of various kinds.

The Bank One approach assumes a parallel shift of the term structure. A parallel shift in the term structure is an equal change in all interest rates. Events that create difficulties for banks often involve changes in the level as well as in the shape of the term structure. For example, if the Federal Reserve raises interest rates, the impact will generally be stronger at the short end of the curve than at the long end. Figure 9.1 shows the example of the dramatic 1979 increase in rates.

Spreads between interest rates of same maturity can also change. Some loans might be pegged to LIBOR while other loans might be pegged to T-bill rates. It could be that interest rates increase but that the spread between the T-bill rates and LIBOR falls.

One way to deal with changes in the shape of the term structure and in spreads is to consider the impact on earnings of past changes in rates corresponding to specific historical events. This is called a **stress test**. Chase reports results of stress tests in its 1999 annual report. It measures the impact on earnings of a number of scenarios. Some of these scenarios are hypothetical, corresponding to possible changes in the term structure that are judged to be relevant. Other scenarios are historical. In 1994, the Federal Reserve increased interest rates sharply. One of the historical scenarios corresponds to the changes in rates in 1994. Chase concludes that the "largest potential NII stress test loss was estimated to be approximately 8% of projected net income for full-year 2000." These stress tests represent an extreme outcome, in that they assume an instantaneous change in rates followed by no management response for one year.

We saw in Chapter 8 that Monte Carlo simulation offers a good way to estimate exposures. We could estimate the exposure of earnings to interest rates by simulating earnings using a forecast of the joint distribution of interest rates. The advantage of such an approach over the stress test approach is that it can take into account the probabilistic nature of interest rate changes.

In general, a bank will want to compute a CaR or earnings-at-risk (EaR) measure that takes into account other risk factors besides interest rates. If it simulates earnings or cash flows, then it can measure its exposure to interest rates of earnings or cash flows by estimating their covariance with relevant interest rates in the way we measured foreign exchange exposures in Chapter 8.

Figure 9.1

Example of a Federal Reserve monetary policy tightening

Note that while rates on all maturities increased, proportionally, the increase in short-term rates was more dramatic.

Panel A. Term structure in March 1979.

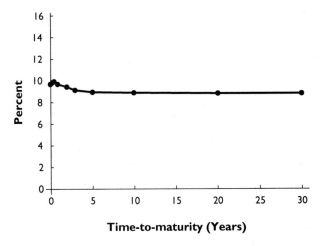

Panel B. Term structure in March 1980.

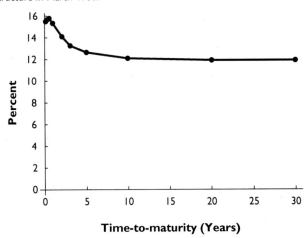

9.3. Measuring and hedging interest rate exposures

Financial institutions or pension fund managers might be more concerned about the value of their portfolio of assets and liabilities than about interest paid or received. This will be the case for assets and liabilities that are marked to market. For an investment bank with a large trading book marked to market daily, a large drop in the value of its marked-to-market assets and liabilities not only represents a loss of shareholder wealth, but it also can create a regulatory capital deficiency, financing problems, and possibly other difficulties. A pension fund manager has to make certain that the fund can fulfill its commitments.

How does an institution such as a pension fund or an investment bank measure the interest rate risks of its portfolio of assets and liabilities? It wants to compute how the market value of assets and liabilities changes for a given change in interest rates.

The tools we develop to measure the interest rate exposure of securities and portfolios of securities would have allowed Orange County in early 1994 to answer questions like: Given our portfolio of fixed-income securities, what is the expected impact of a 100 basis increase in interest rates? What is the maximum loss at a 95 percent confidence interval? When we can measure these impacts of interest rate changes, we can figure out how to hedge a portfolio against interest rate changes.

One fundamental difficulty in evaluating interest rate exposures of fixed-income securities is convexity. Consider the present value of the future payments made by a fixed-income security. If the future payments are non-stochastic, its present value is the sum of the present value of each payment. Interest rates are in the denominator of the present value formula, so that the present value of a fixed income security is a non-linear function of interest rates. Present values of non-stochastic cash flows fall as interest rates increase. However, for non-stochastic cash flows, the reduction in value resulting from an increase in interest rates is smaller than the increase in value resulting from a decrease in interest rates. Consequently, whenever a fixed-income security has non-stochastic cash flows, its value is a convex function of interest rates, as shown in Figure 9.2.[2] A fixed-income security whose sensitivity to interest rate changes falls as interest rates increase is said to exhibit positive convexity. Fixed-income securities whose cash flows are stochastic can exhibit negative convexity for some interest rate changes.

Figure 9.2   **Bond price as a function of yield**

This figure shows the price of a bond paying coupon annually of $5 for 30 years with principal value of $100.

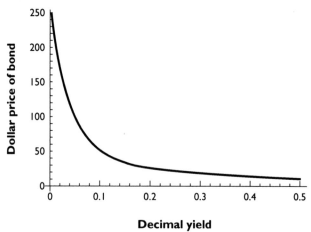

---

2   Remember that in a convex function, a straight line connecting two points on the function is above the function. For a concave function, the line is below.

The economic reason for this is that the yield discounts future payments, so that the greater the yield, the lower the current value of future payments. As the yield increases, payments far in the future become less important and contribute less to the bond price. Payments near in the future contribute more to the bond price when the yield increases, but because they are made in the near future, they are less affected by yield changes.

Ideally, we would like to find an estimate of exposure so that exposure times the change in yield gives us the change in the bond value whatever the current level of the yield or the size of the change in yield. Since the exposure of a bond changes with the yield, we cannot do this. For small yield changes, however, the exposure is not very sensitive to the size of the yield change, so we can reasonably keep exposure constant as we evaluate their impact. We start with that approach, discuss its limitations, and show how to improve it.

9.3.1. Measuring yield exposure

Consider a coupon bond with price B that pays a coupon c once a year for N years and repays the principal M in N years. The price of the bond is equal to the bond's cash flows discounted at the bond yield:

$$B = \sum_{i=1}^{i=N} \frac{c}{(1+y)^i} + \frac{M}{(1+y)^N} \tag{9.1}$$

In the bond price formula, each cash flow is discounted to today at the bond yield. A cash flow that occurs farther in the future is discounted more, so that an increase in the yield reduces the present value of that cash flow more than it reduces the value of cash flows accruing sooner. Consequently, a bond whose cash flows are more spread out over time is more sensitive to yield changes than a bond of equal value whose cash flows are received sooner.

A measure of exposure, duration, exploits this insight. **Duration** measures how the cash flows of a bond are spread over time. It is equal to the weighted average time to receipt of cash flows, where the weight is the present value of the cash flow as a proportion of the bond value:

$$\text{Duration} = \left[\frac{\sum_{i=1}^{i=N} \frac{i \times c}{(1+y)^i} + \frac{N \times M}{(1+y)^N}}{B} \right] \tag{9.2}$$

A bond with yearly coupon payments has a duration in years. If there are n coupon payments per year, the discount rate for one payment period is $(1 + y/n)$ rather than $(1 + y)$. Consequently, we replace $(1 + y)$ in equations (9.1) and (9.2) by $(1 + y/n)$. The resulting duration is one in terms of payment periods. To get a duration in terms of years, we divide the duration in terms of payment periods by n. It is important to note that duration depends on the yield. As the yield increases, the early coupon payments receive more weight, so that the bond's duration falls.

Since a bond with a greater duration has interest payments spread over more time, its value is more sensitive to yield changes. We can quantify this effect. The change in the bond price for an infinitesimal change in the yield is equal to:[3]

Change in bond price for a change in yield of Δy

$$= -\text{Duration} \left[\frac{B}{(1 + y)} \right] \Delta y = -B \times M_D \times \Delta y \qquad (9.3)$$

For an infinitesimal increase in yield, a bond price falls more if it has a longer duration. By inspecting equation (9.3), we can see that the change in the bond price is linear in duration. A bond with twice the duration of another bond falls by twice the amount of the other bond. Duration divided by one plus the yield, $D/(1 + y)$, is called the **modified duration**, which we write M_D.

In Chapter 8, we introduced the delta exposure of cash flow to a risk factor. The delta exposure of a cash flow is the change in cash flow for an infinitesimal change in the risk factor. This measure of exposure is useful when cash flow is a nonlinear function of the risk factor. Using delta exposure, the change in cash flow for a given change in the risk factor is approximated by delta exposure times the change in the risk factor. With delta exposure, we find the exact effect of a change in the risk factor when the change is infinitesimally small. For larger changes, delta exposure is used to approximate the effect.

We can use the delta exposure approach to approximate the change in a bond price for a given change in the yield. The yield delta exposure of a bond is the change in the bond price per unit change in the yield, $\Delta B/\Delta y$, evaluated for an infinitesimal change in the yield. The yield delta exposure of a bond is $-B \times M_D$. Consequently, the change in the bond price for a change in yield of Δy using the bond's yield delta exposure is $-B \times M_D \times \Delta y$.

If we compute the change in bond price per dollar of bond price, the change in the bond price is simply $-M_D \times \Delta y$. The negative of the modified duration is the yield delta exposure of a bond per dollar value of the bond; it measures the change in the bond price per dollar for an infinitesimal change in the yield. Since the percentage change in the bond price is the change in the bond price per dollar times one hundred, the percentage change in the bond price is $-M_D \times 100 \times \Delta y$.

Using duration or the yield delta exposure provides us with an exact estimate of the impact on the bond price of an infinitesimal change in the yield. We can use these tools to approximate the impact on the bond price of a noninfinitesimal change in the yield. When we do so, however, we have to remember that we are using an approximation.

Let's look at an example. Suppose that we have a 25-year bond paying a 6 percent coupon selling at 70.3571. The yield is 9 percent. The modified duration of

3 Technical argument: The impact of the yield change is obtained by taking the derivative of equation (9.1) with respect to the yield. For example, taking the derivative of the present value of the i-th coupon with respect to yield gives us $-i \times c/(1 + y)^{i+1}$.

that bond is 10.62. Using equation (9.3), we can obtain the price impact of a 10 basis point change as $-10.62 \times \$70.3571 \times 0.001$, or $-\$0.747$. The percentage change in price is $-10.62 \times 100 \times 0.001$, or -1.062 percent. Computing the percentage change in price directly using the bond price formula, we get -1.05 percent. Duration works well for small yield changes. For a 200 basis point change, however, duration would imply a fall of 21.24 percent compared to the true fall in the bond price of 18.03 percent

The duration and yield delta approximations work better for small yield changes than for large ones. Figure 9.3 shows the bond price as a function of the yield. Both yield delta exposure and duration use a linear approximation to approximate a nonlinear function. More precisely, they use the slope of the tangent at the point of approximation as shown in Figure 9.3.[4] The bond price following a change in yield obtained using yield delta exposure plots on the tangent for any change in yield. If we move up or down this tangent line, we are close to the bond price function for small changes in yields, so using the yield delta exposure works well. For larger changes the point on the tangent line can be far off the bond pricing curve, so that the approximation is poor, as can be seen in Figure 9.3. For a large increase in yields, we get a substantially lower bond price than the actual bond price. The same is true for a large decrease in yields. This is because the line that is tangent to the bond price at the point of approximation is always below the function that yields the bond price because of the convexity of this function.

The mistake made using delta exposure or duration for large yield changes   *Figure 9.3*

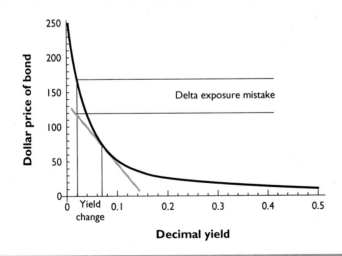

---

4   Technical point: The yield delta exposure of a bond is obtained by taking a first-order Taylor-series expansion of the bond pricing function around the current value of the yield. The tangent line corresponds to the straight line given by the first-order Taylor-series expansion as we vary the yield. Let $B(y)$ be the bond price as a function of the yield and y^* be the yield. A first-order Taylor-series expansion is $B(y) = B(y^*) + B_y(y^*)(y - y^*) + \text{Remainder}$, where $B_y(y^*)$ is the derivative of the bond price with respect to y evaluated at y^*. Ignoring the remainder, the first-order Taylor-series expansion of the bond price is given by a straight line with slope $B_y(y^*)$. $B_y(y^*)$ is the bond yield delta exposure.

The change in value of a portfolio is always the sum of the changes in the value of the investments that compose the portfolio. With a flat term structure, all future cash flows to the portfolio are discounted at the same interest rate. In this case, the yield on a bond must equal that interest rate and all bonds have the same yield. Consequently, when we compute duration, we use the same yield for all bonds. We can then compute the portfolio impact of a change in that yield. This assumes that the new term structure is also flat. To use duration to compute the change in value of a portfolio associated with a change in yields, we can use duration to estimate the change in the value of each bond in the portfolio given the change in yields. In practice, the computation will also be done for parallel changes in yields when the term structure is not flat. In this case, different yields are used in the duration computation, but the change in yields is the same for all bonds.

Suppose a portfolio has assets and liabilities. We have a parallel shift in the term structure. Denote by A the value of the assets and by L the value of the liabilities, so that the value of the portfolio is A − L. Using modified duration, the value of the assets changes by $-A \times M_D(A)\Delta y$ and the value of the liabilities changes by $-L \times M_D(L)\Delta y$. Consequently, the change in the value of the portfolio is:

$$\text{Change in value of portfolio} = \left[-A \times M_D(A) - \left(L \times M_D(L) \right) \right]\Delta y \qquad (9.4)$$

where $M_D(A)$ is the modified duration of assets, $M_D(L)$ is the modified duration of liabilities, and Δy is the parallel shift in yields.

In equation (9.4), we compute the change in value of the portfolio using the modified durations of the assets and liabilities that form the portfolio. We could have computed the duration of the portfolio instead. The value of the portfolio is A − L, or W. The modified duration of the portfolio is the weighted average of the modified durations of the investments in the portfolio, with each weight being the portfolio weight of the investment. In our portfolio with assets A and liabilities L, the portfolio weight of assets is A/W and the portfolio weight of liabilities is (−L/W). Consequently, the modified duration of the portfolio is:

$$\text{Modified duration of portfolio} = \frac{A}{W}M_D(A) + \left(-\frac{L}{W} \right) M_D(L) \qquad (9.5)$$

Suppose Investbank Corp. has assets of $100 million with a modified duration of five years and liabilities of $80 million with a modified duration of one year. The bank's equity is thus $20 million. The modified duration of the bank's equity is $(100/20) \times 5 - (80/20) \times 1$, or 21. The market value of its equity falls by $20M $\times 21 \times 0.01 = \$4.2$ million if the interest rate increases by 100 basis points.

To hedge the value of the bank's balance sheet with futures contracts using the duration approach, we want to take a futures position that pays $4.2 million if the interest rate increases by 100 basis points. The duration of a futures contract is measured by the duration of the underlying bond discounted at the yield that equates the value of the underlying bond to the futures price. If there is a futures contract with a modified duration of five years, we would have to go short that futures contract by $84 million. In this case, the impact of a 100 basis point increase on the balance sheet would yield a futures gain of $84M × 5 × 0.01 = $4.2 million. Hence, the 100 basis point increase in interest rates would leave the value of equity unchanged.

Suppose we have a portfolio with value W and a security with price S we want to use to hedge the portfolio against interest rate risk. To hedge, we need to take a position in security S with a duration that cancels out the duration of the unhedged portfolio. The portfolio has modified duration $M_D(W)$ and the security has modified duration $M_D(S)$. Therefore, we need to take a position of *n* units of the security, so that:

$$W \times M_D(W) + n \times S \times M_D(S) = 0$$

Typically, we will want to sell the security with price S short, so that we will receive cash for *n*S (assuming full use of proceeds from short sale). We can invest that cash in a money market account. A money market account that pays every day the market interest rate for that day has no duration because its value at the start of a day does not depend on the interest paid that day: $100 invested in the fund earns interest at the rate R for the day, so that the value of the investment at the beginning of the day is $100 × (1 + R)/(1 + R) = $100 whatever the value of R. We denote by K the value of the investment in the money market account and assume that we can short the money market account costlessly. In this case, we must have W + *n*S + K = W. Solving for *n*, we get the volatility-minimizing duration hedge.

Volatility-minimizing duration hedge

The volatility minimizing hedge of a portfolio with value W and modified duration $M_D(W)$ using a security with price S and modified duration $M_D(S)$ involves taking a position of *n* units in the security:

$$\textbf{Volatility-minimizing hedge} = n = -\ \frac{W \times M_D\ (W)}{S \times M_D\ (S)} \qquad \textbf{(9.6)}$$

Having *n*, we can then find the money market position K. For Investbank, we have assets of $100 million with a modified duration of five years and liabilities of $80 million with a modified duration of one year. The portfolio has a value of $20 million and its modified duration is 21. Our hedging instrument is a security S with a price of $92 and a modified duration of five years. Using our formula, we get:

$$n = -\ \frac{W \times M_D\ (W)}{S \times M_D\ (S)} = -\ \frac{\$20M \times 21}{\$92 \times 5} = \text{-0.913043M}$$

To construct this hedge, we go short 913,043 units of the security with a price of $92, for proceeds of $84 million. We invest these proceeds in a money market account that has no duration to ensure that our hedged portfolio has no duration.

Let's now consider the case where we hedge with futures. In this case, S in equation (9.6) is the futures price, but we pay nothing when we enter the contract (assuming we can use some portfolio assets for the margin account) so that we do not need the money market account. The futures contract we use has a price of 92 and modified duration of five years. The size of the contract is $10,000. In this case, a change in yield of Δy changes the value of a futures position of one contract by $-\$4.6M \times \Delta y$, or $-\$0.92M \times 5\Delta y$. We want a position of n contracts so that $-n \times 0.92M \times 5\Delta y - 20M \times 21\Delta y = 0$. S in equation (9.6) is the futures price times the size of the contract and is therefore equal to $920,000. $S \times M_D(S)$ is equal to $0.92 million $\times 5$, or $4.6 million. n is the size of our futures position expressed in number of contracts. Dividing $-W \times M_D(W)$ by $S \times M_D(S)$ gives us $-420M/4.6M$, or a short position of 91.3043 contracts.

The duration hedge formula is nothing more than the minimum-volatility hedge formula derived in Chapter 6 when the risk factor is the interest rate and its impact on a security is given by the duration formula. To see this, note that the change in portfolio value if the interest rate risk is the only source of risk is equal to the yield delta exposure times the change in the interest rate, $-W \times M_D(W)\Delta y$, and the change in the value of the security is equal to the yield delta exposure of the security times the change in the interest rate, $-S \times M_D(S)\Delta y$. If the change in the interest rate is a random variable, we can use the minimum-volatility hedge ratio formula. This formula gives us a hedge ratio, which is $\text{Cov}[-W \times M_D(W)\Delta y, -S \times M_D(S)\Delta y]/\text{Var}[-S \times M_D(S)\Delta y]$. This hedge ratio is equal to $[W \times M_D(W)]/[S \times M_D(S)]$. Using our result from Chapter 6, we would go short $[W \times M_D(W)]/[S \times M_D(S)]$ units of asset with price S to hedge.

The duration approximation makes it possible to obtain a VaR measure based on duration. Since the change in the portfolio value is $-W \times M_D(W)\Delta y$, we can interpret Δy as the random change in the interest rate. If that random change is distributed normally, the volatility of the change in portfolio value using the duration approximation is $W \times M_D(W) \times \text{Vol}[\Delta y]$. Using the formula for VaR, there is a 5 percent chance that the portfolio value will be below its expected value by more than $1.65 \times W \times M_D(W) \times \text{Vol}[\Delta y]$. Applying this to our example, we have $1.65 \times \$420M \times 0.005$, or $3.465 million.

Technical Box 9.2, Orange County and VaR, shows how the duration-based VaR discussed in this section would have provided useful information to the officials of Orange County.

9.3.2. Improving on traditional duration

When we estimate the change in value of a portfolio using modified duration, we assume a small parallel shift in a flat term structure. The term structure is rarely

---

Technical Box 9.2   Orange County and VaR

To see that a VaR computation using duration can provide extremely useful information, let's look at the case of Orange County. In December 1994, Orange County announced that it had lost $1.6 billion in an investment pool. The investment pool collected funds from municipalities and agencies and invested them on their behalf. The pool kept monies to be used to finance the public activities of the county. The amount in the pool had been $7.5 billion and was managed by the county treasurer, Bob Citron. As of April 30, 1994, the portfolio had an investment in securities of $19.860 billion with reverse repo borrowings of $12.529 billion. The securities were mostly agency fixed rate and floating rate notes with an average maturity of about four years. The fund was therefore heavily leveraged. The investment strategy was to borrow short term using the repo market discussed in Chapter 2 to invest in securities with longer duration to take advantage of the slope of the term structure. The problem with such a strategy is that as interest rates increase, the value of the assets falls while the liabilities do not. Valuing the securities held on April 30 at cost, we have $19.789 billion worth of assets. The duration of the pool was estimated at 7.4 in a subsequent analysis. The yield of the five-year note went from 5.22 percent in December 1993 to 7.83 percent in December 1994. Let's assume that 7.4 is the appropriate duration for December 1993 and that the portfolio value of $7.5B applies at that time. Assuming further that this duration measure is modified duration and that the yield of the five-year note is the appropriate yield given the duration of the pool, we have an estimate of the loss to the pool for a 261 basis point change in rates:

$$7.5B \times 7.4 \times 0.0261 = \$1.449B$$

This is close to the actual loss reported of $1.6 billion. Let's assume that percentage changes in yields are normally distributed. Using monthly data from January 1984 to December 1993, the volatility for the percentage change in the yield of the five-year note is 4.8 percent per month. Applying the square-root rule, this gives us a yearly proportional volatility of 16.63 percent. The five-year note had a yield of 5.22 percent in December 1993, so that 16.63 percent of 5.22 percent is 0.868 percent. There was therefore a 5 percent chance that the five-year yield would increase by more than 1.65×0.868 percent over the coming year, or more than 1.432 percent. The loss corresponding to an increase of 1.432 percent is given by the duration formula:

$$\text{One-year VaR} = 1.65 \times 7.5B \times 7.4 \times 0.01432 = \$1.31135B$$

In other words, as of December 1993, the one-year VaR of the Orange County pool was $1.31135 billion. There was therefore a 5 percent chance Orange County would lose at least $1.31135 billion given its investment strategy based on the assumptions of this calculation. Obviously, many refinements could be made to this calculation. However, it shows that the duration VaR tool can be sufficient to understand risk well enough to avoid big mistakes. It is hard to believe that the officials of Orange County would have used the investment strategy they chose had they known the VaR estimate we just constructed.

Sources: The Orange County debacle is described in Philippe Jorion, *Big bets gone bad: Derivatives and bankruptcy in Orange County*, Academic Press, 1995. Professor Jorion also maintains a web site that includes a case on Orange County involving various VaR computations for December 1994 and useful other materials: http://www.gsm.uci.edu/~jorion/oc/case.html.

flat, shifts in the term structure are not always parallel, and yield changes are not always small. Does this mean that the duration strategy is worthless? The answer is no. However, we show three ways to improve on modified duration to make the duration strategy perform better.

9.3.2.A. Taking into account the slope of the term structure in computing duration

Since a coupon bond is a portfolio of zero-coupon bonds, the duration of a coupon bond is the duration of a portfolio of zero-coupon bonds. Each coupon's duration has a weight in that portfolio given by the present value of the coupon as a fraction of the present value of the coupon bond.

When we use modified duration, we do not use the present value of the coupons at the appropriate market rates to compute the bond price, but rather compute the bond price using the bond yield as a discount rate. We therefore discount all coupons at the same rate. This is not a problem if the term structure is flat since the market discount rate is also the yield of the bond. When the term structure is not flat, however, this presents a difficulty.

Suppose the term structure slopes upward and we are using duration with a 30-year zero-coupon bond. The bond's yield will be higher than the discount rate appropriate for coupons paid early and will be lower than the discount rate for coupons paid close to maturity. Modified duration, however, will treat all coupons as if they have the same discount rate. Consequently, it will discount the late coupons at a lower rate than they should be discounted and the early coupons at a higher rate. Since the duration of a bond falls with the yield, using too low of a yield for the late coupons amounts to overstating the duration associated with these coupons. Simultaneously, using too high of a yield for the early coupons amounts to understating the duration associated with these coupons. Hence, with an upward-sloping term structure, modified duration overstates duration for the coupons most sensitive to the discount rate and understates duration for the coupons least sensitive to the discount rate.

To avoid these errors, the best approach is to treat each bond cash flow separately and discount it at the appropriate rate from the term structure. Let $r_t(t + i)$ be the continuously compounded rate at which a zero-coupon bond maturing at $t + i$ is discounted, where today is t. The value of a coupon payment c paid at $t + i$ is consequently:

$$\text{Current value of coupon paid at } t + i = ce^{-r_t(t+i) \times i} \qquad (9.7)$$

The impact on the value of the coupon of a small change in the discount rate is:

$$\text{Change in current value of coupon paid at}$$
$$t + i \text{ for interest rate change } \Delta r(t + i)$$

$$= -i \times e^{-r(t+i) \times i} \times c \times \Delta r(t + i)$$

$$= -i \times \text{Current value of coupon paid at } t + i \times \Delta r(t + i) \qquad (9.8)$$

The proportional change is the change given in equation (9.8) divided by the current value coupon, which amounts to $-i \times \Delta r(t + i)$. With continuous compounding, there is no difference between duration and modified duration. The duration of a zero-coupon bond using a continuously compounded discount rate is the time to maturity of the zero-coupon bond. Using equation (9.8), we can estimate the change in the bond price from a change in the whole term structure by adding the changes in the present value of the coupons. Assume the bond pays coupon yearly, matures in N years, and has price B. If $\Delta r(t + i)$ is the change in the rate for maturity $t + i$, the change in the bond price is:

$$\textbf{Change in bond price } = \qquad\qquad (9.9)$$

$$\sum_{i=1}^{N} -i \times e^{-r(t+i)\times i}\, c \times \Delta r(t+i) - N \times e^{-r(t+N)\times N} M \times \Delta r(t+N)$$

The approximation in equation (9.9) is exact for each coupon payment when the change in the interest rate is very small (infinitesimal). It does not eliminate the approximation error resulting from the convexity of bond prices for larger changes in interest rates. Expressing this result in terms of duration for a shift in the term structure of Δ for all rates, we have:

$$\frac{\Delta B}{B} = \left[\frac{\sum_{i=1}^{N} -i \times P(t+i) \times c - (N) \times P(t+N) \times M}{B} \right] \times \Delta$$

$$= -D_F \times \Delta \qquad\qquad (9.10)$$

The above term in brackets, written D_F, is called the **Fisher-Weil duration**, after the people who proposed the formula, Lawrence Fisher and Roman Weil. It is actually what Frederick Macaulay, the father of duration, had in mind when he talked about duration. The duration of each zero-coupon bond used to discount the coupon and principal payments is weighted by the portfolio weight of the current value of the payment in the bond portfolio. For instance, the i-th coupon payment's duration has weight $ce^{-r_t(t+i)} \times i/B$. This formula, which can be used for any term structure, gives the exact solution for a very small parallel shift of the term structure.

Let's consider an example showing the difference between the modified duration and the Fisher-Weil duration. We have a bond with a cash flow of $50 in five years and $50 in ten years. The five-year zero-coupon bond yield is 5 percent and the ten-year zero-coupon bond yield is 10.76315 percent. The value of the bond is $55.9825. The continuously compounded yield of the bond is 8 percent. Let's compute the modified duration of the bond:

$$M_D \text{ (Bond)} = \frac{5 \times 50e^{-0.08 \times 5} + 10 \times 50e^{-0.08 \times 10}}{55.9825} = 7$$

With this modified duration, an increase in all interest rates of 100 basis points decreases the value of the bond by $-7 \times \$55.9825 \times 0.01$, or $-\$3.92$.

Now, let's estimate the bond price change using the Fisher-Weil duration. We have:

$$D_F \text{ (Bond)} = \frac{5 \times 50e^{-0.05 \times 5} + 10 \times 50e^{-0.1076315 \times 10}}{55.9825} = 6.52$$

With the Fisher-Weil duration, the bond price falls by \$3.65. There is almost a 10 percent difference in the estimated price changes. Why is that? With the modified duration, we put more weight on the cash flow that has a higher duration because we discount it at 8 percent when it should be discounted at 10.76315 percent and we put less weight on the cash flow with a lower duration. This means that here we overstate the true exposure to interest rate changes.

9.3.2.B. Taking into account convexity

We know the duration approximation is not exact for larger interest rate changes. We can obtain a more precise approximation of the bond price change associated with an interest rate change by taking into account the curvature of the bond price function. Remember that the bond price function is approximated by a straight line when we use duration (see Figure 9.3). The straight line on which we compute the bond price following a change in the yield is below the bond price function, but the distance from the bond price function to the straight line increases as the bond price function is more convex. When using duration, we therefore would like to make an adjustment that decreases the price drop associated with an increase in yield to reflect the convexity of the bond price function.

This adjustment term uses the bond's convexity. **Bond convexity** measures the curvature of the bond pricing function for an infinitesimal change in yield. The convexity of a zero-coupon bond is duration squared. Convexity is expressed in the same units as the duration.

Bond price change using Fisher-Weil duration and convexity

Consider a zero-coupon bond maturing at $t + i$ with price at t of $P_t(t + i)$ and continuously compounded interest rate $r_t(t + i)$. The duration of that bond is i and its convexity is i^2. Using the bond's duration and convexity, the change in the bond price for a change in the interest rate of Δ is:

$$\Delta P_t(t + i) = -i \times P_t(t + i) \times \Delta + 0.5 \times i^2 \times P_t(t + i) \times \Delta^2 \qquad \text{(9.11.a)}$$

The percentage change in the bond price using modified duration and convexity is:

$$\text{Percentage price change} = -\text{Modified duration} \times \Delta y + 0.5 \times \text{Convexity} \times (\Delta y)^2 \qquad \text{(9.11.b)}$$

Modified duration uses discrete compounding and yields. The convexity is:

$$\text{Convexity} = \left[\frac{\sum_{i=1}^{i=N} \dfrac{(i + 1) \times c}{(1 + y)^{i+2}} + \dfrac{N(N + 1) \times M}{(1 + y)^{N+2}}}{B} \right] \qquad \text{(9.12)}$$

The convexity measure corresponding to duration in coupon payment periods has to be divided by the square of the number of payment periods per year to get convexity in years. So, if convexity is 100 when it is computed using semiannual coupon payment periods, it becomes 25 in years.

For default-free bonds with no options attached, convexity is positive. Using convexity and duration, we add a positive term to the expression for the percentage bond price using duration only, so that we increase the bond price following a change in the interest rate. Suppose we have a 30-year zero-coupon bond. The continuously compounded discount rate is 10 percent. The bond price is $e^{-0.1 \times 30}$, or \$0.0497871. Using duration, a 100 basis point change in the interest rate decreases the bond price by $-30 \times \$0.0497871 \times 0.01$, or \$0.0149361. The true price change obtained by using the bond price formula to compute the new bond price is \$0.012903. Using duration, we therefore overstate the price drop by \$0.00203. We can use equation (9.11.a) to compute the bond price change. In this case, i is equal to 30, and i^2 is equal to 900. Consequently, the bond price change obtained is:

$$\Delta P_t(t + i) = -i \times P_t(t + i) \times \Delta + 0.5 \times i^2 \times P_t(t + i) \times \Delta^2$$

$$= -30 \times 0.0497871 \times 0.01 + 0.5 \times 900 \times 0.0497871 \times 0.0001$$

$$= -0.0126957$$

With the convexity adjustment, we now understate the price fall by \$0.000207. Using convexity reduces the absolute value of the mistake by a factor of 10 in this case.

Duration captures the first-order effect of interest rate changes on bond prices. The duration hedge eliminates this first-order effect. Convexity captures the second-order effect of interest rate changes. Setting the convexity of the hedged portfolio equal to zero eliminates this second-order effect. To eliminate both the first-order and the second-order effects of interest rate changes, we therefore want to take a hedge position that has the same duration and the same convexity as the portfolio we are trying to hedge.

To understand how convexity can affect the success of a hedge, let's go back to Investbank Corp., but now we assume that it has a duration of 21 years and a convexity of 500 using the Fisher-Weil duration instead of the modified duration. Suppose that we hedge with the 30-year zero-coupon bond. This zero-coupon bond has a duration of 30 and a convexity of 900. The bank's equity is worth \$20 million. If we use only the 30-year bond, we have to go short \$$h$ of the zero-coupon bond, so that \$$h \times 30 \times \Delta r$ is equal to $21 \times \$20M \times \Delta r$. The short position in the zero-coupon bond must therefore be for $0.7 \times \$20M$, or \$14 million. The convexity of Investbank Corp. is $500 - 0.7 \times 900$, or -130. In this case, the hedged bank has negative convexity.

To see how interest rate changes affect the value of the bank, suppose the current interest rate is 5 percent and the bank earns 8 percent on its equity over the next year if interest rates do not move. In this case, the hedged bank's value one year from now as a function of the interest rate then prevailing is given in Figure 9.4 assuming that the bank has no duration and negative convexity of 130 in one year. In this figure, the value of the bank is a concave function of the interest rate.

Figure 9.4 Value of hedged bank

This figure shows the value of the hedged bank when the unhedged bank has a duration of 21 years and a convexity of 500. The bank is hedged with a zero-coupon bond with maturity of 30 years. This zero-coupon bond has a duration of 30 years and a convexity of 900. The hedged bank has no duration at the current rate but has negative convexity. (Note that the present value of the hedged bank cannot be $20 million. The present value of the hedged bank is the present value of the payoff represented in this figure. Hence, the bank will be worth more than expected if rates do not change and will be worth less if they change by much.)

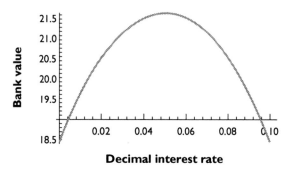

This value reaches a maximum of $21.6657 million at the current interest rate, which we take to be 5 percent. At that rate, the slope of this function is zero if the bank is still hedged so that it has no duration. The current value of the hedged bank's equity, $20 million, is the present value of its hedged payoff one year from now. Since the bank value is highest if rates do not change this means that if rates do not change, the bank value is higher than expected, and if rates change by much in either direction the bank value is lower than expected. Hence, for the bank to earn a fair rate of return, it has to earn more than the risk-free rate of 5 percent if interest rates do not change.

To improve the hedge, we can construct a hedge so that the hedged bank has neither duration nor convexity. This requires us to use an additional hedging instrument so that we can make the convexity of the hedged bank equal to zero. Let h be the short position in a zero-coupon bond with maturity i and k be the short position in a zero-coupon bond with maturity j. We invest the proceeds of the short positions in a money market instrument so that the value of the bank is unaffected by the hedge. In this case, the hedge we need is:

Duration of unhedged bank
= (h/Value of bank) $\times$ i + (k/Value of bank) $\times$ j

Convexity of unhedged bank
= (h/Value of bank) $\times$ i^2 + (k/Value of bank) $\times$ j^2

Let's use a zero-coupon bond of 30 years and one of 5 years. We then need to solve:

$$21 = (h/20) \times 30 + (k/20) \times 5$$

$$500 = (h/20) \times 900 + (k/20) \times 25$$

The solution is to have h equal to 10.5333 and k equal to 20.8002.[5] In this case, the duration is $-(10.5333/20) \times 30 + 21 - (20.8002/20) \times 5$, which is zero. The convexity is $-(10.5333/20) \times 900 + 500 - (20.8002/20) \times 25$, which is also zero.

We can estimate VaR using duration and convexity. Since any fixed-income portfolio of default-free bonds (with no options attached) can be decomposed into a portfolio of investments in zero-coupon bonds, we can model the random change in the value of the portfolio in a straightforward way using the Fisher-Weil formulas for duration and convexity.

$C_t(t + i)$ represents the portfolio cash flow in year $t + i$. For example, if the portfolio holds one coupon bond which makes a coupon payment at date $t + i$ equal to c, $C_t(t + i)$ is equal to c. In this case, the value of the portfolio W is given by:

$$W = \sum_{i=1}^{N} P_t(t + i) \times C_t(t + i)$$

If we make zero-coupon bond prices depend on one interest rate only, r, then we have:

$$\Delta W = \sum_{i=1}^{N} C_t(t + i) \, \Delta P_t(t + i)$$

$$= \sum_{i=1}^{N} C_t(t + i) \Big[i \times \Delta r - 0.5 \times i^2 \times (\Delta r)^2 \Big] \tag{9.13}$$

Using this equation, we can then simulate the portfolio return by generating random changes in r and use the fifth percentile portfolio value from the simulation as our VaR estimate.

9.3.2.C. "Maturity bins" to protect against changes in the slope and shape of the term structure

Duration protects a portfolio against changes in the level of the term structure. Level term structure changes explain a large fraction of bond yield changes—at least 60 percent across countries. In the United States, level changes in the term structure explain more than 75 percent of the bond yield changes for U.S. government bonds, about 10 percent less for high grade corporate bonds, and still less for riskier corporate bonds. In other words, we can expect to eliminate a substantial fraction of the volatility of a bond portfolio through a duration hedge even though not all interest rate changes correspond to level shifts in the term structure.

If all changes in yields for the assets and liabilities of a portfolio are brought about by parallel shifts in the yield curve, the portfolio is hedged against small changes in interest rates if we make the duration of the hedged portfolio zero. To hedge against larger changes in interest rates, we would choose a hedge portfolio

---

5 We obtain this solution by substitution. We first solve the first equation for h in terms of k to get $h = 14 - k \times 5/30$. We then substitute the solution for h in the second equation. This gives us the value for k. Substituting k in the first equation gives us h.

that has a convexity of zero. With parallel shifts in the term structure, the duration of the securities we use to hedge does not matter. This is a strength of duration, since it allows us to use the most liquid bonds to hedge. Suppose a portfolio of $100 million has a 10-year duration. We can hedge that portfolio by going short $1 billion of securities with one-year duration. In this case, the duration of the hedged portfolio is 10 × ($100M/$100M) − 1 × ($1B/$100M), or zero. Alternatively, we could hedge by going short $50 million of securities with a duration of 20. Whatever the duration of the hedge, a 100 basis point increase in yields has no effect on the value of the portfolio when its impact is evaluated using duration.

If changes in the slope and shape of the term structure are a concern, it is no longer the case that the duration of the security used to hedge does not matter. Suppose that we have a steepening of the term structure associated with an increase in rates. The short term increases by 100 basis points while the medium- and long-term rates increase by 200 basis points. The yield of our portfolio goes from 5 to 7 percent. Using duration, we lose 10 × $100M × 0.02, or $20 million. If we hedged with a security that had a one-year duration, we were short $1 billion of that security. Its yield increases only by 100 basis points. Therefore, we gain only $10 million on our hedge, 1 × $1B × 0.01, and our hedged portfolio loses $10 million. Yet, had we hedged with the security that has a duration of 20 years, the yield of that security would have increased by 200 basis points. Consequently, we would have gained 20 × $50M × 0.02, or $20 million, so that we would have been perfectly hedged.

One way to construct a hedged portfolio whose value is insensitive to changes in the slope and shape of the term structure is to start from the cash flows of the portfolio. We can then assign cash flows to maturity bins. For example, all cash flows that are received or paid in a five-year period starting five years from now are put in one bin. Now, instead of hedging the whole portfolio directly, we choose a hedging instrument that reflects zero-coupon bond rates for maturities corresponding to the bin we are hedging and then set the duration of the bin equal to zero using that instrument. This way the yield of the hedging instrument will move by the same amount as the yield of the cash flows hedged.

To implement this approach, one has to have appropriate hedging instruments. In many countries, such instruments are not available, while duration hedges can be implemented.

9.4. Measuring and managing interest rate risk without duration

Duration makes it possible to evaluate exactly the impact of an infinitesimal parallel shift in the term structure. Duration requires a parallel shift and becomes less precise as the size of the shift increases. Whether we use duration only or duration plus convexity, we have only an approximation for interest rate changes that are not infinitesimal.

To estimate VaR, we have to use a distribution for interest rate changes. With a distribution fitted to actual data, there is some possibility of large changes in rates for which duration works poorly. Further, changes for rates of different maturities are not perfectly correlated, so that we have to be able to evaluate the impact of shifts in the term structure, which cannot be done with simple duration approaches. Consequently, if we use duration to measure VaR, we ignore a potentially important source of risk, namely risks associated with changes in the shape of the term structure. We ignore changes in spreads among rates when we apply duration to bonds with credit risks, too. As rates change, credit spreads can change. There is empirical evidence that credit spreads fall as interest rates increase. Bonds often have embedded options—for example, the issuer can call the bond, the holder can exchange the bond for another bond or stock, the holder can put the bond, and so on. Whereas an institution with only high-grade bonds with no embedded options may not miss much if it uses duration, this is not the case for institutions that hold bonds with embedded options or bonds with significant default risks.

The alternative to duration is direct consideration of the impact of interest rate changes on prices. To see how an interest rate change affects the value of a fixed-income position, we simply compute the value of the position given the new interest rates. For example, we can evaluate the impact on the portfolio of a one basis point change in rates by recomputing the value of the portfolio for that change. This approach is becoming increasingly common.

A good example is the Chase Manhattan Bank. In 1999, Chase stopped reporting the gap measures represented in Table 9.2 and started reporting the basis point value for its portfolio (BPV). The BPV gives the change in the market value of a portfolio for a one basis point change in rates. Before 1999, Chase used BPV for its trading portfolio only. Since 1999, it has used it more broadly to include other assets and liabilities. Chase considers two different BPVs. First, it estimates the impact of a one basis point change in interest rates. It reports that at the end of December 31, 1999, the BPV for a one basis point change in rates was –$6.4 million. Second, it computes the impact of a one basis point change in spreads between liabilities and assets (basis risk). It reports that the BPV of a one basis point change in spreads is –$10.7 million.

Recomputing the portfolio value for different interest rates, we can compute the portfolio's VaR as well as construct minimum-volatility hedges. Computing power is the key. For example, we can estimate a joint distribution for the interest rates one is interested in, and use Monte Carlo simulation to obtain draws of interest rates. For each draw of the interest rates, we compute the value of the position. After a large number of draws, we end up with a simulated distribution of the value of the position given the joint distribution of the interest rate changes. We can then use the fifth percentile of that simulated distribution as our VaR and use the distribution to construct minimum-volatility hedges. Alternatively, we could use historical changes in interest rates to obtain simulated values of the position. This type of approach was out of reach when Macaulay introduced his duration measure. Repricing a fixed-income portfolio can now be implemented within minutes or hours.

A model in which all rates depend on only one random variable is called a one-factor model of the term structure. In a one-factor model of the term structure, all rates depend on a single random variable and are therefore perfectly correlated. The duration model is a one-factor model of the term structure; it allows only identical changes to all rates. To allow for rates to be imperfectly correlated, we must allow for more sources of variation in rates. If we make the rates depend on two random variables or sources of risk, we have a two-factor model of the term structure.

When we allow more sources of risk to affect interest rates, a wider range of changes in the shape of the term structure becomes possible. Three alternate approaches to modeling interest rate risk are possible. The first approach considers the distribution of the zero-coupon bond prices. The second approach models spot interest rates as functions of factors. The third approach uses the distribution of forward rates.

9.4.1. Using zero-coupon bond prices as risk factors

The simplest way to model the risk of a fixed-income portfolio without using duration is to use the joint distribution of the returns of the securities in the portfolio. If returns are normally distributed, we know how to compute a VaR analytically. Knowing the joint distribution of the returns of the securities, we could construct minimum-volatility hedges using the covariances and variances of the returns of these securities.

This approach is a natural use of modern portfolio theory, but it runs into some difficulties. The first is that, if we proceed this way, there are likely to be arbitrage opportunities among our fixed-income securities. The portfolio might have many different bonds, each with its own return. We know that to avoid arbitrage opportunities the law of one price must hold: There can be only one price today for a dollar delivered for sure at a future date. This means that if 20 different bonds pay a risk-free cash flow in 30 years exactly, all 20 bonds must discount that risk-free cash flow at the same rate. This does not happen if we allow all bonds to have imperfectly correlated returns.

To eliminate arbitrage opportunities, we can start by generating zero-coupon bond prices and use these bonds to price other bonds. This ensures that all risk-free payoffs have the same prices across bonds. Since any default-free fixed-income security with no options attached is a portfolio of zero-coupon bonds, we can transform any portfolio of such fixed-income securities into a portfolio of zero-coupon bonds. We know how to compute the analytical VaR of stock portfolios when stock returns are normally distributed. We can therefore compute an analytical VaR of portfolios of zero-coupon bonds if zero-coupon bond returns are normally distributed and if we know the volatilities and correlations of the zero-coupon bond returns. RiskMetrics™ assumes that zero-coupon bond returns are normally distributed and provides volatilities and correlations of zero-coupon bond returns. As explained in Chapter 4, the risk model proposed by RiskMetrics™ is widely used. Consequently, with the information provided by RiskMetrics™ we can estimate the VaR of a portfolio of fixed-income securities as we would estimate the VaR of a portfolio of stocks. In addition, since we know the distribution of the return of the portfolio, we can also manage the risk of the portfolio by constructing a minimum-volatility hedge.

The second difficulty is that there are too many securities if we treat each separately. This makes it impractical to compute the distribution of each possible zero-coupon bond. To cope with this difficulty, RiskMetrics™ makes available correlations and volatilities of the returns of selected zero-coupon bonds. To use the RiskMetrics™ approach, we have to transform a fixed-income security into a portfolio of zero-coupon bonds. If the six-year zero-coupon bond is not in the dataset, we have to find a solution where we can know the distribution of the return of the six-year zero-coupon bond. The approach recommended by Risk-Metrics™ involves an interpolation method that is described in Technical Box 9.3, RiskMetrics™ and bond prices.

9.4.2. Reducing the number of sources of risk: Factor models

A different approach is to assume that a few risk factors explain changes in all bond prices. The simplest such model assumes that returns on bonds depend on two factors, such as a short rate and a longer maturity rate or a spread between long maturity and short maturity. The short rate is intended to capture the level of the term structure, and the spread or the long maturity rate is intended to

---

RiskMetrics™ and bond prices   *Technical Box 9.3*

The RiskMetrics™ approach to evaluating interest rate risk involves two steps. The first step consists in mapping cash flows from fixed-income securities to the cash flows available from RiskMetrics™. RiskMetrics™ calls these cash flows vertices. In our language, this operation amounts to matching the cash flows of default-free fixed-income securities to the cash flows of zero-coupon bonds. Through this operation, the portfolio of fixed-income securities is transformed into an equivalent portfolio of zero-coupon bonds. Its return then becomes the return of a portfolio of zero-coupon bonds. RiskMetrics™ makes available the volatilities and the correlations of the returns of these zero-coupon bonds. We can therefore compute an analytical VaR using this information and using as portfolio weights the investments in the zero-coupon bonds of the transformed portfolio.

The complication with the RiskMetrics™ approach is that there are at most 14 vertices available: 1, 3, 6, and 12 months, and 2, 3, 4, 5, 7, 9, 10, 15, 20, and 30 years. Obviously, a portfolio will have cash flows with maturities that do not correspond to the vertices. For example, a portfolio might have a cash flow that matures in 6 years. The solution is then to attribute that cash flow to the two adjoining vertices, 5 year and 7 year, in a way that does not affect the risk of the portfolio compared to what it would be if we had the 6 year vertex. This means that (1) the total value of the cash flow must not be affected by the split, (2) the market risk must be preserved, and (3) the sign is preserved.

The implementation of the approach works by first interpolating the yields linearly. In our example, the 6-year yield is half the 5-year and half the 7-year yields. With the interpolated 6-year yield, we can compute the present value of the 6-year cash flow. The volatility of the 6-year return is computed by taking a linear interpolation of the 5-year and 7-year volatilities. We then solve for weights on the 5-year and the 7-year zeroes so that the variance of this portfolio of two zeroes has the same variance as the 6-year return and the same value. These weights are then used to split the 6-year cash flow into a 5-year and a 7-year cash flow. The following table reproduces an example from the Risk-Metrics™ manual.

(continued)

Technical Box 9.3 (continued)

RiskMetrics™ mapping of cash flows.

Problem: On July 31, 1996, we expect a cash flow occurring in 6 years of USD 100.

Data from RiskMetrics™:		
$r_t(t+5)$	5-year yield	6.605%
$r_t(t+7)$	7-year yield	6.745%
$1.65\text{std}(r_t(t+5))$	RiskMetrics™ volatility on the 5-year bond price return	0.5770%
$1.65\text{std}(r_t(t+7))$	RiskMetrics™ volatility on the 7-year bond price return	0.8095%
$\rho(r_t(t+5), r_t(t+7))$	Correlation between the 5-year and the 7-year bond return	0.9975%
Interpolation of yields	$0.5 \times 6.605\% + 0.5 \times 6.745\%$	6.675%
Standard deviation of $r_t(t+6)$	$0.5 \times (0.5770\%/1.65) + 0.5 \times (0.8095\%/1.65)$	0.4202%
Variance of		
$r_t(t+6)$		$1.765*10^{-3}\%$
$r_t(t+5)$		$1.223*10^{-3}\%$
$r_t(t+7)$		$2.406*10^{-3}\%$
Computation of weight α of 5-year bond and $(1-\alpha)$ of 7-year bond	$1.765 = \alpha^2 \times 1.223 + (1-\alpha)^2 \times 2.406 + 2 \times \alpha \times (1-\alpha) \times (0.5770\%/1.65) \times (0.8095\%/1.65) \times 0.99751$	**Solution:** One solution of this equation is $\alpha = 5.999$ and the other is $\alpha = 0.489$. The first solution does not preserve the sign. The second solution is chosen. The 6-year cash flow is worth USD 93.74. 48.9% of that corresponding to a 5-year bond.

capture the steepness of the curve. When two risk factors are used to explain the term structure, we have a two-factor model. A two-factor model explains returns on bonds better than the duration model, where returns depend on only one factor. A two-factor model explains about 10 percent to 20 percent more of the returns of government bonds than the one-factor model.

Factor analysis also can identify common factors that influence returns of zero-coupon bonds. Suppose we have time-series information for a cross-section of variables, say returns for bonds with different maturities. Factor analysis is a statistical technique that extracts from the data explanatory variables, or factors, that explain bond returns in a regression. Using this technique, analysts extract factors from the data rather than pre-specify them. Litterman and Scheinkman (1991) find that three factors explain at least 95 percent of the variance of the return of zero-coupon bonds. The three factors extracted this way roughly correspond to a level effect, a steepness effect, and a curvature effect. The level or duration effect explains at least 79.5 percent of the variance of the return of zero-coupon bonds. With a time series of factor returns, we can estimate the exposure of each zero-coupon bond using a regression of zero-coupon bond returns on factor returns.

A three-factor model like Litterman and Scheinkman's can be used to hedge. They consider a portfolio with a duration of zero as shown in Table 9.3. That portfolio is bought on February 5, 1986, and sold on March 5, 1986. This portfolio has short positions in the first and third bond and a long position in the second bond. Interest rates fall over that period, so that the portfolio loses money on the short positions and makes profits on the long positions. Over that month, it loses $650,000. Using their three factors, they find that the portfolio loses $84,010 for a one standard deviation (monthly) shock to the level factor, gains $6,500 for a one standard deviation shock to the steepness factor, and loses $444,950 for a one standard deviation in the curvature factor. During the month, the level factor changes by −1.482 standard deviations, the steepness factor by −2.487 standard deviations, and the curvature factor by 1.453 standard deviations. To compute the total impact of these changes on the value of the portfolio, we add these effects:

$$\text{Total change in portfolio value} = -1.482 \times (-\$84,010)$$
$$-2.487 \times \$6,500 + 1.453 \times (-\$444,950) = -\$538,175$$

Since the portfolio has a duration of zero, we would predict no change in its value with a change in rates. The problem is that duration ignores the effect of changes

Examples from Litterman and Scheinkman (1991)				*Table 9.3*
Face value ($)	Coupon	Maturity	Price on February 5, 1986	Price on March 5, 1986
−118,000,000	12 3/8	8/15/87	106 5/32	106 9/32
100,000,000	11 5/8	1/15/92	112 12/32	115 20/32
−32,700,000	13 3/8	8/15/01	130 16/32	141 14/32

in the curvature of the term structure on the value of the portfolio. The three-factor model captures this effect.

To hedge the portfolio with the three-factor model, we would have to go short portfolios that mimic the factors. For example, we would take a position in a portfolio that mimics the curvature factor so that we gain $444,950 for a one standard deviation move in the curvature factor. To hedge a portfolio that is exposed to the three factors, we would therefore have to take positions in three factor mimicking portfolios to set the exposure of the hedged portfolio to each one of the factors equal to zero.

Knowing the exposure of a position to the factors is useful for three reasons. First, if we know the joint distribution of the factors, we can use this joint distribution to compute VaR. If the factor returns are normally distributed, we can take a fixed-income position and compute an analytical VaR. If the factors are normally distributed returns, and we have three factors, the return on a fixed-income position is equivalent to the return of a three-security portfolio, where each security corresponds to a factor. We already know how to compute the VaR analytically in this case.

Second, knowing the exposure of a position to the factors allows us to construct a hedge against this exposure. All we have to do is take a position in securities or futures contracts that have factor loadings that cancel out the factor loadings of our fixed-income position.

Finally, exposure to factors can be an active management tool. We may feel that exposure to one of the factors is rewarding while exposure to the other factors is not. In this case, our understanding of the factor exposures of our position and of individual securities allows us to make sure that we are exposed to the right factor.

9.4.3. Forward curve models

The duration, zero-coupon bond, and factor model approaches do not guarantee that discount rates are distributed so that there cannot be arbitrage opportunities. This is unfortunate because we do not expect to find pure arbitrage opportunities in the markets. If a term structure allows for arbitrage opportunities, one ends up with prices that do not correspond to prices one expects to find in actual markets, and hence the value of the position one obtains is not right. A key requirement for a term structure to exhibit no arbitrage opportunities is that if we have a zero-coupon bond that pays $1 at time $t + i$ with price at t of $P_t(t + i)$, and a zero-coupon bond that pays $1 at time $t + j$ with price $P_t(t + j)$, it must be the case that $P_t(t + j) < P_t(t + i)$ as maturity date $t + i$ takes place before maturity date $t + j$. If $P_t(t + i)$ is the less expensive bond, we can buy that bond and sell the other bond short. We then make a profit today of $P_t(t + j) - P_t(t + i)$ that we get to keep. At date $t + i$, we keep the proceeds from the bond that matures in the risk-free asset. At date $t + j$, we use these proceeds to reverse the short sale.

The problem is that if we are not careful in generating draws of the term structure of interest rates, we can end up with a zero-coupon bond that is more expensive than a zero-coupon bond that matures sooner. For example, if the one-day returns of two zero-coupon bond prices are normally distributed and not perfectly correlated, there is always some probability that the bond with a short maturity ends up being less expensive since one bond could increase in price and the other could fall. To avoid this problem, we must impose some restrictions on how term structures are generated.

A straightforward way to avoid arbitrage opportunities is to use the forward curve. Let $f_t(t + i)$ be the forward rate at t for delivery of a one-year zero-coupon bond at $t + i$. Using continuous compounding, $f_t(t + i)$ is equal to the logarithm of $P_t(t + i)/P_t(t + i + 1)$. The forward rates $f_t(t + i)$, for all i's, define the forward curve. This curve differs from the term structure obtained using yields of zero-coupon bonds or using coupon bonds. The traditional term structure curve is given by the yields of coupon bonds. It is generally called the par curve since it gives the coupon yield of bonds issued at par.

With the forward curve, we could use forward rates for delivery of zero-coupon bonds with a shorter maturity than a year. For example, we could construct a forward curve using the forward rates for delivery of three-month zero-coupon bonds. The procedure to construct the curve would be the same.

Figure 9.5 shows the curves for an upward-sloping term structure. For such a term structure, the zero-coupon bond yield curve, usually called the zero (for zero-coupon) curve, is above the par curve. The par curve has the yields of par bonds. The yield of a par bond is a weighted average of the yields of the zero-coupon bonds that compose the portfolio of zero-coupon bonds. The yield of the zero-coupon bond with the same maturity as the coupon bond is the zero-coupon bond in that portfolio that has the highest yield when the term structure is upward sloping. The forward rate for a six-month zero-coupon bond corresponding to the maturity of the zero-coupon bond is the six-month forward rate implied by that zero-coupon bond and the one maturing six months later. With an upward-sloping term structure, the forward rate is higher than the yield of the zero-coupon bond because the yield of the zero-coupon bond increases as the maturity lengthens, which can be achieved only through a higher implied yield for the next

Term structures   *Figure 9.5*

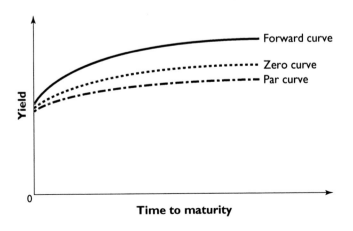

period of time. Figure 9.5 shows how the forward curve, the zero curve, and the par curve relate to each other for an upward-sloping term structure.

From the forward curve, we can compute the value of any bond. To show that this is correct, it is sufficient to show that we can use the forward curve to compute the present value of one coupon. Consider the coupon c paid at $t + i$. We can enter today a forward contract such that, at $t + i - 1$, we take delivery of c zero-coupon bonds that each pay \$1 the next period. With this contract, we agree to buy zero-coupon bonds at $t + i - 1$ for face value c for a price of $F_t(t + i - 1)c$ per coupon. The present value of the coupon today is therefore $P_t(t + i - 1)F_t(t + i - 1)c$. To price the coupon using the forward curve, we have to replace $P_t(t + i - 1)$ by forward prices.

We can enter a forward contract that allows us to buy zero-coupon bonds at $t + i - 2$, so that we can use these zero-coupon bonds to pay for delivery of the zero-coupon bonds we receive at $t + i - 1$. To do that, we need to enter a forward contract that delivers zero-coupon bonds for face value $F_t(t + i - 1)c$ at $t + i - 2$. The price today of a zero-coupon bond that pays \$1 at $t + i - 1$ to be delivered at $t + i - 2$ is $F_t(t + i - 2)$. Therefore, at $t + i - 2$ we will have to pay $F_t(t + i - 2)F_t(t + i - 1)c$. With this forward contract, we then get the $F_t(t + i - 1)c$ face value zero-coupon bonds at $t + i - 2$. At $t + i - 1$, we have $F_t(t + i - 1)c$ that we use to take delivery on the forward contract that matures at that date. We then have zero-coupon bonds with face value of c. At $t + i$, we therefore have c.

The value at t of the coupon to be paid at $t + i$ is therefore $P_t(t + i - 2)F_t(t + i - 2)F_t(t + i - 1)c$. We can keep entering forward contracts, so that we have a forward contract maturing at each date. When we do that, the value of the coupon is $F_t(t)F_t(t + 1)F_t(t + 2)...F_t(t + i - 2)F_t(t + i - 1)c$. $F_t(t)$ is the forward price for immediate delivery, which is the zero-coupon bond price for a bond maturing at $t + 1$. If we know the forward curve, we know the price of each forward contract. Therefore, we can price a bond from the forward curve.

Another way to show that the value at t of the coupon to be paid at $t + i$ is given by the forward curve is to use the definition of the forward price, $F_t(t + j) = P_t(t + j + 1)/P_t(t + j)$:

Value of coupon today

$$= P_t(t + i)c$$

$$= \left[\frac{P_t(t + 1)}{P_t(t)}\right]\left[\frac{P_t(t + 2)}{P_t(t + 1)}\right]...\left[\frac{P_t(t + i - 2)}{P_t(t + i - 3)}\right]\left[\frac{P_t(t + i - 1)}{P_t(t + i - 2)}\right]\left[\frac{P_t(t + i)}{P_t(t + i - 1)}\right]c$$

$$= F_t(t) \times F_t(t + 1) \times F_t(t + 2)...F_t(t + i - 2) \times F_t(t + i - 1) \times c$$

$$= ce^{-r_t(t)}e^{-f_t(t + 1)}e^{-f_t(t + 2)}...\bar{e}^{f_t(t + i - 2)}e^{-f_t(t + i - 1)}$$

$$= ce^{-r_t(t) - f_t(t + 1) - f_t(t + 2)...- f_t(t + i - 2) - f_t(t + i - 1)} \tag{9.14}$$

$P_t(t)$ is the price of a zero-coupon bond that pays \$1 at t and is therefore 1. The discount rate in the last line is the sum of the one-period forward rates plus the current spot rate. If we know the joint distribution of forward rates, we can simulate forward curves and value the portfolio for each simulated forward curve.

There is an important difference between the forward curve approach and the approaches that use zero-coupon bond prices or rates for various maturities. With continuous compounding, equation (9.14) shows that the discount rate that applies to a bond maturing at $t + i$ is the sum of the forward rates. Hence, a shock to the forward rate for maturity $t + i$ has a one-for-one effect on the discount rate of all zero-coupon bonds that mature later and has no effect on the discount rate of zero-coupon bonds that mature earlier. If we instead simulate zero-coupon bonds using the joint distribution of zero-coupon bond returns, a price realization of the price of a zero-coupon bond for one maturity could be high without affecting the price of the zero-coupon bonds maturing later on because of the risk of the bond uncorrelated with the risk of other bond prices. The same could be the case if one uses discount rates instead of zero-coupon bond prices. The forward rate approach therefore ensures that the no-arbitrage condition holds for the term structure.

We can obtain simulated forward curves in essentially two ways. One way is to use the historical changes in the forward curve. To do that, we compute either absolute changes or proportional changes of the forward curve over past periods. If we want to estimate a one-month VaR, we use monthly changes. Whether we use absolute or proportional changes depends on whether we believe that the distribution of absolute or proportional changes is more stable. There are good arguments to use proportional changes since, when interest rates are low, we would think that a 100 basis point change in rates is not as likely as when rates are high.

Computing changes using past history allows us to construct a database of changes. We can then apply these changes to the current term structure to obtain simulated term structures for which we compute portfolio values. The fifth percentile of these portfolio values gives us the VaR.

Alternatively, we can estimate the joint statistical distribution of changes in the forward curve using past data. For example, we could assume that proportional changes are jointly normally distributed and then estimate the parameters for this joint distribution. Then we could use that distribution for a Monte Carlo analysis. With this analysis, we would draw forward curves and price the portfolio for these forward curves to get a VaR. We could also assume that forward rate changes follow a factor model, so that the whole forward curve changes depend on relatively few sources of risk.

9.5. Summary

A firm's mix of floating and fixed rate debt is a risk management tool. If the firm at a particular time sees it has the wrong mix, it can change the mix by refinancing or by using derivatives. We can transform floating rate debt into fixed rate debt using the eurodollar futures contract. A financial institution's interest rate exposure can be evaluated in terms of the effect of interest rate changes on income or on value. We show how one can compute CaR for a financial institution. To compute VaR for a financial institution, we have to understand how changes in interest rates affect the value of the securities held by that institution. Traditionally, duration has been the most popular tool for such an assessment. There are various ways to implement the duration. Modified duration is computed using bond yields. With the Fisher-Weil duration, we transform a coupon bond into a portfolio of zero-coupon bonds and use the interest rates of these zero-coupon bonds to compute duration. Finally, we can add convexity to duration to take into account the nonlinear relation between bond prices and interest rates. Whatever duration we use, we can compute a duration-based VaR. In the last section of the chapter, we consider ways of computing VaR and evaluating interest rate risk that do not rely on duration but rather evaluate the impact of interest rate changes on the value of fixed-income securities directly. One approach, proposed by RiskMetrics™, treats zero-coupon bond prices as risk factors. Another approach treats interest rates as risk factors. The last approach treats forward rates as risk factors.

Key Concepts

asset sensitive, 267
bond convexity 282
dollar maturity gap, 267
duration, 273
Fisher-Weil duration, 281
forward rate agreement, 265

liability sensitive, 266
LIBOR, 259
modified duration, 274
percentage maturity gap, 267
stress test, 270

Review Questions

1. What is floating rate debt?

2. What is LIBOR?

3. What is the reset date?

4. What is an FRA?

5. How do you interpret a eurodollar futures index of 92?

6. What does it mean to say that a bank is liability sensitive?

7. How do you define the dollar maturity gap for the period from one to five years?

8. What is a stress test?

9. How do you estimate the impact of a change in yield on a bond price using modified duration?

10. How does Fisher-Weil duration differ from modified duration?

11. How does the additional use of convexity affect your estimate of the impact of a change in yield on a bond price obtained using modified duration only?

12. What is BPV?

13. What is a factor model for interest rates or zero-coupon bond returns?

14. What is a forward curve model?

15. Which approach in modeling the risk of a fixed-income portfolio guarantees that there are no arbitrage opportunities between the zero-coupon bond prices generated through a draw of a Monte Carlo simulation?

Questions and Exercises

1. A firm has fixed-income of $10 million per year and debt with face value of $100 million and 20-year maturity. The debt has a coupon reset every six months. The rate that determines the coupon is the six-month LIBOR. The total coupon payment is half the six-month LIBOR on the reset date in decimal form times the face value. Today is the reset date. The next coupon has just been set and is to be paid in six months. The six-month LIBOR at the reset date is 5.5 percent annually. The volatility of six-month LIBOR is assumed to be 100 basis points annually and the term structure is flat. What is the one-year CaR for this firm assuming that the only risk is due to the coupon payments on the debt?

2. What is the value of the debt at the reset date if the debt has no credit risk? What is the duration of the debt at the reset date if the debt has no credit risk?

3. A position has modified duration of 25 years and is worth $100 million. The term structure is flat. By how much does the value of the position change if interest rates change by 25 basis points?

4. Suppose that you are told that the position has convexity of 200 years. How does your answer to question 3 change?

5. Consider a coupon bond of $100 million that pays coupon of $4 million and has no credit risk. The coupon payments are in 3, 9, and 15 months. The principal is paid in 15 months as well. The zero-coupon bond prices are $P_t(t + 0.25) = 0.97531$, $P_t(t + 0.75) = 0.92427$, and $P_t(t + 1.25) = 0.82484$. What is the current bond price? What is the forward price today for a six-month zero-coupon bond delivered in nine months? What is the forward rate associated with that forward price?

6. Using the Fisher-Weil duration, compute the impact of a parallel shift in the yield curve of 50 basis points for the data in question 5. How does your answer compare to the change in the bond price you obtain by computing the new bond price directly and subtracting it from the bond price before the parallel shift?

7. Compute the yield of the bond and then compute the modified duration using the data in question 5. What is the impact of a 50 basis points change in the yield using the modified duration? How does it compare to your answer in question 6? How does your answer compare to the change computed directly from the new and the old bond prices?

8. How does your answer to question 7 change if you also use convexity?

9. Assume that the volatility of the zero-coupon bond prices expressed per year in question 5 is 1 percent for the 3-month bond, 3 percent for the

9-month bond, and 5 percent for the 15-month bond. The correlation coefficients of the bonds are 0.9 between all bonds. Ignoring expected changes in value of the bonds, what is the volatility of the bond price? Assuming that the returns of the zero-coupon bond prices are normally distributed, what is the one-day VaR of the bond?

10. Show how the par curve, the zero curve, and the forward curve relate to each other if the term structure is downward sloping.

Literature Note

There are a large number of useful books on fixed-income markets. Fabozzi (1996) provides the ideal background. More advanced books include Ho (1990) and Van Deventer and Imai (1997). Van Deventer and Imai (1997) have a more formal treatment of some of the arguments presented here. Their book also covers some of the topics discussed in Chapter 14. Duffie (1994) reviews the issues involved in interest rate risk management and presents the forward rate approach that we discuss in this chapter. The paper by Litterman and Scheinkman (1991) addresses the key issues involved in factor models. Ilmanen (1992) presents an empirical assessment of duration that supports our discussion. Bierwag, Kaufman, and Toevs (1983) provide a collection of papers evaluating duration in a scientific way. Ingersoll, Skelton, and Weil (1978) provide the Fisher-Weil duration measure discussed in the text and relate it to the work of Macaulay. The RiskMetrics™ manual provides complete information on how RiskMetrics™ deals with interest rate risks. Duffee (1998) shows that credits spreads are negatively related to interest rates.

Chapter 10

Hedging with Options

Chapter **10** *Objectives*

At the end of this chapter, you will:

1. Be able to choose between forwards and options as hedging instruments.

2. Know how to use options to hedge complicated contingent exposures.

3. Be able to determine whether a firm should buy or sell options on itself.

4. Know how to set bounds on option prices.

A **static hedge** is a hedge position that is put in place at one time and is not changed until maturity of the exposure. Export Inc. puts on a static hedge when it sells forward Swiss francs it will receive three months later. Unfortunately, exposures to a risk factor often depend on the level of the risk factor. We saw in Chapter 8 the example of Motor Inc., which exports from the United Kingdom to the United States. It has a dollar exposure that increases as the dollar appreciates. We saw in Chapter 9 that the exposure of a bond to interest rates increases as interest rates fall. Static hedges with futures and forwards can lead to large hedging mistakes when exposures change over time. In the worst case, where exposures change sign, a static hedge with forward and futures can make us worse off than not having hedged at all.

Options permit us to create static hedges for exposures that depend on risk factors that perform dramatically better than static hedges with forwards and futures. Consumer Credit Inc. has a portfolio of consumer loans. The risk manager is asked to hedge the credit risk of the portfolio. If the economy does well, the loans will get paid back. No matter how well the economy does, however, Consumer Credit cannot receive more than the principal and interest on its loans, so that it makes little difference to it whether the economy is doing well or spectacularly well. However, if the economy does poorly, people who are laid off have trouble paying back loans, so that Consumer Credit incurs losses. If economic conditions become sufficiently bad, Consumer Credit might have to file for bankruptcy. Consumer Credit's loan portfolio has an exposure to economic conditions that is high when the economy is doing poorly but low when the economy is doing well. Buying a put on the S&P 500 helps Consumer Credit hedge its business cycle risk. The put makes money if the economy's prospects worsen, but it does not lose increasing sums of money as the economy improves—the most money Consumer Credit loses with its hedge is the put price.

Now suppose Consumer Credit used a static hedge consisting of a short position in the S&P 500 futures contract instead of the option hedge. If the S&P 500 falls, the hedge works because Consumer Credit makes money on the futures position but expects to incur losses on loans because the economy is expected to worsen. With the hedge, Consumer Credit can escape bankruptcy if the economy does poorly. If the S&P 500 increases, the more it increases, the more money Consumer Credit loses on its hedge, but its profits on its loans do not increase. Consequently, Consumer Credit's net income falls more and more as the economy does better and better. With the futures hedge, Consumer Credit might have to file for bankruptcy if an economic boom takes place.

With Consumer Credit, the risk manager who uses the futures hedge shifts bankruptcy risk from bad to good economic times. The risk manager who uses the put hedge eliminates the bankruptcy risk altogether.

In this chapter, we introduce options. In the first section, we describe the payoffs of options and how options are used to reduce risk in a variety of circumstances. We examine when a firm should write or buy options on itself. We conclude the first section showing that almost any payoff can be hedged using options. In the second section, we survey the markets for options and their evolution. In the third section, we discuss some fundamental properties of options that do not depend on the distribution of the price of the asset on which an option is written.

10.1. Using options to create static hedges

We examine first the purchase of puts to hedge a stock portfolio. We then use puts to hedge a fixed exposure to a currency. We compare the impact on the firm's risk of a put hedge versus a forward hedge and show how options can hedge exposures that involve quantity risks.

10.1.1. Options as investment insurance contracts

Consider Ms. Chen, who invested all her wealth in Amazon.com except for $150,000, which she holds in cash. As she sees the volatility of the stock increase, she becomes concerned that she could lose a large fraction of her net worth. She would like to purchase "insurance" that pays her the loss in net worth she incurs if the stock price falls below some threshold level. She can do this using options. Say Ms. Chen has 10,000 shares of Amazon.com and the price of a share is $58 1/2, which is the closing price on May 5, 2000. On May 5, her net worth is $735,000. She is acutely aware that five months before, when Internet stocks were still flying high, her net worth was about double what it is now. To make sure she does not lose much more, she could sell her shares, but she believes that Amazon.com has substantial upside potential.

To avoid giving up this upside potential, Ms. Chen decides to buy puts on her shares. Remember that a put option on a stock gives you the right to sell the stock at the exercise price. Consequently, if a put has an exercise price of K and the stock price is S, you get K − S if you exercise the put. Since it would not make sense for you to exercise the put if the stock price exceeds the exercise price, the payoff upon exercise is Max(K − S, 0). This is called the **intrinsic value** of the put option. A call option gives you the right to buy shares at the exercise price. The intrinsic value of a call option with exercise price K is Max(S − K, 0).

The market value of the option generally differs from its intrinsic value at least for one reason: Unless the option is at maturity, you can always exercise later. Having the opportunity of exercising later is generally valuable, but not always. An example of why this opportunity has value is the case where the stock price exceeds the exercise price. In this case, the put has no intrinsic value and if you could exercise, you would obviously not do so. However, if the option has time to maturity left, there is some chance that the value of the stock will fall and hence that the option will eventually have value. This can be the case only if there is some probability that the stock price will fall, which requires the stock return to be random. If a stock that pays no dividends is risk-free and trades above the exercise price of a put, the put will never have intrinsic value since a risk-free asset that pays no dividends increases in value at the risk-free rate. In this example, therefore, stock return volatility creates value for the option holder. If the opportunity to exercise later has no value, you would want to exercise immediately. Remember that the difference between American and European options is that American options can be exercised at any time before maturity, while European options can only be exercised at maturity. Ms. Chen goes to the Chicago Board

Options Exchange web site to investigate put prices. The puts she finds there are American puts. Using the free delayed quote information, she finds that a large number of options are traded on Amazon.com. In particular, there are options maturing in four different months during 2000 as well as options maturing in 2001.

Ms. Chen investigates options maturing in January 2001. She finds four different quotes for puts maturing in January 2001 with an exercise price of $55. The quotes are shown in Table 10.1. Each quote is for a different exchange identified by the last letter identifying the option. Let's consider the first quote. The next column gives us the last price traded, which is $14 1/4. Next come the bid and the ask. Since Ms. Chen wants to buy, she needs to know the ask, which is $13 7/8. If she buys a put contract on Amazon.com with exercise price of $55 and maturity in January 2001, she gets to sell 100 shares of Amazon.com at $55 per share on or before the maturity in January 2001. CBOE options expire at 11:59 PM Eastern Time on the Saturday immediately following the third Friday of the maturity month. The expiration calendar available on the CBOE web site tells us that the last trading day of the put is January 19, 2001. To protect all the shares in her portfolio, Ms. Chen would have to buy 100 contracts for a total cost (remember that a contract allows you to sell 100 shares at the exercise price) of $100 \times 100 \times \$13\ 7/8$, or $138,750. In addition to this, Ms. Chen would have to pay a commission to her broker. Ignoring commissions, Ms. Chen could guarantee that her wealth in January would be at least $550,000 plus the cash left over after she pays for the options, $150,000 − $138,750, or $11,250, plus the interest on that cash, say 3 percent of $11,250, or at least $561,587.50.

Table 10.1 Calls and puts on Amazon.com maturing in January 2001

The quotes are from the Chicago Board Options Exchange web site for May 5, 2000. The last sale is the price at which the last sale took place. The bid price is the price at which options can be sold and the ask price is the price at which options can be bought. Volume is the number of contracts traded during the day. Open interest is the number of option contracts outstanding for that maturity.

Puts	Last Sale	Bid	Ask	Vol	Open Int
01 Jan 55 (ZCR MK-E)	14 1/4	12 7/8	13 7/8	0	4273
01 Jan 55 (ZCR MK-A)	17 1/2	12 3/8	13 1/8	0	4273
01 Jan 55 (ZCR MK-P)	11 1/8	12 5/8	14 7/8	0	4273
01 Jan 55 (ZCR MK-X)	13 1/4	12 1/4	13	0	4273

Calls	Last Sale	Bid	Ask	Vol	Open Int
01 Jan 55 (ZCR AK-E)	14	18	19	0	1997
01 Jan 55 (ZCR AK-A)	16 3/8	18 1/8	18 7/8	0	1997
01 Jan 55 (ZCR AK-P)	50 1/2	17 5/8	19 7/8	0	1997
01 Jan 55 (ZCR AK-X)	16 5/8	18 1/8	19	0	1997

To see that Ms. Chen could guarantee that her wealth is at least $561,587.50 on January 19, 2001, note that on that day Amazon.com closed at $19.94. In this case, she could sell her puts on that day or exercise. To exercise, Ms. Chen has to tender her options to the exchange before 4:30 PM on January 19 (her broker may impose an earlier time in the day for the tendering of the options). If she exercises, she knows that she will receive $55 per share of Amazon.com. Hence, when she receives the $55 per share, her wealth will be exactly $561,587.50. Without the puts, her wealth on that day would have been the value of the shares, $199,400, plus $150,000, plus interest of 3 percent on $150,000, or $353,900.

We might conclude that the insurance that Ms. Chen buys this way is extremely expensive. However, before we reach this conclusion, it might be useful to compute the one-day VaR of Amazon as of May 5, 2000. To do that, Ms. Chen goes to the web site of E*TRADE, where she can look up volatilities for free. She finds that the annual volatility of Amazon.com is 110 percent. The one-day VaR is 11.5 percent. This means that if we are willing to believe that Amazon.com's return is normally distributed, Ms. Chen has a 5 percent chance of losing about $67,000 the next day!

Ms. Chen might decide that the insurance is worth it. However, she needs to better understand the quote tables. She sees that there was no trade in the put option she wants to buy on May 5; there is a 0 under the volume heading. Further, she notices that the existing open interest is 4,273 contracts, so that investors have the right to sell 427,300 shares of Amazon.com for $55 per share on or before January 19, 2001. The absence of trades concerns her. It suggests that this put contract is not very liquid. This is consistent with the wider bid-ask spread for January options than for the May or June options. For example, a June option with about the same price has a spread of $0.75 rather than $1 for the January option (13 7/8 – 12 7/8). She learns from her broker that the stock itself has a much smaller bid-ask spread of 1/8. Looking at this data, she wonders whether it would be cheaper for her to get exposure to the upside potential of Amazon.com by selling all her shares and using the proceeds to buy call options and to invest in a money market account. She therefore looks at call options with an exercise price of $55. As seen in Table 10.1, she finds that she can buy a call at $19. If she buys 100 call contracts, she would have $545,000 (10,000 × 58 1/2 + 150,000 – 100 × 100 × 19) that she could invest in the money market account ignoring commissions. This is less than she would have buying the put. However, she would earn interest on $545,000 until January 19, 2001, and she gets the right to exercise the calls until expiration. If she exercises the calls, she receives the shares in exchange of $55 per share three business days after she tenders her exercise notice.

For Ms. Chen to make the right decision, she has to know how the price of a put should relate to the price of a call. We will see how the price of an American put relates to the price of an American call in section 10.3.6. The pricing of puts and calls is our main subject in the next two chapters.

10.1.2. Options as exchange rate insurance contracts: The case of Export Inc.

In Chapter 6, we considered the problem of Export Inc., which expects to receive one million Swiss francs on June 1. We saw that Export can make its cash flow riskless by selling one million Swiss francs forward at the forward exchange rate, which we assume to be equal to the current spot exchange rate, $0.75. Suppose Export Inc. wants to figure out ways to hedge that protect it against downside risk but enable it to benefit from an appreciation of the Swiss franc.

If Export buys a put that gives it the right to sell one million Swiss francs at the forward exchange rate, Export gets to exercise the put if the spot exchange rate falls below $0.75 so that by delivering its Swiss francs to the put writer, it gets $0.75. Consequently, having bought the put, the worst Export receives on June 1 is $0.75 million. However, if the Swiss franc exchange rate exceeds $0.75 on June 1, Export receives one million times the Swiss franc exchange rate minus the cost of the put.

Export must pay an option premium when it buys the put. To compare the payoff of the option strategy with the payoff of the forward hedge strategy, we have to consider the value of the option premium as of the maturity of the hedge.

Let's assume that Export borrows at the risk-free rate to pay the option premium and repays the loan at maturity of the hedge. Let S be the dollar price of one Swiss franc on March 1 and $p(S, F, \text{June } 1, \text{March } 1)$ be the option premium paid on March 1 for a put option on one Swiss franc maturing on June 1 with an exercise price equal to the forward exchange rate on March 1 for the Swiss franc for delivery on June 1, F. The premium paid by Export Inc. is $0.01111 per Swiss franc, or slightly more than one cent. Using our notation, if Export buys a put option on one million Swiss francs today, borrows the option premium and repays the loan at maturity of the hedge, it will have to pay $1\text{M} \times p(S, F, \text{June } 1, \text{March } 1)/P_{\text{March } 1}(\text{June } 1)$ at maturity of the hedge, where $P_{\text{March } 1}(\text{June } 1)$ is the price on March 1 of a zero-coupon bond that pays $1 on June 1. Using a continuously compounded annual interest rate of 5 percent, the price of a zero-coupon bond that matures on June 1 is $0.987578. Consequently, the loan reimbursement on June 1 is equal to $1\text{M} \times 0.01111/0.987578$, or $11,249.70.

Figure 10.1 compares the payoffs of three strategies: the put hedge, the forward hedge studied in Chapter 6, and the unhedged cash position. When Export does

---

Figure 10.1   **Difference in firm income between put option and forward hedges**

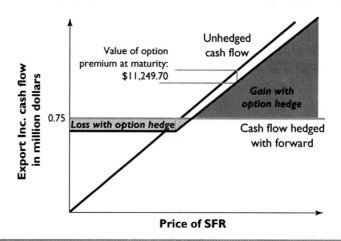

not hedge, it has one million Swiss francs on June 1 that it converts to dollars at the spot exchange rate on that date. With the forward hedge strategy, Export receives 1M Swiss francs × $0.75, or $0.75 million at maturity. When it buys a put with an exercise price equal to the forward rate, the payoff at maturity depends on whether the spot exchange rate is higher or lower than the exercise price of the option.

If the spot exchange rate is lower than the exercise price of the option, and Export has the right to sell Swiss francs at the forward price, it exercises its put. Therefore, denoting the spot exchange rate on June 1 by $S_{June\ 1}$, it receives at maturity:

Cash position + Payoff from put option
– Repayment of loan used to pay put premium

$$1M \times S_{June\ 1} + (1M \times F - 1M \times S_{June\ 1})$$
$$- 1M \times p(S, F, June\ 1, March\ 1)/P_{March\ 1}(June\ 1)$$

$$= 1M \times F - 1M \times p(S, F, June\ 1, March\ 1)/P_{March\ 1}(June\ 1)$$

$$= \$750,000 - \$11,249.70$$

$$= \$738,750.30$$

This is less than it would get with the forward hedge because it has to pay back the loan it took out to pay for the option premium.

If the spot exchange rate exceeds the forward exchange rate, Export chooses not to exercise the option at maturity. If it made the mistake of exercising the option, it would be selling one million Swiss francs for $1M \times F$ when it could get $1M \times S_{June\ 1}$ for them. Consequently, its payoff at maturity if it exercises optimally is:

Cash position – Repayment of loan used to pay put premium
$$1M \times S_{June\ 1} - 1M \times p(S, F, June\ 1, March\ 1)/P_{March\ 1}(June\ 1)$$

If the spot exchange rate is $0.80, Export receives $800,000 – $11,249.70, or $788,750.30. This payoff is less than if it had not hedged by $11,249.70 because it purchased insurance against an unexpected fall in the Swiss franc exchange rate that it ended up not needing. The payoff of the insurance at maturity is the maximum of 0 or $F - S_{June\ 1}$, which we denote by $Max(F - S_{June\ 1}, 0)$. Putting together the payoff of the position when Export Inc. exercises the put and when it does not results in the payoff of the hedged position:

Payoff of hedged position = Cash position + Payoff of put
– Repayment of loan used to pay the premium
$$= 1M \times S_{June\ 1} + 1M \times Max(F - S_{June\ 1}, 0)$$
$$- 1M \times p(S, F, June\ 1, March\ 1)/P_{March\ 1}(June\ 1)$$

In summary, the firm earns more with the put strategy than with the forward strategy if the Swiss franc appreciates sufficiently to offset the cost of the put and earns less otherwise since it has to pay for the put. To decide which strategy to use, Export must trade off the benefit from the put strategy if the Swiss franc appreciates sufficiently against the cost of the put strategy if it does not.

Why would Export choose the put strategy over the forward strategy? There are at least three reasons. First, Export might be more optimistic about Swiss franc appreciation than the market. Second, Export might face an increased need for funding if the Swiss franc appreciates. It therefore wants to have a greater cash flow if the Swiss franc appreciates. For example, Export might sell more in Switzerland following an appreciation of the Swiss franc, so that it has to invest more. Third, there might be tax or accounting considerations that make option strategies more advantageous. Box 10.1, Hedging at Hasbro, shows how accounting rules affect the choice of hedging instrument for some firms.

Box 10.1   **Hedging at Hasbro**

Hasbro is a global toy company with headquarters in the United States. Its classic game is Monopoly, but its lines include Teletubbies and Mr. Potato Head. It sources products in five currencies and sells toys in 30 currencies. In 1997, it had revenues of $3.2 billion dollars. It estimated an adverse effect of foreign exchange fluctuations of $92 million on its net revenues due to the strengthening of the dollar. Revenues for toy manufacturers are highly seasonal—more than 60 percent of the sales take place in the second half of the year. However, prices are set early in the year and then the firm loses its flexibility to deal with changes in costs because of exchange rate changes. Faced with increasing concerns about foreign exchange exposure, Hasbro hired a treasurer in October 1997 who had experience in international treasury and foreign exchange risk management. He immediately developed a hedging program to hedge transaction and anticipated exposures. By the end of 1997, Hasbro had hedged a considerable fraction of its estimated 1998 foreign currency transactions using forwards and options. It had forwards in place for a notional amount of $35 million and options for $135 million. In mid-April 1998, the corporation disclosed that a 10 percent unfavorable movement in exchange rates would affect its operating revenue by only $10 million.

Let's consider now how Hasbro made the choice to use options rather than only forwards. Accounting considerations played a key role in the firm's practice. Forward contracts had to be marked to market when a forward position did not meet the conditions for hedge accounting, which typically was the case for hedges of anticipated exposures. At the time Hasbro made its choice, option premiums for options used to hedge anticipated transactions could be amortized over time and cash flows from the options hit the income statement when they accrue. As a result, if a firm entered a forward contract expiring the next quarter because it expected to have a transaction next quarter, its earnings this quarter were affected by the change in value of the forward contract. The forward hedge therefore affected earnings in a way that the option hedge did not. If the transaction was one that the firm was committed to, this problem did not arise because the forward contract qualified for hedge accounting, so that the loss on the forward was directly matched with a gain on the transaction. Importantly, these accounting issues did not affect the firm's economic cash flow. Yet they affected the reasoning of Hasbro's treasurer substantially:

"We are sensitive to mark-to-market risk as a company, which is driven by the seasonality of our business cycle. We've historically had lower earnings in the first quarter and higher earnings in the fourth quarter. But unfortunately, when we hedge, we are typically hedging for the whole year. So the time we are asked to mark-to-market our forward hedges is typically when our earnings are weakest on a cyclical basis. Purchased options are a way to deal with that mark-to-market issue. We use options for commitments further in the future, and forwards for near-term commitments that already qualify for hedge accounting." Hasbro used options in eight critical currency markets and factored the premiums into the budgeting process as a cost of doing business.

The point of this case is that the accounting treatment of derivatives can affect hedging choices. This accounting treatment of derivatives changes over time and is often complex. The newest FASB ruling on derivatives accounting, FASB 133, which is discussed in Chapter 19, makes options less advantageous from an accounting perspective than they were when Hasbro made its decision.

Note: Hasbro's foreign exchange hedging strategies are presented in "Managing risk in toyland," William Falloon, *Risk*, May 1998, 40–43.

Firms often take positions on their own stock. On May 22, 1997, the *Wall Street Journal* reported that Intel, Microsoft, Boeing, and IBM had all sold puts on their stock.[1] In contrast to the foreign currency hedging examples, however, selling puts generates cash for firms. The article explained that more than 100 firms had sold puts on their own stock. IBM sold puts to hedge a convertible debt issue. At that time, Intel had puts on $1 billion of its stock and had received $423 million in proceeds from selling puts. By 2000, Microsoft had received premiums worth $2.1 billion on puts it had sold. No put had been exercised by 2000, but afterwards puts were exercised and Microsoft lost money on them.

In the fall of 2001, Enron revealed the existence of a large number of off-balance sheet positions. A number of these positions involved puts on Enron's stock. The way that some of these positions worked is that Enron had created companies that it financed by its own stock and by a promise of additional stock if the price of stock fell. The promise of additional stock amounts to writing a put where the payment of the exercise price takes place in shares rather than cash. Puts written on its stock therefore played a role in the downfall of Enron. Though executives sometimes think that writing puts on the firm's stock is free money because they do not think the stock price will fall substantially, Enron provides a sobering lesson.

Firms that sell puts have to buy back equity from the put holders. Firms that issue options to employees regularly issue shares to employees as the options are

---

1 See "More firms use options to gamble on their own stock," E. S. Browning and Aaron Lucchetti, the *Wall Street Journal*, May 22, 1997, C1.

exercised. They typically buy back shares to avoid the dilution that results from having to issue shares to employees. In some cases, institutional shareholders impose dilution limits on firms, so that they have to repurchase shares if employees exercise options. Such firms often sell puts with the reasoning that they will buy shares back anyway. Technology firms use option compensation more than other firms. They also typically sell puts on their stock. If the stock price falls enough, however, employee stock options are worthless and there is no reason to buy back stock to prevent dilution. When a firm sells puts on its equity, however, it increases its risk. If it experiences an adverse shock, its resources are further depleted by having to pay the holders of the puts.

From a risk management perspective, it can make sense for firms to buy puts on themselves. This increases the firm's resources when it is doing poorly. Generally, firms are averse to doing this. One view often expressed is that it amounts to selling equity when it is cheap since the firm has to deliver its shares when it exercises the puts. Firms that have to invest more following good news could buy calls on themselves. Box 10.2, Cephalon Inc., describes how one firm did that.

10.1.3. Options to hedge contingent exposures

Let's look at one more example. Consider a situation where a firm, Nonlinear Exports Inc., exports goods to France. In three months, it will have completed production of one million widgets that it can sell in the United States for $1 each or in France for €1 each. Ignoring transportation costs, it will sell in France if the euro is worth more than $1. Hence, its euro exposure is a nonlinear function of the exchange rate or is contingent on the exchange rate: If the euro is less than $1, Nonlinear Exports Inc. receives no euros; if the euro is more than $1, it receives one million euros in 90 days. Its payoff in 90 days if it does not hedge is:

$$\$1M + €1M \times Max(S_{t+0.25} - 1, 0)$$

To understand this payoff, note that if the euro spot exchange rate at $t + 0.25$ is less than $1, it does not export and it gets $1M. If the spot exchange rate is greater than $1, it exports and gets $€1M \times S_{t+0.25}$. Using the previous formula for the payoff, it gets $\$1M + €1M \times (S_{t+0.25} - 1)$, which is $€1M \times S_{t+0.25}$.

With an option strategy, Nonlinear Export Inc. can eliminate its exchange rate exposure completely. By writing a call instead of buying one, we take on the obligation to sell when the call option buyer exercises. This means that we sell when the spot price exceeds the exercise price. Consider a euro call option with an exercise price of $1. If Nonlinear Exports writes this option, it sells euros for the exercise price if the spot exchange rate at maturity exceeds $1. The option expires unexercised if the spot exchange rate is below $1. The payoff of the option at maturity for the option holder is $Max(S_{t+0.25} - 1, 0)$ and it is $-Max(S_{t+0.25} - 1, 0)$ for the seller. Suppose the firm sells a call option for €1M with exercise price of $1 per euro. It receives the option premium now, $c(S, 1, t + 0.25, t)$ per euro, and can invest it until maturity. Its payoff at maturity is:

Payoff of unhedged position + payoff of option position

$$\$1M + €1M \times Max(S_{t+0.25} - 1, 0)$$
$$+ €1M \times c(S, 1, t + 0.25, t)/P_t(t + 0.25) - €1M \times Max(S_{t+0.25} - 1, 0)$$
$$= \$1M + €1M \times c(S, 1, t + 0.25, t)/P_t(t + 0.25)$$

Cephalon Inc.   *Box 10.2*

On May 7, 1997, Cephalon Inc. acquired derivatives on its own stock, paying for them with newly issued common stock. These derivatives were not publicly traded derivatives; they were engineered by an investment bank. The derivatives had the following payoff: If the share price on October 31, 1997, was below $21.50, Cephalon would get nothing. If the share price was between $21.50 and $39.50, it would get a standard call payoff, namely the difference between the stock price and $21.50. If the share price was above $39.50, the firm would get $18, or the difference between $39.50 and $21.50. Such derivatives are called *capped calls*. Suppose that the stock price at maturity is $50. In this case, we can think of the payoff to Cephalon as receiving the payoff of a call with exercise price of $21.50, which would be $28.50, and having to pay the payoff of a call with exercise price of $39.50, which would be $10.50, so that on net it gets $28.50 − $10.50, or $18. Hence, the payoff to Cephalon of the capped call is the payoff of having a long position in a call with exercise price of $21.50 and writing a call with exercise price of $39.50. Cephalon bought capped calls on 2,500,000 shares and paid for them a total premium of 490,000 shares. The price of a share at that time was close to $20.

Why would Cephalon enter such a transaction? Cephalon entered this transaction just before the FDA was supposed to decide whether a drug developed by the firm, Myotropin, was ready for commercial distribution. If the drug was approved, the stock price would increase sharply. Taking the position would therefore have been a good bet for Cephalon if it thought that approval was more likely than the market thought it was. In that case, the stock price would have been too low and Cephalon could have gotten the capped calls cheap. Straight calls would have generated more profits for Cephalon if it was right, but would have required more shares to be issued since with capped calls, Cephalon sold some calls also.

Cephalon justified its transaction on risk management grounds rather than speculative grounds. If the drug was approved, Cephalon had a large need for cash. Cephalon had sold the rights to the drug to a partnership, but had an option to buy back these rights. With approval, it would become profitable to buy back the rights. This would require Cephalon to raise funds to pay for the repurchase of the rights. If external financing is expensive for Cephalon, then it might face difficulties in raising funds externally. The capped options, though, would pay off precisely when Cephalon would require the funds. Viewed this way, one could argue that Cephalon's purchase of calls amounts to hedging so that it has funds available when it has attractive investment opportunities. This motivation for hedging was discussed in Chapter 4.

Immediately after Cephalon entered this derivatives transaction, the FDA announced that the drug was not ready for commercialization. The stock price fell and the capped calls expired out of the money.

Source: Peter Tufano, Markus Mullarkey, and Geoffrey Verter, 1998, Cephalon Inc., Harvard Business School Case Study, 298–116; George Chacko, Peter Tufano, and Geoffrey Verter, 2002, Cephalon Inc. Taking Risk Management Theory Seriously, *Journal of Financial Economics* 60, 2001, 449–486.

In this case, the option hedge creates a perfect hedge. The payoff from the position hedged by writing call options is shown in Figure 10.2.

A static forward hedge cannot eliminate the exchange rate exposure of Nonlinear Exports. First, suppose that the forward exchange rate is less than $1. In this case, the firm does not use a static hedge because at that exchange rate it does not make a profit exporting to France. In three months, it will want to export to France if the exchange rate is favorable, so it still has exchange rate exposure. Second, suppose the forward exchange rate is greater than $1, say $1.20. If the spot exchange rate is $1.30, the firm can export to France and earn $1.20 per euro through the forward contract. If it chooses not to export instead, it incurs a loss of $0.10 per euro sold forward, so that its net income per unit sold in the United States is $0.90, namely the U.S. selling price minus the foreign exchange loss. Consequently, in that case the firm exports. If the spot exchange rate is $0.90, the firm again can export and earn $1.20 per euro through the forward contract. In this case, even though it has a short forward position, Nonlinear Exports is better off not exporting because it earns net $1.30 per unit sold instead of $1.20. This is because it gets $1 per unit sold in the United States and makes a $0.30 cent gain by buying euros and delivering them on the forward contract. In neither case can a forward strategy eliminate Nonlinear Exports' exposure to the exchange rate.

Some corporations have policies against writing options because they fear that writing options could expose the firm to large losses. If Nonlinear Export had such a policy, it would not have been able to implement a hedge that completely eliminates its exposure.

10.1.4. How we can hedge (almost) anything with options

Options are an incredibly versatile hedging instrument: They can be used to create static hedges for almost anything. When we have options available to con-

---

Figure 10.2   Payoffs to Nonlinear Exports Inc.

Nonlinear Exports Inc. produces one million widgets. It can sell them to France for €1 or in the U.S. for $1 in three months. Since it sells the widgets for the highest proceeds, it receives $1 million if the euro is worth less than $1 and one million euros otherwise. The figure shows the payoff of Nonlinear Exports Inc. if it is unhedged, if it hedges by selling euros forward at the price of $1 per euro, and if it hedges by writing a call on €1 million.

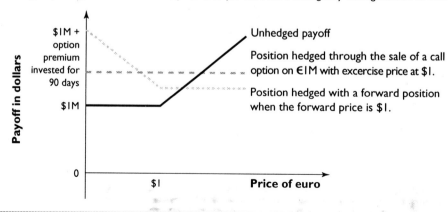

struct static hedges, we no longer need forward contracts to construct such hedges. This is because we can replicate a forward contract with a static portfolio of options but we cannot replicate an option with a static portfolio of forward contracts. Let's see why. Suppose we have a forward contract to buy 100,000 shares of GM stock at date T for F and we want to replicate that contract with options that mature at T. With the forward contract, we have one of two outcomes. First, the stock price at T, S_T, exceeds the forward price so that $S_T - F$ is positive. This payoff increases linearly with the price of GM stock as long as the price exceeds the forward price. Hence, this payoff is $Max(S_T - F, 0)$. This is the payoff of a call option with exercise price equal to F. Second, the stock price is lower than the forward price. In this case, $S_T - F$ is negative. This is equivalent to the payment we would have to make had we written a put on GM stock with exercise price F, $-Max(F - S_T, 0)$. Consequently, buying a call with exercise price F and selling a put with exercise price F has the same payoff as a forward contract.

Remember though that a forward contract has no value when entered into. Consequently, the portfolio long one call and short one put with exercise price equal to the forward price has no value if bought at the initiation date of the forward contract. Let S be the price of the asset on which the forward contract is written, F the forward price for a contract initiated at t, and T the maturity date of the forward contract. At t, the portfolio long a call with price $c(S, F, T, t)$ and short a put with price $p(S, F, T, t)$ is worth zero only if the call price equals the put price:

$$c(S, F, T, t) = p(S, F, T, t) \qquad (10.1)$$

If this equation does not hold, there is an arbitrage opportunity. Suppose the call is worth more than the put. We make money for sure by writing the call, buying the put, and hedging the option position with a short forward position. The option position has the same payoff as a long forward position, but since the call is worth more than the put, we make money when we put this position on even though it has the payoff of a forward contract. We take no risk because we are hedged.

After initiation of the forward contract, say at date t', the value of the forward contract is $c(S, F, T, t') - p(S, F, T, t')$. Since one can hedge a long forward position with a short forward position, it follows that going short the call and long the put hedges a long forward position. We already know that we cannot hedge a nonlinear payoff like the payoff of a put option with a static forward position.

Consider now an arbitrary payoff function like the one represented in Figure 10.3: a payoff to be received at date T that is a function of the price of an underlying asset. Let $G(S_T)$ be the payoff at time T when the underlying asset has price S_T. This payoff function is chosen to make a point, namely, that even a payoff function as unusual as this one can be hedged with options. This function is not linear, but piecewise linear. It has straight lines connected at angles. We cannot use a static hedge composed of futures or forward positions to hedge this payoff. A short forward position could be used to hedge the part of the payoff that increases with the price of the underlying asset, but when the payoff falls with the price of the underlying asset, a short forward position aggravates the exposure of the hedged payoff. Between a and b in Figure 10.3, an increase in the price of

Figure 10.3   Arbitrary payoff function where $G(S_T)$ is the payoff function and S_T is the price of the underlying asset

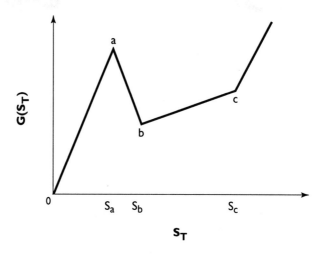

the underlying asset reduces the payoff and reduces the value of the short forward position.

It is possible to use a portfolio of options to replicate the payoff corresponding to the straight line segment from *a* to *b* on Figure 10.3 exactly. To see this, note that the straight line segment represents a payoff that falls as the price of the underlying asset increases. To hedge this payoff, we need a financial position that has a positive payoff when the price at maturity exceeds S_a. With the straight line, every dollar increase in the price of the underlying asset results in a decrease of two dollars in the payoff. A long position of two units of the underlying asset pays off two dollars for each dollar increase in the price of the underlying asset, whatever the price of the underlying asset. A portfolio of two call options on the underlying asset with exercise price S_a pays off two dollars per dollar increase in the price of the underlying asset when the price equals or exceeds S_a since its payoff is:

$$2 \times Max(S - S_a, 0)$$

The problem with the call is that it pays off even if the price exceeds S_b. If we additionally sell two calls on the underlying asset with exercise price S_b, the payoff of the long call position and the short call position is:

$$2 \times Max(S - S_a, 0) - 2 \times Max(S - S_b, 0)$$

This portfolio of calls pays two dollars per dollar increase in the price of the underlying asset as long as the price of the underlying asset is higher than S_a and lower than S_b. Suppose now that the price of the underlying asset is S_b plus one dollar. In this case, the calls with exercise price S_a pay off $2 \times (S_b + 1 - S_a)$ and we have to pay $2 \times (S_b + 1 - S_b)$ to the holders of the calls we sold. The net payoff of the call portfolio when the price of the underlying asset is $S_b + 1$ is therefore $2 \times (S_b + 1 - S_a) - 2 \times (S_b + 1 - S_b) = 2 \times (S_b - S_a)$. Therefore, for each dollar change of the price of the underlying asset between S_b and S_a the call portfolio has a gain that exactly offsets the loss in the cash position. For price changes outside the range from S_a to S_b, the call portfolio pays off nothing. We created a perfect hedge for the payoff function between the points *a* and *b* on Figure 10.3.

Using the same method, we can create a perfect hedge for any straight line segment of the payoff function. For each segment, we need to find the slope of the payoff function. The slope of the payoff function dictates the size of the option position. From *b* to *c*, the slope is 0.5. This means that the payoff function increases as the price of the underlying asset increases. To hedge, we need to take a position that falls in value by 50 cents whenever the price of the underlying asset increases by one dollar. Selling half an option on the underlying asset with exercise price S_b provides this hedge. However, the written call has a negative payoff for any price greater than S_b. Since for a price of the underlying asset equal to or greater than S_c the slope of the payoff function of the cash position is different, we buy half a call option with exercise price S_c. This way we have created a perfect hedge for payoffs between *b* and *c*. Continuing this way, we can hedge the entire payoff function.

What if the payoff function does not have straight lines? We can still use calls and puts to construct a static approximate hedge by using a linear approximation of the payoff function. Figure 10.4 provides an example of a payoff function that does not have straight lines. We can compute the exposure at each point using the delta exposure discussed in Chapter 8, and create a piecewise linear function that is arbitrarily close to the payoff function. Figure 10.4 shows one such possible approximation. We can then proceed as we did with the piecewise linear function of Figure 10.3.

Piecewise linear approximation of arbitrary payoff function where   *Figure 10.4*
$G(S_T)$ **is the payoff function and** S_T **is the price of the underlying asset**

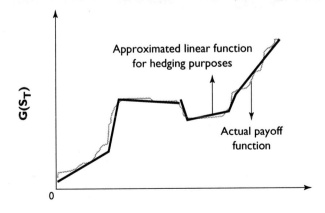

A more precise approximation involves more but shorter straight lines. Since two options are needed to replicate the payoff corresponding to a straight line segment, it follows that more precise approximations require more options. One limitation to hedging this way is that it may be difficult in real-world markets to buy options with suitable exercise prices. However, as we will discover later, one possible (but not perfect) solution is to manufacture options on our own.

10.2. A brief history of option markets

Options have a long history, not all of it illustrious. They were used extensively in the 17th and in the early 18th centuries. A famous financial event at the beginning of the 18th century, the South Sea Company bubble, involved extensive use of options as an incentive device. The South Sea Company's history is complicated to say the least, but to succeed the Company had to obtain approval of the British Parliament for an exchange of public debt for common stock of the company. To help in the approval process, the Company gave options to various members of Parliament. The options would have expired out of the money had Parliament not approved the exchange the Company wanted to make. Eventually, share prices of the Company increased to prices that seemed to have little relation with the future cash flows the Company could generate and then collapsed. In the aftermath of the collapse of the South Sea bubble, England's Parliament banned options with Sir John Barnard's Act and the ban stayed in place for more than one hundred years.

Options have been traded in the United States for a long time. Newspapers in the 1870s carried quotes for options offered by brokerage houses. The Securities Act of 1934 empowered the Securities and Exchange Commission to regulate options on stocks. Until 1973, options were traded over the counter, and there was little secondary trading. All this changed in the early 1970s. In 1973, the Chicago Board Options Exchange, or CBOE, became the first registered exchange to trade options. Trading grew quickly, and options on a stock could at times have higher trading volume than the stock itself.

Until the beginning of the 1970s, the formulas to price options required knowledge of the expected return of the underlying asset, which limited their practical use. This changed in 1973 with the publication of a paper by Fischer Black and Myron Scholes. Their formula for the pricing of options did not require knowledge of the expected return of the underlying asset and has since proven of great practical use. It quickly became the pricing tool of traders on the CBOE. Texas Instruments sold a calculator with the formula preprogrammed.

In the 1970s, economic events provided the impetus for a dramatic extension of options markets. In 1974, the industrialized market economies switched from a regime of fixed exchange rates to exchange rates determined by market forces. Exchange rate volatility quickly became a concern of corporations and investors. Futures contracts on currencies became available. Soon thereafter, over-the-counter option contracts on currencies became available also. Eventually, the Philadelphia Options Exchange started trading foreign currency options. However, most of the trading in currency options remains over the counter.

Another important event in the 1970s was the increase in the volatility of interest rates. This created a demand for instruments to hedge against interest rate changes. Some of these instruments were futures contracts. Other instruments took the form of various options. Options on bonds became available. Options paying the difference between a stated interest rate and the market interest rate at fixed dates over a period of time became popular. These options are called caps. We consider options on bonds and interest rates in Chapter 14.

Since the 1980s, innovation in the options markets has taken two directions. First, options on new underlyings have been introduced. We now have options on futures contracts, on stock indices such as the S&P 500, on electricity, and so on. Second, new types of options, so-called exotic options, were introduced. Exotic options are not standard puts or calls. They can be options on one or many underlyings. Examples of exotic options are Bermudan options, which can be exercised at fixed dates; barrier options, which can be exercised only if the underlying crosses a barrier (or does not cross a barrier for other types of barrier options); and rainbow options, which give the right to buy one of several underlyings at a given price. Chapter 13 discusses index options and Chapter 17 discusses exotic options.

To gain a sense of the size of the options market, we can turn to the estimates of the Bank for International Settlements. The Bank surveys major banks and dealers across the world to collect data on their positions with other institutions and individuals. At the end of June 2000, the Bank estimated that the reporting institutions had options positions with nonreporting institutions for a total amount of underlying of $2,385 billion for currencies, $9,361 billion for interest rate options, $1,527 billion for equities, and $154 billion for commodities. The value of the options outstanding was much less. The total value of currency options written by dealers and held by nondealers was $55 billion. The total value of fixed-income options computed the same way was $145 billion. Finally, the total value of equity options was $231 billion.

10.3. Some properties of options

Certain properties of options hold whatever the distribution of the underlying asset and as long as the underlying asset is a financial asset. A financial asset is a security that pays off only in cash or in a form that can be converted into cash. Stocks and bonds are financial assets. Currency is not a financial asset: It earns a convenience yield, which is the benefit of carrying cash in a wallet—it saves trips to the ATM. A foreign currency zero-coupon bond that pays one unit of foreign currency at maturity is a financial asset. We assume to begin that the underlying asset has no cash payouts until maturity of the option. This means that all its return accrues in the form of capital gains.

10.3.1. Upper and lower bounds on option prices
There exist upper and lower bounds on option prices that hold whatever the underlying of the option and its return distribution. Remember that a call option allows the holder to buy the underlying asset at a fixed price. The most the holder can ever get out of a call option contract is the underlying asset. The upper bound on a call option price is therefore the price of the underlying asset. A put contract

allows the holder to sell the underlying asset at the exercise price. This means that the upper bound on the price of a put contract is the exercise price.

A call option cannot have a negative price. We can get a higher lower bound for call options than that. If the call option is an American option, its value cannot be less than S – K, where S is the price of the underlying asset and K is the exercise price. If the price of the option is lower than S – K, we can buy the option, exercise it, and make a profit equal to S – K minus the call price. This result does not apply to European options since they cannot be exercised early.

We can find a lower bound for European options such that if the call sells for less we can make money for sure. Consider a European call with three months to maturity on a stock that does not pay a dividend. The price of the stock is $50, the exercise price, K, is $40, and the price of a zero-coupon bond paying $1 in three months is $0.95. Suppose the option premium is $10. In this case, we can buy the stock for delivery in three months by paying $10 today and setting aside 0.95 × $40 in zero-coupon bonds, or $38. In three months, we can exercise the option and get the asset by paying $40, which we will have from our investment of $38 in zero-coupon bonds. If we do not exercise in three months because the option is out of the money, we can buy the asset for less than $40 and have money left over, so that our effective cost of buying the asset is at most $48 today. If we want the stock in three months, we are therefore better off buying it using a call option and setting aside the present value of the exercise price than buying it today.

To make money for sure, we construct the following arbitrage portfolio: We sell the stock short, buy the call, and set aside the present value of the exercise price in zero-coupon bonds. This gives us $2 today. At maturity, if the stock price is higher than $40, we get the stock with the call, use the proceeds from the zero-coupon bonds to pay the exercise price, and use the stock to settle the short-sale. If the stock price is lower than $40, the call is worthless, and we use the proceeds from the zero-coupon bonds to buy the stock we need to close the short sale. In this case, we have some money left over.

With this arbitrage portfolio, we make money for sure today and possibly also at maturity. The only way the arbitrage opportunity disappears is if the stock price does not exceed the call price plus the present value of the exercise price. In this case, it is not cheaper to buy the stock for deferred delivery through the call.

The opposite transaction may seem like an arbitrage opportunity but it is not. Suppose the stock price is less than the call price plus the present value of the exercise price. Buying the stock and selling the portfolio of the call and the zero-coupon bonds does not make money for sure. If the call is in the money at maturity, we get nothing at maturity and make money today. If the call is out of the money, we have to repay K (the exercise price is the principal amount of zero-coupon bonds sold short) but the stock is worth less than K so that we lose money at maturity. Potentially, we could lose K if the stock price is zero. Hence, we could make money today but lose much more at maturity.

While there is an arbitrage opportunity if the call price plus the present value of the exercise price is lower than the stock price, which is if $c(S, K, T, t) + P_t(T)K < S_t$, where $P_t(T)$ is the price at t of a zero-coupon bond that pays $1 at

T, there is no arbitrage opportunity when $c(S, K, T, t) + P_t(T)K \geq S_t$. This analysis implies that the call price must exceed the difference between the stock price and present value of the exercise price:

$$c(S, K, T, t) \geq S_t - P_t(T)K \qquad (10.2)$$

In words, we have:

> **Property 1.** The European call price cannot be less than the current price of the underlying asset minus the present value of the exercise price.

The opposite is true for put options. If a put option is an American put option, we can always exercise immediately, so that its value must be at least $K - S_T$. If the put option is a European put option, note that we can get K at maturity by investing the present value of K or at least K by buying the asset and the put. When we buy the asset and the put, we get more than K if the put is out of the money at maturity because we have the asset and its price exceeds K. Consequently, a portfolio of the put and the asset must be worth more than the present value of the exercise price. This implies that the relationship is:

$$p(S, K, T, t) \geq P_t(T)K - S_t \qquad (10.3)$$

In words, we have:

> **Property 2.** The European put price cannot be less than the present value of the exercise price minus the current price of the underlying asset.

This property must hold to avoid the existence of arbitrage opportunities. If it does not hold, we make money today buying the put, buying the asset, and borrowing the present value of K. At maturity, if the put is out of the money, we have $S_T - K$, which is positive. If the put is in the money, the value of the position is zero. Hence, we make money today and never lose money later.

10.3.2. Exercise price and option values

There are relationships between an option's value and its exercise price that hold whatever the distribution of the return of the underlying asset. Consider two calls on the same underlying asset that have the same maturity. One call has exercise price of $40 and one has exercise price of $50. If the asset price is greater than $50 at maturity, the call with the lower exercise price pays $10 more than the call with the higher exercise price. If the asset price is between $40 and $50, the call with the lower exercise price pays something and the other nothing. Finally, if the asset price is below $40, neither call is in the money. Consequently, the call with the lower exercise price never pays less than the call with the higher exercise price, so its value cannot be any less. More generally, if we have a call with exercise price K and one with exercise price K', where K' > K, it must be that:

$$c(S, K, T, t) \geq c(S, K', T, t) \qquad (10.4)$$

This result is the third property of option prices:

> **Property 3.** All things equal, the price of a European call option is a decreasing function of its exercise price.

If both options are in the money, the difference between the two options' payoffs is K' – K. At maturity, one option pays $S_T - K$ and the other pays $S_T - K'$, so that $S_T - K - (S_T - K')$ is equal to K' – K. If K' > S_T > K, one option pays nothing and the other pays $S_T - K$ < K' – K. If S_T < K, each option pays zero. Therefore, the maximum difference between the payoff of the two options is K' – K. By investing the present value of K' – K, one always gets at least the payoff of being long the option with exercise price K and short the option with exercise price K'. Consequently, it must be the case that:

$$c(S, K, T, t) - c(S, K', T, t) \le P_t(T)[K' - K] \tag{10.5}$$

The case for puts is the reverse since we receive the exercise price. Consequently, it must be that:

$$p(S, K', T, t) \ge p(S, K, T, t) \tag{10.6}$$

$$p(S, K', T, t) - p(S, K, T, t) \le P_t(T)[K' - K] \tag{10.7}$$

In words, equation (10.6) tells us that:

Property 4. All things equal, the price of a European put option is an increasing function of the exercise price.

Finally, for both puts and calls:

Property 5. The absolute value of the difference in price of two otherwise identical European put options or call options cannot exceed the absolute value of the difference in the present values of the exercise prices.

Let's demonstrate these properties using a numerical example. Let's use the two call options with exercise prices of $40 and $50. If the price of the call with exercise price of $40 satisfies Property 1, a satisfactory price would then be $20. Property 1 must also hold for the call with exercise price of $50. Consequently, $5 would be an acceptable price for that call, but $1 would not be. If the call with exercise price of $50 sells for $5 and the call with exercise price of $40 sells for $20, the present value of the difference in the exercise prices of $9.50 (remember that $P_t(T)$ = 0.95, so that $9.50 = 0.95 × $10) is exceeded by the absolute value of the difference in option prices, which is $15.

These option prices violate Property 5. To take advantage of this violation, we buy the call with exercise price of $50, sell the call with exercise price of $40, and invest the present value of the difference in exercise prices. The cash flow associated with establishing this portfolio is –$5 + $20 – 0.95 × $10, or $5.50. At maturity, if the stock price is below $40, both options expire unexercised and we have $10, which is the value of our investment in zero-coupon bonds. If the stock price expires between $40 and $50, say at $45, we have to pay $5 on the option we wrote, get nothing from the option we bought, and still have the $10, so on net we have $5. Finally, if the stock price is above $50, say at $55, we have to pay

$15 on the option we wrote, get $5 on the option we bought, and still have the $10, so that on net the portfolio is worthless.

Consequently, the worst that can happen with our portfolio strategy is that we get $5.50 today and have a portfolio that has no value at maturity. This means that we make money for sure, and demonstrates that when Property 5 does not hold, there is an arbitrage opportunity.

10.3.3. The value of options and time to maturity

Option values also depend on time to maturity. Consider two American calls that are equivalent except one has a longer time to maturity. The call with a longer time to maturity cannot be worth less than the one with the shorter time to maturity. If we hold the call with the longer maturity, we can exercise it at the maturity of the call with the shorter time to maturity. If we do this, we make the two calls equivalent. If we choose not to do that, it is because we benefit from not exercising, which must mean that our call has an advantage that the call with the shorter maturity does not have. The same reasoning applies to American puts. This reasoning does not apply in the case of European calls and puts because they cannot be exercised before maturity. In summary:

Property 6. The value of American options increases with time to maturity.

If the underlying asset does not pay a dividend, this result applies also to European call options, but not to European put options. The value of a European put option can fall with an increase in time to maturity if it is sufficiently deeply in the money. Suppose that the stock price is very close to zero, so that the put is deeply in the money. In this case, if we could exercise, we would get the exercise price. We cannot exercise now. Anything that happens subsequently can only reduce the payoff of the option at maturity. The most we can get at maturity is the exercise price, so that the longer we have to wait to exercise, the lower the present value of what we will get and hence the lower the value of the option. However, if the option is not very much in the money, we could gain by holding on to the option since we have little to lose if the stock price increases but much to gain if it falls.

10.3.4. Put-call parity theorem

Put prices and call prices are related. This is because, if there is a market for European calls, we can manufacture European puts on our own. Suppose that we want to buy a put with an exercise price of $40 that matures in three months, but no such puts can be bought. However, we find that we can buy a call with exercise price of $40 that matures in three months. Consider the strategy of buying the call, investing the present value of the exercise price in zero-coupon bonds, and selling the stock short. If the call price is $15, a zero-coupon bond that pays $1 in three months costs $0.95, and the stock price is $50, this strategy costs us $15 + $38 − $50, or $3. Let's see what we have at maturity.

First, if the stock price is below $40, the call is worthless. Hence, we have $40 from the sale of the zero-coupon bonds and have to buy the asset to settle the short-sale. On net, the value of our portfolio is $40 − S_T. This is the payoff of a put with an exercise price of $40 when it is in the money. Second, if the stock price is above $40, the call pays $S_T − $40. We use the zero-coupon bonds to pay the exercise price, get the stock and deliver it to settle the short-sale. On net, the value of our portfolio is zero. This is the payoff of a put with an exercise price of $40 when it is out of the money. We manufactured the payoff of the put at a cost of $3 by buying the call, investing the present value of the exercise price in zero-coupon bonds, and selling the stock short.

We would expect $3 to be the price of the put, since the production cost of the put to us is $3. This result is called the **put-call parity theorem**. It states that the price of a European put is equal to the value of a portfolio long the call, long an investment in zero-coupon bonds for the present value of the exercise price of the call and same maturity as the call, and short the underlying asset:

Put-call parity theorem

$$p(S, K, T, t) = c(S, K, T, t) + P_t(T)K - S_t \qquad (10.8)$$

The put-call parity relationship holds, or otherwise we could make money for sure by creating an arbitrage position. The theorem does not hold for American puts and calls, however. We will see why next.

Let's consider a numerical example of a money machine when the put-call parity theorem does not hold. Assume put and call options mature in 90 days. The underlying asset is worth $50, the put is worth $10, the exercise price is $55, and a zero-coupon bond that matures in 90 days and pays $1 is worth $0.97. This means that $S_t = 50$, $K = 55$, $p(50, 55, t + 0.25, t) = 10$, $P_t(t + 0.25) = 0.97$. Using the put-call parity theorem, the call price must be:

$$c(50, 55, t + 0.25, t) = 10 + 50 - 0.97 \times 55 = 60 - 53.35 = 6.65$$

Suppose that the call sells for $7 instead of $6.65. We therefore want to sell the call because it is too expensive relative to the put. Since we do not want to take the risk of an unhedged short call position, we hedge the short call by buying a portfolio that does not include the call but has the same payoff. The put-call parity theorem tells us that this portfolio is long the put, long the underlying asset, and short zero-coupon bonds that mature at T and have face value of $55. Buying this hedge portfolio creates a cash outflow of $6.65 ($10 plus $50 minus the present value of the exercise price). This cash outflow is financed by selling the call for $7, so that we have $0.35 left. The thirty-five cents is our arbitrage profit, because no cash is needed at maturity. This is shown in Table 10.2.

Suppose that instead the call is worth $6. In this case the call is too cheap. Now we want to buy it, and sell the portfolio that has the payoff of the call. This means that we short the asset, write the put, and invest in zero-coupon bonds with a face value of $55 that mature in three months. This means that we have a cash flow of $-$6 - $53.35 + $50 + $10, or $0.65. At maturity, we get $\text{Max}[S_T - K, 0] - S_T + K - \text{Max}[K - S_T, 0]$. If the call is in the money, the put is not. In this case, we get $S_T - K - S_T + K$, or zero. If the put is in the money, we get $-S_T + K - (K - S_T)$, or zero.

Note that with this strategy we never make or lose money at maturity. We gain $0.65 today and pay nothing at maturity. Hence, there is an arbitrage opportu-

| Arbitrage table to exploit departures from put-call parity | *Table 10.2* |

In the example, $c(50, 55, t + 0.25, t) = 7$, $p(50, 55, t + 0.25, t) = 10$, $S_t = 50$, $K = 55$, and $P_t(t + 0.25) = 0.97$. Put-call parity does not hold since $7 > 10 + 50 - 53.35 = 6.65$.

Position at t	Cash outflow at t	Cash outflow at t + 0.25 if $S_{t + 0.25} < 55$	Cash outflow at t + 0.25 if $S_{t + 0.25} > 55$
Long put	−10	$55 - S_{t + 0.25}$	0
Long underlying asset	−50	$S_{t + 0.25}$	$S_{t + 0.25}$
Borrow K	53.35	−55	−55
Write call	7	0	$-(S_{t + 0.25} - 55)$
Total	0.35	0	0

nity whenever we make money today. If we are not to make money today, the call price has to be at least $6.65. Yet if the call price exceeds $6.65, we are back to the too high call price, where we make money by writing the call as we already noted. Consequently, there is an arbitrage opportunity whenever put-call parity does not hold.

Put-call parity does not hold exactly when there are transaction costs. We saw with the example of Ms. Chen that the bid-ask spread for options can be substantial. Can we rely on put-call parity at all in markets with significant transaction costs? Whenever one of the two strategies used to exploit discrepancies from put-call parity makes money today net of transaction costs, there is an arbitrage opportunity. However, with transaction costs, there is a range of put prices for a given call price where there are no arbitrage opportunities net of transaction costs. Consequently, put-call parity does not need to hold exactly to prevent arbitrage opportunities with transaction costs. It just has to hold closely enough so that exploiting discrepancies from put-call parity does not make enough money to recover transaction costs.

10.3.5. Option values and cash payouts
Things change somewhat when the underlying asset makes cash payouts before the maturity of the option. If the underlying asset is a stock, it may pay dividends. If the underlying asset is a coupon bond, it may make coupon payments before maturity of the option.

If we hold a European call option on a stock, we get to buy the stock at maturity for the exercise price. The dividends the stockholder receives between the time we buy the call and the time it matures do not belong to us unless the option contract includes some provision decreasing the exercise price at maturity by the amount of dividends paid. These dividends reduce the value of our option. If the firm were to pay a liquidating dividend the day after we bought the European call, the call would become worthless unless there is some protection against dividend payouts. Consequently, in the absence of such protection, the results discussed in section 10.2. hold for European options for the stock price minus the present value of dividends to be paid between now and maturity of the option.

In the presence of dividends, it is easy to see why it could be the case that a European call option that matures at $t'' > t'$ is worth less than the option that matures at t'. If the firm pays a liquidating dividend between t' and t'', the call option that matures at t' has value, but the option that matures at t'' does not. With an American call option, the call option that matures at t'' is worth at least as much as the option that matures at t' because one can always exercise the option maturing at t'' at the earlier time t'. With an American call option, if we knew that tomorrow the stock will pay a liquidating dividend, we would exercise the option today. This would give us the stock and thereby the right to collect the liquidating dividend. The American call option therefore has a benefit that the European call option does not have. Consequently, the American call option has to be worth at least as much as the European call option. The early exercise provision of American options is a right, not an obligation. It therefore cannot hurt us.

Suppose we have a call option on a stock that never pays a dividend. Would we ever exercise an American call option on that stock early? The answer is no for a simple reason. Exercising early has a cost and a benefit. The benefit is that we get S_t now. The cost is that we must pay the exercise price K now. If the stock does not pay a dividend, there is no reason to want the stock before maturity of the option. What we get now by exercising is simply the present value of the stock at maturity, but we are worse off paying the exercise price now than at maturity. By paying now, we lose the opportunity to invest our money until maturity. If we exercise at date t, we therefore lose the gain from investing the exercise price from t to T, $K/P_t(T) - K$. We also lose the limited liability feature of the option. Note that by exercising, we receive $S_t - K$. If the stock price falls, we could end up losing money on the exercised position that we would not have lost had we kept the option.

This means that exercising an American call early on a stock that does not pay a dividend is unambiguously a mistake (in the absence of counterparty risks). The American call therefore increases in value with time to maturity. An American call that is never exercised is equivalent to a European call. The price of a European call on a stock that does not pay a dividend must therefore increase with time to maturity.

The reasoning is different if the stock pays a dividend. If the stock pays a dividend and we exercise early, we receive the dividend. So, suppose that the stock pays a dividend just after we exercise at t and that it does not pay a dividend again until maturity. Say that the dividend is D_t. If we exercise just before the dividend payment, we get D_t that we would not otherwise have but lose $K/P_t(T) - K$ and the limited liability feature of the option. Whether we exercise or not depends on the magnitude of D_t relative to the costs of exercising the option. If the dividend payment is large enough, we exercise.

Would we ever exercise at some time other than just before a dividend payment? No. By postponing exercise until just before the dividend payment, we get the benefit of investing the exercise price and there is no cost to us from not exercising since no payout takes place. Consequently, American call options on stocks are exercised just before a dividend payment or not at all.[2]

What about American put options? With a put option, a dividend payment increases the payment we receive upon exercise since it reduces the stock price. Therefore there is no reason to exercise a put option before a dividend payment. When we exercise an American put option, we receive the exercise price, which we then get to invest. Also, we lose the limited liability feature of the option position, which will protect us if the stock price increases to exceed the exercise price. In this case, the short position will keep incurring losses if the stock price increases further, but the put option will not. For a sufficiently low stock price, this limited liability feature does not have much value compared to the benefit of receiving the exercise price now and investing it until maturity. Hence, when the stock price is low, it pays to exercise because there is nothing to gain from waiting until maturity: the lost interest on investing the exercise price overwhelms the possible gain from further declines in the stock price.

10.3.6. American options and put-call parity

The put-call parity theorem does not hold for American options. The reason is straightforward. We had an example where a call's price was too low according to put-call parity, so that we bought the call and hedged it by shorting the stock worth $50, investing in the present value of the exercise price, and writing the put. The put and the call both have exercise price of $55 and the present value of the exercise price is $53.50. We saw that this strategy generates a cash flow today of $0.65 when the options are European options and a cash flow of zero at maturity of the options. Suppose now the options are American. To take an extreme example, suppose tomorrow the stock price is down to one cent. The put is exercised, so that we have to pay $55. The call is worthless. Our only asset is the present value of the exercise price. Since only one day lapsed, the value of that investment is close to $53.50. To avoid default on the put, we have to come up with more money. The strategy is not an arbitrage strategy—we could have a negative cash flow later on that exceeds the initial cash inflow. In this example, we have a cash outflow close to $1.50 tomorrow and a cash inflow of $0.65 today, so that we lose $0.85. Suppose, however, that the mispricing of the call is bigger. Say that the call trades for $5 instead of $6. In this case, our cash inflow is $1.65. We can never lose that much because of early exercise since early exercise means that we have to pay at most $55 and have at least $53.50 available to pay for it, so that our greatest possible loss is only $1.50, which is less than our initial cash flow of

---

2 A word about foreign exchange options, analyzed in detail in Chapter 12. It can be valuable to exercise an American foreign exchange call option early. Foreign currency cash does not pay a dividend in cash, but it pays a convenience yield equal to the foreign interest rate. This convenience yield is the benefit from not having to go to the ATM machine. Whenever we hold cash, the cost of holding cash is the interest rate. The convenience yield of foreign cash is equivalent to a dividend payment that we receive in kind rather than in cash. The foreign exchange call option holder does not receive the convenience yield in the same way that the holder of a call on a dividend paying stock does not receive the dividends paid before maturity if he does not exercise the option. By not exercising early, the holder of the call gives up the convenience yield, (the foreign interest rate on the cash he receives when exercising) but keeps the right to invest the money at the domestic interest rate he would otherwise have to use to pay the exercise price. When the foreign interest rate is high enough compared to the domestic interest rate, it pays to exercise the foreign currency call option early.

$1.65. Consequently, as long as the initial cash inflow exceeds the maximum possible loss we can make because of early exercise, we have an arbitrage strategy.

With this reasoning, we know that we have an arbitrage opportunity as long as the mispricing of the options is large enough. Consequently, there exist bounds on the call price that must be satisfied to avoid the existence of arbitrage opportunities. These bounds are:

Bounds on American call prices

$$P(S, K, T, t) + S_t - K \le C(S, K, T, t) \le P(S, K, T, t) + S_t - P_t(T)K \quad (10.9)$$

Let's look at an example. Let the stock price be $50, the exercise price $40, the put price $5, and the price of a zero-coupon bond paying $1 in three months $0.95. The price of the call must be less than $5 + $50 - 0.95 × $40, or less than $17. It must also be more than $5 + $50 - $40, or $15. Suppose the price of the call is $13. We can buy the call and hedge it.

To hedge the call, we would like to have a position that offsets the payoff of the call. Since the call makes money when the stock price exceeds the exercise price, we want a position that loses money in that case. Being short the stock will result in losses when the stock price increases. However, if the stock price falls, a short position makes gains when we gain nothing from the call. Consequently, we have to write a put to eliminate these gains.

If we write an American put, however, it can be exercised at any time. Consequently, if we want our hedge portfolio to have no cash flow requirements during its life, we have to set aside the exercise price and invest it. This implies that to hedge the call, we sell the stock short, write a put, and invest the exercise price. The proceeds from this hedge portfolio are $50 + $5 - $40, or $15. Since we paid $13 for the call, we make $2 out of buying the call and hedging it. Since we bought the call, we only exercise at maturity. Consequently, suppose that the stock price goes to $55. In this case, we have $15 from the call at maturity and our hedge portfolio is worth -$55 - $0 + $40/0.95, or -$12.8947 since the put is worthless. On net, we have $2.1053. Alternatively, suppose the stock falls to $35 by tomorrow and stays there. In this case, the call is worthless and the put has value. The issue that we have to face is that the holder of the put could exercise tomorrow or at any time until maturity. If the holder exercises at maturity, the hedge portfolio is then worth -$35 - $5 + $40/0.95, or $2.1053. If the holder exercises tomorrow, the hedge portfolio is worth tomorrow -$35 - $5 + $40, or zero. The hedge portfolio will never make a loss when the stock price falls below the exercise price of the put. Further, if the stock price increases, the loss of the hedge portfolio will never exceed the value of the call. As a result, we always make money buying the call and hedging it with the hedge portfolio.

10.4. Summary

Options can be used to hedge just about anything. A forward contract is equal to a portfolio of a long position in a European call and a short position in a European put where both options have the maturity of the forward contract and an exercise price equal to the forward price. A piecewise linear payoff function can be hedged exactly with a portfolio of options, but not with a forward contract.

Whatever the distribution of the return of the underlying asset of an option, option prices must satisfy some properties. Call option prices fall with the exercise price; put option prices increase with the exercise price. American options increase in value with time to maturity. A European call on a dividend-paying stock and a European put can decrease in value with time to maturity. European put and call prices are related to each other through the put-call parity theorem. American calls are exercised only immediately before a dividend payment, whereas American puts are exercised when the price of the underlying asset is low enough. The put-call parity theorem does not apply to American options because they can be exercised early.

Key Concepts

intrinsic value, 301
put-call parity theorem, 320
static hedge, 300

Review Questions

1. Where could you buy an option on a stock?

2. How does the cash flow of Export Inc. differ if it hedges by buying a put on one million Swiss francs and if it hedges by selling one million Swiss francs forward?

3. Why is it possible to construct a static hedge of a contingent exposure with options when it is not possible to do so with forwards or futures contracts?

4. How does one replicate a forward contract with options?

5. Why could it make sense for a firm to buy calls on its stock?

6. What is the minimum price greater than zero that a European call price must exceed?

7. How is the value of an option related to its exercise price? Does it depend on whether the option is a put or a call?

8. Why can time to maturity have a different impact on European and American options?

9. Why would you want to exercise an American call early?

10. Does put-call parity hold for American options?

Questions and Exercises

1. You are the treasurer of a large multinational corporation. The company's competition is mostly Japanese, but you do not produce in Japan and have no assets or liabilities denominated in yen. The board looks at your

derivatives portfolio and finds that you have puts on the yen, so that you get to sell yen for a fixed dollar price. You are accused of speculating. Is there a plausible reason why you would have these puts if you are only hedging?

2. Consider a car manufacturer. In six months, the firm has to start producing 100,000 cars. It can produce them in Europe or in the United States. After the cars are produced, they are sold in the United States at a fixed price. The cost of producing a car in Europe is fixed in euros and is equal to €30,000. This cost is to be paid when production starts. The cost of producing a car in the United States is fixed at $20,000. The current price of a Euro is $0.60. The forward price of a euro for delivery in six months is also $0.60. The firm can decide where it will produce at any time between today and six months from now. You work for this company and the CEO tells you that he wants to decide today because this way the firm can hedge its foreign exchange rate risk. Looking at the forward rate, he finds out that producing in Europe is cheaper. Assuming that production takes six months and cars are sold immediately, what is the net present value of producing 100,000 cars for the company after having hedged exchange rate risk assuming that the continuously compounded dollar risk-free interest rate is 10 percent?

3. Suppose that you did what the CEO wanted you to do and six months from now the euro is selling for $1. The CEO comes to you and says that it no longer makes sense to produce in Europe. Since you hedged, is the company better off to produce in Europe or in the United States?

4. Can you show the CEO how the firm can eliminate foreign exchange rate risk but still choose to produce in six months in the country where the cost per car evaluated in dollars is the lowest?

5. Suppose that you recommend to the CEO to decide in six months. He tells you that he does not understand your recommendation because he does not see the value of waiting. He argues that all that can happen by waiting is that the firm could lose the benefit of producing in Europe at current exchange rates. How could you provide him with an estimate of the value of waiting by comparing the firm's profits if it waits and if it does not wait?

6. Many firms include options to their managers as part of their compensation. It is often argued that a side effect of this practice is that if management wants to pay out funds to shareholders, it prefers to do so in the form of a share repurchase than an increase in dividends. What is the rationale for this argument?

7. Your broker recommends that you buy European calls on a nondividend paying stock maturing in one year. The calls are worth $50, the stock is worth $100, and the exercise price is $49. He tells you that these calls are a great buy. His reasoning is that if they were American calls, you could exercise them and immediately gain $51. He admits that these calls are European calls, but his argument is that since the stock pays no dividends, there is no difference. Should you buy the calls?

8. Consider a European put and a European call on a stock worth $50. The put and the call mature in one year, have the same exercise price of $50, and have the same price. Can you make money from a situation like this if interest rates are 0 percent per annum? What would you do to make money if interest rates are 10 percent?

9. A European put is worth $5 and matures in one year. A European call on the same stock is worth $15 and matures in one year also. The put and the call have the same exercise price of $40. The stock price is $50. The price of a zero-coupon bond that matures in one year is worth $0.90. How do you make risk-free profits given these prices?

10. You hold an American call on a nondividend paying stock. The call has a two-year maturity. The exercise price is $50 and the stock is now worth $70. Your broker calls you and tells you that you should exercise. He argues that the benefit of the call is the downward protection, but that you don't need this protection anymore because the stock price is so high relative to the exercise price. Should you exercise? How do you justify your decision?

11. You wrote an American put with an exercise price of $50. The stock price is now $1 and the option has one year to maturity. Do you gain if the put holder does not exercise today?

Literature Note

The results on option prices that do not require assumptions about the distribution of the underlying asset are classic results first published in Merton (1973). The put-call parity theorem is due to Stoll (1969). Cox and Rubinstein (1985) discuss the use of options to hedge and also have some historical material on options. The role of options in the South Sea bubble is explained in Chancellor (1999). Valerio and Kayris (1997) discuss the option markets in the 1870s. A good description of the use of put options in conjunction with employee option plans is provided by Dwight Cass, "Hedging option plans," *Risk Magazine*, September 2000, 81–83. Dilution limits and their role in the use of derivatives by firms to repurchase shares are discussed in "UK firms consider option scheme," by Nicholas Dunbar, *Risk Magazine*, March 2001, p. 14. McDonald (2002) provides an analysis showing that selling puts is tax-disadvantaged for corporations.

Chapter 11

Option Pricing, Dynamic Hedging, and the Binomial Model

Chapter **11** *Objectives*

At the end of this chapter, you will:

1. Have seen how stock prices evolve if returns follow the binomial distribution.

2. Be able to hedge options with the binomial model.

3. Understand how to price options with that model.

4. Know how to hedge complex payoffs using that model.

Consumer Credit Inc. makes consumer loans. If the economy does poorly, some loans do not get repaid, which endangers Consumer's future. If the economy does well, few loans fail, but Consumer's net income is relatively insensitive to how well the economy is doing. Consumer has an exposure to economic activity that decreases as the economy improves. A put on the S&P 500 can help hedge Consumer against the adverse effect of economic downturns (see Chapter 10). Suppose, however, that Consumer serves mostly employees from the auto industry. Its profits are tied closely to that industry. A put option on an index of auto manufacturers would be a better hedge, but such options are not traded on exchanges. Can Consumer improve on the S&P 500 option hedge?

To improve on the S&P 500 hedge, Consumer has to do some work. It has to figure out how to manufacture a put option on an index of auto manufacturers on its own. Alternatively, it could convince an investment bank to manufacture such a put option. To decide between these two courses of action, Consumer has to determine whether manufacturing the put on its own is cheaper than buying it from the investment bank. This means that Consumer has to find out how much it would cost it to manufacture the put on its own.

In this chapter, we show how firms in Consumer's situation can use a model, the binomial option pricing model, to manufacture options on their own, to assess option prices, and to hedge options. The binomial model is built on a simple assumption about how the price of the underlying asset of an option evolves through time. Taking this asset to be a common stock for concreteness, the binomial model assumes that, given its price today, the common stock price can have only one of two values after one period has elapsed. For example, if the price is $10 today and the period is one week, in one week the stock price can either be $12 or $9. With this simple approach to modeling the evolution of the stock price over time, we can construct a portfolio of the stock and the risk-free zero-coupon bond that exactly replicates the payoff of a call option. A portfolio that replicates the payoff of a security without containing the security is called a replicating portfolio. If a replicating portfolio has the same payoff as a call option, it must have the same price as the call option to avoid the existence of arbitrage opportunities. If we can price the replicating portfolio, we can therefore price the call option by arbitrage. As long as the stock price evolves in this simple way, we can price any derivative whose payoff depends on the stock price. We will show how this is done.

We know how to price forward contracts by arbitrage. There is a crucial difference when we price options by arbitrage. With forward contracts, we have a static replicating portfolio—we set it up and hold onto it. With options, the replicating portfolio changes over time. Look at a European call option on IBM with an exercise price of $100 and maturity in one year. At maturity, the option is worth either one share of IBM minus $100 or nothing. Suppose that after some time in the life of the option, the price of a share has increased so much that it is sure that the option will be in the money at maturity. At that point, holding one share of IBM and borrowing the present value of $100 forms the perfect replicating portfolio. Or, if it is sure that the option will not be in the money at maturity because the share price is so low, the replicating portfolio has to be worth nothing irrespective of changes in the stock price. This can happen only if the replicating portfolio holds no shares of IBM at that point.

At some point, the portfolio either holds a long position of one share in IBM or holds no shares, depending on the price of a share. To achieve this outcome, the portfolio's investment in IBM stock has to be adjusted over time so that it holds one share if exercise is sure and no shares when it is certain that the option will not be exercised. That is, we need a dynamic trading strategy that produces the right outcome.

In section 11.1, we price options in a simple one-period model. This allows us to understand the main components of the binomial model. In section 11.2, we extend the model to incorporate additional periods and obtain a general formula for the pricing of stock options. Section 11.3 uses the binomial model to price American options and other contingent claims. Section 11.4 shows how to use the binomial model to hedge complicated payoffs that do not need to be option payoffs.

11.1. Arbitrage pricing and the binomial model

Suppose we want to price an option on a share of Rubinstein.com. The option has just one period to maturity. The share price of Rubinstein.com follows the binomial model, in that over the period the stock price can go up to a known price or fall to a known price. At date 0, the stock price is $100. At date 1, the share price is $200 if the economy is in a boom and $50 if the economy is in a recession. The call option has an exercise price of $100. The price of a zero-coupon bond that pays $1 at date 1 is $0.90 at date 0. To price the option by arbitrage, we construct a portfolio at date 0 that pays the same as the option at date 1.

11.1.1. The replicating portfolio approach to price an option

We know that the replicating portfolio of a share of Rubinstein.com has to pay the stock price minus $100 if the option is in the money. At maturity of the option, the payoff of the option depends on one random variable, namely, the stock price. If we were sure that the option will be in the money at maturity, we would hold the stock and borrow the present value of $100. Holding the stock and borrowing the present value of $100 cannot be the correct replicating portfolio if there is some chance that the option will expire out of the money. Can some other combination of borrowing and investment in the stock provide the correct replicating portfolio? The correct replicating portfolio must pay $100 if the stock price is $200 and $0 otherwise. Let z be the number of shares in the replicating portfolio. We borrow the present value of B, so that we have to repay B at date 1. In this case, we want the choice of z and B to be such that:

Payoff of replicating portfolio in boom state
= Payoff of call option in boom state

$$z \times 200 - B = 100 \qquad \text{(11.1.A)}$$

Payoff of replicating portfolio in recession state
= Payoff of call option in recession state

$$z \times 50 - B = 0 \qquad \text{(11.1.B)}$$

If we can find z and B so that these two equations are satisfied, we have a replicating portfolio for the option on one Rubinstein.com share.

From equation (11.1.B), we know that z must be equal to B/50. We can therefore eliminate z from equation (11.1.A) to find that B is equal to $100/3. Substituting for B in equation (11.1.B), we discover that z is equal to 2/3. Consequently, to create a portfolio that replicates the option, we have to buy 2/3 of a share and borrow the present value of $33.33.

To verify that we have the correct replicating portfolio, all we need to do is to show that with our solution for z and B, equations (11.1.A) and (11.1.B) hold:

$$z \times 200 - B = (2/3) \times 200 - 33.33 = 100 \qquad \text{(11.2.A)}$$

$$z \times 50 - B = (2/3) \times 50 - 33.33 = 0 \qquad \text{(11.2.B)}$$

By holding 2/3 of a share and borrowing the present value of $33.33, we obtain the same payoff as if we had bought the call option. The value of the call option must be the value of the replicating portfolio which is:

$$\textbf{Value of call option} = 2/3 \times 100 - 0.9 \times 33.33 = \$36.67 \qquad \text{(11.3)}$$

Figure 11.1 shows how the replicating portfolio is purchased at date 0 and how its payoff at date 1 matches the payoff of the option.

Figure 11.1   Evolution of stock price and replicating portfolio for the one-period case

The call option matures at date 1 and has an exercise price of $100. The price of a zero-coupon bond that pays $1 at date 1 is $0.90 at date 0.

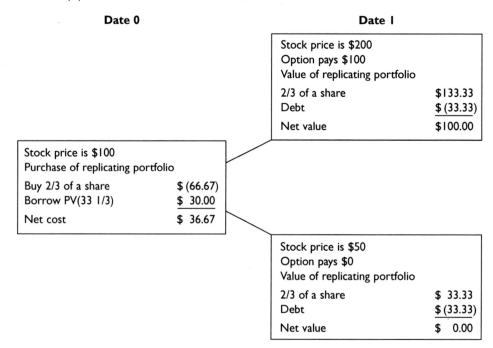

Suppose we find that we can buy the option for $30. In this case, the option is too cheap relative to the theoretical price of $36.67. Since we priced the option by arbitrage, we can take advantage of the price discrepancy without bearing any risk. We would like to buy the option because it is too cheap. This costs us $30 and we are exposed to the risk resulting from stock price changes on the value of the option. To eliminate that risk, we short the replicating portfolio. This means that we short 2/3 of a share and invest the present value of $33.33 in the riskless asset—zero-coupon bonds that pay $1 for sure at maturity. We know that the replicating portfolio is worth $36.67, so that shorting that portfolio creates an inflow of $36.67. We spend $30 to buy the call, so that we are left with $6.67. This amount of $6.67 is our profit because the long call and the short position in the replicating portfolio have offsetting payoffs at maturity, so that we neither receive a cash inflow nor do we have to make a payment at maturity.

Let's check that our arbitrage position pays nothing at maturity. At maturity, we have the payoff of the call, but we have to buy a share to offset the short-sale and have $33.33 from our investment in the riskless asset. If the stock price is $200, our position pays $100 from the call, but buying 2/3 of a share at $200 and selling our investment in the risk-free asset worth $33.33 creates a cash outflow of $100 that exactly matches the inflow from the call. Hence, if the stock price is $200, our position pays nothing at maturity. Similarly, if the stock price is $50, we receive nothing from the call, but the value of the short position in the replicating portfolio requires no payment because 2/3 of a share at $50 is equal to the proceeds of $33.33 from selling the risk-free asset.

11.1.2. Pricing options by constructing a hedge

We can also obtain the value of the option using a different approach that helps our intuition and checks our understanding. Suppose that we have a long position in a call on a Rubinstein.com share but we want to hedge that position so that we bear no risk. The payoff of the option depends on only one risk factor, the stock price. Since the option payoff increases with the stock price, we need to construct a hedge that makes money as the stock price falls. This means that we have to short the stock.

Let h be the hedge ratio. The hedge ratio is the number of units of the hedge instrument sold short to hedge one unit of cash position. Here, we sell h units of stock short to hedge one call. We would have a perfect hedge if a long position in the call and a short position of h shares has the same value whether the stock price is $200 or $50. This means that the perfect hedge is one that satisfies the following equation:

Value of hedged portfolio if stock price is $200
= Value of hedged portfolio if stock price is $50

$$[\$200 - \$100] - h \times 200 = [\$0] - h \times 50 \qquad (11.4)$$

In equation (11.4), the terms in brackets represent the payoffs of the call option. Equation (11.4) has one unknown, the number of shares we go short. Solving the equation we find that h is equal to 2/3. By going short 2/3 shares, we get $-(2/3) \times 50$, or $-\$33.33$, whatever the stock price at maturity of the option. A negative payoff is a debt, so that we have to borrow to finance that portfolio and repay $33.33 at maturity. Note that the number of shares we go short to hedge the call is the number of shares we hold in the replicating portfolio. We have a perfect hedge of the call option. Using our hedging analysis, the exposure of the call to the stock is 2/3 of a share. By hedging, we go short this exposure.

With the hedging approach, we construct a portfolio that pays −$33.33 for sure but is long the call. The present value of the portfolio is the payoff of the portfolio, −$33.33, discounted at the risk-free rate. Therefore, we can price the option by noting that:

$$\text{Call price} - h \times \text{Share price} = \text{PV}[-\$33.33]$$

$$\text{Call price} - (2/3) \times \$100 = -0.9 \times \$33.33 \tag{11.5}$$

Solving for the call price, we get $36.67.

11.1.3. Why the stock's expected return does not affect the option price

We have now seen two ways of finding the call price: the replicating portfolio method and the hedge portfolio method. Neither method uses the probability distribution of the return of the stock. We do not need to know how likely it is that the stock price will be $200. With the replicating portfolio method, we create a portfolio that always pays exactly the same as the option irrespective of the payoff of the option. The probability that the stock price will be $200 is therefore irrelevant because the replicating portfolio pays $100 irrespective of whether this case has a high or low probability. More generally, with the replicating portfolio method, we set the value of the replicating portfolio equal to the payoff of the option for each possible outcome irrespective of its probability. Because of this property of the portfolio, its value must equal the value of the option irrespective of the expected payoff or the probability distribution of the payoffs. With the hedging method, we eliminate all risk and the hedged portfolio always pays the same. Again, the probability of the stock price reaching $200 cannot matter because the payoff of the portfolio is independent of the stock price.

Since we never specify the probability distribution for the stock price at date 1, it could be anything consistent with the absence of arbitrage opportunities without changing the call price we derived. The only probabilities of the stock price reaching $200 that would lead to arbitrage opportunities are 0 and 1. With these probabilities the stock either earns more than the risk-free rate for sure, so that we make infinite profits by going long the stock and borrowing, or earns less than the risk-free rate for sure, so that we make infinite profits by going short the stock and lending at the risk-free rate. A probability of the stock price reaching $200 of 0.99 does not create arbitrage opportunities even though in this case the expected return of the stock is 98.5 percent. Similarly, there is no arbitrage opportunity if the probability that the stock price will reach $200 is 0.01. In this case, the expected return of the stock is −48.5 percent.

The ability to create a replicating portfolio consisting of the investment in the stock and the risk-free zero-coupon bond that pays the same as the option for each possible outcome of the option depends crucially on the assumption we made about possible stock prices. If there are three outcomes for the stock price instead of two, we cannot price the option by constructing a replicating portfolio that consists only of an investment in the stock and borrowing. To see this, suppose that the stock price could also go to $120. In this case, the call pays $20. Now, three outcomes are possible. To construct a replicating portfolio, we would need to find a portfolio such that its payoff matches the payoff of the option for each of the three outcomes:

$$z \times \$200 - B = \$100 \tag{11.6.A}$$

$$z \times \$120 - B = \$20 \tag{11.6.B}$$

$$z \times \$50 - B = \$0 \tag{11.6.C}$$

An investment of 2/3 of a share and borrowing the present value of $33.33 solves equations (11.6.A) and (11.6.C). However, the left-hand side of equation (11.6.B) is $46.67 instead of $20. Consequently, the replicating portfolio that works with two possible outcomes does not work in this case. This is not surprising. We now have three equations with two unknowns. Unless we can obtain one of the equations from the other two, a system of three equations with two unknowns has no solution.

11.1.4. The binomial model

Suppose now that we have many periods and each period the stock price can move to only one of two values. We can determine these values by letting the stock have one of two returns. If the returns the stock can take are the same every period, then the distribution of the returns is identically independently distributed (i.i.d.). Returns then follow a binomial distribution. To understand the binomial distribution, think of an urn from which you can draw a black or a red ball. For each draw, you have probability p of drawing a black ball and a probability $(1 - p)$ of drawing a red ball. The **binomial distribution** is the probability distribution of getting j black balls and $q - j$ red balls when drawing q balls such that each ball has probability p of being a black ball. Now, let the return of the stock take one value if we draw a black ball and another value if we draw a red ball. More precisely, the stock price can earn more than the risk-free rate (an up move) or less than the risk-free rate (a down move). We call period i the time interval from date i to date $i + 1$. S_i is the stock price observed at date i. An up move multiplies the stock price by u, so that the stock price goes from S_i at date i to uS_i at date $i + 1$ with an up move. A down move multiplies the stock price by d, so that the stock price goes from S_i at date i to dS_i at $i + 1$. With the growth rate i.i.d., u and d are always the same. Let's assume further that the probability of an up move is p and the probability of a down move is $1 - p$. These probabilities are constant through time with the i.i.d. assumption.

Figure 11.2 shows how the stock price evolves over time. It looks like a tree. The root of the tree is at date zero and the tree expands each period. A point in the figure where the tree expands into two branches is called a node. Such a figure is called a binomial tree. The shape of the tree depends critically on the i.i.d. assumption. To see this, let's look at the possible prices after two periods. Let the

Figure 11.2

Evolution of stock price when the stock price follows a binomial distribution

The stock price is multiplied each period by u for an up move that has probability p and by d for a down move that has probability $1 - p$.

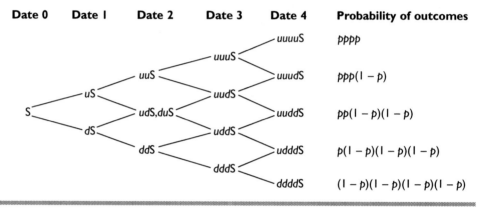

price at date 0 be S. After two periods, the possible prices are uuS, $udS = duS$, and ddS. If the u and d values are not i.i.d. but are time-dependent, so that u_i indicates the up move from date i to date $i + 1$, we would have instead $u_1 u_2 S$, $u_1 d_2 S$, $d_1 u_2 S$, and $d_1 d_2 S$. Without the i.i.d. assumption, $u_1 d_2 S$ is not equal to $d_1 u_2 S$, so that after two periods, we have four distinct possible values. In this case, after n periods, we would have 2^n possible stock prices. In contrast, with the i.i.d. assumption, we have $n + 1$ possible values after n periods. The i.i.d. assumption therefore reduces the number of outcomes in the tree. This is because with the i.i.d. assumption, an up move followed by a down move always leads to the same price as a down move followed by an up move. For convenience, we also assume that the interest rate is constant and use the notation r to denote one plus the one period interest rate. Deterministic changes in the interest rate would change nothing of substance in the following.

We assume that:

$$u > r > d \qquad (11.7)$$

To understand this assumption, suppose that $r > u > d$. In this case, the risk-free asset always pays more than the stock. If we short the stock and invest in the risk-free asset, we make money for sure. Alternatively, if $u > d > r$, the stock always earns more than the risk-free asset. In this case, we make money for sure by borrowing at the risk-free rate and investing in the stock.

Consider now a call option sold at date 0 that allows us to buy the stock at date 1 for K when the stock price follows the binomial distribution. To know whether the price of that call option is fair, we can price the call option by constructing a hedged portfolio that has no risk as we did when we priced a call option on a Rubinstein.com share. Again we have only two states of the world at date 1, the up state where the stock is up and the down state where it is down. Let's write c_u for the payoff of the option in the up state and c_d for its payoff in the down state. These payoffs are known since we know the exercise price of the option and the stock price in each state. We can form a risk-free portfolio that holds one unit of the call and is short h shares of stock:

Payoff of portfolio in up state = Payoff of portfolio in down state

$$c_u - huS = c_d - hdS \qquad (11.8)$$

To form a risk-free portfolio that has one call option, we must short h units of the stock. We can find h by solving the equation (11.8):

$$h = \left(\frac{c_u - c_d}{uS - dS} \right) \qquad (11.9)$$

h is positive because we know that $u > d$ and $c_u - c_d > 0$. We can hedge a call option on one share perfectly by shorting at most one share. The option is always exercised, never exercised, or exercised only in the up state. If the option is exercised for sure, h is equal to one because in that case the numerator in parentheses is equal to the denominator since $c_u = uS - K$ and $c_d = dS - K$, so that $c_u - c_d = uS - dS$. The numerator is equal to zero if the option is never exercised because c_u and c_d are equal to zero. If the option is exercised only in the up state, the numerator is less than the denominator, so that h is between zero and one.

Denote by $c(S, K, 1, 0)$ the price at date 0 of a European call on common stock with price S, exercise price K, and maturity at date 1. We can price the call by remembering that the value of the risk-free portfolio at date 0 is the present value of its payoff at date 1:

$$c(S, K, 1, 0) - hS = \frac{1}{r} \left[c_u - huS \right] \qquad (11.10)$$

Remember that h is known from equation (11.9). Consequently, the only unknown in equation (11.10) is the call price. After substituting our formula for h into equation (11.10), we can solve the equation for the call price to get a formula for the price of an option that matures at date 1:

Formula for a call option that matures in one period

$$c(S, K, 1, 0) = \frac{1}{r} \left\{ \left[\frac{r - d}{u - d} \right] c_u + \left[\frac{u - r}{u - d} \right] c_d \right\} \qquad (11.11)$$

Note that, as we would expect by now, the probability of an up move does not enter the formula.

What do we need to know to apply the formula? The interest rate, u, d, and the payoff of the option in each state. As an example, let $r = 1.1$, $u = 1.2$, $d = 0.9$, $c_u = 100$, and $c_d = 0$. In this case, we have:

$$c(S, K, 1, 0) = \left(\frac{1}{1.1} \right) \left[\frac{1.1 - 0.9}{1.2 - 0.9} \right] 100 = 60.6061 \qquad (11.12)$$

The formula discounts the term in braces in equation (11.11) at the risk-free rate. This term looks like a weighted average of the option payoffs with the term in the first square brackets multiplying the option payoff if the stock price goes up and the term in the second square brackets multiplying the option payoff if the stock price goes down. The expected payoff of the option is a weighted average of the payoffs also, namely $pc_u + (1 - p)c_d$, but the weights are the true probabilities, that is, in this case p and $(1 - p)$. Hence, the term in braces looks like an expected value, but the weights are the terms in brackets, which are *not* the true probabilities.

Probabilities must sum to one. If we sum the weights in equation (11.11), the terms in square brackets, we find that they sum to one like probabilities:

$$\frac{r - d}{u - d} + \frac{u - r}{u - d} = 1 \tag{11.13}$$

Further, each weight has a value between 0 and 1 because, as discussed earlier, $u > r > d$.

Define the term in the first square brackets, $(r - d)/(u - d)$, to be equal to π. With this definition, the term in the second square brackets, $(u - r)/(u - d)$, has to be equal to $1 - \pi$. Noting that π and $1 - \pi$ are positive but less than one, we can think of them as artificial, or pseudo-probabilities. Rewriting the formula for the option price, we have:

$$c(\mathbf{S, K, 1, 0}) = \frac{1}{r}\left[\pi c_u + (1 - \pi)c_d\right] \tag{11.14}$$

With these probabilities, the term in square brackets is the expected payoff of the option. It just is not the expected payoff of the option using the real-world probability of an up move, p, but instead using this made up probability π. The call option price is therefore equal to the expected payoff of the option computed using the probability of an up move π discounted at the risk-free rate.

Applying equation (11.14) to our numerical example, $\pi = 2/3$. We then have:

$$c(\mathbf{S, K, 1, 0}) = \frac{1}{1.1}\left(\frac{2}{3}\right)100 = 60.6061 \tag{11.15}$$

What is the interpretation of π and $1 - \pi$? They are the probabilities that would describe the distribution of the stock return if investors did not care about risk. If investors do not care about risk, they are called risk-neutral. Risk-neutral investors do not require a risk premium to be compensated for taking on risk, so they are willing to hold any asset if its expected return equals the risk-free rate.

To see that π is the probability of an increase in the stock price if investors are risk-neutral, all we have to do is show that the expected return with that probability is equal to the rate of interest. This is the case since:

$$\pi(u\mathbf{S}) + (1 - \pi)d\mathbf{S} = \left[\frac{r - d}{u - d}\right]u\mathbf{S} + \left[\frac{u - r}{u - d}\right]d\mathbf{S}$$

$$= \left[\frac{ru - du + ud - rd}{u - d}\right]\mathbf{S}$$

$$= r\mathbf{S} \tag{11.16}$$

r is one plus the interest rate. If the stock price has a probability π of going up and a probability $1 - \pi$ of going down, the expected stock price is rS, so that the expected return of the stock is the risk-free interest rate ($rS/S - 1 = r - 1$). As a shortcut, π and $1 - \pi$ are called **risk-neutral probabilities**. The risk-neutral probabilities are the probabilities that, given the financial asset's payoffs, make its expected return equal to the risk-free rate, which is the expected return the asset would have if investors were risk-neutral.

We can then state our option pricing formula as follows:

The call price is equal to the call's expected payoff discounted at the risk-free rate when the risk-neutral probabilities are used to compute the expected payoff.

To understand why this result makes sense, remember that our option pricing formula holds for any probability distribution. Consequently, we can make the probability distribution anything we want without changing the option price. In general, having a license to choose the probability distribution is not useful. However, the one case where it is useful is when we choose a probability distribution that corresponds to the case where the expected return of the stock is the risk-free rate. This probability distribution is useful because we know that if investors are risk-neutral, any asset is expected to earn the risk-free rate and we can discount any expected payoff at the risk-free rate. All this works because stock option prices do not depend on the true probability distribution of the stock return. We can therefore choose the probability distribution that makes our analysis the easiest to deal with.

Having priced the call, we also know how to price a put with an identical maturity and exercise price because of the put-call parity theorem discussed in Chapter 10.

11.2. The binomial approach with multiple periods

We first extend the analysis of section 11.1 to the case when the option matures in two periods. The general case where the option matures in n periods is then presented.

11.2.1. The binomial approach with two periods

Suppose we have a call option that expires in two periods. Its value at date 0 is written $c(S, K, 2, 0)$. Figure 11.3 shows the stock prices and option values for a two-period tree. Remember that the stock price evolves each period in the same way, either up by a factor of u or down by a factor of d. Since we know the possible stock prices at date 2, we also know the payoff of the option for each possible outcome. At that date, there are three states of the world. The option price takes value c_{uu} if the stock price went up twice, $c_{ud} = c_{du}$ if the stock price went up once and down once, and finally c_{dd} if the price went down twice. The option values at date 2 are all determined by the stock price at that date and by the exercise price.

Pricing the options at date 1 is straightforward for us because then the options have one period to go to maturity and we already know how to price options that have one period to go to maturity. At date 1, we have two possible option values,

Figure 11.3   Two-period trees for the stock price and the option price

The stock price is S at date 0; it is multiplied each period by either u with probability p or d with probability $1 - p$. The call option has price c at date 0 and matures at date 2. Its exercise price is K. $c_u (c_d)$ is the call price at date 1 if the stock price went up (down).

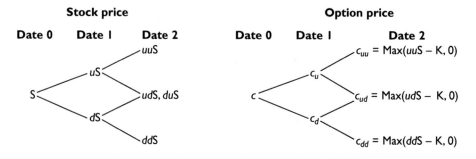

c_u and c_d. We construct a hedged portfolio to find c_u. From c_u, the option can either go to $c_{uu} = \text{Max}(uuS - K, 0)$ or to $c_{ud} = \text{Max}(udS - K, 0)$. Since from date 1, the option value can only become c_{uu} or c_{ud}, the option can take one of two values and so too the stock price. The stock price from date 1 to date 2 has either a (net) return of $u - 1$ or $d - 1$. Hence, it has the same possible returns as from date 0 to date 1. Consequently, since nothing is different except that the stock price is uS instead of S, the value of the option at date 1 if the stock price increased from date zero must be the expected payoff of the option looking forward from that node in the tree discounted at the risk-free rate:

$$c_u = \frac{1}{r}\left[\pi c_{uu} + (1 - \pi)c_{ud}\right] \tag{11.17}$$

Remember that we assume that the interest rate is constant and that the distribution of the growth rate of the stock is i.i.d. Consequently, the probabilities that make the expected return of the stock equal to the risk-free rate are always the same. This holds whatever the number of periods in the tree.

The same reasoning applies if the stock price falls from date 0 to date 1. In this case, the option price is:

$$c_d = \frac{1}{r}\left[\pi c_{du} + (1 - \pi)c_{dd}\right] \tag{11.18}$$

We now know the value of the option at date 1 for each stock price at that date. The option has value c_u if the stock price increased from date 0 and c_d otherwise. We know from section 11.1.4 that the value of the option at date 0 is the expected value of the option at date 1 computed using risk-neutral probabilities discounted at the risk-free rate:

$$c = \frac{1}{r}\left[\pi c_u + (1 - \pi)c_d\right] \tag{11.19}$$

Using this approach, we can price any option. Regardless of the maturity of the option, the current value of the option is the expected value of the option at a future date computed using risk-neutral probabilities discounted at the risk-free rate. The reason for this is that the stock price can go to only one of two values from any node of the binomial tree. Consequently, if we compute the value of the option at the date before the maturity date, the option is a one-period option. We can then work backwards along the tree, knowing how to price the option at each point along the tree.

We know already that we can compute the value of an option using the hedging method or the replicating portfolio method. It is important to understand how the replicating portfolio method works when there is more than one period because in that case the replicating portfolio changes over time. For the value of the option to be the value of the replicating portfolio, it has to be that no cash infusion is required over time when we replicate the option. We therefore now show that trading dynamically the replicating portfolio yields the option payoff at maturity of the option without requiring additional cash.

To construct a replicating portfolio at date 0, we invest in shares and borrow. Since the option can be hedged by shorting h shares, we can obtain the same exposure to the stock with a purchase of h shares or with the call. We therefore buy h shares and borrow $hS - c(S, K, 2, 0)$, so that our portfolio has the same value as the option. At date 1, our portfolio is worth $hS(1) - (hS - c(S, K, 2, 0))r$. The value of our portfolio at date 1 has to be equal to the value of the option at that date. Let's check that this is right for the case when the stock price increases:

Value of stock position – Amount borrowed plus interest

$$= huS - \left(hS - c(S, K, 2, 0)\right)r$$

$$= \left(\frac{c_u - c_d}{uS - dS}\right)(u - r)S + \left(\frac{r - d}{u - d}c_u + \frac{u - r}{u - d}c_d\right)$$

$$= c_u \qquad\qquad\qquad\qquad\qquad\qquad\qquad\qquad \text{(11.20)}$$

The replicating portfolio has the same value as the option if the stock goes down also and can be checked in the same way.

At date 1, we have to trade so that the replicating portfolio has the right payoff at date 2. If the stock price increased from date 0 to date 1, we have to buy $h(1, c_u) - h(0)$ shares at a cost of $(h(1, c_u) - h(0))uS$, where $h(1, c_u)$ is the hedge ratio at date 1 if the stock price increased between date 0 and date 1. We find $h(1, c_u)$ by solving:

$$c_{uu} - h(1, c_u)uuS = c_{ud} - h(1, c_u)udS \qquad\qquad \text{(11.21)}$$

The hedge ratio is:

$$h(1, c_u) = \left(\frac{c_{uu} - c_{ud}}{uuS - udS}\right) \qquad\qquad\qquad \text{(11.22)}$$

We pay for these shares by borrowing more. The price of the option at date 1 when the stock goes up is $c_u = c(uS, K, 2, 1)$ since the option has one period to maturity and the stock price is uS. This gives us a replicating portfolio that has $h(1, c_u)$ shares and has borrowed $h(1, c_u)uS - c(uS, K, 2, 1)$. To understand why we borrow this amount, note that the portfolio is worth $c(uS, K, 2, 1)$ but we hold shares for $h(1, c_u)uS$. Consequently, we have to borrow the difference between the value of the shares and the value of the option.

At maturity of the option, we want the replicating portfolio with $h(1, c_u)$ shares at date 1 to pay $c_{uu} = \text{Max}(uuS - K, 0)$ if the stock price increases from date 1 and $c_{ud} = \text{Max}(udS - K, 0)$ if it falls from date 1. Let's check that this is the case if the price increases from date 1. We have to compute the value of the replicating portfolio at date 2 if the stock price at date 1 is uS. We then substitute the value of the replicating portfolio at date 2, $h(1, c_u)$, from equation (11.22) and $c(uS, K, 2, 1)$ from equation (11.20) to obtain the value of the replicating portfolio as of date 2:

$$h(1, c_u)uuS - \left(h(1, c_u)uS - c(uS, K, 2, 1) \right)r$$

$$= \left(\frac{c_{uu} - c_{ud}}{uuS - udS} \right)uuS$$

$$- \left(\left(\frac{c_{uu} - c_{ud}}{uuS - udS} \right)uS - \frac{1}{r}\left[\frac{r - d}{u - d}c_{uu} + \frac{u - r}{u - d}c_{ud} \right] \right)r$$

$$= c_{uu} \tag{11.23}$$

We have now shown that we can buy a replicating portfolio at date 0, trade at date 1 without using or receiving additional cash, and end up at date 2 with the payoff of the option if the stock price went up twice. Exactly the same demonstration can be carried on for the three other possible price paths.

All the values in the call option formula, equation (11.23), can be computed directly if we know u, d, r, S, and K. Assuming that $u = 1.2$, $d = 0.9$, $r = 1.1$, $S = 500$, and $K = 500$, we can compute the value of a call that matures in two periods using the above formula. Figure 11.4 shows the binomial tree for the stock for two periods. From that tree, we can get the payoffs of the option. First, to get c_{uu}, note that $Suu = 500 \times 1.2 \times 1.2 = 720$. Consequently, the option pays 220 if the stock price goes up in both periods. Second, to get c_{ud}, we need to compute $Sud = 500 \times 1.2 \times 0.9 = 540$. In this case, the option pays 40. Finally, c_{dd} requires the computation of $Sdd = 500 \times 0.9 \times 0.9 = 405$. Hence, $c_{dd} = 0$ since the option is not exercised in that state. Using these values, we can get the option prices for the tree:

$$c_u = (1/1.1)[(2/3)220 + (1/3)40] = 160/1.1 = 145.45 \tag{11.24.A}$$

$$c_d = (1/1.1)[(2/3)40 + (1/3)0] = 24.242 \tag{11.24.B}$$

$$c(500, 500, 2, 0) = (1/1.1)[(2/3)145.45 + (1/3)24.242] = 95.50 \tag{11.24.C}$$

Stock price evolution and option payoff

Figure 11.4

For an up move, the stock price is multiplied by 1.2. For a down move, it is multiplied by 0.9. The option matures at date 2 and has exercise price of $500.

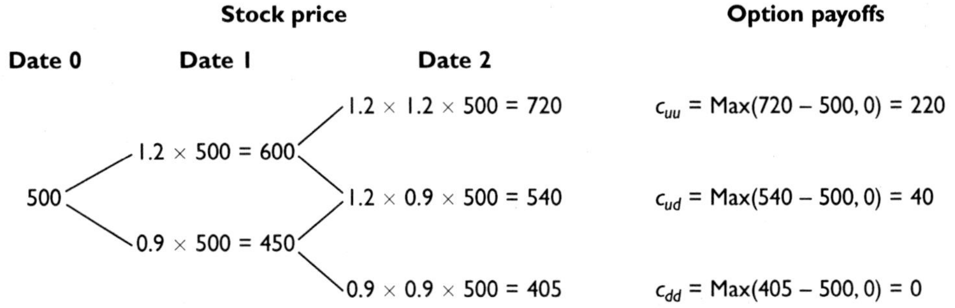

Stock price			Option payoffs
Date 0	**Date 1**	**Date 2**	

$$1.2 \times 1.2 \times 500 = 720 \qquad c_{uu} = \text{Max}(720 - 500, 0) = 220$$

$$1.2 \times 500 = 600$$

$$500$$

$$1.2 \times 0.9 \times 500 = 540 \qquad c_{ud} = \text{Max}(540 - 500, 0) = 40$$

$$0.9 \times 500 = 450$$

$$0.9 \times 0.9 \times 500 = 405 \qquad c_{dd} = \text{Max}(405 - 500, 0) = 0$$

Suppose we find that the option is priced at 100 instead of 95.50. Since the option is too expensive, we want to sell it—which means we want to write the option—and hedge it by taking a long position in the replicating portfolio. This strategy has no risk and makes an immediate profit of $4.50. The cash flows from the arbitrage strategy are shown in Figure 11.5. To hedge the option, we have to buy h shares, where h is the hedge ratio at date 0:

$$h = \frac{c_u - c_d}{uS - dS} = \frac{145.45 - 24.242}{1.2 \times 500 - 0.9 \times 500} = 0.8081 \qquad (11.25)$$

This purchase costs us 404.05. Remember that the option should be worth 95.50. Selling the call, we receive 100. We pocket 4.50 and use the remainder to finance the stock position. In addition, we have to borrow $404.05 - 95.50 = 308.55$.

If the stock price increases, the value of our share position goes from 404.05 to 484.86. At date 1, we owe $308.55 \times 1.1 = 339.41$. Since the stock price changes, we have to adjust our hedge ratio to $h(1, c_u)$:

$$h(1, c_u) = \frac{c_{uu} - c_{ud}}{uuS - udS} = \frac{220 - 40}{720 - 540} = 1 \qquad (11.26)$$

The hedge ratio increases to 1 because if the stock price reaches $600 at date 1, the option is always in the money at date 2. Our stock position is worth $484.86 and we spend an additional $115.14 to have one share. Let's borrow an additional $115.14. At date 2, we need $339.41 \times 1.1 = 373.35$ to repay what we borrowed at date 0 and $115.14 \times 1.1 = 126.65$ to repay what we borrowed at date 1. The total we need to repay is therefore $373.35 + 126.65 = 500$. Suppose the stock price is at $720. In this case, we give the stock to the option holder and receive $500 that we use to repay what we borrowed plus the interest. If the stock price is at $540 instead, we proceed in the same way. Consequently, at date 2, we neither make nor lose money. Remember, however, that we made a gain at date 0 of $4.50 that we get to keep no matter what.

Figure 11.5   Cash flows of arbitrage strategy

This figure shows the cash flows of an arbitrage strategy making a profit out of the fact that the call price is $100 instead of $95.50. The strategy consists in writing a call and hedging it by using a replicating portfolio.

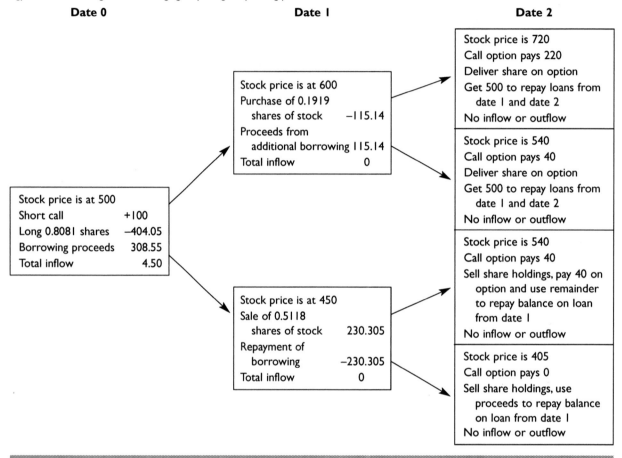

Let's now look at the case where the stock price at date 1 is $450. In this case, the hedge ratio becomes:

$$h(1, c_d) = \frac{c_{du} - c_{dd}}{Sud - Sdd} = \frac{40}{540 - 405} = 0.2963 \qquad (11.27)$$

Now the stock position is worth $363.645. With the new hedge ratio, we need to have $0.2963 \times 450 = 133.34$ invested in the stock. At date 1, we owe $339.41 on our borrowings from date 0. We sell stock for $363.645 - 133.34 = 230.305$, using the cash to reduce the size of the amount borrowed as of date 1 to 109.105. At date 2, the amount we need to repay is $109.105 \times 1.1 = 120$. At that date, our stock position is worth $0.2963 \times 405 = 120$ if the stock price went down to $405. In this case, we sell the stock and use the proceeds to repay the amount we borrowed plus interest. Alternatively, if the stock increases to $540, our stock position is worth $0.2963 \times 540 = 160$. We sell the stock, pay $40 to the option holder and use the remaining of $120 to repay the amount we borrowed plus interest. Irrespective of the outcome at date 2, we neither make nor lose money.

11.2.2. Pricing a European option that matures in *n* periods

To price an option expiring in *n* periods, we compute its expected payoff using the risk-neutral probabilities and discount it at the risk-free rate. To obtain the expected payoff, we must be able to assign a risk-neutral probability to various stock prices at maturity. Remember that a possible stock price at maturity is the stock price at date 0 multiplied by *j* times *u* and *n* − *j* times *d*, for *j* taking values from zero to *n*. The probability of *j* up moves out of *n* moves is obtained from the binomial distribution. Let *n*! be *n* factorial or $n \times (n-1) \times (n-2) \ldots \times 2 \times 1$. With this notation, this probability is:

Probability of *j* up moves in *n* moves $= \left(\dfrac{n!}{j!\,(n-j)!} \right) \pi^j (1 - \pi)^{n-j}$ **(11.28)**

The option payoff corresponding to *j* up moves is:

Payoff if the stock price increases *j* times out of *n* changes $=$

$$\mathbf{Max}\!\left(u^j d^{n-j} \mathbf{S} - \mathbf{K}, 0 \right) \qquad \text{(11.29)}$$

Multiplying the probability of an outcome with the option payoff, we get the expected value of that payoff:

$$\left(\frac{n!}{j!(n-j)!} \right) \pi^j (1 - \pi)^{n-j} \, \mathbf{Max}\!\left(u^j d^{n-j} \mathbf{S} - \mathbf{K}, 0 \right) \qquad \text{(11.30)}$$

Adding up the expected payoffs across all outcomes and discounting at the risk-free rate yields the option price at date 0. We can then write the option price for a call option with *n* periods to go at date 0 as:

$$c(\mathbf{S}, \mathbf{K}, \mathbf{n}, 0) = \mathbf{S} \left[\sum_{j=a}^{n} \left(\frac{n!}{j!(n-j)!} \right) \pi^j (1 - \pi)^{n-j} \frac{u^j d^{n-j}}{r^n} \right]$$

$$- \mathbf{K} r^{-n} \left[\sum_{j=a}^{n} \left(\frac{n!}{j!(n-j)!} \right) \pi^j (1 - \pi)^{n-j} \right] \qquad \text{(11.31)}$$

where *a* is the smallest nonnegative integer such that the option is in the money at maturity if the stock price has at least *a* upward moves and if it does not, the option expires unexercised. Hence, we want *a* to be the smallest integer so that $u^a d^{n-a} S > K$. Using logs, we have $a \ln u + (n-a)\ln d + \ln S > \ln K$, so that we can get *a*.

Equation (11.31) has an interesting interpretation. It is composed of two terms. The first term is multiplied by the current stock price. The term in brackets that multiplies the stock price is the expected growth of the stock price using the risk-neutral probabilities provided that the option is in the money at maturity. The discount factor implies that the first term is the discounted expected stock price using risk-neutral probabilities if the option is in the money at maturity. The second term has the interpretation of the discounted exercise price times the probability (using risk-neutral probabilities) that the option will be in the money at maturity.

Both bracketed terms in equation (11.31) correspond to the complementary binomial distribution function. The second bracketed term is the complementary binomial distribution function $\Phi[a : n, \pi]$. The first bracketed term is the complementary binomial function $\Phi[a : n, \pi']$ where:

$$\pi' = (u/r)\pi \text{ and } 1 - \pi' = (d/r)(1 - \pi) \tag{11.32}$$

With this notation, we can write:

Binomial option pricing formula

$$c(S, K, n, 0) = S\,\Phi[a : n, \pi'] - Kr^{-n}\Phi[a : n, \pi] \tag{11.33}$$

Let's look at an example. Consider a call option that matures in one year on a stock worth 100 at the beginning of the year, date 0. The exercise price is 100. We assume that the price can move up by a factor of 1.02 or down by a factor $1/1.02$ each period. A risk-free investment is assumed to grow by a factor of 1.001 each period. We divide the year into 100 periods. With this, we have $n = 100$, $S = 100$, $K = 100$, $u = 1.02$, $d = 0.980392$, and $r = 1.001$. First, we have to compute:

$$\pi = \frac{r - d}{u - d} = \frac{1.001 - 0.980392}{1.02 - 0.980392} = 0.520299$$

$$\pi' = \frac{u}{r}\pi = \left(\frac{1.02}{1.001}\right)\pi = 0.530175 \tag{11.34}$$

Next, we have to find a, which is the smallest integer such that $u^a d^{n-a}S > K$. In this case:

$$\ln\left(K/Sd^n\right)/\ln(u/d) = \ln\left(100/\left(100 \times 0.980392^{100}\right)\right)$$

$$/\ln\left(1.02/0.980392\right) = 50.00 \tag{11.35}$$

Consequently, $a = 50$. Using the formula for the option value, we have:

$$c(100, 100, 100, 0) = 100\Phi\big[50{:}100, 0.530175\big]$$

$$- 100\left(1.001^{-100}\right)\Phi\big[50{:}100, 0.520299\big]$$

$$= 100(1 - 0.306565) - 90.4883(1 - 0.379334)$$

$$= 13.18 \tag{11.36}$$

In Excel, the binomial cumulative distribution is BINOMDIST. To get the complementary binomial distribution, one subtracts the binomial cumulative distribution from 1 as we do in the second line of the derivation of the call price.

To compute the value of a European call option on a nondividend-paying stock using the binomial approach, we need to know the stock price S, the exercise price K, the number of periods to maturity n, the size of an up move u, the size of a down move d, and one plus the rate of interest per period r. If we price a call, we know the exercise price of the call K. We can find the stock price easily. The same applies to the interest rate. Finding n, u, and d is a bit more difficult.

One might be tempted to say that it should be a trivial task to find n, since it is simply the number of periods remaining in the life of the option. The problem is to define the period appropriately. If there is continuous trading of the stock, we could use a period of one minute. If we did that, our tree would quickly grow to huge dimensions—after one day, we would have more than one billion states of the world. Pricing an option that matures in a number of weeks would be computationally infeasible using periods of one minute. At the other extreme, we could use a period of one year. In this case, it would be kind of silly to use this approach because after one year the binomial model would do an extremely poor job of approximating the true distribution of the stock return and we would not be able to price options that expire within a year. A good starting point in choosing the length of a period is therefore to choose the period so that the true distribution of the stock price at maturity is well-approximated by the binomial distribution but also easy to obtain using a computer. Monthly periods are appropriate if the option matures in a number of years, weekly periods if it matures in a number of months, and daily periods otherwise. Technical Box 11.1, The binomial distribution as an approximation for the lognormal distribution, shows that under some conditions the binomial distribution becomes the lognormal distribution as the length of a period becomes infinitesimally small.

For a European put, we can use the same approach, namely compute the expected payoff using risk-neutral probabilities and discount this expected payoff using the risk-free rate. Remember that the risk-neutral probabilities are stock specific and not option specific. Consequently, we can use the same risk-neutral probabilities to compute the value of any option on a stock.

Let's look at a numerical example. We take the same stock as in the numerical example for the pricing of a call option. The European put option matures in two periods and has an exercise price of $600. Denote by $p(S, K, T, t)$ the value of a European put option. We then have:

$$P(500, 600, 2, 0)$$

$$= \frac{1}{r^2} \left[\pi^2 p_{uu} + 2\pi (1 - \pi) p_{ud} + (1 - \pi)^2 p_{dd} \right]$$

$$= \frac{1}{1.1^2} \left[\left(\frac{2}{3}\right)^2 0 + 2 \left(\frac{2}{3}\right) \left(\frac{1}{3}\right) (600 - 540) + \left(\frac{1}{3}\right)^2 (600 - 405) \right]$$

$$= 39.9449 \tag{11.37}$$

11.3. The binomial model and early exercise

The binomial model is extremely useful to price and hedge options that can be exercised early. When the stock pays a dividend, the early exercise feature of an American call has value. We first show how to use the binomial model to price a European call on a dividend-paying stock. We then study American options.

11.3.1. Using the binomial approach to price a European call on a dividend paying stock

The critical property of the stock price dynamics that makes the binomial model work is that, from every node, the stock price can only go to one of two stock prices. As long as this property is preserved, we can price options starting from

The binomial distribution as an approximation for the lognormal distribution

Let's suppose we want to value an option that matures in one year. We divide the year into n periods, so that $1/n$ is the length of a period. The next step is to find out u and d. Suppose we know that the true distribution of the stock price is such that the continuously compounded rate of return has mean μ and variance σ^2. In this case, the mean over one year is μ and the variance σ^2. The log of u and log of d correspond to the continuously compounded return of the stock if it has an up or a down move over a period. μ_n is the mean stock return per period when we use n periods and the variance σ_n^2 is the variance of the stock return per period when we use n periods. We would like the mean return μ_n and the variance σ_n^2 of the continuously compounded return of the stock as the period becomes small, that is, as n becomes large, to approach the true continuously compounded mean μ and variance σ^2.

Consider the stock price change from date t to date $t + 1$. Over n periods, $S_{t+1}/S_t = u^j d^{n-j}$. Using logs, we have:

$$\ln\left(S_{t+1}/S_t\right) = j\ln(u) + (n - j)\ln(d) = j\ln(u/d) + n\ln(S)$$

Over n periods, the number of up moves, j, is a random variable. However, we know that it has mean np and variance $np(1 - p)$ since the moves follow a binomial distribution. Consequently, the expected value and variance of $\ln(S_{t+1}/S_t)$ are:

$$\mu_n = E\left[\ln\left(\frac{S_{t+1}}{S_t}\right)\right] = E(j)\ln(u/d) + n\ln(nd) = \left[p\ln(u/d) + n\ln(nd)\right]n$$

$$\sigma_n^2 = E\left[\left(\ln\left(\frac{S_{t+1}}{S_t}\right) - \mu_n\right)^2\right] = \text{Var}(j)\left[\ln(u/d)\right]^2 = p(1 - p)\left[\ln(u/d)\right]^2 n$$

We already know how to estimate means and variances using historical data. Suppose that we now have these estimates for the annual mean and variance of the log price increments, defined as μ and σ^2. Can we choose u, d, and p so that the log price increments are normally distributed for sufficiently small periods of time? The answer is yes. Let T be measured in years and be divided into n periods. In our discussion so far, T = 1, but we allow T to differ from one to have a general formula. Let's choose u, d, and p as follows:

$$u = e^{\sigma\sqrt{T/n}}$$

$$d = 1/u$$

$$p = \frac{1}{2} + \frac{1}{2}\left(\frac{\mu}{\sigma}\right)\sqrt{\frac{T}{n}}$$

If u, d, and p satisfy this equation, log price increments are distributed normally as $n \to \infty$. What do our choices of u and d in our application of the binomial formula imply for the volatility of the stock? Using the equation for u, we have $\ln u = \sigma(T/n)^{0.5}$, so that $\ln u$ is 0.01980. Multiplying $\ln u$ by the inverse of $(1/100)^{0.5}$, which is 10, we get $\sigma = 0.1980$, or about 20 percent. If u, d, and p are given by the equation, it can be shown that:

$$\mu_n n = \mu T \text{ and } \sigma_n^2 = \left[\sigma^2 - \mu^2(T/n)\right]T$$

Irrespective of the choice of n, our choice of u, d, and p leads to the correct continuously compounded return. Further, the variance of the continuously compounded return per period converges to the true variance as n becomes large. Our choice for u and d allows us to choose a binomial process that converges to the true distribution as n becomes large. In this sense, we can think of the binomial model as an approximation which gets better as the number of periods until maturity of the option becomes large.

the tip of the branches of the tree working toward its root. Some firms have dividend policies whereby they pay a fixed dollar dividend at a future date regardless of the stock price. In this case, we can still price options by arbitrage since we still have only two outcomes from each node. However, with such a policy, the tree is no longer recombining. To see this, suppose that in the two-period example shown in Figure 11.5, we get to date 1. Absent the dividend, the stock price at date 1 is either $600 or $450. A down move from $600 brings the stock price to $540 and an up move from $450 brings the stock price to $540 so that the tree is recombining. Suppose now that immediately after the close of trading at date 1, the firm pays a dividend of $50. In this case, if the stock price is $600 before the dividend, it becomes $550 afterwards. The down move from $550 multiplies the price by 0.9, so that it becomes $495. If the stock price is $450 before the dividend, it falls to $400 after the dividend payment and the up move from $400 brings the stock price to $400 × 1.2, or $480. Consequently, with a fixed dollar dividend the tree is no longer recombining. This is not a problem in valuing the option. From each stock price, we always face two possible outcomes that we can hedge so that we can always apply the arbitrage strategy discussed in section 11.1.

Some firms have dividend policies whereby the dollar dividend varies, but the dividend yield (dollar dividend divided by stock price) is roughly constant. In this case, the tree remains recombining. We use a constant dividend yield to price a European call and then an American call. Using our two-period example, we suppose that the stock pays a dividend equal to 8 1/3 percent of the stock price at date 1.

Figure 11.6 shows the binomial tree adjusted for the dividend payment. We can still compute the value of the call for each state at date 1 in exactly the same way as before. This is the case because the dividend payment is expressed as a percentage of the stock price. If, instead, the dividend payment were expressed as a fixed dollar amount, then the tree would not be recombining at date 2. If this

Figure 11.6   Binomial tree when the stock pays a dividend

This figure uses the same stock price dynamics as Figure 11.5, except that a dividend payment of 8 1/3 percent of the price is made at date 1. Consequently, the price at date 2 is the ex-dividend price at date 1 times 1.2 for an up move and the ex-dividend price at date 2 times 0.9 for a down move.

Stock price

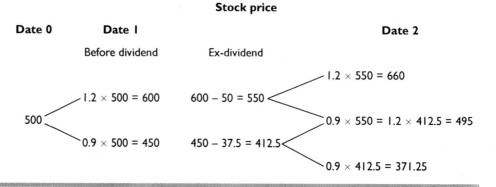

Date 0	Date 1		Date 2
	Before dividend	Ex-dividend	

1.2 × 550 = 660

1.2 × 500 = 600   600 − 50 = 550

500

0.9 × 500 = 450   450 − 37.5 = 412.5

0.9 × 550 = 1.2 × 412.5 = 495

0.9 × 412.5 = 371.25

were the case, we could still price the call option by working from the tips of the branches towards the root of the tree.

With the scenario shown in Figure 11.6, the option pays only if the stock price increases both periods to reach 660, so that the option holder gets 660 − 500 = 160 at maturity. In the other cases, the option holder gets nothing. The risk-neutral probabilities are unchanged. Consequently, we can easily compute the option price:

$$c(S, K, 2, 0) = \frac{1}{r^2} \left\{ \pi \left[\pi c_{uu} + (1 - \pi)c_{ud} \right] + (1 - \pi) \left[\pi c_{ud} + (1 - \pi)c_{dd} \right] \right\}$$

$$= \frac{1}{1.1^2} \left(\frac{4}{9} \right) 160 = 58.77 \tag{11.38}$$

Not surprisingly, the dividend payment reduces the value of the option since the option holder gets the right to buy the stock after the dividend payment.

11.3.2. Using the binomial approach to price an American call on a dividend paying stock

In the case of an American call, we have the additional difficulty of deciding whether we want to exercise early. The binomial model makes it easy to decide. Denote by $C(S, K, 2, 0)$ the value of an American call option at date 0 on stock with price S, with exercise price K, and maturity at date 2. Using the binomial approach, we can compute the value of the American option if we do not exercise at date 1 if the stock price goes up:

$$C_u = \left(\frac{1}{r} \right) \left[\pi C_{uu} \right] = \frac{1}{1.1} \left(\frac{2}{3} \right) 160 = 96.97 \tag{11.39}$$

Hence, if the option holder does not exercise, he owns an asset worth 96.97. If he exercises at that node, he gets the stock price before the dividend payment less the exercise price, namely 100. Since the option unexercised is worth less than the option exercised, the option holder exercises. The value of the European option at date 0 when a dividend of 8 1/3 percent is paid at date 1 is:

$$c(S, K, 2, 0) = \frac{1}{1.1} \left(\frac{2}{3}\right) 96.97 = 58.77 \qquad (11.40)$$

The value of the American option where one exercises at date 1 is:

$$C(S, K, 2, 0) = \frac{1}{1.1} \left(\frac{2}{3}\right) 100 = 60.61 \qquad (11.41)$$

The advantage of being able to exercise early makes the American option's value exceed the European option's value by 1.84.

The binomial approach to pricing American options is straightforward. We look at all the nodes when a dividend is paid. To do this, we have to work backward from maturity since otherwise we do not know the value of the right to exercise early in future periods. At each node where a dividend is paid, we compare the value of the option exercised at that node with its value unexercised. The value of the option is then computed assuming that along the branches of the tree the option is exercised the first time it is optimal to do so along a branch.

11.3.3. Using the binomial approach to price American puts

We price an American put that matures in two periods and has an exercise price of $600. We assume that there are no dividend payments. To price the American put option, we have to look at both nodes at date 1 to see whether it is worthwhile to exercise. First, look at the node corresponding to the stock price $uS = 600$. In this case, we get nothing if we exercise. If we do not exercise, we get:

$$P_u = \frac{1}{1.1} \left[\frac{2}{3} 0 + \frac{1}{3} 60 \right]$$

$$= 18.18 \qquad (11.42)$$

Obviously, we do not exercise in this case. If the stock price is at $dS = 450$, we get $150 by exercising. If we do not exercise, we get:

$$P_d = \frac{1}{1.1} \left[\frac{2}{3} (600 - 540) + \frac{1}{3} (600 - 405) \right]$$

$$= 95.4545 \qquad (11.43)$$

We therefore choose to exercise at date 1 if the stock price is $450. Consequently, the value of the American put is:

$$P(500, 600, 2, 0) = \frac{1}{1.1} \left[\left(\frac{2}{3}\right) 18.18 + \left(\frac{1}{3}\right) 150 \right]$$

$$= 56.4727 \qquad (11.44)$$

This approach to evaluate puts works irrespective of the number of periods we have. All we need to know is that we have to start from the last period and at each node evaluate whether the put is worth more exercised or unexercised. The value of the American put is the discounted value of each payoff times the probability of that payoff. A payoff along one branch of the tree is either the first time it becomes optimal to exercise the put or the terminal payoff.

11.4. Back to hedging everything and anything

With the binomial model, we can value a complicated payoff function and create a dynamic trading strategy that hedges that payoff function as long as (1) the payoff does not depend on a random variable other than the underlying and (2) the law of motion of the price of the underlying is such that we can construct a binomial tree.

To understand why the binomial approach can be used to price and hedge anything rather than just plain vanilla calls and puts, it is important to make sure we understand how this approach works. The fundamental result of this approach is that, since we can hedge the contingent claim perfectly by replicating the payoff at maturity, the value of a contingent claim is simply its expected payoff computed using the risk-neutral probabilities discounted at the risk-free rate. This fundamental result holds irrespective of the payoff of the contingent claim as long as we can replicate that payoff. To hedge the payoff with a position in the underlying and borrowing or lending, it has to be that the value of the payoff depends only on the value of the underlying.

To see this, let's consider our one-period model for simplicity. Remember that equation (11.8) which allows us to find the hedging portfolio, is:

Payoff of portfolio in up state = Payoff of portfolio in down state

$$c_u - huS = c_d - hdS$$

With this equation, the payoff of the portfolio has to be known if the price of the underlying is known. As long as this is the case, it does not matter what c_u and c_d are. They can be anything. That is, as long as we know for sure what the payoff of the contingent claim is for each price of the underlying, we can hedge the contingent claim and hence price it using the binomial model.

To demonstrate the range of applications of the binomial model, suppose that in two periods we receive a payoff that is simply the square of the stock price at that time. This is a special case of a power option. Power options pay $Max(S^2 - K, 0)$, where S is a stock price and K is the exercise price. Our example involves a power option with an exercise price of zero.

Figure 11.7 compares the payoff of a call with the payoff of a power option. The payoff of a power option is not a straight line when it is in the money. There is no way that we could hope to hedge that payoff using a static hedge with a forward or a futures contract. We can hedge such a payoff through a dynamic hedge using the binomial model. To see how, let $G(S, i)$ be the price of the contingent claim at date i. We know that to price the payoff, we have to start from maturity.

Figure 11.7

Payoff of a power option compared to payoff of a call option

The exercise price of the call option is $5.

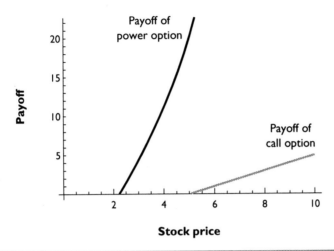

At date 2, we receive one of three possible payoffs: $(uuS)^2, (udS)^2,$ or $(ddS)^2.$ From uS at date 1, we can get either $(uuS)^2$ or $(udS)^2.$ We therefore have to price the contingent claim at date 1 if the stock price is $uS.$ In that case, we need to have $h(uS)$ so that:

$$\left(uuS\right)^2 - h\left(uS, 1\right) \times uuS = \left(udS\right)^2 - h\left(uS, 1\right) \times udS \qquad (11.45)$$

This is one equation with one unknown. We can solve it for $h(uS, 1)$:

$$h\left(uS, 1\right) = \frac{\left(uuS\right)^2 - \left(udS\right)^2}{uuS - udS} \qquad (11.46)$$

Using this equation, we know that the value of the hedged portfolio at date 1 is the present value of the hedged portfolio payoff at date 2. This gives us:

$$G\left(uS, 1\right) = \left(\frac{1}{r}\right)\left[\left(uuS\right)^2 - h\left(uS, 1\right) \times uuS\right] + h\left(uS, 1\right) \times uS \qquad (11.47)$$

where we have already solved for $h(uS, 1)$. In the same way, we get:

$$G\left(dS, 1\right) = \left(\frac{1}{r}\right)\left[\left(duS\right)^2 - h\left(dS, 1\right) \times duS\right] + h\left(dS, 1\right) \times dS \qquad (11.48)$$

To get the price at date 0, we need to construct a hedge at date 1 for a long position in the contingent claim. The hedge ratio at date 0, $h(S, 0)$, must satisfy:

$$G\left(uS, 1\right) - h\left(S, 0\right) \times uS = G\left(dS, 1\right) - h\left(S, 0\right) \times dS \qquad (11.49)$$

Solving for the hedge ratio, we get:

$$h(S, 0) = \frac{G(uS, 1) - G(dS, 1)}{uS - dS} \qquad \text{(11.50)}$$

Solving for G(S, 0), we obtain:

$$G(S, 0) = \frac{1}{r} \left[G(uS, 1) - h(S, 0) \times uS \right] + h(S, 0) \times S \qquad \text{(11.51)}$$

We know G(uS, 1) from equation (11.47) and G(dS, 1) from equation (11.48). We know h(S, 0) from equation (11.50). Consequently, we know all the variables on the right-hand side of equation (11.51), so that we can compute G(S, 0).

Let's see how this works with actual numbers. We use our two-period example from section 11.2. Figure 11.5 gives us the binomial tree and u = 1.2, d = 0.9, r = 1.1, and S = 500. Using these numbers, we can compute the payoffs at date 2. When the stock price is $720, the payoff is $518,400. The payoff is $291,600 if the stock price is $540. Finally, when the stock price is $405, the payoff is $164,025. From equation (11.46) we have:

$$
\begin{aligned}
h(uS, 1) &= \frac{(uuS)^2 - (udS)^2}{uuS - udS} \\
&= \frac{(1.2 \times 1.2 \times 500)^2 - (1.2 \times 0.9 \times 500)^2}{1.2 \times 1.2 \times 500 - 1.2 \times 0.9 \times 500} \\
&= 1{,}260 \qquad \text{(11.52)}
\end{aligned}
$$

To hedge the payoff if the stock price is at $600 at date 1, we need to short 1,260 shares. Alternatively, if the stock price is at $450, we need 945 shares. We can then price the contingent claim if the stock price is $600 at date 1:

$$
\begin{aligned}
G(uS, 1) &= \left(\frac{1}{r} \right) \left[(uuS)^2 - h(uS, 1) \times uuS \right] + h(uS, 1) \times uS \\
&= \left(\frac{1}{1.1} \right) \left[(1.2 \times 1.2 \times 500)^2 - h(1.2 \times 500, 1) \times 1.2 \times 1.2 \times 500 \right] \\
&\quad + h(1.2 \times 500, 1) \times 1.2 \times 500 \\
&= 402{,}545 \qquad \text{(11.53)}
\end{aligned}
$$

Proceeding the same way for G(dS, 1), we get $226,432. Using equation (11.50), we then find the hedge ratio at date 0, which is 1,174.09. This allows us to find the price at date 0, which is $312,582.

Suppose now that our firm receives a payoff at date 2 which is the square of the stock price used in our example. We want to hedge this payoff. If we short the contingent claim, we have a perfect hedge. We can short the contingent claim by following a dynamic strategy that produces at date 2 the negative of the payoff. To do that, we short 1,174.09 shares at date 0 and invest the proceeds in excess of $312,582 in the risk-free asset. Since we are effectively selling the contingent claim, we get to pocket its price of $312,582. Suppose that at date 1 the stock price is $600. In this case, our short portfolio is worth $-1,174.09 \times 600 + (1,174.09 \times 500 - 312,582) \times 1.1$, which is the option price at that date. At date 1, we need to have a short position of 1,260 shares. This gives us additional proceeds of $51,546 that we invest in the risk-free asset. Suppose the stock is $720 at date 2. In this case, the portfolio is worth $-$518,400. The negative value of the portfolio exactly offsets the payoff we receive, so that we are perfectly hedged.

We have shown that the binomial model allows us to create a dynamic trading strategy to hedge payoffs that are known functions of an underlying asset for which a binomial tree can be constructed. The function that yields the payoff can be any function as long as for each price of the underlying asset the payoff is known for sure. This makes the binomial approach an extremely powerful tool for hedging. In general, however, the binomial tree provides only an approximation of the price of the underlying at maturity. This means that the hedge obtained with the binomial model is as good as that approximation.

11.5. Summary

The arbitrage method and some assumptions about the distribution of the underlying asset combine to produce a highly efficient tool for pricing derivative assets. We assume that the stock's return can take one of two values every period, so that the distribution of the stock return is i.i.d. With this assumption, the stock price follows the binomial distribution. In such a setting it is possible to construct a risk-free portfolio holding a long position in the call and a short position in the stock. Since this portfolio is risk-free, its value does not depend on the probability of the stock going up or down and hence it does not depend on the expected stock price. Since we can compute the present value of the portfolio by discounting its payoff at the risk-free rate, we can compute the value of the option.

One way to interpret the option pricing formula is in terms of the expected payoff of the option using risk-neutral probabilities. The risk-neutral probabilities are the probabilities of up and down moves that ensure that the expected return on the stock is the risk-free rate. With these risk-neutral probabilities, the call price is the expected payoff of the call discounted at the risk-free rate. This reasoning allowed us to obtain the binomial option pricing formula.

With the binomial model, we know how to hedge an option and how to replicate an option. Therefore, Consumer Inc. can use the binomial model to manufacture an option on an index of stock prices of car manufacturers. It can also use the model to assess whether the price of such an option offered by an investment bank is reasonable.

An important advantage of the binomial approach is that it makes it easy to compute the value of American call and put options. To value these options, we simply construct a binomial tree. Starting from the end of the tree, we compute the value of the option if exercised and the value of the option if unexercised. Comparing the two values, we decide whether to exercise or not. This can be done on a spreadsheet.

The binomial approach can be used to hedge arbitrary payoff functions. This means that the binomial approach allows us to construct dynamic trading strategies that produce the payoffs we are trying to hedge. With this discovery, we do not need banks and derivatives dealers to hedge. We can, on our own, create a contingent claim that we can short to hedge a complicated nonlinear payoff function.

Key Concepts

arbitrage pricing, 331   binomial model, 335
binomial distribution, 335   risk-neutral probabilities, 339

Review Questions

1. What is a replicating portfolio?

2. What is the key difference between using a replicating portfolio strategy to price a forward contract and a replicating portfolio strategy to price an option?

3. What is the binomial model?

4. If the stock price follows the binomial model, how many securities are there in the replicating portfolio for an option at any point in time?

5. Assuming in all following questions that the binomial model holds, how does the replicating portfolio for a European call option differ from the replicating portfolio for a put option?

6. What happens to the replicating portfolio for a European call option if the stock price increases?

7. What is a binomial tree for the stock price?

8. What is the key to pricing options if the stock price evolution can be described with a binomial tree?

9. How do dividends affect the pricing of options in the binomial model?

10. Why can we price and hedge an arbitrary payoff that depends on the stock price and time only?

Questions and Exercises

1. The stock price next period can be either $100 or $200. The stock price today is $150. You have a put option that expires next period. The exercise price of the put option is $150. The price of a discount bond that matures next period is 0.8. What is the value of your put?

2. What is the portfolio that hedges the put option so that the hedged portfolio has no risk?

3. Is there a portfolio of the stock and the risk-free asset that you could buy today so that the hedged portfolio has no downside risk but has upside potential? What is the cost of that portfolio?

4. As you are reviewing your hedged position, somebody argues that it is not right to assume that the stock price will be either $100 or $200. She wants you to assume that it will be either $50 or $250. From our discussion of the implementation of the binomial model, how does the distribution of the stock return differ when the possible stock prices are $50 or $250 instead of $100 or $200?

5. How does the assumption that the stock price can be $50 or $250 change the price of the put from your answer in question 1?

6. Suppose that you had assumed that the stock price can be $100 or $200, but it turns out that it can be either $50 or $250. Had you used the hedge derived in question 2, what would be your hedging mistake if the stock price is $50 and if it is $250?

7. Your firm expects to receive 100 million euros in two periods. The euro interest rate is 10 percent per period and the U.S. interest rate is 5 percent per period. The current exchange rate is $0.50 per euro. The exchange rate follows a binomial tree where $u = 1.2$ and $d = 0.8$. You want to hedge with a put so that you are sure to have at least $45 million. How much does this put cost? (*Hint:* To hedge, what asset should you use? Not cash, but a foreign currency zero-coupon bond.)

8. Does your answer to question 7 change if the put is an American put? Make sure to check the node at date 1 where the exchange rate falls.

9. Your boss believes that transaction costs on buying a large put are too high. He argues that you can create the put on your own. Create the appropriate replicating portfolio and show how it evolves if the exchange rate falls each period.

10. Suppose that you have devised your hedging strategy but before you can implement it your boss comes back to you and says that your firm receives 120 million euros if the spot exchange rate is above $0.60, 100 million euros if it is at or below $0.60 but above $0.45, and 80 million euros if the spot exchange rate at date 2 is below $0.45. He wants you to devise a hedging strategy that forms a perfect hedge. Describe such a strategy.

Literature Note

That one can price derivatives using the risk-neutral probabilities was first shown by Cox and Ross (1976). The binomial approach was developed by several authors. However, Cox, Ingersoll, and Rubinstein (1979) provide the first complete treatment of that approach. Cox and Rubinstein (1985) expand on the article. Cox and Ross (1976) discuss alternate stochastic processes for the stock price. Leland (1985) extends the binomial approach to the case where there are transaction costs. Broadie and Glasserman (1998) have a collection of recent papers on hedging using trees.

Chapter 12

The Black-Scholes Model

Chapter **12** *Objectives*

At the end of this chapter, you will:

1. Know how to use the Black-Scholes formula to price options.

2. Understand the determinants of the value of an option when the Black-Scholes formula is used.

3. Have a sense of the limitations of the Black-Scholes formula.

4. Understand how the Black-Scholes approach can be used to price other contingent claims.

Mr. Highland, Principal at Private Bank, wants to sell his high net worth clients puts on their stock portfolios. These clients would like to insure their portfolios, but they cannot buy puts on their portfolios either on exchanges or with other banks. Mr. Highland is aware that this new venture is dangerous for his firm because the puts may be exercised, but he expects to be able to charge enough for the puts to make the venture worthwhile as long as he can eliminate most of the risks. He therefore wants to take advantage of the fact that markets for stocks trade continuously during the day to adjust his hedges whenever stock prices move enough to make these hedges imprecise.

The **Black-Scholes formula**, discovered by Fischer Black and Myron Scholes, provides the solution that Mr. Highland is looking for as long as the assumptions required for the formula hold. The Black-Scholes formula provides prices of options on common stock as well as other financial assets when trading in the risk-free asset and in the underlying takes place continuously throughout the day. In addition to providing Mr. Highland with put prices throughout the day, the Black-Scholes formula also tells him how to hedge his puts.

In section 12.1, we present the Black-Scholes formula. In section 12.2, we discuss the determinants of the option price in the Black-Scholes model. This turns out to be simple: When the Black-Scholes formula holds, the option price depends on the stock price, the exercise price, the time to maturity, the price of a zero-coupon bond with the same maturity as the option, and the volatility of the stock. In section 12.3, we show how to cope with various problems that arise in option pricing that require adjustments to the Black-Scholes formula or the use of different option pricing formulas. We review some of the empirical evidence on option pricing in section 12.4. Though we focus on using the Black-Scholes formula to price options on common stocks, it can be used to price options on many different underlyings. In section 12.5, we show how to use the Black-Scholes formula when the underlying is not a stock but instead a currency, a commodity, or a futures contract. Finally, an important result with the binomial model is that it can be used to price complicated exotic payoffs. The same is true with the Black-Scholes model. With the Black-Scholes model, Monte Carlo simulation can be used to price options as well as other payoffs. We show how this is done.

12.1. The Black-Scholes model

Think of an old-fashion movie reel. Each frame of the reel is a period in the binomial option pricing model. The frames are still photographs, yet when you look at the movie, you see all sort of action. This trick is achieved by moving through the frames quickly. If the time you look at a frame is the length of the period in the binomial model, the world that Black and Scholes modeled is a world where the frames go by so quickly that you see a movie rather than individual frames. With the Black-Scholes model, each period is infinitesimally short. If the stock's return distribution in the binomial model is i.i.d., the stock's continuously compounded return is distributed normally if some technical conditions presented in Technical Box 12.1, From the binomial model to the Black-Scholes formula, are satisfied. If S_t is the stock price at t, the continuously compounded return of the stock from t to T is $\ln(S_T/S_t)$. If this log price ratio is distributed normally, the stock price is distributed lognormally.

From the binomial model to the Black-Scholes formula   *Technical Box 12.1*

In our discussion of the implementation of the binomial model, we showed how we can make the continuously compounded return of the stock have mean μ and variance σ^2 as the number of periods becomes large. If n is the number of periods, we argued that if u, d, and p satisfy:

$$u = e^{\sigma\sqrt{T/n}} \qquad d = 1/u \qquad p = \frac{1}{2} + \frac{1}{2}\left(\frac{\mu}{\sigma}\right)\sqrt{\frac{T}{n}}$$

the mean and variance of the return per period converge to μ and σ^2 as n becomes large. In our discussion, we did not address the issue of the distribution followed by the stock price return as n goes to infinity. We know that for each finite value of n, the stock price distribution is the binomial distribution. Given our choice of u, d, and p, the continuously compounded return of the stock is normally distributed as n goes to infinity. Remember that a random variable whose logarithm is normally distributed follows the lognormal distribution. Consequently, as the length of the period of the binomial model becomes infinitesimally small, stock prices follow a lognormal distribution. With the binomial model, we assume that we can trade each period. Consequently, as n goes to infinity, trading takes place continuously. Although some markets are open 24 hours a day (for instance, the currency markets), continuous trading is a useful abstraction rather than a description of reality. This abstraction works well when trading is frequent.

Consider now the distribution of the stock price at date T. The stock price is S_t at t and S_T at T. If the stock's expected continuously compounded return is μ, the expected stock price at T is given by $S_t e^{\mu(T-t)}$. If we choose the continuously compounded return of the stock from t to T to be a normally distributed random variable with mean $\mu(T-t)$ and variance $\sigma^2(T-t)$, the stock price at T will be $S_t e^{\mu(T-t) + \sigma(T-t)\epsilon}$, where ϵ is a standard normal random variable. Taking the expectation of the stock price at T will give us a stock price that exceeds $S_t e^{\mu(T-t)}$. This is because the exponential function is a convex function. A mathematical result called Jensen's Inequality states that the expected value of a function of a random variable is greater than the value of the function evaluated at the expected value of the random variable, so that $S_t E[e^{\text{return}}] > S_t e^{E[\text{return}]}$. To see why this is the case, suppose that the stock return over the next period has mean of 10 percent and can take values of 0 and 20 percent with equal probability. For simplicity, the stock price at time t is $1. The expected stock price is then $0.5 \times e^0 + 0.5 \times e^{0.2}$, which is 1.1107, yielding a continuously compounded return of 10.499 percent. In other words, if we use an expected continuously compounded stock return of 10 percent, the expected stock price corresponds to a greater return. This is because an unexpected positive return of 10 percent has a greater stock price impact in absolute value than an unexpected negative return of 10 percent. Suppose we take the expected return to be 10 percent. The expected stock price is 1.10517. If the return is 20 percent, the stock price is $1.2214, while if it is 0, it is $1. The unexpected gain if the return is 20 percent, $0.11623, is greater than the unexpected loss if the return is 0 percent, $0.10517. Since both outcomes are equally probable, the expected stock price must correspond to an expected

(continued)

return greater than 10 percent. This effect is due to uncertainty in the stock return. To get an expected stock price that corresponds to an expected continuously-compounded return of 10 percent, we therefore have to reduce the expected return to account for the effect on the expected stock price of the uncertainty of the return. This requires the natural log of S_T/S_t to be distributed normally with mean $(\mu - 0.5 \times \sigma^2) \times (T - t)$. Consequently, the stock price at T is given by:

$$S_T = S_t E\left[e^{\left(\mu - 0.5\sigma^2\right)(T - t) + \sigma(T - t)\epsilon}\right]$$

where ϵ is a standard normal random variable with mean zero and variance of 1.

When we discussed the binomial formula for the call option price, we showed that the price of the call option is the expected payoff computed using the risk-neutral distribution of the stock price at maturity discounted at the risk-free rate. In a risk-neutral world, the continuously compounded expected rate of return of the stock is R, where R is the continuously compounded rate of return on the risk-free asset. This means that we can price the option by setting μ equal to R. The continuously compounded return over the interval from t to T is then normally distributed with an expected value of $R(T - t)$ $-0.5 \times \sigma^2(T - t)$ and a volatility of $\sigma(T - t)$. We can therefore compute the value of the call option by using the following expectation:

$$c(S, K, T, t) = P_t(T) \times E^*\left[\text{Max}(S_T - K, 0)\right]$$

where the expectation has an asterisk to denote the fact that it is taken with respect to the risk-neutral distribution. Computing this expectation yields the famed Black-Scholes formula.

With the binomial model, we can price a call option by computing the expected payoff of the option if investors are risk-neutral and discount that expected payoff at the risk-free rate. We can do that because we can hedge the option exactly, so that the attitude of investors towards risk cannot matter in the pricing of the option. Remember that to hedge the option exactly, the interest rate cannot change unexpectedly. No part of this argument depends on the number of periods we have before maturity of the option. Therefore, the Black-Scholes world is just a special case of the binomial model and everything we know about the binomial model still applies. When each period is infinitesimally short, trading is continuous—we can trade all the time. Yet we can hedge the option exactly over each period because the binomial model still applies. When we look at the movie that shows how the stock price evolves, we want to remember that each frame still corresponds to a period in the binomial model.

Because the binomial model still holds when periods are infinitesimally short and the stock price is lognormally distributed, we can price the option by arbitrage. We compute the call price by taking the expected value of the payoff of the call assuming that the expected return on the stock is the risk-free rate and discount that expected payoff at the risk-free rate of interest. The Black-Scholes formula is the result of this calculation:

Black-Scholes formula for the price of a European call option

Let $c(S, K, T, t)$ be the price of a European call option on a stock with price S_t at t and the volatility of the continuously compounded return of the stock over one year is a constant σ. The option has exercise price K and time to maturity $T - t$. $P_t(T)$ is the price of a zero-coupon bond that pays one dollar at date T. If financial markets are perfect, trading is continuous, and the stock price is lognormally distributed, the price of a call option that pays $Max(S_T - K, 0)$ at T is:

$$c\left(\mathbf{S, K, T}, t\right) = \mathbf{SN}(d) - \mathbf{P}_t(\mathbf{T})\, \mathbf{KN}\left(d - \sigma\sqrt{\mathbf{T} - t}\right)$$

$$d = \frac{\ln\left(\mathbf{S}/\mathbf{P}_t\mathbf{K}\right)}{\sigma\sqrt{\mathbf{T} - t}} + \frac{1}{2}\,\sigma\sqrt{\mathbf{T} - t}$$

$$\mathbf{N}(d) = \textbf{Cumulative standard normal distribution evaluated at } d \qquad (12.1)$$

To use the Black-Scholes formula, we need to know the current stock price, S_t, the exercise price, K, time to maturity $T - t$, the volatility σ, and the price of a zero-coupon bond that pays \$1 when the option matures, $P_t(T)$. This is the same information that we need to use the binomial formula when the stock price following an up move and the stock price following a down move are determined by the volatility of the stock. Suppose we want to use the Black-Scholes formula to price the option we valued with the binomial formula in the previous chapter (equation 11.33). The option matures in one calendar year and the year has 100 equal periods. We further assume that S = 100, K = 100, $u = 1.02$, $d = 0.98$, and $r = 1.001$. The value of the option with the binomial formula is \$13.18. This choice of u and d implies a σ of 0.1980 in the Black-Scholes world. (The technical details of this calculation are in Technical Box 11.1, The binomial distribution as an approximation for the lognormal distribution.) To implement the Black-Scholes formula in this case, we need to find $P_t(t + 1)$, the price of a zero-coupon bond that pays \$1 in one year. The continuously compounded interest rate corresponding to $r = 1.001$ is 9.95 percent (since $1.001 = e^{0.0995/100}$). Using the Black-Scholes formula, we have:

$$
\begin{aligned}
\mathbf{C}\left(100, 100, 1, 0\right) &= 100\mathbf{N}(d) - 0.90529 \times 100\mathbf{N}\left(d - 0.1980\right) \\
&= 100\mathbf{N}(0.601525) - 90.529\mathbf{N}\left(0.601525 - 0.1980\right) \\
&= 100\mathbf{N}(0.601525) - 90.529\mathbf{N}\left(0.403525\right) \\
&= 100 \times 0.7263 - 90.529 \times 0.6567 \\
&= 13.18
\end{aligned}
$$

$$d = \frac{\ln\left[100(0.90529 \times 100)\right]}{0.1980} + \frac{1}{2}\,0.1980 = 0.601525 \qquad (12.2)$$

The Black-Scholes formula gives us the same value as the binomial formula. Even though the binomial formula is an approximation if the true distribution of the stock price is lognormal, it performs well in a situation like this because we have a large number of periods.

Figure 12.1 shows the call price as a function of the stock price for our numerical example. The call price is a convex function of the stock price. As the stock price increases, the call price increases more for a given change in the stock price. This makes the call price a nonlinear function of the stock price.

In practical applications of the Black-Scholes formula, there cannot be any difficulty in finding S, K, and the time to maturity. There can be some argument as to how to measure the risk-free rate. Some favor euro rates over the T-bill rates because they correspond to market borrowing rates. Nevertheless, once one has settled on the risk-free rate, it is readily observable. If one uses the T-bill rates as we will in the following, then $P_t(T)$ is the price of a T-bill at t paying \$1 at T. There is a difficulty in finding the volatility. The volatility used in the Black-Scholes formula is the volatility we expect the stock to experience during the life of the option, which we assume to be constant. If log price changes are i.i.d., we can compute the variance of log price changes using past data, assuming that the future will be like the past. If we compute weekly log price changes, we get a measure of the weekly variance of log price changes. To get the annual measure of variance, we multiply the weekly variance by 52. If instead we compute daily log price changes, we multiply the variance of the daily log price changes by the 252 trading days in a year to obtain the yearly variance. Once we have the yearly variance, we can get the yearly volatility, which is just the square root of the yearly variance.

Figure 12.1 Call price as a function of the stock price

The figure shows the price of the Black-Scholes call with maturity in one year and exercise price of \$100. The stock price is \$100 and its volatility is 19.80 percent.

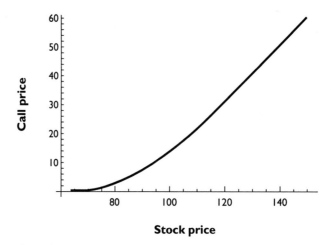

There is an alternative to this procedure. Suppose that we know the price of an option at some date but do not know the volatility of the stock return. Before, we wanted to use the Black-Scholes formula to find the call price based on our knowledge of the right-hand side variables. Now we know the call price but do not have one of the right-hand side variables, namely, the volatility. We could proceed as follows. We start by making a guess for the volatility and compute the value of the option and compare it to the market price of the option. The price based on our guess is either higher or lower than the market price. We then adjust our guess until the market price of the option coincides with the Black-Scholes price. The volatility we obtain is the market's expectation of the volatility assuming that the Black-Scholes formula is the correct pricing model for options. We can then use this volatility, called the **implied volatility**, to price options whose price we do not know. Though the Black-Scholes model assumes constant volatility, this is stretching things. If volatility changes, we want the best possible forecast of volatility over the life of the option. There is empirical evidence showing that the implied volatility is a better forecast of the volatility over the life of the option than a volatility estimated from historical data.

Generally, there are many option prices available from which we can obtain an implied volatility. Because of noise in the data and because the Black-Scholes model is not perfect, different options on the same stock will have different implied volatilities. Three approaches are generally used to combine the different implied volatilities into one that is used for the purpose of pricing options. The simplest approach is to use an equally weighted average of the various implied volatilities. In this case, we might want to eliminate the deep-out-of-the-money options and the deep-in-the-money options. These options are not very sensitive to volatility and are often traded in thin markets. A second approach is to find the implied volatility that minimizes the absolute deviations of traded options from the Black-Scholes formula prices. A final approach is to use the implied volatility of options whose specifications are closest to those of the option one is trying to price.

The first two approaches yield a single implied volatility that can then be used to forecast future volatility. They make a lot of sense for somebody who believes that the Black-Scholes formula has no biases and that the fact that different options have different implied volatilities is due to noise in the data. The last approach is the right one for those who believe that the Black-Scholes formula has biases. We discuss possible biases later in this section.

With the Black-Scholes model, each period of the binomial model is infinitesimally short. The model holds only if we can trade every period. This is because the option is priced by arbitrage like it is in the binomial model. We construct a dynamic trading strategy where we trade every period to replicate the option perfectly. When Black and Scholes first derived their formula, they did not proceed from the binomial model. Rather, they started directly from a world where investors can trade continuously and showed how investors can hedge options in such a world. Technical Box 12.2, Black-Scholes: The beginning, summarizes their argument.

We already know the number of shares we have to sell short to hedge one call in the binomial model. The hedge ratio in the Black-Scholes model is the hedge

Technical Box 12.2 Black-Scholes: The beginning

When Black and Scholes discovered their formula, there was no binomial model. Their approach proceeded as follows. Suppose that we try to hedge a call option. Let $c(S, K, T, t)$ be the price of the call option, which depends on the stock price S, the exercise price K, and time to maturity $T - t$. We make the assumption that markets are perfect, trading is continuous, the distribution of the return of the stock is i.i.d., and the interest rate is constant. Over an interval of time of length Δt, the stock price changes by ΔS. We can approximate the change in the call price using a second-order expansion around its current value with remainder:

$$\Delta c(S, K, T, t) = c_s(S, K, T, t)\Delta S + c_t(S, K, T, t)\Delta t$$

$$+ 0.5c_{ss}(S, K, T, t)\Delta S^2 + \text{Remainder}$$

where a subscripted variable indicates that we are taking the partial derivative of the option price with respect to the subscripted variable. In this equation, we take S, K, and T to be given in the option formula. The random change in the option price comes from the change in the stock price ΔS and the random change in the remainder. When they discovered their formula, Black was a financial consultant in Boston who had a Ph.D. in applied mathematics but was interested in financial economics and Scholes was an assistant professor at the Sloan School of Management at MIT. They had the advantage of interacting with another assistant professor at the Sloan School of Management, Merton, who had introduced into finance mathematical techniques that made it possible to deal with stochastic processes in continuous time. These techniques were crucial in enabling Black and Scholes to price options. Using these techniques, it can be shown that over an infinitesimal amount of time, if the stock price follows a geometric Brownian motion, the remainder can be ignored because it vanishes. A geometric Brownian motion is a stochastic process where a random variable has a normally distributed return in the limit of continuous time. In this case, the change in the stock price return in the limit of continuous time is given by:

$$dS = \mu S dt + \sigma S dz$$

where dz is the increment of a normally distributed random variable with mean zero and volatility of one and dt is the continuous time limit of Δt. With this notation, the stock price has an expected return of μ and a volatility of σ in the limit of continuous time. Consider now a portfolio long one call hedged with h shares. The change in value of this portfolio over Δt is given by:

$$c_s(S, K, T, t)\Delta S + c_t(S, K, T, t)\Delta t + 0.5c_{ss}(S, K, T, t)(\Delta S)^2 - h\Delta S$$

If we choose h to be equal to $c_s(S, K, T, t)$, we can eliminate the random change of the stock price from the return of the hedged portfolio, but we still have the square of the random change. It turns out that in the limit of continuous time, the square of the random change is not a random variable, but is equal to the variance times the squared stock price times dt. As a result, with the appropriate choice of n, the change in value of the portfolio is not random in the limit of continuous time. This means that the portfolio must earn the risk-free rate R since it has no risk. Otherwise, there would be arbitrage profits. Therefore, the change in the portfolio must be equal to the risk-free rate times the value of the portfolio. The value of the portfolio is $c(S, K, T, t) - hS$. Consequently, in the limit of continuous time we have:

$$c_t(S, K, T, t)dt + 0.5c_{ss}(S, K, T, t)\sigma^2 S^2 dt$$

$$= \left(c(S, K, T, t) - c_s(S, K, T, t)S \right)R dt$$

We can divide by dt to get our final expression:

$$c_t(S, K, T, t) + 0.5c_{ss}(S, K, T, t)\sigma^2 S^2 + c_s(S, K, T, t)SR$$

$$= c(S, K, T, t)R$$

This expression is a partial differential equation. It can be solved for $c(S, K, T, t)$. Black and Scholes found the solution for this partial differential equation. It is their famed formula for the pricing of options.

ratio that obtains when the length of a period becomes infinitesimally small. It is:

The hedge ratio for the Black-Scholes formula

$$h_t = N(d) \text{ where } d = \frac{\ln\left(S/P_t(T)K\right)}{\sigma\sqrt{T-t}} + \frac{1}{2}\sigma\sqrt{T-t} \qquad (12.3)$$

In our numerical example, the hedge ratio is 0.7263, so we must short 0.7263 shares to hedge the call option. Figure 12.2 shows how the hedge ratio changes with the stock price. As the stock price becomes large relative to the exercise price, d in equation (12.3) becomes large so that $N(d)$ becomes close to 1. The opposite happens when the stock price falls. In that case, d becomes small, so that $N(d)$ becomes close to 0. This means that the hedge ratio becomes close to 1 when one is almost sure that the option will be exercised at maturity and close to 0 when one is almost sure that it will not be exercised. Whenever the stock price changes, the hedge ratio changes also. Since the stock price changes continuously, so does the hedge ratio.

12.2. The determinants of the call option price

With the Black-Scholes formula, to compute the call price we need the stock price S_t, the zero-coupon price $P_t(T)$, the exercise price K, the time to maturity $T - t$, and the standard deviation of the continuously compounded stock return, σ. In this section, we show how the Black-Scholes call option price depends on these five variables. With the Black-Scholes model, the zero-coupon bond price

Figure 12.2   Hedge ratio of Black-Scholes call as the price of the stock changes

The call price has maturity of one year and exercise price of $100. The stock's volatility is 19.80 percent.

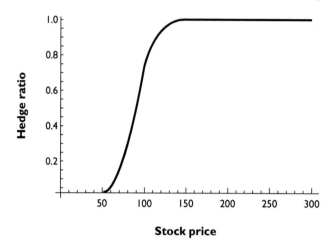

and the stock's volatility cannot change unexpectedly. In practice, they do. Suppose that we have an option on a stock that we value using the Black-Scholes call price. We want to know how unexpected changes in the stock price, the zero-coupon bond price, and volatility affect the Black-Scholes value of the option. In the language of risk management, we want to know the exposure or sensitivity of the Black-Scholes call price to changes in these variables. Knowing these exposures, we can hedge the Black-Scholes price of the option against unexpected changes in the stock price, the zero-coupon bond price, and the volatility.

We can use the Black-Scholes formula to compute these exposures. Because the call price is a nonlinear function of these variables, the exposures we measure are delta exposures. They are evaluated for a small (infinitesimal) change in the variable (see Chapter 8). We call these exposures the **Greeks** of the derivative because all of these exposures but one are associated with a letter from the Greek alphabet that is the same across derivatives.

Let's look at the Greeks of the Black-Scholes formula:

1. Delta (δ): The exposure of the option price with respect to the stock price. The call price is a nonlinear function of the stock price. A change in the stock price therefore has a different impact on the call price depending on the level of the stock price. We know that an approach to hedge when the exposure changes with the risk factor against which we are hedging is to use delta hedging. With delta hedging, we go short the delta exposure, which is the position's exposure per unit change (here $1) in the risk factor evaluated for a small change in the risk factor. Remember that in hedging, we try to choose the hedge ratio so that the change in the option price resulting from a change in the stock price ΔS is matched by the change in the value of h shares. We have a perfect hedge if:

$$c(S + \Delta S, K, T, t) - c(S, K, T, t) - h\Delta S = 0 \qquad (12.4)$$

We can approximate the change in the option value as the stock price changes using the change in the call price for a very small change in the stock price. This change in the call price measured for a dollar change in the stock price is the call's stock price delta exposure, $c_s(S, K, T, t)$. Using this delta exposure, the change in the call price is:

$$c(S + \Delta S, K, T, t) - c(S, K, T, t)$$

$$= c_s(S, K, T, t)\Delta S + \text{Approximation error} \qquad (12.5)$$

Hence, going short the stock delta exposure of the option, $h = c_s(S, K, T, t)$, the change in value of the hedge portfolio is:

$$c(S + \Delta S, K, T, t) - c(S, K, T, t) - h S$$

$$= c_s(S, K, T, t)\Delta S + \text{Approximation error} - h\Delta S$$

$$= \text{Approximation error} \qquad (12.6)$$

We have a perfect hedge as long as the approximation error can be ignored.

The Black-Scholes model gives us a formula for the stock price delta exposure of the call. It is equation (12.3). The call option's delta exposure is $N(d)$, the cumulative standard normal distribution evaluated at d, where:

$$d = \frac{\ln\left(S/P_t(T)K\right)}{\sigma\sqrt{T - t}} + \frac{1}{2}\sigma\sqrt{T - t}$$

$N(d)$ is called the option's delta.

Figure 12.3 shows graphically how a delta hedge performs as a function of the change in the stock price. With delta hedging, our hedge ratio is the slope of the tangent at the point of approximation. The slope of the tangent is $c_s(S, K, T, t)$ if we hedge the call value that holds for a stock price S. The tangent line gives us the value of a portfolio of $c_s(S, K, T, t)$ shares of stock. Since we are short this portfolio to hedge, the gap between the call price function and the tangent line evaluated at a given stock price is the value of the hedged portfolio for that stock price. Since this tangent line is always below the call price function since that function is convex, our hedge overstates the fall in value of the option when the stock price falls and understates the increase in the value of the option when the stock price increases. For small changes in the stock price, the hedge using delta exposure can work well. For larger changes, the hedging mistake becomes large.

Let's look at an example. The option we price in equation (12.2) has a price of $13.18 and a hedge ratio of 0.7263. If the stock price increases from $100 to $101, the option price goes from $13.18 to $13.91, an increase of 73 cents. Using the δ reported above of 0.7263, the value of our stock position falls by about 73 cents. Our hedge is just about perfect. Note that when the stock price is $101, delta is almost the same as when the stock price is $100. Consider, however, a fall in the stock price of $10. In this case, the option price falls to $6.86, a fall of $6.32, but our short stock position increases in value by $7.263. The

Figure 12.3   Performance of the delta hedge

In this figure, the option delta is the slope of the dotted line that is tangent to the option price function for the stock price S*. Using delta to hedge the option works well if there is a small stock price change, but if the stock price falls to S**, the value of the hedge falls more than the option because the slope of the option pricing function falls as the stock price falls. When the stock price is at S**, the value of the delta shares falls to H while the option price falls only to C(S**). Since the hedged option writer is short delta shares, he would therefore make a gain in his hedged position because the delta hedge is not a perfect hedge for large stock price changes.

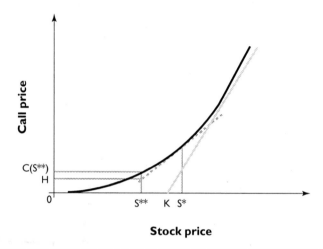

change in value of the call minus the change in value of the short stock position is –$6.32 – (–$7.263), or $0.943. This is a hedging mistake. We might think that this mistake is not a problem since it increases the value of the hedged portfolio. However, the point of hedging is to diminish risk—a hedge with random outcomes leaves us exposed to risk. The hedge ratio when the stock price is $90 is 0.53, which is quite different from the hedge ratio when the stock price is $100. For large changes, our hedge is not as good.

With continuous trading, the lognormal distribution assumed in the Black-Scholes model implies that changes over small periods of time are small in the following sense: If we were to draw the stock price path assuming continuous trading, we would never lift the pen. Figure 12.4 shows a stock price path obtained when the lognormal distribution holds and compares it to a distribution that allows for large changes, or jumps, in the stock price. The property that with the lognormal distribution delta hedging is exact over infinitesimal periods of time is the foundation of the original derivation of the Black-Scholes formula discussed in Technical Box 12.2, Consequently, when the assumptions of the Black-Scholes model are not valid, large hedging errors can occur because the stock price can move away substantially from its value before the hedge can be changed.

2. Vega (Λ): Exposure of the call option with respect to the volatility. What happens if volatility increases? It becomes more likely that the stock price will assume values far from the mean. This means that both high and low values become more likely. If a stock price is below the exercise price for a call option at maturity, we don't care; the fact that the stock price becomes even lower does not affect the value of the option at that time. If the stock price is above the exercise

Path A describes the evolution of a stock price that is lognormally distributed. Path B shows the possible evolution of a stock price whose distribution allows for jumps.

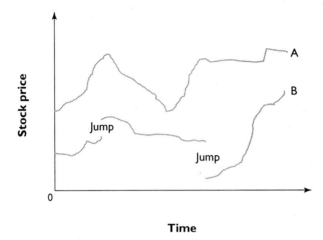

price at maturity and becomes higher, though, the option value at maturity increases. If the volatility of the stock increases, the holder benefits from the greater likelihood of really high values and is not hurt by the greater probability of really low values. The exposure of the Black-Scholes price of a call with respect to volatility is:

$$\Lambda = S\sqrt{T-t}\, N'(d) > 0$$

$$d = \frac{\ln\big(S/P_t(T)K\big)}{\sigma\sqrt{T-t}} + \frac{1}{2}\sigma\sqrt{T-t} \tag{12.7}$$

where $N'(d)$ is the standard normal density function evaluated at d.

Figure 12.5 plots vega as a function of the stock price and shows that it first increases and then falls as the stock price increases. If the option is way out of the money, it is unlikely that it will be exercised, so changes in volatility are not important. If the option is way in the money, it almost certainly will be exercised. In this case, the option holder gets the stock almost for sure, but the value of the stock does not depend on its volatility. Consequently, volatility matters little for either very low or very high stock prices.

Let's compute vega for the call option example:

$$\Lambda = S\sqrt{T-t}\, N'(d) = 100 \times \sqrt{1} \times N'(0.601525) = 33.29 \tag{12.8}$$

To see the impact of a change in volatility on our numerical example, let's double the volatility from 0.198 to 0.4. The change in the call price can be approximated using vega times the change in volatility. Here, the change in volatility is

Figure 12.5

Vega as a function of the stock price for a call option with exercise price of $100, one year to maturity, and a stock with return volatility of 20 percent

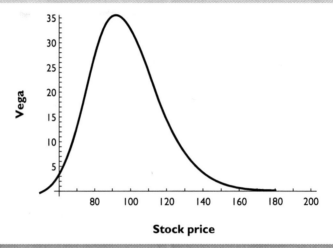

assumed to be 0.4 – 0.198, so that the change in the call price is vega × 0.202, or 33.29 × 0.202 = 6.72. Computing the Black-Scholes formula for a volatility of 0.4, we get an option value of $20.30. The actual increase in the option price is $7.12, which is forty cents more than our estimate using vega.

3. Rho (ρ): The exposure of the option price with respect to the interest rate. The easiest way to understand the impact of an increase in the interest rate on the option price is to divide the Black-Scholes formula into two parts as we did in the binomial approach. The first part is positive. It is the present value of getting the stock price at maturity if the option is in the money. Remember that the expected return of the stock is the risk-free rate. Hence, if the risk-free rate rises, the expected stock price at maturity rises, but the present value of the stock price is unaffected because the discount rate rises also. The second part is negative. It is the present value of the payment of the exercise price if the option is exercised. For this second part, the increase in the interest rate decreases the present value of the exercise price. Since we have to pay the exercise price, the decrease in the present value of what we have to pay increases the value of the option. In addition, the increase in the interest rate increases the probability of exercise of the option, but the impact of this effect on the positive part of the option pricing formula is cancelled out by its impact on the negative part of the formula. Consequently, the value of the option increases as the interest rate rises because the present value of the exercise price falls as the interest rate increases.

In summary, therefore, an increase in the interest rate increases the value of the option. The exposure with respect to the interest rate is:

$$\rho = (T - t)KP_t(T)N\left(d - \sigma\sqrt{T - t}\right) > 0$$

$$d = \frac{\ln\left(S/P_t(T)\right)}{\sigma\sqrt{T - t}} + \frac{1}{2}\sigma\sqrt{T - t} \qquad (12.9)$$

The computation of ρ in the numerical example is as follows:

$$\rho = (T - t)KP_t(T)N\left(d - \sigma\sqrt{T - t}\right)$$

$$= 1 \times 100 \times 0.90529 \times N(0.403525) = 59.4521 \qquad (12.10)$$

Let's look at the impact of an increase in the interest rate on our numerical example. If we double the interest rate from 9.95 percent to 20 percent, our estimate of the change in option value using rho is rho $\times$ decimal interest rate change, or $59.4521 \times 0.1005 = 5.9749$. The actual change in the option price obtained by recomputing the formula is \$6.40.

4. Theta (θ): The exposure of the option price with respect to time to maturity ($T - t$). Time to maturity cannot change unexpectedly. Since it changes over time, though, it is useful to know how this change affects the value of the option. If the time to maturity falls by half in the numerical example, so that the call option now matures in half a year instead of one year, the value of the call becomes \$8.21 instead of \$13.18. With the Black-Scholes formula, a reduction in time to maturity always reduces the value of the option. Since theta measures the impact of an increase in time to maturity, we have:

$$\theta = \frac{SN'(d)\sigma}{2\sqrt{T - t}} - P_t(T)K \times h\left(P_t(T)\right)N\left(d - \sigma\sqrt{T - t}\right)/(T - t) > 0 \qquad (12.11)$$

where $N'(d)$ is the density of the normal distribution evaluated at d.

Why does the call option fall in value as time to maturity decreases? Again, it becomes less likely that the option will be in the money at maturity and have a significant payoff. With the binomial tree, when there is less time to maturity, the tree expands less. As a result, the highest possible stock price is lower and the lowest possible stock price is higher. The two effects do not offset because, if the option does not pay off, we do not care how low the stock price is. Hence, we are hurt by decreases in the highest price the stock can reach but do not benefit from increases in the lowest price.

Let's look at how we compute theta in the numerical option example:

$$\theta = \frac{SN'(d)\sigma}{2\sqrt{T - t}} - P_t(T)K \times h\left(P_t(T)\right)N\left(d - \sigma\sqrt{T - t}\right)/(T - t) > 0$$

$$= \frac{100 \times N'(0.601525) \times 0.1980}{2\sqrt{1}} + 90.529 \times 0.0995$$

$$\times N\left(0.601525 - 0.1980 \times \sqrt{1}\right)$$

$$= 9.211 \qquad (12.12)$$

If we halve the time to maturity, our estimate of the change in the price of the call option is $\theta \times (-0.5)$, or a drop in value of \$4.6055. We could also obtain the change in option value by recomputing the Black-Scholes formula for time to maturity equal to 2. This is the previous calculation that we did to get a change in value from \$13.18 to \$8.21 corresponding to a drop in value of \$4.97. The true change in value is more than our estimate using theta. As the change in time to maturity becomes small, the estimate using θ becomes more precise.

5. Impact of a change in the exercise price on the call option price. There is no greek letter for this impact. All other variables we have looked at can actually change in the normal course of the life of an option—the stock price can increase, time to maturity can fall, the interest rate can change, and so on. However, the exercise price is given. Nevertheless, for completion, we investigate how a change in the strike price affects the value of the option. The formula is:

Change in call price per dollar change in exercise price $=$

$$-P_t(T)N\left(d - \sigma\sqrt{T - t}\right) < 0$$

$$d = \frac{\ln\left(S/P_t(T)K\right)}{\sigma\sqrt{T - t}} + \frac{1}{2}\sigma\sqrt{T - t} \qquad (12.13)$$

Not surprisingly, the call price falls as the exercise price increases. We can compute the impact of a dollar change in the exercise price for the call we are using for our numerical examples. Remember that it is a call with an exercise price of \$100 on a stock worth \$100. Suppose we increase the exercise price by \$1. Using the formula, we have:

Change in call price per dollar change in exercise price $=$

$$-P_t(T)N\left(d - \sigma\sqrt{T - t}\right)$$

$$= -0.90529 \times N\left(0.403525\right)$$

$$= -0.594504 \qquad (12.14)$$

We therefore expect that the call price falls by \$0.594504 if the exercise price increases by \$1. Consequently, the call price falls from \$13.18 to \$12.59. Note that the call price does not fall by the entire amount of the exercise price for two reasons. First, the expected payoff of the call is discounted. Second, we may never pay the exercise price. Computing the call price directly for the lower exercise price, we get the same price.

In summary, the call option price increases as the stock price, the time to maturity, the volatility, and the interest rate increase, and falls as the exercise price increases.

12.3. Extensions and limitations of the Black-Scholes formula

In this section, we look at extensions and limitations of the Black-Scholes formula still using common stock as the underlying. In section 12.5., we consider extensions where the underlying is no longer a stock.

12.3.1. Pricing puts

Let $p(S, K, T, t)$ be the price at t of a European put on a stock with price S, exercise price K, and maturity at T. We can use put-call parity to obtain a formula for the pricing of put options. To see this, substitute the Black-Scholes formula for the call price in the put-call parity formula (equation 10.8) to get:

$$p(S, K, T, t) = c(S, K, T, t) + P_t(T)K - S$$

$$= SN(d) - P_t(T)KN\left(d - \sigma\sqrt{T - t}\right) + P_t(T)K - S$$

$$= S[N(d) - 1] + P_t(T)K\left[1 - N\left(d - \sigma\sqrt{T - t}\right)\right]$$

$$\text{where } d = \frac{\ln\left(S/P_t(T)K\right)}{\sigma\sqrt{T - t}} + \frac{1}{2}\sigma\sqrt{T - t} \qquad (12.15)$$

Remember that with the standard normal distribution, $1 - N(d)$ is equal to $N(-d)$. Consequently, we have the formula for the price of a put option:

Formula for the price of a European put option

$$p(S, K, T, t) = -S\,N(-d) + P_t(T)KN\left(-d + \sigma\sqrt{T - t}\right)$$

$$\text{where } d = \frac{\ln\left(S/P_t(T)K\right)}{\sigma\sqrt{T - t}} + \frac{1}{2}\sigma\sqrt{T - t} \qquad (12.16)$$

Suppose we have a put maturing in one year with an exercise price of $100 on the stock used in our numerical example. The stock is priced at $100 with a volatility of 19.80 percent. The price of a zero-coupon bond paying $1 in one year is $0.90529. Using the formula, we have:

$$p(100, 100, 1, 0) = -100N(-d) + P_t(T)100N\left(-d + \sigma\sqrt{T - t}\right)$$

$$= -100N(-0.601525) + 90.529N(-0.403525)$$

$$= 3.70238 \qquad (12.17)$$

Figure 12.6 shows the price of the put as a function of the stock price. The put price falls in value as the stock price increases, but the put price drops less for a given fall in the stock price as the stock price increases. The put is a convex function of the stock price. The put and the call are linked by the put-call parity formula given in the first line of equation (12.15). This formula implies that:

$$\textbf{Put delta = Call delta } -1 \qquad (12.18)$$

It immediately follows that the exposure of the put to the stock price is negative or zero since the call's delta never exceeds one. Figure 12.7 plots the put's delta. The put becomes insensitive to the stock price as the stock price becomes large relative to the exercise price. This is not surprising since for a large stock price relative to the exercise price, it is unlikely that the put will be exercised and its value is small. Since the delta of the call in our numerical example is 0.7263, the delta of the put must be -0.2737.

In the put-call parity relation, only the put and the call depend on volatility—neither the stock price nor the exercise price discounted at the risk-free rate do.

Figure 12.6   Price of put as a function of the stock price

The put has a maturity of one year and the exercise price is $100. The stock volatility is 19.80 percent.

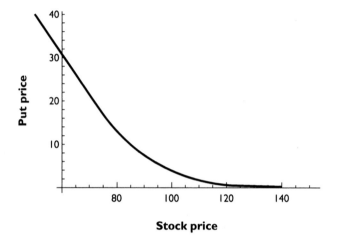

Consequently, an increase in volatility has to increase the value of the put by exactly the same value as the value of the call with similar terms:

$$\text{Vega of the put} = \text{Vega of the call} \qquad (12.19)$$

An increase in the interest rate affects the right-hand side of the put-call parity relation by increasing the price of the call and decreasing the present value of the exercise price. The net effect is positive:

$$\text{Put rho} = \text{Call rho} - (T - t)K \times P_t(T) > 0 \qquad (12.20)$$

Figure 12.7   Hedge ratio of put

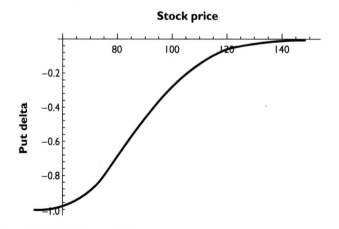

Let's consider the theta of the put. Remember that it may be optimal to exercise an American put early. Early exercise is worthwhile when having a longer time to maturity destroys value in the put. As a result, if we would want to exercise a put early but cannot, we would be better off if the put had a shorter time to maturity and therefore the value of the put must fall as time to maturity is increased. This means that the put can increase or decrease in value as time to maturity increases:

$$\text{Put theta = Call theta} -r \times K \times P_t(T) \tag{12.21}$$

where r is the continuously compounded rate of interest.

Figure 12.8 shows how the value of the put depends on time to maturity and the stock price. The key point of Figure 12.8 is that the put price can fall as the time to maturity increases. This happens in the figure when the stock price is close to zero.

Finally, the impact of an increase in the put's exercise price follows directly from put-call parity:

Impact of increase in exercise price on put

= Impact of increase in exercise price on call + $P_t(T)$

$$= -P_t(T)N\left(d - \sigma\sqrt{T - t}\right) + P_t(T) - 1 \tag{12.22}$$

This confirms that an increase in the exercise price increases the value of a put.

12.3.2. Taking dividends into account

So far, we have assumed that the stock pays no dividends until the option matures, but often we have to price options on common stock that pays dividends. Dividends are incorporated in a straightforward way in the binomial approach. The option gives the holder a claim on the stock price at maturity. The holder

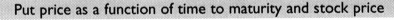

Put price as a function of time to maturity and stock price   *Figure 12.8*

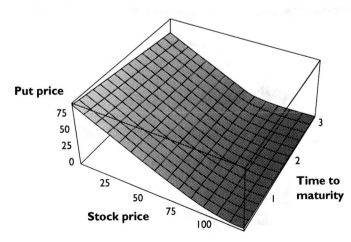

does not receive the dividend. Consequently, dividend payments make options less valuable.

The present value of the dividend payment is subtracted from the present value of the underlying asset when the holder of the option has no right to the dividend payment. If the stock price net of the dividend is distributed lognormally, we can apply the Black-Scholes formula to the stock price net of the dividend. We can apply this both to continuous dividends and dividends paid at discrete times.

12.3.2.A. Continuous dividend payments
With continuous dividends, the return to the stock comes in the form of capital appreciation and dividend payments. We know that the total expected rate of return has to be the risk-free interest rate in a risk-neutral world. Let z be the dividend rate per unit of time and assume that z is certain. In this case, the expected rate of share appreciation is the interest rate minus the dividend rate in a risk-neutral world. The holder of a share expects to get the interest rate minus the dividend rate through share appreciation and z from dividends. The stock price minus the present value of the dividends to be paid until the option matures is $Se^{-z(T-t)}$.

This is the relevant stock price to use in the option pricing formula, and we have to adjust the formula accordingly. A constant dividend rate does not affect the volatility. Remember that we compute the volatility of the log price changes. If we take the log of the stock price adjusted for the dividend payments, we get $\ln(Se^{-z(T-t)}) = \ln(S) - z(T - t)$. The dividend term does not affect the variance because it is nonstochastic. The resulting formula is called Merton's formula:

**Merton's formula for the price of a call option
on a stock that pays a continuous dividend**

$$c(S, K, T, t) = Se^{-z(T-t)}N(d) - P_t(T)KN\left(d - \sigma\sqrt{T-t}\right)$$

$$d = \frac{\ln\left(Se^{-z(T-t)}/P_t(T)K\right)}{\sigma\sqrt{T-t}} + \frac{1}{2}\sigma\sqrt{T-t} \qquad (12.23)$$

Let's look at an example. We want to price a call that pays a dividend at the rate of 2 percent per year. The stock price is \$100, the exercise price is \$100, volatility is 19.80 percent, and the price of a zero-coupon bond paying \$1 in one year is \$0.90529. The call price is:

$$c(100, 100, 1, 0) = Se^{-z(T-t)}N(d) - P_t(T)KN\left(d - \sigma\sqrt{T-t}\right)$$

$$= 100e^{-0.02}N(0.500515) - 90.529N(0.302515)$$

$$= 100 \times 0.980199 \times 0.691644 - 90.529 \times 0.61887$$

$$= 11.7692$$

$$d = \frac{\ln\left[100e^{-0.02}/(0.90529 \times 100)\right]}{0.1980} + 0.5 \times 0.1980 = 0.500515 \qquad (12.24)$$

Note that the option price falls by less than the dividend. This is because, although we do not get the dividend if we exercise at maturity, the dividend does not affect the option payoff if the option expires out of the money.

12.3.2.B. Discrete dividend payments   Consider an option maturing at date T on a stock that pays a certain dividend D at date t' before the maturity of the option. In this case, the relevant stock price is the current stock price minus the present value of the dividend, $P_t(t')D$. If we can assume that the distribution of the stock price minus the present value of the dividend is lognormal, then we can use $S - P_t(t')D$ in the Black-Scholes formula:

**Formula for the pricing of a call option
on a stock that pays a discrete dividend**

$$c(S, K, T, t) = \left[S - P_t(t')D\right]N(d) - P_t(T)KN\left(d - \sigma\sqrt{T - t}\right)$$

$$d = \frac{\ln\left(\left[S - P_t(t')D\right]/P_t(T)K\right)}{\sigma\sqrt{T - t}} + \frac{1}{2}\,\sigma\sqrt{T - t} \qquad (12.25)$$

This formula implies that the price of the stock is not relevant—the relevant price is the stock price minus the present value of the dividends. Hence, call options with same time to maturity and exercise price on stocks with same volatility and same price can have different values because these stocks pay different dividends. Let's assume the stock has a price of $100 and pays a dividend of $2 at the end of the year. The call matures an instant after the dividend payment. A zero-coupon bond that pays $1 at the end of the year is worth $0.90529. The exercise price of the call is $100. The volatility of the stock is 19.80 percent. In this case, the present value of the dividend is 0.90529×2, or $1.81058. Applying the option pricing formula, we then have:

$$(100 - 1.81058)N(0.509244) - 90.529N(0.311244)$$

$$= 98.18942 \times 0.694709 - 90.529 \times 0.622192$$

$$= 11.8867$$

$$d = \frac{\ln\left((100 - 1.81058)/(0.90529 \times 100)\right)}{0.1980} + 0.5 \times 0.1980 = 0.509244$$

$$(12.26)$$

The option price is slightly higher than when the stock pays a continuous dividend. This is not surprising: a 2 percent dividend paid continuously over the next year results in a lower stock price net of the present value of future dividends than a 2 percent dividend paid in one year. With Merton's formula, the stock price net of the present value of dividends is 98.0199, whereas here it is 98.18942.

12.3.3. What if volatility changes over time?

If the volatility changes over time, the option value at time t will not depend on the volatility at time t but rather on the volatility of the option over its life. Remember that the volatility affects the option value because it determines the expected payoff of the option. This expected payoff depends on the total volatility between now and the maturity of the option. Let's denote this total volatility by σ_T. Consequently, if we know exactly how the volatility will change over time, all we have to do is use as the volatility the total volatility over the period $T - t$, σ_T, rather than the current volatility multiplied by the square root of the time to maturity, $\sigma\sqrt{(T - t)}$, which is the total volatility if σ is constant.

With a volatility that changes deterministically each period, we can price the option in the binomial model because for each period the volatility is known. Hence, we still have a perfect hedge each period. Nothing changes as the length of a period becomes infinitesimally short. This means that we can still compute the value of the option by taking the expected payoff using the risk-neutral distribution.

Things get more complicated if volatility changes, but does so randomly. We can think of two different random volatility cases. In the first case, the volatility depends only on the stock price. As a result, it fluctuates randomly over time because the stock price changes randomly over time. In the second case, the volatility depends on other variables. We look at these cases in turn.

12.3.3.A. The volatility is a function of the stock price

There is empirical evidence showing that there is a negative relation between stock prices and volatility for small firms. Leverage could be an explanation for this evidence since equity becomes riskier as leverage increases. If firm value drops, leverage rises and stock return volatility rises. The Black-Scholes model has been modified to allow for a negative relation between volatility and the stock price. This is done by making volatility a function of the stock price. With this modification, the volatility is given when we know the stock price. This means that each period we know the volatility and can hedge the option. We can therefore price the option. When the length of a period of time becomes infinitesimally small, the option formula is called the "constant elasticity of variance option pricing formula."

There is one problem in assuming that the volatility depends on the stock price. With the binomial model, this means that the distribution of the return on the stock for the period ahead depends on the stock price and hence depends on past returns. As a result, the binomial tree is no longer recombining. This makes implementation of the binomial model more challenging.

12.3.3.B. The volatility changes randomly

When volatility is a function of the stock price, it is perfectly correlated with the stock price. When volatility changes randomly but is not perfectly correlated with the stock price, the binomial model no longer works. There are many reasons why volatility could change randomly. Suppose a firm has just announced its earnings. One would expect the stock's volatility to drop regardless of whether the announcement was good or bad news because there is less uncertainty about future cash flows. If volatility changes are a significant possibility, the Black-Scholes delta hedge no longer hedges the option—it leaves the option unprotected against changes in volatility. If the option cannot be hedged against all risks over each period, we cannot price it by arbitrage.

Suppose we want to hedge an option against both volatility and stock price risk. To do so, we need to find some asset that is correlated with volatility. Since option values depend on volatility, the asset that we can use to hedge volatility is another option. Suppose that we have two options with identical maturities, but exercise prices K and K'. We are trying to eliminate the volatility and stock price risks associated with holding the option with exercise price K. We write the price of the call as $c(S, K, T, t, \sigma)$ to emphasize its dependence on volatility. We can hedge the option against volatility and stock price changes by forming a hedged portfolio that has a stock price exposure of zero and a volatility exposure of zero. Since the stock price does not depend on the stock's volatility, we use an option to hedge against volatility changes. To form the hedged portfolio, we have to short the stock to get rid of stock-price exposure and short the option with exercise price K' to get rid of volatility exposure.

To figure out the positions of the hedged portfolio, we compute the exposures of the option with respect to the stock price as well as with respect to the volatility. Denote the call's exposure with respect to the stock price, the option's delta, by $c_S(S, K, T, t, \sigma)$, and the call's exposure to volatility, the option's vega, by $c_\sigma(S, K, T, t, \sigma)$. Even though the Black-Scholes formula does not apply when both the stock price and volatility change randomly, it is common to estimate an option's exposure to the stock price and the volatility by using the delta and vega from the Black-Scholes formula. However, the hedges we solve for would hold if we used a different option pricing formula. To hedge the call we hold, we want to choose the number of shares held short in the stock, h, and the number of options with exercise price K' held short, h_c, so that the hedged portfolio has no exposure to the stock price and no exposure to volatility. The portfolio holds one call with exercise price K, h shares, and h_c calls with exercise price K'. We therefore require the exposure of the portfolio to be zero:

$$c_S(S, K, T, t, \sigma) - h - h_c c_S(S, K', T, t, \sigma) = 0 \tag{12.27}$$

We also want the volatility delta exposure of the portfolio to be zero. The stock price has no volatility delta exposure. Consequently, we require that:

$$c_\sigma(S, K, T, t, \sigma) - h_c c_\sigma(S, K', T, t, \sigma) = 0 \tag{12.28}$$

We have two equations with two unknowns, h and h_c. Since the stock has no volatility risk, the second equation can only be satisfied if:

$$h_c = \frac{c_\sigma(S, K, T, t, \sigma)}{c_\sigma(S, K', T, t, \sigma)} \tag{12.29}$$

The expression on the right-hand side of equation (12.29) is the ratio of the vega of the option with exercise price K to the vega of the option with exercise price K'. Since we know how to compute vega, we know how to compute this ratio. This gives us h_c, the number of options with exercise K' we have to write. Having solved for h_c, we can substitute the solution for h_c in equation (12.27):

$$c_S(S, K, T, t, \sigma) - h - h_c c_S(S, K', T, t, \sigma)$$
$$= c_S(S, K, T, t, \sigma) - h - \frac{c_\sigma(S, K, T, t, \sigma)}{c_\sigma(S, K', T, t, \sigma)} c_S(S, K', T, t, \sigma)$$
$$= 0 \tag{12.30}$$

Solving equation (12.30) for h, we get:

$$h = c_S(S, K, T, t, \sigma) - \frac{c_\sigma(S, K, T, t, \sigma)}{c_\sigma(S, K', T, t, \sigma)} c_S(S, K', T, t, \sigma) \qquad (12.31)$$

It is therefore possible to hedge an option both against the effect of unanticipated changes in the stock price and unanticipated changes in volatility. Since hedging the option against volatility risk requires a short position in an option, we have to change the stock position from the Black-Scholes delta hedge because now we have two option positions that are affected by unanticipated changes in the stock price.

Suppose that we want to hedge the call option we priced in section 12.1 against volatility exposure as well as against stock price exposure. Remember that the call has a maturity of one year and an exercise price of $100. The stock has a price of $100 with volatility of 19.80 percent. We know from section 12.2 that the vega of that option is 33.29. Suppose that there is a second call available with the same maturity but exercise price of $90. This option costs $19.91, has a delta of 0.8715, and a vega of 20.98. To hedge our option position against stock price delta exposure and volatility delta exposure, we need to find h and h_c. Using equations (12.29) and (12.31), we get:

$$h_c = \frac{c_\sigma(S, K, T, t, \sigma)}{c_\sigma(S, K', T, t, \sigma)} = \frac{33.29}{20.98} = 1.5867$$

$$h = c_S(S, K, T, t, \sigma) - \frac{c_\sigma(S, K, T, t, \sigma)}{c_\sigma(S, K', T, t, \sigma)} c_S(S, K', T, t, \sigma)$$

$$= 0.7263 - 1.5867 \times 0.8715 = -0.6565 \qquad (12.32)$$

In other words, we go short 1.5867 options with the exercise price of $90 and long 0.6565 shares to hedge the option with exercise price of $100 against both stock price risk and volatility risk. The reason we end up with a long position in the stock is that we have to short so much of the option with the lower exercise price to eliminate the volatility risk.

12.3.4. What if the option is an American option?

We already know that American call options are exercised only, if at all, before dividend payments. Consequently, we can use the Black-Scholes formula to price an American call option on a stock that does not pay a dividend. We cannot, however, use the Black-Scholes formula to price an American put option on a stock that does not pay a dividend. Remember that for a put option, there is a stock price that is low enough that it pays to exercise the put option.

If the stock pays a dividend, we can take advantage of our knowledge that an American call option is exercised immediately before a dividend payment if it is exercised early to develop Black's formula for an American call option. Suppose that the stock pays one dividend before maturity of the option at date t'. We therefore know that the option will either be exercised at t', at T, or not at all. We can price the option assuming it is exercised at T using the European call option formula on a stock that pays a dividend before maturity of the option. We can also price the option assuming it is exercised at t'. The price of an option exercised at t' is obtained from the Black-Scholes formula for a stock that does not pay a dividend. Black's formula gives as the value of the option, $C^{Black}(S, K, T, t)$, the highest value of these two European options:

Black's formula for the pricing of an American call option on a stock that pays one dividend before maturity

$$C^{Black}(S, K, T, t) = Max \left\{ c\big(S - P_t(t')D, K, T, t\big), c\big(S, K, t, t\big) \right\}$$

This formula is only an approximation. The maximum option value might be today the one of the option with maturity t'. Yet, as time evolves, the stock price might fall so that at time t' the option is out of the money before the dividend payment. At that point, exercise does not make sense. Hence, Black's formula ignores the value to the option holder of the ability to reconsider the exercise decision depending on how the stock price evolves. It therefore provides only a lower bound to the American call price.

To apply Black's formula, suppose that we want to value an American call option maturing in one year with exercise price of \$100 on a stock worth \$100. The volatility of the stock is 19.80 percent. The price of a zero-coupon bond paying \$1 in one year is \$0.90529. The stock pays a dividend of \$2 shortly before the option expires. In this case, if we exercise just before the dividend payment, we get the stock before the dividend payment. Hence, the value of the option is given by equation (12.2) and is \$13.18. If the option is not exercised early, we get the stock after the dividend is paid. This is the price of an option on a dividend-paying stock, so that the price of the underlying asset in the Black-Scholes formula is the stock price minus the present value of the dividend. The value of this option is given by equation (12.25) and is \$11.8867. In this case, the maximum of the two values is \$13.18, which corresponds to the case when the option is exercised early. If the dividend is paid earlier, the value of the option exercised early falls because the option has a shorter maturity. In fact, if the dividend is paid immediately after the option is bought, exercising early would not be worthwhile because the stock would fall from \$100 to \$98 after the payment of the dividend, but the exercise price is \$100. Depending on the date of the dividend payment, therefore, the value of the option if no exercise takes place will be greater or smaller than the value of the option if exercise takes place.

We examine a more exact approach for the pricing of options on dividend-paying stocks later when we discuss exotic options. It is important to note, however, that the method for valuing American options on dividend paying stocks when the stock price follows the binomial distribution works irrespective of the length of the period of time between stock price changes. Since, when this period gets infinitesimally small, the Black-Scholes formula holds, it follows that we can use the binomial model for American options on dividend paying stocks to get an option value when the Black-Scholes assumptions hold.

12.3.5. What if the stock price is not distributed lognormally?
The foundation of the Black-Scholes model is that the option can be hedged exactly. If the stock price is not lognormally distributed, it is likely that the effect of

the change in the stock price on the option cannot be hedged exactly. To understand why, let's go back to Figure 12.3, which shows the performance of the delta hedge as a function of the stock price. We saw that the Black-Scholes hedge ratio works well for small changes in the stock price, and that with the lognormal distribution all changes in the stock price are small over small intervals of time. We also saw that we make hedging mistakes when large changes in the stock price take place over a short interval of time.

Is there anything we could do to make the hedge exact if large stock price changes take place? The answer is no if we construct the hedge holding only the stock. Suppose we increase the hedge ratio above its value with the Black-Scholes model. In this case, the hedge will be better if there is a large increase in the stock price, but if such an increase does not take place, the hedge will be worse than if we had used the Black-Scholes hedge ratio.

Jumps in stock prices can lead to extremely large losses or gains in a hedge portfolio. As an example, consider the call maturing in one year with exercise price of $100 on a stock price worth $100. Suppose that we wrote the call and are hedging it. Let's look at the case where the stock price unexpectedly drops to zero. The call option is worth $13.18 before the jump. We are long 0.7263 units of the stock to hedge it, which amounts to a stock position worth $72.63. As the stock falls to zero, our stock holding is wiped out, so we lose $72.63. The call we wrote becomes worthless, so that we gain $13.18. On net, we lose $59.45. Hence, we lost a lot more than the call we wrote was worth before the stock price jump.

The problem arises because the price of the call option is a convex function of the stock price, which means that a straight line tangent to the price function of the call option is everywhere below that function except at the point of tangency. The value of the call's replicating portfolio, which has a long position in the stock and borrowing, is given by such a straight line. This portfolio has a value equal to the call for one stock price and a value below the call price for every other stock price. If the stock price changes by a small amount, the replicating portfolio works well, but if the stock price changes by more, the replicating portfolio can make a substantial mistake. This means that if we hedge by shorting the replicating portfolio, we have a poor hedge. To avoid such a mistake, one would like the value of the replicating portfolio to be a convex function of the stock price if the stock price changes by a significant amount. One way to make the payoff of the replicating portfolio convex in the stock price is to take positions in other options. Since the payoff of these options is convex in the stock price, the resulting replicating portfolio can be made to have payoffs that are convex in the stock price also. In general, going short such a replicating portfolio will not produce a perfect hedge, but it will insure the hedge portfolio against large hedging mistakes. There are some cases, though, where using the stock and other options in the replicating portfolio creates a perfect hedge when the stock price can jump.

When the assumptions for the Black-Scholes formula apply, it is a matter of indifference whether we hold a call option or replicate it dynamically. However, this is no longer the case when stock price jumps are possible and no exact hedge can be achieved. In this case, the payoff of the option and of the replicating portfolio will differ whenever the stock price experiences jumps over the life of the option.

Options can be priced even if they cannot be hedged perfectly, however. When an option can be hedged perfectly, we saw that its value is the present value of the expected payoff using the risk-neutral distribution. Suppose that the jumps in the stock price constitute diversifiable risk. This means that no risk premium is associated with the jumps. Consequently, we can still compute the expected payoff and discount it at the risk-free rate.

12.4. Empirical evidence on the pricing of options on stocks

Many researchers have investigated the performance of option pricing models. The first articles used estimates of historical volatility. The problem with such estimates is that they reflect the past history of the stock, when the relevant volatility is the one that the market expects to hold over the life of the option. More recent papers use implied volatility, which requires an option pricing model to be computed.

Whaley (1982) provides a comprehensive empirical study of the pricing of stock options. He proceeds as follows. He uses options written on 91 dividend-paying stocks for 160 weeks from January 17, 1975, through February 3, 1978. Each week, he computes the implied volatility that minimizes the squared errors of the option pricing model. He then uses that implied volatility to price options the following week and studies the biases of the resulting option prices. He uses the Black-Scholes formula, Black's model for the pricing of American options, and an additional model that provides an exact formula for the pricing of an American call on a stock that will pay one dividend before the maturity of the option. Over 15,582 call prices, Whaley finds that the average mistake is 3.16 cents for the Black-Scholes formula with an average call price of $4.1388. The average mistake of the other two formulas considered are smaller. In relative terms, the Black-Scholes average mistake is 2.15 percent with a standard deviation of 25.24 percent. Taking into account the early exercise feature of American options leads to better results. In terms of relative prediction errors, the exact American call formula has an average prediction error of 1.08 percent with a standard deviation of 23.82 percent. However, irrespective of the formula considered, the option formulas perform well.

The three models Whaley examines have particular biases. All models overprice options on high volatility stocks and underprice options on low volatility stocks. Whatever the model, Whaley does not find a significant relation between underpricing and the degree of moneyness (i.e., by how much an option is in the money) of the option. He finds, however, that the Black-Scholes model and the Black model relative pricing errors fall with the dividend yield and increase with time to maturity. Consequently, these models underprice options on high-dividend stocks and overprice options with a long time to maturity. These last two biases do not exist with the exact American call option valuation formula.

The other extensive study of stock option prices is a study by Rubinstein (1985) of options that have a very low or zero probability of early exercise. He focuses directly on the Black-Scholes formula. He uses a transactions database that allows him to consider the prices of two options on the same stock that differ along some dimension. For example, one option might have a higher price than another option. With the Black-Scholes formula, both options should have the same implied volatility. If the option with the higher exercise price has a higher implied volatility, this would imply a bias in the Black-Scholes formula. Examining option prices this way, Rubinstein found that there are statistically significant differences in implied volatilities.

Rubinstein finds that the implied volatility of out-of-the-money options increases as time to maturity becomes shorter. In other words, short-maturity options are valued more than implied by the Black-Scholes model. When Rubinstein divides his sample into two periods, he finds that the other biases he documents change between the two periods. In the first subperiod, the implied volatility generally increases as the strike price falls. The opposite is true in the second subperiod. Finally, for at-the-money calls, implied volatility increases with time to expiration in the first subperiod and falls with time to expiration in the second subperiod. Rubinstein investigates a number of alternative option pricing models, including the Merton (1976) model with jumps, and finds that none can explain the biases observed in Black-Scholes option prices consistently.

The biases documented by Rubinstein change over time. Important changes in the biases of the Black-Scholes model took place after the stock market crash of 1987. These changes have generated much analysis and led to new option pricing approaches. Most of that analysis has focused on index options, such as options on the S&P 500. These options can be priced by the Black-Scholes formula—we can treat the index as a stock for the purpose of option pricing. Before the crash, a graph of implied volatilities of index options against the extent to which options are in the money (i.e., the index exceeds the exercise price) would typically look like a smile as seen in Figure 12.9. Deep in the money and deep out of the money options would have higher implied volatilities. After the crash, the smile disappears; instead, the implied volatilities fall as the exercise price increases as seen in Figure 12.10. This means that deep-in-the-money calls are valued more—the ones on the left of the figure. Because of the put-call parity theorem, this also means that deep-out-of-the-money puts are valued more. In an important paper, Rubinstein (1994) describes this as "crash-phobia"—investors value the insurance provided by deep-out-of-the-money puts more because they fear the recurrence of a crash. Because of the limitations of dynamic hedging, it is difficult for put writers to hedge against stock price crashes. It may therefore not be surprising that when the probability of large downward jumps in stock prices is not trivial, those who provide puts will want to be compensated for the unhedgeable risk they bear.

What can we do if options are valued so that the Black-Scholes formula does not hold? One approach is to let the data tell us how to price options. Instead of constructing a binomial tree with constant volatility, we could deduce the volatility at each node of the tree from existing option prices. Since we have many nodes, we have many unknowns. Consequently, to find the volatility at each node, we need lots of option prices. Such approaches are now used in practice, but they are controversial. Some, like Bakshi, Chen, and Cao (1997), show that the biases of the Black-Scholes formula can be eliminated by models that allow for stochastic volatility. Others, such as Dumas, Fleming, and Whaley (1998), argue that models that allow for volatility to change over time do not perform any better than the Black-Scholes formula adjusted to take into account the known

Typical smile before the crash of 1987   *Figure 12.9*

This graph from Rubinstein (1994) shows the implied volatilities of S&P 500 index options on July 1, 1987.

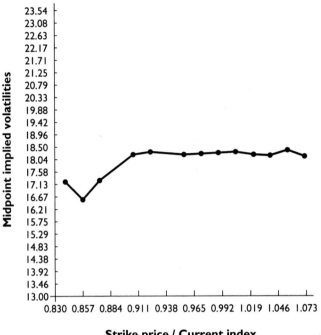

biases. They argue that to take into account the known biases of the Black-Scholes formula, one should use an implied volatility that reflects the terms of the option one attempts to price. Consequently, if deep-out-of-the-money calls have higher implied volatilities, one should use a higher implied volatility to price a deep-out-of-the-money call. Such an "empirical" or "ad hoc" version of the Black-Scholes model seems to perform well and is easy to implement.

12.5. Beyond plain vanilla Black-Scholes

So far, we have valued and hedged options on common stock. We show how we use the Black-Scholes model to price options on other underlyings, such as futures contracts and currencies, as well as derivatives with more complicated payoffs. Some key assumptions must apply. Let's review the three key assumptions to remember if we want to apply the Black-Scholes formula to price and hedge options when the underlying is not a common stock:

1. **Perfect markets.** With Black-Scholes, we obtain prices for options using a replicating portfolio or a perfect hedge. Therefore, we cannot price options that we cannot hedge. This means that if we cannot trade the underlying or a financial asset that yields the underlying at maturity of the option in markets that are well-approximated by the perfect markets assumption, we cannot price the option using Black-Scholes. The binomial

Figure 12.10 **Typical smile after the crash of 1987**

This graph from Rubinstein (1994) shows the implied volatilities of S&P 500 index options on January 2, 1990.

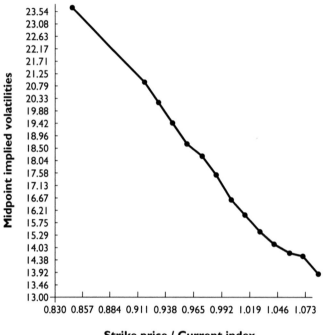

model, however, can be extended to take into account market imperfections. For example, Leland (1985) and others show how to take into account transaction costs.

2. **The underlying can be replicated with a portfolio of financial assets.**
Remember that the replicating portfolio for a call is long the stock and short zero-coupon bonds maturing when the option matures. The stock is a financial asset in that all its return is a pecuniary return. A painting is not a financial asset because we get to enjoy it and therefore it has a convenience yield. Since, with the option, we do not get the benefit of the convenience yield from having possession of the underlying, we have to form a replicating portfolio that has no convenience yield either. We know that if we buy the underlying using a forward contract, we do not get the convenience yield of the underlying until maturity of the forward contract. Consequently, the simplest way to form a replicating portfolio is to use as the underlying a forward contract that matures when the option matures plus an investment in the risk-free asset corresponding to the present value of the forward price.

3. **Lognormal distribution.** The Black-Scholes formula assumes that the price of the underlying at maturity of the option is distributed lognormally. If this assumption does not hold, we cannot use the Black-Scholes formula.

If we can use the Black-Scholes approach, then there is no difficulty in pricing options when the underlying is not a common stock. Instead of using common stock as the underlying, we use a portfolio that pays the underlying at maturity. If we can apply the Black-Scholes approach, this means we can hedge and create a replicating portfolio. As a result, the present value of a payoff is the expected payoff using the risk-neutral distribution discounted at the risk-free rate. This means that we can use the Black-Scholes approach to price complicated nonlinear payoffs as well as to hedge them.

The difficulty of using the Black-Scholes approach instead of the binomial model, however, is that with the Black-Scholes approach we have to compute the expectation of the payoff using the lognormal distribution, and this is difficult. In contrast, with the binomial model we just compute the expected payoff using the binomial tree.

One way to obtain values as well as exposures of contingent claims when the Black-Scholes assumptions hold is to use the Monte Carlo approach. Since the value of a derivative is the present value of the expected payoff using the risk-neutral distribution, we can simulate possible payoffs and take the expectation of these possible payoffs. To do that, however, one has to assume that the expected rate of growth of the price of the underlying is the risk-free rate. In other words, one does not simulate payoffs using the true distribution of the return of the underlying. This is because the pricing result require the use of the risk-neutral distribution.

12.5.1. Pricing currency and futures options

If we consider an option on a foreign currency, we use as the underlying the present value of the foreign currency delivered at maturity if the option is in the money. Now, S denotes the exchange rate. For an option on a foreign currency, the underlying is $S \times P_t^{FX}(T)$, where S is the price of the foreign currency in dollars at date t and $P_t^{FX}(T)$ is the price of a T-bill in foreign currency at date t that pays one unit of foreign currency when the option matures at date T. The volatility is simply the volatility of the log change in the spot exchange rate since the change in the price of the T-bill is not random.

Our reasoning gives us the formula for currency options:

Black-Scholes formula for the price of a
European call option on a foreign currency

$$c(S, K, T, t) = SP_t^{FX}(T)N(d) - P_t(T)KN\left(d - \sigma\sqrt{T - t}\right)$$

$$d = \frac{\ln\left(SP_t^{FX}(T)/P_t(T)K\right)}{\sigma\sqrt{T - t}} + \frac{1}{2}\sigma\sqrt{T - t} \qquad (12.33)$$

Everything in this formula is the same as in equation (12.1), the Black-Scholes formula for the pricing of a call option on a common stock, except that now the underlying asset is the domestic currency value of a foreign bond. Suppose we have an option on a foreign currency with maturity in six months. The foreign risk-free rate is 10 percent and the domestic interest rate is 5 percent. The volatility of the exchange rate is 20 percent. The exercise price is 0.6 and the current exchange rate is 0.5. In this case, $S = 0.5$, $K = 0.6$, $\sigma = 0.2$, $T - t = 0.5$, $P_t(T)$ $= e^{-0.05 \times 0.5} = 0.97531$, and $P_t^{FX}(T) = e^{-0.10 \times 0.5} = 0.951229$. We then obtain:

$$c(S, K, T, t) = SP_t^{FX}(T)N(d) - P_t(T)KN\left(d - \sigma\sqrt{T - t}\right)$$

$$= 0.5 \times 0.951229 \times N(-1.395) - 0.97531 \times 0.6 \times N(-1.5364)$$

$$= 0.5 \times 0.951229 \times 0.0815 - 0.97531 \times 0.6 \times 0.0622 = 0.0024$$

$$d = \frac{\ln\left[SP_t^{FX}(T)/P_t(T)K\right]}{\sigma\sqrt{T - t}} + \frac{1}{2}\sigma\sqrt{T - t}$$

$$= \ln\left[0.5 \times 0.9512299/(0.97531 \times 0.6)\right]$$

$$/(0.2 \times 0.7071) + 0.5 \times 0.2 \times 0.7071 = -1.395 \qquad (12.34)$$

With foreign currency options, delta hedging involves holding the foreign currency zero-coupon bond. Here, δ is 0.0815, so that a hedge for a long position in the option requires selling short 0.0815 units of the foreign currency zero-coupon bond.

The pricing of American calls on currencies is more complicated than the pricing of American calls on nondividend-paying stocks. This is because, by exercising a call option, one receives a fixed number of units of foreign currency immediately. The benefit of exercising immediately is that one gets to invest the face value of the foreign currency bond used in the option pricing formula immediately. The cost of exercising early is that one has to pay the exercise price now. If the foreign interest rate is low compared to the domestic interest rate, the cost of exercising early dominates the benefit from exercising early. If the foreign interest rate is high, the opposite is the case, and early exercise can be profitable if the call option is sufficiently in the money. It may therefore be optimal to exercise an American foreign currency call option early.

The approach that we used to price options on currencies can be used to price options whenever the underlying is not a financial asset, that is, whenever part of its return comes in the form of a convenience yield. Let's say we want to price an option on silver that way. We first have to find the price of a portfolio that pays the appropriate quantity of silver at maturity of the option. The underlying asset is then the price of that portfolio. If there exists a forward contract that matures when the option matures, we can create such a portfolio by taking a position in zero-coupon bonds for a face value equal to the forward price and a long position in the forward contract.

Consider an option that matures at date T. Let's assume that the interest rate is constant. Let $F_t(T)$ be the forward price of one unit of silver today for delivery at date T. In this case, a bond that pays one unit of silver is equivalent to a position in a zero-coupon bond that pays $F_t(T)$ at T and a long position in the forward contract. At maturity, we use the proceeds of the zero-coupon bond to pay for the delivery of silver on the forward contract. In this case, the underlying asset in the option pricing formula is $P_t(T)F_t(T)$. If $P_t(T)F_t(T)$ evolves over time so that the distribution of the forward price at date T is lognormal, we can use the Black-Scholes formula with $P_t(T)F_t(T)$ as the underlying asset.

We know from Chapter 5 that with fixed interest rates, the futures price is equal to the forward price. Consequently, we can use a futures price instead of a forward price. Let G be the futures price. A portfolio with an investment of $P_t(T)G$ in zero-coupon bonds and a long futures position of $P_t(T)$ contracts is a financial asset that replicates the payoff of the futures contract. We can therefore use this portfolio as the underlying for an option that gives us the right to open a futures contract at maturity. The resulting formula is Black's formula for the pricing of options on futures:

Black's formula for the pricing of options on futures

$$c(G, K, T, t) = P_t(T)GN(d) - P_t(T)KN\left(d - \sigma\sqrt{T - t}\right)$$

$$d = \frac{\ln(G/K)}{\sigma\sqrt{T - t}} + \frac{1}{2}\sigma\sqrt{T - t} \qquad (12.35)$$

The hedging of an option on futures is straightforward, since it involves a position of $N(d)$ in the underlying asset. We can create a portfolio that replicates the underlying asset with a position in zero-coupon bonds equal to the present value of the futures price and a long position of $P_t(T)$ units of the futures contract.

12.5.2. The Monte Carlo approach

To see how this approach works to price contingent claims, let's use it to price the call option maturing in one year with an exercise price of $100 on the stock worth $100. The volatility of the stock is 0.1980 and the continuously compounded risk-free rate is 0.0995. The stock price at maturity is $100 \times e^{\text{return}}$ where "return" is the stock's continuously compounded return over the life of the option. To use the risk-neutral approach, we have to set the stock's continuously compounded expected return equal to the risk-free rate, which is 9.95 percent. If the expected rate of return equal of the stock is the risk-free rate over the next instant, r, the continuously compounded rate of return of the stock over the interval from t to T is distributed normally with mean $r(T - t) - 0.5 \times \sigma^2(T - t)$ and volatility $\sigma(T - t)^{0.5}$ (see Technical Box 12.1, From the binomial model to the Black-Scholes formula, for an explanation of the technical reason).

With our example, the continuously compounded return of the stock from time t to T is distributed normally with an expected value of $[0.0995 - 0.5 \times 0.0392](T - t)$ and a volatility of $0.1980 \times (T - t)$. This gives us an expected rate of return of $0.0799 \times (T - t)$. Using a random number generator, we can simulate returns by generating random numbers that follow a normal distribution with a mean of 0.0799 and volatility of 0.1980. For each simulated return value, we compute the value of the option payoff and discount that payoff at the risk-free rate: $0.90529 \times \text{Max}(100 \times e^{\text{return}} - 100, 0)$. Averaging over 100,000 return values to get the present value of the expected option payoff, the option price is $13.173 versus the Black-Scholes formula price of $13.18. When we use a large number of trials in the Monte Carlo analysis, we therefore find an option price which is close to the option price one obtains from an analytical formula.

In Chapter 11, we price a contingent claim that pays the square of the stock price at maturity. Using Monte Carlo analysis to price this contingent claim, we find a value of $11,487.49 using 10,000 simulations. If we wanted to hedge this contingent claim or create a replicating portfolio, we would need to know the stock price delta exposure of the contingent claim. To find this exposure, we can simulate the option price using two different stock prices. One stock price is the actual stock price of $100, and the other stock price is a slightly higher stock price, say $101. With this second stock price, we find a value of $11,718.35. A one dollar increase in the stock price therefore increases the present value of the payoff by $230.86. To hedge the claim, we therefore need to go short 230.86 shares, since a one dollar increase in the stock price reduces the value of 230.86 shares by $230.86.

The bottom line from this is that using the Monte Carlo approach to price contingent claims when the Black-Scholes assumptions hold works well.

12.6. Summary

The Black-Scholes formula is a limiting case of the binomial formula. It holds when trading is continuous, so that the periods in the binomial model are infinitesimally short, and when the stock price is lognormally distributed. Because the reasoning of the binomial model still holds with the Black-Scholes formula, we can hedge the option exactly. However, this requires that we change the hedge after each period—since the periods are infinitesimally short, this means that we have to change the hedge continuously. The requirement that the stock price is lognormally distributed means that the stock price cannot jump for the Black-Scholes model to apply. When we plot the stock price over time, the Black-Scholes model holds only if we can plot the price without lifting the pen.

We showed how to implement the Black-Scholes formula. To implement the Black-Scholes formula for a call on a common stock, we need to know the maturity of the option, the exercise price, the stock price, the price of a discount bond that matures when the option does, and the stock's volatility. One useful way to obtain an estimate of the stock's volatility over the life of the option is to use an implied volatility. The implied volatility is the volatility that makes the known price of a call option match its Black-Scholes price. The Black-Scholes model performs well, but it has a number of problems. We showed how to cope with these problems in practice. The key recommendation is that we should use implied volatilities from options whose terms match most closely the terms of the option we are pricing. The Black-Scholes approach can be used to price options when the underlying is not a stock price. Finally, the Monte Carlo approach can be used to compute the value of derivatives with complicated payoffs when the Black-Scholes assumptions hold.

Key Concepts

Black formula for the pricing of American calls, 383
Black formula for the pricing of options on futures, 391
Black-Scholes formula, 360

Greeks, 368
implied volatility, 365
option delta, 368
option vega, 370

Review Questions

1. How is the Black-Scholes formula related to the binomial option pricing formula?

2. What types of options are priced by the Black-Scholes formula?

3. What are the key assumptions required for the Black-Scholes formula to hold?

4. What are the five variables required to apply the Black-Scholes formula?

5. If you know the five variables that enter the Black-Scholes formula, what else do you need to compute the Black-Scholes value of an option?

6. How does the option delta change if the stock price increases?

7. How can we still use the Black-Scholes formula if we assume that the stock pays a continuous dividend?

8. Why does the Black-Scholes approach to pricing options not work if the stock price can jump?

9. How can we price an option on a foreign currency using the Black-Scholes approach?

10. How can we use a Monte Carlo simulation to price an option?

Questions and Exercises

1. Consider the numerical example in section 12.1. Suppose that the stock price and the exercise price at maturity are always half of what they would be with this numerical example. What is the payoff of the option at maturity compared to what it is with the assumptions of the numerical example? Suppose now that the stock price and the exercise price in the numerical example fall by half at date t. How does this reduction in these values affect the Black-Scholes value for the option? Can you generalize from your result? Why?

2. Check the formula for the hedge ratio. What happens to the hedge ratio in your experiment of question 1?

3. Using the normal distribution from a spreadsheet, can you compute the probability that the stock price will exceed the exercise price for our numerical example using the risk-neutral probability distribution? With the risk-neutral probability distribution, the stock price at maturity is given by $S_t e^x$, where x is distributed normally with a mean equal to the interest rate R minus 0.5 times the variance of the return of the stock, and a volatility equal to the volatility of the stock return. How does this probability compare to the hedge ratio?

4. Going back to the spreadsheet and the normal distribution, suppose that the true expected rate of return of the stock is 15 percent instead of R. What is the probability that the stock price will be below \$90 on the last trading day of the month if a month has 21 trading days?

5. You have just created a portfolio to replicate dynamically the option priced in section 12.1. The stock price doubles before you have a chance to trade because of a takeover announcement. How does the option price after the stock price doubles compare to the value of your replicating portfolio?

6. Using the put-call parity formula, construct a replicating portfolio for a put option on the stock used in the numerical example of section 12.1 with an exercise price of $100.

7. You own a call with a delta of 0.815 and a vega of 40.16. The call is on the same stock as the one used in the numerical example. Using the call in the numerical example as well as the stock, hedge the call you own against stock price and volatility risk.

8. You have two European calls on foreign currencies that have the same spot exchange rate. The calls have the same maturity and exercise price. The U.S. interest rate is 10 percent. One call is on foreign currency A. The interest rate in that currency is 20 percent. The other call is on foreign currency B where the interest rate is 5 percent. Which call is more valuable and why?

9. Suppose that question 8 is changed so that both calls are American calls. Is one call more likely to be exercised and why?

10. How could you use Monte Carlo simulation to find the exposure to the volatility of the contingent claim that pays the square of the stock price analyzed in section 12.5.2?

Literature Note

The original derivation of the Black-Scholes formula is to be found in Black and Scholes (1973). Merton (1973) provides additional results and clears up some mistakes in the original proof of the formula. Cox, Ross, and Rubinstein (1979) show that the Black-Scholes formula is a limiting case of the binomial model. Figlewski (1989) provides a detailed examination of how option prices are affected when the Black-Scholes assumptions do not hold. Merton (1976) shows how to price options when the price of the underlying can jump. Jones (1984) shows how one can hedge jumps with options. For a recent examination of how alternative option pricing models perform, see Bakshi, Cao, and Chen (1997). Rubinstein (1985) develops the approach where one extracts volatility dynamics from observed option prices. Garman and Kohlhagen (1983) and Grabbe (1983) developed currency option pricing formulas. The formula for pricing options on futures is in Black (1976). Clewclow and Strickland (1999) show in great detail how to implement the Monte Carlo approach discussed in the chapter as well as how to implement various numerical approaches.

Latané and Rendleman (1976) provide cross-sectional tests showing that stocks with greater implied volatilities have greater future volatility. In more recent tests, authors use time-series tests, focusing often on options on the S&P 100. Initially, for example in Canina and Figlewski (1993), these tests showed that implied volatilities were not as useful as expected. However, more recent tests using more data and better methods show that implied volatility outperforms past volatility in forecasting future volatility. Christensen and Prabhala (1998) find in some of their tests that past volatility offers no useful information to forecast future volatility given implied volatility for the S&P 100 index options.

Chapter 13

Risk Measurement and Risk Management with Nonlinear Payoffs

Chapter **13** *Objectives*

At the end of this chapter, you will:

1. Know how to measure the risks of nonlinear payoffs.

2. Be able to evaluate risks of portfolios of derivatives.

3. Understand the tradeoffs involved in choosing a method to compute VaR for a portfolio of derivatives.

4. Have tools to build static hedges of nonlinear payoffs using options.

Barings was the Queen of England's bank. It collapsed because of trades undertaken by Nicholas Leeson in Singapore. As we will see in this chapter, it is possible that a simplification in Barings' approach to compute value-at-risk could have led it to believe that its operations in Singapore had little risk even though these operations were the cause of Barings' collapse. Barings apparently approximated the risk of an option book on a single underlying by the risk of a position in delta units of the underlying, where delta is the delta of the option book. When Leeson had a book with a delta of zero, his option positions had no risk using that approximation. This was true only for infinitesimal changes in the price of the underlying.

Whenever a portfolio has options or other derivatives, computing risk becomes trickier. In Chapter 10, we showed that options can be used to hedge almost any payoff function that depends on the price of an underlying asset at a particular time. We need to know how to price and hedge options in order to understand how to hedge nonlinear payoffs and evaluate the risk of such payoffs. In this chapter, we start by discussing how to measure and hedge the risk of nonlinear payoffs. This leads us to an extended analysis of how to compute value-at-risk (VaR) for portfolios that include options and other derivatives.

We know that the return of portfolios that have options and other derivatives is not normally distributed. Consequently, to estimate the VaR of such portfolios, we cannot use an approach that assumes normally distributed returns. The **delta-VaR** approach transforms a portfolio of options into a portfolio of the underlying assets of the options using the delta of the options. If the underlying assets have normally distributed returns, we can then compute VaR for a portfolio of options. This and other methods we discuss have different advantages and disadvantages. There are trade-offs involved in deciding which method to use, so there is no method that is always the best. Remember that a risk measure is a tool that we use to maximize shareholder wealth; it is not an end by itself. A risk measure that is more precise may not be useful if it is extraordinarily expensive or time-consuming to compute. Different firms have different portfolios of derivatives, so for some firms the simplest method may be adequate while for others more complicated methods may be required to avoid problems.

We finish the chapter using our newly acquired tools to understand when it pays to use options to hedge. We consider two examples: portfolio insurance and hedging the exchange rate risk in a bid made in foreign currency by a firm concerned about cash flow at risk (CaR).

13.1. Estimating the risk of nonlinear payoffs using delta

In Chapter 6, we learned how to measure risk when the exposures do not depend on risk factors, such as when an exporter expects to receive a fixed number of units of foreign currency. In this case, the exporter's risk is a multiple of the risk of a unit of foreign currency and does not depend on the exchange rate. The stand-alone risk of a unit of foreign currency can be measured by the volatility of its increments and its value at risk. In the case of an option, the exposure is not fixed. For example, if an exporter holds a currency option, her exposure increases with the price of the foreign currency, which means the payoff is a nonlinear payoff. In Chapter 10, we saw that a portfolio of options can approximate a nonlinear payoff function. It follows that techniques to estimate the risk of portfolios of options allow us to evaluate the risk of nonlinear payoffs. We start by measuring the risk of options, portfolios of options, and portfolios that include positions in options as well as in the underlyings of the options.

A useful approximation for measuring nonlinear exposures is the delta exposure. The delta exposure of a position is the change in its value resulting from a unit change in the risk factor evaluated for an infinitesimal change in the risk factor. (In mathematical terms, the delta exposure is the derivative of the value of the position with respect to the risk factor.) The delta exposure of a call option with respect to the stock price is the change in the call price evaluated for an infinitesimal change in the stock price. The delta exposure of a position with respect to a risk factor is an exact measure of the exposure of the position to that risk factor for an infinitesimally small change in the risk factor. For small enough changes in the risk factor, multiplying the delta exposure by the change in the risk factor provides an accurate estimate of the change in the position due to the change in the risk factor.

When the assumptions required for the Black-Scholes formula are satisfied, the delta exposure of an option to the underlying is the option's delta, δ, given by the Black-Scholes formula. In this case, an option is exposed to only one risk factor: the price of the underlying. We measure the risk of the option by evaluating its exposure to the price of the underlying using delta. For concreteness, we assume that the underlying is a common stock, but the analysis holds whatever the underlying is.

13.1.1. The risk of an option: The delta-VaR method

With the assumptions made in Chapter 12 to obtain the Black-Scholes formula, the return on a European call option is the same over a sufficiently short interval as the return on a portfolio of δ shares of the stock plus borrowing at the risk-free rate. Over an interval of time sufficiently short that it is reasonable to assume that δ is constant, the interest payment on the amount borrowed does not affect the volatility of the return of the portfolio because the value of the investment in the risk-free asset is not random. Therefore, the volatility of the return of the call option is the volatility of the return of a portfolio with δ shares invested in the stock and value equal to the price of the call. The distribution of the return of the stock is normal over an infinitesimal period of time if the Black-Scholes formula applies. Therefore, the VaR of an option over a sufficiently small period of time is 1.65 times the return volatility of the portfolio that replicates the option times the value of the portfolio. This method of computing VaR is called the **delta-VaR method**.

To apply the delta-VaR method, we create a portfolio that has the same value as the option and whose change in value over a period of time of length Δt will become the same as the change in value of a call option when Δt becomes infinitesimally small. Let S be the stock price at t, K the exercise price, T the maturity date, and $c(S, K, T, t)$ the value of the European call at time t. The portfolio consists of an investment worth δS of stock and an investment in the risk-free asset equal to $c(S, K, T, t) - \delta S$. One dollar invested in the risk-free asset for a period of length Δt earns $R\Delta t$ for sure. The change in value of the portfolio is the sum of the gain from the investment in the risk-free asset, $[c(S, K, T, t) - \delta S]R\Delta t$, plus the gain from holding δ shares, $\delta\Delta S$:

**Change in value of call approximated
by change in value of replicating portfolio**

$$= [c(S, K, T, t) - \delta S]R\Delta t + \delta\Delta S \qquad (13.1)$$

This expression gives us the change in value of an option position as a linear function of the change in value of the stock price. Since the first term in equation (13.1) is not risky, the only source of risk in the return of the portfolio is the change in the stock price. We can therefore simply treat the option position as a stock position for the purpose of risk measurement. If a portfolio includes a call, then the call can be treated as having the same risk as δ shares, so that the portfolio has an investment in the stock worth δS at time t in addition to its other investments. Remember, however, that δ changes as the stock price and time change.

Suppose a call has a delta of 0.7263. Consider a portfolio that has 1,000 such calls and 500 shares. Using the reasoning developed here, the portfolio that includes the call options is equivalent to a portfolio that has $1,000 \times 0.7263 + 500$ shares, or 1,226.3 shares.

To compute the VaR of a call option position, we want to know the position's expected gain and volatility. Using equation (13.1), we can obtain an estimate of the expected change in value of the option price over the next period of length Δt as well as an estimate of the volatility of this change in value:

Expected change in option price from replicating portfolio

$$= [c(S, K, T, t) - \delta S]R\Delta t + \delta E(\Delta S) \qquad (13.2)$$

Volatility of the change in the option price from replicating portfolio

$$= \text{Vol}[(c(S, K, T, t) - \delta S)R\Delta t + \delta\Delta S] = \delta\text{Vol}(\Delta S) \qquad (13.3)$$

where $E(\Delta S)$ and $\text{Vol}(\Delta S)$ are, respectively, the mean and volatility of the stock price change for a short period of time from t to $t + \Delta t$. If we know $\text{Vol}(\Delta S)$, we can compute the delta-VaR of the option, but we know that $\text{Vol}(\Delta S)$ is $\text{Vol}(\text{Stock return})$ times S over a small interval of time. The delta-VaR at the 95 percent confidence level of the option is 1.65 times the value of the stock position represented by the option multiplied by the volatility of the stock return, or $1.65\delta S \times \text{Vol}(\text{Stock return})$, if the stock return is normally distributed.

We compute the one-day delta-VaR using a call option with exercise price of $100 with one year to maturity on a stock with price of $100 and volatility of 19.80 percent. The interest rate is 9.95 percent. The option is worth $13.17, and δ is 0.7263. Applying our formula for the expected price change over one day, we get:

Expected option price change over one day using replicating portfolio

$$= [c(S, K, T, t) - \delta S]R\Delta t + \delta E(\Delta S)$$

$$= [13.17 - 0.7263 \times 100] \times [\text{Exp}(0.0995/365) - 1] + 0.7263E(\Delta S) \qquad (13.4)$$

To find the expected price change of the option, we need to know the expected stock price change. We require this information because the expected stock price increment depends on the true probability distribution of the stock price. Suppose that the continuously compounded expected return of the stock is 20 percent. We know from Chapter 12 that if the stock price follows a lognormal distribution, the expected stock price after n days when the expected continously-compounded return is 22 percent per year and the volatility of the stock return is 19.80 percent per year is $100 \times e^{[(0.22 - 0.5 \times 0.1980^2) \times n/365]}$ or $100e^{(0.2 \times n/365)}$. In this case, we get:

Expected option price change using replicating portfolio

$$= [13.17 - 0.7263 \times 100] \times [\text{Exp}(0.0995/365) - 1]$$
$$+ 0.7263 \times 100 \times [\text{Exp}(0.2/365) - 1] = 0.0236 \qquad (13.5)$$

The investment of an amount equal to the value of the call in the stock would have an expected price change of $0.007, or $13.17 \times [\text{Exp}(0.2/365) - 1]$. Note that the percentage expected return from investing in the option for one day, 0.18 percent, is much higher than the percentage return of investing in the stock, 0.05 percent.

Although interest is paid daily and returns accrue daily, volatility of an option price is assumed to accrue per trading day. Using the formula, we have:

Volatility of call option price change using replicating portfolio = $\delta\text{Vol}(\Delta S)$

$$= 0.7263 \times 100 \times 0.1980/\sqrt{252}$$

$$= 0.9059 \qquad (13.6)$$

This compares to investing $13.17 in the stock, where the volatility of the change in value would be $0.1643, or $13.17 \times 0.1980/\sqrt{252}$. Hence, while the option investment has a greater expected gain than a comparable investment in the common stock, it also has more volatility. This is because the option has an exposure to the stock equivalent to holding 0.7263 shares, while an investment of $13.17 in the stock has an exposure equivalent to holding 0.1317 shares.

This approach allows us to compute the VaR because the change in the value of the option over the next day is just the change in value of the replicating portfolio. The only source of risk in the replicating portfolio is the position in the stock. Ignoring the expected change in value of the portfolio, the delta-VaR of the option is therefore simply the VaR of a portfolio holding 0.7263 shares of common stock. If we take into account the expected change in value of the portfolio, we obtain the 5 percent VaR by multiplying the volatility of the change in value of the portfolio given in equation (13.6) by 1.65 and subtracting the expected change in value given in equation (13.5):

Delta-VaR of the Call Option = 1.65 (Volatility of change in option value estimated using the replicating portfolio) – Expected change in option value estimated using the replicating portfolio

$$= 1.65 \times 0.9059 - 0.0236$$

$$= \$1.471 \qquad (13.7)$$

For the daily VaR computed here, the expected change in the value of the option is less than 2 percent of the VaR. The expected return is typically ignored in one-day VaR computations. Equation (13.7) shows that the delta-VaR does not require much in the way of computation. The delta-VaR on an option ignoring the expected return is 1.65 times the delta of the option times the volatility of the stock.

This is a simple formula for estimating VaR, which is the main benefit of the delta-VaR approach. The method is applied in the same way for put options, since a put option is equivalent to an investment in the risk-free asset plus a short position in the stock given by the delta of the put. The approach can be used for options on any kind of underlying for which the Black-Scholes pricing approach is appropriate. When the Black-Scholes pricing approach is not appropriate, the exposure to the underlying is given by the delta exposure, so that the approach discussed here still works, but the delta exposure is computed differently.

13.1.2. The risk of a portfolio of options written on the same stock

The delta-VaR method for measuring the risk of options applies equally well to portfolios of options written on the same stock. In this case, the change in value of the replicating portfolio becomes the sum of the changes in value of the replicating portfolios of the individual options times the position in each option:

$$\Delta \textbf{Portfolio value} = \sum_{i=1}^{i=N} n_i \left[\left(c_i(\textbf{S, K}_i, \textbf{T}_i, t) - \delta_i \textbf{S} \right) \textbf{R} \Delta t + \delta_i \Delta \textbf{S} \right] \quad \textbf{(13.8)}$$

where the subscript i denotes an option with a specific maturity and exercise price, n_i is the number of units of that option held in the portfolio, δ_i is the δ of that option, and R is the rate of interest. If an option is written instead of bought, n_i is negative. The volatility of the change in value of that portfolio is:

$$\textbf{Volatility} \left(\Delta \textbf{Portfolio value} \right) = \left[\sum_{i=1}^{i=N} n_i \delta_i \right] \textbf{Vol} \left(\Delta \textbf{S} \right) \quad \textbf{(13.9)}$$

Over short intervals of time, this formula allows us to obtain the VaR of the portfolio of options since the VaR at the 95 percent confidence level is 1.65 times the volatility of the change in value of the portfolio.

The delta method works equally well for puts and for combinations of puts and calls as it does for calls. More generally, it works for any derivative whose value can be written as the value of a portfolio of the risk-free asset and of delta units of the underlying.

13.1.3. The risk of a portfolio of options written on different underlying assets

We can use this same approach to evaluate the risk of portfolios with options written on different underlying assets. An example is a portfolio of positions in options of different types written on different stocks. We know that an option on a stock can be replicated with a portfolio with positions in the underlying stock and the risk-free asset. Adding up the replicating portfolio for each option gives us a portfolio that is invested in stocks and in the risk-free asset. Over a sufficiently short period of time, the return on the option portfolio is the same as the return of the portfolio with positions in stocks and the risk-free asset. When we can express a portfolio of stock options as a portfolio of positions in stocks and in the risk-free asset, we already know how to compute the volatility of the return of the portfolio. The VaR of the portfolio at the 95 percent confidence level is then simply 1.65 times the volatility of the portfolio multiplied by the value of the portfolio.

To compute the VaR of a portfolio of derivatives on risky assets when these assets are not common stocks, we simply have to be able to construct a portfolio whose return is the same as the return of the derivatives portfolio and has positions in the underlyings of the derivatives and in the risk-free asset. For instance, we saw that the value of a currency option is equivalent to the value of a portfolio invested in delta units of a foreign currency bond and borrowing in the risk-free asset. Our approach to computing the VaR of a portfolio of options would therefore work if some of the options in the portfolio are currency options.

Suppose that we have a portfolio with two options. One option is a call on 100 shares of common stock and the other is a call on 10,000 Swiss francs. To apply the approach, we transform the stock option into a stock position and borrowing, and the Swiss franc option into a Swiss franc position and borrowing. We then use the formula for the volatility of the return of a portfolio. Since we have two assets in the portfolio, we have to know the volatility of the return of each asset as well as the covariance of the return of the two assets.

We assume that both calls have a maturity of one year. The risk-free rate is 6 percent. The exercise price of the call on common stock is $100 and the stock price is $100. The volatility of the common stock return is 25 percent. The price of a Swiss franc is $0.52 and the call has an exercise price of $0.52. The Swiss franc interest rate is assumed to be 6 percent also. The volatility of the exchange rate is assumed to be 15 percent.

The call on the stock is worth $1,285. Its delta is 0.6424 per share. Consequently, holding the call has an exposure to the stock of 64.24 shares. Since 64.24 shares cost $6,424, we have to borrow $5,139 to create a portfolio that replicates the call on the stock. The call on the Swiss franc is worth $293 and has a delta of 0.53 per Swiss franc. The Swiss franc call has the exposure of 5,300 Swiss francs. We therefore have to borrow $0.52 × 5,300 − $293, or $2,463, to create the replicating portfolio for the call on the Swiss franc. As a result, we have a portfolio worth $1,285 + $293, or $1,578.

To use the portfolio return formula, equation (2.1), we need the portfolio weights. The weight for the stock, w_{stock}, is $6,424/$1,578, or 4.07. The weight for the Swiss franc, w_{SFR}, is $2,756/$1,578, or 1.75. Finally, the weight for the risk-free asset, w_{RF}, is −[(4.07 + 1.75) −1], or −4.82, since the weights have to sum to one. Let R_{stock}, R_{SFR}, and R_{RF} be respectively the returns on the stock, the Swiss franc, and the risk-free asset. The return of the portfolio is:

$$\textbf{Return of portfolio} = w_{stock}R_{stock} + w_{SFR}R_{SFR} + w_{RF}R_{RF}$$

$$= 4.07R_{stock} + 1.75R_{SFR} - 4.82R_{RF} \qquad (13.10)$$

To compute the volatility of the portfolio return, note that the volatility of the return of the risk-free asset is zero. Let $Var(R_{stock})$, $Var(R_{SFR})$, and $Cov(R_{stock},R_{SFR})$

be, respectively, the variance of the common stock returns, the variance of the Swiss franc return, and the covariance between the common stock return and the Swiss franc return. Let's assume that the correlation between the stock return and the Swiss franc return is –0.3. We compute the variance of the return ignoring the risk-free asset since its variance is zero:

$$
\begin{aligned}
\textbf{Variance of the return} = {} & \textbf{4.07} \times \textbf{4.07} \times \textbf{Var(R}_\textbf{stock}\textbf{)} \\
& + \textbf{1.75} \times \textbf{1.75} \times \textbf{Var(R}_\textbf{SFR}\textbf{)} \\
& + \textbf{2} \times \textbf{4.07} \times \textbf{1.75} \times \textbf{Cov(R}_\textbf{stock}\textbf{,R}_\textbf{SFR}\textbf{)} \\
= {} & \textbf{4.07} \times \textbf{4.07} \times \textbf{0.25}^\textbf{2} + \textbf{1.75} \times \textbf{1.75} \times \textbf{0.15}^\textbf{2} \\
& - \textbf{2} \times \textbf{4.07} \times \textbf{1.75} \times \textbf{0.3} \times \textbf{0.25} \times \textbf{0.15} \\
= {} & \textbf{0.94}
\end{aligned}
\tag{13.11}
$$

The volatility of the return is the square root of the variance, or 0.97. Let's look at the VaR for one trading day. Using the square root formula, the volatility over one trading day is 0.97 times the square root of 1/252, or 0.061. The VaR of the portfolio is 1.65 × Portfolio return volatility × Portfolio value, or 1.65 × 0.061 × \$1,578, which is \$158.83.

13.2. Beyond delta-VaR

Remember that δ is an exact measure of the exposure of a call option to changes in the price of the underlying only for infinitesimal changes in the price of the underlying. Consequently, the delta-VaR becomes less accurate as it is computed over longer periods because over longer periods there is a greater probability of large changes in the price of the underlying. There is more to this, however. Over longer periods of time, it is no longer the case that the return on the option is normally distributed. The reason for this is that δ changes over time, so that the return on the option is the return on a portfolio with portfolio weights that change over time as a function of the return of the stock. The return on the option cannot therefore be i.i.d. and cannot be normally distributed. In fact, we do not know what distribution the option return follows over longer periods of time. We present alternative methods to computing VaR. Finally, we show how these various methods assess the risk of option positions of Barings in Singapore.

13.2.1. Measuring the risk of a portfolio of options over longer periods of time

The delta-VaR method has a wonderful simplicity and elegance to it. To implement it, we take a portfolio that contains derivatives as well as other positions, transform the derivatives into positions in the underlying assets, and then use traditional portfolio analysis to compute VaR. We know, however, that the delta exposure measure works exactly only for infinitesimal changes in the price of the underlying. With the Black-Scholes assumptions, the probability of large changes in the price of the underlying increases as the observation interval lengthens. So, how does the delta method work when changes in the price of the underlying can be large?

To understand how the delta method works over longer periods of time, it is useful to compare the distribution of the gain from an option position implied by the delta approximation and the distribution of the gain obtained from using the pricing formula. Suppose we have a call option maturing in one year with exercise price of $100 on a stock worth $100 with volatility of 50 percent. The interest rate is 6 percent. For this option, we have a Black-Scholes value of $22.21 with a delta of 0.64. We simulate the distribution of the gain on a long position in the call option over two time periods. The first time period is one day.

Figure 13.1 shows the distribution of the gain from the simulation. For the simulation, we draw 1,000 possible stock prices. We then compute the gain on the position using both the delta approximation of the option price and the option price computed using the Black-Scholes formula. The two distributions are indistinguishable in Figure 13.1. Remember that the 5 percent VaR is given by the loss corresponding to the fifth percentile of the distribution of the gain from a position. The fifth percentile of the distribution is a loss of $2.80 when we use the delta approximation and of $2.75 when we use the Black-Scholes formula. The mistake we make with the approximation over one day is therefore less than 2 percent.

What if we have a one-year holding period for the option? At the end of the year, we price the option on its maturity day. We use a simulation again. Figure 13.2 shows the distribution of the gain from the simulation. With a one-year holding period, we see that there is a substantial difference between the

Option gain distribution using the delta approximation and the pricing formula: one-day period   *Figure 13.1*

The option is on a stock with price $100, has an exercise price of $100, and a maturity of one year. The stock has a volatility of 50 percent. The risk-free rate is 6 percent. The figure shows two option gain distributions for a one-day holding period for 1,000 possible stock prices drawn assuming an expected stock return of 15 percent per year. The first option gain distribution approximates the change in the option price using the delta approximation. The second option gain distribution uses the option price formula to compute the change in the option price.

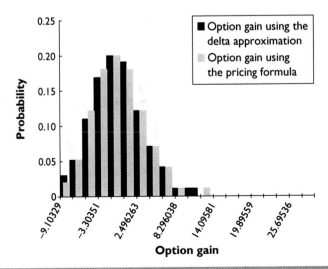

Figure 13.2 — Option gain distribution using the delta approximation and the pricing formula: one-year period

The option is on a stock with price $100, has an exercise price of $100, and a maturity of one year. The stock has a volatility of 50 percent. The risk-free rate is 6 percent. The figure shows two option gain distributions for a one-year holding period for 1,000 possible stock prices drawn assuming an expected stock return of 15 percent per year. The first option gain distribution approximates the change in the option price using the delta approximation. The second option gain distribution uses the option price formula to compute the change in the option price.

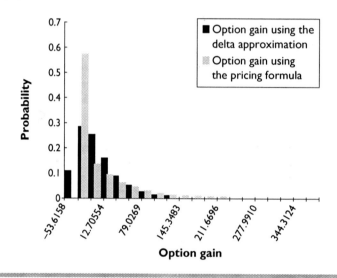

distribution of the gain using the delta approximation and the distribution of the gain using the pricing formula. The delta approximation over such a long period of time shows that we can lose more than what we paid for the option, which is obviously impossible because of the limited liability of options. Computing the delta-VaR analytically, the option has a delta of 0.64 and the stock has an expected return of 15 percent and a volatility of 50 percent, so that the delta-VaR taking into account the expected return is $1.65 \times 0.64 \times 0.5 \times 100 - 100(e^{0.15} - 1)$, or $36.6166. In other words, the delta-VaR approximation tells us that there is a 5 percent chance that we will lose 50 percent more than the option premium, which is impossible.[1]

The fifth percentile of the distribution for the delta approximation is a loss of $38.03, which exceeds what we paid for the option. The fifth percentile of the

---

1 The reader may notice that if the volatility of a portfolio is high and the period over which the VaR is computed is long enough, the VaR obtained by taking 1.65 × volatility × value of portfolio could exceed the value of the portfolio. When computing the VaR over a period significantly longer than one day when volatility is high, it is important to use the lognormal distribution directly, so that if the portfolio value S is distributed lognormally with continuously-compounded expected return μ and volatility σ, the fifth quantile of the portfolio price distribution over a period of length τ is $Se^{(\mu - 0.5\sigma^2)\tau - 1.65\sigma\tau}$. The VaR computed this way is S minus the fifth quantile and it can never be more than the portfolio price. This is not an issue when computing daily or weekly VaRs, but can be an issue when computing a VaR for one year.

distribution using the pricing formula is a loss corresponding to what we paid for the option.

When large changes are possible, we make mistakes, and these mistakes make the delta-VaR inaccurate. In some cases, the mistakes can be trivial. In others, they can destroy the entire value of a firm. The option pricing function is a non-linear function of the price of the underlying, and this nonlinearity makes the delta exposure measure only an approximation.

Consider a portfolio of derivatives on an underlying. If the value of that portfolio is almost linear in the price of the underlying, the delta exposure measure will be fairly accurate. This could be the case if the portfolio has deep-out-of-the-money options or deep-in-the-money options. If the value of the portfolio is poorly approximated by a straight line, the mistakes of the delta exposure method can end up obscuring a firm's risk—sometimes understating it, and other times overstating it.

13.2.2. Alternative methods to computing the VaR of an option or portfolio of options

The delta-VaR approach approximates the distribution of the option gain with the distribution of the gain from a portfolio that has delta shares and risk-free borrowing. To obtain a more precise VaR estimate, a better approximation uses convexity, which the delta exposure ignores. To take into account the curvature of the option pricing function, we have to adjust for how delta changes as the stock price changes. The impact on delta of a small change in the stock price, the exposure or derivative of delta with respect to the stock price, is called the option's gamma. The formula for a call option's gamma is:

$$\gamma = \frac{\dfrac{e^{-x^2}}{\sqrt{2\sigma}}}{S\sigma\sqrt{T-t}}$$

$$x = \frac{\ln\left(S/P_t(T)K\right)}{\sigma\sqrt{T-t}} + \frac{1}{2}\,\sigma\sqrt{T-t} \qquad \textbf{(13.12)}$$

Using gamma as well as delta, the change in the option price for a change in the stock price of ΔS is:[2]

$$c(S + \Delta S, K, T, t) - c(S, K, T, t) = \delta\Delta S + 0.5\gamma(\Delta S)^2 \qquad \textbf{(13.13)}$$

Using the known distribution for the stock price, we can then compute the mean and volatility of the call option price in the same way as when we introduced the delta-VaR. There is one substantial complication. The expression $(\Delta S)^2$ is part of

---

2 *Technical note.* To obtain this result, one uses a second-order Taylor-series expansion of the option price around the stock price S. This gives us:

$$c(S + \Delta S, K, T, t) = c(S, K, T, t) + c_S(S, K, T, t)\Delta S + 0.5c_{SS}(S, K, T, t) \times (\Delta S)^2 + \text{Remainder}$$

where c_S is δ, the derivative of the option price with respect to the stock price, and c_{SS} is γ, the second derivative of the option price with respect to the stock price.

the dollar increment of the option, and to compute the mean and the volatility of the dollar increment of the option, we have to know the distribution of the square of the change in the stock price. In a portfolio that includes other assets besides the option, one has to take into account the covariance of $(\Delta S)^2$ with the other assets. The best way to do this is to represent the option's dollar increment in the portfolio by equation (13.13) and then use a Monte Carlo analysis to generate the asset prices including the price of the stock underlying the option. Risk-Metrics™ calls this method the **structured Monte Carlo method**. We show later how to compute the delta-gamma VaR in a detailed example comparing the various ways of computing the VaR for a portfolio of options.

Figure 13.3 compares the distribution of the gain of the option position using the delta approximation, the delta-gamma approximation, and the pricing formula for an option whose holding period is one year. The delta-gamma approximation produces a gain distribution that is closer to the true distribution. The fifth percentile of the distribution using the delta-gamma approximation is a loss of $27.89, which is about halfway between the loss using the true distribution of $22.21 and the loss of $38.03 with the delta approximation.

We can compute the VaR without using the delta approximation or the delta-gamma approximation by computing the option price explicitly for possible stock prices using the option pricing model that is appropriate. For each stock price, we use the option pricing formula to obtain the option price. The VaR is then obtained by computing the loss corresponding to the fifth quantile of the distribu-

---

Figure 13.3   **Option gain distribution using the delta approximation, the delta-gamma approximation, and the pricing formula**

The option is on a stock with price $100, has an exercise price of $100, and a maturity of one year. The stock has a volatility of 50 percent. The risk-free rate is 6 percent. The figure shows three option gain distributions for a one-year holding period for 1,000 possible stock prices drawn assuming an expected stock return of 15 percent per year. The first option gain distribution approximates the change in the option price using the delta approximation. The second distribution uses the delta-gamma approximation. Finally, the third distribution uses the option price formula to compute the change in the option price.

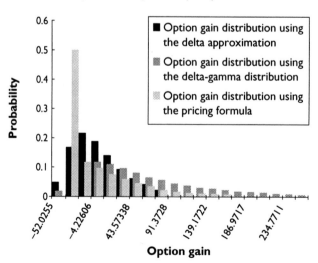

tion of option prices. With the binomial distribution, the number of possible stock prices is finite if the number of steps is finite. We can therefore compute option prices for each possible stock price at the date corresponding to the end of the period for which we estimate VaR. If the stock price follows a lognormal distribution, the number of possible stock prices is not finite. We can nevertheless generate a sample of stock prices for that date using Monte Carlo simulation.

To do so, we proceed as in the simulations for Figures 13.1 through 13.3. If the stock price is lognormally distributed and we know the expected return and the volatility of the return of the stock, we can generate stock price realizations using the stock's return distribution. For each one of the stock price realizations generated, we can compute the option price. Once we have a large number of stock price and option price realizations, we can use the distribution of portfolio values obtained from these stock and option price realizations to compute the loss corresponding to the fifth quantile of the distribution of the portfolio values.

This use of the Monte Carlo method is called the **full valuation Monte Carlo method**, since we value the option for each stock price generated through the simulation. Given the distribution of the option prices, the VaR is simply the fifth quantile of the generated distribution.

This Monte Carlo method is the same as in Chapter 12 except for one difference. To value options, we use the risk-neutral distribution, while the VaR depends on the actual distribution of the stock price. This difference is generally not important for a one-day VaR, but it can become important when the period over which VaR is computed becomes longer.[3] The Monte Carlo method works equally well if we have a portfolio of options written on the same stock. In this case, for each realization of the stock price, we have an associated portfolio value. We can then use the fifth quantile of the generated distribution of the portfolio values to obtain the VaR of the portfolio. The same method applies if we have options as well as other assets in the portfolio, but we have to generate joint realizations of all the asset prices.

A final method is to use past history to generate prices. Instead of generating a sample of prices based on assumptions about the distribution of these prices, we use a historical sample. Consequently, we do not have to take a stand on statistical distributions. If we assume that returns are i.i.d., we form our sample to compute VaR from past returns. With this sample, we generate possible prices by applying past returns to the current prices to obtain a generated distribution of portfolio values. This method is called the **historical VaR**. We could use historical VaR with the delta-method or with the full valuation method. An important decision in applying the historical VaR is the length of the period of time we use to form our sample of past returns. Often, firms (for example, JP Morgan Chase) use one year of daily returns.

The various methods to compute VaR work if there is more than one risk factor. For example, if we believe that changes in interest rates affect option prices

---

3 With the lognormal distribution, the variance of the stock return is the same for the risk-neutral distribution and for the actual distribution. Consequently, if we were to compute the VaR of a stock over one day ignoring the expected return, we would get exactly the same estimate whether we use the risk-neutral distribution or the actual distribution.

in an important way, we might use as risk factors the stock price and the interest rate on a zero-coupon bond with the same maturity as the option. The first decision we would have to make in this case is whether we want to stick to the Black-Scholes model, which assumes constant interest rates, or use a model that allows for stochastic interest rates. In practice, the Black-Scholes model is used most often. Irrespective of the option pricing model we use, however, we can use the VaR methods discussed here. With the delta method, we have to allow for the delta exposure of the option with respect to the stock price as well as with respect to the interest rate. The volatility of the dollar return on the option will then depend on the covariance between the two risk factors. With the Monte Carlo method, we have to use a joint distribution of stock price returns and interest rate changes. With the historical method, we have to use past stock price returns as well as interest rate changes.

We might be tempted to conclude that the more precise the VaR measure, the better. The problem with this view is that a VaR measure is useless if it takes too much time to compute. If a financial firm uses VaR to measure and manage risk over a day, any measure that cannot be computed overnight is useless. This means that there is a trade-off between accuracy and speed. This trade-off changes over time as computers become faster and better algorithms are developed, but it cannot be ignored. A firm might decide to use the delta-VaR even though it is less accurate than a full valuation VaR because the full valuation VaR could not be produced quickly enough to be useful. Whatever method we use, we have to start by specifying a valuation model. We could have used a different model, but nothing fundamental in the discussion changes with the model. VaR is the product of assumptions, approximations, and statistical estimation—a significant issue for VaR users. How can we compare the different VaR methods? Pritsker (2001) examines the delta method, several different implementations of the delta-gamma method, and the full valuation Monte Carlo method from the perspective of accuracy as well as computational time for large portfolios of options. He focuses on currency options, assuming that the exchange rates and interest rates are stochastic but the implied volatilities are not. For the variance-covariance matrix of the risk factors, he uses RiskMetrics™ data. His main simulation exercise uses 500 randomly chosen portfolios of options. The performance of the portfolios is then simulated 10,000 times. The benchmark is the full valuation Monte Carlo. Pritsker is able to use a measure of statistical significance of the difference between the VaR computed according to a specific method and the full Monte Carlo VaR across the 10,000 trials. He finds that the delta-VaR significantly understates or overstates the VaR at the 1 percent confidence level in almost half of the trials. The delta-gamma VaR using the Monte Carlo method significantly understates or overstates at the 1 percent level in about 25 percent of the trials. These methods still make an average absolute mistake of about 10 percent of the VaR. In a separate exercise, Pritsker evaluates computational time by computing the VaR for a randomly chosen portfolio of 50 foreign exchange options using a workstation. The delta method takes 0.07 seconds, the delta-gamma Monte-Carlo method takes 3.87 seconds, and the full valuation Monte Carlo method requires 66.27 seconds. For a portfolio of 10,000 options, it would therefore take more than 3 hours to compute the VaR using the full simulation method, but under five minutes using the delta method. Since his paper, progress in the implementation of the full valuation Monte Carlo simulation have reduced the time that it would take to perform his simulation exercises, but it is still the case that Monte Carlo simulation on real-world portfolios can take a long time (days in some cases).

Pritsker (1996) investigates only parametric approaches to estimate VaR. Those are approaches where the joint distribution of the risk factors is specified. All approaches except the historical approaches are parametric approaches. With the Monte Carlo method, one has to select a distribution for the risk factors. Hendricks (1996) examines sixteen different approaches to estimate VaR. His study does not consider portfolios of derivatives like Pritsker (1996), but only foreign currency portfolios. He considers three types of approaches: an approach like RiskMetrics™ that estimates the variance weighting more recent observations more heavily, an approach where all sample observations to estimate the variance are weighted equally, and the historical approach. For each approach, he then varies the window over which the volatility is estimated or the window from which the historical sample is obtained from a short window of 125 days to a long one of 1,250 days. He then considers how well each approach performs over time from 1983 through 1994. The bottom line from his study is that these approaches make little difference at the 95 percent confidence interval. The approaches relying on estimates of the variances and covariances tend to understate the risk at the 1 percent confidence interval compared to the historical VaR. Such a result could occur if the distribution of a random variable has fat tails, namely the probability of outcomes at the tails is greater than with the normal distribution.

13.2.3. Leeson, Barings, delta-VaR, delta-gamma VaR, and Monte Carlo VaR

Nick Leeson arrived in Singapore in the spring of 1992 to manage the local futures operation for Barings Bank. He developed an arbitrage business, trading on differences between futures prices in Singapore and in Osaka for the Nikkei 225. This business appeared to be highly profitable and to have little risk. During 1994, auditors reviewed the operations of Singapore and concluded that "The success of the derivatives arbitrage business carried on from Singapore has apparently been achieved without the acceptance of high levels of exposure to changes in the Nikkei 225 index." In an internal Barings report, executives of Barings wrote at the time that "we are not as yet convinced that there is enough work for a full-time treasury and risk manager" in Singapore.

Any trader can look good if he succeeds in revealing only his winning trades. Leeson was hiding some of the losses he made. At the end of 1994, the hidden losses were £205 million and kept increasing. Leeson could do that because he was both making and recording trades in Singapore. He was free to do whatever he wanted provided the London office did not look at him too closely. They did not want to look too closely because they thought he was making a lot of money with apparently little risk. In 1994, Leeson accounted for £30 million of revenues for Barings Structured Products Group, well over half the revenues of that group.

To keep hiding the losses, Leeson apparently had to generate cash to make various margin payments to keep futures positions open so that losses would not have to be recognized. One way a trader can generate cash is to sell options. By doing so, he increases the firm's risk. Leeson used this method to raise cash, but with a twist. He sold short straddles on the Nikkei 225 index. A short straddle involves the sale of a put and a call with the same strike price. Consider a short at the money straddle when the Nikkei is at 19,000. As Figure 13.4 shows, a short straddle forces the option writer to make payments on the put if the index is lower than 19,000 and on the call if the index is above 19,000. On January 17, an earthquake rocked Kobe in Japan, killing 5,000 people. By January 23, the Nikkei was at 17,785. The Nikkei fell, so that Leeson had to deal with the prospect of having to make large payments on the puts he had written. He went on a futures buying spree, going long 55,399 contracts expiring in March. He behaved as if he wanted to prop up the falling Nikkei. That buying spree would cost £384 million to Barings and the losses on the options were £51 million by February 27. By then, Leeson was gone. He sent a fax from a hotel in Kuala Lumpur where he wrote "My sincere apologies for the predicament that I have left you in." He signed it "Apologies, Nick." Barings was measuring its market risk. Yet, on the day Barings discovered what Leeson had been up to, it discovered also that its Nikkei exposure was such that a 1 percent fall in the Nikkei before it could close its positions would cost it $70 million.

It is possible to measure market risk and conclude that a short straddle has no risk. Consider the delta-VaR of a short straddle. Say that the Nikkei is currently at 18,759, the volatility is 15 percent, the dividend yield is assumed to be zero for simplicity, the interest rate is 4 percent, and the maturity is in 90 days. Using the Black-Scholes formula to price the put and the call, the current value of the position is:

$$-(\text{Value of put} + \text{Value of call}) = -p(\text{Nikkei}, 19{,}000, t + 0.25, t)$$
$$- c(\text{Nikkei}, 19{,}000, t + 0.25, t) \qquad (13.14)$$

Figure 13.4   Payoff of short straddle

The straddle has a short position in a call with exercise price at 19,000 and a short position in a put with the same exercise price. Note that this figure does not take into account the initial receipt of cash for the premiums of the options sold.

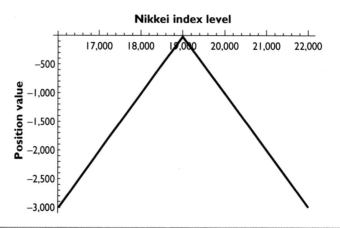

Remember that we denote by $P_t(t + 0.25)$ the price of a zero-coupon bond at t that pays \$1 at $t + 0.25$. Note that equation (10.8), the put-call parity theorem, implies:

$$p\textbf{(Nikkei, 19,000, } t + 0.25, \, t\,) = c\textbf{(Nikkei, 19,000, } t + 0.25, \, t\,)$$

$$- \textbf{Nikkei} + \textbf{19,000} \times \textbf{P}_t\textbf{(}t + 0.25\textbf{)} \qquad \textbf{(13.15)}$$

Consequently, the value of the position is also:

$$-2c\textbf{(Nikkei, 19,000, } t + 0.25, \, t\,) + \textbf{Nikkei} - \textbf{19,000} \times \textbf{P}_t\textbf{(}t + 0.25\textbf{)} \qquad \textbf{(13.16)}$$

The price of the call is ¥536.33 when the underlying corresponds to the Nikkei index, which makes the value of the position:

$$-\textbf{(2} \times \textbf{¥536.33} - \textbf{¥18,759} + \textbf{¥18,810.9) = −¥1,124.56} \qquad \textbf{(13.17)}$$

Because of put-call parity, the δ of the put is equal to the δ of the call minus the δ of the Nikkei, which is one.[4] With our assumption that the value of the Nikkei is at 18,759, the δ of the call is exactly 0.5. Consequently, the δ of the short straddle is zero since it is two times 0.5 minus the δ of the Nikkei. This means that the delta-VaR of the short straddle for that value of the Nikkei is zero.

This delta-VaR we just computed ignores the fact that the option price is a convex function of the price of the underlying asset. To take this curvature into account is to extend the computation of the VaR to take into account gamma, so that the change in the value of the option is:

$$\Delta c\textbf{(S, K, T, } t\textbf{)} = \delta\Delta\textbf{S} + \textbf{0.5 } \gamma\textbf{(}\Delta\textbf{S)}^2 \qquad \textbf{(13.18)}$$

The variance of the change in the value of the option is:[5]

$$\textbf{Var}\big(\Delta c\textbf{(S, K, T, } t\textbf{)}\big) = \delta^2 \, \textbf{Var}\big(\Delta\textbf{S}\big) + \textbf{0.5}\gamma^{\,2}\big[\textbf{Var}\big(\Delta\textbf{S}\big)\big]^2 \qquad \textbf{(13.19)}$$

---

4 To see this, note that differentiating the put-call parity equation of (13.15) with respect to the Nikkei level, we have:

$$\frac{\partial p(\text{Nikkei, 19,000, } t + 0.25, \, t\,)}{\partial \text{Nikkei}} = \frac{\partial c(\text{Nikkei, 19,000, } t + 0.25, \, t\,)}{\partial \text{Nikkei}} - 1$$

The term on the left-hand side of this equation is the δ of the put and the first term on the right-hand side of this equation is the δ of the call.

5 To obtain the variance of the change in the value of the call, we take the variance of the change given in equation (13.18):

$$\text{Var}(\Delta c \text{ (S, K, T, } t\,)) = \text{Var } (\delta\Delta S + 0.5\gamma(\Delta S)^2)$$
$$= \delta^2 \text{Var}(\Delta S) + 0.25\gamma^2 \text{Var}[(\Delta S)^2] + \delta\gamma \text{Cov}[\Delta S, \, (\Delta S)^2]$$
$$= \delta^2 \text{Var}(\Delta S) + 0.25\gamma^2 \text{Var}[(\Delta S)^2] + \delta\gamma E[(\Delta S)^3]$$

With the normal distribution, $\text{Var}[(\Delta S)^2] = 2[\text{Var}(\Delta S)]^2$, and the expected value of $(\Delta S)^3$, which corresponds to the third moment of ΔS, is equal to zero. Substituting these results in the last line yields equation (13.19).

We can now compute the delta-gamma VaR of the option. γ is equal to 0.000283. The annual variance of ΔS evaluated at 18,759 is the square of the volatility of the return times 18,759, namely $(0.15 \times 18{,}759)^2$. Consequently, the variance of the change in the stock price over one trading day is $(0.15 \times 18{,}759)^2/252$ which is 31,419.7.

To compute the VaR at the 95 percent confidence level using the delta-gamma method, remember that the short straddle position is equivalent to having written two calls, having a long position in the Nikkei, and having borrowed the present value of the exercise price. Consequently, the variance of the position is:

$$
\begin{aligned}
\textbf{Variance of position} \ &= \ \textbf{Var}(-2\Delta c(18{,}759,\ 19{,}000,\ t + 0.25,\ t) + \Delta S) \\
&= \ \textbf{Var}\left[-2\delta\Delta S - \gamma(\Delta S)^2 + \Delta S\right] \\
&= \ \textbf{Var}\left[-\gamma(\Delta S)^2\right] \\
&= \ 2 \times 0.000283^2 \times 31{,}419.7^2 \\
&= \ 158.13
\end{aligned}
\tag{13.20}
$$

To go from the second line to the third one, remember that δ is equal to 0.5 with our assumptions. While the delta-VaR of the position is zero, the delta-gamma VaR is 1.65 times the square root of 158.13, or is 20.75. By taking into account the nonlinearity of the option pricing formula, the delta-gamma method recognizes in this case that the short straddle is a risky position.

How reasonable is the risk assessment of the short straddle obtained with the delta-gamma method? We can evaluate this by simulating the change in value of the position over one day for a given distribution of the stock price. In other words, we use the full valuation Monte Carlo method to generate possible values for the short straddle and use the fifth quantile of the distribution of the simulated outcomes as our VaR. This method best takes into account the nonlinearity of the option pricing formula. It involves no approximation of the pricing formula since it computes the actual value of the short straddle for possible option prices. Like the delta-gamma method, however, the Monte Carlo method we implement assumes that the Black-Scholes formula is the appropriate pricing formula for options.

Figure 13.5 shows the distribution of the simulated values of the short straddle when we simulate the value of the short straddle 10,000 times assuming the continuously compounded return of the stock price is distributed normally with a mean of 0.20 per year and a standard deviation of 0.15.[6] With these assumptions, we find that the fifth percentile of the distribution of the value of the short straddle the next day is $-¥1,158.98$. This means that the VaR is $-¥1,125.54$ minus $-¥1,158.98$, which amounts to ¥33.44. In this case, the Monte Carlo VaR is even higher, 61 percent higher, than the delta-gamma VaR.

---

6 The approach we use is to assume that the Nikkei of the next day is distributed $18{,}759 \times$ Exp$(0.2/252 + \epsilon)$ where $\epsilon \sim N(0, 0.00009))$. $N(0, 0.00009)$ denotes a normally <u>distributed random</u> variable with mean zero and variance of 0.00009. The standard deviation is $0.15/\sqrt{252}$, or $\sqrt{0.00009}$.

Simulated values of the short straddle assuming that the Nikkei is at 18,759

Figure 13.5

The put and the call have an exercise price of 19,000 and maturity in 90 days. The Nikkei volatility is assumed to be 15 percent, the dividend yield is zero for simplicity, and the interest rate is 4 percent.

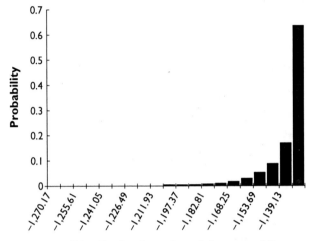

Distribution for value of short straddle

Suppose the Nikkei is at 17,000 instead. In this case, the straddle position is worth –¥1,920.63. Using the delta-gamma VaR, note that the delta of the call option is 0.0947. Hence, the position's delta using put-call parity is 0.81. In other words, a fall of the Nikkei by 100 basis points creates a loss of 81 basis points. The gamma of the call is 0.000132. The gamma of the position is twice the gamma of the call using put-call parity, so that it is two times 0.000132, or 0.000264. Finally, the daily variance of the stock price is the square of 0.15 × 17,000 divided by 252, or 25,803.6. In this case, the variance of the position becomes:

$$
\begin{aligned}
\textbf{Variance of position} \ &= \ \textbf{Var}(-2\Delta c(17{,}000, 19{,}000, t + 0.25, t) + \Delta S) \\
&= \ \textbf{Var}\!\left[-2\delta\Delta S - \gamma(\Delta S)^2 + \Delta S\right] \\
&= \ \textbf{Var}\!\left[0.81\Delta S - \gamma(\Delta S)^2\right] \\
&= \ 0.81^2 \times 25{,}803.6 + 2 \times 0.000132^2 \times 25{,}803.6^2 \\
&= \ 16{,}952.9 \hspace{4cm} \textbf{(13.21)}
\end{aligned}
$$

The VaR of the position is 1.65 times the square root of 16,952.9, namely ¥214.84. If we had neglected to take gamma into account, our estimate of the VaR would have been ¥214.69, which is almost the same number. The reason for the similarity is straightforward: there is little curvature in the value of the position when the Nikkei is 17,000. The contribution of gamma to the VaR of the position is trivial in this case. Computing the VaR with a Monte Carlo simulation, we get instead ¥209.29, which is almost the same number. Figure 13.6 shows the 10,000 simulated values for the short straddle.

Figure 13.6   Simulated values of the short straddle when the Nikkei is at 17,000

The put and the call have an exercise price of 19,000 and maturity in 90 days. The Nikkei volatility is assumed to be 15 percent, the dividend yield is zero for simplicity, and the interest rate is 4 percent.

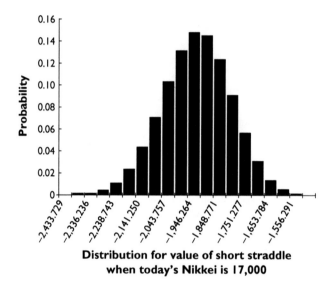

**Distribution for value of short straddle
when today's Nikkei is 17,000**

13.2.4. Stress tests

As in the case of Barings, nonlinear payoffs can make VaR estimates spectacularly wrong. A VaR estimate can be wrong for many reasons. For example, we could have made the wrong assumptions, taken an unwise shortcut, or made a computational mistake. Even if we do everything right, though, VaR can fail to tell us about what some risk managers call black holes. In black holes, the portfolio's exposure to one risk factor or several risk factors is extraordinarily large, leading to extremely large losses.

Suppose a trader has bought 10 calls on IBM with exercise price of $101 and sold five calls with exercise price of $100 and five calls with exercise price of $102. Figure 13.7 plots the payoff of that position. If the price of IBM shares tomorrow is less than $100 or higher than $102, the trader owes nothing. If the price of IBM is $101, the trader owes $5, which is his maximum possible loss. The trader could scale such a position—say, multiply the size of the trades by $1 million, in which case he would owe $5 million. For a VaR estimate to pick up this black hole, it requires the trader's book to be valued for stock prices between $100 and $102. Such stock prices may have an extremely low probability of occurring, so that they may have no impact on VaR.

We know that the firm should eliminate risks it does not have a comparative advantage in bearing. It should therefore seek out and eliminate black holes, and VaR is not enough to do this. The firm would be able to spot such black holes if it plotted the value of the trader's book tomorrow against the price of IBM as in Figure 13.7. Plots of positions like this are called stress tests. Stress tests are computations of the value of portfolios for specific values of risk factors. Here, we

A trader's black hole   *Figure 13.7*

This example has the payoff of a position where a trader sells five calls on IBM maturing tomorrow with exercise price of $100, buys 10 calls with exercise price of $101, sells five calls with exercise price of $102.

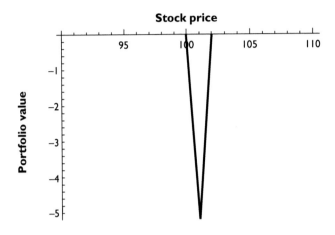

compute the value of the portfolio for a range of values. An alternative is to study a scenario we are concerned about. For example, we might compute the value of the trader's book if the events of the stock market crash of October 1987 were to repeat themselves.

Stress tests are routine in risk management. Chase describes its stress testing in its 1999 annual report for the corporation as a whole. It states that its "corporate stress tests are built around changes in market rates and prices that result from pre-specified economic scenarios, including both historical and hypothetical events." It then goes on to explain that each stress test involves the specification of more than 11,000 individual shocks to market rates and prices involving more than 60 countries. As of the end of 1999, Chase had six historical and five hypothetical stress tests scenarios. These scenarios included the 1994 bond sell-off, the 1994 Mexican peso crisis, and the 1998 Russian bond default crisis. Chase performs such stress tests monthly or whenever it has concerns that it wants to investigate. In 1999, its average stress test loss for its trading portfolio was pre-tax $186 million. Its largest stress test loss was $302 million for the Russian crisis scenario, compared to the VaR of its portfolio of only $23.2 million at the end of 1999. Chase used the historical VaR computed using one trading year of data. At the end of 1999, the Russian crisis played no role in the historical VaR computation since it had taken place sixteen months before the end of 1999. Chase also performs weekly stress tests at the trading desk level.

Let's go back to Barings. Suppose that it had a stress test asking: What would happen if the Nikkei falls by 10 percent and Nikkei volatility increases by 10 percent? The value of the puts and calls that they were short in would have increased by 80 percent.

13.3. Portfolio insurance

A **portfolio insurance** strategy makes the investor's payoff at maturity of the strategy the maximum of his initial wealth or of the value of a diversified portfolio. If the diversified portfolio does well, the investor gains from exposure to risky assets, but if the diversified portfolio does poorly, the investor does not lose principal. Such a strategy implies that the investor obtains a nonlinear payoff at maturity since it does not depend on the value of the diversified portfolio at maturity if the value of that portfolio at maturity has fallen below the principal and otherwise increases dollar for dollar with the value of the diversified portfolio.

Such a payoff can be replicated using options, or we can replicate the payoff by trading dynamically in the risk-free asset and the diversified portfolio. Consequently, a money manager could offer such a payoff to his clients whether options are traded or not. Since the probability of a loss is zero but the probability of no gain is generally greater than 0.05, it follows that the 5 percent VaR of a portfolio insurance strategy is usually 0. Hence, portfolio insurance strategies allow us to reduce the VaR of a portfolio to zero.

Let's see how we could implement portfolio insurance. Consider an investor who has available 1 million Swiss francs. This investor wants to invest in the Swiss market for 12 weeks but wants to be sure that in 12 weeks his wealth will be at least 1 million Swiss francs. If the investor simply invests in the Swiss market portfolio, there is no guarantee that in 12 weeks his wealth will be at least 1 million Swiss francs. The investor wants us to create an investment strategy that allows him to invest in the Swiss market portfolio but also insures him against losses. The Swiss value-weighted market index, SMI, has a value of 1,577 when the investor comes to us.

Let the investor hold n shares of the Swiss market portfolio at a price of 1,577 Swiss francs a share and n European put options on the SMI index with exercise price of K. The current value of the portfolio must be 1 million Swiss francs:

$$n \times p(\text{SMI, K, T, } t) + n \times 1{,}577 = 1\text{M} \qquad (13.22)$$

where T is the date of the end of the insurance period and $p(\text{SMI, K, T, } t)$ is the price of the European put. We assume that the put price is given by the Black-Scholes formula. In this case, we have two unknowns, K and n, and one equation. We also have to impose the constraint that at T the investor has at least 1 million Swiss francs:

$$n \times \text{Max}(\text{K} - \text{SMI, 0}) + n \times \text{SMI} \geq 1\text{M} \qquad (13.23)$$

If K is smaller than $1\text{M}/n$, there is always some chance that the SMI will fall enough that this inequality will not be satisfied. For instance, if nK is 999,999, the equation will not be satisfied if the SMI is equal to zero. If we choose K = $1\text{M}/n$, the equation is always satisfied. We therefore have to use this value of K. Then, we can substitute it in equation (13.22), which becomes:

$$n \times p(1{,}577, 1{,}000{,}000/n, \text{T, } t) + n \times 1{,}577 = 1\text{M} \qquad (13.24)$$

With our example, we have 84 days to maturity. The volatility of the index is 21.04 percent and the risk-free rate is 6.5 percent. The number of shares of the index that solves equation (13.24), obtained by iteration, is 584.70. This leads to an exercise price per share of 1,710.28 Swiss francs. The price of a put option with that exercise price is 133.281 Swiss francs. If the options can be purchased, then wealth can be insured without manufacturing the options synthetically.

Table 13.1 shows how wealth evolves when it is insured with a put option and when it is not over the next 12 weeks. Not surprisingly, the uninsured wealth falls more than the insured wealth as the SMI falls initially. Since the SMI ends above its initial level, the insured portfolio does not get all the gain in the index because the investor pays a premium for the puts.

Suppose next that the options cannot be purchased directly. We know that a put can be replicated by shorting the underlying and investing in the risk-free asset. The formula for a put, equation (12.15), is:

$$p(S, K, T, t) = S\big[N(d) - 1\big] + P_t(T)K\Big[1 - N\big(d - \sigma\sqrt{T - t}\big)\Big]$$

$$\text{where } d = \frac{\ln\big(S/P_t(T)K\big)}{\sigma\sqrt{T - t}} + \frac{1}{2}\,\sigma\sqrt{T - t} \tag{13.25}$$

Portfolio insurance for 12 weeks	*Table 13.1*

An investor has SFR 1 million which he wants to invest in the Swiss index, SMI, in such a way that after 12 weeks his wealth will be at least SFR 1 million. The SMI is initially at 1,577. Its volatility is 21.04 percent. The risk-free rate is 6.5 percent.

			Wealth with portfolio insurance when the put is replicated dynamically					
			Before rebalancing				After rebalancing	
Week	Wealth without portfolio insurance	Wealth with portfolio insurance: Put purchased	Index investment	Risk-free asset investment	Total wealth		Index investment	Risk-free asset investment
0	1,000,000	1,000,000			1,000,000		253,108	746,892
1	985,796	996,533	249,513	747,822	997,335		195,247	802,088
2	970,831	993,943	192,283	803,088	995,371		139,737	855,634
3	966,709	993,540	139,143	856,700	995,843		114,898	880,945
4	947,495	992,154	112,614	882,043	994,657		62,903	931,754
5	996,006	997,574	66,124	932,915	999,039		159,432	839,607
6	1,030,657	1,004,748	165,299	840,653	1,005,952		281,751	724,201
7	1,030,438	1,003,141	281,145	725,104	1,006,249		246,845	759,404
8	1,054,217	1,008,473	252,542	760,350	1,012,892		348,970	663,922
9	1,039,252	1,002,714	344,016	664,749	1,008,765		224,808	783,957
10	1,070,197	1,009,467	231,502	784,933	1,016,435		404,586	611,849
11	1,083,766	1,011,361	409,716	612,612	1,022,328		515,243	507,085
12	1,108,117	1,021,763	526,820	507,717	1,034,537			

The first term of the put formula gives us the value of the position in the stock required to replicate the put and the second term gives us the value of the position in the risk-free asset. Using this formula, to replicate a put on one share we go short $1 - N(d)$ shares and invest $p(S, K, T, t) - S(t)[1 - N(d)]$ in the risk-free asset. With traded puts, we had an investment in n puts and n shares of the index. Replicating the puts dynamically, we achieve the right number of shares of the index by selling $n[N(d) - 1]$ shares so that we are left with $n \times N(d)$ shares. Remember that $N(d)$ is the call's δ, so that the strategy involves investing $n\delta$ shares in the index, where n is determined when the strategy is initiated. As the index rises, we know that δ increases. Table 13.1 shows the investments in the stock and the risk-free asset over time when the put option is manufactured synthetically.

Table 13.1 also tells us that the portfolio of stocks and risk-free investment puts 25.31 percent of its funds in the market. Consequently, the return volatility of the portfolio using the delta method is 0.2531×0.2104, or 5.33 percent. The VaR using the delta approximation is therefore $1.65 \times 0.0533 \times 1M$, or \$87,945. Using the delta-VaR, we would find that the portfolio has a positive VaR. Yet, we know that the true VaR is zero.

This example makes two points. First, for a static portfolio where portfolio insurance is implemented by buying puts, the delta-VaR overestimates the true VaR. Second, if a dynamic strategy is implemented, the VaR computed using portfolio weights at a particular time is an inaccurate measure of the risk over a period of time over which the weights change. With portfolio insurance, the weights are changed to reduce risk. The opposite could take place, though. Hence, if we compute VaR over a period of time which involves portfolio changes, it is not enough to know the portfolio at the start of the period. We must also take into account the firm's trading strategies.

Dynamic replication of the put option involves trades in the underlying asset. In the case of an index, this means trading the components of the index. Such a strategy will be expensive if rebalancing takes place often. In the example of Table 13.1, rebalancing takes place once a week. A rule that requires rebalancing at fixed intervals of time generally can be improved upon. Suppose that after one week the index has changed little. In this case, it probably does not make sense to rebalance if there are significant transaction costs. Remember that delta hedging becomes less accurate as the underlying asset changes more in value. Therefore, a better approach is to rebalance only when the index changes by a large enough amount. For example, one could choose a threshold of 2 percent, and rebalance whenever the index changes by 2 percent.

It will be cheaper to trade in futures than in the underlying asset if there are futures or forward contracts on the underlying asset. Suppose first that we have a forward contract. We know that investing the present value of the forward price in the risk-free asset and taking a long forward position amounts to taking a synthetic position in the underlying asset. The only difference with using a futures contract instead of a forward contract is that the futures contract is marked to market, so the futures position has to be tailed appropriately. One also has to be prepared to make payments when the futures position evolves adversely.

13.4. Using options to hedge quantity risk

Quantity risk shows up when we have an exposure to a risk factor but do not know the size of this exposure because it depends on future developments. An example of quantity risk is the case where a firm makes a bid in foreign currency. If the firm gets the bid, it has exposure in foreign currency for the amount of the bid. If it fails, it has no foreign currency exposure. It is often argued that a good use of options is to hedge bids made in foreign currency.

To investigate this, we consider the simplest possible example. Bidder Inc. makes a bid on January 15 to deliver goods on September 15 for 10 million Swiss francs. Assume for simplicity that on the same day the firm finds out whether it won the bid, delivers the goods, and gets paid. Let's assume that on January 15 the forward rate for delivery on September 15 is $0.52 per Swiss franc.

If Bidder uses a forward contract to hedge and sells 10 million Swiss francs forward on January 15 for delivery on September 15, it guarantees receipt of $5.2 million on September 15 if the bid succeeds. The problem with selling forward 10 million Swiss francs is that Bidder has to deliver 10 million Swiss francs on September 15 that it has to buy in the market if the bid does not succeed. If, at that time, the Swiss franc is worth more dollars than the forward price agreed upon on January 15, Bidder makes a loss on its forward contract. This loss is potentially unbounded—there is no limit on how much the dollar price of the Swiss franc could increase between January 15 and September 15.

The traditional argument is that a firm like Bidder should hedge with options to avoid the possibility of a large forward loss if it does not get the contract. Suppose that instead of selling 10 million Swiss francs on the forward market, Bidder buys a European put option to sell 10 million Swiss francs maturing on September 15 with exercise price set equal to the forward price of $0.52 per Swiss franc. If the bid fails, the firm can simply sell the put option. With the option position, the maximum loss Bidder can incur is equal to the premium paid for the put option plus the opportunity cost of the money invested in the option.

Suppose Bidder wants to minimize cash flow at risk, CaR, and has no other cash flow than the one it will receive from the bid and, possibly, from its hedges. Intuition suggests that the put strategy should be advantageous for a firm concerned about CaR since the put strategy limits the worst loss—i.e., the loss that occurs when the firm does not get the bid and further loses on its hedge. We show that this intuition is not correct with our assumptions. Not only may the firm be better off not hedging, but the put hedge is never the firm's best strategy for our example.

To understand when a firm using CaR may find that it does not pay to hedge a bid, we consider the CaR at the 95 percent confidence level computed on January 15 for cash flows available on September 15. Since the put hedge requires payment of a premium on January 15, we borrow on January 15 the price of the put premium and repay that amount on September 15. Let's assume that whether the firm succeeds in the bid or not does not depend on the exchange rate and that the probability of success is 0.8. We assume further that the expected spot exchange rate for September 15 is equal to the forward price, so that there is no risk premium attached to foreign exchange risks by the capital markets; a currency expected payoff can thus be discounted at the risk-free rate. Finally, to simplify the analysis, we assume that the spot exchange rate is lognormally distributed with a volatility of 15 percent and an expected rate of change of zero. The continuously compounded risk-free rate is assumed to be 6 percent in the United States and in Switzerland.

We can use Monte Carlo analysis to obtain estimates of CaR. We have to use two distributions: the assumed lognormal distribution for the exchange rate and a distribution for the bid outcome.[7] The cash flow for the firm if it does not hedge is:

$$S \times 10M \qquad \text{with probability 0.8}$$
$$0 \qquad \text{with probability 0.2}$$

where S is the price of a Swiss franc on September 15.

If the firm sells 10 million Swiss francs at the forward exchange rate of $0.52, its cash flow is:

$$\$5.2M \qquad \text{with probability 0.8}$$
$$(\$0.52 - S_{September\ 15}) \times 10M \qquad \text{with probability 0.2}$$

The firm's cash flow if it does not get the bid is the gain from the forward position. The forward position makes a profit if the spot exchange rate is lower than $0.52 per Swiss franc and makes a loss otherwise.

Finally, we consider the cash flow if the firm uses a put to hedge. With the put, the firm acquires the right to sell 10 million Swiss francs at $0.52 per Swiss franc. The price of such a put on January 15 is $243,959 using the Black-Scholes formula with our assumptions. At 6 percent interest, the firm has to pay $253,915 (compounding continuously) on September 15 to reimburse the loan it took out to pay for the put. The firm's cash flow if it gets the bid is equal to the proceeds from selling 10 million Swiss francs minus the amount paid to reimburse the loan plus the put payoff. The put payoff is $Max(0.52 - S, 0) \times 10M$. Consequently, the firm's cash flow with the put hedge is:

$$S \times 10M - \$253,915 + Max(0.52 - S, 0) \times 10M \qquad \text{with probability 0.8}$$
$$- \$253,915 + Max(0.52 - S, 0) \times 10M \qquad \text{with probability 0.2}$$

Figure 13.8 shows the distribution of the cash flows for the three hedging strategies. The first result to notice is that the distribution is bimodal for all strategies. This is perhaps not surprising: the firm either gets the bid or it does not. The second result is that the firm's cash flow can be negative if it hedges but not otherwise. Without hedging, the worst outcome for the firm is that it earns nothing.

---

7 In @Risk, we use RiskDiscrete({1,0},{80,20}). S(September 15) is distributed as 0.52Exp(Risk-Normal(−0.5 × 0.15², 0.15).

Distribution of cash flow under alternate hedging strategies   *Figure 13.8*

The figure gives cash flow in million dollars. It shows that with hedging cash flow can be negative while absent hedging it can never be negative.

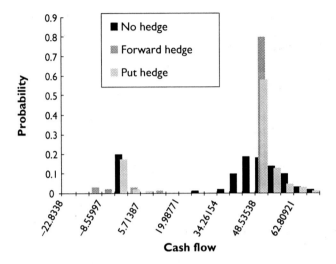

With a forward or put position, the worst outcome is that the firm loses on the hedge when it does not succeed with the bid. Under our assumptions, the probability of not receiving the bid and losing on the hedge is greater than 0.05. As a result, the worst cash flow at the 95 percent confidence interval is a negative cash flow for a firm that hedges, but zero for a firm that does not hedge. The estimates for CaR from the Monte Carlo analysis are $4.16 million for the case where the firm does not hedge, $4.63 million for the forward hedge, and $4.67 million for the put hedge. The firm has the lowest CaR when it does not hedge.

The CaR depends on the probability that the bid will succeed. If we assume instead that the probability of success is 0.96, the CaR is $1.36 million if the firm does not hedge, zero if the firm hedges with the forward contract, and $100,000 if the firm hedges with the put. When success in the bid is highly likely, the firm minimizes its CaR by using the forward contract to hedge. The reason is that unsuccessful bid outcomes are irrelevant for CaR because the probability of not succeeding is too small, so that the firm's CaR depends on what happens when it is successful. The firm can eliminate all risk for the outcomes when it gets the bid by selling the currency proceeds forward.

With our assumptions, the put hedge is never the firm's CaR-minimizing strategy regardless of the probability of success of the bid. The reason for this is straightforward: It does not pay to hedge if the CaR corresponds to the firm's cash flow when it does not get the bid and loses on the hedge. If the CaR corresponds to the firm's cash flow when it does not get the bid but makes a profit on the hedge, the payoff of the forward contract and of the put are the same at maturity, but the firm must still reimburse the loan it took on to pay for the put, so that it is better off with the forward contract than with the put. Finally, if the CaR corresponds to the firm's cash flow when it receives the bid, it has a perfect hedge only with the forward contract, so that the forward strategy minimizes CaR in that case.

Risk management does not mean that the firm should always hedge. It should hedge only when doing so increases shareholder wealth. Knowing how to analyze the impact of a hedge on CaR is crucial in figuring out whether a hedge reduces CaR or not. Monte Carlo estimation of CaR lets us analyze the impact on CaR of alternative hedging strategies.

13.5. Summary

Measuring and hedging the risk of nonlinear payoffs is at the heart of risk management. And nonlinear payoffs can be approximated well with a number of option pricing tools to measure and hedge their risk. Armed with an option pricing formula, we can measure the risk of options using a number of different methods. The simplest method, the so-called delta-VaR method, uses the delta-exposure approximation. This method can find risk when there is none (in the case of portfolio insurance) and can also conceal risk when there is plenty (as in the case of Leeson's straddles). In full-valuation Monte Carlo VaR methods, option values are computed for each possible outcome. Such methods can be implemented using binomial trees, Monte Carlo analysis, or historical data. VaR can be computed for individual options, for portfolios of options on one underlying asset, and for portfolios of options on multiple underlying assets. The methods we develop can also be applied when option prices are affected by multiple risk factors. In the last two sections, we applied our techniques of measuring and hedging the risk of nonlinear payoffs to portfolio insurance and to the hedging of a bid made in foreign currency. Surprisingly, and contrary to popular beliefs, a firm can have a lower CaR if it does not hedge the currency risk of a bid than if it does.

Key Concepts

delta-VaR, 398
delta-VaR method, 399
full valuation Monte Carlo method, 409

historical VaR, 409
portfolio insurance, 418
structured Monte Carlo method, 408

Review Questions

1. How is an option's delta useful in computing the VaR of an option?

2. How can you transform a portfolio of option positions into a portfolio of positions in the underlyings?

3. Why could delta-VaR lead you to believe that a portfolio has no risk when in fact it has substantial risk?

4. Why are stress tests useful?

5. What is the delta-gamma VaR?

6. Why is the delta-gamma VaR difficult to compute?

7. How does one compute the full valuation historical VaR for a portfolio of derivatives?

8. How could you insure a portfolio if you cannot buy the appropriate put options?

9. Why is a bid hedged with a forward contract risky?

10. Why could you be better off not hedging the currency exposure in a bid?

Questions and Exercises

1. Consider a portfolio of 1,000 shares and 100 call options on a stock with price $50. The call options have an exercise price of $75 and a maturity of six months. The volatility of the stock is 30 percent and the interest rate is 5 percent. Using the delta-VaR method, what is the one-day VaR of this portfolio?

2. Suppose that in question 1 the portfolio has a short position of 1,000 shares instead of a long position. The proceeds from the short-sale are invested in the risk-free asset. How does the VaR differ from the VaR you computed in question 1?

3. Compute the VaR for a portfolio that has a long position in the euro. It holds an investment in euro zero-coupon bonds that mature in six months with an annualized continuously compounded interest rate of 6 percent. The face value of the investment is euro 1 million. The spot exchange rate is assumed to be $0.40. It is assumed that the German interest rate is constant and that the U.S. interest rate of 5 percent is also constant. In addition to the euro zero-coupon bonds, the portfolio holds puts on the euro for a total of euro 1 million with exercise price of $0.50 and has short call positions for a total of euro 0.5 million with an exercise price of $0.60. The puts and calls have a maturity of six months. The volatility of the euro exchange rate is assumed to be 10 percent. What is the dollar value of the portfolio today? By how much does that value change if the exchange rate increases by $0.01?

4. Using the data in question 3, compute the delta-VaR of the portfolio.

5. Compute gamma, γ, for the call option priced in question 1.

6. Using the result in question 1, compute the change in the option price using the delta-gamma approximation for a change in the stock price of $1 and a change in the stock price of $10. Does gamma allow you to get a better estimate?

7. Compute the delta-gamma VaR for the portfolio in question 1 using the γ computed in question 5.

8. In section 13.3, we show that using the delta-VaR method implies that an insured portfolio has a positive VaR. Would using the delta-gamma VaR method solve this problem?

9. In 1998, observers were arguing that the market turmoil would have been less damaging had investors used portfolio insurance more. However, the general assessment was that it was not used more because it was too expensive. What determines the cost of portfolio insurance? What does an increase in the cost of portfolio insurance imply for the payoff of the insured portfolio?

10. An importer bid on a shipment of materials. The bid is in yen and the firm will discover whether it owns the materials in two months. What is the exchange rate exposure that results from the bid? Should the firm hedge it? How?

Literature Note

The methods to compute VaR described in this chapter are discussed extensively in the RiskMetrics™ technical manual. Picou (1997) provides a more advanced discussion of using Monte Carlo to compute VaR. Pritsker (2001) discusses some problems with historical simulation. The portfolio insurance example comes from Stucki, Stulz, and Wasserfallen (1989). Leland (1985) provides an analysis of who should buy portfolio insurance. Rubinstein (1985) shows alternative ways to implement portfolio insurance. Etzioni (1986) and Bookstaber and Langsam (1988) discuss some of the issues associated with dynamic replication of insured portfolio payoffs. Dufey and Giddy (1995) discuss uses of currency options by corporations. The Risk book titled *VaR: Understanding and applying value-at-risk* has a good collection of classic papers on VaR (1997, Risk Publications, London). Duffie and Pan (1997) provide a technical survey of issues concerning the estimation of VaR. Jorion (2001) has a book focused on VaR, including the implications of Leeson's straddles for delta-VaR estimates. The facts concerning Barings and Leeson come from Rawnsley (1995).

Chapter 14

Options on Bonds and Interest Rates

Chapter **14** *Objectives*

At the end of this chapter, you will:

1. Understand how to hedge with caps, floors, and bond options.

2. Know how to price and evaluate the risk of caps, floors, and bond options.

3. Become an informed user of fixed income derivative pricing models.

There is no derivative that is more commonly used than an option on a bond, but most of the time, that derivative is embedded and disguised. Consider Mortgage Emporium, a bank that mostly writes mortgages. All its mortgages can be prepaid without penalty for the principal balance of the mortgage plus the interest due. Absent transaction costs, if interest rates fall so that the present value of the mortgage payments exceeds the mortgage principal balance plus the interest due, the borrower benefits from refinancing. Let $M(t)$ be the value of the mortgage at time t without prepayment option and $K(t)$ the mortgage principal balance plus the interest due. It is optimal for the borrower to prepay when $M(t)$ exceeds $K(t)$. If the borrower exercises the prepayment option, she pays $K(t)$ and receives $M(t)$, making a gain of $M(t) - K(t)$. This gain the borrower receives is the payoff of a call option on $M(t)$ with exercise price $K(t)$, $\text{Max}[M(t) - K(t), 0]$, since $M(t) - \text{Max}[M(t) - K(t), 0] = K(t)$ in that case. The value of the mortgage with prepayment option for Mortgage Emporium is therefore equal to the value of a mortgage without prepayment option minus the value of a call option on that mortgage with exercise price equal to the mortgage principal balance plus the interest due.

The borrower owes Mortgage Emporium the present value of the mortgage payments on a mortgage that cannot be prepaid, but in addition she has an asset, the prepayment option, that reduces the present value of her liability. Since the prepayment option can be exercised at any time, the borrower holds an American call option on $M(t)$ with exercise price $K(t)$. The present value of the mortgage is equivalent to the present value of the interest payments on an amortizing callable bond issued by the mortgage borrower and the prepayment option of the mortgage is equivalent to a bond call option. All mortgage borrowers are therefore long the equivalent of a call option on a bond in their portfolio.

The prepayment option creates important risk management issues for Mortgage Emporium. Absent the call option, a bond price is a convex function of interest rates. However, the call option reduces the value of the bond since the borrower may prepay when the value of the bond exceeds the exercise price of the call option. Consequently, to hedge the mortgage against changes in interest rates, Mortgage Emporium has to take into account the impact of interest rate changes on the value of the prepayment option of the mortgage. To do that, it has to know how the prepayment option is valued and how its value depends on interest rates. In a world without transaction costs where everybody prepays when it is optimal to do so, Mortgage Emporium has to value a call option on the mortgage with exercise price equal to the mortgage principal balance and interest due. Since the real world has transaction costs and since individuals do not always prepay when they might benefit from doing so, valuing the prepayment option is generally more complex than valuing a call option on a bond, but valuing a call option on a bond is the starting point for valuing the prepayment option.

To see why interest rate options might be useful, consider Steady Inc. that has $100 million of floating-rate debt indexed to LIBOR. With such debt, the interest payment over a payment period is determined on the reset date shortly before the start of the payment period, so that the firm does not know its debt service payments beyond the current payment period. Unexpectedly high interest payments could force the firm into financial distress. Suppose Steady Inc. wants to reduce the risk of financial distress but still benefit from higher cash flows if rates fall. To achieve its risk management objective, the firm would most likely buy a cap. A **cap** pays the difference between the floating rate payment and what the payment would be at a contracted fixed rate, the **cap rate**, whenever this difference is positive during the life of the cap. We show in this chapter how caps are used to hedge and present a simple and popular approach to price caps that uses the Black-Scholes approach to pricing options.

The Black-Scholes formula assumes that the price of the underlying asset follows a lognormal distribution and that the interest rate does not change randomly. Neither of these two assumptions makes much sense when pricing bond options. Because nominal interest rates cannot be negative, the highest price a zero-coupon bond can ever have is the bond's par value. If the bond price is lognormally distributed, there is always some probability that its value at maturity of the option will exceed par. Further, bond prices change randomly only if interest rates change randomly.

As with the pricing of options on stocks, bond options can be priced using two approaches. First, we can construct a binomial tree. Second, we can apply pricing formulas that hold when trading can take place continuously. Both of these approaches can be used to price bond options avoiding the problems created by the assumptions that have to be satisfied for the Black-Scholes formula to hold. To do that, we generally obtain the distribution of bond prices by allowing the discount rate for bond cash flows to evolve randomly. The distribution of bond prices is then derived by assessing the distribution of the present value of bond cash flows given the process followed by discount rates. This approach ensures that bond prices are at par at maturity. To obtain the distribution of bond prices, we therefore have to start with a model of how discount rates, that is, interest rates, evolve.

Various models based on the binomial approach have been developed to price fixed-income claims. For these models, the construction of bond price trees generally involves a two-step procedure. First, we construct a tree for the spot interest rate or the forward rates. Second, we use this tree to discount the payoffs of the bonds using risk-neutral probabilities. We explain this process in detail.

For interest rates, there is no distribution that is as commonly used as the lognormal distribution for stock prices. We therefore consider the most popular distributions. As with the binomial model for options on stocks, we can consider the limiting case where periods are infinitesimally short. For this case, a number of formulas based on different distributions of interest rates have been provided. We show that the choice of a distribution for interest rates affects how one hedges securities against interest rate changes. We also show that using the wrong model can have dramatic implications for VaR estimates. We discuss some empirical evidence that is helpful in assessing the various models discussed in this chapter.

Throughout the chapter, we assume that bonds are default-free. Bonds with default risk are considered in Chapter 18.

14.1. Caps and floors

We first show how caps can be used and then proceed to discuss how they can be priced using the formula presented in Chapter 12 for the pricing of options on futures. We also show how a floor can be priced. A **floor** is a contract that promises for each payment period to pay the difference between the floor and the contractual interest rate times the principal.

14.1.1. Hedging with caps

Consider Steady Inc. that has $100 million of face value of floating rate debt. The interest rate on the debt is reset every three months at LIBOR prevailing on the reset date. The three-month payment period starts two business days after the reset date. For instance, if LIBOR is 10 percent on the reset date that we assume to be two business days before the end of March, the firm pays $0.25 \times 0.10 \times$ $100M, or $2.5 million on the last business day of June. Two business days before the end of June, LIBOR is at 8 percent. The 8 percent rate determines the payment to be made at the end of September but is irrelevant for the payment to be made at the end of June.

Suppose that Steady Inc. concludes that it wants to benefit from low interest rates, but would be in trouble if it had to make payments at an annual rate that exceeds 8 percent. The firm would like to pay at most $0.25 \times 0.08 \times$ $100M per quarter, or $2 million. To make sure that it does not pay more than $2 million on interest payment dates, the firm can buy a cap at 8 percent for the life of the debt. Figure 14.1 shows the cap rate and the cap payments for an interest rate path assuming eight payment periods. For each interest payment date, the cap pays $0.25 \times Max(RL - 0.08, 0) \times$ $100M, where RL is the decimal LIBOR on the reset date. For the second payment period, LIBOR on the reset date is 10 percent, so that RL is 0.10. Steady Inc. receives a payment from the cap of $0.25 \times$ $Max(0.10 - 0.08, 0) \times$ $100M, or $0.5 million. The firm pays $2.5 million to the bondholders, but after its cap payment of $0.5 million, the net debt service is $2 million, or 8 percent at an annual rate.

Steady Inc. makes the interest payment three months after the reset date. To have a perfect hedge, the firm must receive the payment from the cap when it has to pay interest on its debt, but the value of the payment must be determined at the reset date that is three months before the payment and must equal $0.25 \times$ $Max(RL - 0.08, 0) \times$ $100M, where RL is LIBOR at the reset date. For example, Steady Inc. must receive $0.5 million at the end of June, but that amount must be determined at the end of March. A cap makes payments on the interest payment date based on the interest set at the reset date, so that the firm receives $0.5 million at the end of June even though at that time LIBOR is 8 percent. A cap provides a perfect hedge, given Steady Inc.'s risk management objective.

14.1.2. Pricing caps and floors

An **interest rate call option** pays upon exercise the difference between the current interest rate and a contracted interest rate, the strike, computed on a given amount of principal. Since the principal on which the interest rate payment is computed is not exchanged in the transaction, it is called a notional amount. A European interest rate call option with payment in arrears is an interest rate call option where the payoff is paid not at maturity of the option but at maturity of

Cap payments *Figure 14.1*

In this figure, the firm has a cap at 8 percent for eight payment periods on debt of $100 million with interest rate reset every three months at LIBOR. The interest rate is set at the beginning of a payment period for payment at the end of the period. The cap makes three payments over the eight payment periods. It pays at the end of payment periods 2, 3, and 7.

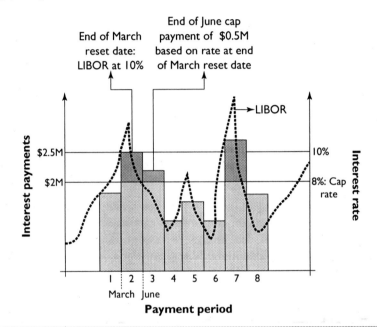

the period over which the interest rate on which the option is written is earned. For instance, a European call option maturing on the last day of March on three-month LIBOR pays LIBOR on that day minus the strike. However, if the option pays in arrears, the payment will be made three months later on the last day of June since that is when a contract entered into at the end of March paying three-month LIBOR would mature. The payoff of a cap for a payment period is equal to the payoff of a European interest rate call option paid in arrears that matures on the reset date for that payment period.

The value of a cap is the present value of its future payments and is therefore the value of a portfolio of European interest rate call options paid in arrears where the portfolio has an option maturing on each date on which a cap payment is determined. The options in this portfolio of options are called caplets. A **caplet** is the claim to a single cap payment.

The underlying in a caplet or in an interest rate option is not a financial asset but an interest rate. We already know that to price an option, we need to be able to construct a portfolio whose value becomes equal to the underlying when the option is exercised. To construct a portfolio that pays an amount equal to an interest rate at maturity, we can use interest rate futures with the futures price computed so that the futures price at maturity is equal to the interest rate. In this case, the current value of the underlying at maturity is the futures price discounted at the risk-free rate.[1] We can therefore look at the present value of a cap payment as a call option on a futures contract on the interest rate with payment in arrears. Since the payments are determined on the reset date, the cap payment as of that date is the present value of the payment received at the end of the payment period. We can therefore value the caplet as an option that pays the cap payment discounted to the reset date.

The Black formula (equation 12.35 in Chapter 12) enables us to price an option on a futures contract. The assumptions require that the futures price follows a lognormal distribution and that the interest rate is constant. It is not unreasonable to assume that the implied futures yield follows a lognormal distribution—the yield cannot be negative and a lognormally distributed variable cannot be negative. Obviously, if we assume that the implied futures yield moves randomly through time, it seems contradictory to assume that the spot interest rate is constant. This compromise is often made in practice because the resulting pricing formula works well. Later in this chapter, we will show how to price fixed income contingent claims without making this compromise.

To compute the payoff of the caplet at the reset date, we must discount the payment of the caplet received on the interest payment date back to the reset date. The amount on which the interest is computed is called the notional amount of the cap, which we denote by NA. Consider a cap with a cap rate of K. The payment based on reset date T is $\tau \times \text{Max}(RL_T - K, 0) \times NA$, where τ is the length of the interest payment period expressed as a fraction of a year (e.g., 0.25 for a quarterly interest payment period). $\text{Max}(RL_T - K, 0)$ is the payoff of a call option on RL_T with exercise price K. The cap payment is made at $T + \tau$. Consequently, at reset date T, the value of the payment to be received at $T + \tau$ is:

$$\left[\frac{1}{1 + \tau RL_T}\right] \tau \times \text{Max}\left(RL_T - K, 0\right) \times NA \qquad (14.1)$$

The term in brackets is the discounting factor. Because of the discounting, the value of the payment at T is a fraction of the payment received at $T + \tau$. As a result, the value of the caplet is equal to the value of receiving a fraction $1/(1 + \tau RL_T)$ of the cap payment at T. We can therefore value the caplet by valuing $1/(1 + \tau RL_T)$ interest rate call options that mature at T.

Typically, we would want to be able to compute the value of the caplet at some date t, $t < T$, when we do not know RL_T. To compute the number of interest rate call options $1/(1 + \tau RL_T)$, we have to guess what RL_T will be. The practice is to use the implied futures yield to compute that number in equation (14.1). A caplet maturing at T is therefore worth $1/[1 + \tau G_t(T)]$ options on the futures

---

1 To see that this works, we need to use what we learned in Chapter 6. We showed there that a tailed position in a futures contract pays an amount at maturity equal to the value of the underlying of the contract at maturity. Suppose that there is a futures contract that pays LIBOR on reset date T and a zero-coupon bond that pays $1 at date T. The futures price at t is $G_t(T)$ and the zero-coupon bond price is $P_t(T)$. A long position of $P_t(T)$ units of the futures contract and an investment of $G_t(T)P_t(T)$ in zero-coupon bonds maturing at T constitute a portfolio that is worth LIBOR on reset date T. To have LIBOR at maturity, we invest all the settlement variation in zero-coupon bonds maturing at date T and the size of the futures position changes as the price of the zero-coupon bond maturing at T changes.

yield of a contract maturing at T, where $G_t(T)$ is the implied LIBOR from the futures market. We can price the caplet using the Black model. The explicit formula is:

Black formula for the pricing of a caplet

Let RL_T be LIBOR at date T, $P_t(T)$ the price at t of a zero-coupon bond that matures at T, $G_t(T)$ the implied LIBOR (100 minus the futures price) from the futures contract that pays RL_T at time T, K the cap rate or strike price of the option, NA the notional amount, T the reset date, τ the length of the payment period (so that the cap payment is made at $T + \tau$), $N(d)$ the cumulative normal distribution evaluated at d, and σ the volatility of the implied futures yield. The price of a caplet is:

$$\textbf{CAPLET }(\textbf{RL, K, NA, T, }t) = \frac{\tau \textbf{NA}}{1 + \tau G_t(T)}\, P_t(T)\big[G_t(T)N(d_1) - KN(d_2)\big]$$

$$d_1 = \frac{\ln\big(G_t(T)/K\big) + \sigma^2(T-t)/2}{\sigma\sqrt{(T-t)}}$$

$$d_2 = \frac{\ln\big(G_t(T)/K\big) - \sigma^2(T-t)/2}{\sigma\sqrt{(T-t)}} \qquad \textbf{(14.2)}$$

Let's look at the pricing of a caplet bought by Steady Inc. We price the caplet at the start of the first payment period. In this example, the cap rate is at 8 percent, the notional amount is $100 million, the maturity of the caplet is three months, and the length of the payment period is three months. The futures index for a contract maturing in three months is assumed to be at 92.5, so that the current implied futures yield is 7.5 percent. Let's say that the volatility of the implied futures yield is 15 percent annually and that a bond that pays one dollar in three months sells for $0.9814. With our notation, we have NA = 100M, $P_t(t + 0.25)$ = 0.9814, $G_t(t + 0.25)$ = 0.075, K = 0.08, σ = 0.15, τ = 0.25, and T = t + 0.25. It follows that the price of the caplet is given by:

$$\textbf{CAPLET }(\textbf{RL, 0.08, 100M, }t + \textbf{0.25, }t)$$

$$= \frac{0.25 \times 100M}{1 + .0.25 \times 0.075} \times 0.9814 \times \big[0.075N(-0.8230) - 0.08N(-0.8980)\big]$$

$$= \$15,091.3 \qquad \textbf{(14.3)}$$

If the futures yield is 8.5 percent, so that the caplet is in the money, we have a price of $137,715. Figure 14.2 shows how the value of the cap payment depends on maturity and volatility. For short maturities, the value of the cap payment is not very sensitive to volatility, but as maturity increases, it becomes much more sensitive to volatility.

This approach can be used for the case where a financial institution has made a floating rate loan and is concerned about its revenue from the loan. If revenue is low, the financial institution could have insufficient income to finance its expenses. An alternative to hedging with futures is to use a floor. When it buys a

Figure 14.2   Cap value as a function of maturity and volatility

The assumptions made for this figure are that the cap is for only one quarterly interest payment on a notional amount of $100 million with a cap rate of 8 percent. The Black futures formula is used as explained in the text. The interest rate and the implied futures yield are both at 7.5 percent annually.

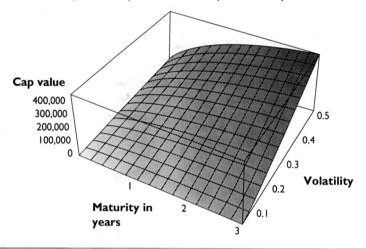

floor, the financial institution effectively receives the payment of a put on the interest rate on each payment date:

$$NA \times Max(K - RL_T, 0) \tag{14.4}$$

where NA is the notional amount, K is the floor rate, and T is a reset date on the loan contract. A **floorlet** is a claim to one payment of a floor. The value of a floor is the value of the portfolio of floorlets that compose the floor. Using put-call parity (remember that the underlying here is the present value of the futures price using the risk-free rate as the discount rate), we can price a floorlet from a caplet. We have:

Black's formula for the pricing of a floorlet

Let RL_T be LIBOR at date T, $P_t(T)$ the price of a zero-coupon bond at time t that pays \$1 matures at T, $G_t(T)$ the implied LIBOR (100 minus the futures price) from the futures contract that pays RL_T at time T, K the cap rate, NA the notional amount, T the reset date, τ the length of the payment period (so that the cap payment is made at $T + \tau$), $N(d)$ the cumulative normal distribution evaluated at d, and σ the volatility of the implied futures yield. The price of a floorlet is:

$$\text{FLOORLET}(RL, K, NA, T, t) = \frac{\tau NA}{1 + \tau G_t(T)} P_t(T)\Big[KN(-d_2) - G_t(T)N(-d_1)\Big]$$

$$d_1 = \frac{\ln\big(G_t(T)/K\big) + \sigma^2(T - t)/2}{\sigma\sqrt{(T - t)}}$$

$$d_2 = \frac{\ln\big(G_t(T)/K\big) - \sigma^2(T - t)/2}{\sigma\sqrt{(T - t)}} \tag{14.5}$$

Consider again Steady Inc. that borrowed at a floating rate and wants to protect itself against high interest rates. Purchasing a cap requires that the firm pays a premium. One way to reduce the cash outlay associated with the purchase of a cap is to simultaneously sell a floor. The simultaneous purchase of a cap and sale of a floor is called a **collar**. Suppose that the firm sells a floor at 7 percent. If the rate in three months is 6 percent, the firm will have to pay $0.25 \times 100M \times 0.01$, which amounts to $250,000. For simplicity, we assume that the cap and floor make only one payment.

To compute the cash outlay if the firm buys this collar, we have to price the floor. This is straightforward using the Black floor formula:

FLOORLET$(RL, 0.07, 100M, t + 0.25, t)$

$$= \frac{0.25 \times 100M}{1 + 0.25 \times 0.75} \times 0.9814\left[0.07 \times N\left(-0.8824\right) - 0.075 \times N\left(-0.9574\right)\right]$$

$$= \frac{0.25 \times 100M}{1 + 0.25 \times .075} \times 0.9814\left[0.07 \times 0.188779 - 0.075 \times 0.169181\right]$$

$$= \$12,665.82$$

$$d_1 = \frac{\ln\left(0.075/0.07\right) + 0.15^2\left(0.25\right)/2}{0.15\sqrt{0.25}} = 0.9574$$

$$d_2 = \frac{\ln\left(0.075/0.07\right) - 0.15^2\left(0.25\right)/2}{0.15\sqrt{0.25}} = 0.8824 \tag{14.6}$$

We already know that the price of the cap in this case is $15,091.30. Consequently, if the firm sells a floor at 7 percent, it has a collar with cost of $15,091.30 – $12,666.80, which is $2,424.50. By raising the strike of the floor, we could end up with income from the floor that equals the cost of the cap, a costless collar, so that Steady Inc. can protect itself against high interest rates without a cash outflow.

14.2. Hedging with options and measuring the interest rate exposure of bond options

Suppose that a mutual fund manager, Mr. Kaufman, is concerned about threats to the value of his fund, the Safe Bond Fund, which includes bonds only. The value of the Safe Bond Fund portfolio at today's prices is $120 million. Mr. Kaufman would like to make sure that in one year the value of the portfolio is not less than $100 million. Coupon payments are paid out to investors in the fund as they accrue, so that the value of the portfolio at the end of the year does not include the reinvested coupon payments. Mr. Kaufman wants portfolio insurance for a bond portfolio. We saw with stocks that one way to guarantee that the value of a portfolio will not fall below some amount is to buy a put on the portfolio. In the case of Safe Bond Fund, the equivalent strategy is to buy a put on the bond portfolio with an exercise price of $100 million.

We know how to price options if the underlying asset is a financial asset whose value follows a lognormal distribution. Let's assume here that the value of the bond portfolio follows a lognormal distribution with a dividend payment equal to the coupon payment of the portfolio. Consequently, we can apply the Black-Scholes formula as follows:

The Black-Scholes formula to value call and put options on a bond or bond portfolio

Let W be the value of a bond portfolio, PVC the present value of coupons to be paid by the portfolio before time T, K the exercise price, T the maturity, $N(d)$ the cumulative normal distribution evaluated at d, and $P_t(T)$ the current value of a zero-coupon bond that pays \$1 at T. The prices at t of a call and a put on the portfolio with exercise price K and the maturity T are, respectively:

$$c(W - PVC, K, T, t) = (W - PVC)N(d_1) - P_t(T)KN(d_2)$$

$$p(W - PVC, K, T, t) = P_t(T)KN(-d_2) - (W - PVC)N(-d_1)$$

$$d_1 = \frac{\ln\left[(W - PVC)/(P_t(T)K)\right] + 0.5\sigma^2(T - t)}{\sigma\sqrt{(T - t)}}$$

$$d_2 = \frac{\ln\left[(W - PVC)/(P_t(T)K)\right] - 0.5\sigma^2(T - t)}{\sigma\sqrt{(T - t)}} \quad \text{(14.7)}$$

Let's apply the formula to price the put that would insure the mutual fund manager's portfolio for one year. We assume that the volatility of the return of the bonds is 10 percent. In this case, we know that W is \$120, K is \$100M, $T - t$ is equal to one, and σ is equal to 0.1. We have to compute the present value of the coupon payments. Let's say that the portfolio pays coupons worth \$2.5 million in three and nine months. Assume that the price of a zero-coupon bond maturing in three months is \$0.98 per dollar, in nine months is \$0.95 per dollar, and in 12 months is \$0.93. The present value of the coupon payments is therefore:

$$0.98 \times \$2.5M + 0.95 \times \$2.5M = \$4.825M \quad \text{(14.8)}$$

Using the put formula, we have:

$$p(W - PVC, K, T, t) = 0.93 \times 100M \times N(-2.08853)$$

$$- (120M - 4.825M)N(-2.18853) = \$0.06$$

$$d_1 = \frac{\ln\left[(120M - 4.825M)/(0.93 \times 100M)\right] + 0.5 \times 0.1^2}{0.1} = 2.18853$$

$$d_2 = \frac{\ln\left[(120M - 4.825M)/(0.93 \times 100M)\right] - 0.5 \times 0.1^2}{0.1} = 2.08853 \quad \text{(14.9)}$$

In this case it would cost \$0.06 million to hedge the portfolio so that its value does not fall below \$100 million.

Instead of buying a put, Mr. Kaufman can insure the portfolio by dynamically replicating the put. To do that, he has to initially sell 1.43 percent of the portfolio of bonds, since the delta of the put option is –0.0143, and invest the proceeds in the risk-free asset to create the payoff of the insured portfolio without actually purchasing the put. The portfolio could of course be a single bond, so the approach can be applied to pricing options on individual bonds.

The delta of an option on a bond allows us to evaluate the exposure of the option with respect to the value of the portfolio. Here, a $1 increase in the value of the portfolio decreases the value of the put by $0.0143. The modified duration (discussed in Chapter 9) of the portfolio, MD, tells us that the change in the value of the portfolio, ΔW, is equal to $-MD \times W \times \Delta r$, where W is the value of the portfolio and Δr is the decimal change in the interest rate. Hence, if the modified duration of the portfolio is 10, a 100 basis points increase in the interest rate decreases the value of the portfolio by $-10 \times \$120M \times 0.01$, or $12 million.

Using delta, the change in the value of the put for a given change in the interest rate is the delta of the put times the change in the value of the bond portfolio induced by the change in the interest rate:

Change in put value = Delta of put $\times$ (–MD of bond portfolio

$\times$ W $\times$ Change in interest rate)   **(14.10)**

where the term in parentheses is the change in the value of the bond portfolio. For our example, this is $-0.0143 \times (-10 \times \$120M \times 0.01)$, or $0.1716 million. The modified duration of the put is such that $-(MD$ of the put $\times$ Put price $\times \Delta r)$ is equal to the change in put value from equation (14.10). Solving for the modified duration of the put, we see that it is equal to:

Modified duration of the put = Delta of the put $\times$ MD of bond portfolio

$\times$ Value of bond portfolio/Put price   **(14.11)**

For our example, the modified duration of the put is $-0.0143 \times 10 \times 120/0.06$, or –286. Note that the put has a negative duration, so that an increase in the interest rate increases the value of the put because it decreases the value of the bond portfolio.

If we have the modified duration of the put, we can compare the duration of the insured portfolio to the duration of the uninsured portfolio. The duration of a portfolio is the weighted average of the durations of the securities included in the portfolio, where the weights are the portfolio weights of these securities. Since the put is worth $0.06 million, the insured portfolio is worth $120.06 million. The weight of the uninsured portfolio is $120M/$120.06M and the weight of the put is $0.06M/$120.06M. This gives us a duration for the insured portfolio that is 9.852. The impact of the portfolio insurance on duration is small in this case because the put option is out of the money.

Suppose that the portfolio of Mr. Kaufman is worth $100 million instead. In this case, the value of the put is $2.76 million and its delta is –0.3893. The duration of the put is then $-0.3893 \times 10 \times 100/2.76$, or -141.05. The duration of the insured portfolio becomes 5.94. It should be noted, once more, that duration is an exact measure of interest rate exposure only for infinitesimal interest rate changes; further, the delta exposure of an option to changes in the underlying works for only small changes in the underlying. As the bond price falls, the delta of the put increases in absolute value. This means that using delta leads us to underestimate the impact of interest rate increases on the value of the put. Since the portfolio is insured, its value cannot fall below $100 million regardless of the magnitude of interest rate changes, but because we underestimate the impact of interest rate increases on the value of the put, we might conclude otherwise when using the duration formula for the put.

We could use the approach to compute the duration of a callable bond. Panel A of Figure 14.3 plots the price of a coupon bond that is not callable and Panel B plots the price of the same bond callable at $100. The bond pays a coupon once a year of $10. The value of the call provision is the value of a call option on the bond with the exercise price set at the call price—in this case, $100. The option is American if the bond can be called at any time. The value of the callable bond is the value of the bond if it is not callable minus the value of the call option—remember that the borrower gets to exercise the call option and does so to minimize the value of its payments to the lender. The duration of a call option on a bond is computed the same way as the duration of a put option on a bond (see equation (14.11)): the duration of the call is the delta of the call times the duration of the underlying bond times the value of the bond divided by the value of the option. The duration of the call is positive since the value of the call falls when the interest rate increases as an increase in the interest rate decreases the value of the bond. Since the callable bond has a short position in the call option, the duration of a callable bond must be less than the duration of the underlying bond. The duration of a callable bond computed taking into account the impact of interest rate changes on the value of the call option embedded in the bond is often called the option-adjusted duration since it adjusts for the embedded option. Since a mortgage is similar to an amortizing callable bond, the duration of a mortgage is less than the duration of an amortizing noncallable bond.

We have implicitly assumed that the call option is exercised optimally by the borrower. Borrowers do not always behave that way—think of how inertia can set in for mortgage borrowers, so that they do not refinance when it would make sense for them to do so. Suppose you know that the call option will be exercised late by the borrower. In this case, the callable bond is more valuable to you. If you write an option and it is not exercised optimally by the purchaser, the purchaser of the option leaves money on the table that reduces the value of the option for him. With mortgages, the value of a portfolio of mortgages depends crucially on assumptions made about when borrowers will choose to refinance. The valuation of mortgages therefore requires a model of the refinancing behavior of borrowers—a model that we can use to predict when borrowers will exercise their call option.

Figure 14.3, Panel B, shows clearly why ignoring the call option can lead to dramatic mistakes in assessing the interest rate exposure of a bond. The bond is called when the interest rate is 10 percent. Consider the interest rate exposure of the bond at 10.1 percent. At that rate, the bond has a duration of 9.36 and a price

Callable and noncallable bonds

Figure 14.3

The bond pays a yearly coupon of $10 for thirty years. In Figure 14.3.A., the bond is not callable. In Figure 14.3.B., the bond is callable at $100.

Panel A

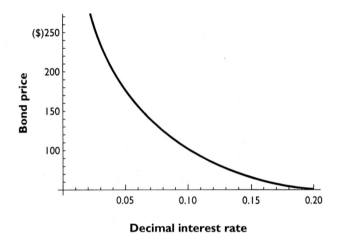

Panel B

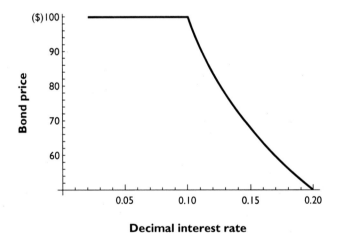

of $99.06. For that rate, using duration ignoring the call option, a 100 basis point decrease in the interest rate would increase the value of the bond by 9.36 × 99.06 × 0.01, or $9.27. This is not possible since the bond will be called at $100, so that if the interest rate falls by 100 basis points, the bond holder gains only $0.94. To evaluate the interest rate exposure of the callable bond, we therefore have to take great care in taking into account the impact of the call provision on the interest rate exposure. Ignoring the call option could lead us to conclude that interest rate shocks have a much larger impact on bond values than they have in reality, whether we perform a traditional duration analysis or we estimate VaR.

14.3. Beyond Black-Scholes

The Black-Scholes approach has important limitations in pricing fixed-income derivatives. The binomial model can be used to avoid these limitations.

14.3.1. The limitations of the Black-Scholes approach

When we use the Black-Scholes approach to price caps and floors, we use the Black model that assumes both that the implied futures yield is random and that the risk-free rate is constant. The assumption means that the interest rate on a bond that matures when the option matures does not change randomly, but that the interest rate at maturity of the option for a bond that matures at some later date does change randomly. Such an assumption is hard to justify when pricing one caplet. When we price multiple caplets, it forces us to use assumptions that are inconsistent across caplets.

Suppose that we need to price two caplets: one that matures in three months and one that matures in six months. Both caplets are for interest payments over a three-month period. To price the six-month caplet with the Black formula, we have to assume that the short-term interest rate will not change randomly over six months. Yet, when we price the three-month caplet, we are assuming that the same interest rate will not change randomly over three months but will then change randomly. The three-month rate three months from now is therefore assumed to be random when pricing the three-month caplet but not when pricing the six-month caplet.

Assuming a constant interest rate also affects the use of the Black-Scholes formula to price options on bonds. This amounts to making the contradictory assumptions that the short-term rate is constant but the yield of the bonds on which an option is written evolves randomly.

Another problem is the Black-Scholes assumption of constant volatility. There is no uncertainty about the dollar payoff at maturity of a U.S. government bond. This means that the volatility of the bond price immediately before maturity is zero, so that the constant volatility assumption of the Black-Scholes formula is necessarily violated with bonds.

Some times, these problems are not very important. In fact, the Black formula typically does a reasonable job in pricing caps and floors. It is the most widely used approach to price these derivatives. The Black-Scholes approach works reasonably well when the maturity of the underlying bonds is not close to the maturity of the bond option.

Consider the case where the term structure is flat and the continuously compounded interest rate for any maturity is 5 percent. The volatility of the rate of return of the three-year bond is 10 percent. The price of a three-year zero-coupon bond paying $100 at maturity is $86.07. If we assume that the bond price has a lognormal distribution, so that the Black-Scholes assumptions are satisfied, we are effectively assuming that there is a 25 percent chance that two years from now the zero-coupon bond price will have a value that exceeds $100. The value of a 30-year bond paying $100 at maturity is $22.31. Since a 30-year bond would have a longer duration, we would expect it to be much more volatile. Suppose that the return volatility is 25 percent for the 30-year bond. Because the value of the 30-year bond is low relative to par, the probability that the bond will have a value that exceeds par in two years is zero. In this case, the assumption of log-normal distribution is not unreasonable.

To price a two-year option on a 30-year bond, it is therefore not unreasonable to assume that the bond price is lognormally distributed. If the bond is a coupon bond, it can sell for more than par in two years; if the bond is a zero-coupon bond, its value is low relative to par so that the probability that its value will exceed par in two years with the lognormal distribution is likely to be trivial. Pricing a two-year option on a three-year zero-coupon bond with the Black-Scholes formula would make little sense because the value we obtain would assign a significant probability to price outcomes—the prices above par—that cannot possibly occur.

Another limitation of the Black-Scholes approach arises when a financial institution has to estimate the risk of portfolios with many different fixed income instruments. In this case, using the Black-Scholes approach to estimate the VaR of a portfolio of fixed income instruments requires assumptions which are inconsistent with the assumptions we make when evaluating risk.

To see this, suppose we want to estimate the one-day VaR of a portfolio that has bonds as well as puts and calls on bonds. Suppose, for simplicity, that the portfolio only has a six-month bond and a six-month call on a 20-year bond. In computing the VaR, we take into account the volatility of the return of the six-month bond and the covariance of that return with the return of the call option. In computing the price of the option, however, we assume that the six-month interest rate does not evolve randomly. In a simulation VaR, we could evaluate the return on the option assuming that both the six-month bond interest rate and the price of the 20-year bond evolve randomly. In this case, the joint distribution of the risk factors is inconsistent with the pricing model we use.

Should we be concerned about this inconsistency? The answer is yes, for at least two reasons. First, risk measurement systems have to be robust to manipulation. Pricing models that ignore risks we care about open the door to manipulation. Suppose that we want to monitor the risk of a trader. We tell the trader that the value of his book cannot fall by more than $1 million if the three-month T-bill rate increases by 300 basis points. By using the Black-Scholes formula, we do not measure the exposure to the short-term rate correctly because we price the call option ignoring the true distribution of the short-term rate. If the trader wants to maximize his true exposure (not the one we measure) to the short-term rate while satisfying the constraint we impose on his exposure, he can choose the portfolio of options that meets the exposure requirement but has the highest true exposure to the short-term rate. Second, the simulation VaR should give us an unbiased estimate of the fifth quantile of the distribution of the value of the portfolio given the distribution of the risk factors we use. However, when we use the Black-Scholes formula, we do not let the price of the call option reflect correctly changes in the short-term interest rate since the formula assumes that such changes do not take place. Therefore, our VaR estimate cannot be unbiased—unless we are lucky.

In Chapter 12, we assume that the price of a particular stock follows a lognormal distribution, but make no assumption about how other stock prices evolve in relation to that stock price. Assuming a stochastic process for one price without paying attention to the stochastic process followed by other prices presents problems with bonds. If one simply posits a stochastic process for each bond separately, nothing prevents bond prices from evolving so that at some future date there are arbitrage opportunities.

Suppose, for example, that we have two zero-coupon bonds with different maturities, say 10 and 20 years, and that we assume that each bond price follows a lognormal distribution over the coming year. There is thus a positive probability that at some point during the coming year the bond with the shorter maturity will sell for less than the bond with the longer maturity. This presents an arbitrage opportunity. Yet, when we use the Black-Scholes approach to price various bond options, we assume that each bond price follows a lognormal distribution. Hence, when we simulate the value of a portfolio with puts and calls on bonds using the distribution for bond prices assumed in the Black-Scholes approach, the simulated values of the bonds may admit arbitrage opportunities. This means that in measuring risk we assign some probability to outcomes that could not occur in the real world. Alternate approaches make it possible to avoid this problem.

14.3.2. Alternate approaches

We now show how to build a binomial tree for bond prices. To do that, we need to figure out how to construct a binomial tree for bond prices so that each zero-coupon bond price reaches par at maturity and does not sell for more than par along the way.

Let's assume that we can price bonds by arbitrage. This means that if we are pricing a bond, we can always construct a portfolio that has the same payoff as the bond we are pricing but does not include that bond. Since we can replicate an *n*-period zero-coupon bond by taking a position in a one-period zero-coupon bond and forward contracts, the assumption that we can price bonds by arbitrage will generally be satisfied. When we can price by arbitrage, we know from Chapter 11 that the price of any financial asset is its expected payoff computed using risk-neutral probabilities and discounted at the risk-free rate.

If we have an interest rate tree for the one-period risk-free rate and risk-neutral probabilities for the evolution of the one-period risk-free rate along that tree, we can compute the price of any bond and construct a bond price tree. A **bond price tree** shows how bond prices evolve when the interest rate has a binomial distribution, so that each period a bond price can move to only one of two new prices. At maturity, the bond price is par. One period before par, the bond price is simply the bond price at maturity discounted at the risk-free rate at that time in the tree. Once we have the bond prices one period before maturity, we can work backwards. This is because the bond price at a node of the bond price tree has to be the expected bond price next period using risk-neutral probabilities discounted at the risk-free rate at that node. The expected next period bond price using risk-neutral probabilities is obtained by multiplying the bond price at each of the two nodes succeeding the current node by their risk-neutral probabilities. Using this approach, we can price all existing bonds at each date along the tree in such a way that no bond price can exceed par along the tree as long as the one-period risk-free rate is nonnegative and that each bond pays par at maturity.

Today's prices for zero-coupon bond prices can be obtained from a number of vendors—for example, Bloomberg or Reuters. These vendors provide the zero curve—that is, the term structure of interest rates for zero-coupon bonds. When constructing the bond price tree, we want to obtain bond prices close to today's zero curve. Hence, we must choose the binomial process for the interest rate so that we price today's zero-coupon bonds. If we can price zero-coupon bonds, we can price coupon bonds that do not have a call provision since such bonds are portfolios of zero-coupon bonds.

Once we have a binomial tree for bond prices, we can then price any derivative whose payoff depends on bond prices in the same way that we can price any derivative whose payoff depends on a stock price once we have a binomial tree for the stock price.

14.4. Spot interest rate models

A **spot interest rate model** specifies how the interest rate for the shortest maturity evolves over time. We can construct an interest rate tree that fits the current zero-coupon bond prices. In section 14.4.1, we describe how to construct an interest rate tree. In section 14.4.2, we present the three most important models of interest rate dynamics used to construct interest rate trees.

14.4.1. Building interest rate and bond price trees

Suppose we want to construct a tree for a zero-coupon bond that pays $1,000 for sure in one year. We use six-month periods, so that we have dates 0, 1, and 2. The current rate for one year is 3.75 percent. Since reinvestment can take place only at the end of a period, the bond price is therefore $1,000/(1 + 0.0375/2)^2$ or $963.529. We have to specify the evolution of the interest rate for one period. Let's say that the six-month rate is 3.25 percent at date 0, and that it can be either 3.5 or 4.5 percent at date 1 with equal probability. For now, we take this to be a given, and do not worry about how it is obtained. Since we are pricing a one-year bond, we can price it at each node with the information we have. There are two nodes at date 1 and three nodes at date 2. The price of the bond at date 2 is $1,000 for each node. At date 1, the bond is worth either $1,000/(1 + 0.035/2)$, which is $982.801, or $1,000/(1 + 0.045/2)$, which is $977.995. Figure 14.4 shows the interest rate tree and the bond price tree.

For one tree, we know the true probability of each outcome. Consequently, we can compute the expected price of the bond at date 1. This expected price is $0.5 \times 982.801 + 0.5 \times 977.995$, or $980.398. This price is the expected price of a bond with six months to maturity at date 1. Since we have the price of a six-month bond and the price of a twelve-month bond, we can compute the forward price of a six-month bond at date 1. To compute this forward price, we need the price of a six-month bond at date 0, which is $1,000/(1 + 0.0325/2)$, or $984.01. Using the formula for the forward price of a bond, we get a price of $979.183, which is equal to the ratio of the twelve-month bond price and the six-month bond price. The expected price of the six-month bond price at date 1 differs from its forward price. This occurs when there is a risk premium for bearing the risk associated with the underlying of the forward contract. Consequently, our tree implies that the expectation hypothesis does not hold—the forward price of a bond is not the expected value of the bond.

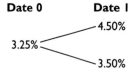

Figure 14.4   Two-period interest rate and three-period bond binomial trees

Tree for six-month interest rate

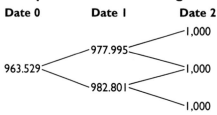

Tree for price of bond maturing at date 2

Let's use our bond tree to price a call option on a bond by arbitrage. This call option matures at date 1 and has an exercise price of \$980. Consequently, the call pays \$2.801 if the bond price is \$982.801 and zero otherwise. To price the call by arbitrage, we need to construct a portfolio that does not include the option but pays the same as the option. We therefore solve for the number of bonds that mature at date 1, n, that we invest in and the number of bonds that mature at date 2, m, that we invest in to ensure that the portfolio replicates the payoff of the call:

$$n \times 1{,}000 + m \times 982.801 = 2.801$$

$$n \times 1{,}000 + m \times 977.995 = 0 \qquad (14.12)$$

The solution is to hold long 0.582813 units of the bond that matures at date 2 and to short 0.569988 units of the bond that matures at date 1. The value of this portfolio is $0.582813 \times 963.529 - 0.569988 \times 984.01$, or \$0.683. This gives us the price of the call.

When we can price by arbitrage, the value of a derivative is the expected payoff of the derivative discounted at the risk-free rate assuming that investors are risk-neutral. Let π be the risk-neutral probability that the interest rate will fall from date 0 to date 1. If investors are risk-neutral, the current price of the bond that matures at date 2 must be equal to its expected price at date 1 computed using the risk-neutral probabilities discounted at the risk-free rate. Consequently, the price of the bond that matures at date 2 must be:

$$963.529 = 0.98401 \times [\pi \times 982.801 + (1 - \pi) \times 977.995] \qquad (14.13)$$

The solution for π is 0.247854. Using this solution we can price the option by taking the expected payoff with risk-neutral probabilities and discounting it at the risk-free rate:

$$0.683 = 0.98401 \times [\pi \times 2.801 + (1 - \pi) \times 0]$$

$$= 0.98401 \times 0.247854 \times 2.801 \qquad \textbf{(14.14)}$$

When building a bond price tree, we must choose the risk-neutral probabilities at each node to ensure that the resulting bond prices correspond to the market prices at date 0 as we just did when building a two-period bond price tree. Let's build the bond price tree for a bond that matures in three periods, at date 3. To build such a tree, we first need to extend our interest rate tree. Remember that the one-period rate is 3.25 percent and the two-period rate is 3.75 percent. We assume that the interest rate can move up or down by 50 basis points. We further assume that the three-period rate is 4 percent, which implies that the current price of a bond that matures at date 3 is $1,000/(1 + 0.04/2)^3$, or \$942.322. Figure 14.5 shows the interest rate and the bond price trees. The bond price tree represents the evolution of the price of the bond that matures at date 3. This bond pays \$1,000 at date 3. Since we know the six-month rates at date 2 for each node, we can price the bond at date 2 for each node by discounting its date 3 payoff at the risk-free rate. We also know the price of the bond at date 0 from the current term structure.

To complete the bond price tree, we have to find the bond price for the two nodes at date 1. This price will depend on the evolution of the interest rate from date 1 to date 2 from each node. The probability of an interest rate increase from date 1 to date 2 need not be the same as the one of an interest rate increase from

---

Three-period interest rate and four-period bond binomial trees   *Figure 14.5*

P(up, 3) [P(down, 3)] is the price of a zero-coupon bond at date 1 that matures at date 3 following a down [up] move in the interest rate from date 0.

Tree for term structure

Tree for price of bond maturing at date 3

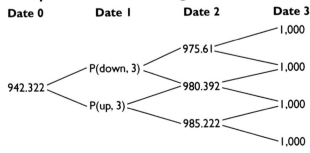

date 0 to date 1. Let's assume that the interest rate tree is such that at date 1 the risk-neutral probability of an interest rate increase from each node is the same, $1 - q$. This means that there is a risk-neutral probability q of a bond price increase.

The bond prices at date 1 must satisfy three equations. First, the price of the bond maturing at date 3 following a price increase (decrease in interest rate), P(up, 3), must equal the expected price of the bond at date 2 viewed from the node up at date 1 discounted at the risk-free rate at that node:

$$[q \times 985.222 + (1 - q) \times 980.392]/(1 + 0.035/2) = P(up, 3) \qquad (14.15)$$

Second, the bond price following a down move (up move in the interest rate), P(down, 3), must equal the expected price at date 2 viewed from the node down at date 1 discounted at the risk-free rate at that node:

$$[q \times 980.392 + (1 - q) \times 975.61]/(1 + 0.045/2) = P(down, 3) \qquad (14.16)$$

Finally, the price of the bond at date 0 must be equal to the expected price of the bond at date 1 using risk-neutral probabilities discounted at the risk-free rate. We have already computed the risk-neutral probabilities of the tree over the first period and found that the probability of an up move is 0.247854. Consequently, we require that:

$$942.322 = [0.247854 \, P(up, 3)$$
$$+ (1 - 0.247854) \, P(down, 3)]/(1 + 0.0325/2) \qquad (14.17)$$

We have three equations and three unknowns. The unknowns are q, P(up, 3) and P(down, 3). Solving for these unknowns, we find that q is equal to 0.24838, that P(up, 3) is equal to \$964.709, and that P(down, 3) is equal to \$955.303.

We can use this approach to keep building bond trees for bonds that mature later than one and a half years. We first require a model that shows how the one-period interest rate evolves so that we can obtain an interest rate tree and the current zero curve. This information allows us to compute the risk-neutral probabilities from each node and then the bond price for each node. Once we have the bond price tree, we can price contingent claims along the tree.

This approach is equivalent to the approach using the binomial model to price options on stocks, but it is a bit more complex. We must make sure that bond prices do not exceed par. To insure that bond prices do not exceed par, our example started from an interest rate tree which we took as a given. We now need to specify how to build the interest rate tree.

14.4.2. Spot interest rate models and tree building

To build an interest rate tree, we start from an interest rate model that specifies how the spot interest rate evolves over time. We discuss two of the most important models for the construction of trees in this section.

14.4.2.A. The Ho-Lee model

Ho and Lee (1986) apply the binomial distribution to interest rate changes. The model differs from the common stock binomial model in an important way. The common stock model has a *multiplicative shock*; the stock price at a node is multiplied by a random variable that can take one of two values. The Ho-Lee model has an *additive shock*, in that a random variable is added to the current interest rate. The interest rate at a node is the interest rate at the previous node plus a variable that takes a higher value for an up move than for a down move.

If r is the current one-period interest rate on an annualized basis, $\mu\tau$ is the expected change in the rate, τ is the length of a period expressed as a fraction of a calendar year, and $\sigma\sqrt{\tau}$ is the volatility of the change in the rate, the Ho-Lee model specifies that the next interest rate on the tree is:

$$r + \mu\tau + \sigma\sqrt{\tau} \quad \textbf{following up move}$$

Interest rate next period =

$$r + \mu\tau - \sigma\sqrt{\tau} \quad \textbf{following down move}$$

The only difference between an up and a down move is that we add $\sigma\sqrt{\tau}$ for an up move and subtract it for a down move. To estimate $\sigma\sqrt{\tau}$, we can use historical data on interest rate changes and then use the square root rule to get the annualized volatility. An alternative is to obtain a volatility estimate using current option prices or a view on volatility.

Ho and Lee assume that the volatility of the change in the interest rate is constant along the tree. The tree must be constructed so that it provides the current market value of existing bonds. To price bonds of different maturities, the expected change in the interest rate must change as we move along the tree, or we would not have enough flexibility. Ho and Lee specify only one mean change for all nodes at one time. This means that irrespective of the rate reached at date 2, the expected change in the interest rate from date 2 to date 3 is the same. With this assumption, the tree is recombining and manageable, so that we could then proceed to build the tree using their interest rate dynamics. Technical Box 14.1, Constructing the Ho-Lee tree, gives more details for those interested.

There are two problems with the Ho-Lee model. The first is that, if σ is large enough, a succession of down moves along the tree could lead to a negative interest rate. In our example, the random variable takes values of +0.353553 percent or −0.353553 percent. We start with an interest rate of 3.25 percent. If the expected change is zero along the tree, the lowest interest rate in the tree after ten periods will be negative and the tree will have an increasing number of such negative rates afterward. The negative rates mean that bonds which expire the following period have a value above par.

The other problem is that the volatility of the interest rate shock does not depend on the rate. Since the shock is additive, the volatility of the percentage change in the interest rate falls as interest rates increase. One would not expect this to be true since it would imply that the percentage volatility would become trivial as interest rates become large.

14.4.2.B. The Black, Derman, and Toy (1990) model

The Black, Derman, and Toy (BDT) model maintains the multiplicative shock of the common stock model. The interest rate at the next node is obtained by multiplying the interest rate at the current node by a positive variable that is larger for an up move than for a down move. Since the interest rate is multiplied by a positive variable, it can

Technical Box 14.1 Constructing the Ho-Lee tree

In section 14.4.1, the price of a two-period bond is equal to the present value of the expected bond price after one period using the risk-neutral probability distribution. In the Ho-Lee model, the interest rate dynamics specify the interest rate after one period for an up move and a down move. Knowing the interest rate, we can compute the bond prices. We then need to solve for the risk-neutral probability. If we assume we know σ, we need to find the value of μ and π. Since we have one equation, we cannot solve for both μ and π. We have to fix one of these two values. Instead of fixing the interest rates following an up and a down move like we did in section 14.4.1, Ho-Lee set π equal to 0.5 and solve for the μ that prices current bonds.

Given the current rate r and the volatility, we choose μ so that we price the existing two-period bond. In the two-period example of Figure 14.4, we have a bond maturing at date 2 that sells for \$963.529 at date 0. Let's choose σ to be 0.5 percent. Solving for μ requires us to solve the following equation:

$$963.529 = \frac{0.5\left(\dfrac{1{,}000}{1 + 0.0325/2 + \mu/2 + 0.005 \times \sqrt{1/2}}\right) + 0.5\left(\dfrac{1{,}000}{1 + 0.0325/2 + \mu/2 - 0.005 \times \sqrt{1/2}}\right)}{1 + 0.0325/2}$$

The solution for μ is 0.01. This means that the one-period interest rate next period is either 4.10355 or 3.39644 percent with equal probability.

Ho and Lee assume that the volatility of the change in the interest rate is constant along the tree. As we extend the tree, we add a bond that we have to price, namely, the bond that matures in eighteen months. To price bonds of different maturities, the expected change in the interest rate must change as we move along the tree, or we would not have enough flexibility.

We could actually choose a mean rate of change $\mu^\wedge$ when the interest rate is 3.39644 percent and a mean change $\mu^{\wedge\wedge}$ when it is 4.10355 percent. In this case, the tree would not be recombining. The rate following a down move from 4.10355 percent would be $4.10355\% + \mu^{\wedge\wedge}/2 - 0.353553\%$, while the rate following an up move from 3.39644 percent would be $3.39644\% + \mu^\wedge/2 + 0.353553\%$. Nonrecombining trees are difficult to handle computationally because they lead to many more nodes than recombining trees. If we divide a year into 12 periods, we have 8,191 nodes with a nonrecombining tree and only 91 with a recombining tree.

Ho and Lee specify only one mean change for all nodes at one time. This means that irrespective of the rate reached at date 2, the expected change in the interest rate from date 2 to date 3 is the same. We could then keep building the tree. The tree would match the existing term structure and allow us to price any contingent claim.

never be negative. This resolves the problem that interest rates can become negative in the Ho-Lee model.

The other advantage of the BDT model is that it allows volatility to change along the tree. This enables the model to be consistent with the empirical result that the volatility of rates is inversely related to the maturity of rates. For example, from 1971 to 1990, changes in the one-month rate have an annualized volatility of 0.91 percent but changes in the 13-week rate have a volatility of 0.351 percent.[2] The gap between the volatility of the yield of the 30-year bond and the one-year bill was surprisingly large at the beginning of the 1980s. Estimating volatilities of percentage changes in rates using periods of 24 months, the volatility of the 30-year yield peaked early in the 1980s at close to 20 percent while the proportional volatility of the one-year yield peaked at slightly more than 40 percent. After that, these volatilities fell so that the 30-year volatility oscillates between 10 and 15 percent and the one-year volatility is about 5 percent higher.[3]

Figure 14.6 shows how the interest rate evolves along the BDT tree. We can make the volatility change over time. This means that we can decide on how the volatility should change and then fit the tree to that volatility curve. The volatility that is relevant in the BDT model is the volatility of the percentage change in the interest rate, called the **proportional volatility**, unlike the volatility of the level of the interest rate, or **level volatility**, used in the Ho-Lee model. An important issue with building a BDT tree is to make it recombining. For those interested, this is discussed in Technical Box 14.2, Making the BDT tree recombining.

14.4.3. Interest rate models and derivatives pricing

The tree models posit how the interest rate changes through time. A model that describes how the interest rate changes over time is an interest rate model. From

The Black, Derman, and Toy tree   *Figure 14.6*

In this tree, r is the interest rate at date 0. The rate at 0 is multiplied by a shock to get the rate at date 1. $\mu\tau$ and $\mu'\tau$ are, respectively, the expected rate of change of r from date 0 to date 1 and from date 1 to date 2. $\sigma\sqrt{\tau}$ and $\sigma'\sqrt{\tau}$ are, respectively, the volatility of the rate of change of r from date 0 to date 1 and from date 1 to date 2. τ denotes the length of a period, expressed as a fraction of a year.

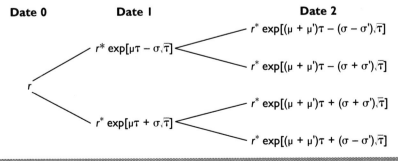

2   See Brenner, Harjes, and Kroner (1996).
3   See Koenigsberg, Showers, and Streit (1991).

Technical Box 14.2 Making the BDT tree recombining

The problem in choosing the volatility curve and having to fit the existing term structure is that the tree will not be recombining unless we allow the expected rate of change of the interest rate to vary between up and down moves. We want a recombining tree to simplify computations. This means that we require that the down move from the high rate equal the up move from the low rate:

$$r \times \text{Exp}\left[(\mu + \mu')\,\tau + (\sigma - \sigma')\sqrt{\tau}\right]$$

$$= r \times \text{Exp}\left[(\mu + \mu'')\,\tau - (\sigma - \sigma')\sqrt{\tau}\right]$$

This equation only can be satisfied if:

$$(\mu'' - \mu')\,\tau = 2\,(\sigma - \sigma')\sqrt{\tau}$$

μ' cannot equal μ'' if the volatility is changing across periods. To ensure that the tree is recombining, it is necessary to let the expected percentage of change of the interest rate differ between up and down moves. With the BDT model, the proportional volatility at a node is equal to $0.5\ln[r(\text{up})/r(\text{down})]$. To construct a tree, we therefore have to impose the following conditions: (1) we must price the zero curve, (2) we must fit the volatility curve, and (3) volatility must be the same for all nodes at a date.

---

an interest rate model, we can price bonds and derivatives. As the period of the binomial model becomes infinitesimally short, we have the case of continuous trading.

Define Δr_t as $r_{t+\Delta t} - r_t$, where Δt is the length of a period, ϵ_t is an i.i.d. random variable with mean zero and volatility of one, and ϕ, λ, k, σ, β are model parameters that we will define in our discussion of the model. As period length becomes shorter, the distribution of ϵ_t converges to the normal distribution. A fairly general model of interest rate dynamics with one source of risk is:

$$\Delta r_t = \left[\phi + \lambda\left(k - r_t\right)\right]\Delta t + \sigma r_t^{\beta}\, \epsilon_t \tag{14.18}$$

This model gives the change in the interest rate over a period. The change is the sum of two terms. Over the period from t to $t + \Delta t$, the only random variable that affects the change in the interest rate is ϵ_t. The first term in the equation is deterministic and the second one is random. The deterministic term corresponds to the expected change in the interest rate. An important feature of interest rates is that neither very high nor very low rates seem to persist forever. This suggests that rates exhibit mean reversion. Equation (14.18) accommodates mean reversion by allowing the expected change in the interest rate to depend on the current level of the interest rate. If λ is equal to zero, the expected change in the interest rate does not depend on the interest rate and there is no mean reversion. This is the case of the Ho-Lee model. If λ is positive, an interest rate below k has a higher expected change than one above k. Consequently, the part of the equation that depends on λ captures the mean reversion of interest rates. The higher the value of λ, the faster the interest rate goes back to its long-run value of k, so that λ is a measure of the speed of mean reversion. The volatility of the rate over the next period is σr_t^β.

The interest rate model in equation (14.18) allows the volatility of the change in the interest rate to depend on the interest rate. If β is equal to zero, the volatility does not depend on the interest rate. The equation captures the interest rate dynamics of the Ho-Lee model when we set λ and β equal to zero. Note that in this case, changes in the interest rate are normally distributed with mean ϕ and volatility σ. Negative values of ϵ_t can therefore make the interest rate negative.

If β is equal to zero and λ is a constant, we have a classic model of interest rate dynamics called the Vasicek model. This model allows for mean reversion in rates, because the expected change in the interest rate falls as the interest rate increases. Like the Ho-Lee model, the Vasicek model implies normally distributed rates, so that negative rates are possible. Setting β equal to 0.5, we get the Cox-Ingersoll-Ross (CIR) square-root model, which allows for the volatility of the change in the interest rate to increase as the interest rate increases. Hull and White (1990) show that these models can be fitted to the initial term structure of interest rates and to the current term structure of interest rate volatilities by choosing appropriate values for the parameters of the model, but to do so one must make these parameters be functions of time.

The interest rate model in equation (14.18) is the subject of considerable investigation. In a classic paper, Chan, Karolyi, Longstaff, and Sanders (1992) provide evidence that β should be 1.5 and that models where β is set above one perform better than models where β is set below one. With β set at 1.5, the proportional volatility of interest rates increases as the level of rates increases. Their estimate of λ is 0.59 with a t-statistic of 1.55, which provides weak evidence of mean reversion. Some authors have argued that these conclusions are not robust because they do not hold up if the stock market crash of 1987 and a period in the early 1980s are eliminated from the data set. Other authors have made technical econometric arguments that have important implications for the results. Brenner, Harjes, and Kroner (1996) conclude that β should be 0.5 and that there is no economically significant mean reversion in rates. Recent evidence suggests that if there is mean reversion, it is noticeable only when rates are extremely high or extremely low.

The models discussed here make the assumption that only one source of risk affects changes in all the rates. There is evidence that one-factor models have trouble explaining both the short end of the term structure and the long end at the same time. The economic importance of this limitation seems to depend on the derivatives considered and on the sample period considered, but researchers have developed a number of models allowing for two or more sources of risk to affect changes in rates. Examples of additional sources of risk are the slope of the term structure, the long maturity rate, or the short rate volatility. The most recent models assume that each rate is essentially its own risk factor, so that there are as many factors as there are rates. It is too early to know much regarding the usefulness of these models.

The basic question is how much the choice of model matters. The answer is that one has to be quite careful! The current term structure has a lot of information about interest rate dynamics and ignoring that information is a poor idea. If we choose the parameters of a model so that it does a good job of pricing current zero-coupon bond prices, though, the choice of a model matters most for out of the money options.

The difficulty is that the models make the biggest differences when one is the least certain what the right model is. For example, the speed at which rates revert back to their long-run value is especially important when rates are far from their long-run value. Since it is rare for the rates to be far away from their long-run mean, it is difficult to be confident about interest rate dynamics at such a time. In these cases, we generally have to appeal to economic arguments to motivate the model of interest rate dynamics we are using.

The empirical evidence on the various models shows clearly that models that use one factor cannot explain bond prices along the whole yield curve. Models allowing two or more sources of risk are generally required to explain changes in bond prices across the whole curve. When we use more complicated models, however, more estimation is required. This creates two dangers. First, imprecisely estimated parameters can play a big role in the predictions we make. Second, as we keep making models more complicated and adding sources of risk, we can end up explaining the past—not because we have a good model but rather because we just fit the model to the data we have. This model could fail miserably outside the estimation period.

The bottom line for risk management is that it would be a fundamental mistake to take what the computer spits out at face value. The valuations one obtains for fixed-income securities are model-sensitive. It is important to check for the extent of this sensitivity when considering the value and the risk of a portfolio of fixed-income securities.

14.4.4. The Vasicek model and risk management

As discussed, Vasicek's model is an example of a model of bond and derivatives pricing that starts from equation (14.18). This model is quite popular in practice because it is fairly easy to deal with, yet produces formulas for bond prices and some derivatives prices. It is useful to see specifically how the use of an interest rate model affects risk management and how it permits the pricing of derivatives.

Vasicek builds a zero curve starting from the interest rate dynamics. Because there is only one source of risk, ϵ_t, one bond can be hedged with another one, so we can price bonds by arbitrage when we make the assumptions of the Vasicek model. The price of bearing risk must be the same for all bonds per unit of risk—unit of volatility of ϵ_t.

Let Ω be this price of risk. Using this definition and letting the period length become infinitesimally short, the Vasicek model leads to a formula for a zero coupon bond price at date t maturing at date T assuming that short maturity interest rate at t (in the model, short maturity means over an infinitesimally short period) is r_t:

$$P_t(T) = A(T)e^{-B(T)r_t}$$

$$B(T) = \frac{\left(1 - e^{-\lambda(T - t)}\right)}{\lambda}$$

$$A(T) = \exp\left(\frac{\left(B(T) - T + t\right)\left(\lambda\theta - 0.5\,\sigma^2\right)}{\lambda^2} - \frac{\sigma^2 B(T)^2}{4\lambda}\right)$$

$$\theta = \lambda k + \theta - \Omega\sigma \tag{14.19}$$

Using this formula, we can compute the exposure of bond prices to changes in r_t. Mean reversion dampens the impact of a change in r on bond prices. This is because the interest rate is expected to move toward the long-term rate k, so that an interest rate shock is not permanent. The exposure of bond prices to changes in r takes into account this dampening effect with the Vasicek formula.

As a result, the modified duration discussed in Chapter 9 overstates the impact of an interest rate change with the Vasicek model because it does not take into account the fact that an interest rate shock is not expected to be permanent. If the Vasicek model holds, we therefore should use the Vasicek duration formula. For a zero-coupon bond, the Vasicek duration formula is:

$$\textbf{Vasicek duration } = \frac{1}{\lambda}\left(1 - e^{-\lambda T}\right) \tag{14.20}$$

Remember that since the duration of a portfolio is a value-weighted average of the duration of the securities comprised in the portfolio, we can use the duration formula for a zero-coupon bond to compute the duration of any default-free fixed-income bond with no options attached since such a security is equivalent to a portfolio of zero-coupon bonds.

Consider a 30-year zero-coupon bond using continuous compounding. The modified duration of that bond is 30. The Vasicek duration is only 9.5 using a λ of 0.1; it is 25.9 using a λ of 0.01. These two durations lead to markedly different changes in bond values for a given change in interest rates. With the duration approximation, a 1 basis point change in the shortest maturity rate (it is r in equation 14.19) reduces the value of a bond with a duration of 9.5 by 0.095 percent and a bond with a duration of 25.9 by 0.259 percent. The Vasicek duration increases as mean reversion becomes less important. If there is no mean reversion, the modified duration formula applies. If the interest rate model is such that the modified duration formula applies, one can go short $30 of the one-year bill to hedge a $1 investment in the 30-year zero-coupon bond. In contrast, if the Vasicek interest rate model holds and λ is 0.1, the duration of the one-year T-bill is 0.95. One would have to go short only 9.5/0.95 dollars, or $10, of the one-year bill to hedge a $1 investment in the 30-year zero-coupon bond.

Using the wrong interest rate model can have dramatic implications for hedging effectiveness and for value at risk estimates. With our example, somebody using the modified duration formula to hedge the 30-year zero-coupon bond with the one-year T-bill when the Vasicek model applies would be sharply over-hedged. In fact, the value at risk of the hedged position when using the modified duration formula in that case would exceed the value at risk of the unhedged position. To see this, let's assume that interest rate changes are normally distributed. Using the duration approximation as discussed in Chapter 9, the 5 percent VaR of the hedged position for a $1 investment would be 19 × 1.65 × Short interest rate volatility. The 19 is the result of being long the 30-year bond with a duration of 9.5 and short $30 of the one-year T-bill with a duration of 0.95 (the duration with equation 9.5). In contrast, the VaR of the unhedged position is 9.5 × 1.65 × Short interest rate volatility, which is 50 percent of the VaR of the hedged position. If, instead, one uses the correct interest rate model, the duration VaR of the hedged portfolio is zero.

If we accept the assumptions of the Vasicek model, there is a formula for a call option on a zero-coupon bond that looks like the Black-Scholes formula. Let's consider a call option on a zero-coupon bond:

Vasicek formula for a call option on a zero-coupon bond

Let $P_t(t^*)$ be the price of a zero-coupon bond that matures at t^*, $P_t(T)$ the price of a zero-coupon bond that matures at T, $t^* > T$, T the maturity of the call, $N(d)$ the cumulative normal distribution evaluated at d, σ the volatility of the interest rate, and λ the mean-reversion parameter of the interest rate model. The Vasicek model for a call option on $P_t(t^*)$ maturing at T with exercise price K is:

$$C(P, K, T, t) = P_t(t^*)N(d) - KP_t(T)N(d - \sigma_p)$$

$$d = \frac{1}{\sigma_p} \ln \frac{P_t(t^*)}{P_t(T)K} + 0.5\sigma_p$$

$$\sigma_p = \sqrt{\frac{\sigma^2\left(1 - e^{-2\lambda(T - t)}\right)}{2\lambda} \left[\frac{1 - e^{\lambda(t^* - T)}}{\lambda}\right]} \qquad (14.21)$$

Remember that λ is the speed at which the interest rate reverts to its long-run value in equation (14.18). We have assumed that the interest rate dynamics are fitted to the term structure, so that they price the bonds correctly. The volatility that enters the formula differs from the volatility in the Black-Scholes model, where it is a constant. In equation (14.21), the volatility depends on time to maturity of the underlying bond and of the option. It can be verified that if the bond and the option have the same maturity, the volatility term is zero since we know the payoff of the option exactly in that case. In addition, in the formula given here, $P_t(t^*)$ replaces the price of the common stock in the Black-Scholes formula. The Vasicek bond call option pricing formula—or for that matter, any call option pricing formula for a bond call option—can be used to evaluate the interest rate exposure of a call option in the same way we used the Black-Scholes formula to evaluate the interest rate exposure of a call option.

14.5. Building trees from the forward curve: The Heath-Jarrow-Morton (HJM) model

With the risk-neutral distribution, the expected price of a bond for date $t + i$ is equal to its forward price for delivery at $t + i$. Consider a zero-coupon bond that matures at $T > t + i$. Remember that the current price of that bond is equal to the expected price of the bond for $t + i$ using the risk-neutral distribution discounted at the risk-free rate, $P_t(t + i)E^*[P_{t+i}(T)]$ where E^* denotes the expectation using the risk-neutral distribution. This is a general version of what we saw in equation (14.13). However, if we have a forward contract for delivery of the bond at $t + i$, we also know from Chapter 5 that the forward price discounted at the risk-free rate must be equal to the current price of the bond, $P_t(t + i)F$, where F is the forward price at t for delivery at $t + i$ of the bond maturing at T. Consequently, the forward price must be equal to the expected bond price using the risk-neutral distribution, $F = E^*[P_{t+i}(T)]$. Heath, Jarrow, and Morton (1992) have built a pricing model, the HJM model, that is based on forward prices and uses the fact that with the risk-neutral distribution, the forward price is equal to the expected bond price using the risk-neutral distribution. We first discuss the key insights of this model using the binomial approach and then consider the model when periods become infinitesimally short.

14.5.1. The forward rate tree

We define by $F_t(t + i)$ the forward price at t for delivery of a one-period bond at $t + i$. The price of that bond at $t + i$ is $P_{t+i}(t + i + 1)$. With the risk-neutral distribution, we have that:

$$F_t(t + i) = E^*\left[P_{t+i}(t + i + 1)\right] \tag{14.22}$$

The continuously compounded forward rate $f_t(t + i)$ is defined so that $F_t(t + i)$ is equal to $e^{-f_t(t+i)}$. Let's look at continuously compounded rates and let's assume that rates change every period. The length of a period is equal to one year for simplicity. At date $t + i$, $f_{t+i}(t + i)$ is the forward rate for immediate delivery, which is the spot interest rate. We can rewrite equation (14.22) using forward rates as follows:

$$e^{-f_t(t+i)} = E^*\left[e^{-f_{t+i}(t+i)}\right] \tag{14.23}$$

The forward price of a zero-coupon bond is a nonlinear function of the forward rate. Since the forward price of a bond is equal to the expected future price of the bond using the risk-neutral distribution, it cannot be the case at the same time that the forward rate is equal to the expected spot interest rate.[4] The result that the forward price of a bond equals the expectation of the future price of the bond under the risk-neutral distribution strongly restricts the distribution of the

---

4 Remember that $E^*[e^{-f_{t+i}(t+i)}]$ is different from $e^{E^*[-f_{t+i}(t+i)]}$ because the exponential function is not a linear function.

change in the forward rates from one date to the next. To see this, it is best to consider a specific model of how the forward rates evolve over time.

In the Ho-Lee model, a single random variable affects the interest rate. In addition, with that model, the volatility of interest rate changes is constant. The Ho-Lee model is therefore a one-factor constant volatility model. We assume that forward rates for all maturities (all i's) evolve as follows under the risk-neutral distribution:

$$f_{t+i}(t+i) = \begin{cases} f_t(t+i) + \mu + \sigma & \text{up move} \\ \\ f_t(t+i) + \mu - \sigma & \text{down move} \end{cases} \tag{14.24}$$

As with Ho-Lee, the probability of an up move is 0.5. With equation (14.24), the volatility of the change in a forward rate is σ, irrespective of maturity since the only uncertainty concerning the change in the rate is whether it moves up by σ or down by σ. Equation (14.24) therefore implies that all forward rates experience the same random shock, the same expected change μ, and have the same volatility σ.

Substituting the right-hand side of equation (14.24) in equation (14.23), we have that:

$$e^{-f_t(t+i)} = \left[0.5e^{-f_t(t+i)+\mu-\sigma} + 0.5\bar{e}^{\,f_t(t+i)+\mu-\sigma} \right] \tag{14.25}$$

The forward prices at t are known. Consequently, we know $f_t(t+i)$ in equation (14.25). This means that if one knows σ, one knows μ. For example, if the volatility is 0.1, then $\mu = 0.005$. From the equation describing the change for the forward rate, we know that μ is the expected change in the forward rate and that σ is the volatility of the change. It follows that the absence of arbitrage opportunities has a crucial implication for the dynamics of forward rates:

> The absence of arbitrage opportunities implies that the expected change in continuously compounded forward rates is uniquely determined by their volatility.

The analysis implies that if we specify the volatility of forward rates, we specify their expected change. Heath, Jarrow, and Morton (1992) describe the precise conditions that relate the volatility of forward rates to the expected change of forward rates in the absence of arbitrage. We therefore call the model used here the Heath-Jarrow-Morton (HJM) model. Having specified the volatility of changes in forward rates, we can then derive the expected change in forward rates using equation (14.23). Technical Box 14.3, Building HJM trees, shows how we can build trees in this model.

14.6. HJM models as periods become shorter

When the volatility of changes in the forward rate is constant, there is a pricing formula for a call option on a zero-coupon bond. As periods become infinitesi-

Building HJM trees   *Technical Box 14.3*

Since we assume that forward rates can only move up or down by a fixed amount, we can construct a binomial tree describing the evolution of forward rates that we can use to price contingent claims.

Say we start from zero-coupon bond prices at a specific date. Table 1 shows the prices at date 0 of zero-coupon bonds maturing at the end of years 1, 2, 3, 4, and 5. From these prices, we get forward prices for one-period zero-coupon bonds. For example, the forward price at date 0 for a one-period bond maturing at date 4 is $P_0(4)/P_0(3) = 0.79014/0.84312 = 0.937162$. From the forward bond price, we can get the forward rate, remembering that we are using continuously compounded forward rates, so that $\ln(1/0.937162) = 0.0648991$ is the forward rate from today's term structure for a one-period zero-coupon bond delivered at date 3 maturing at date 4. We write such a forward price as $f_i(j, T)$ where i stands for the pricing date, j for the delivery date, and T for the maturity date of the bond delivered. Hence, using our notation, we have that $f_0(3, 4) = 0.0648991$. We get forward rates at date 0 for bonds maturing at date 1 through 5. The forward rate $f_0(0, 1)$ is the forward rate for a bond maturing next period and therefore is the current spot interest rate.

To construct the tree of forward rates, we have to choose the volatility σ. We choose $\sigma = 0.005$. When we get to date 1, the bond maturing at date 1 no longer exists. Consequently, we now have four forward rates. One of these four forward rates is for the bond maturing at date 2 and hence is the spot interest rate at that date. Forward rates can experience an up move, namely a move such that ϵ is equal to 1, or a down move, such that ϵ is equal to -1. Given

Table 1   Implementation of Heath-Jarrow-Morton model in discrete time: Data

The bond prices are obtained from the *Wall Street Journal* (December 12, 1996). They are arithmetic averages of bid-ask prices for the T-bill and strips maturing last in each of the five following years. $P_0(T)$ denotes the price of a zero-coupon bond at date 0 that pays \$1 at T. $f_0(i)$ denotes the forward rate at 0 for the zero-coupon bond with one period to go at date i.

Maturity	1	2	3	4	5
Zero-coupon bond prices at date 0	$P_0(1) =$ 0.94815	$P_0(2) =$ 0.89625	$P_0(3) =$ 0.84312	$P_0(4) =$ 0.79014	$P_0(5) =$ 0.74027
Forward one-period zero-coupon bond prices		0.945262	0.94072	0.937162	0.936885
Forward rates	$f_0(0) =$ 0.0532426	$f_0(1) =$ 0.0562931	$f_0(2) =$ 0.0611097	$f_0(3) =$ 0.0648991	$f_0(4) =$ 0.0651947

(continued)

Technical Box 14.3 *(continued)*

our choice of σ, each up move corresponds to 0.005 added to the forward rate of the previous period and each down move results in subtracting 0.005 from the previous period. We use the superscripts *u* to denote an up move and *d* to denote a down move. The forward rates following an up move are:

$$f_1^u(1, 2) = 0.056 + 0.005 = 0.061$$

$$f_1^u(2, 3) = 0.061 + 0.005 = 0.066$$

$$f_1^u(3, 4) = 0.065 + 0.005 = 0.070$$

$$f_1^u(4, 5) = 0.065 + 0.005 = 0.070$$

We can proceed in the same way for the down move. For example, $f_1^d = 0.056 - 0.005 = 0.051$. The whole tree construction proceeds then by getting the next set of forward rates from a node by adding 0.005 for an up move and subtracting 0.005 for a down move. At each node, the number of forward rates falls by one since a bond matures. Table 2 has the whole tree of forward rates.

This example uses a one-factor constant volatility model of forward rates, but we could choose a different model. The HJM approach applies irrespective of the model assumed for the forward rates as long as that model is consistent with the absence of arbitrage opportunities. For example, we could assume that volatility depends on the level of the forward rates or that there are two sources of uncertainty that affect forward rates (a two-factor model). Depending on the model used to generate changes in forward rates, the tree might not be recombining, making the analysis computationally unmanageable as the number of periods is extended.

mally short, changes in the forward rate become normally distributed. This implies that zero-coupon bond prices follow a lognormal distribution. However, in contrast to the distribution for stock prices, the distribution for bond prices has to change over the life of the bond because volatility has to be zero immediately before maturity since at maturity the bond price must be par. This important difference between stocks and bonds affects the pricing formula, but otherwise the pricing formula is similar to the Black-Scholes formula.

Consider a European call option maturing at T with exercise price K on a zero-coupon bond paying \$1 at t^* with price today of $P_t(t^*)$. $\sigma(t^* - T)$ is the volatility of the forward price of the bond with maturity t^* for delivery at T. Using our notation, the price of the option is $c[P_t(t^*), K, T, t]$. In this case, the closed-form solution is:

$$c\left[P_t\left(t^*\right), K, T, t\right] = P_t\left(t^*\right)N(h) - KP_t(T)N\left[h - \sigma\left(t^* - T\right)\sqrt{(T - t)}\right]$$

$$h = \left[\ln\left(P_t\left(t^*\right) / KP_t(T)\right) + (1/2)\sigma\left(t^* - T\right)^2(T - t)\right]\left[\sigma\left(t^* - T\right)\sqrt{(T - t)}\right]$$

(14.26)

Table 2 · Implementation of Heath-Jarrow-Morton in discrete time: Forward yield tree

We use a volatility of 0.005. The value for the expected rate of change of the forward yields with this volatility is trivial and is therefore ignored. $f(i)$ denotes the forward rate at t for the zero-coupon bond with one period to go at date i. Superscripts u and d denote up and down moves respectively. For example, $f^{uu}(2,3,4)$ is the forward rate at date 2 for a zero-coupon bond at 3 paying \$1 at 4 following an up move from date 0 to date 1 and an up move from date 1 to date 2.

Date 0	Date 1	Date 2	Date 3	Date 4
				$f^{uuuu}(4) = 0.085$
			$f^{uuu}(3) = 0.080$	
			$f^{uuu}(4) = 0.080$	
		$f^{uu}(2) = 0.071$		$f^{uuud}(4) =$
		$f^{uu}(3) = 0.075$		$f^{uudu}(4) =$
		$f^{uu}(4) = 0.075$		$f^{uduu}(4) =$
				$f^{duuu}(4) = 0.075$
	$f^u(1) = 0.061$		$f^{uud}(3) =$	
	$f^u(2) = 0.066$		$f^{udu}(3) =$	
	$f^u(3) = 0.070$		$f^{duu}(3) = 0.070$	
	$f^u(4) = 0.070$		$f^{uud}(4) =$	
			$f^{udu}(4) =$	
			$f^{duu}(4) = 0.070$	
$f(0) = 0.053$		$f^{ud}(2) =$		$f^{uudd}(4) =$
$f(1) = 0.056$		$f^{du}(2) = 0.061$		$f^{udud}(4) =$
$f(2) = 0.061$		$f^{ud}(3) =$		$f^{uddu}(4) =$
$f(3) = 0.065$		$f^{du}(3) = 0.065$		$f^{dduu}(4) =$
$f(4) = 0.065$		$f^{ud}(4) =$		$f^{duud}(4) =$
		$f^{du}(4) = 0.065$		$f^{dudu}(4) = 0.065$
	$f^d(1) = 0.051$		$f^{udd}(3) =$	
	$f^d(2) = 0.056$		$f^{dud}(3) =$	
	$f^d(3) = 0.060$		$f^{ddu}(3) = 0.060$	
	$f^d(4) = 0.060$		$f^{udd}(4) =$	
			$f^{dud}(4) =$	
			$f^{ddu}(4) = 0.060$	
		$f^{dd}(2) = 0.051$		$f^{uddd}(4) =$
		$f^{dd}(3) = 0.055$		$f^{ddud}(4) =$
		$f^{dd}(4) = 0.055$		$f^{dddu}(4) =$
				$f^{dudd}(4) = 0.055$
			$f^{ddd}(3) = 0.050$	
			$f^{ddd}(4) = 0.050$	
				$f^{dddd}(4) = 0.045$

where, as before, N(h) is the cumulative normal distribution function evaluated at h. This closed-form solution is similar to the Black-Scholes formula with the price of the zero-coupon bond, $P_t(t^*)$, replacing the stock price. The crucial difference, however, is that with the Black-Scholes formula the volatility would be the volatility of the bond price. Here, this volatility is the volatility of the forward price of the bond. This volatility goes to zero as t^* approaches T. The difference between the two volatilities is best illustrated by the example of a two-year option on a bond that now has a two-year maturity. In this case, $t^* = T = t + 2$. The volatility of the forward price is zero, but the volatility of the bond price return is not. The formula gives the correct option price in that case because the option payoff is not stochastic.

Let's apply the closed-form formula to a call option maturing in three years on a five-year zero-coupon bond with exercise price of 0.88. The prices for zero-coupon bonds paying $1 in five years and three years are, respectively, $0.60651 and $0.756994. The volatility is 8 percent. With these data, we have T = 5, t^* = 3, K = 0.88, σ = 0.08, $P_t(t^*)$ = 0.756994, and $P_t(T)$ = 0.60651. The formula yields a call option price per dollar of $0.0442637. If the option is on $1 million of face value for the zero-coupon bond instead of $1, the option price is obtained by multiplying $0.0442637 by $1 million, or $44,263.7.

Figure 14.7 shows call option prices as a function of the time to maturity of the underlying bond price keeping the exercise price of the option fixed at 0.88. As the maturity lengthens, the bond price falls but its volatility increases. Figure 14.7 shows that initially the volatility effect dominates if volatility is not too small, so that the call option value increases as maturity increases. Eventually, however, the maturity effect dominates so that the option falls in value as the maturity increases.

Figure 14.7 **HJM call price as a function of volatility and maturity of underlying bond**

We assume that the call option matures in three years; the price of a zero-coupon bond paying $1 in three years is 0.756994. The bond prices are given by P(T) = exp[−(0.08125 + 0.004(T − t) − 0.00005(T − t)²)T], where P(T) is the price for a zero-coupon bond that pays $1 at T.

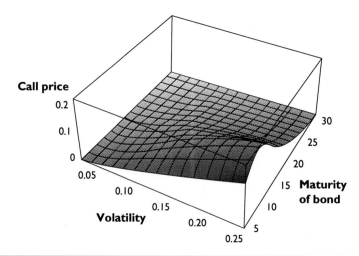

As with the Black-Scholes formula, we can obtain the delta and the gamma of the call option. Knowing delta allows us to replicate the payoff of the call option through a dynamic trading strategy as well as to hedge the option. The formula for delta is:

$$\delta = -P_t\left(t^*\right)N(h) + KP_t(T)N\left[h - \sigma(T - t^*)\sqrt{(T - t)}\right] \quad \text{(14.27)}$$

This formula has one more term than the formula of the delta with Black-Scholes. The reason is that with options on zero-coupon bonds the present value of the exercise price changes randomly because of changes in interest rates. Hence, one has to hedge the impact on the option of changes in the price of the underlying as well as changes in the present value of the exercise price. Since there is only one source of uncertainty for changes in bond prices, shocks that affect the value of the underlying asset also affect the present value of the exercise price.

The put-call parity theorem applies for options on zero-coupon bonds. We can therefore obtain the price of a put option by applying the theorem. Let the price of a put on a zero-coupon bond with price $P_t(t^*)$, exercise price K, and maturity T be $p[P_t(t^*), K, T, t]$. The theorem yields a formula for the put option which is:

$$p\left[P_t\left(t^*\right), K, t, T\right] = KP_t(T)N\left[-h + \sigma\left(t^* - T\right)\sqrt{(T - t)}\right] - P_t\left(t^*\right)N(-h)$$

$$h = \left[\ln\left(P(t, t^*)/KP_t(T)\right) + (1/2)\sigma\left(t^* - T\right)^2(T - t)\right] \sigma\left(t^* - T\right)\sqrt{(T - t)}$$

$$\text{(14.28)}$$

We can use the put option formula to price a cap. Remember that for quarterly interest payments the cap paid $\text{Max}(0.25 \times (RL_{T + 0.25} - K)/(1 + 0.25 \times RL_{T + 0.25}), 0)$, where K is the cap rate. Let K' be $1/(1 + \tau \times K)$. We can then express the payoff of the cap as $(1 + \tau RL_T)\text{Max}(K' - P_T(T + \tau), 0)$ since:

$$\frac{\tau(RL_T - K)}{1 + \tau RL_T} = \frac{1 + \tau RL_T}{1 + \tau RL_T} - \frac{1 + \tau K}{1 + \tau RL_T}$$

$$= 1 - \frac{1 + \tau K}{1 + \tau RL_T}$$

$$= (1 + \tau K)\left[K' - P_T(T + \tau)\right]$$

$$= (1 + \tau K)\left[K' - P_T(T + \tau)\right]$$

$$\text{(14.29)}$$

We can therefore price the cap using the put option formula. Per dollar of notional, we buy $(1 + \tau K)$ puts with exercise price K' on a zero-coupon bond that matures at date $T + \tau$. Note that here we assume that the interest rate on which the cap is written is the same as the one used to compute the price of the zero-coupon bond. Since the Eurodollar rate is not a risk-free rate, this is not exactly true, but without this approximation, we have to model how a rate with credit risk compares to a rate without credit risk.

Let's apply this approach to pricing the first cap we considered, which had a strike of 8 percent on a notional amount of $100 million. The interest payments are quarterly and the cap is for the interest payment to be determined one quarter from now. Consequently, we have $\tau = 0.25$ and $K = 0.08$. K' is equal to $1/(1 + 0.25 \times 0.08)$, or 0.980392. Per dollar of notional, we therefore buy 1.02 puts with exercise price of 0.980392 on a bond that matures in half a year. Let's assume a flat term structure with a continuously compounded yield of 7.5 percent. We need to make a volatility assumption to compute the cap value. If the volatility is 1 percent, a one standard deviation proportional change in the futures implied yield (15 percent of the yield given our earlier assumption) implies roughly a one standard deviation proportional change on the zero-coupon bond on which the cap is written. With these assumptions, we obtain a cap price of $17,601.70 compared to $15,091.30 using the Black formula.

14.7. Some empirical evidence

Amin and Morton (1994) compare the pricing of Eurodollar futures option contracts from 1987 to 1992 using a variety of models. They compute the implied volatilities on one day and price the contracts using these implied volatilities on the following day. For the 18.5 contracts they price on average each day, the average absolute pricing error is one-and-a-half to two basis points. To put this in perspective, the typical at-the-money puts and calls have a value of about 30 basis points.

The linear proportional model of volatility fits the Amin-Morton data the best when looking one day ahead. With this model, volatility depends on the forward rate, but less so for longer maturities. This amounts to allowing mean reversion. With mean reversion there is less uncertainty about forward rates of long maturities because mean reversion kicks in for these rates, so that they are more likely to be close to the mean. The linear proportional model has the lowest average absolute pricing error of 1.57 basis points, while the absolute model in which volatility does not depend on forward rates has an average absolute pricing error of 2.23 basis points. The average pricing error of these models is −0.13 basis points for the absolute model and −0.06 basis points for the linear proportional model, indicating that these models do not suffer from significant biases. The evidence indicates further that the pricing errors exhibit some persistence.

So should we jump to use the linear proportional model because it has the smallest absolute pricing error? The catch is in the number of parameters to be estimated. The linear proportional model requires estimating more parameters. Because a model with more parameters is more flexible, it fits better in-sample. The problem is that it may overfit by fitting incorrect or mistaken prices. A model with fewer parameters might not be able to fit incorrect prices because it is less flexible.

One way to assess models is to find out whether we can use them to make money. Amin and Morton devise a trading strategy that takes advantage of mispriced options. If the model prices options correctly, buying an option that is too cheap according to the model and hedging it with a delta hedge should make money. Amin and Morton find that all models can be used to make money to some extent, but that one-parameter models make more money. In particular, the absolute volatility model makes money consistently across puts and calls. The linear proportional model, even though it fits prices better over one day, produces significant profits only for puts. Simple models may appear to be less realistic, but they often have the benefit of being more robust. When we are evaluating alternative models, it is useful to simulate the models in the context in which they will be used.

In another study, Bühler, Uhrig, Walter, and Weber (1999) evaluate fixed income derivatives pricing models for the valuation of interest rate options in Germany. This study differs from the Amin and Morton study in two useful ways. First, it considers interest rate options that have a maturity of up to two-and-a-half years. Second, it investigates both HJM models and models that are based on the dynamics of the short-term interest rate (spot rate).

As Amin and Morton, they find that out-of-sample the simplest HJM model performs better than the more complicated HJM models. The one-factor spot interest rate models perform poorly but a two-factor model taking one factor as the short rate and the other factor as the spread between the long and the short rate performs well and possibly better than the simplest HJM model.

Finally, Driessen, Klaassen, and Melenberg (DKM, 2000) examine the pricing of caps. Their database has weekly implied volatilities on caps with maturities from one through ten years from January 2, 1995, to June 7, 1999. They examine the performance of HJM models with one, two, and three factors for pricing and hedging. The HJM models can be implemented in one of two ways. With HJM, only volatilities matter for the pricing of caps. We can therefore forecast volatilities from historical data. Alternatively, we can obtain volatilities from existing cap prices. DKM use volatilities obtained from cap prices two weeks before the pricing date. They find that using volatilities from cap prices leads to significantly smaller pricing mistakes. The absolute pricing mistake is on average 8 percent when forecasting volatilities from past date, but is less than 4 percent when using volatilities from cap prices. The best model in their study is a three-factor model, where the factors correspond roughly to the level, steepness, and curvature of the term structure. The problem with the one-factor models is that they do not allow for a hump in the forward volatility curve.

After having examined the pricing of caps, they consider the dynamic hedging of caps. DKM proceed in two ways. The first approach is to construct a delta hedge based on the number of factors in the pricing model. With a one-factor pricing model, there is only one source of risk. Therefore, in theory, one zero-coupon bond is enough to implement delta hedging and any zero-coupon bond will do. For a two-factor pricing model, we would need two zero-coupon bonds, and so on. DKM call this approach the factor hedging approach. The second approach takes into account the maturity of the caplets. For each caplet, it uses as the hedging instrument a zero-coupon bond that matures when the caplet matures. They call this approach the bucket approach. They find that the choice of model matters a great deal with the factor hedging approach. With that approach, 65 percent of the volatility is eliminated when they use the three-factor model, but only 46 percent of the volatility is eliminated when they use the one-factor model. With the bucket approach, the choice of model does not seem to matter.

Regardless of the model, hedging eliminates roughly 65 percent of the volatility of the cap. The bucket approach seems remarkably robust.

14.8. Summary

Interest rate risk is pervasive; it affects all firms. Options can be used to hedge interest rate risk. Caps, in particular, permit firms to bound their interest rate payments on floating rate debt since they pay the excess of debt service over what it would be at a stated rate, the cap rate. We show that the Black formula can be used to price caps. We explain when the Black-Scholes model can be used to price and hedge options on bonds. We show how we can use a call option formula to evaluate the interest rate risk of a callable bond. The Black-Scholes model has severe limitations for pricing and hedging derivatives whose payoff depends on bond prices because bond prices cannot have a lognormal distribution: At maturity, a default-free bond pays par. The arbitrage approach that leads to the Black-Scholes formula can be used to price fixed-income derivatives; however, no approach to price fixed-income derivatives has had the success of the Black-Scholes formula. Each approach we reviewed has advantages and disadvantages.

Key Concepts

bond price tree,   442

cap,   429

cap rate,   429

caplet,   431

collar,   435

floor, 430

floorlet,   434

interest rate call option,   430

level volatility,   449

proportional volatility,   449

spot interest rate model,   443

Review Questions

1. What is a cap?

2. What is a floor?

3. Why is the Black model useful to price caps?

4. How does one use the Black-Scholes formula to price a call option on a coupon bond?

5. Why is it that prices of bonds near maturity cannot have a lognormal distribution?

6. What is the main benefit from constructing a bond binomial tree from an interest rate binomial tree?

7. What is an important deficiency of the Ho and Lee model?

8. What are the key assumptions of the Black, Derman, and Toy model?

9. What do we mean by a one-factor model of interest rates?

10. What is mean reversion for interest rates?

11. What is the fundamental difference between models such as Ho and Lee and Black, Derman, and Toy on the one hand, and the model of Heath, Jarrow, and Morton on the other hand?

Questions and Exercises

1. It is December 30. A firm has borrowed on the euro market for one year with the first quarterly interest rate period starting on January 1. The first interest payment is set on December 30, two days before the payment period, at the current rate for three months of 7.5 percent annually. The interest rate is reset quarterly at the three-month euro-rate two days before the start of each payment period. The firm wants to make sure that it does not have to pay a quarterly rate in excess of 8 percent. Explain carefully how the firm would achieve this objective with caps.

2. Suppose that the firm buys caps to hedge its interest rate risk and decides to price these caps using the Black formula. Can you explain exactly how the assumptions it would make to price the different caps are inconsistent?

3. Use Figure 14.5. Consider a firm that has committed to borrow at date 2 for one period at the interest prevailing at that date. The interest rate is an add-on rate, so that the firm pays the rate at date 3 and repays the principal. It wants to buy a cap so that the interest paid at date 3 plus the payoff of the cap does not exceed 4.5 percent annually. What does the cap pay and when?

4. Using the interest rate tree of Figure 14.5 and the risk-neutral probabilities, price the cap described in question 3.

5. Using the interest rate tree and the bond price tree of Figure 14.4, price a put option maturing at date 2 with exercise price of $980 on the bond maturing at date 3.

6. Show how you could replicate the payoff of the put described in question 5 using a dynamic trading strategy.

7. Using the equation that specifies how the interest rate evolves in the Ho-Lee model, choose the interest rate dynamics to price the two-period bond in Figure 14.4.

8. Suppose you hedge a 30-year zero-coupon bond with a 25-year zero-coupon bond using modified duration. The true interest rate model is the Vasicek model. The shortest maturity interest rate has a volatility of 0.5 percent. What is the value at risk of your hedged position using the duration approximation?

9. Suppose you have a ten-year zero-coupon bond. The volatility of the return of the bond is 10 percent per year. Using the duration approximation, what is the volatility of the one-month interest rate if the correct interest rate model is such that the modified duration formula (using continuous compounding) can be used? What is the volatility of the same interest rate if the correct interest rate model is the Vasicek model with λ equal to 0.2?

10. You are asked to estimate a one-month VaR of a fixed income portfolio. You decide to do so using the Vasicek model. You assume that the period in equation (14.18) is one month. How would you proceed next to obtain a Monte Carlo VaR?

Literature Note

The first model with stochastic interest rates is Merton (1973). In that model, bonds are assumed to have a lognormal distribution. During the 1970s and 1980s, a number of interest rate models were developed. The most prominent of these models are the Vasicek (1977) and the Cox, Ingersoll, and Ross (1985) model. The Cox, Ingersoll, and Ross model is a so-called equilibrium model. It makes assumptions about production and preferences of investors to derive the equilibrium interest rate and the risk premium for bearing interest rate risk. Having the equilibrium interest rate and the risk premium for bearing interest rate risk, the whole term structure can be derived as a function of the spot interest rate. Brennan and Schwartz (1979) develop the arbitrage approach using two-factor models. Following Ho and Lee (1986), a number of papers provide interest rate models for trees. The papers using trees emphasized the importance of pricing the current bonds with the tree. This led to the same concern within the literature that focuses on the limit of continuous time. Hull and White (1990) show how the models of Vasicek and Cox, Ingersoll, and Ross can be extended to fit the current term structure. A prominent more recent model is Longstaff and Schwartz (1992). They show how their model can be fitted to the existing term structure in Longstaff and Schwartz (1993). The Heath, Jarrow, and Morton (1992) model led to the emergence of a large literature focused on arbitrage models using the forward curve. They provide a discrete-time implementation in Heath, Jarrow, and Morton (1990). An approach that has a different source of risk for each interest rate, the so-called string approach, is presented in Goldstein (2000) and Santa Clara and Sornette (2000). Longstaff, Santa Clara, and Schwartz (2000) show that this approach is useful to price caps and swaptions. A number of textbooks have extensive presentations of fixed-income derivatives pricing models. Tuckman (1995) has a good presentation of trees. A technical but useful book that focuses on results for the limit of continuous-time is Deventer and Imai (1997). The book by Hughston (1996) collects many of the most important academic papers.

Part 3

Beyond Plain Vanilla Risk Management

Chapter 15

The Demand and Supply for Derivative Products

Chapter **15** Objectives

At the end of this chapter, you will:

1. Understand the issues involved in taking positions in more complex derivatives.

2. Be able to choose among many different ways of obtaining a similar payoff.

3. Know the comparative advantages of different derivatives producers.

4. Be able to investigate when it is optimal to produce derivatives on your own.

5. Understand the costs and benefits associated with using new financial products.

In 1994, Procter & Gamble took positions in highly customized derivatives and lost about $200 million. These were not the conventional calls, puts, forwards, and futures contracts that we call **plain vanilla derivatives**. Plain vanilla derivatives are like commodities—they are generally traded on exchanges or on liquid over-the-counter (OTC) markets. In contrast, Procter & Gamble's derivatives were designed and priced using the proprietary model of Procter & Gamble's counterparty, Bankers Trust. The derivative position that caused most of Procter & Gamble's losses had a payoff that obeyed a complicated formula depending both on short-term and long-term interest rates. These losses led to an investigation from the Securities and Exchanges Commission (SEC), expensive litigation, and considerable adverse publicity for Procter & Gamble. Bankers Trust also fared poorly because of adverse publicity. In this chapter, we discuss the issues that users of derivatives must resolve before they decide whether or not to take positions in derivatives that are not plain vanilla derivatives.

Some critics argue that corporations are foolish to enter transactions involving customized or **exotic derivatives**—derivatives with payoffs that cannot be created through a portfolio of plain vanilla derivatives. Arguing that firms should not use exotic derivatives because some firms have had problems with them is like saying that one should not step into a jet because jets sometimes crash. Firms have exposures that cannot be hedged by putting on a static hedge involving plain vanilla derivatives. To hedge such exposures, they have to use dynamic strategies or exotic derivatives that are already traded or others that are created explicitly for firm-specific needs. However, hedging with exotic or customized derivatives does require derivatives users to think about a number of issues they can ignore when hedging with plain vanilla derivatives.

Suppose a derivatives user wants to take a position that produces a particular payoff, say, she wants to benefit from S&P 500 appreciation so that her portfolio will not be worth less in two years than today. There are many different ways to produce this payoff. She could achieve the desired outcome by investing in a portfolio that replicates the S&P 500, and buying a put option on that portfolio. A second choice is to invest in a two-year zero-coupon bond and buy a call option on the S&P 500. Third, she might choose to put her money in a two-year zero-coupon bond, take a long forward position on the S&P 500, and buy a put option on the S&P 500. Fourth, she could reproduce the payoff of the insured portfolio using dynamic replication with investments in the risk-free asset and a basket of stocks that replicates the S&P 500. Fifth, she could use an investment in the risk-free asset and holdings of the S&P 500 futures contract to replicate the payoff of the insured portfolio dynamically. Sixth, she could buy a two-year CD with a participation in the S&P 500. And so on. Different technologies can be used to produce the same promised payoff, and the producers of payoffs also differ. The CD is produced by a bank, while the put might be purchased from an exchange.

When she considers these various approaches to obtaining an insured investment in the S&P 500, the investor has to figure out which problems might crop up with the various approaches and has to evaluate which approach is most advantageous, taking these problems into account. She might also decide that no standard approach is satisfactory and design a new approach that meets her requirements.

At the very least, there are four issues in evaluating the alternate approaches to obtaining an insured portfolio on the S&P 500:

1. The likelihood that the required payoff will be obtained through a particular approach. Derivatives have a promised payoff. In many cases, the promised payoff is easy to understand. Many other times the payoff is complicated enough that understanding it correctly requires substantial effort. Since the derivatives user might misunderstand the payoff a derivative promises to deliver, she has to make sure that, if she gets the promised payoff, it will be what she expects. However, she also has to understand how likely it is that she will get the promised payoff. Many factors might prevent the derivatives user from receiving the promised payoff. For example, dynamic replication might fail because the wrong model is used, or the counterparty in a derivatives transaction might default.

2. The cost of the various approaches. The derivatives user has to be able to understand the cost of the various approaches and estimate the value of the position over time. She has to be able to take into account the subtle differences across approaches. The CD might have a penalty for early withdrawal, or the put might be an American put, so that the position has to be monitored over time to make sure that the put is exercised optimally. She also has to think about the markets in which she would trade. For example, if the two-year put trades in a very illiquid market, she will move prices against her by trading in that market, so that her cost will be higher.

3. The need for pricing models. The derivatives user has to figure out whether she needs to use pricing models to assess the various approaches and whether she is comfortable with these models. If there is competition for a derivative, the market determines the price, and a derivatives user can obtain a good estimate of a derivative's value without using pricing models. In a perfectly competitive market for cars, knowing the dealer cost is irrelevant—a car buyer cannot affect the price. In a less competitive market, knowing the dealer cost is an important bargaining tool. In the case of derivatives, the model price is the equivalent of the dealer cost.

If a derivatives user is negotiating with a single counterparty that is offering a derivative that nobody else offers, she has to understand the production cost of the derivative to be an effective negotiator. This requires an understanding of the pricing model. As derivatives become more complex and more customized, evaluating them becomes more complicated. A derivatives user therefore has to figure out whether she knows enough about the production cost of the derivatives to assess their pricing and whether it makes sense for her to buy derivatives if she does not understand their production cost.

4. The cost of getting out of the position. A derivatives user has to think about how she could get out of the position. Does the seller make a market for the derivative? Does she face a competitive market if she chooses to get out of her position or is she at the mercy of the issuer of the derivative? Does she have to pay penalties? Can she assess whether the price offered is a reasonable price?

Each derivatives position we consider entering is different. We cannot analyze separately the almost infinite number of variations in derivatives positions. We can, however, learn how to think about the costs and benefits of derivatives solutions to risk management problems. To do this, we focus on the technologies used to produce payoffs and on the suppliers of derivatives products. We first explore the properties of different technologies to produce payoffs. In the second section, we investigate which suppliers are the most efficient producers of various types of payoffs. We discuss the role of financial institutions in manufacturing payoffs and when they have a comparative advantage in doing so. A financial institution can supply a payoff in three different ways: dynamic replication, static replication, and underwriting. We explain which approach a financial institution uses in specific cases. In the third section, we discuss why and how the menu of financial products changes over time. In section four, we address when it makes sense for a firm to issue new securities with complicated payoffs. Finally, we discuss how to assess the tradeoffs between various possible hedging instruments using VaR.

15.1. Comparing payoff production technologies

Let's say that the treasurer of XYZ, Mr. Careful, wants to hedge 10 million Swiss francs by acquiring a payoff like the payoff of a European put option on the Swiss franc. We know how to price and dynamically replicate such a put option using the Black-Scholes approach. We also know that there is some debate as to whether the Black-Scholes approach is the best approach to price such an option and that other models have been proposed. Mr. Careful has a number of possible choices. We consider these solutions in turn.

15.1.1. Exchange-traded option

Exchange-traded options are standardized, with well-defined exercise prices and maturities. Mr. Careful might not be able to find options on an exchange with exactly the right maturity or the right exercise price. There is nothing that an exchange will or can do to accommodate Mr. Careful if his exposure has a different maturity from the maturity of traded options or if the required exercise price does not correspond to a multiple of the exercise price of traded options. We call the costs resulting from the standardization of exchange-traded financial products standardization costs.

Using an exchange, Mr. Careful incurs three different types of transaction costs. First, there are commissions to be paid, generally to a broker and to the exchange. There is also a bid-ask spread. If the treasurer buys the option and wants to sell it the next instant, XYZ loses the bid-ask spread. Finally, there is a **market impact cost**, which is the additional cost resulting from the impact of the trade on prices. As the treasurer places the order to buy options, his order may increase prices, so that it can be filled only at prices that are higher than those that prevailed before the order. In an illiquid market, the price of the options might have to increase to induce an increase in the supply.

Option prices on an underlying are closely tied to the price of the underlying. A typical option order would not affect the spot price of a currency for a developed country, but when the market for the underlying—the asset on which the option is written—is thin, such as the market for a stock with low volume or an emerging market currency, a large option trade is likely to convey information about the price of the underlying. The market could interpret a large purchase of a call as an indication that somebody has favorable information about the future price of the underlying asset. The market would immediately incorporate this implication of the purchase in the price of the underlying asset. Further, in an illiquid market, investors have to be induced to take the opposite position to the trade by pricing that is advantageous to them.

Derivatives exchanges have clearinghouses so that Mr. Careful does not buy the option from the option writer directly. The clearinghouse stands between the option writer and the option buyer. Therefore, Mr. Careful does not have to worry about not receiving the promised payoff from an exchange-traded option acquired on a reputable exchange. However, he still has to worry that he might not be able to trade the option when he wants to because the exchange is closed or because the market for the option is not liquid. The NYSE has well-defined procedures to stop the trading of a common stock, and numerous such trade suspensions take place each year. Futures exchanges establish price limits for some contracts so that trading stops for the day when the price changes reach the day's limit. Trading can stop because nobody wants to trade. If we believe that a counterparty wants to sell us a security because it has inside information that leads it to believe that the security is overvalued, we are willing to trade only at a price that protects us against the counterparty's information advantage, but then the counterparty may not want to trade at that price. If Mr. Careful wants to sell the option he bought, he may find the market to be extremely illiquid. The likelihood of such an event might be small for a Swiss franc option, but might be large for an option on an emerging market currency.

15.1.2. Over-the-counter option

Mr. Careful has to buy an over-the-counter option from a specific option writer, such as a bank. The direct advantage of buying an option over the counter is that standardization costs are low. Mr. Careful can buy over the counter an option that exactly meets his needs. If the bank goes bankrupt, XYZ may get only a fraction of the promised payoff. Counterparty risks are the risks that the opposite side in a derivatives contract will not pay the contractual amount specified from the derivatives contract. The direct purchase of an option from an option writer could result in Mr. Careful not receiving the promised payoff because of a default of the option writer (credit risk) or because the counterparty fails to deliver even though it is not in default (other counterparty risks). Both credit risk and other counterparty risks are typically trivial for exchange-traded products.

15.1.2.A. Credit risk　　The option buyer has to pay attention to the credit of the option writer when he buys the option. Not all option writers have the same credit. An AAA bank is quite unlikely to default on its commitments in the near future. As of the fall of 2001, Standard and Poor's had an AAA rating for only one bank that is not state owned, Rabobank of the Netherlands. Typically, Mr. Careful will not have the option to deal with an AAA bank, so that there will be some probability of default. Table 15.1 shows the credit ratings of Standard and Poor's for some major U.S. and foreign banks and U.S. investment banks in the fall of 2001. Credit risk makes a hedging strategy riskier since the derivative can become worthless if the counterparty defaults. We will discuss the determinants of credit risk in Chapter 18.

Table 15.1	Standard and Poor's ratings of banks and investment banks (Fall of 2001)
Bank of Montreal	AA–
Canadian Imperial Bank of Commerce	AA–
BNP Paribas	AA–
Credit Lyonnais	A–
Societe Generale	AA–
Deutsche Bank AG	AA
Bank of Tokyo-Mitsubishi	A–
Dai-Ichi Kangyo Bank	BBB+
ABN Amro	AA
Rabobank Netherlands	AAA
Credit Suisse	AA
UBS	AA+
Barclays Bank	AA
HSBC	A+
National Westminster Bank	AA–
Bank One Corp.	A+
Bank of America Corp.	A+
Citicorp	AA–
JP Morgan Chase	AA–
Wells Fargo and Co.	A+
Goldman Sachs Group	A+
Lehman Brothers Inc.	A+
Merrill Lynch & Co.	AA–
Morgan Stanley Dean Witter & Co.	AA–

Firms typically adopt one of four ways to deal with the problem of credit risk: (1) deal only with counterparties that have a sufficiently high rating; (2) limit their exposure to a counterparty; (3) require collateral, a margin agreement, or a credit enhancement; and (4) purchase protection against default.

Firms often have policies on the rating of counterparties. An example is the General Electric Capital Corporation. Its policy is to accept only counterparties that are rated AA or better for short-dated derivatives and AAA for transactions with maturities of five years or longer.

To reduce the credit risk presented by derivatives trades, market makers often set up specialized subsidiaries that are highly capitalized so that they can have an AAA rating even if the parent does not. In this case, Mr. Careful could deal with the highly rated subsidiary or with the parent company. The pricing of the transaction with the subsidiary would be more advantageous to Mr. Careful because of the reduced credit risk.

Salomon's Swapco is an example of an AAA subsidiary. Swapco, with a minimum capital of $175 million, can trade derivatives with any investment grade counterparty. Each transaction with a counterparty is mirrored with the parent company, Salomon. This means that if Swapco sells a put to the treasurer, it simultaneously buys a put from Salomon, so that it incurs no market risk. Swapco's capital is increased depending on the size and nature of its derivatives portfolio.

An interesting feature is that Swapco liquidates if some trigger events occur. Examples of such events are a downgrading of Swapco, bankruptcy of Salomon, or capital in Swapco falling below $175M. If a trigger event occurs, all derivatives are marked-to-market and liquidated.

By adopting the second approach, a firm that limits its exposure to any counterparty naturally diversifies across sources of credit risk. Instead of buying one option with a single counterparty, Mr. Careful buys options from several counterparties; if one counterparty defaults, he still gets the payoff from the other counterparties.

An example of the third solution would be if Mr. Careful requires that the bank establish collateral in the form of foreign currency T-bills. The T-bills might be deposited with a trustee and belong to XYZ if the bank defaults on its option contract. Such an arrangement will be costly for a capital-constrained option writer. To reduce the option writer's costs, Mr. Careful might agree that the amount set aside by the option writer depends on the extent to which the option is in the money. As the option gets deeper in the money, the collateral increases so that the amount corresponding to the option payoff will be available at maturity. This is like a margin account that grows as profits are made on the financial contract.

Finally, XYZ could purchase insurance against the default of the option writer. In this case, Mr. Careful would purchase a **credit derivative**—a derivative whose payoff is a function of the credit of a firm. We consider credit derivatives in Chapter 18.

15.1.2.B. Other counterparty risks

Not all counterparty risks are credit risks. XYZ might not receive the promised payoff even though the counterparty is solvent simply because the treasurer and the counterparty interpret the derivatives contract differently. For example, the option buyer might think he has an American option while the option seller might think he sold a European option. As we see in Chapter 17, there are many opportunities for misunderstandings to arise with more complicated derivatives. It is therefore crucial for the derivatives user to be sure that she has a complete understanding of the attributes of the derivatives she buys.

There are other reasons why a buyer might have trouble receiving the payoff of the option. The person who wrote the option contract might not have been authorized to do so by her firm. Box 15.1, Swap defaults by English local councils, presents an example. Alternatively, a contract could have some legal problems that enable the option writer to avoid paying. These problems are less likely to occur with firms that are active derivatives market makers. These firms generally gain from being viewed as reliable and from having a reputation of honoring the letter as well as the spirit of contracts. However, if Mr. Careful buys an option from a firm with few other derivatives positions, the gain to that firm from behaving opportunistically could exceed its reputation loss.

Buying an option over the counter creates a counterparty risk. The benefit of buying an option over the counter for Mr. Careful is that he can buy an option that precisely satisfies his needs; he can purchase an option with an unusual maturity and an unusual strike price. In this case, however, there is no market where

---

Box 15.1 **Swap defaults by English local councils**

In the 1980s, the local borough of Hammersmith in England was extremely active in sterling-denominated derivatives. It entered into 592 different swap transactions. Hammersmith wrote contracts whereby it promised to make floating rate payments in exchange for receiving fixed rate payments computed on a fixed amount of pounds. The fixed interest rate payments were agreed upon when the contract was signed. The fixed rate was set below market, so that to make the transaction fair, a fee had to be paid immediately to Hammersmith to compensate it for receiving fixed rate payments at a below market rate. The advantage of these transactions for the local borough of Hammersmith was that they provided it with a source of income in the form of fees. These transactions were risky. An increase in interest rates increased the payments that Hammersmith had to make without affecting the payments it received. Unfortunately, interest rates did increase and the borough was exposed to large losses on the swaps. One estimate of the losses was of £186 million over five years.

In fact, British local authorities are legally allowed to enter derivatives transactions only for hedging purposes. The transactions that Hammersmith did were not for hedging but to generate fee income. The House of Lords therefore concluded in the case of *Hazell v. Hammersmith & Fulham London Borough Council and others* that Hammersmith had no legal authority to enter the swaps and that these swaps were therefore void.

Sources: Andrew J. C. Clark, "Derivatives litigation in the United Kingdom," in *Derivatives Handbook*, Robert J. Schwartz and Clifford W. Smith, eds., John Wiley & Sons, Inc., New York, 1997; Norma Cohen, "When fingers get burned," *Financial Times*, September 6, 1989.

---

he can check the price of the option. This creates a pricing risk—the seller might take advantage of the buyer.

In an organized market, Mr. Careful knows he can sell the option at the bid price and buy it at the offer price. This means that the option is worth at least what he can sell it for. Over the counter, the pricing is not as transparent. Mr. Careful must therefore assess whether the price asked by the writer is reasonable. The simplest approach is to ask several different banks for quotes on the option he wants. In fact, firms often have a well-developed routine to obtain different bids. They may even have a formal bidding process. Mr. Careful would call several banks and explain the option he is trying to buy. He would then ask the banks to make a bid before some deadline. If the credit risk of all the banks is similar, he might then buy the option that has the lowest price. The Internet has become an efficient way for treasurers to obtain bids.

Sometimes, however, a prospective buyer may be unable to obtain more than one bid. Say Mr. Careful wants to buy a derivative that has some unusual features that only one bank is willing to supply. Maybe the time to maturity is long enough that most banks will choose not to bid. In this case, Mr. Careful cannot get competition among banks to help set the price. Instead, he has to judge the price requested by the seller according to some other benchmarks.

There are three ways for a buyer to better understand the price offered by a seller. First, a buyer can use a negotiating strategy that leads the seller to reveal information about the pricing. Mr. Careful, the treasurer, would want to discover whether the seller makes a two-way market—that is, whether he buys as well as sells—and what his price would be if the treasurer wanted to sell the option that he is seeking to buy. Often, a buyer might inquire about prices from a bank not specifying whether he wants to buy or sell a particular derivative. This approach is not possible when providing a price for a complex derivative involves substantial work on the part of the bank.

Second, we know that options must be priced so that there are no arbitrage opportunities. For example, a call on a stock cannot be worth more than the stock. Using no-arbitrage bounds provides a first approach to evaluating the reasonableness of the requested price. No-arbitrage bounds are available for more exotic derivatives.

Third, the buyer can use pricing models. In the case of the currency option Mr. Careful wants to buy, he could evaluate the price of the option using a particular formula. He might not have the right model, though. He might then find the option too expensive when it is not. If a derivative seems expensive, given the model price, the first question to ask is whether we are using the right model.

Suppose we conclude that we have the right model. This would mean that the derivative seller added a substantial markup to the model price. The markup on a derivative can be high only when there is no competition. Competition can come from other dealers, from substitution of another product through dynamic trading, or from the creation of a static portfolio strategy. When the markup is high, the derivative buyer likely has no substitutes—or the seller thinks the buyer has no substitutes. No derivative seller will provide a payoff below cost, but if the seller has some monopoly power, he can take advantage of this power and sell the derivative at a price that exceeds its production cost. The buyer must assess the price relative to the benefit of hedging. The buyer can also try to use some other derivative to substitute for this one or try to replicate the payoff of this one dynamically.

Finally, what happens when somebody with a position in an OTC product wants to get out of that position? With an exchange-traded product, there is a market where the position can be undone at quoted prices. With an OTC product, the solutions are to either take an offsetting position or go to the institution that sold the product in the first place. When the approach of taking an offsetting position is feasible, we can obtain quotes from a number of institutions, so that we are not at the mercy of a single institution. However, when there is no way to take an offsetting position, perhaps because the derivative is customized, then we have no choice but to go back to the issuing institution to undo the position. This creates the possibility for a hold-up. If the product is such that one might have to make payments, the issuing institution may not let us sell it to some other party, arguing that the credit of the new party is not as good as ours. The issuing institution may also quote an unfavorable price. For example, Mr. Scott Fullman, chief options strategist for Swiss American Securities, summarizes the problem of an option writer as follows: "Say you are a writer and it comes time to buy back. You will feel better in a competitive marketplace, whereas in the OTC you can only go back to the person you originally traded with, and that's a negative. A lot of people perceive that as an opportunity to be squeezed."[1]

Another example of difficulties is provided by the hedge fund manager David Askin, whose fund collapsed in 1994. This collapse involved various lawsuits. In an affidavit accompanying one lawsuit, Askin states: "A broker made a margin call on a security, which the broker valued at 33.5. ACM [the fund management company] immediately tried to auction the security to another firm and immediately received an oral bid of 36. When this bid was relayed to the broker, the firm refused to release the security to the higher bidder."[2]

15.1.3. Dynamic replication

Provided some conditions are met, we can create the payoff of an option by taking a position in the underlying asset and the risk-free asset. Dynamic replication is one way that Mr. Careful can obtain the option payoff that he wants. The first problem Mr. Careful faces with dynamic replication is that trades have to be made frequently. He therefore has to decide who trades and what rules that person has to follow. In the case of a put, dynamic replication involves an investment in a risk-free asset and a short position in the underlying asset, here a Swiss franc zero-coupon bond. Whenever a trade is made as part of the dynamic replication strategy, firm XYZ incurs transaction and market impact costs.

For the dynamic replication strategy to make economic sense, XYZ has to use a strategy that limits the number of trades. By choosing to trade only when the exchange rate varies by a sufficient amount, XYZ takes the risk that its dynamic replication strategy approximates the payoff of the put imperfectly. Dynamic replication also requires market data and computer software to be available. If XYZ decides to trade whenever the price of the underlying asset moves by 2 percent, XYZ would be foolish to decide to trade on the basis of newspaper prices. This means that XYZ must have some form of online access to data. XYZ must also be able to implement the formula that prescribes the hedge ratio.

If it adopts a dynamic replication strategy, XYZ does not know how often it will have to trade and what the market conditions will be when it trades. The firm might have to trade at a time when the market for the Swiss franc zero-coupon bond is very illiquid. Crises that are accompanied by very illiquid markets sometimes occur in currency markets. Trades can become very expensive. In some extreme cases, the market shuts down because nobody wants to trade. This would be extremely unlikely in a market such as the Swiss franc market, but in times of great uncertainty dealers do not want to carry inventories.

We call **liquidity risk** the risk that we might have to trade in an illiquid market with the approach we are using to obtain a particular payoff. Liquidity risk is typically low in highly liquid markets. However, even for the most liquid markets, there are times when everybody rushes to the exits and few trades are feasi-

---

1 *Derivatives Strategy*, vol. 2 (1), 11.

2 See Jack Willoughby, "Askin accuses Street firms of improper dealing at end," *Investment Dealers Digest*. 60(20) May 16, 1994, 6–7.

ble. For example, during September 1998, trades in the Treasury bond market were difficult at times, which is not typically the case.

This liquidity issue played an important role in the collapse of a Wall Street hedge fund managed by David Askin that relied on dynamic hedging. Granite Partners was pursuing a strategy of exploiting arbitrage opportunities in the market for mortgage-backed securities. The fund would lever its equity to buy securities that were cheap and hedge them dynamically. In 1994, the market for mortgage securities went through substantial turmoil and Granite Partners collapsed. In mid-February, one month before the collapse, David Askin was still saying that the mortgage securities market "is deep and broad. In the macro picture [our funds] could be ten times as big and have ten to 20 other competitors the same size without being too big." Yet, when the bear market developed, the liquidity of the market evaporated. Askin could no longer sell securities close to his model prices.

An *Institutional Investor* article argues that "An oversight that killed Askin, many managers now argue, was his complete failure to take into account the huge imbalance between supply and demand that would develop in a bear market."[3] The article quotes a Wall Street mortgage trader that: "The major Wall Street dealers are distributors, not holders and accumulators of securities. If the market is bullish and dealers can't find investors to buy bearish securities, they don't want them either. And if the market is bearish, they don't want bullish pieces. They may be obliged to make a quote, but not for a fair economic value."

A dynamic trading strategy exposes XYZ to model risks that it does not have if it buys a put outright on an exchange or over the counter. Model risks are the risks that arise because we are using the wrong model in a financial strategy. Box 15.2, Model risks and finance professors, provides an example of model risks. Suppose XYZ uses the Black-Scholes approach, which requires that the exchange rate be distributed lognormally with a constant volatility. If these assumptions do not apply, XYZ could end up with tracking error resulting from the use of the wrong model. When there are jumps in the exchange rate, the hedge ratio Mr. Careful is using is no longer correct. Consequently, at maturity, the value of the replicating portfolio of XYZ may be quite different from the value of the put XYZ tried to replicate.

Dynamic replication may not work out for more prosaic reasons. Somebody has to implement the strategy and that person can make mistakes. What if the person is sick and nobody performs his function during that time? What if someone inputs the wrong number into the computer? A famous example is the clerk at Salomon who bought 11 million shares instead of buying shares for $11 million. With homemade dynamic replication, XYZ bears the cost of all these mistakes. These risks are operational risks. Operational risks are the risks that the firm incurs as a result of mishaps in its operations. The loss incurred by a firm when it has the right dynamic strategy that it does not implement correctly because of mistakes in execution is an operational risk. Obviously, XYZ can reduce

---

3 See Alyssa A. Lappen, "Did dealers gang up on David Askin?" *Institutional Investor*, July 1994, 84–85.

Box 15.2   Model risks and finance professors

An important discovery of the late 1970s in finance is that small firm stocks earn higher returns than large firms. This discovery was refined in the early 1980s by Don Keim, a professor at the Wharton School, who showed that the superior returns on small stocks are earned in January, the so-called January effect for small stocks. This led Jay Ritter, a professor at Wharton at the time, to devise a strategy to benefit from the January effect. The Value Line index reflects the returns of small firms relative to the S&P 500 index. Consequently, by going long the futures contract on the Value Line index and shorting the futures contract on the S&P 500 index, Professor Ritter expected to make money from the January effect while being protected against overall market movements. This is an example of using risk management techniques to implement a trading strategy that would be too risky otherwise. Without the S&P 500 hedge, Professor Ritter would have had to bear all the market risk of the Value Line index. He might have made losses on his position even though the Value Line index might have outperformed the S&P 500 index because stocks in general fell in value.

Professor Ritter and his partners made significant amounts of money on this strategy in January 1984 and January 1985. By that time, Professor Ritter was classified as a large futures trader with the Commodity Futures Trading Commission and he was making more money as a futures trader than from his day job of teaching students and doing research. In May 1986, Professor Ritter and his partners were offered an extremely large position in the Value Line futures contract maturing in March 1987. They decided to take that position and to hedge it with the contract maturing in December 1986. They expected the price of the March contract to be bid up relative to the December contract as traders started to try to take advantage of the January effect by taking long positions in the March contract.

In June, things started to go wrong. The March contract started falling relative to the December contract. Professor Ritter could not understand what was going on. It made no sense to him. After asking various Wharton colleagues, he realized that the pricing model he and everybody else was using for the Value Line index was not the right one. We know that, ignoring the marking to market, the cash market value of a stock portfolio is the present value of its futures price using the risk-free rate minus the dividend rate as the discounting factor (equation 5.13). This formula works for the S&P 500 futures because the S&P 500 is constructed like a portfolio of stocks. Unfortunately, the Value Line index is not constructed like a portfolio of stocks. It is a geometric index rather than a value-weighted index like the S&P index. We cannot buy a portfolio that is a geometric index. A geometric index of two stocks would be the square root of the product of the stock prices. To replicate a geometric index, we have to implement a complicated dynamic trading strategy. It turns out that, ignoring the technical details, a geometric index earns less than an equally weighted index of the stocks included in the index. Hence, it is as if replicating the index has an additional cost. This additional cost depends on the volatility of the index. Ignoring this additional cost, one overstates the futures price.

The market and Professor Ritter had ignored this peculiarity of geometric indices. Hence, the futures price was too high. However, a former finance professor, Fisher Black, had become a partner at Goldman Sachs. He noticed that the contract was overpriced and got the traders to start taking advantage of the overpricing. In the process of doing so, Goldman Sachs sold a large position in the March contract to Professor Ritter. When Professor Ritter realized that the market was moving towards the correct pricing of the March contract, he and his partners owned the whole long position of the contract. They could not get out of the position easily—the size of their position made it illiquid. They therefore decided to hedge the position by going long the December 1987 contract and short the September 1986 contract. This helped. They further recovered some of their losses when the March 1986 contract was bid up in December by traders trying to take advantage of the January effect. However, all in all, Professor Ritter lost more from futures trading in 1986 than he gained from his day job.

The lesson from all this is that model risk spares no one.

Source: Jay Ritter, "How I helped to make Fisher Black wealthier," *Financial Management*, Winter 1996; 104–107.

operational risks by putting in place a variety of monitoring mechanisms. This increases the costs of dynamic replication.

Dynamic replication can have important advantages, however. Obviously, when Mr. Careful cannot buy the option and cannot find a close substitute, dynamic replication allows him to hedge effectively. Also, if the option is available, but too expensive, dynamic replication enables the firm to hedge at lower cost. Finally, with dynamic replication, XYZ trades in a market that in general is much deeper than the market for the put option. This has several benefits. First, XYZ's hedging has much less of a price impact. Second, XYZ's trades are more likely to be anonymous and hence XYZ is less likely to reveal information about its currency exposure to third parties. Information about XYZ's exposure can make the firm less competitive in product markets. For example, a direct competitor may infer XYZ's production plans from its exposure.

15.1.4. Static replication

With the simple payoff of a put option on the Swiss franc, we cannot usefully discuss static replication. Suppose instead that Mr. Careful wants to finance the cost of the put by giving up some of the upside potential of XYZ's exposure, so he buys a put and sells a call with different exercise prices. This is called a collar. The current value of the collar is the value of the put minus the value of the call. Mr. Careful could buy a collar directly or replicate the collar dynamically. Another portfolio strategy provides a static replication of the collar, namely, buying the put and selling the call. A **static portfolio replicating strategy** is one that takes a position in a portfolio that yields the desired payoff and requires no trading after the portfolio is purchased.

Mr. Careful can purchase a collar from a bank or make two transactions—a purchase of a put and the sale of a call. With the static replication, Mr. Careful can buy the put from one counterparty and sell the call to another counterparty. If the market for puts and calls is deeper than the market for collars, Mr. Careful might be able to construct a cheaper hedge through static replication than by buying a collar directly. Alternatively, Mr. Careful might be able to buy a put and sell a call on an organized exchange, while he could not buy a collar directly on an organized exchange.

If Mr. Careful is trying to replicate a complicated nonlinear payoff instead, we know that he can do so with a portfolio of options. Taking a position in a portfolio of options to replicate a nonlinear payoff is an example of static replication.

15.1.5. Comparison
Table 15.2 compares the costs and risks of the various approaches to obtaining a payoff discussed in this section. The table should be read to compare approaches rather than as an indication of the absolute value of these costs and risks.

15.2. The suppliers of derivatives

A firm treasurer like Mr. Careful could obtain the payoff he wants from an exchange, from a financial intermediary such as a bank, or he could produce the payoff himself. Each one of those potential producers has a comparative advantage in producing the payoff along some dimension.

Table 15.2   The costs and risks of alternate approaches to obtaining a payoff

The costs and risks should be interpreted in relative terms, so that low standardization costs for OTC products means low relative to organized exchange products.

	Organized exchange	OTC	Dynamic replication using exchange-traded products	Static replication using exchange-traded products
Standardization costs	High	Low	Low	Medium
Transaction costs	Low	Medium	High	Medium
Fixed costs	Low	Low	High	Medium
Credit risks	Low	High	Low	Low
Pricing risks	Low	High	Low	Low
Operational risks	Low	Low	High	Medium
Model risks	No	No	High	Medium

15.2.1. Exchanges

An exchange serves as a place for individuals and firms who want to sell a payoff to meet those who want to buy that payoff. An exchange must make some investments to trade a financial instrument. It sets up and monitors a trading pit or a computerized trading mechanism; it organizes a system to record and process trades, establishes a mechanism to distribute quotes, and so on. Some of these costs are fixed costs—they are incurred whether there are many or few trades of the financial instrument. It is not profitable for an exchange to incur these costs for financial instruments that trade infrequently. When it designs an exchange-traded product, the exchange wants to make sure there will be enough trades to enable it to recover its fixed costs. This means the instrument cannot be designed for a single counterparty, but instead must be standardized so that it is useful to many different counterparties.

Exchanges can do many things to ensure that a product will appeal to many counterparties, but sometimes they fail. On futures markets, contracts sometimes die for lack of trades. An example is the GNMA CDR futures contract. This contract on Government National Mortgage Association (GNMA) Collateralized Depository Receipts (CDR), which are mortgage-backed securities, was one of the first interest rate futures contracts. It was introduced in 1975. In 1980, annual trading volume was over 2.3 million contracts, but by 1987, volume had fallen to 8,000 contracts, and trading quotations were no longer listed in the financial press.

There is a straightforward explanation for the failure of this contract: it stopped being useful. Mortgage bankers used it to hedge current coupon mortgages. During the 1980s, its hedging effectiveness deteriorated, and eventually the Treasury bond contract became a better hedge for current coupon mortgages. The demand for the GNMA CDR contract fell and eventually disappeared.

When a payoff is useful for a small number of counterparties, there will not be an active organized market for it. As a payoff becomes more specialized in its usefulness, the organized market has no longer a comparative advantage in producing it. Organized markets have costs that are too high to produce payoffs that are useful to only few individuals or firms.

15.2.2. Financial intermediaries

Financial intermediaries can produce a payoff useful to only few individuals or firms at lower cost than an exchange or than the derivative user. The financial intermediaries have valuable firm-specific assets that they can use to produce the put, such as a trading operation and a financial engineering staff. However, financial intermediaries lose out to an exchange when the exchange can harness economies of scale to produce a payoff useful to very large numbers of investors and firms.

To understand why a financial intermediary could have a comparative advantage in producing a payoff, suppose Derivatives Bank (DB) is approached by treasurer Careful, who wants to purchase a put option payoff. DB can sell the put option to Mr. Careful, but it now has a short position in a Swiss franc put. This means that if the Swiss franc falls, Mr. Careful does not lose money; DB loses money. DB's risk changes when it sells the put. DB cannot let its risk increase each time it makes a transaction; or its promised payoffs would have little value.

Let's suppose DB does not want its VaR to increase. In this case, the sale of the put will be profitable for DB only if the price paid covers DB's entire costs in producing the put, including the cost of the transactions required to offset the impact of the sale of the put on its VaR.

15.2.2.A. The intermediary as market maker

DB could sell the put to Mr. Careful and immediately turn around and buy the same put from a third party. In this case, DB would have no net position in the put. Whether the complete trade affects the risk of DB depends on the counterparty risk resulting from the purchase of the put. If DB buys the put from a highly reliable counterparty, the complete trade has almost no effect on the riskiness of DB. If the counterparty is not as reliable, DB could eliminate the risk resulting from the trade by buying a credit derivative that insures the put against default.

To avoid making a loss on the transaction, DB would have to charge Mr. Careful for the price of the put bought plus the price of the credit derivative. It would also have to incorporate the various costs incurred in providing the payoff—back office costs, the time of the trader, and so on. Note that to make this complete trade, DB must be able to find a counterparty. This means it needs a trader who has information about who might want to sell a put. If the put is traded on an exchange, DB can go to the exchange and buy the put. In this case, there is no credit risk and DB can buy the put easily, but it just acts as a broker and Mr. Careful could do the same at close to the same costs. With a trading operation and no organized market, DB has a comparative advantage over Mr. Careful in producing the payoff. It is better able than Mr. Careful to obtain information about potential suppliers of puts.

In general, the purchase and sale of the put will not be simultaneous. After selling the put, the intermediary must bear the position's risk until it can find a put to buy. DB therefore has to estimate the risk it will bear while waiting to buy the put. This risk will depend on the proficiency of its trading room and sales force.

15.2.2.B. The intermediary as producer

Derivatives Bank may not find a supplier for the put. In that case, DB can produce the payoff of a long position in the put through a dynamic trading strategy. Its balance sheet will show a short position in a put and a long position in a synthetic put. On net, DB will have no exposure if the dynamic replication is perfect—that is, it produces the payoff for sure. Mr. Careful, as we saw earlier, could produce a put synthetically also, but DB has several advantages over Mr. Careful in replicating this payoff. First, it has a trading operation; it is therefore more likely to get good execution on the trades. Second, it has the knowledge and the experience to pursue such a trading strategy. Third, it can save on transaction costs because there might be offsetting trades within DB, and trades could be combined into larger trades that would have lower transaction costs. Hence, in general one would expect a financial intermediary to be able to implement a dynamic trading strategy more efficiently than Mr. Careful.

By manufacturing the payoff of the put synthetically, DB assumes model risks, liquidity risks, and operational risks. Some of these risks may be diversified within the firm. For example, if the possibility of jumps in prices is not correctly taken into account in the models used by the firm, jumps may create profits for some products and losses for other products. If a nonfinancial firm were to dynamically replicate one put, there is much less room for the risks of that strategy to be diversified.

How would the financial intermediary price the put sold to Mr. Careful? The minimum price it can charge needs to take into account the anticipated trading costs of the dynamic replication strategy. Hence, this minimum price will generally exceed the Black-Scholes price even if the other assumptions that lead to the Black-Scholes formula hold since that price assumes no transaction costs. Various formulas are available to price options with transaction costs. It may also be, though, that this minimum price differs from the Black-Scholes price for other reasons, for example because volatility changes randomly. Whatever the theoretical option pricing model that is appropriate to price the put option, this model provides only a lower bound on the price the financial intermediary charges to the buyer. Depending on its competitive position, the financial intermediary may charge substantially more than this minimum price.

15.2.2.C The intermediary as hedger   An intermediary can trade without hedging individual transactions, focusing instead on the risk of the firm as a whole. In this case, Derivatives Bank buys and sells products and separately hedges its current equity value to make sure its capital is sufficient to guarantee that it can deliver on its promises. It will constantly review its aggregate exposure to risk factors and manage this exposure.

DB might use the delta approach to evaluate the risk of derivatives, in which case each derivative is represented by a position in an underlying security. The firm's risk is thus like the risk of a portfolio, but the weights of the securities in the portfolio depend on the deltas of the derivatives as well as on the size of the derivative positions. Let's assume DB has a portfolio of equity options written on different stocks. It could dynamically hedge each option separately, or it could hedge the portfolio. The firm could effectively have the equivalent of a diversified portfolio of stocks and use only index futures to eliminate the market risk of this portfolio. It would assume that firm-specific risks are diversified within the portfolio. The advantage of this approach is that it requires fewer trades than dynamically hedging each derivative in the firm's portfolio.

This approach does not provide an exact hedge, however. Even if a portfolio has low volatility because of diversification, there is always a small chance that the portfolio may incur a large loss. While a portfolio has many uncorrelated risks, so that positive and negative outcomes will typically roughly cancel each other because of diversification, it could always happen that they do not. An exact hedge of each exposure, if feasible, would avoid the possibility of such a large loss, but would be more expensive. With a portfolio of uncorrelated risks, an exact hedge would go short each risk so as to eliminate the firm's exposure to that risk. Consequently, even if the outcomes for all risks were adverse to the firm, it would not suffer with an exact hedge.

15.2.2.D. The intermediary as packager   A financial institution that sells a product could buy a portfolio of financial instruments that provides a hedge and not have to trade dynamically. Derivatives Bank might not be able to buy a put that would offset the put it sells to Mr. Careful, but it might find that it can buy a call easily. In this case, DB could use put-call parity to hedge the put it sells to Mr. Careful by hedging the put with a portfolio long a call and short the underlying asset. DB might find that it cannot buy a put or buy a call, but there is a demand for a structured note that pays a fixed amount at maturity minus the payoff of a put on the Swiss franc. If the put were for a sufficiently large amount, DB could issue such a structured note and hedge the put sold to Mr. Careful.

Say that Mr. Careful wants a put on 10 million Swiss francs that has a maturity of 10 years and an exercise price of $0.50 per Swiss franc. In this case, DB could sell a structured note that pays the principal in 10 years minus ($5M – the dollar value of 10M Swiss franc) if that amount is positive. Let S_{t+10} be the spot rate in 10 years. If X is the principal, the payoff of the structured note is:

$$X - Max(\$5M - \$10M \times S_{t+10}, 0)$$

Since in 10 years DB must pay $Max(5M - 10M \times S_{t+10}, 0)$ to Mr. Careful, the structured note is a perfect hedge. All DB has to figure out is how to price the note at date t. With what we have learned so far, this is not hard:

$$\text{Present value of} \left[X - Max\left(\$5M - \$10M \times S_{t+10}, 0\right) \right]$$
$$= P_t(t + 10)X - p(S, 5M, t + 10, t)$$

where $P_t(t + 10)$ is the price of a dollar to be paid in 10 years and $p(S, 5M, t + 10, t)$ is the current value of a European put option on the Swiss franc with exercise price of $5 million at maturity in 10 years.

The point of this example is that when it knows what investors are looking for, a financial intermediary may be able to create a package of securities that is attractive to some investors and resolves its own risk management problem.

15.2.3. The "do it yourself approach"

In general, Mr. Careful can find his put payoff at lower cost on an exchange (if it is traded on an exchange) or from a financial intermediary such as a bank. Financial intermediaries have trading rooms, computer resources, financial engineering talent, and experience that they can use to implement individual transactions efficiently. Even a large firm outside the financial services industry has only a staff with limited experience and will not have traders with up-to-date intelligence about market conditions. Mr. Careful will therefore generally use a financial services firm or an exchange to provide him with the payoffs he wants. There will be exceptions to this, but probably not for a simple derivative like the Swiss franc put.

If Mr. Careful wants to obtain complicated payoffs that are path-dependent, he could end up having to create these payoffs synthetically on his own. Suppose Mr. Careful wants to hedge XYZ's exposure to the Swiss franc, but this exposure changes frequently and in ways that cannot be easily described. The effect of an unexpected change in the Swiss franc exchange rate on the value of XYZ might depend on the evolution of the exchange rates of several other currencies as well as interest rates in complicated ways. As the dynamic strategy required to synthesize the payoff that hedges the exposure becomes complicated to explain to third parties and depends on frequent transfers of information, it can become more cost-effective for XYZ to design and implement the strategy on its own. Further, the third party may require information to act efficiently that XYZ does not want to provide.

15.3. Financial innovation and financial engineering

So far, we have seen that Mr. Careful will acquire a derivative on an exchange when that derivative is a standardized high-volume financial product. If Mr. Careful requires a more specialized product, he will go to a financial intermediary. Finally, if the product Mr. Careful wants is complex and unique to firm XYZ, he may find it most efficient to manufacture the product in-house.

An important activity of financial intermediaries is to provide efficient solutions to risk management problems. If Mr. Careful's overall risk management problem is extremely complicated, a bank such as Derivatives Bank might hope it has products that are useful to at least partly solve XYZ's risk management problem. If it does not have such products, it may want to design them. The menu of financial products is not fixed over time. New technologies become available, computers become more powerful, risk becomes better understood, and so on. When DB attempts to find more efficient solutions for Mr. Careful's risk management problem, it practices financial engineering. As Robert Merton defines it, "Financial engineering . . . is a systematic approach used by financial-service firms to find better solutions to specific financial problems of their customers."[4]

Investors and firms have many reasons to hedge. Their hedging needs may be complicated. Financial service firms satisfy these hedging needs by creating new financial products that enable firms to hedge efficiently.

15.3.1. The life-cycle of financial products

The first step in the creation of any financial product is the identification of a problem that cannot be solved efficiently with the financial products at hand. The problem could be a risk management problem of a particular firm or of an individual. It might take the form of a risk that has to be hedged or a risk that has to be taken efficiently.

Suppose a Derivatives Bank customer, Ms. Smith, the treasurer of ABC Inc., comes to it with a specific problem that she cannot solve on her own. Say she is concerned about having to make a payment at the end of next year that depends on the interest rate at that time. The payment to be made is $100M $\times r^2$, where r is the decimal interest rate, provided that r exceeds 0.04. Otherwise, the payment is $0.16 million. Figure 15.1 shows ABC's payment. Ms. Smith noticed that the payment does not increase linearly with the interest rate. She is used to buying caps, but she knows that a cap cannot solve her problem. She would like DB to propose a solution to her hedging problem.

DB turns to a financial engineer. With the tools developed so far in this book, the financial engineer would be able to design and price a financial instrument

---

4 See Robert C. Merton, "A functional perspective of financial intermediation," *Financial Management*, vol. 24 (2), Summer 1995; 23–41.

Figure 15.1   ABC's payment

ABC Inc. has to pay \$0.16 million if the interest rate is below 4 percent. Otherwise, it has to pay \$100M $\times$ r^2 where r is the decimal interest rate.

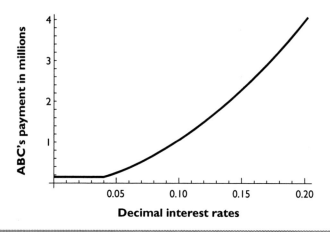

that is an exact hedge for ABC. To hedge the random part of the payment, ABC must earn \$100M $\times$ r^2 if the interest rate is greater than 4 percent. Consider an option on the square of the interest rate with exercise price equal to 0.0016. This option pays Max[r^2 – 0.0016, 0]. The payoff of that option is r^2 – 0.0016 if the interest rate is above 4 percent and zero otherwise. Hence, if we take a position of \$100 million notional in such an option, we get \$100M $\times$ (r^2 – 0.0016) when the interest rate is higher than 4 percent, which is \$100M $\times$ r^2 – \$0.16M. This payment is lower than the required interest payment by \$0.16 million. Hence, if we take a position of \$100 million notional in the option and then invest in a bond that pays off \$0.16 million, we get \$100M $\times$ r^2 when the interest rate is higher than 4 percent and \$0.16 million otherwise.

Having found a solution to the problem, the financial engineer has to figure out the production costs and understand the demand for the product. Once she has designed the product, the design costs are sunk. The production costs for a unit of the product are now simply the replication costs. She can use an interest rate tree as in Chapter 14 to price the product, taking into account transaction costs.

The next step is to decide the markup DB wants to charge. To decide this, DB has to know its customer. DB also has to decide whether it will attempt to market this new product to other customers. At this point, DB has a unique product. In the very short run, it does not have to worry about competition, but when competitors find out about the product, they can replicate it. They have the same technology DB has. The fact that competitors will enter the market if DB charges too high a price may lead it to choose to limit the markup. Another factor that will make DB choose a lower markup is if it is trying to increase the market for the product.

Finally, an important issue in the markup decision has to do with DB's reputation. DB's customers know neither how to produce the product it is selling nor its production costs. If it turns out that later the same product is sold at a much lower price, will they still trust DB?

Initially, the product will have one or a handful of customers. Over time, however, competitors will step in to undercut DB or even offer a better product. Competitors will move in more quickly if DB's price includes a high margin. By choosing a lower margin, DB reduces its profit per unit but increases its volume and delays the entry of competition. Eventually, though, the product will be produced by many financial services firms competing aggressively for the business. DB will no longer make abnormal profits on the product, and the product will be priced to just cover the production costs of the most efficient producers. If DB is not among the most efficient producers, it will be driven out of the market for the product. As the market for the product keeps expanding as the price falls, it may even become profitable for an exchange to start trading a standardized version of the product. This standardized version of the product can then become a building block of portfolios and other products.

In this hypothetical example, DB's financial engineer knows how to solve the customer's risk management problem. There is no product available and DB can create one. DB makes a profit by being the first to create the product. If the product succeeds, DB can sell it to more customers and the market for it increases. If the product becomes standardized, it ceases to be a source of abnormal profits for DB. For a financial services firm to be successful in making profits, it must keep innovating.

15.3.2. The profits from innovation

As the Japanese Nikkei index was close to its peak in 1990, American investment banks were aware that they could profitably sell Nikkei puts to retail investors. Goldman Sachs and Co. was the first firm to succeed. A Harvard Business School case shows that Goldman looked carefully at what investors wanted. It realized that American investors did not want exchange rate risk, did not want credit risk, but wanted a product they could trade, wanted an American-style option, and wanted a maturity of about three years. It designed an instrument with these features that it could list on an exchange. Goldman could not issue and list such a product directly because SEC disclosure requirements for publicly issued securities would force disclosure of information about the Goldman partnership. Goldman therefore made a deal with the Kingdom of Denmark. To produce the warrants, it used puts from its inventory. These puts were in yen and had a longer maturity than investors wanted. Hence, it had to dynamically hedge its supply of puts against exchange rate risks. Goldman priced the first issue of warrants on January 12, 1990, at $4.05 and the second one on January 17 at $5.375. The volatility of the Nikkei increased slightly during that period and the Nikkei level fell slightly, but these changes do not appear to explain the substantial increase in the price. Competition surfaced almost immediately. Salomon issued warrants on January 17 and Bankers Trust on February 1.

Why did Goldman behave the way it did? Most likely, it was uncertain about the demand curve. If the demand for the product turns out to be lower than expected, the product fails. This can diminish the reputation of the issuing firm and impair its ability to introduce new products later. Goldman may therefore have made the equivalent of an introductory offer where the product is priced low enough to gather information about demand. An "introductory offer" can also be profitable for a different reason. Investors need to study a new product. Investors who wait to buy a product until it is more seasoned can "free-ride" on the experience of investors who buy the product first. A low price attracts investors to a product early in its lifecycle.

Large-sample empirical evidence shows that the concept of the introductory offer seems to apply to financial innovations. In a study of 58 financial innovations from 1974 to 1986, Tufano (1986) finds that firms do not charge a higher price for a new product to take advantage of their monopolistic position. He even finds evidence that in the long run innovators charge prices below those of imitators. This may seem to indicate that innovators learn through innovation and that this enables them to manufacture the product at lower cost. The reward to the innovators is therefore not higher margins initially, but rather greater market share over time. In other words, innovators make their profit on volume.

In a complementary study, Tufano (1996) examines the experience of the investors who buy the products. A striking result is that it pays for investors to buy new products: investors who buy the first issue of a new product earn on average 8 percent more than investors who buy subsequent issues, although they face substantial volatility for the returns of first issues of new products. In other words, while investors in the first issue of new products earn more on average, there is considerable dispersion in their experience across new products. In this sense, new products are risky for investors. The firms that use new products proposed by investment bankers do not appear to make significant gains from doing so. Tufano investigates the stock returns of these firms around the announcement of their use of a new product and finds no significant difference between the firms that are first in using a product and firms that use it subsequently.

What is the bottom line of all this evidence? Producers of derivatives have few incentives to take advantage of customers when they introduce new products. It can happen that one individual may take advantage of a firm's customers because the incentives of individuals working for a firm may differ from those of the firm. If an employee's bonus depends on the profits he brings to the firm and he does not plan on staying there a long time, he can increase his income by charging more now. He will not be around later when customers do not deal with the firm anymore.

In general, when a product is broadly marketed, this circumstance is unlikely to arise because much information about the product will circulate to potential buyers. With a product marketed to one or few customers, employees have taken advantage of buyers. Buyers of derivatives have to remember that the legal obligations of the seller of derivatives are quite limited, especially when its derivatives do not qualify as securities as discussed in the Box 15.3, Buyers beware.

15.4. Embedded derivatives

A company might want to hedge its yen exposure because a yen appreciation makes it worse off. It could hedge by buying a call on the yen, or consider a

Buyers beware   *Box 15.3*

In 1993, two companies in Cincinnati, Ohio, entered into complicated derivatives transactions with Bankers Trust (BT). Both companies lost large amounts of money on their derivatives transactions. One company, Procter & Gamble (P&G), had losses close to $200 million; the other company, Gibson Greetings, a much smaller company, had losses in excess of about $21 million. These derivatives losses led to SEC investigations and lawsuits.

In the Gibson Greetings case, fraudulent behavior was found. A BT salesman gave incorrect valuations for the company's derivatives positions. BT taped all conversations of its traders with clients as well as with other traders. After the value of the transaction started to become significantly negative, the salesman understated the losses. A taped conversation of the salesman with a BT trader has him stating: "I think we should use this [downward market price movement] as an opportunity. We should just call [Gibson] and maybe chip away at the differential a little more. I mean, we told him $8.1 million when the real number was 14. So now if the real number is 16, we'll tell him that it is 11." This is illegal.

The litigation following these derivatives losses has important implications for buyers of derivatives. P&G argued that BT somehow had a fiduciary duty to P&G because it had a relationship of trust with BT and BT had superior knowledge concerning the transactions. P&G meant that BT had to take care of the financial interests of P&G and hence had to make sure that the transaction was appropriate for P&G. Such fiduciary responsibilities exist under some circumstances. If BT had acted as an advisor to P&G and if there had been an established advisory relationship, it would have had fiduciary responsibilities. Had it then been established that BT had breached these responsibilities, the derivatives contracts would have been voided and P&G would have sustained no losses.

BT recorded BT traders commenting that P&G did not understand well the derivatives it had entered into. At the same time, however, P&G had a sophisticated treasury in constant contact with investment banks, seeking out information about financial products that would enhance P&G's profits. The judge in the case dismissed P&G's claims concerning the breach of fiduciary duty. He concluded that P&G employed its own expertise in evaluating the transactions and that therefore the transactions were done at arms-length. In other words, in derivatives trades between nonfinancial corporations and dealers, the disclosure duties of the dealer are extremely limited. A buyer of derivatives should therefore not expect the dealer to have any responsibility to protect the buyer's financial interests unless an advisory relationship has been clearly established. At the same time, however, dealers have to consider their reputation if their customers feel that they were taken advantage of. Perhaps because of this consideration, BT ended up agreeing to a settlement with P&G that eliminated most of the losses of P&G from its derivatives positions.

Source: Carol J. Loomis, "Untangling the derivatives mess," *Fortune*, March 20, 1995, 50–68. John M. Quitmeyer, "P&G v. Bankers Trust delivers another blow to fiduciary duty claims," *Derivatives*, September/October 1996, 28–32.

different solution. It could raise funds so that its debt servicing becomes less onerous if the yen appreciates. One way is to borrow and make the principal repayment depend on the yen/$ exchange rate. The Ford Motor Credit Company, a subsidiary of the Ford Motor Company, made such an issue in 1987. It issued reverse PERLS™. PERLS™ stands for Principal Exchange Rate Linked Securities, a security introduced by Morgan Stanley. It pays interest in dollars. In the case of the Ford issue, Ford paid 11 percent interest on a face value of $100 million. The repayment at maturity (May 19, 1992) is $200 million minus the U.S. dollar equivalent of ¥13,920 million.

Figure 15.2 shows the repayment as a function of the exchange rate. At the exchange rate of ¥139.2 per dollar, the security repays its principal value of $100 million. If the yen is worth less than that, the security repays more than its principal value. Otherwise, it repays less. As the dollar price of the yen increases, the repayment falls in value. PERLS™ have limited liability, so that the investors in the security owe nothing at maturity. However, suppose that at maturity a dollar is worth ¥33. In that case, the formula for the repayment would indicate a repayment of $200M – ¥13,920M/33, which would be –$221.82 million. Obviously, in this case, the formula does not apply and the repayment is zero. Consequently, the exact formula for the repayment is:

Max($200M – Dollar value of ¥13,920M, 0)

With this formula, there is no repayment if the dollar value of the yen is more than $0.0143678 or, equivalently, if a dollar is worth less than ¥69.6.

Why would a company choose to take a long yen position in this way? As we know, it could take a long yen position in many different ways. In this case, it bundles a hedging transaction with a financing transaction. Bundling like this

---

Figure 15.2   Repayment due on the Ford PERLS™

The promised payment by Ford is $200 million minus the U.S. dollar equivalent of ¥13,920 million if that amount is positive and zero otherwise.

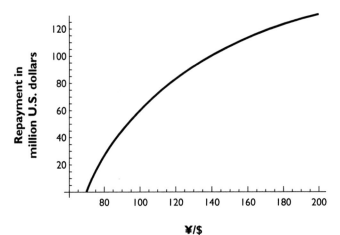

¥/$

might enable Ford to raise funds more cheaply than if it issued fixed-rate debt and/or to hedge more cheaply than if it purchased calls. Let's consider these benefits in turn.

15.4.1. Bundling can reduce credit risks associated with the issuer's debt

By issuing a security as opposed to buying one, Ford does not take on credit risk. The investors take on the credit risk instead, in that Ford might default on the securities it sells. If indeed Ford is trying to hedge a short yen exposure, these securities also have an advantage over straight debt in terms of default risk. Note that if Ford has a short yen exposure, it will be weaker when the yen is strong—that is precisely when it will have to repay the least.

Consequently, the Ford PERLS™ promise to pay the least when Ford might be short of resources and promise to pay the most when Ford is in the best situation to pay. Such securities cost less than straight debt because of their hedging function.

15.4.2. Bundling can offer new investment opportunities to investors

Although Ford has easy access to forward markets to take positions in the yen, small investors do not. By issuing the securities, Ford enables small investors to take a short position in the yen. To the extent that investors were unable to take this exact position before, they might be willing to pay for this benefit by requiring a lower coupon. This would reduce Ford's cost of funds.

15.4.3. Bundling can eliminate difficulties with counterparties

Ford can take a long yen position for an extremely large amount, ¥13,920 million. It might not be able to find a bank that is willing to be the counterparty to such a forward position with a five-year maturity. A bank might consider the counterparty risk excessive. Consequently, Ford might have to split the forward position among a number of different banks, requiring more attention to more transactions. Banks would monitor Ford's credit quite carefully. At times, they might ask Ford to post collateral. This means that during the life of the contracts, Ford would have to deal with bank requests. If it issues securities, the security holders cannot require anything unless Ford is in default.

15.4.4. Bundling can reduce transaction costs

If Ford wants to raise funds anyway, the marginal cost of hedging through bundling is the difference in issuance costs resulting from having the repayment depend on the yen exchange rate. This marginal cost is likely to be fairly small. If Ford hedged without bundling, it might have had to deal with a number of banks, and in each transaction it would have faced transaction costs in the form of the bid-ask spread on forward contracts. For long-maturity forward contracts, this spread can be substantial. If long-dated forward contracts are not feasible, Ford might have had to take positions in short-dated futures contracts and design a dynamic trading strategy that replicates the payoff of a long-dated forward contract, incurring higher transaction costs and involving risks.

We assumed that Ford issued these securities because it wanted to hedge, but it could have done so for other reasons. It is tempting to say that Ford almost surely entered the transaction for other reasons, because one would expect an American automobile manufacturer to be naturally long yen—an increase in the dollar value of the yen makes Japanese imports more expensive and hence benefits American companies. Exposures of companies are typically complicated, though, and Ford might have been short yen until maturity of the debt. Nevertheless, it may have issued the security to reduce its cost of funds. It could have done so for two reasons.

First, it might have tried to satisfy some investor clientele. We have noted that some investors may want to short the yen but cannot do so efficiently through futures, options, or forwards because their trades are too small. A corporation might benefit from acting as an intermediary by issuing low-denomination notes that have the desired payoff for these investors and hedging the issue on the forward and options markets. In fact, some firms did just that. Sallie Mae issued reverse PERLS™, and then completely hedged the issue so that the hedged issue had no foreign exchange risk. Obviously, such a transaction makes sense if it reduces the cost of funds for the issuing company.

Another reason a company may issue securities whose payoff is directly linked to risk factors is that the company believes it has information about future changes in risk factors. In the case of reverse PERLS™, Ford might have believed that the yen would appreciate more than the market thought it would. Hence, it viewed the securities as advantageous because its estimate of the expected repayment is less than the investors.

When the notes matured, the yen exchange rate was 129.10 per dollar. Ford had to repay roughly $200M − $107,823,393 = $92,176,607. Because the yen had appreciated, it had to repay less than the face value of the PERLS™.

15.5. Assessing the trade-offs

A firm or an individual considering hedging a particular risk faces choices. At one extreme, the hedge is perfect, and at the other extreme the hedge is so poor as to be useless. We might be tempted to decide that we should hold the most effective hedge. Upon reflection, this makes little sense. A firm always has to think about how to maximize its shareholders' wealth. Hedges have different transaction costs and different attributes, though. A perfect hedge might be extremely costly, so purchasing it could eliminate the benefits from hedging in the first place. Tolerating some risk from a hedged position might increase shareholder wealth if doing so reduces transaction costs sufficiently.

We can assess the trade-off between transaction costs and risk by explicitly comparing the cost of a hedge and the benefit of reducing VaR (or CaR). This approach applies generally to all the situations we considered in this chapter. Look at Mr. Careful's comparison of various ways of taking a position equivalent to being long a Swiss franc put. Exchange-traded options, over-the-counter options, and dynamic replication all have different costs and lead to a different outcome. For each possible hedging strategy, Mr. Careful can compute the cost of the hedging strategy and the reduction in the VaR resulting from the hedge. If he can estimate the value of reducing VaR for the various hedging options, he can then choose the hedging strategy that is the most valuable.

Let's be more specific. Let's assume that the Swiss franc is worth $0.50, the exposure is a one-year exposure of 10 million Swiss francs, the expected rate of depreciation of the Swiss franc is zero, the volatility of the exchange rate is $0.05, and the VaR of the unhedged position is $825,000. Suppose we have a put strategy using an over-the-counter put that costs $0.15 million and reduces the VaR to $0.1 million, versus an exchange-traded put that matures after the exposure but costs only $0.1 million and reduces the VaR to $0.15 million. With this example, hedging reduces the VaR considerably. If the cost of VaR is 15 percent a year for Mr. Careful, he would choose to hedge. The VaR gain of $0.05 million from using the over-the-counter put, however, is not enough to justify the additional cost of $0.05 million. Consequently, Mr. Careful would choose the exchange-traded option even though he could obtain a hedge that reduces the VaR more.

VaR provides us with the appropriate tool to evaluate potential hedges if VaR measures risk appropriately. The example should make it clear that the best hedge is not the one that minimizes VaR. The best hedge is the one that creates the most value.

15.6. Summary

We have examined the issues we face when deciding where and how to purchase a particular payoff. We saw that payoffs could be obtained on an exchange, from a financial intermediary, and finally using a "do-it-yourself" approach. Exchanges provide standardized payoffs; financial intermediaries and the "do-it-yourself" approach provide customized payoffs. Customized payoffs are more expensive. When bought from a third party, customized payoffs suffer from counterparty and pricing risks. Producing payoffs using the "do-it-yourself" approach exposes us to model, operational, and liquidity risks. There is no technology producing payoff that is the best under all circumstances, but rather there are always trade-offs. VaR allows us to evaluate the trade-offs and choose among possible hedges.

Key Concepts

credit derivative, 475
exotic derivatives, 470
liquidity risk, 478
market impact cost, 472

plain vanilla derivatives, 470
static portfolio replicating
  strategy, 482

Review Questions

1. What is a plain vanilla derivative?

2. What is an exotic option?

3. What are the issues you should think about before taking a position in an exotic or customized option?

4. What is the main advantage of using the OTC market instead of an exchange? What is the main disadvantage?

5. How can derivatives users reduce counterparty risk?

6. What type of payoffs can be produced more efficiently by an exchange than by a financial firm?

7. When is it that homemade production of a derivative position is more efficient than using an exchange or a financial firm to produce that position?

8. How are new products priced?

9. Why might a firm issue securities to hedge rather than take positions in derivatives?

10. Why might a derivatives user not choose the hedge that reduces VaR the most?

Questions and Exercises

1. Consider two insurance companies that sell seven-year annuities that promise a minimum guaranteed return of 3 percent plus half the appreciation in the S&P 500 over the life of the annuity on an investment equal to the initial annuity payment. One company, Short-term Inc., hedges using options on the S&P 500 with maturity of one year or less while the other company, Long-term Inc., hedges by buying seven-year options on the S&P 500. How will these two companies most effectively obtain the options they require for hedging?

2. On average, which company in question 1 would you expect to be most profitable? Why?

3. Suppose that the volatility of the S&P 500 is constant over time. Is it possible for Short-term Inc. to have a more precise hedge than Long-term Inc. ex post? Why?

4. Suppose that the volatility of the S&P 500 doubles overnight. What are the implications for the hedging program of Short-term Inc. and for the hedging program of Long-term Inc.?

5. Suppose that the volatility of the S&P 500 doubles. As a result, the terms of new annuities have to be changed and the annuity buyers receive one quarter of the appreciation of the return of the S&P 500. You find that the customers of your company do not want annuities with a small participation in the increase of the S&P 500 because they primarily want these annuities to make sure that if the market does extremely well, they do well also. Instead, with the lower participation, they feel that they will never do really well. Can you design annuities that are attractive to your clients?

6. Consider a firm that has an unhedged VaR of $100 million. It has a choice between two hedging programs. One is a perfect hedge and eliminates all risk so that the VaR is zero. The other program has tracking error, so that the firm ends up with a VaR of $10 million. The firm can raise equity that has a net cost of 15 percent annually. The perfect hedge costs $5 million to implement and the hedge with tracking error costs $4 million. What should the firm do?

7. Consider a money manager who is implementing a large dynamic hedging strategy to insure a portfolio indexed to the S&P 500. The strategy is such that the end-of-year value of the portfolio should be at least equal to its beginning of year value. The money manager uses futures contracts to implement his strategy. A consultant advises him to announce his intent of making large trades one or two hours in advance. Can you explain why the consultant is making this recommendation?

8. You work for a large manufacturing firm. Your firm has a difficult hedging problem. Your investment bank proposes that you solve the problem by purchasing a complicated derivative. As you figure out what to do, you check whether the bank will make a two-way market for the derivative. You are told that the bank will not promise to make a two-way market. How does this information affect your decision?

9. You purchased the derivative discussed in question 8. Two months later you want to sell it. You call up several investment banks to get quotes. The purchase price was $20 million and market conditions now are similar to what they were when you purchased the derivative. Yet, you find that the quotes you get range from $5 million to $40 million. How can you explain this wide price range?

10. Suppose that a bank is constrained—perhaps because of regulation—so that its derivative operations are not allowed to make a two-way market on a derivative with a bid-ask spread in excess of 6 percent of the bid-ask midpoint. The derivative is on a currency where neither you nor the bank have any kind of inside information. The bank is unwilling to make a two-way market at a 6 percent bid-ask spread. How could that be?

Literature Note

Miller (1992) provides a good review of the issues surrounding financial innovation. Allen and Gale (1994), Duffie and Jackson (1989), and Ross (1989) provide theoretical models of financial innovation. Merton (1992) discusses the role of financial intermediaries and the innovation process. Merton (1993) provides a theory of financial intermediation where financial intermediaries have a comparative advantage in trading over nonfinancial customers. Tufano (1989) provides an empirical investigation of financial innovation. For a good description of derivatives product companies such as Swapco, see "Risk assessment of derivatives subsidiaries," *Asiamoney*, Derivatives Guide Supplement, May 1994: 34–43. Johnston and McConnell (1989) analyze the GNMA CDR contract and why it disappeared. The policy of GE Capital Corporation on the rating of counterparties is reported by Bensman (1993).

Chapter 16

Swaps

At the end of this chapter, you will:

1. Know the main types of swaps.

2. Understand the determinants of swap pricing.

3. Have analyzed the benefits of swaps.

4. Have seen forward swaps, options on swaps, and exotic swaps.

Mr. Sharp, treasurer of Multi Inc., keeps scanning the globe for good financing deals. He realizes that he could raise funds cheaply in euros through a subsidiary located in the Netherlands Antilles. If he does that, Multi takes on euro exposure, which increases the firm's risk and negates the benefit of the deal he is contemplating. However, Mr. Sharp realizes that if he can hedge the exposure, he may be able to raise funds cheaply without having to take on more risk. The euro debt would have annual coupons for 15 years plus a principal payment in 15 years. This means that to hedge the euro exposure with forward contracts, Mr. Sharp should buy euros forward for 15 different maturities. He quickly realizes that there is no liquidity for most of the contracts required, so that the forward contract approach would be expensive since he would have to convince bankers to offer such contracts by providing them with appropriate financial inducements.

A swap could resolve Mr. Sharp's problem. In this case, the swap would make the interest and principal payments of an investment in a par euro bond that matures in 15 years minus the interest and principal payments on borrowing in the form of a par U.S. dollar bond with the same maturity. With such a swap, the cash flows from the long euro bond position would provide Mr. Sharp with the cash to service the euro debt, but to pay for that he would incur the debt service associated with a U.S. dollar bond of same maturity. Hence, Mr. Sharp would have substituted dollar debt for euro debt. As long as the swap is priced so that the benefit of borrowing in euros does not go away, Mr. Sharp will want to borrow in euros and take the swap position. The swap therefore allows Mr. Sharp to borrow cheaply without taking on additional risks.

Swaps are exchanges of cash flows. When two parties agree to a swap, one party pays a cash flow stream to the other party and receives a cash flow stream from that party, both payments being pegged to the same reference amount called the notional amount. Swaps are uniquely suited to alter the risk of a stream of cash flows. A common use of swaps is to transform fixed rate debt into floating rate debt. A firm that has just issued a par bond paying a fixed rate can enter a swap allowing it to pay a floating rate on a notional amount equal to the bond's par and to receive fixed rate payments computed on the same amount. The fixed rate payments the firm receives flow through to the investors who bought the newly issued bond and the firm has to make floating rate payments to the swap counterparty. As a result, the net payments the firm makes are floating rate payments even though it has issued fixed-rate debt.

Swaps are not only useful to change the risk of interest payments; their uses are almost limitless. Mr. Sharp could have used 15 forward contracts to eliminate the risk of raising funds in euros. Swaps are therefore equivalent to packages of simple derivatives. The advantage of a package is that one transaction, entering the swap, substitutes for a large number of transactions. By using a financial intermediary's swap product, Mr. Sharp achieves his objective of eliminating euro risk with one transaction and avoids all the risks associated with implementing multiple derivatives transactions.

We start this chapter with a detailed discussion of the swap between IBM and the World Bank in 1981. This swap represents the coming of age of the swap market and shows neatly why firms can benefit from swaps. We then show how the swap market has evolved since that famous swap. Our analysis of interest rate swaps demonstrates how to price and hedge these swaps and then considers how they can increase firm value.

There has been considerable innovation in swaps over the last fifteen years. We will talk about various types of innovative nongeneric swaps and their uses in risk management. Swaps are not restricted to interest rate and currency swaps. There are also equity swaps and commodity swaps. We use the tools developed in the chapter to study the swap responsible for about two-thirds of the well-publicized derivatives losses of Procter & Gamble.

16.1. The swap market and its evolution

In the 1970s, IBM developed a worldwide program to raise funds. It issued Deutsche mark (DM) and Swiss franc debt in 1979 and exchanged the funds for dollar funds. In 1981, IBM had large DM and Swiss franc exposures because of the debt it had issued in these currencies. At the same time, the World Bank was raising funds in low interest rate currencies, such as the DM and the Swiss franc. It had large funding requirements relative to the size of these capital markets that made it difficult for it to meet its funding targets.

A smart investment banker realized that a **currency swap** would solve the problems of the World Bank and of IBM. In a currency swap, one party agrees to make interest payments in currency A at a fixed rate on a notional amount N and to pay that notional amount in currency A at maturity of the swap to a counter-party in exchange for receiving from it all interest rate payments in currency B on a notional amount N* and receiving N* in currency B at maturity. The notional amounts are chosen to have an identical value in a common currency at initiation, so that they do not have to be exchanged (but could be since the parties might want inflows and outflows in the currencies used for the swap); the value of the notional amounts in a common currency necessarily differs at maturity, so that the notional amounts are exchanged then (or the difference is paid).

The World Bank did not want U.S. dollar debt. To get out of its dollar-denominated debt, the World Bank agreed to make all Swiss franc and DM payments on IBM's debt, including the principal payments. In exchange, IBM committed to making all the payments on the dollar debt of the World Bank, including the principal payment. The World Bank took the IBM payments and gave them to the holders of the debt, serving as a conduit for the payments. In exchange, IBM received from the World Bank the payments on the Swiss franc and DM debt, serving as a conduit for these payments. The end result for IBM was as if IBM did not have Swiss franc and DM debt but instead had dollar debt. The swap enabled IBM to eliminate its exposure to the Swiss franc and DM exchange rates. Figure 16.1 shows the cash flows resulting from the transaction for the World Bank and IBM.

The IBM-World Bank swap shows how a swap can allow a firm or an investor to completely change its exposure to some risk. Here, IBM starts from an exposure to the Swiss franc and the DM and succeeds in eliminating it. Yet, it does so without altering its original debt. The DM and Swiss franc bond issues of IBM are still outstanding after the swap.

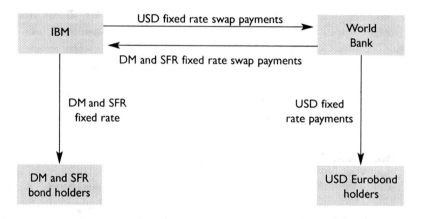

Figure 16.1 **The IBM-World Bank Swap**

IBM could have eliminated its exposures by buying back its Swiss franc and DM debt and then issuing U.S. dollar debt, but repurchasing debt is expensive. It involves additional unnecessary transaction costs and, if the debt is not callable, the holders of the debt may try to force the repurchasing firms to pay a higher price by holding out. With the swap transaction, there is only one debt issue taking place, namely the one of the World Bank. If instead IBM had repurchased the foreign currency debt and issued dollar debt, there would have been a total of two debt issues (one by IBM and one by the World Bank).

In the swap we are describing, IBM and the World Bank exchange cash flows. There are no payments initially. The payments take place when coupon and principal payments are due. The only way that such an arrangement makes sense is if the present value of the payments that IBM must make equals the present value of the payments that IBM is promised at initiation of the swap. As a result, the World Bank does not make a substantial investment in IBM as it would have if it had purchased IBM debt. Nor does the World Bank provide capital to IBM, so the credit risk is less than if it had purchased IBM debt.

The World Bank could lose on its swap with IBM because of credit risk only if, at some point, the present value of the net payments IBM has to make to the World Bank is positive but IBM no longer makes net payments. If IBM goes bankrupt, its debtholders lose money, but its swap counterparty does not necessarily lose money. The bankruptcy of IBM would not cost anything to its swap counterparty if the swap is such that the present value of the net payments the counterparty has to make is positive.[1]

---

1 Generally, bankruptcy leads to early termination of a swap. In this case, the solvent party is due a payment equal to the market value of its position if positive and zero otherwise. Litzenberger (1992) discusses the difference in bankruptcy proceedings between a position long a fixed rate bond and short a floating rate note versus a swap receiving fixed payments and requiring floating payments.

Let's look at the details of the transaction. IBM had to make Swiss franc payments of 12.375 million Swiss francs on March 30 from 1982 through 1986 when it also had to repay the principal of 200 million Swiss francs. In DM, IBM had to make payments of DM 30 million on the same dates and the principal payment was DM 300 million. Through the swap, IBM wanted to receive these payments from the World Bank.

The World Bank had to figure out the dollar payments from IBM that would be equivalent in value to the DM and Swiss franc payments it would have to make. This requires the computation of the present value of the foreign currency payments the World Bank had promised to make. Suppose term structures are flat for simplicity and that the interest rates when the transaction settled on August 11, 1981 were 8 percent in Switzerland and 11 percent in Germany. The settlement date of the swap was August 25, 1981. With these assumptions, the discounted value of the payments for the Swiss franc debt is Swiss franc 191,367,478 as of August 25, 1981. The terms of the swap were agreed to on August 11, 1981. Consequently, forward contracts for August 25 were used to convert foreign currency amounts into dollar amounts. On the 14-day forward market, the U.S. dollar was then worth 2.18 Swiss francs, so the dollar value of this Swiss franc amount was $87,783,247. Discounting the DM payments at 11 percent, we then have a present value for the DM payments in dollars of $117,703,153 since one dollar was worth DM 2.56 on the 14-day forward market. The dollar value of the payments (rounded to the nearest $5,000) that the World Bank would have to make is therefore $205,485,000.

The World Bank could borrow a present value of $205,485,000 with a payment schedule matching the payment schedule of the IBM debt. The World Bank had to issue the debt and had to pay commissions and expenses of 2.15 percent of par. Consequently, to get a net present value of $205,485,000, it could issue debt at par for $210 million with a coupon of 16 percent. The first period for the bond would have 215 days rather than 360 days since the first coupon would have to be paid on March 30, 1982. The World Bank would receive 97.85 percent of $210 million, which amounts to $205,485,000. Table 16.1 shows the payments exchanged at each date.

The IBM–World Bank swap is a currency swap. The first currency swap was in 1976. Goldman Sachs and Continental Illinois arranged a transaction between a Dutch company, Bos Kalis Westminster, and a British company, ICI Finance, involving the Dutch Florin and the British Pound. Early swaps were predominantly currency swaps because currency swaps are a natural evolution of then current foreign currency transactions. Foreign exchange transactions were highly restricted following World War II in many countries, preventing firms from financing investment in foreign subsidiaries. With foreign exchange restrictions, a U.S. firm wanting to finance investment in its subsidiary in the United Kingdom would have had trouble acquiring pounds. One solution that eventually developed was for a U.K. firm to lend to the U.S. subsidiary and then for the U.S. firm to lend in the United States to a subsidiary of the U.K. firm. Such a transaction is called a parallel loan. Unfortunately, this transaction involves credit risk; the U.K. subsidiary of the U.S. parent could default, but the U.S. subsidiary of the U.K. firm would still have to pay back the loan made by the U.S. firm. A swap eliminates this credit risk.

Table 16.1	Cash flows exchanged through the IBM-World Bank swap

The first dollar amount is reduced because the payment period is incomplete. IBM pays the US$ amounts to the World Bank and receives from it the Swiss franc and DM amounts.

Exchange date	Swiss franc amount	DM amount	US$ amount
3.30.82	12,375,000	30,000,000	20,066,667
3.30.83	12,375,000	30,000,000	33,600,000
3.30.84	12,375,000	30,000,000	33,600,000
3.30.85	12,375,000	30,000,000	33,600,000
3.30.86	212,375,000	330,000,000	243,600,000

The interest rate swap is a natural evolution from this currency swap structure. In the prototypical interest rate swap, one party (conventionally, the short side) pays cash flows corresponding to floating rate payments on a notional amount and receives cash flows corresponding to fixed rate payments on the same notional amount for the duration of the swap. Since the notional amount used to calculate the interest rate payments is the same for the floating rate and the fixed rate payments, there is no reason to exchange the notional amounts at maturity. This is different from a foreign currency swap, where the principal amounts have to be exchanged at maturity because their value in one currency need not be the same at maturity even though it was the same at initiation of the swap.

The first interest rate swap was in 1981. Since then, the interest rate swap market has grown much faster than the currency swap market. At the end of June 2001, the notional amount of interest rate swaps outstanding was $57,220 billion compared to $4,302 billion for currency swaps.

The swap markets have changed considerably since their beginning. Early transactions were highly specific to the counterparties, so that swap contracts could not be traded effectively. Standardized swap contracts have evolved since. In 1985, the International Swap Dealers Association (subsequently renamed as International Swaps and Derivatives Association, ISDA) introduced the Code of Standard Wording, Assumptions, and Provisions for Swaps, which ensures swap contract terms are well understood. Some parties simply adopt the Code in its entirety as the basis of a contract; others may change some terms. There is now considerable trading taking place in standardized contracts, and the bid-ask spreads for these contracts are generally extremely small—of the order of five or so basis points. In 2001, the turnover in notional amount of dollar interest rate swaps was about $331 billion per day compared to $7 billion per day for currency swaps. In some countries, the market for swaps can be more liquid than the market for bonds of similar maturity.

Initially, swaps were driven by firms trying to exploit temporary advantageous fund raising opportunities. A firm might find that borrowing in fixed rate Swiss franc debt at ten year maturity was advantageous, but did not want to have an exposure to the Swiss franc and preferred to borrow in the form of floating rate debt denominated in dollars. The firm could sell Swiss franc debt and then enter a swap to convert the Swiss franc debt into dollar floating rate debt. Many swaps took place when a corporation financed in the Eurobond market and then swapped into some preferred form of financing.

As the market evolved, however, swaps unrelated to security issues became more important. Rather than issuing debt and then using a swap to transform the cash flows into the desired type of debt cash flows, firms use swaps to change the riskiness of cash flows to which they have already contracted. Whether a debt issue is associated with a swap or not, the swap is effectively used for risk management purposes in that it allows a firm to exchange one cash flow for another whose risk characteristics are more appropriate for the firm. There is no reason for the cash flows to be exchanged to be only cash flows associated with debt. As the swap market has grown, swaps involving commodities, stocks, and portfolios of many assets have become common.

16.2. Interest rate swaps

The key characteristic of a simple **interest rate swap** is that one party receives fixed rate payments equal to the notional amount times the quoted fixed interest rate. In exchange for receiving the fixed rate payments, the party pays the floating rate times the notional amount. Intuitively, this is functionally equivalent for the party that pays fixed rates to buying an asset that makes fixed rate payments and financing the purchase at a floating rate. The floating rate is determined at regular intervals on reset dates and applies to the payment period following the reset date. We assume that there are no default risks on the fixed rate payments and that the default risk of the floating rate payments is the one corresponding to LIBOR.

A dealer can quote a swap in two different ways. One way is the all-in quote. The **swap rate** is the interest rate paid on the fixed interest rate leg of the swap. In a fixed-for-floating swap where the floating rate is six-month LIBOR, the dealer could quote a swap rate of 7.25–7.05. This quote would mean that the dealer receives 7.25 percent fixed and pays LIBOR or pays 7.05 percent fixed and receives LIBOR.

The alternative way of quoting a swap is to quote a swap spread. The **swap spread** is the difference between the fixed rate paid on the swap and the fixed rate on a par default-free bond of same maturity. A dealer could quote a five-year swap at a spread of 60–65. The 60–65 quote means that the dealer pays the five-year T-note rate plus 60 basis points and receives LIBOR, or receives the five-year T-note rate plus 65 basis points and pays LIBOR.

In both cases, the dealer makes a market and is willing to pay either the fixed rate or the floating rate. The date on which the agreement is reached is called the trade date. For swaps involving euro rates, the effective date (the starting date of the first payment period) is usually two London business days after the trade date. Payment periods are generally chosen so that there are no incomplete payment periods. The first reset date is the trade date, and subsequent reset dates are determined by the market conventions for the floating rate instrument. For example, if the floating rate is a six-month rate, every payment period will be a six-month period.

The day count specifies how days are counted for interest payments. This important contractual feature of swaps is always mentioned explicitly. For floating rate payments, the day count is normally the actual number of days using a 360-day year. For example, the LIBOR interest payment over a 253-day period is (253/360) × LIBOR. For fixed rate payments, the day count depends on the reference instrument. The day count and the computation of interest differ for euro bonds and domestic U.S. bonds. Eurobond interest is computed on a 30-day month basis and is paid once annually. U.S. Treasury bond interest is paid semiannually, and the day count is actual/actual, meaning the actual number of days as a fraction of the actual number of days in the year. Consequently, a Treasury bond with a stated annual coupon of 10 percent actually earns an annual interest rate comparable to the interest rate of a euro bond paying a coupon of 10.25 percent since:

$$(1 + 0.1/2)^2 - 1 = 0.1025$$

16.2.1. Pricing a new swap

Let us first consider the pricing of a new fixed-for-floating swap, where one party pays fixed rate and receives floating rate payments. In perfect markets, there is an equivalent bond market transaction that produces exactly the same net cash flows as the swap. This transaction involves selling fixed rate debt at par and buying floating rate debt so that the principal payments and the interest payment dates of the bonds are the same.

To see that a bond market transaction replicates a swap, consider a ten-year swap where the fixed rate is 10 percent paid semiannually and the floating rate is six-month LIBOR determined two London business days before the start of the payment period. The notional amount of the swap is $100 million. In this case, there is no exchange of cash flows at origination; the fixed rate payer must pay $5 million and receive LIBOR every six months, and there is no exchange of principal at maturity. The fixed-rate payer can get exactly the same cash flows by selling ten-year fixed rate debt at par with a 10 percent coupon and investing the proceeds at LIBOR.

At initiation, the proceeds from selling the debt are $100 million and are invested in LIBOR, so that the fixed rate payer receives no cash flow. At the end of the first six-month period, the fixed rate payer pays $5 million on the fixed rate debt and receives LIBOR on $100 million. The net cash flow is therefore LIBOR on $100 million minus $5 million, which is also the net cash flow of the swap.

At the end of the first six-month period, LIBOR is reset for the next six months. This is the rate at which the $100 million is reinvested. At maturity, the floating rate investment pays $100 million plus LIBOR determined six months earlier. The fixed rate payer takes the $100 million to pay off the fixed rate debt. Consequently, the last cash flow to the fixed rate payer is LIBOR on $100 million minus $5 million. We have therefore shown that the fixed rate payer can obtain the same cash flows as those of the swap by issuing $100 million debt at par at fixed rate and investing the proceeds at LIBOR.

Since the cash flows of a swap paying fixed and receiving floating are equivalent to the cash flows of a long position in an asset receiving floating and a short position in a bond paying fixed, we can find the terms of the swap by arbitrage:

Interest rate swap pricing condition in perfect markets (bond equivalent approach)

At initiation of a swap, the swap rate must be equal to the yield of a par bond that has face value equal to the notional amount of the swap and coupon payments at the same dates that the swap payments must be made.

Note that the bond yield approach to pricing an interest rate swap requires that we are able to observe the yield on a par bond with the appropriate maturity. If such a bond exists, then failure of the interest rate swap pricing condition to hold means that we face an arbitrage opportunity. To see this, suppose that the swap rate is 12 percent when the coupon rate is 10 percent as in our example. In this case, it pays to enter the swap to receive fixed and pay floating. We can then hedge our swap position by selling fixed rate debt for a 10 percent coupon and investing the proceeds in LIBOR. Having done this transaction, we earn 2 percent of the notional amount of the swap every year and have no risk. We have no risk because we pay LIBOR on the swap but receive LIBOR on our investment. The fixed rate coupon payments we make of 10 percent are more than matched by the swap fixed rate payments we receive of 12 percent. Consequently, if the swap rate exceeds the coupon rate of the par bond, there is an arbitrage opportunity. Similarly, we can make money if the swap rate is below the yield of the par bond by promising to pay fixed and hedging our position.

The present value of the swap transaction for the fixed rate payer is the present value of the floating rate payments minus the present value of the fixed rate payments. The fixed rate payer is only willing to enter the transaction if its present value is not negative:

Value of swap for fixed rate payer

= Present value of floating rate payments

– Present value of fixed rate payments ≥ 0   (16.1)

The floating rate payer is the counterparty to the fixed rate payer. The present value of the swap transaction for the floating rate payer is equal to the present value of the fixed rate payments minus the present value of the floating rate payments, which is the negative of the present value of the swap to the fixed rate payer. The floating rate payer is also only willing to enter the transaction if its present value is not negative:

Value of swap for floating rate payer =

– (Value of swap for fixed rate payer)

= Present value of fixed rate payments

– Present value of floating rate payments ≥ 0   (16.2)

Since the positive value of one is the negative of the other, the only way that no present value is negative is that both swap values are equal to zero since zero is the only number that is equal to its negative. The following result states how swaps must be priced with the present value approach:

The present value approach to price swaps

A swap must be priced so that the present value of the fixed rate payments equals the present value of the floating rate payments.

The present value approach can be implemented even if we do not observe a par bond outstanding with the appropriate maturity. The present value of the fixed rate payments is equivalent to the present value of the payments from a fixed rate bond. We already know how to value a default-free fixed rate bond and can therefore compute the present value of the fixed rate payments. The present value of the floating rate payments is the present value of a bond with floating rate payments. The best way to determine the value of the floating rate bond is to value it first at the start of the last payment period. At that date, the bond's value is the present value of the payment in six months of the principal and six months of interest. With LIBOR, the day count is actual/360. Let us assume for our example that six months correspond to 183 days. If $PV(x)$ denotes the present value of x, the bond's value is:

Value of floating rate bond = PV($100M × [1 + LIBOR × (183/360)]) (16.3)

If the interest payment is determined using LIBOR, one expects the risk characteristics of the payment to be those of LIBOR. Consequently, the appropriate discount rate is LIBOR. Discounting a payment to be made in six months of $100M[1 + LIBOR × (183/360)] at LIBOR yields $100M[1 + LIBOR × (183/360)]/[1 + LIBOR × (183/360)], which is the par value of the bond. To obtain the value of the bond one year before maturity, we discount for six months the value of the bond just before the interest payment six months (183 days) before maturity. Say that LIBOR then is LIBOR'. Immediately before the bond reverts to par six months before maturity, its value is $100M × [1 + LIBOR' × (183/360)]. Discounting this amount back six months at LIBOR', we get an amount equal to $100 million. Hence, immediately before the start of a payment period, the bond is worth par. The same reasoning applies to any payment period, so that the floating rate bond's value immediately before the start of an interest payment period is always equal to par.

We have now shown that the present value of the floating rate bond corresponding to the floating rate payments of the swap is equal to the par value of the bond, which is the notional amount of the swap. The present value of the fixed rate payments including the principal payment must therefore be equal to $100 million. Let c be the fixed rate semiannual interest payment and i denote the ith semiannual interest payment. There are twenty semiannual interest payments in the swap. $P(t + i × 0.5)$ is the price of a zero-coupon bond paying $1 when the ith semiannual interest payment is made at $t + i × 0.5$. Consequently, we have to choose c so that:

$$100M = \sum_{i=1}^{i=20} P_t(t + i \times 0.5)c + P_t(t + 0.5 \times 20)100M \qquad (16.4)$$

To find out the fixed rate payments, all we need is the price of the zero-coupon bonds paying $1 at the various payment dates. This way of proceeding gives us a general approach for pricing a fixed-for-floating swap:

Formula for the pricing of a default-free fixed for floating swap with N semi-annual payment dates and notional amount M

$$M = \sum_{i=1}^{i=N} P_t(t + 0.5 \times i)c + P_t(t + 0.5 \times N)M \qquad (16.5)$$

There is an alternative way of computing the interest payment c. Suppose that the yield-to-maturity of the fixed rate bond is known to be y per payment period. There are N periods. In this case, the price of a fixed-rate bond paying a semi-annual coupon c is the present value of the coupon and principal payment discounted at the rate y per payment period. Using the yield, the formula in equation (16.5) is:

$$M = \sum_{i=1}^{i=N} \frac{c}{(1+y)^i} + \frac{M}{(1+y)^N} \qquad (16.6)$$

Let us apply this formula to a ten-year swap with semiannual payments and notional amount of $100 million. Let's assume that y is 5 percent per payment period. Hence, we have:

$$100,000,000 = \sum_{i=1}^{i=20} \frac{c}{(1+0.05)^i} + \frac{100,000,000}{(1+0.05)^{20}} \qquad (16.7)$$

Solving for c, we find that the interest payment is equal to $5,000,000.

When the fixed rate payment has some default risk, the discount rate has to reflect that default risk. For example, if the fixed rate payer is a firm with an A rating, it would be more appropriate to use the yield of an A bond than the yield of government securities. This means that the appropriate swap rate for the fixed rate payer is higher than the yield on a default-free par bond if the fixed rate payer has default risk but the floating-rate payer has no default risk.

An alternative is for the firm to post collateral and mark to market the swap at pre-specified dates or following large moves so that the swap is close to default-free for the counterparty. This practice has become much more common over time. Yet, despite this practice, there is a swap spread—the fixed rate exceeds the comparable Treasury rate. This swap spread was of the order of 50 basis points in 1996 and 1997 for a ten-year swap, but it increased sharply in the fall of 1998 and has been mostly high since, averaging 100 basis points in 2000. Much research has been gathered to explain this swap spread. Research found evidence supportive of the view that spreads compensate for counterparty risk. More recently, attention has been paid to the role of liquidity in the determination of spreads. He (2001) argues that credit risk cannot explain spreads with the current practice of the market where swaps tend to be collateralized and marked to market. He points out that a swap where one receives fixed and pays floating is functionally equivalent to buying an asset and financing the purchase through borrowing; for example, a Treasury bond or note can be purchased with financing on the repo market. The cost of repo financing is lower than LIBOR. With repo financing, the borrowing is collateralized with the Treasury security, while LIBOR reflects the credit risk of large London banks. For somebody to be indifferent between financing the purchase of a Treasury security through a swap and financing the purchase through a repo, that investor has to receive a premium over the yield of the Treasury security since if he pays LIBOR, his financing cost is higher than with a repo. This fact explains the existence of a spread for default-free swaps, but does not explain the changes in the spread over the last few years.

We have seen two approaches to pricing a swap: the bond equivalent approach and the present value approach. There exists a third approach which uses futures prices. This approach is described in Technical Box 16.1, Using eurodollar futures to price and hedge a swap.

16.2.2. Pricing an outstanding swap

We now look at pricing of a swap that has been outstanding for some period of time. Say that we entered a swap where we pay fixed and receive floating on a notional of $50 million that has four more payments before maturity. One payment is in three months, and the other payments are every six months after the

---

Technical Box 16.1   Using eurodollar futures to price and hedge a swap

With our pricing analysis, a swap is a portfolio long in one bond and short in another bond such that its value at inception is zero. This means that both the hedging and the risk measurement of a simple swap are straightforward. The risk of the swap is simply the risk of a bond portfolio; we have already seen how such risk can be measured. If we take a position in a swap and want to hedge it, we can do so by taking bond positions that offset the swap position. We can also, however, hedge the swap position using forwards and futures. Suppose that we are a swap dealer and are considering taking a swap position where we pay floating and receive fixed. Abstracting from credit risks, we know exactly what we will receive over time but we do not know the size of the payments we will have to make since they will depend on the reference rate on future reset dates. There is, however, a futures contract that is helpful in hedging our future payments. Remember that the eurodollar futures contract that we talked about in Chapter 9 is a contract whose payoff depends on LIBOR at maturity. The eurodollar futures contract can therefore be used to lock in today payments that correspond to the payments that have to be made on the swap provided that the reset dates match the maturity dates of the futures contracts. A swap with dates tailored to take advantage of the eurodollar contract is called an IMM swap (where IMM stands for the International Monetary Market where the eurodollar contract is traded).

(continued)   *Technical Box 16.1*

To understand how a dealer can price and hedge the swap using eurodollar futures contracts, we look at an example of a one-year swap with quarterly payments. The first floating rate payment is determined when the swap is agreed to and the payment period starts two business days later. There are three additional floating rate payments and they are chosen so that a futures contract can be used to hedge each payment. We assume that the futures prices are for contracts maturing in March, June, and September. The prices for these contracts are respectively 95, 94.5, and 94. Three-month LIBOR when the swap is agreed to is 4.8 percent. The notional amount of the swap is $100 million. The implied futures LIBOR rates are 5, 5.5, and 6 percent, respectively. Suppose that the payment periods are respectively 90, 91, 92, and 91 days. The implied futures yield of a contract corresponds to our cost of funds for the payment period following the maturity of the contract. We therefore use the implied futures yields to compute the present value of the fixed rate payments. Hence, if c is the coupon payment, we want the present value of the fixed rate payments including the notional amount to be:

$$100 = \frac{c}{1 + 0.048 \times (90/360)}$$

$$+ \frac{c}{\left[1 + 0.048 \times (90/360)\right] \times \left[1 + 0.05 \times (91/360)\right]}$$

$$+ \frac{c}{\left[1 + 0.048 \times (90/360)\right] \times \left[1 + 0.05 \times (91/360)\right]}{\times \left[1 + 0.055 \times (92/360)\right]}$$

$$+ \frac{c + 100}{\left[1 + 0.048 \times (90/360)\right] \times \left[1 + 0.05 \times (91/360)\right]}{\times \left[1 + 0.055 \times (92/360)\right] \times \left[1 + 0.06 \times (91/360)\right]}$$

We can solve for the fixed rate payment corresponding to the implied futures yields. Doing so, we obtain that c is equal to $1.32987 million. This corresponds to an interest payment of 5.32 percent paid quarterly.

This example helps us understand how to hedge the swap. We can recompute the value of the swap if the futures price for March falls by 10 basis points so that the implied futures yield goes from 5 to 5.1 percent and nothing else changes. In this case, we lose $24,400 on the swap. To offset this loss, we have to create a futures position that generates a gain of $24,400 if the March futures price falls by 10 basis points. A fall of 10 basis points in the futures price pays $250 per contract held short, namely 2.5 basis points times the notional amount of the contract position of $1 million. We therefore require 24,400/250 contracts short, which amounts to 97.6 contracts. We can then proceed to hedge the swap by evaluating the impact of changes in the other futures contracts on the swap value.

first payment. We are therefore valuing the swap in the middle of a payment period.

First, we have to value the floating rate bond. The next interest rate payment is to be made in three months. Suppose that three months ago six-month LIBOR was at 4 percent. LIBOR is an add-on rate so that in three months the swap payment will be $1 million, that is, 2 percent of $50 million. Say that now LIBOR has increased to 5 percent.

What is the value of the floating rate bond equivalent to the floating rate leg of the swap given that LIBOR has increased from 4 to 5 percent? To value the floating-rate bond, note that at maturity of the floating rate bond, we receive $50 million plus the interest payment corresponding to the last interest payment period. The value of that payment at the start of the last interest payment period is therefore the discounted value of $50 million plus the interest payment, which must be $50 million. The floating rate bond is therefore worth $50 million immediately after the next to the last interest payment. We can then work backward to show that this is true immediately after any interest payment, so that the value of the floating rate bond at any time is the present value of the floating rate bond's value immediately after the next interest payment date plus the present value of the interest payment to be made then. The value of the floating rate bond after three months is therefore $51M/(1 + 0.0125) = $50.37037 million (assuming that the three-month period is a quarter of a year).

Consider now the value of the fixed rate bond. Say that the six-month payments are $1.5 million. We have to obtain the prices of zero-coupon bonds paying $1 at the dates of each of the next four payments. Let's assume that these prices are $P_t(t + 0.25) = 0.99$, $P_t(t + 0.75) = 0.95$, $P_t(t + 1.25) = 0.90$, $P_t(t + 1.75) = 0.84$. With these numbers, the value of the fixed rate bond in millions of dollars is:

$$P_t(t + 0.25) \times 1.5 + P_t(t + 0.75) \times 1.5 + P_t(t + 1.25)$$
$$\times 1.5 + P_t(t + 1.75) \times 1.5 + P_t(t + 1.75) \times 50$$
$$= 0.99$$
$$\times 1.5 + 0.95 \times 1.5 + 0.90 \times 1.5 + 0.84 \times 1.5 + 0.84 \times 50$$
$$= 47.52 \tag{16.8}$$

The value of the swap is therefore $50.37037M – $47.52M = $2.85037 million.

This swap is quite valuable to us. Since the counterparty has to make payments to us, the swap's value to the counterparty must be –$2.85037 million. Remember that the swap was worth zero when we entered it. Our gain on the swap is the counterparty's loss.

We can figure out why the swap became valuable for us by reverse engineering. Suppose that the swap is a ten-year swap at inception. The fixed rate payment is $3 million per year, which amounts to an annual par yield of 7.02 percent. Now, however, the annualized yield is 10.36 percent. In other words, interest rates have increased since the inception of the swap. Since the swap requires fixed rate payments to be made in exchange for receiving floating rate payments, the floating rate payments received increase with the interest rate whereas the fixed rate payments to be made do not. Hence, on net, the swap holder receives more but pays the same.

In present value terms, the present value of the payments to be made has fallen whereas the present value of the payments to be received is unchanged. As a result, the value of the swap has increased.

16.2.3. Measuring the risk of an interest rate swap

We have now seen that an interest rate swap where we pay fixed and receive floating is equal to a long position in a floating rate bond and a short position in a fixed rate bond. At initiation of the swap, the two bonds have exactly the same value. Subsequently, the value of the two bonds diverges.

Define t to be the origination date and t' the valuation date. Let r_B be the decimal rate of return of the fixed rate bond with price $B_t(T)$ at t from t to t' and r_L be the decimal rate of return of the floating rate bond with current price $L_t(T)$ over the same period. Both bonds have par equal to M. The gain from a long position in the swap over a period is therefore:

$$\text{Gain from long swap position} = L_t(T)r_L - B_t(T)r_B \qquad (16.9)$$

Say that we entered a swap where we pay fixed and receive floating on a notional of $50 million that has four more payments before maturity. One payment is in three months, and the other payments are every six months after the first payment. No interest payments have been made. The fixed rate bond is worth $47.52 million and the floating rate bond is worth $50.37037 million. At origination of the swap, both bonds were trading at $50 million. The decimal rate of return of the fixed rate bond since origination is –$2.48M/$50M, or –0.0496, and the decimal rate of return of the floating rate bond is $0.37037M/$50M, or 0.00741. Applying our formula, we have:

$$L_t(T)r_L - B_t(T)r_B = -\$50M \times 0.0496$$

$$= \$50M \times 0.00741 + \$50M \times 0.0496 = \$2.85037M \qquad (16.10)$$

Absent interest payments during the evaluation period, the gain from a swap position is equal to the change in value of the swap position. In the case considered here, where there are no interest payments during the evaluation period, the formula produces a loss from a long position in the swap that is exactly the negative of the change in value for the fixed rate payer computed earlier. With interest payments made during the evaluation period, the net interest rate payment is part of the gain from the swap position.

If we have the joint distribution of r_B and r_L, we can compute the volatility of the gain from the swap position. Let $\text{Var}(r_B)$ be the variance of r_B, $\text{Var}(r_L)$ be the variance of r_L, and $\text{Cov}(r_B, r_L)$ be the covariance between the two returns. In this case, the volatility of the gain in value of the swap position is:

$$\text{Volatility of change in value of the swap} = \qquad (16.11)$$

$$\left[B_t(T)^2 \times \text{Var}(r_B) + L_t(T)^2 \times \text{Var}(r_L) - 2B_t(T) \times L_t(T) \times \text{Cov}(r_B, r_L) \right]^{0.5}$$

The variance of r_L will be small since it corresponds to the variance of the return of a bond with a very short duration—it will be zero immediately before a reset date since on that date the floating leg is valued at par. As a result, the volatility of the gain from the swap position will be close to the volatility of the change in value of a fixed rate bond that matures when the swap matures.

With normally distributed returns, the 5 percent VaR of the swap position is 1.65 times its volatility. We want to compute the VaR of the swap position used in our example as of the valuation date, t'. Suppose then that for one month starting at t', the decimal volatility of the return of the fixed rate bond in our example is expected to be 0.0288, the decimal volatility of the return of the floating rate bond is expected to be 0.005, and the decimal covariance between the two is expected to be 0.0000576. Using our formula, the one-month VaR of the swap whose value we just computed is:

VaR of the swap =

$$1.65\left[B_t(T)^2 \times \text{Var}(r_B) + L_t(T)^2 \times \text{Var}(r_L) - 2B_t(T) \times L_t(T) \times \text{Cov}(r_B, r_L)\right]^{0.5}$$

$$= 1.65\left[\begin{array}{l} 47.52\text{M}^2 \times 0.0288^2 + 50.37037\text{M}^2 \times 0.005^2 \\ - 2 \times 47.52\text{M} \times 50.37037\text{M} \times 0.0000576 \end{array}\right]^{0.5}$$

$$= 1.65 \times \$1.288676\text{M} = \$2.126316\text{M}$$

16.2.4. Do swaps make something out of nothing?

Early on in the swap market, financial economists were unclear why corporations thought swaps were so valuable. After all, a firm could replicate swap payoffs with transactions in other financial instruments; if markets are close to perfect, swaps do not enable firms to do things that they could not do without swaps. One argument made to explain the benefits of swaps is that swaps enable firms to exploit their financing comparative advantage. Consider two firms—Gold-Plated Inc. has an AAA rating and Shaky Inc. has a B rating. Both companies want to borrow $10 million for five years. Gold-Plated would like to borrow floating, and Shaky would like to borrow fixed. Gold-Plated can borrow on the fixed rate market at 8 percent or on the floating rate market at LIBOR plus 30 basis points. Shaky can borrow on the fixed rate market at 9 percent or on the floating rate market at LIBOR plus 80 basis points. Shaky has a narrower credit spread on the floating rate market than on the fixed rate market because the credit risks are different. One reason for this is that the fixed rate debt is sold to public investors while floating rate debt is typically bank debt where the bank can require repayment of the loan if the firm becomes significantly less creditworthy.[2]

A swap arranged by a dealer might enable both firms to borrow at lower cost. Suppose Gold-Plated borrows fixed but enters a swap where it pays floating pay-

---

2 Chapter 9 notes another reason firms might have lower credit risks with floating rate debt than with fixed rate debt. This is because firms that issue floating rate debt might choose to do so because interest rates are low when their cash flows are low, so that they are better able to make debt payments than if they borrowed fixed.

ments and receives fixed. In this case, Gold-Plated pays 8 percent fixed on the debt it issued. Let us assume that the swap is such that the firm pays LIBOR flat and receives 7.9 percent from the bank. With this, Gold-Plated ends up having a net cash flow of 7.9 percent – LIBOR – 8 percent. Hence, the firm pays LIBOR + 0.1 percent. This is a floating rate debt cash flow, but by issuing fixed and using the swap, the firm pays less than if it had issued floating (since LIBOR + 10 basis points is less than LIBOR + 30 basis points).

Shaky borrows floating and pays LIBOR plus 80 basis points. Suppose it pays 8 percent to the bank and receives from it LIBOR flat. In this case, Shaky ends up having a net cash flow of –LIBOR – 80 basic points + LIBOR – 8 percent, or 8.80 percent. Hence, Shaky ends up with fixed rate payments that are 20 basis points lower than if it had issued fixed rate debt.

Shaky and Gold-Plated are better off by issuing debt of a type they do not want to issue and using a swap to transform the debt service from the debt they issue into payments from the debt they would want to issue. The two transactions are compared in Figure 16.2.

Financing without a swap versus financing with a swap for Gold-Plated Inc. and Shaky Inc.   *Figure 16.2*

Borrowing on capital markets and no swap

Borrowing on capital markets plus swap

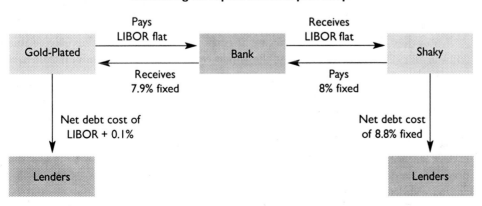

How does the bank make money? It receives LIBOR from Gold-Plated and pays it to Shaky. It also receives 8 percent from Shaky and pays 7.9 percent to Gold-Plated, thereby making a profit of 10 basis points. The bank could make more of a profit and the transaction would still benefit both Gold-Plated and Shaky. The reason is that the credit spread of Shaky over Gold-Plated is 100 basis points on the fixed rate market and only 50 basis points on the floating rate market. The 50 basis points difference in the two credit spreads is the profit that is created through the swap. It can be divided among the three parties to the swap—the two firms and the bank. In this example, the bank gets 10 basis points, Gold-Plated gets 20 basis points, and Shaky gets 20 basis points.

An argument often made to explain the profit generated by the swap is that Shaky has a comparative advantage in borrowing floating because its credit spread on that market is lower than its credit spread on the fixed rate market. The argument is then that Shaky should finance itself where it has this comparative advantage. Sometimes a company can obtain funds at advantageous rates. In the euro bond market, for example, the absence of withholding taxes means investors will buy dollar-denominated bonds with a lower yield than dollar-denominated bonds issued in the United States. A firm might be made better off issuing fixed rate debt on the euro bond market even if it wanted to have floating rate debt. Taking advantage of such windows of opportunity can provide firms with cheaper financing—and the swap market can enable firms to take advantage of such opportunities.

The benefits of comparative advantage in financing are often illusory. Firms usually do not get something for nothing. When Shaky issues public debt, it pays 9 percent with our assumptions. Fixed rate debt provides Shaky with money that it can use for five years as long as it pays the coupon. When Shaky borrows at the floating rate from banks, the firm is a different credit than if it borrows fixed from the public markets. The bankers might have the option to cancel the loan, to increase the spread over LIBOR, or to force Shaky to pay a lower dividend to make sure that the debt remains safe.

In this case, Shaky may well gain nothing from the swap. This is because, when its bankers tighten credit conditions, Shaky can lose valuable investment opportunities. The present value of these lost investment opportunities might exceed the lower debt service cost obtained through the use of the swap. On net, Shaky might therefore have been better off to issue fixed rate debt on the public markets. A careful analysis is required to evaluate where the improvement in a firm's financing costs is really coming from.

If no other claims of either firm are affected by the swap, then the gain of one counterparty has to be the loss of the other. Swaps are a zero-sum game in perfect markets. Market imperfections make it possible for swaps to create value from which both parties can benefit if it allows them to get a more appropriate interest rate exposure. Alternatively, a firm that expects its credit to improve might prefer borrowing short-term and rolling over short-term loans so that when its credit improves it benefits from the narrowing of its credit spread. There is debt service volatility with this strategy and the firm might want to swap the floating rate debt service into fixed rate debt service to avoid this volatility. Swaps facilitate short-term borrowing for such a company. By borrowing short term, the company signals to the markets that it expects its credit to improve, which has an immediate positive impact on its stock price.

16.3. Beyond simple interest rate swaps

We value fixed-for-fixed currency swaps exactly the same way as a fixed for floating interest rate swap. Such a currency swap is equivalent to buying a fixed rate bond in currency A and selling a fixed rate bond in currency B so that at inception of the swap both bonds trade at par and have the same value in currency A and the same maturity. With an exchange of notional amounts at inception, the party making payments in currency A would have an initial outflow of currency A and an inflow of currency B, while the party making payments in currency B would have an initial inflow in currency A and an outflow in currency B. Unless the parties to the swap want the currency inflows and outflows, there is no reason for exchange of payments at inception since the swap has no value then. Throughout the life of the swap, the coupon payments of the two bonds are exchanged. At maturity, the notional amounts are exchanged.

Evaluating the risk of the currency swap position is more complicated. The reason is that the swap can change value because of changes in interest rates in each of the two countries as well as changes in the foreign exchange rate. We examine this difficulty in the first part of this section. We then describe swaps whose notional amount changes over time, total return swaps, swaps with options, forward swaps, and options on swaps.

16.3.1. Pricing, risk evaluation, and hedging currency swaps

We want to price a swap where one party pays the interest on the domestic currency notional amount and receives interest on the foreign currency notional amount. Let $B_t(T)$ and $B_t^{CH}(T)$ be the prices at t of the two coupon bonds maturing at T that comprise the swap, where $B_t^{CH}(T)$ is the price in foreign currency of the foreign currency bond. As before, let S_t be the domestic price of the foreign currency. At inception, $B_t(T) - S_t B_t^{CH}(T) = 0$.

Using this approach, we can price a currency swap in a straightforward way. Suppose we have a fixed U.S. dollar for fixed Swiss franc swap. The term structures are flat in both countries with an 8 percent coupon paid annually in dollars and a 4 percent coupon paid annually in Swiss francs. Payments are made annually for three years, and the dollar notional amount is $100 million. The dollar payments are $8 million each year, except in year three when they are $108 million. The present value of these payments is $100 million. If the dollar is worth 1.3 Swiss francs, the Swiss franc principal amount is 130 million Swiss francs. At maturity, a payment of 130 million Swiss francs plus the Swiss franc coupon is received. We then need to find the Swiss franc interest payment c expressed in millions of Swiss francs:

$$130 = \frac{c}{1.04} + \frac{c}{1.04^2} + \frac{130 + c}{1.04^3} \qquad (16.12)$$

The solution for c is 5.2, which corresponds to a payment of 5.2 million Swiss francs the first two years and of 135.2 million Swiss francs the final year.

The dollar return on the foreign currency swap is the dollar return on a portfolio long one domestic currency bond of value $B_t(T)$ and short one foreign currency bond of value $S_t B_t^{CH}(T)$. If interest rates do not change randomly, the exposure to exchange rate changes is simply the value of the foreign currency bond in foreign currency, $B_t^{CH}(T)$. A \$1 change in the exchange rate changes the domestic currency value of the foreign bond by $B_t^{CH}(T)$.

What makes the computation and the hedging of the risk tricky is that interest rates are not constant, so the exposure to the foreign currency is not constant. Whenever the value of the foreign currency bond changes in foreign currency, the foreign exchange exposure changes. Further, it is important to note that with a foreign position whose value changes over time, we make foreign exchange gains and losses both on the initial exposure and on the changes in the exposure over time.

To better understand the foreign exchange gains and losses associated with a foreign currency swap, let's look at the change in value of a swap where $B_t(T)$ = 100M, S_t = \$0.5, and $B_t^{CH}(T)$ = SFR200M. At t, the swap has no value. Suppose now that over the next six months there are no interest payments so that all the change in value of the swap results from changes in bond prices and in the exchange rate. Let's use the following values for date $t + 0.5$: $B_{t+0.5}(T)$ = \$95M, $S_{t+0.5}$ = 0.55, and $B_{t+0.5}^{CH}(T)$ = SFR206M. The value of the swap is now:

$$B_{t+0.5}(T) - S_{t+0.5}B_{t+0.5}^{CH}(T) = 95M - 0.55 \times 206M = -\$18.3M \quad \text{(16.13)}$$

We therefore lost \$18.3 million. We can think of this loss as the sum of four components. The first two components are changes in the values of the bonds that constitute the swap due to changes in interest rates. The last two components are the exchange rate loss on the initial foreign currency bond value and the exchange rate loss that applies to the change in value of the foreign bond since inception. First, we lost \$5 million on the domestic currency bond. Second, we lost 6 million in foreign currency units because of the increase in value of the foreign currency bond in foreign currency, which at the initial exchange rate represents a loss of \$3 million. With an initial foreign currency bond value of 200 million in foreign currency, the appreciation of the foreign currency by \$0.05 creates a loss of \$10 million. Adding the first three components, we have $-\$5M - \$3M - \$10M$, which amounts to a loss of \$18 million. This loss is less than the loss computed directly by valuing the swap because we also lost the foreign exchange appreciation on the gain of the foreign bond in foreign currency, namely \$0.05 × SFR6M, which is \$0.3 million. Adding this additional loss, we end up with $-\$18.3$ million, which is the loss we directly computed in equation (16.13). At the end of the period, the swap's exposure to the foreign currency has changed from 200 million to 206 million units of foreign currency.

If we have the return in domestic currency of the domestic bond and of the foreign bond, the computation of the change in value of the swap is straightforward. We define by r_B the decimal return on the domestic bond over the evaluation period. We also define by r_{SBCH} the decimal return of the foreign bond in domestic currency. The change in value of the swap is:

Change in value of a currency swap

$$= r_B B_t(T) - r_{SB^{CH}} S_t B_t^{CH}(T) \qquad (16.14)$$

We can also compute the value change of the swap using the foreign currency return of the foreign bond, r_B^{CH}, and the decimal exchange rate return over the evaluation period, $r_S = S_{t+\Delta t}/S_t - 1$. In this case, the change in value of the swap is given by:

Change in value of currency swap

$$= r_B B_t(T) - \left[\left(1 + r_B^{CH}\right)(1 + r_S) - 1\right] S_t B^{CH}_t(T)$$

$$= r_B B_t(T) - r_B^{CH} S_t B_t^{CH}(T) - r_S S_t B_t^{CH}(T) - r_B^{CH} r_S S_t B_t^{CH}(T) \qquad (16.15)$$

The cross-product term, $r_{BCH} r_S S_t B_t^{CH}(T)$, is required because of the change in the foreign currency exposure during the period over which the change in value of the swap is evaluated. Using our example, we have $r_B = -0.05$, $r_B^{CH} = 0.03$, and $r_S = 0.10$. Using our formula gives us:

$$-0.05 \times 100M - 0.03 \times 0.5 \times 200M - 0.10 \times 0.5$$

$$\times 200M - 0.03 \times 0.10 \times 0.5 \times 200M = -\$18.3 \qquad (16.16)$$

Had we ignored the cross-product term, we would have found a change in value of the swap of –$18 million.

Computation of the VaR of the swap is straightforward if we start from the formula for the change in value of the swap, which uses the domestic currency return of the foreign bond (equation (16.14)). In this case, the volatility of the change in value of the swap is given by:

Volatility of change in value of the swap

$$= \left[\begin{array}{l} B_t(T)^2 \text{Var}(r_B) + \left(S_t B_t^{CH}(T)\right)^2 \text{Var}\left(r_{SB^{CH}}\right) \\ - 2B_t(T)S_t B_t^{CH}(T)\text{Cov}\left(r_B, r_{SB^{CH}}\right) \end{array}\right]^{0.5} \qquad (16.17)$$

As long as the returns are normally distributed, the VaR of the swap is 1.65 times the volatility of the change in value of the swap.

The computation of the VaR is more involved if we start from the returns of the foreign bond in foreign currency. The reason is that we then have a product of two random variables, r_{BCH} and r_S. If each random variable is normally distributed, their product is not normally distributed. One approach is to assume that these two random variables are normally distributed and then compute a Monte Carlo VaR. As the period over which the change in value of the swap is computed becomes small, the cross-product term becomes unimportant and can be ignored. Hence, if one were to compute the VaR over one day, one could ignore that cross-product term. In this case, the computation of the VaR is again straightforward. It is the VaR when we use the domestic currency return of the foreign bond, but now the domestic currency return of the foreign bond is $r_{BCH} + r_S$.

Hedging the foreign bond is more complicated, but in the presence of well-developed forward markets for foreign currency, the foreign currency bond can be transformed into a domestic currency bond. To do this, note that the foreign currency bond has known payments in foreign currency at future dates. In the swap, we are short the foreign currency bond, so that we have to make the payments. We can buy now the foreign currency corresponding to the payments we will have to make using the forward market.

Say that we have a payment of 5 million Swiss francs to make once a year for ten years and an additional payment of 100 million Swiss francs to make in year ten. Using forward contracts, we can buy forward 5 million Swiss francs for each year and an additional amount of 100 million Swiss francs for the final year. Once we have done that, we know exactly how much we will have to spend in dollars to fulfill our swap obligation. We can buy zero-coupon bonds (strips) that pay the product of 5 million Swiss francs times the forward price for each future payment date. We then hold a portfolio of dollar strips. We already know that a default-free dollar bond is a portfolio of strips, each with a face value equal to the promised payment of the bond. In this case, we have a portfolio of strips whose face values are likely to differ from year to year because forward rates differ from year to year. For example, if the forward rate is $0.6 in year 1 and $0.65 in year two, the strips have face value of $3 and $3.25 million respectively, since the Swiss franc coupon is Swiss franc 5 million. This is like a bond whose coupon payments vary over time in a deterministic way. We know, however, how to hedge a portfolio of strips already.

Currency swaps can provide a useful instrument to compare borrowing costs across countries. To see this, suppose an AAA-rated issuer is deciding whether to borrow in dollars or in euros. It can borrow by issuing a ten-year fixed rate issue in dollars, or it can borrow by issuing a ten-year fixed rate euro issue. These two debt issues are not directly comparable. One way to make them comparable is to swap into floating LIBOR. Suppose that the fixed rate dollar issue can be swapped into LIBOR minus 17 basis points and that the euro issue can be swapped into LIBOR minus 10 basis points. In this case, borrowing in dollars is cheaper by 7 basis points. Tracking these borrowing costs by using the differential in LIBOR floating rates, it turns out that dollar borrowing is almost always cheaper by less than half a dozen basis points.

16.3.2. Swaps where the notional amount changes over time

So far, we have considered swaps whose interest payments are computed using a constant notional amount for the swap. Sometimes a company might want to hedge a position that is equivalent to a bond with a principal that changes over time. One example is an amortizing bond on which the borrower repays a fraction of the principal at various times. Another example might be a mortgage security. There is a large market for securitized mortgages. An investment bank puts together a portfolio of mortgages that it buys from various banks or mortgage issuers. The investment bank then sells securities that have claims against this portfolio of mortgages. The principal of a mortgage is paid back over the life of the mortgage. Further, mortgage borrowers can prepay their mortgages at any time, usually without a penalty. As some of the mortgages in the portfolio are prepaid and the principal is paid back on the mortgages that are not prepaid, the bond entitling the holder to the payment of the interest and principal on a portfolio of mortgages has a face value—that is, the sum of the principal balances outstanding of the mortgages in the portfolio—that falls over time.

A final example is a building or project developer. Such a firm might arrange with a bank a loan whose principal first increases as the building is financed and then the principal starts falling as the debt is amortized.

Assume that a firm has issued debt whose principal changes over time. Say that the bond is an amortizing bond. This firm now wants to change the riskiness of its cash flows. Suppose that the interest payments on the bond are a fixed proportion of the outstanding principal and now the firm would like to change its interest payments to payments equal to LIBOR on the reset date times the outstanding principal. A swap with a constant notional does not work here. An alternative swap called an **amortizing swap** works. With such a swap, the notional amount falls over time according to a well-defined schedule.

To price an amortizing swap, the concept of par for the floating rate is meaningless since the principal outstanding falls over time. We therefore must start by computing the present value of the floating rate payments and principal repayments, given our knowledge of how the notional amount changes over time. Table 16.2 shows how the notional amount changes over time. Using the eurodollar futures contract, we could lock in the implied futures rate for each future payment date. We can discount these locked-in payments to price the swap. The present value of each future floating rate payment is the $25 million plus the implied futures rate times the relevant notional amount discounted to today.

Adding up the present value of the payments in Table 16.2, we obtain (in millions of dollars):

$$25.8796 + 25.3168 + 24.7364 + 24.0672 = 100 \qquad (16.18)$$

Pricing an amortizing swap	*Table 16.2*

The implied futures yields correspond to implied futures yields from the 3-month LIBOR futures contract. On each payment, 25 of outstanding principal is repaid. The amounts are in millions of dollars.

Period	Day count	Notional	Implied futures yield	Discount factor	Present value of floating rate payment
1	90	100	4.8%	0.98827	25.8796
2	91	75	5.0%	0.97607	25.3168
3	92	50	5.5%	0.96269	24.7364
4	91	25	6.0%	0.94846	24.0672

This is not surprising. If we receive $100 million from our bank as proceeds for a loan, in perfect capital markets that amount must be the present value of the loan. We now have to find the relevant interest rate for the fixed rate payments. To do that, we can compute the present value of the fixed rate payments with an unknown interest rate and equate it to $100 million (again in million dollars):

$$0.98827 \times [c \times (90/364) \times 100 + 25] + 0.97607$$
$$\times [c \times (91/364) \times 75 + 25] + 0.96269$$
$$\times [c \times (92/364) \times 50 + 25] + 0.94846$$
$$\times [c \times (91/364) \times 25 + 25] = 100 \qquad (16.19)$$

The solution of this equation is $c = 0.0511296$, which corresponds to an interest rate of 5.11296 percent.

16.3.3. Total return swaps

A swap does not always define payments as fractions of a certain notional amount. A CEO with a large equity stake in the equity of his firm may want to reduce the risk of his portfolio. Lorne Weil, chairman and chief executive of the Autotote Corporation, faced this problem in March 1994. He wanted to reduce his exposure to his corporation by 500,000 shares. He could sell the shares, but he would have had to pay capital gains taxes and would also have lost the voting rights attached to the shares. He could have hedged the shares using index futures and other securities. Unfortunately, a firm's equity has substantial idiosyncratic risk, so that such a hedge would still have left Mr. Weil with significant risk. A third possibility addresses these problems. Mr. Weil could use a swap to exchange the cash flows associated with the shares for cash flows from a safer asset, say, a floating rate note. Mr. Weil used the third possibility, entering a swap for five years with Bankers Trust. Mr. Weil's transaction was one of the first of this kind.[3]

Mr. Weil agreed to pay Bankers Trust the dividends from the shares and at maturity the appreciation of the shares over the life of the swap. In exchange, Bankers Trust promised to pay floating rate interest payments on a notional amount equal to the value of the shares at inception of the swap.

The swap is equivalent to having a long position in a floating rate note with par equal to the present value of the shares and a short position in the shares. Such a portfolio has zero value when it is created, which means that the swap has zero value at inception. At maturity, the portfolio is liquidated, which requires the purchase of shares to close the short stock position and selling the note. The net cash flow of the portfolio at maturity is equal to the difference between the value of the shares when the portfolio was created, which is equal to the par value of the notes in the portfolio, and the value of the shares at maturity. Mr. Weil promised to pay Bankers Trust the total return of the shares over the life of the swap since it receives all dividends plus the capital gains, so swaps like this one are

---

3 See "Keeping votes as stock is sold," *New York Times*, March 29, 1994, D1.

called total return swaps. A **total return swap** requires one party to pay the total return on a reference asset or portfolio to a counterparty in exchange for the total return on another reference asset or portfolio so that the reference assets or portfolios have the same market value at inception of the swap.

When Mr. Weil's swap was agreed to, his shares were valued at $26.78 per share. Consequently, 500,000 shares were worth $13.39 million. Bankers Trust therefore promised to pay the floating rate payments on a notional of $13.39 million. Each subsequent period, Mr. Weil had to pay to Bankers Trust the dividend received on the shares and received the floating rate payments. At maturity, Mr. Weil received a payment from Bankers Trust equal to the final floating rate payment minus the change in the share price times 500,000. If, instead, the swap had involved fixed rate payments, we would have needed to find the appropriate coupon payments given existing interest rates on a bond whose par value is $13.39 million. Note that with such a swap, Mr. Weil may have had to make a large payment to Bankers Trust at maturity of the swap. This would not have been a problem as long as Mr. Weil had the shares and could sell them to make the payment. However, if Mr. Weil no longer had the shares or had incurred debt for which the shares are collateral, he might not be able to make the payment to Bankers Trust. To avoid this counterparty risk, Bankers Trust may have asked to hold the shares as collateral.

Total return swaps can use as the reference asset or portfolio any financial asset or portfolio. A money manager might have all his portfolio invested in the S&P 500, but wants to diversify the portfolio internationally. To achieve this international diversification, he could sell shares and use the cash to buy foreign shares. Or he could simply enter a total return swap. The money manager could promise to pay the total return on his portfolio over the next five years in exchange for receiving the total return on an investment in the world portfolio equal to the current value of his portfolio. Without buying or selling any stock, the money manager could become internationally diversified with one transaction.

This could be a tricky situation for the money manager's clients, however. If his clients invest with him because they see him holding the S&P 500, they might not want to invest with him if they knew that they are effectively investing in the world market portfolio. The lesson is we cannot know the distribution of the return of a portfolio by looking only at the securities it holds—we have to know the swaps too.

16.3.4. Swaps with options

Suppose the swap has options attached to it. We can still price it using the pricing approach developed in this chapter. Earlier, we priced a fixed-for-floating swap. Consider now our counterparty in this swap. The counterparty pays floating and receives fixed. The counterparty may have entered the swap because it believes that interest rates will fall and hence took an interest rate bet. However, the counterparty may be concerned that if interest rates unexpectedly increase, it may have to make extremely large floating rate payments and may therefore choose to buy insurance against large interest rate increases in the form of a cap. The counterparty could buy the cap separately from the swap or could buy it as part of the swap. If the cap is part of the swap, the counterparty continues to receive fixed but pays floating with an upper limit given by the cap rate. Hence, for the swap to be fairly priced, we must have:

Present value of fixed rate payments

= Present value of (floating rate payments – cap payments)   (16.20)

To see that this is correct, consider the tenth payment period. The counterparty receives the fixed rate payment at the end of the period. It pays at the end of the period the rate chosen on the reset date if this rate is below the cap rate. If the rate on the reset date exceeds the cap rate, the counterparty pays the cap rate. Hence, the payment it makes is equal to the floating rate payment it would make in the absence of the cap minus the payment it would receive from having bought a cap. As a result of this arrangement, the present value of the payments received by the fixed rate payer is lower since the floating rate payer never pays more than the cap rate. The present value of the payments received by the fixed rate payer is equal to the present value of the payments on a floating rate bond minus the present value of the payments from a cap. Compared to a simple fixed-for-floating swap, the fixed rate payer receives smaller payments from the floating rate payer and the present value of the difference is equal to the value of a cap. Hence, the fixed rate payments have to be reduced by an amount equal in present value to the current value of the cap.

This approach makes it possible to price any swap with embedded options. The swap is priced so that the present value of the payments made is equal to the present value of the payments received. Any option that affects one stream of cash flows must be incorporated into the present value of that stream of cash flows. In general, we can use option pricing formulas to compute the present value of the option features of a swap.

16.3.5. Forwards and options on swaps

Suppose a firm plans on issuing a fixed rate bond in two years that will mature five years from now and pay interest semiannually. The firm wants to lock in the fixed rate today. How can it do this? It enters a forward swap. In a **forward swap**, fixed rate payments are agreed upon today but the first payment period starts at some future date. Today the firm could enter into a swap, Swap A, so that starting in two years it pays a fixed rate agreed upon today and receives floating. In two years, the firm enters another swap at market, Swap B, whereby it pays floating and receives fixed at the rate prevailing then. The firm can then use the fixed payments it receives from Swap B to pay the debt service on the bond. The floating rate payments on Swap A and Swap B offset each other, so the firm is left with making the fixed rate payments on Swap A. These transactions allow the firm to lock in its interest payments at the fixed interest rate of Swap A, which is known today. The swap entered into today but starting in two years, Swap A, is a forward swap.

Say that the fixed rate payments on Swap A are 10 percent paid semiannually, and that the firm receives LIBOR semiannually in exchange. Two years from now, a swap at market might involve the payment of 11 percent semiannually in exchange of LIBOR. The coupon rate on the bond the firm issues is also 11 percent. Hence, every six months, the firm pays 5.5 percent on the bond. It receives 5.5 percent on the later swap and pays LIBOR. On net, therefore, the firm pays LIBOR. From the forward swap entered into today, the firm must pay 5 percent every payment period to receive LIBOR. Once everything is taken into account, the firm pays 5 percent per payment period, whatever the interest rates are in two years, since the cash flows of the firm are:

–Coupon on debt issued of 5.5% per six months

+ Market swap fixed rate receipt of 5.5%

– LIBOR payment + LIBOR receipt

– Forward swap fixed rate payment of 5%

= Fixed rate payment of 5% **(16.21)**

To price the forward swap, suppose that a two-year swap with semiannual payments trades at 8 percent/7.9 percent today and that the five-year swap with semiannual payments trades at 9.5 percent/9.35 percent. Remember that the firm wants a swap where it pays fixed. Hence, the firm can enter today into a swap where it pays 9.5 percent fixed and receives LIBOR. Starting two years from now, this swap will have exactly the payments the firm wants. However, there is a problem in the first two years since the firm must make payments when it does not want to. Suppose that the firm enters into an offsetting swap where it receives fixed and pays LIBOR for two years. The LIBOR payments cancel out, but the fixed rate payments do not exactly cancel out. The firm pays 9.5 percent and receives 7.9 percent. This means that it must pay 0.8 percent every six months for two years. We now have a forward swap and the cost to the firm is this semiannual payment for two years. This semiannual payment can be eliminated by adding a payment to 9.5 percent starting in two years whose present value is equal to 0.8 percent semiannually for two years. Having done this, we would have a forward swap where payments start in two years.

An alternative for the prospective bond issuer is to enter a swap in two years when it actually issues debt. A **swaption** is an option to enter into a swap with a specified fixed rate payment at maturity of the option. For example, a call swaption could give the right to enter a swap in two years to receive 10 percent fixed semiannually on $100 million and pay floating rate payments on the same notional amount for three years. In one year, the present value of the fixed rate payment will depend on prevailing interest rates at that time. Say that the value of a bond paying 10 percent semiannually on $100 million for three years in one year is $B^\wedge$. Since the swap underlying the call swaption is equivalent to a portfolio long a fixed rate bond and short a floating rate bond, the call swaption gives the right to receive the bond worth $B^\wedge$ for $100 million. This is equivalent to a call option on the fixed rate bond with an exercise price of $100 million. We already know how to price bond options. There is no difference between pricing a call swaption and pricing a bond option. A put option would give the right to pay $B^\wedge$ and receive $100 million. This is equivalent to a put option on a bond, which we also know how to price.

16.4. Case study: The Procter & Gamble levered swap

On November 2, 1993, Procter & Gamble (P&G) and Bankers Trust (BT) entered into a five-year swap that would have guaranteed extremely low financing costs as long as interest rates did not increase much—the 30-day commercial paper rate (CP) minus 75 basis points, which would have been less than 3 percent. Unfortunately for P&G, interest rates increased sharply in 1994 because of a tightening of monetary policy. This swap accounts for about 2/3 of the more than $200 million losses P&G made on exotic derivatives (much of these losses were wiped out when P&G settled with Bankers Trust).

This swap had semiannual settlement and a notional amount of $200 million. With this swap, BT agreed to pay P&G 5.30 percent annually and P&G agreed to pay a rate that is the daily average of the 30-day commercial paper rate minus 75 basis points plus a spread. The spread was set at zero for the first six-month payment period and then was set at an amount equal to:

$$\text{Max}\left[\frac{98.5\left(\dfrac{5\text{-year CMT\%}}{5.78\%}\right) - (30\text{-year T-bond price})}{100}, 0\right] \qquad (16.22)$$

CMT stands for Constant Maturity Treasury. The five-year CMT rate is the rate on a five-year T-note that has five years to maturity.

The swap is called a **levered swap**. We know that a plain vanilla interest rate swap is equivalent to simultaneous long and short positions in bonds with par value equal to the notional. Suppose now that we change the plain vanilla swap so that the size of the short bond position is increased. To maintain the value of the swap at inception equal to zero, we take the proceeds from this increase in the short position and invest them in the risk-free asset. The resulting swap is called a levered swap because its cash flows are those of the plain vanilla swap with additional borrowing. Now, suppose that the bond we are short is a bond with interest payments that depend on some index. The net interest payments of the swap are the interest payments on the short bond position minus the interest earned on the investment in the risk-free asset. When the index is low, the net interest payments could be zero or even negative because of the interest earned on the risk-free asset position. However, if the index increases, the interest payments increase by more than with a plain vanilla swap because the short position in the bond is larger than with such a swap.

With the P&G swap, P&G makes extremely low interest payments when interest rates are low, but the interest rate payment increases by more than the CMT rate if the spread is positive. The CMT rate has a multiplier of 98.5/5.78 or 17.04, so that if the CMT rate increases by 100 basis points when the spread is positive, the spread increases by 17.04×100 basis points, or 1,704 basis points, keeping the T-bond price constant. As the CMT rate increases, P&G ends up paying more than the CMT rate on the notional.

The formula for the spread may appear complicated, but it turns out to be easy to understand. In addition to leverage, the spread has an option component since the spread cannot be negative. At initiation, the five-year CMT rate was 5.02 percent and the 30-year T-bond price was 102.57811 for a yield of 6.06 percent. Substituting these prices in the formula, we have:

$$\text{Max}\left[\frac{98.5\left(\dfrac{5.02\%}{5.78\%}\right) - 102.57811}{100}, 0\right] = \text{Max}(-0.1703, 0) = 0 \qquad (16.23)$$

Accordingly, the initial spread is zero and rates could increase some without affecting the spread. The five-year rate could increase to 5.78 percent and the 30-year T-bond could fall to 98.5 and the spread would still be zero.

The problem for P&G was that interest rates increased dramatically over the six-month period. On May 4, 1994, which was the scheduled date on which the spread would be set, the five-year CMT rate was 6.71 percent and the 30-year T-bond price was 86.84375 for a yield of 7.35 percent. When we substitute these numbers in the formula, we get a spread of 27.50 percent. This spread means that P&G would have had to pay the commercial paper rate (CP) plus 27.50 – 0.75, or CP plus 26.75 percent per year on $200 million, which corresponds to annual interest payments of $53.5 million in excess of the interest payments P&G would have had to make if it had paid the CP rate.

Graphing the payoffs of a derivative is a good tool to study the properties of a derivative. Such an approach is a way to perform a stress test systematically—a stress test estimates the impact of specific changes in risk factors on a derivative. The P&G swap is no exception. It is striking that the range of values is extremely important to understand the properties of this contract. In Figure 16.3, we graph the payoffs twice. In the first case, we assume a narrow range for the five-year CMT rate and for the T-bond price—that is, we assume that large changes cannot occur. In the second case, we assume a wider range of values for the five-year CMT and the T-bond price. The wider range of values shows clearly that the swap could lead to extremely wide spreads for combinations of the five-year CMT rate and the T-bond price. Panel A gives a very different impression of the risks from Panel B. Panel A does not include the spread that eventually P&G had to pay, but Panel B does.

The lesson is that the wrong scale can be extremely misleading in evaluating a derivative. A corporate treasurer seeing the figure in Panel A might conclude that the swap is a good deal; a treasurer seeing the figure in Panel B might reach the opposite conclusion.

Another way to understand the risks of the P&G swap is to compute the VaR in terms of the spread. In other words, we seek to answer the question: What is the number such that 5 percent of the time the spread will be worse than that number? Suppose we assume that both the five-year CMT rate and the T-bond have normally distributed changes. In this case, the term that determines the spread in percent can be written as:

Max[(98.5/5.78) × (5-year CMT + Δ5-year CMT)

– (T-bond price + ΔT-bond price), 0] $\qquad$ **(16.24)**

Figure 16.3

P&G swap spread as a function of 5-year CMT rate and T-bond price

The P&G swap required P&G to pay to BT the average commercial paper rate plus a spread minus 75 basis points. The spread, in percentage terms, was equal to 17.04 times the five-year CMT rate minus the T-bond price, provided that this amount is positive. The two figures graph the spread as a function of the five-year CMT rate and the T-bond price.

Panel A

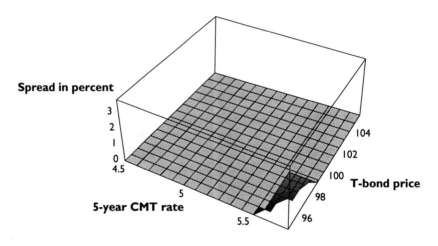

Panel B

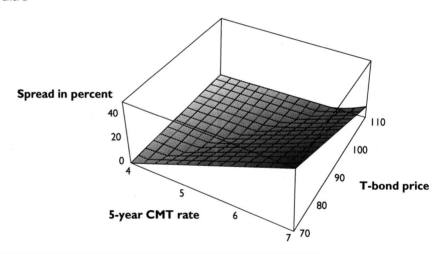

The first term in this expression has a volatility given by:

$$\text{Vol(Spread)} = [17.04^2 \times \text{Var(5-year CMT)}$$
$$+ \text{Var(T-bond price)} - 2\rho \times 17.04$$
$$\times \text{Vol(5-year CMT)} \times \text{Vol(T-bond price)}]^{0.5} \qquad (16.25)$$

where Vol() denotes a volatility, Var a variance, and the ρ correlation between the five-year CMT rate and the T-bond price. The VaR computed over the period of determination of the spread (the 132 days between the start of the swap and the determination of the spread) is the spread corresponding to:

$$\text{Max}[(98.5/5.78) \times (\text{5-year CMT}) - \text{T-bond price}$$
$$+ 1.65 \times \text{Vol(Spread)}, 0] \qquad (16.26)$$

where the volatilities are computed over 132 days. Using historical data for 1993, we can take 0.055 as the daily volatility of the five-year CMT rate, 0.6 as the daily volatility of the T-bond price, and –0.8 as the correlation coefficient between the five-year CMT rate and the T-bond price. In this case, we have:

$$(98.5/5.78) \times 5.02 - 102.57811 + 1.65$$
$$\times (17.04^2 \times 132 \times 0.055^2 + 132 \times 0.6^2 + 2$$
$$\times 132 \times 17.04 \times 0.8 \times 0.055 \times 0.6)^{0.5} = 10.69\% \qquad (16.27)$$

The VaR is 10.69 percent. Because of the multiplier that affects the five-year CMT rate, small changes in that rate can lead to potentially large changes in the VaR. Under our assumptions, the swap would have had a spread exceeding 10.69 percent five years out of one hundred. Any treasurer or analyst considering entering such a swap to take advantage of some view on interest rates should compute the swap's VaR as well as graph the payoffs of the swap.

In computing the VaR, we made assumptions about the joint distribution of the five-year CMT rate and the 30-year T-bond price. To fully understand the risk of the swap, a treasurer should investigate how sensitive the VaR is to changes in these assumptions. Hence, he might want to estimate the VaR using different assumptions.

Finally, if the swap is a hedge, the treasurer would have to estimate how good of a hedge the swap is—he would have to estimate the effectiveness of the swap as a hedge. In this case, the relevant risk measure is not the VaR of the swap as a stand-alone financial instrument but the contribution of the swap to the VaR of the firm or to the position being hedged.

16.5. Summary

The swap market has grown tremendously over time. It is likely to keep growing because swaps are extremely useful. Any cash flow can be transformed into another using a swap.

The simplest swaps are the fixed-for-floating interest rate swap and the currency swap. In a fixed-for-floating swap, one party pays to another a fixed rate on a notional amount and receives from the other party a floating payment on the same notional amount. This interest rate swap enables firms to transform cash flows corresponding to fixed rate interest payments into cash flows corresponding to floating rate payments, or vice versa. In a currency swap, one party pays to another a fixed rate payment on a notional amount in one currency and receives from the other party a fixed rate payment on a notional amount in another currency. A currency swap enables a firm to transform a cash flow in one currency into a cash flow in another currency.

With an interest rate swap, the swap interest payments are computed on a notional amount that is never exchanged. With a currency swap, the notional amounts are in different currencies but equal in value at origination of the swap. At maturity, the notional amounts of the currency swap are exchanged. We saw how these swaps are quoted and priced, and how their risk is measured.

We also saw that not every cash flow can be transformed into another one with interest rate or currency swaps of the type we studied early in the chapter. A firm may not be able to change its cash flows in a way that fits its objectives without using more complicated swaps or using options on swaps. It is therefore crucial that a derivatives user be able to assess the pluses and minuses of more complicated swap transactions. We used the P&G leveraged swap to show how a derivatives user can analyze an exotic swap using some of the tools developed in this book.

Key Concepts

amortizing swap, 521
currency swap, 501
forward swap, 524
interest rate swap, 505
levered swap, 526

swap rate, 505
swap spread, 505
swaption, 525
total return swap, 523

Review Questions

1. What is a swap?

2. What is a fixed-for-floating swap?

3. When and how are the cash flows of a swap equivalent to those of a bond portfolio?

4. What is the swap spread?

5. What is the value of a new swap?

6. What is the bond yield approach to pricing a swap?

7. What is the present value approach to pricing a swap?

8. Is the notional amount exchanged at maturity in an interest rate swap? What about a currency swap?

9. How would you use a forward swap to lock the rate you will pay on debt issued in the future?

10. What is a swaption?

Questions and Exercises

1. Consider the case where an interest rate swap with notional amount of $100 million is initiated at date 0. The bond matures at date 4. LIBOR for one period is at 5 percent. The interest rate per period for a bond maturing at date 1 is 5 percent, for a bond maturing at date 2 is 5.5 percent, for a bond maturing at date 3 is 5.5 percent, and for a bond maturing at date 4 is 5.75 percent. Payments take place at dates 2, 3, and 4. Find the interest payment c that has to be made at dates 2, 3, and 4 for the swap to have no value at initiation.

2. The swap described in question 1 is modified so that the floating rate payer never pays more than 6 percent per period. The price of a cap with exercise price of 6 percent on $100 million notional is $1 million. Find the coupon payment c' that makes the swap have no value at initiation given that the floating rate payments are capped at 6 percent.

3. At date 2, the term structure of zero-coupon bonds is flat at 6 percent. LIBOR for one period is at 6 percent. What is the value of the swap priced in question 1 for the fixed-rate payer?

4. Let's consider again the data in question 1. Now, however, payments take place at dates 3 and 5. The interest rate per period for a bond maturing at date 5 is 6 percent. All the other data is kept the same. Compute the interest payment c that has to be made at dates 3 and 5.

5. At date 1, the term structure is flat at 6 percent. What is the value of the swap of question 4 for the floating rate payer?

6. Consider a currency swap requiring payments at dates 2, 3, and 4. A U.S. coupon bond paying a coupon at dates 2, 3, and 4 selling at par has a coupon of 8 percent. A foreign coupon bond paying a coupon at dates 2, 3, and 4 selling at par has a coupon of 5 percent. The domestic price of the foreign currency is $0.50. The dollar notional amount of the swap is $50 million. What is the foreign currency fixed rate payment?

7. At date 2, the U.S. interest rates are unchanged from date 1. The foreign term structure has shifted up by 100 basis points. The dollar price of the foreign currency is $0.60. What is the value of the swap for the U.S. fixed rate payer?

8. At date 4, the dollar price of the foreign currency is $0.80. What is the net payment that the U.S. fixed rate payer receives?

9. A portfolio manager whose portfolio is fully invested in 30-year bonds wants to shorten the duration of his portfolio to six months for the next five years. He wants to do that through a swap. Describe the transaction he wants to enter into.

10. Go back to the swap in question 1. Now, the swap contract is such that the floating rate payer receives 2 times the fixed rate and pays 2 times the floating rate. Compute the value of the swap at date 1 and at date 2 given that the term structure is flat at 6 percent and that LIBOR is 6 percent per period.

Literature Note

For an analysis of interest rate swap pricing, see Sundaresan (1991). Sundaresan and Ramaswamy (1986) examine the pricing of floating rate notes. Smith, Smithson, and Wakeman (1986) provide an overview of the swap market, its growth, and the valuation principles. Litzenberg (1992) discusses the economics of the swap contracts and of the swap market. Minton (1997) and Sun, Sundaresan, and Wang (1993) provide an empirical study of the interest rate swap market. Das (1994) provides the most extensive resource on the swap market. Jarrow (1996) has some articles from *Risk* on the pricing of exotic swaps. Arak, Estrella, Goodman, and Silver (1988), Turnbull (1987), and Titman (1992) examine the question of the gains from interest rate swaps. Turnbull (1987) provides a lucid analysis of the limitations of the comparative advantage argument. Titman (1992) provides an analysis of when a firm is better off borrowing short term and locking in long-term financing costs. Cooper and Mello (1991) and Jarrow and Turnbull (1997) provide analyses of the credit risks of swaps. The best record of the IBM-World Bank swap is Bock (1986). Since he disguises some of the terms of the transaction, our discussion shows the general components of the transaction. The Bank for International Settlements produces regular surveys of the global derivatives market. Their most recent survey can be downloaded from http://www. bis.org. Smith (1997) reviews the P&G swap.

Chapter 17

Using Exotic Options

Chapter **17** *Objectives*

At the end of this chapter, you will:

1. Be familiar with the most frequently used exotic options.

2. Understand how to use exotic options in a hedging program.

3. Know how to price exotic options.

4. Understand the risks associated with exotic options.

Why do companies all over the world use exotic derivatives? One of the main reasons is that they have exposures that could not be hedged as efficiently with a static hedge. Consider Petroleos de Venezuela (PDVSA), an energy company with assets in excess of $50 billion. On January 28, 2000, its finance subsidiary entered into a currency swap agreement with respect to notes issued in April 1999. In its annual report, the company states that "The agreement provides protection to the Company with respect to interest and principal payments from a possible appreciation of the euro relative to the U.S. dollar during the term of the notes." This agreement looks like a type of swap we previously discussed. However, PDVSA then explains that "The agreement contains a knock-out provision which eliminates protection to the Company with respect to principal payments, above a $1.09/euro exchange rate if during the term of the agreement the U.S. dollar/ euro exchange rate reaches or exceeds 1.2." This provision of the agreement embeds in the swap an exotic option, namely the swap ceases to hedge the company against euro appreciation if during the life of the swap the euro reaches a sufficiently high value against the dollar. The agreement has a so-called **knock-out provision**.

To understand the knock-out provision, note that the agreement has a call option on the euro with exercise price of $1.09. With a plain vanilla call, PDVSA could exercise the call option whenever the dollar price of the euro exceeds $1.09. However, because of the knock-out provision, the call is not a plain vanilla call. It is a barrier option. A **barrier option** is an option that can be exercised only if the price of the underlying during the life of the option satisfies some condition defined by a barrier. In this case, the barrier is an exchange rate of $1.20 per euro and the option cannot be exercised if the barrier is crossed during the life of the call. A call option with such a barrier is called an up-and-out call or a knock-out call if the barrier is higher than the current value of the underlying. When the underlying—the dollar price of the euro—exceeds some level during the life of the option, PDVSA's call no longer exists. Why would PDVSA use a call like this? There are at least three possible reasons: (1) It may not need protection if the euro appreciates that much; (2) it may actually want exposure to the euro if it appreciates that much because it will require more funding for investment; and (3) the market's assessment of the probability that the euro will appreciate that much is too high given PDVSA's beliefs. For any of these three reasons, paying for protection against euro appreciation when the euro exceeds $1.20 during the life of the option is not worth it for PDVSA. If PDVSA requires euro exposure if the euro exceeds $1.20 but wants protection otherwise, no plain vanilla option would enable PDVSA to achieve its risk management objective.

We analyze the uses, hedging, and pricing of the most popular exotic options: we examine digital options, barrier options, options on averages, and options on multiple assets. Exotic options have been the target of intense adverse publicity because of prominent losses at several corporations. Throughout the chapter, we pay special attention to managing the risks of exotic options. We put some of the highly publicized losses into context using the difficulties of Gibson Greetings Inc. as an example.

17.1. Digital options

Digital options are options with a fixed payoff if they are in the money. A **European cash or nothing digital call option** pays a fixed amount of cash if the price of the underlying exceeds the exercise price at maturity. American digital options exist as well. Figure 17.1 compares the payoff of a cash or nothing digital call option to a plain vanilla call option and to a forward contract.

A digital option can meet a hedging need that cannot be solved with a European call option. The Mexican firm Aspe has concluded that if the dollar appreciates to be worth at least 10 pesos in one year, building a new plant costing 1 billion pesos will be a positive NPV project. Aspe wants to make sure that the money required to build the profitable plant will be available. The firm could enter an arrangement today to borrow 1 billion Mexican pesos. Borrowing today might be expensive or perhaps even impossible. The lenders would worry that, having the money, Aspe might build the plant even if it is not likely to be profitable. A conditional loan agreement to make the money available next year if the peso depreciates would solve the problem for the lenders. Yet, if the firm faces financial difficulties in one year, the lenders might choose not to fund the plant. The firm therefore wants to consider taking a derivative position that provides the required funds if the dollar appreciates sufficiently, regardless of its financial condition at that time.

Payoff diagram for a forward contract, a plain vanilla call option, and a cash or nothing digital call option

Figure 17.1

F is the forward price and K is the exercise price of the options.

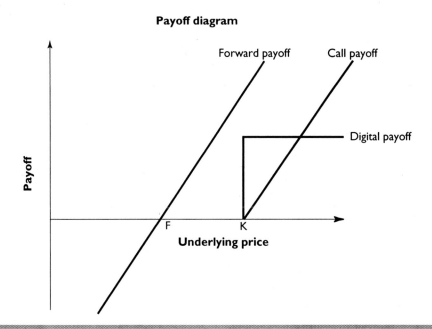

A European call on $100 million with exercise price of 10 pesos per dollar will not work to secure the firm's funding. Define S_{t+1}^{Peso} to be the price of the dollar in pesos in one year. The payoff of the call is $100M \times Max(S_{t+1}^{Peso} - 10, 0)$. If the exchange rate is 10.1 pesos in one year, building the plant is profitable but the option pays only 10 million Mexican pesos, which is insufficient to fund the plant. If the dollar is worth instead 20 Mexican pesos, the firm gets exactly 1 billion Mexican pesos. If the dollar is worth more than 20 Mexican pesos, the firm gets more than 1 billion Mexican pesos. There is no way that a plain vanilla call option will yield a payoff corresponding exactly to the investment the firm has to make.

The solution to the firm's problem is to use a cash or nothing digital call option. The firm buys a European cash or nothing digital call option that pays 1 billion Mexican pesos if the peso price of the dollar exceeds 10 pesos in one year. In one year, the payoff of the option provides the firm with the funding it requires if it is profitable to build the plant.

To price such an option, we can use the Black-Scholes formula. With that formula, the price of a European call option is given by:

$$c(S, K, T, t) = SN(d) - P_t(T)KN\left(d - \sigma\sqrt{T - t}\right)$$

$$d = \frac{\ln(S/P_t(T)K)}{\sigma\sqrt{T - t}} + \frac{1}{2}\sigma\sqrt{T - t} \qquad (17.1)$$

where $c(S, K, T, t)$ is the price of the call at t, S is the price of the underlying asset at t, $P_t(T)$ is the present value of a zero-coupon bond at t that pays one dollar at T, K is the exercise price, and σ is the volatility of the underlying asset. Remember that $N(d)$ is the cumulative normal distribution evaluated at d.

The first term in the formula is the cumulative normal distribution multiplied by the current value of the underlying asset. This is the benefit of receiving the underlying asset if the option expires in the money. The second term in the formula is the cumulative normal distribution multiplied by the present value of the exercise price. This term is the cost of having to pay the exercise price if the option is in the money at maturity.

Under this interpretation of the Black-Scholes formula, the price of a cash or nothing digital call option is simply the present value of receiving a fixed amount of money if the option is in the money at maturity. The value of a fixed amount of money paid if the plain vanilla option is in the money at maturity is given by the second term of the Black-Scholes formula. Following this reasoning, the value of this option is:

Formula for the price of a cash or nothing digital call option

Let $cdc(S, X, K, T, t)$ be the price of a cash or nothing digital call option that pays X if the price of the underlying exceeds the exercise price K at maturity T, S the price of the underlying, σ the volatility of the underlying, and $N(d)$ the cumulative normal distribution evaluated at d. The price of the option is:

$$cdc(S, X, K, T, t) = XP_t(T)N(d)$$

$$d = \frac{\ln(S/P_t(T)K)}{\sigma\sqrt{T - t}} - \frac{1}{2}\sigma\sqrt{T - t} \qquad (17.2)$$

We can use this formula to price the option in our example. To price a currency option we use as the underlying asset the present value of a unit of foreign currency to be paid when the option matures. This present value is the domestic currency value of a foreign currency zero-coupon bond that pays one unit of foreign currency at maturity. Suppose that the Mexican interest rate is 20 percent, the U.S. interest rate is 5 percent, the volatility of the peso is 20 percent, and the current value of the dollar is 8 pesos per dollar. In this case, the price of the underlying is the present value of a dollar to be paid in one year, or $8e^{-0.05}$, which is 7.61. Further, since we value the option in pesos, the risk-free asset is a Mexican T-bill, so that $P_t(T) = e^{-0.20} = 0.818731$. The option is then worth 262.574 million Mexican pesos.

Close to maturity, small changes in the price of the dollar can have a dramatic effect on the value of the digital cash or nothing option. To see this, suppose that an instant before maturity, the price of the dollar is 9.999 Mexican pesos. In this case, the option pays nothing if the price stays the same over the next instant. If the price of the dollar increases slightly to 10.0001 Mexican pesos, however, the option pays 1 billion Mexican pesos. Figure 17.2 shows how the price of the option priced above changes as a function of time to maturity and the price of the

Price of cash or nothing digital call as a function of time to maturity and price of the dollar   *Figure 17.2*

The option pays 1 billion Mexican pesos at maturity if the peso price of the dollar exceeds 10 pesos. The current price of the dollar is 8 pesos, the volatility of the peso is 20 percent, the peso risk-free rate is 20 percent, and the dollar risk-free rate is 5 percent.

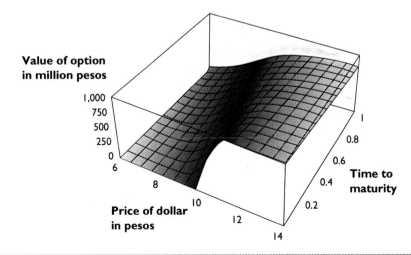

dollar. The delta exposure of the option with respect to the underlying can change dramatically with small changes in the price of the underlying when the option is close to maturity and the price of the underlying is close to the exercise price. This behavior means that delta hedging of a digital option can pose tremendous challenges.

If the price of the dollar is 9.999 Mexican pesos one day before maturity, the price of the option is 652.9 million Mexican pesos. Suppose that the trader who writes the option has to hedge it. He is short a digital option. If, over the next day, the price of the dollar increases by 0.001 Mexican pesos or more, the option is worth one billion Mexican pesos the next day. Otherwise, it is worth nothing. To hedge the option, the trader has to create a portfolio that generates slightly more than 347 million Mexican pesos for an increase in the price of the dollar of 0.001 Mexican pesos and − 652.9 million Mexican pesos for a smaller increase in the price of the dollar.

In this case, to delta hedge the option, the trader would have to be able to trade literally every second since a minuscule change in the price of the dollar has a dramatic impact on the value of the option. This is obviously impossible. Given the inability to hedge the option with a dynamic hedge, the approach used in practice consists of hedging the option by taking large positions in plain vanilla options whose exercise price straddles the exercise price of the digital option.

Another difficulty resulting from the fact that the delta of a digital option can change dramatically for small changes in the price of the underlying is that the delta approximation can yield a very poor estimate of the change in the value of the option for a small change in the price of the underlying. This makes the delta-VaR approach dangerous with this type of option as we could conclude that we have little risk when a small change in the price of the underlying would lead us to a completely different conclusion.

A European **asset or nothing digital call option** pays the underlying if its price exceeds the exercise price at maturity. A call option on one IBM share with exercise price of $100 pays one share of IBM if the share price exceeds $100. For Aspe, an asset or nothing digital call option would pay $100 million if the dollar price exceeds 10 Mexican pesos at maturity since the foreign currency is the asset in this case. The value of an asset or nothing digital call option corresponds to the first term of the Black-Scholes formula:

Formula for an asset or nothing digital call option

Let $adc(S, K, t, T)$ be the price of an asset or nothing digital call option that pays S if the price of the underlying exceeds the exercise price K at maturity T, S the price of the underlying, σ the volatility of the underlying, and $N(d)$ the cumulative normal distribution evaluated at d. The price of the option is:

$$adc(S, K, T, t) = S \times N(d)$$

$$d = \frac{\ln(S/P_t(T)K)}{\sigma\sqrt{T-t}} + \frac{1}{2}\sigma\sqrt{T-t} \tag{17.3}$$

If the option is on a currency, we use as the underlying asset the present value of one unit of foreign currency.

A European cash or nothing digital put option pays a given amount of money if the price of the underlying is below the exercise price at maturity. The put-call parity theorem applies for digital options. A cash or nothing digital put and a cash or nothing digital call with the same terms amount to receiving the cash for sure at maturity, and they must therefore be worth the cash now.

17.2. Barrier options

The payoff of plain vanilla options does not depend on the price path of the underlying. A barrier option is an exotic derivative that pays off if the price path of the underlying during the life of the option crosses some threshold called the barrier. Suppose we have a call option on a share of Fence.com with an exercise price of $50 where the payoff depends on the evolution of the stock price before maturity. The option contract states that the option holder can exercise if and only if the stock price never falls below $40 during the life of the option.

There are three possible outcomes for the exotic option (see also Figure 17.3):

1. The option expires out of the money because the stock price is below the exercise price of $50: The option holder receives nothing.

2. The option expires in the money and the stock price never dropped below $40: The option pays the stock price minus the exercise price.

Graph of down-and-out barrier call   *Figure 17.3*

This is a call option on a stock that is contingent on the stock price staying above the barrier. Here, the barrier is at $40, the exercise price at $50, and the stock price at maturity is $60. This figure shows four price paths that start at $55 and end at $60. A conventional call always pays $10. However, the barrier option pays nothing if the stock price follows the dotted paths. It pays off at maturity only for the paths that do not cross the barrier, so that it does not pay for the paths given by dotted lines.

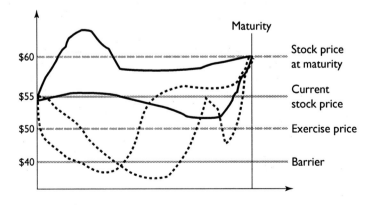

Time

3. The option expires in the money and the stock price dropped below $40: The option holder receives nothing, whatever the stock price at maturity.

In Figure 17.3, a plain vanilla option would pay $10 if the stock price followed any of the price paths, but the exotic option pays nothing if the stock price follows one of the dotted price paths. Since the exotic option does not pay off when the stock price has fallen below $40 during the option's life while a plain vanilla European call does, the option is worth less than the plain vanilla European call. The derivative asset becomes a plain vanilla European call only if the stock price does not fall below $40, so that the barrier option becomes a plain vanilla call for all price paths that do not cross the barrier from above. An option that loses its value if the price of the underlying falls below the barrier is called a **down-and-out barrier option**: the option becomes worthless or gets knocked out if the stock price falls below the barrier. A barrier can be an in or an out barrier. Crossing an in barrier means that the option converts into a plain vanilla option. Crossing an out barrier means that the option to convert into a plain vanilla option is out. Consequently, a **down-and-in option** has value at maturity only if the stock price falls below the barrier at some point before exercise. Down barriers are below the price of the underlying at inception of the option, while up barriers are above. An **up-and-in option** converts into a plain vanilla option if and only if the barrier is exceeded once before maturity. An option can be a knock-in option or a knock-out option depending on whether it can be exercised if the barrier is crossed. Finally, barrier options can have a rebate. The rebate is the amount paid if a knock-out option is knocked out or if a knock-in option is never knocked in.

17.2.1. Why use barrier options?

Plain vanilla options pay off regardless of the price path followed by the underlying before maturity. If a firm does not need protection for some paths, having protection for all paths means paying for protection that is not needed and is potentially harmful. Barrier options are useful hedging tools because they pay off only for the paths where the barrier option has value at maturity.

Suppose an exporting firm, Computer Inc., will produce 1 million computers in each of the following four years and expects to sell them in Japan for ¥100,000 each. Computers are produced throughout the year and sold for immediate payment at the end of the year. The production cost of $900 per computer is fixed in dollars. At an exchange rate of $1 per ¥100, Computer Inc. receives an income of $1 billion and makes a profit of $100 million if it exports the computers. The price of the computer is assumed to be fixed in yen, so the exposure is straightforward. Depreciation of the yen means that the exporting firm receives fewer dollars. Let's say that the current exchange rate is $1 per ¥100. If the value of the yen falls so that ¥100 are worth $0.99 instead of $1, the profits of Computer Inc. fall by $10 million, or 10 percent. Computer Inc. could lock in its yen revenue by selling ¥100 billion forward for each of the next four years.

Computer Inc. wants to hedge so that it recovers its production costs, but it does not want to give up the potential gains from appreciation of the yen. Suppose that Computer Inc. buys plain vanilla put options with an exercise price such that, after paying for the cost of the put, it receives $0.90 per ¥100 at the end of each calendar year so that its gross revenue is at least $900 million per calendar year. If the price of ¥100 falls to $0.70, Computer Inc. receives $700 for each computer sold in Japan but in addition receives $200 per computer from the puts after netting out their cost, so that its net income is $900 per computer, which would cover its cost.

Suppose, however, that Computer Inc. produced the computers and could sell them in the United States for $900 each. At the exchange rate of $0.70 per ¥100, Computer Inc. is better off to sell the computers in the United States even if it bought the puts. By selling the computers in the United States, the company receives $900 per computer sold plus the payoff from the puts. By selling the computers in Japan, the company receives $700 per computer sold plus the payoff from the puts.

If Computer Inc. exports to Japan, it receives $200 million net of the cost of the puts to offset the operating loss resulting from the weak yen. By not exporting the computers, Computer Inc. makes its shareholders wealthier by $200 million. If Computer Inc. does not export, its operating cash flow no longer depends on the yen exchange rate. Its net income *will* depend on the payoff of the puts and will be risky because of them. By hedging with plain vanilla puts, Computer Inc. creates a yen exposure when it does not export. (The same would be true if Computer Inc. hedged with forward contracts since it would also not pay for it to export when the yen's value is too low.)

Suppose that Computer Inc.'s policy is that if, at any time, the dollar price of the yen price of a computer falls below $800, it stops exporting to Japan and redirects the computers it was going to sell in Japan toward the United States where it can sell them for $900. Its argument is that it is worth to sell in Japan at a loss to maintain its sales network, but if the exchange rate falls below $0.80 per ¥100, the probability that it will make money in Japan over time is too low to keep exporting there.

With this policy, Computer Inc.'s exposure to the yen disappears if the price of ¥100 falls below $0.80. A plain vanilla put will be a bad hedge because it could turn out that Computer Inc. has no yen exposure. A down-and-out put on the yen with a barrier at $0.80 for ¥100 would provide a perfect hedge; it would protect Computer Inc.'s production costs as long as it is exporting to Japan, but not if it stops doing so. Further, buying a down-and-out put is cheaper than buying a plain vanilla put with the same exercise price. With the exotic option, Computer Inc. not only gains a more effective hedge but also obtains a cheaper hedge.

In another case, a modified barrier option might be more appropriate. A conventional barrier option ceases to exist if the price of the yen falls below the barrier during the life of the put. Modified barrier options have barriers in place for only part of the life of the option. They can have multiple, decreasing or increasing barriers, or even so-called outside barriers—barriers that depend on variables other than the underlying. A modified barrier option would provide a perfect hedge when Computer Inc. does not export in a year if the price of the yen falls below a barrier over some interval of time at the start of that year. Or Computer Inc. might want to enter a foreign market only if the exchange rate becomes sufficiently advantageous. In this case, the exposure would start if and only if the price of the foreign currency appreciates sufficiently. The efficient hedge would be an up-and-in put.

Barrier options can often be used to reduce the cost of a hedge when the firm has different expectations from the market. If the firm believes some price paths are not going to occur but the market believes that they have some probability of occurring, the firm can use barrier options so that it does not pay for protection corresponding to price paths it does not believe will occur.

The put prices reflect the market's expectations. If Computer Inc. has different expectations, it can take them into account when developing its risk management strategy. Suppose the firm has no flexibility in its export policy and will export to Japan for sure in each of the next four calendar years. It could buy plain vanilla puts to lock in its production costs. In some circumstances, Computer Inc. can reduce the cash cost of the puts it buys by using barrier puts instead of plain vanilla puts.

Suppose the firm believes there is no probability that the yen will appreciate beyond $1.20 per ¥100 before falling so that the puts are in the money at maturity, but that the market assigns some significant probability to such exchange rate paths. In this case, Computer Inc. could buy up-and-out puts. An **up-and-out put** loses all its value if the price of the underlying exceeds a prespecified barrier. If Computer Inc. chooses a barrier of $1.20 per ¥100, the up-and-out puts would lose all value if the yen appreciates beyond $1.20 per ¥100. Since the firm is convinced that the yen will not appreciate beyond $1.20 and then also be below the exercise price at maturity, it does not need protection against such an event. By buying barrier puts with an up-and-out barrier at $1.20 per ¥100, Computer Inc. does not pay for something it does not believe will happen. In 1995, Jim Scalfaro was the senior manager for treasury at RJR Nabisco. He is quoted as saying: "The cheapest thing to do is to do nothing or do a forward contract. It's expensive to do options. But unless you have a clear market view, doing nothing or forwards can be very costly. Given the size of our cash flows, we try to use these structures [knock-in and knock-out options] to average in to more favorable exchange rates."[1]

Barrier options can also be useful to implement portfolio management strategies. Consider a portfolio manager who has invested $100 million in the S&P 500. He thinks that the S&P 500 is undervalued. Over the next year, he believes that if the S&P 500 has a return of more than 25 percent it will be overvalued and he will want to sell immediately. In addition, his clients want to be protected against wealth losses over the coming year. The portfolio manager could achieve his objectives by implementing a dynamic portfolio strategy for portfolio insurance that gets him out of the market if the S&P 500 appreciates by 25 percent. By using exotic options, however, the portfolio manager can transform the dynamic portfolio strategy into a static portfolio strategy. Consider the following portfolio:

1. Invest the present value of $100 million in a default-free bond that matures in one year.

2. Buy an up-and-out barrier option on an investment in the S&P 500 of $100 million with exercise price of $100 million, a barrier at $125 million that triggers immediate exercise, and a rebate equal to $25 million.

---

1 William Falloon, "Hedges for export," *Risk* 8, 1995, 20.

This portfolio achieves exactly what the portfolio manager hopes to achieve with a dynamic trading strategy. First, the risk-free investment guarantees that the portfolio will be worth at least $100 million at the end of the year. Second, if the S&P 500 appreciates by less than 25 percent, the portfolio manager gets the S&P 500 appreciation at the end of the year. Third, whenever the S&P 500 achieves an increase of 25 percent relative to the beginning of the year, the barrier option pays the increase and the investor is out of the market.

Barrier options like this trade at the Chicago Board Options Exchange. They trade under the name of **capped options**. The Chicago Board Options Exchange trades capped options on the S&P 100 and the S&P 500 indices.

17.2.2. Pricing and hedging barrier options

Barrier options can be priced in a straightforward way using the binomial model.[2] To see this, let's look at Figure 17.4. This figure shows the evolution of the price of a financial asset over two periods. We want to price a down-and-out call option where the barrier is set at $19 and the exercise price at $18. For simplicity, let's assume there is no rebate.

With a plain vanilla call with exercise price of $18, the holder would receive $6.20 with probability $0.55 \times 0.55 = 0.3025$; $1.80 with the probability that $19.80 is reached by an up move followed by a down move, $0.55 \times 0.45 = 0.2475$; and $1.80 with the probability that $19.80 is reached by a down move followed by an up move, $0.45 \times 0.55 = 0.2475$. The price of the plain vanilla call is therefore the expected payoff computed using the risk-neutral probability distribution, $2.77, discounted at the risk-free rate. The risk-free rate is 1 percent per period, so that the price of the call is $2.77/(1 + 0.01)^2 = 2.712$.

Binomial approach for pricing barrier options *Figure 17.4*

An up move multiplies the previous price by 1.1. A down move multiplies the previous price by 0.9. The up move has risk-neutral probability of 0.55.

Exercise price = 18; interest rate of 1 percent per period; barrier is at 19.

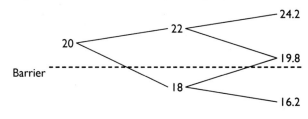

$[0.55 \times 0.55 \times 6.2 + 0.55 \times 0.45 \times 1.8]/(1.01 \times 1.01) = 2.28$
If no barrier: $2.28 + 0.45 \times 0.55 \times 1.8/(1.01 \times 1.01) = 2.72$

---

2 Boyle and Lau (1994) point out an important technical issue when pricing barrier options using a binomial tree. The value of a barrier option is sensitive to the level of the barrier. Depending on the placement of the barrier and on the number of time-steps one uses, there may be no nodes of the tree just below the barrier. In this case, the binomial approach gives inaccurate prices. They therefore point out that when constructing a binomial tree to price barrier options, one has to choose the number of time-steps so that there will be nodes immediately below the barrier.

The barrier option pays $6.20 at the price of $24.20 with probability 0.55 × 0.55 = 0.3025. If the asset price reaches $19.80, the barrier option pays $1.80 only if the asset price reaches $19.80 following a down move since otherwise it crosses the barrier. The probability of the asset price reaching $19.80 following a down move is 0.55 × 0.45 = 0.2475. The expected payoff of the barrier option is therefore 0.3025 × $6.20 + 0.2475 × $1.80, or $2.32. To get the option price, we discount $2.32 at the rate of 1 percent per period, so that the barrier option is worth $2.32/(1.01)^2, or $2.27.

The plain vanilla call option with the same exercise price and the same maturity as the barrier option is worth more than the barrier option because, contrary to that option, it pays off if the asset price reaches $19.80 following an up move. The present value of this additional payoff is its expected value, $1.80 with the probability that $19.80 is reached by a down move followed by an up move, 0.45 × 0.55 × 1.80, discounted at 1 percent for two periods, or $0.44. Consequently, the plain vanilla call option is worth $2.27 + $0.44, or $2.71.

17.2.3. Some surprising properties of barrier options

Remember that the value of a derivative is the expected payoff of the derivative computed using the risk-neutral distribution discounted at the risk-free rate. Once we have the risk-neutral distribution, we can price any type of barrier option whose barrier is either known beforehand or depends on the price of the asset. When the times between price changes become very short, the formulas for the pricing of barrier options are rather complex. Software to price barrier options is easily obtainable, so that there is no need to program these formulas. Technical Box 17.1, Barrier option pricing formulas, provides them for readers who want to see them.

Using the formula for the down-and-in call option, we can price a barrier call. Assume the underlying asset price is $100, the interest rate is 10 percent, the annual standard deviation is 0.2, the barrier is $97, the exercise price is $100, and time-to-maturity is one year. There are no rebates and no dividends. Substituting these values in the formula for the pricing of a down-and-in call option, we get a price for the call of $8.08. The Black-Scholes call would be worth $13.27. The two prices are different because the stock price is initially above the barrier, and if it stays above the barrier the option expires worthless.

A plain vanilla European call option always increases in value as the price of the underlying asset increases. This is not the case with the down-and-in option. In our example, the underlying asset is at $100 while the barrier is at $97. Suppose that the barrier has not been reached and the underlying asset price increases to $110. In this case, the price of the down-and-in call falls to $2.90. The reason is that the probability that the barrier will be crossed falls as the price of the underlying asset increases and the probability that the option holder will be able to exercise at maturity if the option is in the money also falls. This feature means that a portfolio of call options that includes barrier options could fall in value as the value of the underlying increases.

To assess the effect of a change in the price of the underlying financial instrument on a portfolio of options, we need to ascertain whether the options include

Barrier option pricing formulas   *Technical Box 17.1*

Let's consider the formula for a down-and-in call option with a rebate. Remember that a down-and-in call is one that pays off only if the price of the underlying falls below the barrier at some point during the life of the option. Let $d\&ic(S, H, R, K, t, T)$ be the price at t of a down-and-in European call on a financial asset with price S, barrier H, rebate R, exercise price K, and maturity at T. As before, σ is the volatility of the underlying asset's return. The financial asset pays a dividend, so that one plus the dividend rate is d. The resulting formula (from Reiner and Rubinstein (1991)) is:

$$d\&ic\left(S, H, R, K, T, t\right) = S d^{-(T-t)}(H/S)^{2\lambda} N(y)$$

$$-K r^{-(T-t)}(H/S)^{2\lambda-2} N\left(y - \sigma\sqrt{T-t}\right)$$

$$+ R r^{-(T-t)}\left[N\left(x_1 - \sigma\sqrt{T-t}\right) - H/S\right)^{2\lambda-2} N\left(y_1 - \sigma\sqrt{T-t}\right)\right]$$

$$x_1 = \left[\ln(S/H)/\sigma\sqrt{T-t}\right] + \lambda\sigma\sqrt{T-t}$$

$$y = \left[\ln\left(H^2/SK\right)/\sigma\sqrt{T-t}\right] + \lambda\sigma\sqrt{T-t}$$

$$y_1 = \left[\ln(H/S)/\sigma\sqrt{T-t}\right] + \lambda\sigma\sqrt{T-t}$$

$$\lambda = 1 + \left(\ln(r/d) - 0.5\sigma^2\right)/\sigma^2$$

This formula appears quite complicated, but its interpretation is simple. As with the Black-Scholes formula, the option price is the sum of the present value of receiving the underlying financial asset if the option is in the money at maturity minus the present value of having to pay the exercise price. The formula has a third term that the Black-Scholes formula does not have. This third term is the present value of the rebate. Remember that the rebate is paid if the option gets knocked out.

Let's now turn to the pricing of knock-out puts. The formula for the pricing of a down-and-out put (from Reiner and Rubinstein (1991)) is:

$$d\&op\left(S, H, R, K, T, t\right) = -S d^{-(T-t)}N(-x) + K r^{-(T-t)}N\left(-x + \sigma\sqrt{T-t}\right)$$

$$- S d^{-(T-t)}N(-x_1) + K r^{-(T-t)}N\left(-x_1 + \sigma\sqrt{T-t}\right)$$

$$- S d^{-(T-t)}(H/S)^{2\lambda} N(y) + K r^{-(T-t)}(H/S)^{2\lambda-2} N\left(y - \sigma\sqrt{T-t}\right)$$

$$+ S d^{-(T-t)}(H/S)^{2\lambda} N(y_1) - K r^{-(T-t)}(H/S)^{2\lambda-2} N\left(y_1 - \sigma\sqrt{T-t}\right)$$

$$+ R\left[(H/S)^{a+b}\left[N(z) + (H/S)^{a-b}N\left(z - 2b\sigma\sqrt{T-t}\right)\right]\right]$$

(continued)

Technical Box 17.1 *(continued)*

$$x = \left[\ln(S/H)/\sigma\sqrt{T-t}\right] + \lambda\sigma\sqrt{T-t},$$

$$y = \left[\ln\left(H^2/SK\right)/\sigma\sqrt{T-t}\right] + \lambda\sigma\sqrt{T-t},$$

$$y_1 = \left[\ln(H/S)/\sigma\sqrt{T-t}\right] + \lambda\sigma\sqrt{T-t},$$

$$x_1 = \left[\ln(S/K)/\sigma\sqrt{T-t}\right] + \lambda\sigma\sqrt{T-t},$$

$$z = \left[\ln(H/S)/\sigma\sqrt{T-t}\right] + b\sigma\sqrt{T-t},$$

$$a = \mu/\sigma^2, \qquad b = \left[\left(\mu^2 + 2(\ln r)\sigma^2\right)^{0.5}\right]/\sigma^2$$

$$\lambda = 1 + \left(\mu/\sigma^2\right), \qquad \mu = \ln(r/d) - 0.5\,\sigma^2$$

where $d\&op(S, H, K, R, T, t)$ is the price of a down-and-out put at t, maturing at T, on a financial asset with price S, that has a barrier at H, an exercise price of K, and pays a rebate R if the barrier is hit. Again, we end up with a rather forbidding expression, but the intuition is the same as before. The option price is the expected value computed using the risk-neutral distribution of receiving a plain vanilla put option if the financial asset price does not fall below the barrier.

exotics. If they do, we have to compute the deltas of each option and add them up to obtain the delta of the portfolio.

Figure 17.5 graphs the price of the down-and-in call option of our example as the stock price and the barrier change. The call price increases as the price of the underlying asset falls, and increases as the barrier increases as long as the price of the underlying is above the barrier and the barrier has not been crossed. If the barrier has been met, the down-and-in call option becomes a plain vanilla call option and the Black-Scholes formula applies. In this case, the call option value necessarily increases with the price of the underlying.

We can also price the down-and-out call. A portfolio of a down-and-in call and a down-and-out call that have the same barriers and no rebates corresponds to a conventional call since one and only one of the two barrier options can be exercised at maturity. The down-and-in call in our example will convert into a plain vanilla call only if the underlying asset price falls below $97. A down-and-out call with the same exercise price will convert into a plain vanilla call only if the underlying asset price never falls below $97. One call always converts into a plain vanilla call, while the other is worthless. In our example, the down-and-out call would be worth $5.19, which is equal to the price of the European call minus the price of the down-and-in call.

Down-and-in call option   *Figure 17.5*

This figure shows the relation between the price of the down-and-in call option, the underlying asset price, and the barrier. The exercise price is at $100, the dividend yield is 0 percent, the volatility is 20 percent, there is no rebate, the interest rate is 10 percent, and time to maturity is one year.

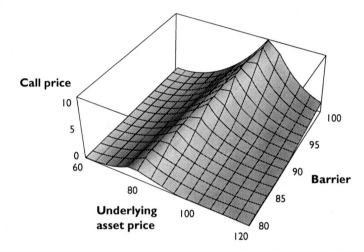

The down-and-out call increases in value as the price of the underlying asset increases because it becomes less likely that the call will lose its value because the barrier is hit. If the barrier options have a rebate, then the portfolio of barrier calls pays a rebate for sure since one option gets knocked out for sure. As a result, in the presence of a rebate, the portfolio is equal to the value of a plain vanilla call plus the rebate discounted at the risk-free rate since it gets paid for sure.

We saw that a barrier call can fall in value as the price of the underlying increases. The value of a down-and-out put option may also fall as the price of the underlying asset falls. When the asset price is close to the barrier, the probability that the barrier will be hit is higher than when the price of the underlying financial asset is higher. Consequently, close to the barrier the value of the put option increases as the price of the underlying asset increases.

Figure 17.6 shows this for a one year down-and-out put option with exercise price of $110 on an asset with volatility of 30 percent and dividend yield of 5 percent. The interest rate is 10 percent. The put option price actually falls when the financial asset price falls close to the barrier. We would expect to see this since when the asset hits the barrier, the put option becomes worthless.

We can use the formula for the down-and-out put option to evaluate the cost saving for Computer Inc. if it uses barrier options rather than plain vanilla options. We compare the price of a plain vanilla put option that insures the production cost of one computer to the price of a down-and-out put that does the same but becomes worthless if the producer stops exporting. In the formula for the down-and-out put, we use as the underlying asset the dollar value of a yen zero-coupon bond that matures when the put matures. We assume that the yen interest rate is 4 percent, the USD interest rate is 6 percent, and the volatility of

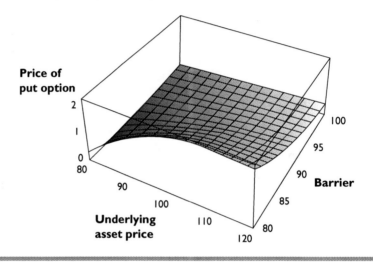

Figure 17.6   Down-and-out put option

This figure shows the relation between the price of the put option, the underlying asset price, and the barrier. The exercise price is $110, the dividend yield is 5 percent, the volatility is 30 percent, the interest rate is 10 percent, the maturity of the option is one year, and there is no rebate.

the exchange rate is 15 percent. With these assumptions, a one-year put option on ¥10,000 with exercise price of $0.90 per ¥100 costs $1.525. The exporter stops exporting if the price of ¥100 falls below $0.80. A down-and-out barrier put with the barrier set at $0.80 would cost $0.357 for ¥10,000. The hedge that protects Computer Inc. against the exposure it actually has costs about a fifth of the cost of the plain vanilla put. The barrier put also provides a much more precise hedge.

Use of barrier put options reduces the cost to the exporter dramatically the first year. The gain is even greater in following years. The reason is that the cost of the barrier put with our assumptions about the exchange rate, the interest rates, and volatility decreases with time to maturity sharply after one year as evidenced by Figure 17.7. As maturity lengthens, there is a higher probability that the barrier will be hit and hence that the put will become worthless.

17.2.4. Some practical issues

Our discussion of barrier options ignores an important practical problem. Not all parties to the option always agree on whether the barrier is crossed or not. Sometimes there is litigation to determine whether a barrier has been crossed. Therefore, it is important to specify precisely who gets to decide when the barrier is crossed and what constitutes a barrier crossing.[3]

Monitoring a barrier means checking whether it is breached or not. Our analysis assumes that the barrier is monitored continuously. In other words, a barrier

---

3   See Hans Hsu, "Surprised parties," *Risk Magazine* (April 1997), 27–29, for a description of the problems and solutions in identifying barrier events.

Relation between barrier put price and time to maturity   *Figure* 17.7

The put option is for one yen. The current exchange rate is $0.01, the domestic interest rate is 6 percent, the yen interest rate is 4 percent, the barrier is 0.008 and the exercise price is 0.009.

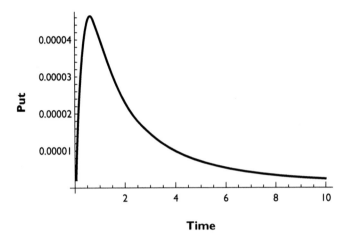

is crossed whenever the price of the underlying is observed on the other side of the barrier. For an underlying that is traded on an exchange, this is not too difficult. We can look at all the transaction prices and see whether there is at least one price that results in a barrier being crossed.

For an underlying that is traded only over the counter, it is not possible to check all prices because transactions will not be recorded. Hence, we need to reach an agreement as to how a barrier crossing will be recorded. This might involve checking quotes published by an online vendor (for example, quotes on a Reuters or Bloomberg page) at the same time every day.

There is little risk of manipulation of the price of the underlying to enhance the value of a plain vanilla option because the payoff from doing so is small. This is not always true for barrier options. Suppose we have an up-and-in call on 10,000 shares of a stock with barrier at $120 and exercise price at $100. Suppose next that the stock price has not crossed the barrier and is at $119.99 immediately before maturity. Buying shares to push the stock price up by $0.02 would increase the payoff of the plain vanilla call by $200 (the $0.02 increase times 10,000 shares). For the barrier option, however, the payoff of a $0.02 increase in the stock price is $200,100 because it leads to a barrier crossing, which then enables the holder to get the full value of a European call.

Because a small push to the price of the underlying has an extremely large payoff, it is more likely that a party to a barrier option might manipulate the price of the underlying. If the holder of the barrier option just happens to place a large order for the stock that pushes its price above $120, there is little that the writer of the option can do. As Box 17.2, The Flaming Ferraris, shows, indices are not protected from manipulation.

Source: "The flaming Ferraris reach the end of the road," *Financial Times*, March 6, 1999.

There are ways to structure contracts so that the option holder is better protected against possible manipulation. When entering a barrier option contract, one has to decide how often the barrier will be monitored. It may make sense to monitor at specified times. If a barrier is monitored at a particular time, it is considered crossed only if at that time the price is on the other side of the barrier. For instance, in our example for Computer Inc., if the firm makes decisions every quarter it might want the barrier to be monitored once every quarter. In this case, at the end of the quarter, the down-and-out option would be out if the dollar price of the yen is below $0.80 and the option would still have value otherwise. The less frequently the barrier is monitored, the more likely it is that the barrier will be crossed by the underlying but the crossing will not count because it is not monitored. Consequently, the less frequently the barrier is monitored, the less valuable is a barrier option with an in barrier and the more valuable is an option with an out barrier.

17.3. Options on the average

What if Computer Inc. is more concerned about its cash flow over some particular period of time? It is not concerned about its monthly foreign exchange gains and losses, but rather about its gains and losses over a year. Similarly, a producer of electricity that buys oil daily as input is not concerned about gains and losses on a daily basis but rather about its gains and losses over a longer period of time.

Suppose Computer Inc. receives payments quarterly but is concerned about the gains and losses over one year. Each quarterly payment corresponds to the sale of 250,000 computers. Computer Inc. could ensure that it does not make a loss for the year by buying puts for each quarter. Doing so, however, would be like buying puts on each stock of a portfolio when one wants to insure the portfolio as a whole. Buying a put for each quarter would amount to buying useless insurance. It could happen that the yen will depreciate in the first half of the year and then appreciate strongly so that the year would be profitable without hedging. In this case, puts for the beginning of the year would pay off, and Computer Inc. would have paid for them even though they paid off when not needed.

Computer Inc. wants to hedge its cumulative monthly net income to insure that it is positive. Without reinvesting the quarterly profits, this is equivalent to wanting the arithmetic average quarterly net income to be positive. The appropriate option to use is an option on the average. An **option on the average** is an option where the underlying at exercise is the arithmetic average of a price over a period of time. In this case, the option would be a put option on the average dollar price of the yen computed from end-of-quarter exchange rates. The payoff of the put per yen would be the exercise price minus the average dollar price of the yen if the put is exercised and zero otherwise.

17.3.1. A binomial example of an option on the average

In a simple example of an option on the average, suppose that a stock price return follows a binomial distribution where an up move multiplies the stock price by 1.1 and a down move by 0.9. The initial stock price is $18. The interest rate is 1 percent per period. The risk-neutral probability of an up move is 0.55. There are four dates including the initial date. We consider first an option on the average maturing at date 4. The average is computed using the stock price at dates 2 and 4. The exercise price is $18.

Table 17.1 provides all possible paths of the stock price with the associated risk-neutral probabilities. In the fourth path, the stock price starts at $18. Next, the stock has an up move that brings it to $19.80. This up move is then followed by two consecutive down moves, so that the stock price ends at $16.038. The probability that this path will occur is 0.111375. If this path occurs, the average stock price computed from prices at dates 2 and 4 is (19.8 + 16.038)/2, which is $17.919. Since the exercise price is $18, the option pays nothing.

Suppose instead the stock price follows the first path. With that path, the stock price at date 4 is $23.958. The probability that this path will take place is 0.166375 (0.55 × 0.55 × 0.55). The average is (19.8 + 23.958)/2, which is $21.879. The payoff of the option if that path is followed is $21.879 − $18, or $3.879. This payoff occurs with probability 0.166375, so that its expected value is 0.645369.

Adding up the expected payoffs for the different paths gives us the expected payoff of the option, which is $1.108467. Discounting this expected payoff at the risk-free rate of 1 percent per period gives us the option value of $1.075867. Averaging dampens the extremes, meaning the average is less volatile than the terminal stock price. Options on the average have less value than a standard European call option. For our example, the value of the European call option is $1.385427, which is 28.77 percent more than the value of the option on the average.

17.3.2. A replicating portfolio for the average

With options on the average, the underlying is the average. The average is not a financial asset. To price options on the average by arbitrage, we need to find a replicating portfolio strategy that allows us to create synthetically a financial asset

Table 17.1   Pricing an option on the arithmetic average

The stock price is $18, the exercise price is $18, the interest rate is 1 percent per period, the option matures at date 4, the average is computed from the prices at dates 2 and 4, the probability of an up move is 0.55, an up move multiplies the stock price by 1.1 and a down move multiplies it by 0.9. The top row of each cell gives the stock price. The second row of each cell gives the probability of that outcome.

Price/Risk neutral probability	Date 2	Date 3	Date 4	Average	Option payoff
18	19.80	21.78	23.958	21.879	3.879
1	0.55	0.3025	0.166375	0.166375	
18	19.80	21.78	19.602	19.701	1.701
1	0.55	0.3025	0.136125	0.136125	
18	19.80	17.82	19.602	19.701	1.701
1	0.55	0.2475	0.136125	0.136125	
18	19.80	17.82	16.038	17.919	0
1	0.55	0.2475	0.111375	0.111375	
18	16.20	17.82	19.602	17.901	0
1	0.45	0.2475	0.136125	0.136125	
18	16.20	17.82	16.038	16.119	0
1	0.45	0.2475	0.111375	0.111375	
18	16.20	14.58	16.038	16.119	0
1	0.45	0.2025	0.111375	0.111375	
18	16.20	14.58	13.122	14.661	0
1	0.45	0.2025	0.091125	0.091125	

whose value at maturity of the option is the average. If we know the current value of the replicating portfolio, we then know the value of the average.

A binomial example helps us understand how we can create a portfolio strategy that pays off the average at maturity and is self-financing (i.e., there are no cash inflows or outflows over time). Since the portfolio strategy is self-financing, the current value of the portfolio that pays off the average at maturity is equal to the present value of the average. We can use the value of this portfolio as the value of the average in the put-call parity formula.

In the binomial example, the average is computed from the price of the underlying asset at date 2, $S(2)$, and the price at date 4, $S(4)$. Suppose we buy today $0.5/(1.01^2)$ units of the underlying asset and sell them at date 2, investing the proceeds at the risk-free rate until date 4. At date 2, we will have $0.5S(2)/(1.01^2)$. Investing this amount until maturity of the option, we end up having $0.5S(2)(1.01^2)/(1.01^2) = 0.5S(2)$. We also buy at date 1 one-half unit of the underlying asset that we hold until maturity. At maturity, we therefore have $0.5S(2)$ plus $0.5S(4)$, which is the arithmetic average used in the computation of the option on the average and hence is the underlying asset. Proceeding this way, we can always compute the present value of the average, A(*t*), by creating a replicating portfolio.

If we have an option on A(*t*), we can apply the put-call parity theorem:

Put-call parity theorem for options on the average

$$p(A, K, T, t) = c(A, K, T, t) - A(t) + KP_t(T) \qquad (17.4)$$

where $p(A, K, T, t)$ is the European put option price on the average with maturity at T and exercise price K, A(*t*) is the present value of the average, $c(A, K, T, t)$ is the European call price, and $P_t(T)$ is the price of a zero-coupon bond that pays \$1 at T.

17.3.3. Pricing options on the average using the Monte Carlo approach

The average of lognormally distributed random variables is not a lognormally distributed random variable, so we cannot use the Black-Scholes formula to price the option on the average. Constructing a binomial tree can be impractical because of computational requirements—the option price depends on the whole path of the price of the underlying rather than only on the price of the underlying at maturity as with plain vanilla options. A more common approach is to perform a Monte Carlo simulation of the paths of the underlying asset. The distribution of the underlying asset is its risk-neutral distribution, so for a common stock that does not pay a dividend, we assume that the expected rate of return is the risk-free rate. If a dividend is paid, the expected rate of return is the risk-free rate minus the dividend yield. For each path, the relevant average is computed and the option payoff is obtained. Averaging across all payoffs gives us an estimate of the expected payoff using the risk-neutral distribution. We can then discount the estimate of the expected payoff at the risk-free rate to obtain the value of the option.

Say that Computer Inc. now wants to make sure that it makes profits over four years rather than each year. To guarantee this with a static hedge using plain vanilla puts, it would have to buy puts maturing at the end of each of the next four years. If the exchange rate is high at the end of the first year, however, it does not require as much protection subsequently. With its puts, Computer Inc. has excess insurance if at the end of the first year the exchange rate is high. To avoid paying for protection it does not need, Computer Inc. can buy a put on the average exchange rate, where the average is computed using year-end exchange rates over four years. If the exchange rate is high at the end of the first year, the put on the average is less likely to expire in the money so that Computer Inc. does not buy protection it does not need.

The Monte Carlo approach gives us an expected payoff of \$0.11855 for a call option on the average with exercise price of \$1 for ¥100. This means that the value of the option is \$0.11855 discounted at the rate of 6 percent for four years, yielding \$0.093903.

To provide some insight into the precision of this approach, Figure 17.8 graphs the payoffs of the option on the average and of a European call option with

Figure 17.8 Payoffs of option on the average and European call option

This example assumes that the options have a maturity of four years and an exercise price of $0.01 per yen. The average is computed using the year-end exchange rate each year for four years. The domestic interest rate is 6 percent. The Japanese interest rate is 4 percent. The yen is at 100 yen per dollar. The volatility of the yen is 15 percent. 10,000 exchange rate paths are simulated.

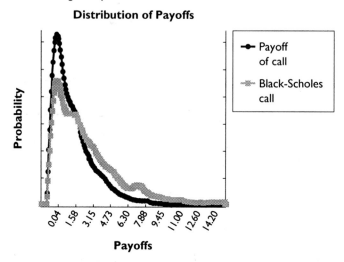

maturity of four years. This shows precisely how the average dampens the extremes. The expected payoff of the European call option is $0.172186, so its discounted value is $0.135446. When we compute the price of the option using the Black-Scholes formula, we get a price of $0.136387. As the number of trials gets large, the Black-Scholes price and the Monte Carlo estimate become indistinguishable.

We can use put-call parity to compute the price of a put on the average with an exercise price of $1 per ¥100. To do this, we need to compute our replicating portfolio for the average. The average here is the average of four exchange rates, so we have to obtain the value at time $t + 4$ of the payoff of 1/4 units of foreign currencies for dates $t + 1$, $t + 2$, $t + 3$, and $t + 4$. Remember that with currencies one does not hold foreign cash but invests it. Let S_{t+1} be the price of the foreign currency at date $t + 1$. To obtain $0.25S_{t+1}$ at date $t + 4$, we want to invest an amount in foreign currency that, at date $t + 1$, gives us the present value of 0.25 S_{t+1} to be paid at $t + 4$. Let $P_{t+1}(t + 4)$ be the price of a zero-coupon bond paying $1 at date $t + 4$ sold at date $t + 1$. We then want to have $0.25P_{t+1}(t + 4)$ S_{t+1} at date $t + 1$. Buying one unit of foreign currency today at S_{t+1} gives us $S_{t+1}/P_t^{FX}(t + 1)$, where $P_t^{FX}(t + 1)$ is the price today of a foreign currency zero-coupon bond paying one unit of foreign currency at date $t + 1$.

Putting this all together, we need to buy today $0.25P_{t+1}(t + 4)P_t^{FX}(t + 1)$ units of the foreign currency. Given a domestic interest rate of 6 percent and a foreign interest rate of 4 percent, we therefore buy 0.20063 units of foreign currency. Proceeding in the same way for each future date, we find that we have to buy 0.827166 units of foreign currency for an option on one unit of foreign currency. In our case, the option is on ¥100, so that we need to buy ¥82.7166.

Applying put-call parity from equation (17.4), we have:

$$p(A, 100, t+4, t) = 0.093903 - 0.827166 + 0.786628$$

$$= 0.053365 \qquad\qquad (17.5)$$

Computer Inc. can benefit by using an option on the average. It wants to make sure that over four years its income from Japan is at least equal to $900 million per year on average. If Computer Inc. wants to guarantee that the exchange rate it receives plus the put on the average payoff correspond to $0.90 per ¥100, it can buy a put on the average on ¥400 billion with exercise price of $3.6 billion. Such a put would cost $87.3954 million. Computer Inc. can achieve the same outcome by buying puts on ¥100 billion that mature at the end of each calendar year with exercise price of $900 million, which would cost $113.557 million. Computer Inc. saves $26.16 million by buying puts on the average instead of plain vanilla puts to get the hedge it wants.

Box 17.3, Beyond Monte Carlo: Some technical arguments, presents an approximation for pricing options on the average that does not rely on Monte Carlo analysis and yields a closed-form formula. Such an approximation shows how the value of the option on the average depends on the number of price observations used to compute the average. If we use only one observation, we get the Black-Scholes formula. This represents the upper bound for the value of an option on the average. Using the approximation, we can evaluate the impact on the option price of using more observations to compute the average.

Beyond Monte Carlo: Some technical arguments   *Box 17.3*

As mentioned already, the Monte Carlo approach described so far is time-consuming to implement. This has led financial economists to try to come up with approximations for options on the average that do not require the use of Monte Carlo analysis.* Let's look at one of these approximations, introduced by Vorst (1992). Vorst's approach works well generally and is simple to implement. The idea is to compute the value of the option using the geometric average instead of the arithmetic average. If we average over n prices at dates t_i, $i = 1, \ldots n$, the arithmetic average is:

$$A = \sum_{i=1}^{i=n} S_{t_i} / n$$

In contrast, the geometric average G is:

$$G = \prod_{i=1}^{i=n} \left(S_{t_i}\right)^{1/n}$$

* See Ton C. F. Vorst, "Average Options," *The Handbook of Exotic Options: Instruments, Analysis, and Applications,* Israel Nelken, ed., Irwin, 1996, Chicago, Ill.

(continued)

Using the fact that the geometric average is a product of lognormally distributed variables and hence is itself lognormally distributed, an option on the geometric average is an option on a lognormally distributed variable and hence the Black-Scholes formula applies:

$$C(G, K, T, t) = e^{-r(T-t)}\left[e^{M+V/2} N(d_1) - KN\left(d_1 - V^{0.5}\right)\right]$$

$$d_1 = \frac{M - \ln(K) + V}{V^{0.5}}$$

$$M = \ln(S_t) + 1/n \sum_{i=1}^{i=n}\left(r - d - \sigma^2/2\right)(T - t_i)$$

$$V = \sigma^2/n^2 \sum_{i=1}^{i=n}\sum_{j=1}^{j=n} Min(i, j)$$

This formula gives us the value of a call option on the geometric average at date *t* with exercise price K and maturity at time T. M is the mean of the logarithm of the average and V is its variance. The volatility of the underlying asset is σ, and its dividend rate is *d*. The interest rate is *r*.

If the call option is on the arithmetic average, then C(G, K, T, *t*) understates the value of the option. To get a better approximation, Vorst (1992) suggests an adjustment to the exercise price. With this adjustment, we compute the option using K' as the exercise price, where K' is the true exercise price of the option minus the value of the difference between the expected arithmetic average and the expected geometric average:

$$K' = K - \left[E\left(\sum_{i=1}^{i=n} S_{t_i}/n\right) - E\left(\prod_{i=1}^{i=n} S_{t_i}\right)^{1/n}\right]$$

To compute K', we need to know how to compute the expected values of the geometric and arithmetic averages. To get the expected value of the arithmetic average, we just need to remember that the average is a weighted sum of future values of the underlying asset, so that we can compute the expected value of each future value and add them up. The formulas to do this are straightforward:

$$E\left(\sum_{i=1}^{i=n} S_{t_i}/n\right) = S_t \sum_{i=1}^{i=n} e^{(r-d)(t_i-t)}/n$$

$$E\left(\prod_{i=1}^{i=n}(S_{t_i})^{1/n}\right) = e^{M+V/2}$$

Let's apply this formula to the example of the call option on the average that we considered in the case of Computer Inc. In this case, the option had a maturity of four years, it was on the yen with exercise price at *t* of $1 per ¥100, the domestic interest rate was 6 percent, the foreign interest rate was 4 percent, the volatility of the yen was 15 percent, and the option was monitored annually. We therefore have $S_t = 1$, $r = 0.06$, $r^* = 0.04$, $T = t + 4$, $t_i = t + i$, $i = 1, 2, 3, 4$, and $\sigma = 0.15$. Let's start by computing the expected values of the arithmetic average:

$$E\left(\sum_{i=1}^{i=n} S_{t_i} / n\right) = 1 \sum_{i=1}^{i=4} e^{(0.06 - 0.04)i} / 4 = 1.05153$$

To compute the geometric average, we first have to compute M and V:

$$M = \ln(1) + 1/4 \sum_{i=1}^{i=4}\left(0.06 - 0.04 - 0.5 \times 0.15^2\right) \times i = 0.021875$$

$$V = \frac{0.15^2}{4^2} \sum_{i=1}^{i=n}\sum_{j=1}^{j=n} \text{Min}(i, j) = 0.0421875$$

We now turn to the computation of the geometric average:

$$E\left(\prod_{i=1}^{i=n}\left(S_{t_i}\right)^{1/n}\right) = e^{0.021875 + 0.0421875/2} = 1.04391$$

We can now compute K' as:

$$K' = 1 - (1.05153 - 1.04391) = 0.0762$$

We now use the option pricing formula given in equation (17.9). This gives us an option value of $0.0877527 for the option on 100 yens, compared to the Monte Carlo value of 0.0895615. We cannot infer from the comparison of the two numbers that the approximation has an error equal to the difference of the two numbers. Remember that the Monte Carlo value is an estimate with a standard error, so that we have to find out whether the Monte Carlo estimate is significantly different from the Vorst approximation. The standard deviation of the payoffs with the Monte Carlo approach is 0.163811. At conventional levels of statistical significance, the difference between the Vorst approximation and the Monte Carlo value is not significant.

The advantage of closed-form formulas such as the Vorst approximation is that they make it possible to compute the greeks of the option in a straightforward way by simply taking the derivative of the formula with respect to the variable of interest. This makes it much easier to hedge the option than using the Monte Carlo approach. With the Monte Carlo approach, one can compute numerical derivatives by evaluating the value of the option for different parameters. However, to do that, one has to evaluate the value of the option using the same simulation data. In our case, this means that using the same 10,000

(continued)

Box 17.3   **(continued)**

exchange rate paths, one evaluates the option for different values of the variables with respect to which one wants to compute the greeks.

Suppose you wanted to hedge the option against changes in the underlying asset. Taking the derivative of the option with respect to the underlying asset, we obtain the option delta. For instance, in the example we have considered with an exercise price of $1 for ¥100, the option delta is 0.526034. In contrast, the delta of the conventional European call is $0.6623579.

Figure 17.9 shows how the price of the call option on the average with exercise price of $1 for ¥100 changes in value as the number of averaging intervals increases from 1 to 48. As the number of prices used to estimate the average increases, the variance of the average falls and the value of the option falls.

17.3.4. Evaluation of options on the average during the averaging interval

We also need to value options on the average after the averaging period starts. Computer Inc. has to be able to value the option it purchases during the life of the option. Viewed from a given time, the underlying of the option at maturity is the average of past and future values. The past values are known; the future ones are not. Suppose that the average is computed using n prices and that m of these prices have already been observed. The arithmetic average of the already ob-

---

Figure 17.9   **Option on the average and monitoring interval**

This example assumes that the options have a maturity of four years and an exercise price of $0.01 per yen. The average is computed using the year-end exchange rate each year for four years. The domestic interest rate is 6 percent. The Japanese interest rate is 4 percent. The yen is at 100 yen per dollar. The monitoring interval is varied from 1 to 48. A monitoring interval of 1 corresponds to the Black-Scholes formula when the monitoring takes place at the end.

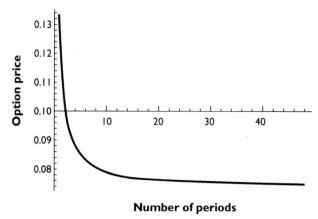

Number of periods

served prices is $B(t)$, and the arithmetic average of the $n - m$ prices not yet observed is $D(t, T)$. With this notation:

$$A(T) = \frac{m}{n} B(t) + \frac{n - m}{n} D(t, T) \qquad (17.6)$$

The payoff of the option is:

$$Max\big[A(T) - K, 0\big] = \frac{n - m}{n} Max\left(D(t, T) - \frac{n}{n - m}\left[K - \frac{m}{n} B(t)\right], 0\right)$$

$$(17.7)$$

An option on the average computed over n prices of which m are known can be viewed as $(n - m)/n$ options on the average $D(t, T)$ with an exercise price set at:

$$\frac{n}{n - m}\left[K - \frac{m}{n} B(t)\right] \qquad (17.8)$$

17.4. Options on multiple assets

If Computer Inc. sells products in multiple countries, it might consider hedging its exposures using a **basket option**, which protects its total income. A basket call option is an option to buy a basket or portfolio of foreign currencies at a given exercise price—for example, a call option giving the right to buy a portfolio of 1 million Swiss francs and 5 million Canadian dollars. Box 17.4, Risk management at Microsoft, shows that Microsoft has used both basket options and options on the average in its risk management strategy. A basket option is an example of an option on multiple assets.

17.4.1. Basket options

Suppose Computer Inc. sells in Europe and has euro exposure similar to its yen exposure. In this case, a depreciation of the yen might not be a problem if at the same time the euro appreciates. Computer Inc. is buying useless protection if it buys puts to protect itself separately against a fall in the yen and a fall in the euro. The put on the yen might pay off even though the euro has appreciated. To avoid buying useless protection, it wants to protect itself against a fall in the value of a yen and euro portfolio. In this case, the portfolio is a weighted average of money market investments in Euroland and Japan. To protect itself, the firm would want to buy a put on the portfolio. A portfolio of two assets does not follow a lognormal distribution. Though it is reasonable to assume that a portfolio of a large number of assets (for example, the S&P 500) follows a lognormal distribution, such an approximation is poor when the portfolio has a small number of assets.

The put option on the portfolio the firm wants to buy is called a basket put. A basket put is similar to an option on the average, except that the averaging is at one date across assets, not across dates for one asset. We can thus use the same pricing approaches to price basket options. We can either use the Monte Carlo approach or approximate their value using the approximation discussed in Box 17.3.

17.4.2. Quantos

A **quanto** (abbreviation for quantity-adjusted option) is an option on a random number of units of foreign currency. Assume an investor believes the dollar value of Sony stock is too low. She wants to take advantage of her belief by purchasing a call option. She could buy a call option on Sony in yen, but her option might expire out of the money even though the dollar price of Sony appreciated if the price of Sony falls in yen when the yen appreciates. To make sure that she profits from an increase in the dollar value of Sony, our investor could buy a call option that gives her the excess of the dollar value of Sony stock over the exercise price. Such a call option pays $\mathrm{Max}(S_T^{\mathrm{Yen}}\,S_T^{\mathrm{Sony\ in\ yen}} - K, 0)$ at maturity, where S_T^{Yen} is the dollar price of the yen at maturity of the option at T, $S_T^{\mathrm{Sony\ in\ yen}}$ is the yen price of a share of Sony at T, and K is the exercise price in dollars. This option is a quanto, in that it is a call on a random number of yen, where the number of yen is the price of Sony shares.

The underlying asset in this option is the dollar value of the foreign stock. A portfolio that replicates the underlying asset is a portfolio consisting of one unit of the foreign stock. For that portfolio you pay $S_t^{Yen} S_t^{Sony \, in \, yen}$ at t. At T, this portfolio is worth $S_T^{Yen} S_T^{Sony \, in \, yen}$.

A useful property of the lognormal distribution is that the product of two lognormally distributed variables is lognormally distributed. Consequently, if the yen exchange rate and the price of Sony in yen are lognormally distributed, then the dollar price of Sony is lognormally distributed also. Consequently, we can value the option using the Black-Scholes formula with the dollar value of Sony as the underlying asset. We then have to find the volatility to use in the Black-Scholes formula. This volatility can be obtained from the volatility of Sony in yen and from the volatility of the exchange rate. Let $Vol[ln(S_T^{Yen} S_T^{Sony \, in \, yen})]$ be the volatility of the continuously compounded rate of return in dollars on Sony from t to T (prices at t are omitted since they do not affect the volatility). In this case:

$$\mathbf{Vol}\left[\ln\left(S_T^{Yen} \, S_T^{Sony \, in \, yen}\right)\right] \tag{17.9}$$

$$= \left[\mathbf{Var}\left(\ln S_T^{Yen}\right) + \mathbf{Var}\left(\ln S_T^{Sony \, in \, yen}\right) + 2\mathbf{Cov}\left(\ln S_T^{Yen}, \, \ln S_T^{Sony \, in \, yen}\right)\right]^{0.5}$$

where $Vol(\ln S_T^{Yen})$ is the volatility of the continuously compounded rate of return on the yen and $Vol(\ln S_T^{Sony \, in \, yen})$ is the volatility of the continuously compounded rate of return on Sony in yen.

17.4.3. Exchange options

Hedging problems sometimes involve an option with a random exercise price. Consider the Riskless Hedge Fund (RHF), which buys stock A with price S_t^A and sells short stock B with price S_t^B because it believes that stock A will gain in value relative to stock B. RHF plans to hold this position until date T, when it will unwind it. It wants to buy insurance so that it does not lose money with its strategy. Traditional portfolio insurance would not work since RHF is long a stock and short another. Without insurance, RHF has $S_T^A - S_T^B$ at maturity. To hedge, it wants to buy an option that pays its loss if it makes a loss. The Fund's loss is $S_T^B - S_T^A$ if the price of stock A is less than the price of stock B, or $Max(S_T^B - S_T^A, 0)$. If RHF can buy an option that pays $Max(S_T^B - S_T^A, 0)$, the most the strategy can lose is the price of the option and the opportunity cost of the funds used to finance the option.

The payoff of the option that RHF wants to buy looks like the payoff of a call option on stock B, but with a twist. Instead of a fixed exercise price, the option has a random exercise price, the price of stock A. An option that pays the difference between the price of stock B and the price of stock A is called an **exchange option**. Its payoff is what we would receive if we had the right to exchange stock A for stock B at T. We would not exercise that right if the price of A is higher than the price of B at T. Consequently, we get the higher of zero and the difference between the price of B and the price of A, which corresponds to $Max(S_T^B - S_T^A, 0)$.

To price exchange options, we rewrite the payoff of the exchange option as follows:

$$\mathbf{Max}\left(S_T^B - S_T^A, 0\right) = S_T^A \, \mathbf{Max}\left(S_T^B / S_T^A - 1, 0\right) \tag{17.10}$$

The right-hand side of this expression states that the payoff of the option is a random number of units of a call on an asset with value S_T^B / S_T^A with exercise price equal to one. Suppose that A and B are two currencies, so that S_T^A and S_T^B are the dollar prices of these currencies. The exchange option gives the right to exchange one unit of currency A for one unit of currency B. In this case, S_T^B / S_T^A is the price of currency B in units of currency A. The option on the right-hand side of equation (17.10) is therefore an option to sell one unit of currency B expressed in units of currency A for one unit of currency A. When we multiply the payoff of that option by the price of currency A, S_T^A, we get its dollar value. The present value in dollars of a payoff in foreign currency is the present value of that payoff in foreign currency times the current price of the foreign currency in dollars (for instance, the dollar price today of a bond in euros that pays one euro in one year is the euro value of the bond times the dollar price of the euro). To value the exchange option, we can therefore value the exchange option by first valuing the foreign currency payoff and then multiplying its value by the current exchange rate. If A and B are not currencies, we can still use this approach—the option on the right-hand side of equation (17.10) is the payoff of an option to buy asset B for one unit of asset A expressed in units of asset A. We can compute the present value of the payoff in units of asset A and then get the dollar value of the option by multiplying the present value by the current price of asset A, S_T^A.

The random variable in the payoff function of the option, S_T^B / S_T^A, is the ratio of two asset prices. If two asset prices have a lognormal distribution, the ratio has a lognormal distribution also. The volatility of the continuously compounded rate of change of the ratio is:

$$\mathbf{Vol}\left[\ln\left(S_T^B / S_T^A\right)\right] = \left[\mathbf{Var}\left(\ln S_T^B\right) + \mathbf{Var}\left(\ln S_T^A\right) - 2\mathbf{Cov}\left(\ln S_T^B, \ln S_T^A\right)\right]^{0.5} \quad (17.11)$$

Note that the ratio S_T^B / S_T^A is the ratio of two asset prices where each asset price has an expected rate of return equal to the risk-free rate when we use risk-neutral valuation. We would expect the risk-free rate to cancel out. Consequently, the exchange option is the value of S_T^A units of an option that pays $\text{Max}[S_T^B / S_T^A - 1, 0]$ at maturity. We can use the Black-Scholes formula to price the option in a straightforward way; set the exercise price equal to S_T^A, the underlying asset equal to S_T^B, the interest rate equal to zero, and the volatility equal to the above expression. With this, the value of an exchange option is:

Formula for the value of an exchange option

Let $ec(S^B, S^A, T, t)$ be the value of an option to exchange S^A for S^B at maturity date T, $N(d)$ the cumulative normal distribution evaluated at d, σ_A (σ_B) the volatility of asset A (B), and ρ the correlation between assets A and B. The value of the option is:

$$ec\left(S^A, S^B, T, t\right) = S^B N(d) - S^A N\left(d - \sigma\sqrt{t}\right)$$

$$\sigma^2 = \sigma_A^2 + \sigma_B^2 - 2\rho\sigma_A\sigma_B$$

$$d = \left[\ln\left(S^B / S^A\right)/\sigma\right] + 0.5\,\sigma\sqrt{t} \quad (17.12)$$

Consider an option to exchange S^B for S^A with a maturity of one year, where S^A and S^B each have value of 100 and volatility of 0.25 and there is no correlation between the two assets. We have $S_t^A = 100$, $S_t^B = 100$, $\sigma_A = 0.25$, $\sigma_B = 0.25$, $\rho = 0$, $t = 1$. In this case, the option is worth 14.

The value of the exchange option increases with the volatility of the ratio S^B/S^A. This means that the option value increases with the volatility of the two assets but falls as the correlation coefficient increases. Note that if both assets have the same volatility, a correlation coefficient of one and the same initial values, the option to exchange is worthless because the two assets always have the same price. As the correlation coefficient falls from one, the values become more likely to differ by a significant amount.

Figure 17.10 shows how the option value is affected by changes in the correlation coefficient and in the volatility of the assets assuming that both assets have the same volatility.

17.5. Risk management and exotic options: The lessons from Gibson Greetings Inc.

Exotic derivatives can be extremely useful. There are so many exotic derivatives that we cannot discuss more than a handful. Box 17.5, More exotic derivatives, describes some additional exotic derivatives.

Because exotic derivatives are complex financial instruments, they can create significant pitfalls for the unwary. The story of Gibson Greetings Inc.'s derivatives transactions shows the need for care when dealing with these financial instruments. Gibson is a card and wrapping paper company located in Cincinnati. It is not a huge company—in 1993, it had sales of $547 million and profits of $20 million. In April 1994, Gibson announced losses of $16.7 million due to two

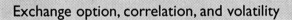

Exchange option, correlation, and volatility   *Figure 17.10*

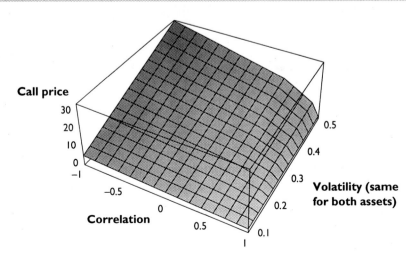
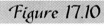

Box 17.5   More exotic derivatives

There is no limit to the number of exotic options. Anybody can come up with a new one. Unfortunately, there is also no standard terminology, so that different names can designate the same payoff. However, in addition to the exotic options we talked about in the text, some other interesting exotic options are briefly defined below.

1. Lookbacks.

A lookback option is one whose payoff depends on the maximum or minimum of the underlying price over a period of time. An example is an option that pays the difference, if positive, between the highest stock price over one year and the current stock price.

2. Options with outside barriers and correlation digitals.

With a correlation digital call, the option pays the asset if some index variable, say the price of an asset, exceeds some level at maturity. For example, a correlation digital call on IBM could pay a share of IBM if at maturity the price of a share of Apple exceeds some strike price.

Outside barriers are barriers defined in terms of some index variable other than the price of the underlying. For instance, a barrier call on IBM with an outside barrier would be one where the call loses all value if the price of a share of Apple exceeds some barrier.

3. Bermuda or Mid-Atlantic option.

Such options allow for exercise at specific dates during the life of the option.

4. Rainbow options.

A rainbow option has a payoff that depends on n assets. The most common is an option that pays the maximum (or minimum) of the n assets minus the strike price if that quantity is positive at maturity.

5. Passport options.

Passport options are options on actively managed portfolios.

swap transactions undertaken with Bankers Trust (BT). Eventually, Gibson owed $19.7 million to BT for its various derivative transactions. Its ultimate settlement with BT required Gibson to pay only $6.2 million.

According to documents from the Commodities Futures Trading Commission, Gibson started with a plain vanilla swap, but then entered into more complicated transactions. Let's look at six transactions that show this evolution:

1. **Plain vanilla swap.** The first swap was entered on November 12, 1991. Gibson was to pay semiannually from June 1, 1992, to December 1, 1993, 5.91 percent times $30 million, while BT paid 6-month LIBOR times $30 million.

2. **Ratio swap.** This swap was entered into on October 1, 1992, and specified that starting on April 5, 1993, until October 5, 1997, Gibson would pay BT six-month LIBOR squared divided by 6 percent times $30 million and BT would pay Gibson 5.50 percent times $30 million.

3. **The periodic floor.** On October 30, 1992, BT and Gibson entered into a contract requiring BT to pay Gibson 6-month LIBOR plus 0.28 percent times $30 million starting on October 6, 1993, and up to October 6, 1997, and Gibson to pay BT six-month LIBOR as long as LIBOR was not more than 0.15 percent points lower than LIBOR on the previous reset date.

4. **Spread lock.** On January 11, 1993, BT and Gibson entered an agreement that starting on May 15, 1995, until November 15, 2001, BT would pay Gibson a fixed payment semiannually equal to $30 million times the sum of the mid-market swap spread and the on-the-run Treasury rate while Gibson would pay BT a fixed payment of $30 million times the sum of 38 basis points and the off-the-run Treasury rate. These rates would be determined on November 15, 1994. This swap was amended numerous times, most notably to add option features.

5. **The Treasury-linked swap.** On February 19, 1993, the two parties agreed for Gibson to pay LIBOR and to receive LIBOR plus 200 basis points on $30 million notional amount over eight months. At maturity, Gibson had to pay BT $30 million and BT would pay:

$$\text{Min}\left(\text{\$30.6M}, \text{\$30M} \times \left[1 - \frac{\dfrac{103 \times 2\text{-year T-note Yield}}{4.88\%} - 30 - \text{T-bond price}}{100}\right]\right)$$

6. **Knock-out call option.** On June 10, 1993, Gibson bought a knock-out call option from BT. The option required BT to pay Gibson at maturity:

Max[(6.876% − Yield to maturity of 30-year T-bond) × 12.5 × $25M, 0]

If, at any time during the life of the option, the T-bond yield fell below 6.48 percent, BT would have to pay nothing.

These six Gibson transactions described here are only some of Gibson's transactions with BT. In 1993, Gibson entered into 18 separate derivative transactions with BT. Gibson's whole derivatives strategy was predicated on the belief that interest rates would drop. In 1993, though, rates increased sharply, and Gibson sustained substantial losses. This prompted more transactions designed to reverse the losses.

On October 11, 1995, Gibson's chief financial officer, Ward A. Cavanaugh, and its treasurer, James H. Johnsen, settled with the SEC for violations "of the reporting and books and records provisions of the federal securities laws in connection with the accounting for and disclosure of certain transaction derivatives purchased by Gibson." The SEC document notes: "Gibson's books and records did not contain quarterly mark-to-market values for the derivatives and did not identify or separate transactions that for accounting purposes amounted to trading or speculation. Gibson also lacked adequate internal controls for ascertaining whether derivatives transactions were consistent with corporate derivatives objectives established by Gibson's Board of Directors. The Board had approved a resolution on April 15, 1992, authorizing the Vice President, Finance, or his designee 'to take such actions as he may deem appropriate from time to time to effectuate interest rate swap transactions relating to the Corporation's obligations upon such terms as he may approve.' This resolution did not authorize transactions beyond interest rate swap transactions relating to the corporation's debt. No specific procedures were put in place to implement that resolution, such as procedures to place limits on the amounts, types or nature of derivatives transactions, or to assess the risks of derivatives transactions."[4]

In other words, Gibson did not know how to track the value and risk of its derivatives positions and did not have procedures to ensure that it only entered into transactions its directors would condone. In tapes from the trading floor of Bankers Trust, one managing director is heard to say "From the beginning [Gibson] just, you know, really put themselves into our hands like 96%. . . . These guys have done some pretty wild stuff. And you know, they probably do not understand it quite as well as they should. . . . And that's like perfect for us."[5]

17.6. Summary

We have analyzed digital options, barrier options, options on the average, quantos, basket, and exchange options.

There are many different types of exotic options, some frequently used and some used only once in an innovative application to resolve an unusual hedging problem. Properly chosen and understood, exotic options can resolve what otherwise would be insurmountable hedging problems. A firm that understands how to use them can enhance shareholder wealth in ways that a firm that does not understand them cannot. Because these options are complex, they have to be treated with care. They can create traps for the unwary. For example, we can have barrier puts that fall in value as the underlying decreases in value and barrier calls that decrease in value as the underlying increases in value. The deltas of exotic options can change dramatically with small changes in the price of the underlying—for example when a digital call is close to maturity and the underlying price is close

---

4 SEC, Accounting and auditing enforcement, Release No. 730, October 11, 1995. This document is available at http://www.sec.gov.
5 Carol J. Loomis, "Untangling the derivatives mess," *Fortune*, March 20, 1995, 131(5), 50–68.

to the strike price. Because the value of exotic options can change so much for small changes in the price of the underlying, the temptation sometimes exists for one of the counterparties to try to manipulate the price of the underlying. Further, the delta-VaR method of estimating VaR can lead to large errors in VaR estimates when a portfolio has exotic options.

Key Concepts

asset or nothing digital call
   option, 538
barrier option, 534
basket option, 559
capped options, 543
digital options, 535
down-and-in option, 540
down-and-out barrier option, 540

European cash or nothing digital call
   option, 535
exchange option, 561
knock-out provision, 534
option on the average, 551
quanto, 560
up-and-in option, 540
up-and-out put, 542

Review Questions

1. What is a cash or nothing digital call option?

2. What is an asset or nothing digital call option?

3. How is the Black-Scholes formula used to price digital options?

4. What is a barrier option?

5. Why are barrier options cheaper than otherwise equivalent plain vanilla options?

6. Why is it that the value of an up-and-out barrier call on IBM could fall as the price of IBM stock increases?

7. What does it mean to monitor a barrier?

8. What is an option on the average?

9. What is a basket option?

10. What is an exchange option?

Questions and Exercises

1. The initial stock price is $41. The up step multiplies the stock price by 1.061837 and the down step multiplies it by 0.941765. The interest rate per step is 1 percent. A plain vanilla call has an exercise price of $40 and matures at date 7. The binomial trees for the stock price and the call price were discussed in Chapter 13 and are reproduced on the following page.

Stock values

Date 1	Date 2	Date 3	Date 4	Date 5	Date 6	Date 7
						58.76651
					55.34421	
				52.12122		52.12122
			49.08591		49.08591	
		46.22737		46.22737		46.22737
	43.5353		43.5353		43.5353	
41		41		41		41
	38.61235		38.61235		38.61235	
		36.36374		36.36374		36.36374
			34.24608		34.24608	
				32.25174		32.25174
					30.37355	
						28.60473

Call option values

Date 1	Date 2	Date 3	Date 4	Date 5	Date 6	Date 7
						18.76651
					15.74025	
				12.90937		12.12122
			10.26231		9.481951	
		7.909537		7.015529		6.227371
	5.928702		4.995663		3.931338	
4.337319		3.458544		2.452514		1
	2.342957		1.515256		0.562661	
		0.928716		0.316588		0
			0.178132		0	
				0		0
					0	
						0

Show the payoffs at date 7 of a cash or nothing digital call option that pays $100 if the stock price exceeds $39.

2. Demonstrate the hedge portfolio at date 6 of the cash or nothing digital call option described in question 1 for each stock price.

3. Find the value at date 1 of the cash or nothing digital call option described in question 1.

4. Consider an up-and-out barrier call option on the stock with exercise price $40 and maturity at date 7. The barrier is $48. Show the payoffs of the barrier call option for each possible stock price at date 7.

5. What is the value of the barrier call option described in question 4 at date 1?

6. Consider a call barrier option with an up-and-in barrier at $48, an exercise price of $40, and maturity at date 7. Find the value of the option using only the information that a plain vanilla option with an exercise price of $40 maturing at date 7 is worth $4.337319 at date 1 and your answer to question 5.

7. Instead of describing a stock price, the binomial tree of question 1 is now assumed to represent the evolution of the price of a foreign currency. The foreign interest rate is 2 percent per period. Price an asset or nothing digital option that pays 100 units of foreign currency at date 7 if the price of the foreign currency exceeds $50.

8. Suppose now that the digital option priced in question 7 is transformed so that it pays off only if the exchange rate never goes below $40 during the life of the option. What is the value of this digital barrier option?

9. Using the data you used to answer question 7, price a call option on the average monitored each period starting at date 2 that matures at date 7 with exercise price of $50.

10. The true probability of an up move in the binomial tree of question one is 0.60. Show the VaR of the plain vanilla call, the digital option, and the barrier options with the stock as the underlying asset computed over seven periods.

Literature Note

There is considerable literature on exotic options. Nelken (1996) has an excellent chapter classifying the various types of exotic options and includes materials on pricing, hedging, and using exotic options. Jarrow (1996) provides a collection of articles on exotic options. For techniques on how to construct static hedges of exotic options, see Carr, Ellis, and Gupta (1998). Gentle (1993) shows how to use the Vorst approximation for basket options.

Chapter 18

Credit Risks and Credit Derivatives

At the end of this chapter, you will:

1. Understand the main approaches to price risky debt.

2. Know how to evaluate credit risks quantitatively for individual credits and for portfolios.

3. Have learned what credit derivatives are and how to use them.

4. Have tools to assess the credit risks of derivatives.

Consider Credit Bank Corp. It makes loans to corporations. For each loan, there is some risk that the borrower will default, in which case Credit will not receive all the payments the borrower promised to make. Credit has to understand the risk of the individual loans it makes, but it must also be able to quantify the overall risk of its loan portfolio. Credit has a high franchise value and wants to protect that franchise value by making sure that the risk of default on its loans does not make its probability of financial distress too high. Though Credit knows how to compute VaR for its trading portfolio, it cannot use these techniques directly to compute the risk of its loan portfolio. Loans are like bonds—Credit never receives more from a borrower than the amounts the borrower promised to pay. Consequently, the distribution of the payments received by borrowers cannot be lognormal.

To manage the risk of its loans, Credit must know how to quantify the risk of default and of the losses it makes in the event of default both for individual loans and for its portfolio of loans. At the end of this chapter, you will know the techniques that Credit can use for this task. We will see that the Black-Scholes formula is useful to understand the risks of individual loans. Recently, a number of firms have developed models to analyze the risks of portfolios of loans and bonds. For example, J.P. Morgan has developed CreditMetrics™ along the lines of its product RiskMetrics™. We discuss this model in some detail.

A **credit risk** is the risk that someone who owes money might fail to make promised payments. Credit risks play two important roles in risk management. First, credit risks represent part of the risks a firm tries to manage in a risk management program. If a firm wants to avoid lower tail outcomes in its income, it must carefully evaluate the riskiness of the debt claims it holds against third parties and determine whether it can hedge these claims and how. Second, the firm holds positions in derivatives for the express purpose of risk management. The counterparties on these derivatives can default, in which case the firm does not get the payoffs it expects on its derivatives. A firm taking a position in a derivative must therefore evaluate the riskiness of the counterparty in the position and be able to assess how the riskiness of the counterparty affects the value of its derivatives positions.

Credit derivatives are one of the newest and most dynamic growth areas in the derivatives industry. At the end of 2000, the total notional amount of credit derivatives was estimated to be $810 billion; it was only $180 billion two years before. Credit derivatives have payoffs that depend on the realization of credit risks. For example, a credit derivative could promise to pay some amount if Citibank defaults and nothing otherwise; or a credit derivative could pay the holder of Citibank debt the shortfall that occurs if Citibank defaults on its debt. Thus firms can use credit derivatives to hedge credit risks.

18.1. Credit risks as options

Following Black and Scholes (1973), option pricing theory has been used to evaluate default-risky debt in many different situations. The basic model to value risky debt using option pricing theory is the Merton (1974) model. To understand this approach, consider a levered firm that has only one debt issue and pays no dividends. Financial markets are assumed to be perfect. There are no taxes and no bankruptcy costs, and contracts can be enforced costlessly. Only debt holders and equity holders have claims against the firm and the value of the firm is equal to the sum of the value of debt and the value of equity. The debt has no coupons and matures at T.

At date T, the firm has to pay the principal amount of the debt, F. If the firm cannot pay the principal amount at T, it is bankrupt, equity has no value, and the firm belongs to the debt holders. If the firm can pay the principal at T, any dollar of firm value in excess of the principal belongs to the equity holders.

Suppose the firm has issued debt that requires it to make a payment of $100 million to debt holders at maturity and that the firm has no other creditors. If the total value of the firm at maturity is $120 million, the debt holders receive their promised payment, and the equity holders have $20 million. If the total value of the firm at maturity is $80 million, the equity holders receive nothing and the debt holders receive $80 million.

Since the equity holders receive something only if firm value exceeds the face value of the debt, they receive $V_T - F$ if that amount is positive and zero otherwise. This is equivalent to the payoff of a call option on the value of the firm. Let V_T be the value of the firm and S_T be the value of equity at date T. We have at date T:

$$S_T = \text{Max}(V_T - F, 0) \qquad\qquad (18.1)$$

To see that this works for our example, note that when firm value is $120 million, we have S_T equal to Max($120M − $100M, 0), or $20 million, and when firm value is $80 million, we have S_T equal to Max($80M −$100M, 0), or $0.

Figure 18.1 graphs the payoff of the debt and of the equity as a function of the value of the firm. If the debt were riskless, its payoff would be the same for any value of the firm and would be equal to F. Since the debt is risky, when the value of the firm falls below F, the debt holders receive less than F by an amount equal to $F - V_T$. The amount $F - V_T$ paid if V_T is smaller than F, Max($F - V_T$, 0), corresponds to the payoff of a put option on V_T with exercise price F. We can therefore think of the debt as paying F for sure minus the payoff of a put option on the firm with exercise price F:

$$D_T = F - \text{Max}(F - V_T, 0) \qquad\qquad (18.2)$$

where D_T is the value of the debt at date T. Equation (18.2) therefore tells us that the payoff of risky debt is equal to the payoff of a long position in a risk-free zero-coupon bond with face value F and a short position on a put option on firm value with exercise price F. This means that holders of risky debt effectively buy risk-free debt but write a put option on the value of the firm with exercise price equal to the face value of the debt. Alternatively, we can say that debt holders receive the value of the firm, V_T, minus the value of equity, S_T. Since the payoff of equity is the payoff of a call option, the payoff of debt is the value of the firm minus the payoff of a call option with exercise price equal to the principal amount of the debt.

Figure 18.1 **Debt and equity payoffs when debt is risky**

F is the debt principal amount and V(T) is the value of the firm at date T.

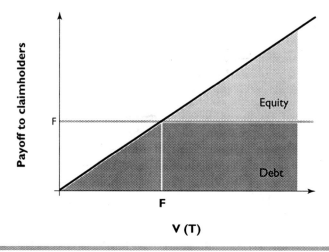

To price the equity and the debt using the Black-Scholes formula for the pricing of a European call option, we require that the value of the firm follow a lognormal distribution with a constant volatility σ, the interest rate r be constant, trading take place continuously, and financial markets be perfect. We do not require that there is a security that trades continuously with value V. All we need is a portfolio strategy such that the portfolio has the same value as the firm at any particular time. We use this portfolio to hedge options on firm value, so that we can price such options by arbitrage. We can write the value of equity as S(V, F, T, t) and use the formula to price a call option to obtain:

Merton's formula for the value of equity

Let S(V, F, T, t) be the value of equity at date t, V the value of the firm, F the face value of the firm's only zero-coupon debt maturing at T, σ the volatility of the value of the firm, $P_t(T)$ the price at t of a zero-coupon bond that pays \$1 at T, and N(d) the cumulative distribution function evaluated at d. With this notation, the value of equity is:

$$S\big(V, F, T, t\big) = VN\big(d\big) - P_t\big(T\big)FN\big(d - \sigma\sqrt{T - t}\big)$$

$$d = \frac{\ln\big(V / P_t\big(T\big)F\big)}{\sigma\sqrt{T - t}} + \frac{1}{2}\,\sigma\sqrt{T - t} \tag{18.3}$$

When V is \$120 million, F is \$100 million, T is equal to $t + 5$, $P_t(T)$ is \$0.6065, and σ is 20 percent, the value of equity is \$60.385 million. From our understanding of the determinants of the value of a call option, we know that equity increases in value when the value of the firm increases, when firm volatility increases, when time to maturity increases, when the interest rate increases, and when the face value amount of the debt falls.

Debt can be priced in two different ways. First, we can use the fact that the payoff of risky debt is equal to the payoff of risk-free debt minus the payoff of a put option on the firm with exercise price equal to the face value of the debt:

$$D(V, F, T, t) = P_t(T)F - p(V, F, T, t) \qquad (18.4)$$

where $p(V, F, T, t)$ is the price of a put with exercise price F on firm value V. F is $100 million and $P_t(T)$ is $0.6065, so $P_t(T)F$ is $60.65 million. A put on the value of the firm with exercise price of $100 million is worth $1.035 million. The value of the debt is therefore $60.65M – $1.035M, or $59.615 million.

The second approach to value the debt involves subtracting the value of equity from the value of the firm:

$$D(V, F, T, t) = V - S(V, F, T, t) \qquad (18.5)$$

We subtract $60.385 million from $120 million, which gives us $59.615 million.

The value of the debt is, for a given value of the firm, a decreasing function of the value of equity, which is the value of a call option on the value of the firm. Everything else equal, therefore, the value of the debt falls if the volatility of the firm increases, if the interest rate rises, if the principal amount of the debt falls, and if the debt's time to maturity lengthens.

To understand the effect of the value of the firm on the value of the debt, note that a $1 increase in the value of the firm affects the right-hand side of equation (18.5) as follows: It increases V by $1 and the call option by δ, where δ is the call option delta. $1 - \delta$ is positive, so that the impact of a $1 increase in the value of the firm on the value of the debt is positive and equal to $1 – δ. δ increases as the call option gets more in the money. Here, the call option corresponding to equity is more in the money as the value of the firm increases, so that the impact of an increase in firm value on debt value falls as the value of the firm increases.

Investors pay a lot of attention to credit spreads. The **credit spread** is the difference between the yield on the risky debt and the yield on risk-free debt of same maturity. If corporate bonds with an A rating have a yield of 8 percent while T-bonds of the same maturity have a yield of 7 percent, the credit spread for A-rated debt is 1 percentage point. An investor can look at credit spreads for different ratings to see how the yields differ across ratings classes. An explicit formula for the credit spread is:

$$\text{Credit spread} = - \left(\frac{1}{T - t} \right) \ln \left(\frac{D}{F} \right) - r \qquad (18.6)$$

where r is the risk-free rate. For our example, the risk-free rate (implied by the zero-coupon bond price we use) is 10 percent. The yield on the debt is 10.35 percent, so the credit spread is 35 basis points. Not surprisingly, the credit spread falls as the value of the debt rises. The logarithm of D/F in equation (18.6) is multiplied by $-[1/(T - t)]$. An increase in the value of debt increases D/F, but since the logarithm of D/F is multiplied by a negative number, the credit spread falls.

With debt, the most we can receive at maturity is par. As time to maturity lengthens, it becomes more likely that we will receive less than par. However, if the value of the debt is low enough to start with, there is more of a chance that the value of the debt will be higher as the debt reaches maturity if time to maturity is longer. Consequently, if the debt is highly rated, the spread widens as time to maturity gets longer. For sufficiently risky debt, the spread can narrow as time to maturity gets longer. This is shown in Figure 18.2.

Helwege and Turner (1999) show that credit spreads widen with time to maturity for low-rated public debt, so that even low-rated debt is not risky enough to lead to credit spreads that narrow with time to maturity. It is important to note that credit spreads depend on interest rates. The expected value of the firm at maturity increases with the risk-free rate, so there is less risk that the firm will default. As a result, credit spreads narrow as interest rates increase.

18.1.1. Finding firm value and firm value volatility

Suppose a firm, Supplier Inc., has one large debt claim. The firm sells a plant to a very risky third party, In-The-Mail Inc., and instead of receiving cash it receives a promise from In-The-Mail Inc. that it will pay $100 million in five years. We want to value this debt claim. If V_{t+5} is the value of In-The-Mail Inc. at maturity of the debt, we know that the debt pays $F - \text{Max}(F - V_{t+5}, 0)$ or $V_{t+5} - \text{Max}(V_{t+5} - F, 0)$. If it were possible to trade claims on the value of In-The-Mail Inc., pricing the debt would be straightforward. We could simply compute the value of a put on In-The-Mail Inc. with the appropriate exercise price. In general, we cannot directly trade a portfolio of securities that represents a claim to the whole firm; In-The-Mail Inc.'s debt is not a traded security.

The fact that a firm has some nontraded securities creates two problems. First, we cannot observe firm value directly and, second, we cannot trade the firm to hedge a claim whose value depends on the value of the firm. We can solve both problems. Remember that with Merton's model the only random variable that affects the value of claims on the firm is the total value of the firm. Since equity is a call option on firm value, it is a portfolio consisting of δ units of firm value plus a short position in the risk-free asset. The return on equity is perfectly correlated with the return on the value of the firm for small changes in the value of the firm because a small change in firm value of ΔV changes equity by $\delta \Delta V$. We can therefore use equity and the risk-free asset to construct a portfolio that replicates the firm as a whole, and we can deduce firm value from the value of traded claims on the value of the firm. To do that, however, we need to estimate the δ of equity.

To compute the δ of equity from Merton's formula, we need to know firm value V, the volatility of firm value, the promised debt payment, the risk-free interest rate, and the maturity of the debt. If we have this information, computing delta is straightforward. Otherwise, we can estimate these variables using information we have. If we have an estimate of δ and we know the value of the firm's equity, then we can solve for firm value and the volatility of firm value as long as we know the promised debt payment and the maturity of the debt. This is be-

Credit spreads, time to maturity, and interest rates   *Figure 18.2*

Panel A has firm value of $50 million, volatility of 20 percent, and debt with face value of $150 million. Panel B differs only in that firm value is $200 million.

Panel A

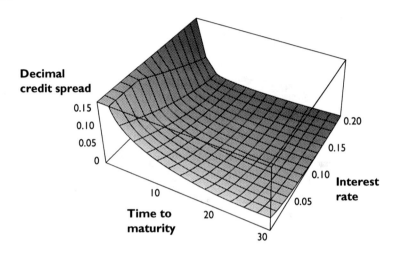

Panel B

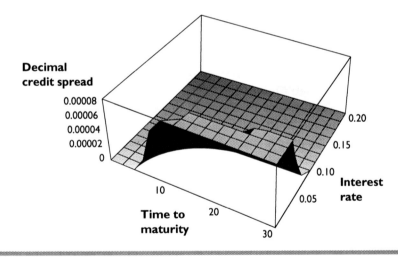

cause, in this case, we have two unknowns, firm volatility and firm value, and two equations, the Merton equation for the value of equity and the Merton equation for the equity's delta. We can solve these equations to find firm volatility and the value of the firm. Having these values, we can then solve for the value of the debt. (In practical applications, the Merton model is often used for more complicated capital structures. In this case, the promised debt payment is an estimate of the amount of firm value over some period of time such that if firm value falls below that amount, the firm will be in default and have to file for bankruptcy.)

Suppose we do not know δ. One way to find δ is as follows. We assume In-the-Mail Inc. has traded equity and that its only debt is the debt it owes to

Supplier Inc. The value of the debt claim in million dollars is D(V, 100, $t + 5$, t). The value of a share is \$14.10 and there are 5 million shares. The value of the firm's equity is therefore \$70.5 million. The interest rate is 10 percent per year. Consequently, in million dollars, we have:

$$S(V, 100, t + 5, t) = 70.5 \qquad (18.7)$$

We know that equity is a call option on the value of the firm, so that $S(V, 100, t + 5, t) = c(V, 100, t + 5, t)$. We cannot trade V because it is the sum of the debt we own and the value of equity. Since the return to V is perfectly correlated with the return on equity, we can form a dynamic portfolio strategy that pays V_{t+5} at $t + 5$. We will see the details of the strategy later, but for now we assume it can be done.

If we know V, we can use equation (18.7) to obtain the firm's implied volatility, but the equation has two unknowns: V and the volatility of the value of the firm, σ. To solve for the two unknowns, we have to find an additional equation so that we have two equations and two unknowns. Suppose that there are options traded on the firm's equity. Suppose further that a call option on one share with exercise price of \$10 and maturity of one year is worth \$6.72. We could use the option pricing formula to get the volatility of equity and deduce the volatility of the firm from the volatility of equity. After all, the option and the equity both depend on the same random variable, the value of the firm.

The difficulty with this is that the Black-Scholes formula does not apply to the call option in our example because it is a call option on equity, which itself is an option when the firm is levered. We therefore have an option on an option, or what is called a compound option. The Black-Scholes formula applies when equity has constant volatility, but the equity in our example cannot have constant volatility if firm value has constant volatility. For a levered firm where firm value has constant volatility, equity is more volatile when firm value is low than when it is high, so that volatility falls as firm value increases. This is because, in percentage terms, an increase in firm value has more of an impact on equity when the value of equity is extremely low than when it is extremely high—even though the equity's δ increases as firm value increases.

A compound call option gives its holder the right to buy an option for a given exercise price. Geske (1979) derives a pricing formula for a compound option that we can use. Geske's formula assumes that firm value follows a lognormal distribution with constant volatility. Therefore, if we know the value of equity, we can use Geske's formula to obtain the value of firm volatility. This formula is presented in Technical Box 18.1, Compound option formula.

18.1.2. Pricing the debt of In-The-Mail Inc.

We now have two equations that we can use to solve for V and σ: the equation for the value of equity (the Black-Scholes formula), and the equation for the value of an option on equity (the compound option formula of Technical Box 18.1). These two equations have only two unknowns. We proceed by iteration.

Suppose we pick a firm value per share of \$25 and a volatility of 50 percent. With this, we find that equity should be worth \$15.50 and that the call price should be \$6.0349. Consequently, the value of equity is too high and the value

Compound option formula   *Technical Box 18.1*

A compound call option gives its holder the right to buy an option on an option for a given exercise price. Since equity is an option on firm value, an option on the stock of a levered firm is a compound option. Geske (1979) provides a formula for a compound option to value a call on the equity of a levered firm. Geske assumes that firm value follows the same distribution as the stock price in the Black-Scholes formula: firm value has constant volatility and the logarithm of firm value is normally distributed.

Let V be the value of the firm and F be the face value of the debt per share. We define T' as the maturity date of the option on equity and T the maturity of the debt, where T' < T. With this, the option holder receives equity at T' if the option is in the money. Let K be the option exercise price. In exchange for paying K at date T', the option holder receives equity which is a call on firm value. Using our notation for equity, the value of this call at T' is S(V, F, T, T'). If S(V, F, T, T') exceeds K, the option is exercised.

With this notation, the value of the compound option is:

$$Ve^{-d(T-t)}N_2\left(a_1, b_1; \left[(T' - t)/(T - t)\right]^{0.5}\right)$$

$$- Fe^{-r(T-t)}N_2\left(a_2, b_2; \left[(T' - t)/(T - t)\right]^{0.5}\right) - e^{-r(T'-t)}KN(a_2)$$

$$a_1 = \frac{\ln(V/V^*) + (r - d + \sigma^2/2)(T' - t)}{\sigma(T' - t)^{0.5}}; \ a_2 = a_1 - \sigma(T' - t)^{0.5}$$

$$b_1 = \frac{\ln(V/F) + (r - d + \sigma^2/2)(T - t)}{\sigma(T - t)^{0.5}}; \ b_2 = b_1 - \sigma(T - t)^{0.5}$$

V^* **is such that, for** $t = T'$, $V^* e^{-d(T-t)}N(b_1) - Fe^{-r(T-t)}N(b_2) - K = 0$

where $N_2(a, b, \rho)$ denotes the cumulative bivariate normal distribution evaluated at a and b for two random variables, each with zero mean and unit standard deviation, that have a correlation coefficient of ρ. The bivariate normal distribution is the distribution followed by two random variables that are jointly normally distributed. The dividend rate is d; it is assumed that dividends are a constant fraction of firm value.

The intuition that we acquired in Chapter 12 about the determinants of the value of a call option works for compound call options. The value of the compound call option increases when the value of the firm increases, falls when the face value of the debt rises, increases when the time to maturity of the debt rises, increases when the risk-free interest rate rises, increases when the variance of the firm rises, falls as the exercise price rises, and increases as the time to expiration of the call rises.

of the call is too low. Reducing the assumed firm value reduces both the value of equity and the value of the call, so that it brings us closer to the value of equity we want but farther from the value of the call we want. We therefore need to change both firm value and some other variable, taking advantage of the fact that equity and a call option on equity have different greeks. Reducing our assumed firm value reduces the value of equity as well as the value of the call, and increases volatility, which increases the value of equity and the value of the call. In this case, we find an option value of $7.03 and a value of equity of $13.30. Now, the value of equity is too low and the value of the option is too high. This suggests that we have gone too far with our reduction in firm value and increase in volatility. A value of the firm of $21 per share and a volatility of 68.36 percent yield the right values for equity and for the option on equity. Consequently, the value of the debt per share is $6.90. The value of the firm is therefore $105 million. It is divided between debt of $34.5 million and equity of $70.5 million.

Once we have the value of the firm and its volatility, we can use the formula for the value of equity to create a portfolio whose value is equal to the value of the firm and thus can replicate dynamically the value of the firm just using the risk-free asset and equity. Remember that the value of the firm's equity is given by a call option on the value of the firm. Using the Black-Scholes formula, we have:

$$S\big(V, F, T, t\big) = VN\big(d\big) - P_t(T)FN\big(d - \sigma\sqrt{T - t}\big)$$

$$d = \frac{\ln\big(V/P_t(T)F\big)}{\sigma\sqrt{T - t}} + \frac{1}{2}\,\sigma\sqrt{T - t} \qquad (18.8)$$

Inverting this formula, the value of the firm is equal to:

$$V = \left(\frac{1}{N(d)}\right)S\big(V, F, T, t\big) + P_t(T)F\left(\frac{N\big(d - \sigma\sqrt{T - t}\big)}{N(d)}\right) \qquad (18.9)$$

Note that we know all the terms on the right-hand side of this equation. Hence, an investment of $1/N(d)$ of the firm's equity and of $N(d - \sigma\sqrt{T - t})F/N(d)$ units of the zero-coupon bond is equal to the value of the firm per share. Adjusting this portfolio dynamically over time insures that we have V(T) at maturity of the debt. We can scale this portfolio so that it pays off the value of the firm per share. With our example, the portfolio that pays off the value of the firm per share has an investment of 1.15 shares, and an investment in zero-coupon bonds worth $7.91.

18.1.3. Subordinated debt

In principle, subordinated debt receives a payment in the event of bankruptcy only after senior debt has been paid in full. Consequently, when a firm is in poor financial condition, subordinated debt is unlikely to be paid in full and is more like an equity claim than a debt claim. In this case, an increase in firm volatility makes it more likely that subordinated debt will be paid off and hence increases the value of subordinated debt. Senior debt always falls in value when firm volatility increases.

To understand the determinants of the value of the subordinated debt, consider then the case where the senior debt and the subordinated debt mature at the same date. F is the face value of the senior debt and U is the face value of the subordinated debt. Equity is an option on the value of the firm with exercise price U + F since the shareholders receive nothing unless the value of the firm exceeds U + F. Figure 18.3 shows the payoff of subordinated debt as a function of the value of the firm. In this case, the value of the firm is:

$$V = D(V, F, T, t) + SD(V, U, T, t) + S(V, U + F, T, t) \qquad (18.10)$$

D denotes senior debt, SD subordinated debt, and S equity. The value of equity is given by the call option pricing formula:

$$S(V, U + F, T, t) = c(V, U + F, T, t) \qquad (18.11)$$

By definition, shareholders and subordinated debt holders receive collectively the excess of firm value over the face value of the senior debt, F, if that excess is positive. Consequently, they have a call option on V with exercise price equal to F. This implies that the value of the senior debt is the value of the firm V minus the value of the option held by equity and subordinated debt holders:

$$D(V, F, T, t) = V - c(V, F, T, t) \qquad (18.12)$$

Having priced the equity and the senior debt, we can then obtain the subordinated debt by subtracting the value of the equity and of the senior debt from the value of the firm:

$$SD(V, U, T, t) = V - c(V, F + U, T, t) - [V - c(V, F, T, t)]$$

$$= c(V, F, T, t) - c(V, F + U, T, t) \qquad (18.13)$$

Subordinated debt payoff   *Figure 18.3*

Both debt claims are zero-coupon bonds. They mature at the same time. The subordinated debt has face value U and the senior debt has face value F. Firm value is V(T).

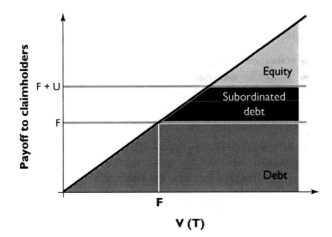

With this formula, the value of subordinated debt is the difference between the value of an option on the value of the firm with exercise price F + U and an option on the value of the firm with exercise price F. Consider a firm with value of $120 million. It has junior debt maturing in five years with face value of $50 million and senior debt maturing in five years with face value of $100 million. The interest rate is 10 percent and the volatility is 20 percent. In this case, we have F = $100 million and U = $50 million. The first call option is worth $60.385 million. It is simply the equity in the absence of subordinated debt, which we computed before. The second call option is worth $36.56 million. The value of the subordinated debt is therefore $60.385M – $36.56M = $23.825 million. Using our formula for the credit spread, we find that the spread on subordinated debt is 4.83 percent, which is more than 10 times the spread on senior debt of 35 basis points.

The fact that the value of subordinated debt corresponds to the difference between the value of two options means that an increase in firm volatility has an ambiguous effect on subordinated debt value. As shown in Figure 18.4, an increase in firm volatility can increase the value of subordinated debt. Subordinated debt is a portfolio that has a long position in a call option that increases in value with volatility and a short position in a call option that becomes more costly as volatility increases. If the subordinated debt is unlikely to pay off, the short position in the call is economically unimportant. Consequently, subordinated debt is almost similar to equity and its value is an increasing function of the volatility of the firm. Alternatively, if the firm is unlikely to ever be in default, then the subordinated debt is effectively like senior debt and inherits the characteristics of senior debt.

The value of subordinated debt can fall as time to maturity decreases. If firm value is low, the value of the debt increases as time to maturity increases because there is a better chance that it will pay something at maturity. If firm value is high and debt has low risk, it behaves more like senior debt.

Similarly, a rise in interest rates can increase the value of subordinated debt. As the interest rate rises, the value of senior debt falls so that what is left for the subordinated debt holders and equity increases. For low firm values, equity gets little out of the interest rate increase because equity is unlikely to receive anything at maturity, so the value of subordinated debt increases. For high firm values, the probability that the principal will be paid is high, so the subordinated debt is almost risk-free, and its value necessarily falls as the interest rate increases.

18.1.4. The pricing of debt when interest rates change randomly

Unanticipated changes in interest rates can affect debt value through two channels. First, an increase in interest rates reduces the present value of promised coupon payments absent credit risk, and hence reduces the value of the debt. Second, an increase in interest rates can affect firm value. Empirical evidence suggests that stock prices are negatively correlated with interest rates. Hence, an increase in interest rates generally reduces the value of debt both because of the sensitivity of debt to interest rates and because on average it is associated with an adverse shock to firm values. When we want to hedge a debt position, we therefore have to take into account the interaction between interest rate changes and firm value changes.

Subordinated debt, firm value, and volatility   *Figure 18.4*

We consider subordinated debt with face value of $50 million and senior debt with face value of $100 million. The two debt issues mature in five years. The risk-free rate is 10 percent.

Panel A. Firm value is $20 million.

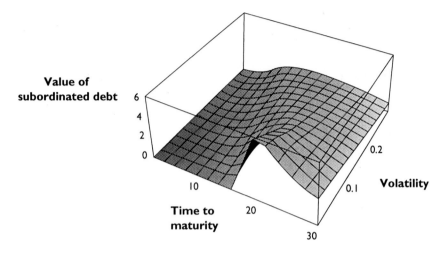

Panel B. Firm value is $200 million.

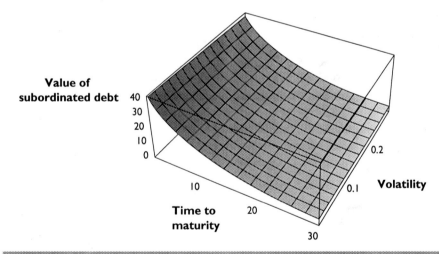

We consider the pricing of risky debt when the spot interest rate follows the Vasicek model discussed in Chapter 14. The change in the spot interest rate over a period of length Δt is:

$$\Delta r_t = \lambda\left(k - r_t\right)\Delta t + \sigma_r \epsilon_t \qquad (18.14)$$

where r_t is the current spot interest rate and ϵ_t is a random shock. When λ is positive, the interest rate reverts to a long-run mean of k. With equation (18.14) describing how the interest rate evolves, the price of a zero-coupon bond at t that pays $1 at T, $P_t(T)$, is given by the Vasicek model.

Suppose value and interest rate changes are correlated. Shimko, Tejima, and van Deventer (1993) show that with these interest rate dynamics the value of risky debt is:

$$D(V, r, F, t, T) = V - VN(h_1) + FP_t(T)N(h_2)$$

$$Q = (T - t)\left(\sigma^2 + \frac{\sigma_r^2}{k^2} + \frac{2\rho\sigma\sigma_r}{k}\right)$$

$$+ \left(e^{-k(T - t)} - 1\right)\left(\frac{2\sigma_r^2}{k^3} + \frac{2\rho\sigma\sigma_r}{k^2}\right)$$

$$- \frac{\sigma_r^2}{2k^3}\left(e^{-2k(T - t)} - 1\right)$$

$$h_1 = \frac{\ln\left(\frac{V}{P_t(T)F}\right) + 0.5Q}{\sqrt{Q}}$$

$$h_2 = h_1 - \sqrt{Q} \tag{18.15}$$

To see how interest rate changes affect the price of debt, we price debt of face value of $100 million maturing in 5 years on a firm worth $120 million as we did before. When we assumed a fixed interest rate of 10 percent and a firm volatility of 20 percent, we found that the value of the debt was $59.615 million in section 18.1. We choose the parameters of the Vasicek model to be such that, with a spot interest rate of 10 percent, the price of a zero-coupon bond that pays $1 in 5 years is the same as with a fixed interest rate of 10 percent. This requires us to assume k to be 14.21 percent, the interest rate volatility 10 percent, and the mean reversion parameter 0.25. The volatility of firm value is 20 percent as before and the correlation between firm value changes and interest rate changes is –0.2. With these assumptions, the debt is then $57.3011 million.

Figure 18.5 shows how the various parameters of interest rate dynamics affect the price of the debt. We choose a firm value of $50 million, so that the firm could not repay the debt if it matured immediately. In Panel A, the value of the debt falls as the correlation between firm value and interest rate shocks increases. In this case, firm value is higher when the interest rate is high, so that the impact of an increase in firm value on the value of the debt is more likely to be dampened by a simultaneous interest rate increase. In Panel B, an increase in interest rate volatility and an increase in the speed of mean reversion reduce debt value. With high mean reversion, the interest rate does not diverge for very long from its long-run mean, so that we are closer to the case of fixed interest rates. However, with our assumptions, the long-run mean is higher than the current interest rate.

Figure 18.6 shows that the debt's interest rate sensitivity depends on the volatility of interest rates. At highly volatile interest rates, the value of the debt is less sensitive to changes in interest rate. Consequently, if we were to hedge debt against changes in interest rates, the hedge ratio would depend on the parameters of the dynamics of interest rates.

Debt value and interest rate dynamics   *Figure 18.5*

In the base case, firm value of $50 million, the promised debt payment is $100 million, the maturity of the debt is 5 years, the interest rate is set at 10 percent, the speed of mean reversion parameter is 0.25, the volatility of the interest rate is 10 percent, the correlation between firm value and the interest rate is −0.2.

Panel A

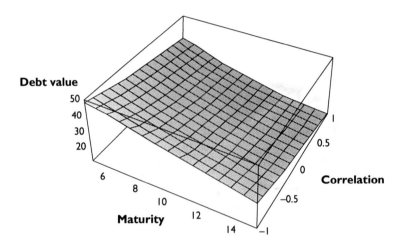

Panel B

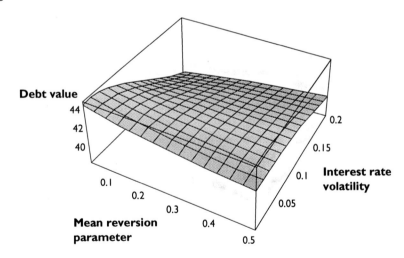

18.1.5. VaR and credit risks

Once we have a pricing model for the valuation of default-risky debt held by the firm, we can incorporate credit risk into the computation of firm-wide risk. Suppose we use the Merton model. Default-risky debt depends on firm value, which itself is perfectly correlated with the debtor's stock price. This makes the debtor's equity one additional risk factor. Suppose we want to compute a VaR measure for the firm, and the firm has just one risky asset: its risky debt. One way is to compute the delta-VaR by transforming the risky debt into a portfolio of the risk-free

Figure 18.6   Interest rate sensitivity of debt

Firm value is $50 million, the promised debt payment is $100 million, the maturity of the debt is 5 years, the speed of mean reversion parameter is 0.25, the correlation between firm value and the interest rate is –0.2.

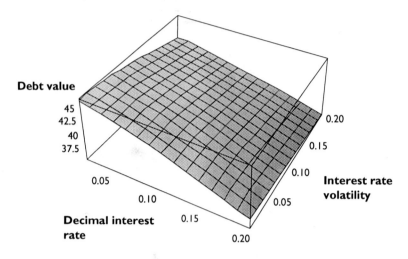

bond and of the debtor's equity if we are computing a VaR for a short period of time. A second way is to compute the Monte Carlo VaR by simulating equity returns and valuing the debt for these equity returns. If the firm has other assets, we must consider the correlations among the asset returns.

Conceptually, the inclusion of credit risks in computations of VaR does not present serious difficulties. All the difficulties are in the implementation—but they are serious. The complexities of firm capital structures create important obstacles to valuing debt, and often debt is issued by firms with no traded equity. There are thus alternative approaches to debt pricing.

18.2. Beyond the Merton model

Corporations generally have many different types of debt with different maturities, and most debt makes coupon payments when not in default. The Merton model approach can be used to price any type of debt. Jones, Mason, and Rosenfeld (1984) test this approach for a panel of firms that include investment-grade firms as well as firms below investment grade. They find that a naive model predicting that debt is riskless works better for investment-grade debt than the Merton model. In contrast, the Merton model works better than the naive model for debt below investment grade. As pointed out by Kim, Ramaswamy, and Sundaresan (1993), however, Merton's model fails to predict credit spreads large enough to match empirical data. They point out that from 1926 to 1986, AAA spreads ranged from 15 to 215 basis points, with an average of 77, while BAA spreads ranged from 51 to 787 basis points, with an average of 198. Yet they show that Merton's model cannot generate spreads in excess of 120 basis points.

There are important difficulties in implementing the Merton model when debt makes coupon payments or a firm has multiple debt issues that mature at different dates. Consider the simple case where debt makes one coupon payment u at t' and pays F + u at T. We know how to value the coupon payment u since it is equivalent to a risky zero-coupon debt payment at t'. Valuing the right to F + u to be received at T is harder because it is contingent on the firm paying u at t'. Taking the viewpoint of the equity holders simplifies the analysis. After the equity holders have paid the coupon at t', their claim on the firm is the same as the claim they have in our analysis in section 18.1, namely a call option on the firm with maturity at T with exercise price equal to the promised payment to the debt holders (which here is F + u). Consequently, by paying the coupon at t' the equity holders acquire a call option on the value of the firm at T with exercise price F + u. The value of equity at t is the present value of the call option equity holders acquire at t' if they pay the coupon. This is the present value of the payoff of a European call option maturing at t', since they get Max($S_{t'} - u$, 0), where $S_{t'}$ is the value of equity at t'. Hence, at t, the equity holders have a call option on the equity value at t' with exercise price u—they have an option on an option, or a compound option. The value of debt at t is firm value minus a compound option. If we had an additional coupon at t'', so that $t' < t'' < T$, we would have to subtract from V at t an option on an option on an option. This creates a considerable computational burden in computing debt value. This burden can be surmounted, but it is not trivial to do so. In practice, this difficulty is compounded by the difficulty that one does not know V because of nontraded debt.

Another difficulty with the Merton model is that default is too predictable. Remember that to obtain prices of debt in that model, we make the Black-Scholes assumptions. We know that with these assumptions firm value cannot jump. As a result, default cannot occur unless firm value is infinitesimally close to the point where default occurs. In the real world, default is often more surprising. For instance, a run on a bank could make its equity worthless even though before the run its equity value was not close to zero.

These problems have led to the development of a different class of models that take as their departure point a probability of default that evolves over time according to a well-defined process. Under this approach, the probability of default can be positive even when firm value significantly exceeds the face value of the debt—this is the case if firm value can jump. The economics of default are modeled as a black box. Default either happens over an interval of time or it does not. Upon default, the debt holder receives a fraction of the promised claim. The recovery rate is the fraction of the principal recovered in the event of default. This recovery rate can be random or certain.

Let's look at the simplest case and assume that the process for the probability of default is not correlated with the interest rate process and recovery in the event of default is a fixed fraction of the principal amount, θ, which does not depend on time. The bond value next period is $D_{t+\Delta t} + u$ if the bond is not in default, where u is the coupon. If the debt is in default, its value is θF. In the absence of arbitrage opportunities, the bond price today, D_t, is simply the expected value of the bond next period computed using risk-neutral probabilities discounted at the risk-free rate. Using q as the risk-neutral probability of default, it must be the case that:

$$D_t = P_t(t + \Delta t)\big[q\theta F + (1 - q)(D_{t + \Delta t} + u)\big] \qquad (18.16)$$

In this equation, the value of the nondefaulted debt today depends on the value of the nondefaulted debt tomorrow. To solve this problem, we therefore start from the last period. In the last period, the value of the debt is equal to the principal amount plus the last coupon payment, $F + u$, or to θF. We then work backward to the next-to-the-last period, where we have:

$$D_{T - \Delta t} = P_{T - \Delta t}(T)[q\theta F + (1 - q)(F + u)] \tag{18.17}$$

If we know q and θ, we can price the debt in the next-to-the-last period and continue to keep working backward to get the debt value.

How can we obtain the probability of default and the amount recovered in the event of default? If the firm has publicly traded debt, we can infer these parameters from the price of the debt. Alternatively, we can infer risk-neutral probabilities of default and recovery rates from spreads on debt with various ratings.

Different applications of this approach can allow for random recovery rates as well as for correlations between recovery rates and interest rates or correlations between default rates and interest rates. The empirical evidence shows that this approach works well to price swap spreads and bank subordinated debt.

18.3. Credit risk models

There are several differences between measuring the risk of a portfolio of debt claims and measuring the risk of a portfolio of other financial assets. First, because credit instruments typically do not trade on liquid markets where we can observe prices, we cannot generally rely on historical data on individual credit instruments to measure risk. Second, the distribution of returns differs. We cannot assume that continuously compounded returns on debt follow a normal distribution. The return of a debt claim is bounded by the fact that investors cannot receive more than the principal payment and the coupon payments. In statistical terms, this means that the returns to equity are generally symmetric, while the returns to debt are skewed—unless the debt is deeply discounted.

The third difference is that firms often have debt issued by creditors with no traded equity. A fourth difference is that typically debt is not marked to market in contrast to traded securities. When debt is not marked to market, a loss is recognized only if default takes place. Consequently, when debt is not marked to market, a firm must be able to assess the probability of default and the loss made in the event of default.

A number of credit risk models resolve some of the difficulties associated with debt portfolios. Some models focus only on default and on the recovery in the event of default. The most popular model of this type is CreditRisk+, from Credit Suisse Financial Products. It is based on techniques borrowed from the insurance industry for the modeling of extreme events. Other models are based on the marked-to-market value of debt claims. **CreditMetrics™** is a risk model built on the same principles as those of RiskMetrics™. The purpose of this risk model is to provide the distribution of the value of a portfolio of debt claims, which leads to a VaR measure for the portfolio. The KMV model is in many ways quite similar to the CreditMetrics™ model, except that it makes direct use of the Merton model in computing the probability of default.[1] All these models can be used to compute the risk of portfolios that include other payoffs besides those of pure debt contracts. For example, they can include swap contracts. As a result, these models talk about estimating the risk of **obligors**—all those who have legal obligations to the firm—rather than debtors.

To see how we can use the Merton model for default prediction, remember that it assumes that firm value is lognormally distributed with constant volatility and that the firm has one zero-coupon debt issue. If firm value exceeds the face value of debt at maturity, the firm is not in default. We want to compute the probability that firm value will be below the face value of debt at maturity of the debt because we are interested in forecasting the likelihood of a default. To compute this probability, we have to know the expected rate of return of the firm since the higher that expected rate of return, the less likely it is that the firm will be in default. Let μ be the expected rate of return of the firm value. In this case, the probability of default is simply:

$$\textbf{Probability of default} \ = \ \textbf{N}\!\left(\frac{\ln(\textbf{F}) \ - \ln(\textbf{V}) \ - \ \mu(\textbf{T} \ - \ t) \ + \ 0.5\sigma^2(\textbf{T} \ - \ t)}{\sigma\sqrt{\textbf{T} \ - \ t}} \right)$$

(18.18)

where N denotes the cumulative normal distribution, F is the face value of the debt, V the value of the firm, T the maturity date of the debt, and σ the volatility of the rate of change of V.

Consider the case where a firm has value of $120 million, debt with face value of $100 million and maturity of five years, the expected rate of change of firm value is 20 percent, the volatility is 20 percent, and the interest rate is 5 percent. The probability that the firm will default is 0.78 percent.

Figure 18.7 shows how the probability of default is related to volatility and firm value. As volatility increases, the probability of default increases. It can be substantial even for large firm values compared to the face value of the debt when volatility is high.

We use the same approach to compute the firm's expected loss if default occurs. The loss if default occurs is often called **loss given default** or **LGD**. Since default occurs when firm value is less than the face value of the debt, we have to compute the expected value of V given that it is smaller than F. The solution is:

$$\textbf{Expected loss} \ = \ \textbf{FN}\!\left(\frac{\ln(\textbf{F}) \ - \ln(\textbf{V}) \ - \ \mu(\textbf{T} \ - \ t) \ + \ 0.5\sigma^2(\textbf{T} \ - \ t)}{\sigma\sqrt{\textbf{T} \ - \ t}} \right) \qquad \text{(18.19)}$$

$$- \ \textbf{V}e^{\mu(\textbf{T} \ - \ t)}\textbf{N}\!\left(\frac{\ln(\textbf{F}) \ - \ln(\textbf{V}) \ - \ \mu(\textbf{T} \ - \ t) \ - \ 0.5\sigma^2(\textbf{T} \ - \ t)}{\sigma\sqrt{\textbf{T} \ - \ t}} \right)$$

---

1 Oldrich A. Vasicek, Credit Valuation, KMV Corporation, 1984.

Figure 18.7   Probability of default

The firm has debt with face value of $100 million due in five years. The firm's expected rate of return is 20 percent.

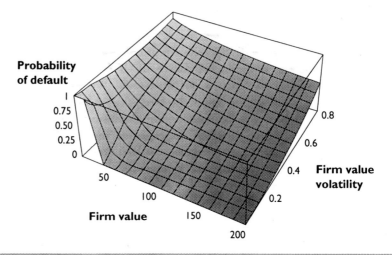

The expected loss is $100,614.

Figure 18.8 shows how the expected loss depends on firm value and its volatility.

18.3.1. CreditRisk+

CreditRisk+ allows only two outcomes for each firm over the risk measurement period: default and no default. If default occurs, the creditor experiences a loss of fixed size. The probability of default for an obligor depends on its rating, the realization of K risk factors, and the sensitivity of the obligor to the risk factors. The risk factors are common across all obligors, but sensitivity to the risk factors differs across obligors. Defaults across obligors covary only because of the K risk factors. Conditional on the risk factors, defaults are uncorrelated across obligors.

The conditional probability of default for an obligor is the probability of default given the realizations of the risk factors, while the unconditional probability of default is the probability obtained if we do not know the realizations of the risk factors. For example, if there is only one risk factor, say, macroeconomic activity, we would expect the conditional probability of default to be higher when macroeconomic activity is poorer. The unconditional probability of default in this case is the probability when we do not know whether macroeconomic activity is poor or not.

If $p_i(x)$ is the probability of default for the ith obligor conditional on the realizations of the risk factors, and x is the vector of risk factor realizations, the model specifies that:

$$p_i(x) = \pi_{G(i)}\left(\sum_{k=1}^{K} x_k w_{ik}\right)$$

(18.20)

The expected loss and its dependence on volatility   *Figure 18.8*

The firm has value of $120 million, the face value of the debt is $100 million, the expected rate of change of firm value is 20 percent, and the interest rate is 10 percent.

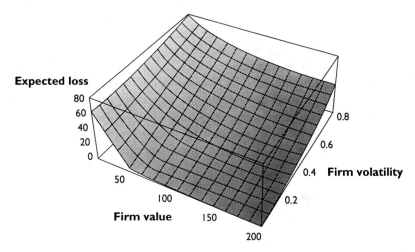

where $\pi_{G(i)}$ is the unconditional probability of default for obligor i given that it belongs to grade G. A natural choice of the grade of an obligor would be its public debt rating if it has one. Often, obligors may not have a rating, or the rating of the company may not reflect the riskiness of the debt. Bank debt has different covenants than public debt, which makes it easier for banks to intervene when the obligor becomes riskier. As a result, bank debt is less risky than otherwise comparable public debt. The bank internal evaluation system often grades loans on a scale from one to ten. A bank internal grading system could be used to grade obligors.

The risk factors can take only positive values and are scaled so that they have a mean of one. The model also assumes that the risk factors follow a specific statistical distribution (the gamma distribution). If the kth risk factor has a realization above one, this increases the probability of default of firm i in proportion to the obligor's exposure to that risk factor measured by w_{ik}.

Once we have computed the probability of default for all the obligors, we can get the distribution of the total number of defaults in the portfolio. The relevant distribution is the distribution of losses. The model expresses the loss upon default for each loan in standardized units. A standardized unit could be $1 million. The exposure to the ith obligor, $v(i)$, would be an exposure of $v(i)$ standardized units. A mathematical function gives the unconditional probability of a loss of n standardized units for each value of n. We can also get the volatility of the probability of a loss of n standardized units since an unexpectedly high realization of the vector of risk factors will lead to a higher than expected loss.

The CreditRisk+ model is easy to use, largely because of some carefully chosen assumptions about the formulation of the probability of default and the distribution of the risk factors. The statistical assumptions of the model are such that an increase in the volatility of the risk factor has a large impact on the tail of the distribution of the risk factor. Gordy (2000) provides simulation evidence on the CreditRisk+ model. His base case has 5,000 obligors and a volatility of the risk factor of 1. The distribution of grades for obligors is structured to correspond to the typical distribution for a large bank according to Federal Reserve Board statistics. He assumes that the loss upon default is equal to 30 percent of the loan for all loans. Losses are calculated as a percentage of outstanding loans. For a low-quality portfolio (the model rating is BB), the expected loss is 1.872 percent and its volatility is 0.565 percent. The distribution of losses is skewed, so the median of 0.769 percent is much lower than the expected loss. There is a 0.5 percent probability that the loss will exceed 3.320 percent. As the volatility of the risk factor is quadrupled, the mean and standard deviation of losses are essentially unchanged, but there is a 0.5 percent probability that the loss will exceed 4.504 percent.

18.3.2. CreditMetrics™

J.P. Morgan's CreditMetrics™ offers an approach to evaluate the risk of large portfolios of debt claims on firms with realistic capital structures. To see how the CreditMetrics™ approach works, we start from a single debt claim, show how we can measure the risk of the claim with the approach, and then extend the analysis to a portfolio of debt claims.[2]

Consider a debt claim on Almost Iffy Inc. We would like to measure the risk of the value of the debt claim in one year using VaR. To do that, we need to know the fifth quantile of the distribution of the value of the debt claim if we use a 5 percent VaR.

Our first step in using the CreditMetrics™ approach is to figure out a rating class for the debt claim. Say that we decide the claim should have a rating BBB. Almost Iffy's debt could remain at that rating, could improve if the firm does better, or could worsen if default becomes more likely. There is a historical probability distribution that a claim with a BBB rating will move to some other rating. Across claims of all ratings, the **rating transition matrix** presented in Table 18.1 gives us the probability that a credit will migrate from one rating to another over one year. Such matrices are estimated and made available by rating agencies. For a debt claim rated BBB, there is a 1.17 percent probability that the debt claim will have a B rating next year.

To obtain the distribution of the value of the debt claim, we compute the value we expect the claim to have for each rating in one year. Using the term structure of bond yields for each rating category, we can get today's price of a zero-coupon bond for a forward contract to mature in one year. Table 18.2 provides an example of one-year forward zero curves. The rows of the table give us the one-year forward discount rates that apply to zero-coupon bonds maturing in the following four years.

We assume coupons are promised to be paid exactly in one year and at the end of each of the four subsequent years. Say that the coupon is $6. We can use the

---

2 The CreditMetrics™ Technical Manual, available on RiskMetrics website, analyzes the example used here in much greater detail. The data used here is obtained from that manual.

One-year transition matrix (%)   *Table 18.1*

Initial rating	Rating at year-end (%)							
	AAA	AA	A	BBB	BB	B	CCC	Default
AAA	90.81	8.33	0.68	0.06	0.12	0	0	0
AA	0.70	90.65	7.79	0.64	0.06	0.14	0.02	0
A	0.09	2.27	91.05	5.52	0.70	0.26	0.01	0.06
BBB	0.02	0.33	5.95	86.93	5.30	1.17	0.12	0.18
BB	0.03	0.14	0.67	7.73	80.53	8.84	1.00	1.06
B	0	0.11	0.24	0.43	6.48	83.46	4.07	5.20
CCC	0.22	0	0.22	1.30	2.38	11.24	64.86	19.79

forward zero curves to compute the value of the bond for each possible rating next year. For example, using Table 18.2, if the bond migrates to a BB rating, the present value of the coupon to be paid two years from now as of next year is $6 discounted at the rate of 5.55 percent.

If the bond defaults, we need a **recovery rate**, which is the amount received in the event of default as a fraction of the principal. Suppose that the bond is a senior unsecured bond. Using historical data, the recovery rate for this type of bond is 51.13 percent.

We can compute the value of the bond for each rating class next year and assign a probability that the bond will end up in each one of these rating classes. Table 18.3 shows the result of such calculations. A typical VaR measure would use the fifth percentile of the bond price distribution, which is a BB rating and a value of $102.02. The mean value of the bond is $107.09, so that the fifth percentile is $5.07 below the mean. Say that the price today is $108. There is a 5 percent chance we will lose at least $5.98.

One-year forward zero curves for various rating classes (%)   *Table 18.2*

Rating class	Year 1	Year 2	Year 3	Year 4
AAA	3.60	4.17	4.73	5.12
AA	3.65	4.22	4.78	5.17
A	3.72	4.32	4.93	5.32
BBB	4.10	4.67	5.25	5.63
BB	5.55	6.02	6.78	7.27
B	6.05	7.02	8.03	8.52
CCC	15.05	15.02	14.03	13.52

Table 18.3	The value of the debt claim across ratings classes and associated probabilities

Year-end rating	Probability (%)	Bond value plus coupon($)
AAA	0.02	109.37
AA	0.33	109.19
A	5.95	108.66
BBB	86.93	107.55
BB	5.30	102.02
B	1.17	98.10
CCC	0.12	83.64
Default	0.18	51.13

If we have many claims, we have to make an assumption about the correlations among the various claims. If we know the correlations, we can measure the risk of a portfolio of debt claims using the distribution of the portfolio value. For example, suppose that we have an AAA bond and a B bond whose migration probabilities are independent. That is, knowing that the B bond migrates from a B rating to a BB rating provides no information about the likelihood that the AAA bond will migrate to an AA rating. We compute the probabilities of the transitions for each bond independently and multiply them to obtain the joint probability. Using the transition probability matrix in Table 18.1, we know that the probability of a B bond moving to a BB rating is 6.48 percent and that the probability of an AAA bond moving to an AA rating is 8.33 percent. The probability of these two events happening at the same time is the product of the probabilities of the individual events, $0.0648 \times 0.0833 = 0.0054$, or 0.54 percent.

We can compute the value of the portfolio for that outcome. Once we have computed the value of the portfolio for each possible outcome as well as the probability of each outcome, we have a distribution for the value of the portfolio, and we can compute the fifth percentile to obtain a VaR measure.

If the probabilities of the two bonds moving to a particular rating are not independent, the probability that the B bond moves to BB given that the AAA bond moves to AA is not the product of the probability of the B bond moving to BB and the probability of the AAA bond moving to AA. We have to know the probability that the two bonds will move that way. In other words, we need to know the joint distribution of bond migrations. Note that the values of the portfolio for each possible outcome are the same whether the bond migrations are independent or not. The probabilities of the various outcomes differ depending on the migration correlations. Once we know the probabilities of each outcome, we can compute a distribution for the bond portfolio and again compute its VaR.

The major difficulty using the CreditMetrics™ approach is computing the joint distribution of the migrations of the bonds in the portfolio. One way is to use historical estimates for the joint probabilities of bond migrations. In other words, we could figure how often AAA bonds move to an AA rating and B bonds move to a BB rating. This historical frequency would give us an estimate of the probability that we seek. Once we have the joint probability distribution of transitions for the bonds in the portfolio, we can compute the probability distribution of the portfolio.

In general, though, the historical record of rating migrations will not be enough. The correlation among the rating migrations of two bonds depends on other factors. For example, firms in the same industry are more likely to migrate together. To improve on the historical approach, CreditMetrics™ proposes an approach based on stock returns. Suppose that a firm has a given stock price, and we want to estimate its credit risk. From the rating transition matrices, we know the probability of the firm moving to various ratings. Using the distribution of the stock return, we can compute ranges of returns corresponding to the various ratings—if there is a 5 percent probability of default, a default event corresponds to all stock returns that have a probability of at least 95 percent of being exceeded over the period over which credit risk is computed. Proceeding this way, we can produce stock returns corresponding to the various rating outcomes for each firm whose credit is in the portfolio. The correlations between stock returns can then be used to compute probabilities of various rating outcomes for the credits. For instance, if we have two stocks, we can compute the probability that one stock will be in the BB rating range and the other in the AA rating range.

With a large number of credits, using stock returns to compute the joint distribution of outcomes is time-consuming. To simplify the computation, CreditMetrics™ recommends using a factor model in which stock returns depend on country and industry indices as well as on unsystematic risk. The CreditMetrics™ technical manual shows how to implement such a model.

18.3.3. The KMV model

KMV derives default probabilities using the "Expected Default Frequency" for each obligor from an extension of equation (18.18). KMV computes similar probabilities of default, but assumes a slightly more complicated capital structure in doing so. With KMV's model, the capital structure includes equity, short-term debt, long-term debt, and convertible debt. KMV then solves for the firm value and volatility.

One advantage of the KMV approach is that probabilities of default are obtained using the current equity value, so that any event that affects firm value translates directly into a change in the probability of default. Ratings change only with a lag. Another advantage is that probabilities of default change continually rather than only when ratings change. An increase in equity value reduces the probability of default. In the CreditMetrics™ approach, the value of the firm can change substantially, but the probability of default may remain the same because the firm's rating does not change.

KMV uses an approach inspired by the CAPM to obtain the expected growth of firm values that is required to implement equation (18.18) and uses a factor model to simplify the correlation structure of firm returns. The assumptions used imply an analytical solution for the loss distribution, so that simulation is not needed to compute a credit VaR with the KMV model.

18.3.4. Some difficulties with credit portfolio models

The credit portfolio models just discussed present an important advance in measuring credit risk. At the same time, however, the models as presented have obvious limitations. Some have addressed some of these limitations in implementing the models and other models have been developed trying to avoid some of these limitations, but these models as described are the most popular. Models in their most common implementations do not take into account changes in interest rates or credit spreads. Yet, we know that the value of a portfolio of debt can change both because of changes in default risk and changes in interest rates or credit spreads. Nor do the models do much to take into account current economic conditions. As the economy moves from expansion to recession, the distribution of defaults changes dramatically. For example, default numbers reached a peak in 1991, a recession year, then fell before reaching another peak in 2001, another recession year. Further, the transition correlations increase in recessions. Models that use historical transition matrices cannot take into account changing economic conditions.

18.4. Credit derivatives

Credit derivatives are financial instruments whose payoffs are contingent on credit risk realizations. For most credit derivatives, the payoff depends on the occurrence of a "credit event" for a reference entity. Generally, a **credit event** is (1) failure to make a required payment, (2) restructuring that makes any creditor worse off, (3) invocation of cross-default clause, and (4) bankruptcy. Generally, the required payment or the amount defaulted will have to exceed a minimum value (e.g., $10 million) for the credit event to occur.[3]

Credit derivatives are designed as hedging instruments for credit risks. Consider a bank that has credit exposure to many obligors. Before the advent of loan sales and credit derivatives, banks managed their credit risk mostly through diversification. The problem with that approach to managing credit risk is that it forces a bank to turn down customers with which it has valuable relationships. With a credit derivative, a bank can make a loan to a customer and then hedge part or all of this loan by buying a credit derivative. A highly visible example of such a way to use credit derivatives is discussed in Box 18.2, Citigroup and Enron. Except for a futures contract discussed later, credit derivatives are not traded on exchanges. They are over-the-counter instruments. However, firms can also issue securities publicly that provide them with credit protection.

The simplest credit derivative is a put that pays the loss on debt due to default at maturity. A put on the firm value with the same maturity as the debt and with an exercise price equal to the face value of the debt is a credit derivative, called a credit default put, that compensates its holder for the loss due to default if such a loss occurs. The put gives its holder the option to receive the exercise price in exchange of the debt claim. Since the put pays the loss incurred by the debt holder if default takes place, a portfolio of the risky debt and the put option is

---

3 For a description of the documentation of a credit derivative trade, see "Inside a credit trade," *Derivatives Strategy*, 1998 (December), 24–28.

| **Citigroup and Enron** | *Box 18.2* |

Citigroup had considerable exposure to Enron in 2000. At that time, Enron was a successful company. It had equity capitalization in excess of $50 billion at the start of the year. Its net income for the year was $979 million. Enron's senior unsecured debt's rating was upgraded, so that it finished the year rated BAA1 by Moody's and BBB+ by Standard and Poor's. Despite all this, Citigroup chose to issue securities for $1.4 billion from August 2000 to May 2001 that effectively hedged Citigroup's exposure to Enron.

Enron's senior unsecured debt kept its ratings until October 2001. In December 2001, Enron's rating was a D; it was bankrupt. Citigroup had a loan exposure of $1.2 billion. It also had some insurance-related obligations. It had collateral for about half of the loan exposure. Most likely, its potential losses were covered by the securities it had issued.

These securities worked as follows. Citibank created a trust. This trust issued five-year notes with fixed interest payments. The proceeds were invested in high-quality debt. If Enron did not go bankrupt, the investors would receive the principal after five years. If Enron did go bankrupt, Citigroup had the right to swap Enron's debt to Citigroup for the securities in the trust.

Citigroup promised a coupon of 7.37 percent. At the time, BAA companies were promising 8.07 percent. However, according to a presentation by Enron's treasurer to Standard and Poor's in 2000, Enron debt was trading above its rating, which led him to pitch a rating of AA. At the same time, he explained that the off-balance sheet debt was not material to Enron.

Source: Daniel Altman, "How Citigroup hedged bets on Enron," *New York Times*, February 8, 2002.

equivalent to holding default-free debt since the risk of the debt is offset by the purchase of the put. We already priced such a put when we valued In-The-Mail's debt, since that debt was worth risk-free debt minus a put. The holder of In-The-Mail debt was short a put on firm value; by buying the credit default put, the holder of the debt eliminates his credit risk by acquiring an offsetting position in the same put.

The most popular credit derivatives involve swap contracts.[4] One type of contract is called a **credit default swap**. With this swap, party A makes a fixed annual payment to party B, while party B pays the amount lost if a credit event occurs. For example, if Supplier Inc. in our example wants to get rid of the credit risk of In-The-Mail Inc., it can enter a credit default swap with a bank. It makes fixed payments to the bank. If In-The-Mail Inc. defaults at maturity, the bank pays Supplier Inc. the shortfall due to default (face value minus fair value of the debt at the time of default). The credit default swap for Supplier Inc. is effectively equivalent to buying a credit default put but paying for it by installment. Note

---

4 Dominic Baldwin, "Business is booming," Credit Risk Special Report, *Risk*, April 1999, 8.

that the debt will in general require interest payments before maturity and covenants to be respected. If the obligor fails in fulfilling its obligations under the debt contract, there is a credit event. With the credit event, the default payment becomes due.

The credit default swap can have physical delivery, so that Supplier Inc. would sign over the loan to the bank in the event of a default and would receive a fixed payment. Physical delivery is crucial for loans that do not have a secondary market, but physical delivery of loans involves tricky and time-consuming issues. Borrowers often object to having their loans signed over. The settlement period for a credit default swap with physical delivery tends to be longer than for a bond trade. If the transfer of a loan faces objections from the borrower, the settlement might extend beyond 30 days.[5]

A credit default exchange swap requires each party to pay the default shortfall on a different reference asset. Two banks might enter a credit default exchange swap for Bank A to pay the shortfall on debt from Widget Inc. and Bank B to pay the shortfall on debt from In-The-Mail Inc. This way, Bank A reduces its exposure to In-The-Mail Inc. and Bank B reduces its exposure to Widget Inc.

Another popular structure is the total return swap. The party seeking to buy insurance against credit risks receives the return on a risk-free investment and pays the return on an investment with default risk. Suppose a bank, the protection buyer, owns a debt claim worth $80 million today that pays interest of $6 million twice a year in the absence of default for the next five years. In a total return swap, the bank pays what it receives from the debt claim every six months. Assuming that the issuer of the debt claim is not in default, the bank pays $6 million every six months. If the issuer does not pay interest at some due date, then the bank pays nothing. In return, the bank might receive six-month LIBOR on $80 million. At maturity, the obligor repays the principal if he is not in default. Suppose the principal is $100 million. In this case, the bank gets a payment at maturity of $20 million corresponding to the final payment of $100 million minus the initial value of $80 million to the swap counterparty. Or, if the obligor is in default and pays only $50 million, the protection buyer receives from the swap counterparty $80 million minus $50 million, or $30 million. This total return swap guarantees to the bank the cash flows equivalent to the cash flows of a risk-free investment of $80 million.

Pricing a total return swap is straightforward, since it is effectively the exchange of a risky bond for a default-free bond. At initiation, the two bonds have to have the same value.

Another credit derivative is a futures contract. The Chicago Mercantile Exchange Quarterly Bankruptcy Index (QBI) futures contract has been traded since April 1998. The QBI is the total of bankruptcy filings in U.S. courts over a quarter. Most bankruptcies are filed by individuals, which makes the contract appropriate to hedge portfolios of consumer debts, such as credit card debt.

The contract is cash settled and the index level is the number of bankruptcy filings in thousands during the quarter preceding contract expiration. At matu-

5 Dwight Case, "The devil's in the details," *Risk*, August 2000, 26–28.

rity, the futures price equals the index level. The settlement variation is the change in the futures price times $1,000. The minimum increment in the futures price is $0.025.

18.5. Credit risks of derivatives

Since the value of an option is never negative whereas a swap can alternate between positive and negative values, it is not surprising that the credit risks of options are easier to evaluate than the credit risks of swaps.

An option with default risk is called a **vulnerable option**. At maturity, the holder of an option receives the promised payment only if the writer can make the payment. Suppose the writer is a firm with value V and the option is a European call on a stock with price S. The exercise price of the call is K. Without default risk, the option holder receives Max(S – K, 0) at maturity. With a vulnerable option, the holder receives the promised payment only if it is smaller than V, so that the payoff of the call is:

$$\text{Max[Min(V, S – K), 0]} \qquad (18.21)$$

The current value of the call with default risk is just the present value of this payment. There is no closed-form solution for such an option, but it is not difficult to evaluate its value using a Monte Carlo simulation. The correlation between the value of the firm and the value of the option's underlying asset plays an extremely important role in valuation of the vulnerable option. Suppose that V and S are strongly negatively correlated. In this case, it could be that the option has little value because V is low when the option pays off. If V and S are strongly positively correlated, the option might have almost no credit risk because V is always high when S is high. If an option has credit risk, it becomes straightforward to write an option contract that eliminates that credit risk. The appropriate credit derivative is one that pays the difference between a call without default risk and the vulnerable call:

$$\text{Max(S – K, 0) – Max[Min(V, S – K), 0]} \qquad (18.22)$$

If we can price the vulnerable call, we can also price the credit derivative that insures the call.

An alternative approach is to compute the probability of default and apply a recovery rate if default occurs. In this case, the option is a weighted average of an option without default risk and of the present value of the payoff if default occurs. Say that the option can default only at maturity and does so with probability p. If default occurs, the holder receives a fraction z of the value of the option. In this case, the value of the option today is $(1 - p)c + pzc$, where c is the value of the option without default risk.

This approach provides a rather simple way to incorporate credit risk in the value of the option when the probability of default is independent of the value of the underlying asset of the option. Say that the probability of default is 0.05 and the recovery rate is 50 percent. In this case, the vulnerable call is worth

$(1 - 0.05)c + 0.05 \times 0.5 \times c$, which is 97.5 percent of the value of the call without default risk.

As we saw in Chapter 16, it is often the case that the counterparties to a swap enter margin arrangements to reduce default risk. Nevertheless, swaps can entail default risk for both counterparties. Netting means that the payments between the two counterparties are netted out, so that only a net payment has to be made. We assume that netting takes place and that the swap is treated like a debt claim. If the counterparty due to receive net payments is in default, that counterparty still receives the net payments. This is called the full two-way payment covenant. In a limited two-way payment covenant, the obligations of the counterparties are abrogated if one party is in default.

With these assumptions, the analysis is straightforward when the swap has only one payment. Suppose a market maker enters a swap with a risky credit. The risky credit receives a fixed amount F at maturity of the swap—the fixed leg of the swap—and pays S. S could be the value of equity in an equity swap or could be a floating rate payment determined on some index value at some point after the swap's inception. Let V be the value of the risky credit net of all the debt that is senior to the swap. In this case, the market maker receives S–F in the absence of default risk. This amount can be positive or negative. If the amount is negative, the market maker pays F–S to the risky credit for sure. If the amount is positive, the market maker receives S–F if that amount is less than V.

The swap's payoff to the market maker is:

$$-\text{Max}(F - S, 0) + \text{Max}[\text{Min}(S, V) - F, 0] \qquad (18.23)$$

The payment that the risk-free counterparty has to make, F, is chosen so that the swap has no value at inception. Since the risk-free counterparty bears the default risk, in that it may not receive the promised payment, it reduces F to take into account the default risk. To find F, we have to compute the present value of the swap payoff to the market maker.

The first term in equation (18.23) is minus the value of a put with exercise price F on the underlying asset whose value is S. The second term is the present value of an option on the minimum of two risky assets. Both options can be priced. The correlation between V and S plays a crucial role. As this correlation falls, the value of the put is unaffected, but the value of the option on the minimum of two risky assets falls because for a low correlation it will almost always be the case that one of the assets has a low value.

Swaps generally have multiple payments, however, so this approach will work only for the last period of the swap, which is the payment at T. At the payment date before the last payment date, $T - \Delta t$, we can apply our approach. At $T - 2\Delta t$, however, the market maker receives the promised payment at that date plus the promise of two more payments: the payment at $T - \Delta t$ and the payment at T. The payment at $T - \Delta t$ corresponds to the option portfolio of equation (18.23), but at $T - \Delta t$ the market maker also has an option on the payment of date T which is itself a portfolio of options. In this case, rather than having a compound option, we have an option on a portfolio of options. Valuation of an option on a portfolio of options is difficult to handle analytically, but as long as we know the dynamics that govern the swap payments in the default-free case as well as when default occurs, we can use Monte Carlo analysis.

18.6. Summary

We have developed methods to evaluate credit risks for individual risky claims, for portfolios of risky claims, and for derivatives. The Merton model allows us to price risky debt by viewing it as risk-free debt minus a put written on the firm issuing the debt. The Merton model is practical mostly for simple capital structures with one debt issue that has no coupons. Other approaches to pricing risky debt model the probability of default and then discount the risky cash flows from debt using a risk-neutral distribution of the probability of default. Credit risk models such as the CreditRisk+ model, the CreditMetrics™ model, and the KMV model provide approaches to estimating the VaR for a portfolio of credits. Credit derivatives can be used to hedge credit risks.

Key Concepts

credit default swap, 597
credit event, 596
credit risk, 572
credit spread, 575
CreditMetrics™, 588
KMV model, 595

loss given default (LGD), 589
obligors, 589
rating transition matrix, 592
recovery rate, 593
vulnerable option, 599

Review Questions

1. Why is equity an option?

2. Why are you doing the equivalent of writing a put when you buy risky debt?

3. What is Merton's model for the pricing of debt?

4. What is a compound option?

5. How can you use the risk-neutral distribution of default to price coupon debt?

6. Why is it not reasonable to estimate the VaR of a portfolio of debt using 1.65 times the volatility of the return of the portfolio?

7. What is CreditRisk+?

8. What is CreditMetrics™?

9. What is a credit-default swap?

10. Why is it more difficult to evaluate the credit risk of a swap than to evaluate the credit risk of a risky zero-coupon bond?

Questions and Exercises

1. Debt can be priced using the Merton model. You are told that an increase in the volatility of firm value can increase the value of senior discount debt on the firm because in some cases debt is like equity and equity increases in value as firm volatility increases. Is this argument correct?

2. Consider a firm with a debt payment due in five years. The debt is not traded, so that firm value does not correspond to a traded asset. The assumptions that make the Merton model work hold. The longest maturity option traded on the firm's equity matures in one year. Assume that you know the volatility of the return of the firm and you know the firm value. How could you form a portfolio strategy that pays the same amount as the debt in five years?

   Extra credit: Provide portfolio weights if firm value volatility is 50 percent, interest rate is constant at 5 percent, firm value is $1 billion, and face value of debt is $1.2 billion.

3. Given your answer in question 2, what are the implications for your portfolio strategy of an unexpected increase in the firm's stock price caused by an increase in firm value?

   Extra credit: Using the data of the previous question, show how the portfolio changes if equity value increases by 10 percent because of a change in firm value.

4. Assume again that the assumptions that make the Merton model work hold, except that the firm pays a known dividend before maturity of its only debt, which is discount debt. How can you quantify the impact of a known future dividend payment on the value of discount debt?

   Extra credit: Using the data in the extra credit portion of question 3, assume a dividend payment of $100 million in three years. What is the impact of that payment on firm value?

5. Suppose that you compute a one-year VaR of a portfolio using the delta-VaR approach. The assumptions that make the Merton model work hold. You want to include in your VaR computation discount debt that matures in sixteen months. Somebody points out to you that your VaR computation has a significant probability that the discount debt will pay more than par. Is that right?

6. Attending a conference on credit risk, an attendee tells you that he computes the probability of default for a firm as the cumulative normal that multiplies $P_t(T)F$ in equation (18.3). Has he discovered a better mousetrap or does he have a biased estimate of the probability of default? If he has a biased estimate, what is the bias?

   Extra credit: Using the data from question 3, compute the probability of default and the expected loss for the debt. How does your answer differ from the one proposed by the conference attendee?

7. At the same conference, you find an old friend. She emphatically declares that, since her firm does not mark loans to market, she uses CreditRisk+

because CreditMetrics™ would be useless for her. What arguments could you make for her to use CreditMetrics™?

8. You are told by your boss that there is no reason for your bank to use a credit risk model because the bank has thousands of obligors, so that default risk is diversifiable. Is this argument correct if Merton's model applies to each of the obligors?

9. In an advertisement for credit derivatives, it is argued that the benefit of a credit default swap for the protection seller is that he "earns investment income with no funding cost."[6] How would you analyze the impact on a bank of selling credit protection through a credit default swap?

10. You want to enter a swap with a bank. The bank does not want to make the trade because their credit risk model implies that the swap has too much credit risk. The bank agrees to enter the swap if it is marked to market, but your boss objects to such an arrangement. Why does the bank find such an arrangement more agreeable than a swap that is not marked to market? What arguments could your boss have to reject the arrangement?

Literature Note

Black and Scholes (1973) had a brief discussion of the pricing of risky debt. Merton (1974) provides a detailed analysis of the pricing of risky debt using the Black-Scholes approach. Black and Cox (1976) derive additional results, including the pricing of subordinated debt and the pricing of debt with some covenants. Geske (1977) demonstrates how to price coupon debt using the compound option approach. Stulz and Johnson (1985) show the pricing of secured debt. Longstaff and Schwartz (1995) extend the model so that default takes place if firm value falls below some threshold. Their model takes into account interest rate risk as well as the possibility that strict priority rules will not be respected. Amin and Jarrow (1992) price risky debt in the presence of interest rates changing randomly using the Black-Scholes approach with a version of the Heath-Jarrow-Morton model.

Duffie and Singleton (1999) provide a detailed overview and extensions of the approaches that model the probability of default. Applications of this approach show that it generally works quite well. Perhaps the easiest application to follow is the work of Das and Tufano (1996). They extract probabilities of default from historical data on changes in credit ratings. Armed with these probabilities and with historical evidence on recovery rates and their correlations with interest rates, they price corporate debt. Instead of using historical estimates of default probabilities and recovery rates, they could have extracted these parameters from credit spreads and their study discusses how this could be done. Jarrow and Turnbull (1995) build an arbitrage model of risky debt where the probability of default can be obtained from the firm's credit spread curve. Jarrow, Lando, and Turnbull (1997) provide a general approach using credit ratings. Another

---

6 Barclays Capital, "Applying credit derivatives to emerging markets," Credit Risk Special Report, Advertising Supplement, *Risk*, November 1998.

interesting application is Duffie and Singleton (1997), who use this approach to price credit spreads embedded in swaps. Madan and Unal (1998) price securities of savings and loan associations. They show how firm-specific information can be incorporated in the default probabilities.

These various approaches to pricing risky claims have rather weak corporate finance underpinnings. They ignore the fact that firms act differently when their value falls and that they can bargain with creditors. Several recent papers take strategic actions of the debtor into account. Leland (1994) models the firm in an intertemporal setting taking into account taxes and the ability to change volatility. Anderson and Sundaresan (1996) take into account the ability of firms to renegotiate on the value of the debt. Deviations from the doctrine of absolute priority by the courts are described in Eberhart, Moore, and Roenfeldt (1990).

Crouhy, Galai, and Mark (2000) provide an extensive comparative analysis of the CreditRisk+, CreditMetrics™, and KMV models. Gordy (2000) provides evidence on the performance of the first two of these models. Jarrow and Turnbull (2000) critique these models and develop an alternative. Johnson and Stulz (1987) were the first to analyze vulnerable options. A number of papers provide formulas and approaches to analyzing the credit risk of derivatives. Jarrow and Turnbull (1995) provide an approach consistent with the use of the HJM model. Jarrow and Turnbull (1997) show how the approach can be implemented to price the risks of swaps.

The CME-QBT contract is discussed in Arditti and Curran (1998). Longstaff and Schwartz (1995) show how to value credit derivatives.

Chapter 19

Recent Developments in the Practice of Risk Management

Chapter **19** Objectives

At the end of this chapter, you will:

1. Know how LTCM got in trouble.

2. Be able to avoid pitfalls in risk management.

3. Be able to evaluate your risk measurement process.

4. Know how new accounting rules affect derivatives.

5. Know about the empirical evidence on derivatives uses by corporations.

The failure of LTCM in 1998 had an extremely significant impact on thinking about risk management. We examine what happened at LTCM and discuss some of the implications for risk management. We review the operational risk of risk management in the second section of the chapter and discuss how to measure it. Operational risk refers to failures in implementation.

LTCM's failure prompted a number of proposals for risk measures different from VaR and CaR or for complementing them. We consider how a firm would evaluate the performance of its VaR or CaR measure and then discuss alternate risk measures that have been proposed.

Innovations in risk management take place every day. Regulations that affect risk management change over time. New products are developed. Statistical techniques improve. Data become available, and contracting arrangements are refined. We review the current state of regulation and discuss its implications for risk management practice in section 19.4. We present evidence on the practice of risk management in general in section 19.5.

19.1. Long-Term Capital Management (LTCM)

In the 1980s, the investment banking firm of Salomon Brothers made large amounts of money through its proprietary trading, most of it from its bond arbitrage group headed by John Merriwether. The group rarely, if at all, engaged in transactions that would meet our academic definition of arbitrage. The positions were built to take advantage of discrepancies between the prices of two securities, and hedges were put on to reduce risks, but there was always some element of risk in the positions taken. Such positions are called "convergence trades" since they are built on the expectation that the prices of two securities will move closer together.

A typical position for the arbitrage group might involve a Government National Mortgage Association (GNMA), or Ginnie Mae, security. The typical Ginnie Mae issue is a security that passes through to the investors the payments made on a pool of mortgages (minus a spread) and is called a Ginnie Mae pass-through certificate. A private issuer—for example, a mortgage company—will put together a pool of mortgages that are government insured or guaranteed. It will then issue securities that give a right to the interest and principal payments from this pool of mortgages. These securities are backed by the full faith and credit of the U.S. government.

A Ginnie Mae pass-through has no default risk because the payment of principal and interest is guaranteed. By stripping the embedded prepayment options of the underlying mortgages from the pass-through, one can create a synthetic portfolio of Treasury bonds that should have a yield that does not exceed the yield of a comparable portfolio of Treasury bonds by more than compensation for the transaction costs involved in creating the synthetic portfolio and shorting the comparable portfolio of Treasury bonds. If the yield on the synthetic portfolio is sufficiently higher than the yield on the matching portfolio of Treasury bonds, an arbitrage opportunity develops.

Salomon held a long position in the synthetic portfolio and a short position in the matching portfolio of Treasury bonds to capture the difference in cash flows between the two portfolios. As a result, it was long Ginnie Mae pass-throughs and short government bonds. If the yield of the synthetic portfolio fell as the price of the synthetic T-bond and the price of the actual T-bond became closer to each other, Salomon would realize a capital gain because the synthetic portfolio would gain in value. The short position in government bonds provides funds to Salomon to implement the strategy and hedged the strategy against changes in interest rates.

Salomon's strategy had little interest rate risk because of the offsetting bond positions. It generated cash because of the difference in coupons, and any narrowing of the spreads would create a capital gain. If the spreads were to widen, however, the marked-to-market value of the position would fall.

While the arbitrage group was making its large profits, there was controversy within Salomon as to the amount of capital used by the group. The group thought it was using little capital since its positions had limited risk. At the same time, however, the rest of the firm thought the capital charge of the group should be high. The profitability of the group was inversely related to the capital allocated to it since it was charged for allocated capital. In 1998, a former Salomon partner was quoted as saying that the bond arbitrage group "was never really profitable, but created the illusion of profitability by creating the illusion it wasn't using much capital."[1]

Eventually, Merriwether left Salomon and founded Long-Term Capital Management (LTCM) to manage a hedge fund, the Long-Term Capital Fund. LTCM was designed to pursue the strategies that the arbitrage group at Salomon Brothers had implemented. Hedge funds are managed pools of money not subject to the regulations controlling mutual funds in the United States. A hedge fund can have only a limited number of investors who meet stringent wealth requirements. Hedge fund management companies typically charge a fee for managing the fund and operate under incentive contracts paying the management a fraction of the profits, often 20 percent. Two famous financial economists—Robert Merton and Myron Scholes, who with Fischer Black are the fathers of derivatives pricing theory—became partners of LTCM.

LTCM was very successful in its first two full years of operations, earning net returns of 43 percent in 1995 and 41 percent in 1996. Figure 19.1 shows the monthly returns of the Fund. Except in 1998, LTCM never had two consecutive months of losses; it operated for as long as 19 months in a row without making a loss. In 1997, its net returns were lower, amounting to 17 percent. At the beginning of 1998, the Long-Term Capital Fund had capital of about $7.4 billion. Had the Fund had half its amount of capital in 1997, its return would have been 34 percent.

To try to recapture results similar to those of 1995 and 1996, LTCM decided to reduce the amount of capital of the fund, returning to investors $2.7 billion.

---

[1] Michelle Celarier, "Citigroup: The last days of Salomon Brothers," *Euromoney*, December 1998, 10–12.

Figure 19.1	The returns of the Long-Term Capital Fund

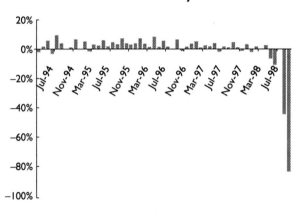

Each dollar of capital was used to borrow roughly $25 after the reduction in the amount of fund capital. The notional amount of its derivatives positions exceeded $1 trillion dollars, but that amount was misleading. Instead of closing swaps, LTCM's practice was to enter an offsetting swap because doing so was generally cheaper since LTCM could seek the best deal on the market. Hence, if it had swaps with $100 billion notional amount and wanted to offset their payoffs, it ended up with $200 billion notional amount of derivatives even though functionally it had no net swap position since all swaps had an offsetting swap. In the summer of 1998, the Fund had convergence trades in a wide variety of markets: Italian bonds, Danish mortgages, U.S. T-bonds, Russian bonds, U.S. stocks and mortgage bonds, Latin American bonds, British bonds, and U.S. swaps.

LTCM wanted volatility not to exceed 20 percent per year. We can compute a monthly 5 percent VaR based on this target assuming normally distributed returns. This VaR is $448 million. The Fund had a loss of $460 million in June 1998. On August 17, Russia restructured its debt, forcing a conversion of its domestic debt securities for new securities with less advantageous terms. On August 21, the Fund lost $551 million in a day. It lost $1.85 billion in the entire month of August. The probability of a loss of such magnitude with normally distributed returns was essentially zero. By the end of August, investors in the Fund had lost more than half of their investment at the beginning of the year, and the leverage ratio had climbed to $50 of assets per $1 of capital. In the first three weeks of September 1998, the Fund lost half a billion dollars per week.

On September 23, the Federal Reserve Bank of New York intervened because it thought that a collapse of the Fund would seriously endanger the financial system. It assembled 14 major banks, which decided to invest $3.6 billion in the Fund. As part of the deal, these banks obtained a 90 percent stake in LTCM. By September 28, the investors had lost 92 percent of their investment at the beginning of the year, and the partners had lost $1.9 billion. Because investors had taken money out of the Fund earlier and some investors had cashed out altogether, most investors who were not partners earned more than the risk-free rate from their investment despite the collapse of the Fund.

The losses of the Fund in August and September of 1998 had essentially a probability of zero of happening, yet they happened. VaR is not designed to estimate the worst possible outcome. Low-probability events happen. If low-probability events happen often, though, there is something wrong with the measurement system. The one-week 5 percent VaR based on an annual volatility of 20 percent and capital of $4.7 billion is $215 million. The fund exceeded this one-week VaR five weeks in a row. With independent weekly returns, such an event has probability of 0.0000003 of occurring.

There are four reasons why VaR estimates for the Fund assuming normally distributed returns with distribution parameters estimated using historical data were biased downward in late August and September 1998:

1. **Fat tails.** There is considerable evidence that large positive and negative daily returns occur more frequently for financial data than one would expect with the normal distribution. This evidence implies that extreme returns—the tails of the density function—have higher probabilities than with the normal distribution. When extreme returns have higher probabilities than with the normal distribution, we say the distribution has **fat tails**. In August and September 1998, large returns occurred repeatedly. This means VaRs were exceeded for large investment banks as well as for the Fund. We discuss in section 3 the implications of fat tails for VaR estimation.

2. **Correlations.** LTCM thought its various trades had uncorrelated outcomes, producing low volatility because of the extensive benefits of diversification. As previously described, the convergence trades were often in different countries and involved different types of assets. However, in August and September 1998 correlations increased dramatically—seemingly unrelated positions all moved in the same direction. In fact, safe and liquid assets increased in value and less safe and less liquid assets lost value across the board. Most of the trades of the Fund were short the safe bonds and long bonds LTCM thought were worth more and had less risk than the market thought. The long positions fell in value at the same time that the bonds sold short increased in value.

3. **Volatilities.** Return volatilities on many financial securities increased sharply towards the end of August. This increase was sharp enough that estimating volatilities using historical data would have understated true volatilities. The RiskMetrics™ approach that puts more weight on recent observations would have understated true volatilities less than an approach that weighs all observations equally, but it would still have understated true volatilities.

4. **Liquidity.** Returns are computed from recorded prices, either transaction prices or indicative quotes. Whether prices are obtained from transactions or quotes, they correspond to typical trade sizes. If markets are liquid, large quantities can be traded without having much of an impact on prices. If we cannot trade out of a portfolio without having a substantial

market impact when we liquidate a portfolio, the VaR can substantially underestimate the risk of the portfolio.

To understand how liquidity can bias VaR estimates, suppose it is highly likely that a large negative return is associated with a drop in liquidity, which means that to liquidate the portfolio, a large price concession is required. The drop in liquidity magnifies the impact of the large negative return on the true value of the portfolio. As a result, the 5 percent VaR underestimates the true loss that is exceeded only with a probability of 5 percent because it ignores the fact that the market impact of trades increases as prices fall.

Suppose an asset was quoted at $10 bid yesterday. It falls 10 percent today, so that the bid for typical trade sizes becomes $9. At the same time, the liquidity of the market for the asset also has fallen, so that an additional concession of 2 percent may be required to make a large trade. Consequently, the return is not really −10 percent if we want to liquidate the portfolio, but −12 percent. The possibility of this additional 2 percent loss is not taken into account in estimates of the distribution of returns using historical data for typical transaction sizes. If there is randomness in the price concession, possibly because the price concession is greater with worse returns as in our example, the volatility of the liquidation value of the position depends on the distribution of the price concession.

In August and September 1998, LTCM could not liquidate positions without affecting prices dramatically. The valuation of the Fund at "screen prices"—the prices recorded by data services that typically reflect bid and ask or transaction prices for small trades—no longer provided a good estimate of the value of positions that were liquidated. As trades were made to reduce the size of the positions, the Fund would lose money because of the market impact of the trades. Dealers would be reluctant to buy from LTCM because they worried that more trades would be coming their way, leading to adverse returns and excess inventory. It was even the case that dealers would not buy today because they thought LTCM would be more desperate later. The problem was worsened by a general flight to quality, making investors and banks reluctant to take on risky positions. Despite all these problems, though, LTCM did very well at managing the details of its business—it never missed a margin call.

Had LTCM (1) accounted for fat tails, (2) taken into account the possibility of increases in correlations, and (3) worried more about liquidity, it would have had more capital or less risk. Even then, such adjustments would not have produced an amount of capital large enough for LTCM to survive. The conjunction of events that took place in August and September 1998 was extremely unusual, it was so unusual that the Secretary of the Treasury stated that "the world is now experiencing the worst financial crisis in 50 years."[2]

If capital is expensive, one would not expect firms to have so much capital that they would never fail. If LTCM had substantially more capital, its performance would not have been stellar in 1995 and 1996. Consequently, it may have made

---

2 Michael Lewis, "How the eggheads cracked," *New York Times Magazine*, January 21, 1999, 30.

perfect sense for LTCM to incur the small risk of things going really wrong to have a large probability of outperforming the market. The same Salomon partner had this to say about LTCM: "If they had been running the operation with $8 billion of equity, which they needed, they wouldn't have been earning 41% returns, but more like 18% or 19%, which would have meant that they did about half as well as the stock market."[3]

The LTCM story is a lesson that it is difficult for everybody to understand how markets change. Statistical analysis is no substitute for economic and financial analysis. To forecast VaR, we have to understand how markets function and how they change over time. We must always try to see whether historical relations still hold or have been altered through innovation. However, risk measurement can go wrong in more pedestrian ways.

19.2. The operational risk of risk management

The **operational risk** of risk management is the risk that things go wrong in the implementation of a risk management measurement system and strategy. We focus on this risk in the context of risk management focused on VaR.

19.2.1. Steps in implementation of VaR

Suppose we decide to use the RiskMetrics™ approach to estimate VaR. The steps to compute a daily VaR using RiskMetrics™ are:

Step 1. Inventory. The firm has to produce an inventory of all the financial positions in the portfolio whose VaR it is trying to estimate.

Step 2. Valuation. Once the firm knows its financial positions, it has to value them. It may have market prices for some positions, but other positions may not have market values and prices might have to be computed using a pricing model.

Step 3. Assignment to RiskMetrics™ assets. Each security in the portfolio has to be approximated by a RiskMetrics™ asset or a portfolio of such assets. This assignment is simple in some cases and complicated in others. A major problem is to decide how derivatives should be treated. To use the parametric VaR (1.65 times portfolio volatility), the firm has to use the delta method. In this case, a derivative can be represented as a position of delta units of the underlying asset, and the underlying asset can be matched to a RiskMetrics™ asset.

Step 4. Computation. After assignment, the firm has transformed its portfolio of financial positions into a portfolio of RiskMetrics™ assets. It can then compute the variance of this new portfolio using the RiskMetrics™ dataset and the formula for the variance of a portfolio. Having obtained the variance of the portfolio, the firm's volatility is the square root of the firm's variance, and the VaR at the 95 percent level is 1.65 times the firm's volatility. The firm therefore has a VaR estimate.

---

[3] Michelle Celarier, "Citigroup: The last days of Salomon Brothers," *Euromoney*, December 1998, 12.

This is a straightforward procedure, but in practice many decisions can affect the outcome in important ways.

19.2.2. What can go wrong with implementation?

Let's consider in turn how VaR estimates could differ across identical firms because of implementation difficulties in each of the four steps.

19.2.2.A. Inventory problems

Computing the risk of the trading positions of a firm involves taking into account both positions that are on the firm's balance sheet and those that are not. If a firm has an off-balance sheet swap, the swap is part of the inventory because it contributes to or detracts from firm value; its cash flows add or detract from firm cash flows. The firm must therefore devise a system that can collect the required information from all its trading desks. This process is often made difficult by software and hardware differences across departments in many firms. The mortgage-trading desk may use a Unix platform, while the bond-trading desk may use a Windows NT platform.

The inventory process apparently played a role in the loss of independence of one of the world's largest banks in 1997. In the fall of 1997, Union Bank of Switzerland (UBS) felt compelled to merge with another large bank, Swiss Bank Corporation (SBC). Although UBS was in many ways the larger bank, this was no merger of equals. SBC executives ended up with almost all the top positions in the new bank, United Bank of Switzerland. Analysts since then have attributed the weakened position of UBS to large derivative losses in its worldwide equity derivatives operation. The Bank had little understanding of its exposures to equity derivatives as a result of poor inventory at the Bank level. Though the operating units knew their inventory and the resulting exposures, this information was not adequately aggregated at the Bank level, so that the Bank had an incomplete understanding of its exposures.

There were at least two reasons for this problem. One reason was that the Bank had shifted in the early 1990s to a geographically decentralized model. Collecting information in a timely manner from regional organizations proved difficult. Another reason is that the equity derivatives group, which was organized on a worldwide basis, contributed a substantial fraction of the profits of the Bank. This gave the head of the group more leeway to do things his way. Unfortunately for the Bank, he was an enthusiast of the Next operating system, that was unused and unknown in the rest of the Bank. As a result of these differences in operating systems, however, it was not possible to incorporate records of positions from the equity derivatives unit in firm-wide assessments of the Bank's exposures.

The greatest difficulty in implementation arises because firms ultimately obtain the data from individuals. Individuals can misunderstand positions, can forget about positions, or can even hide positions. Such risks are called operational risks. Consider the case of Barings Bank that we already talked about several times. A key part of the Barings Bank disaster was that Nicholas Leeson was able to hide losses in an account that the firm viewed as an account used for the reconciliation of small trading errors. Box 19.1, Account 88888, describes the history of this account in more detail. The inventory process of Barings Bank failed in that it produced an inaccurate record of the firm's positions.

Account 88888   *Box 19.1*

After his trading day was done on Simex, Leeson was in charge of the back office. He had to deal with 37 different accounts. Once positions were entered into Barings Futures' computer system, they were communicated to Simex. If Simex showed that Barings had different futures positions from those Barings thought it had, Barings would have to enter the compensating positions the next day. The gains and/or losses from doing this would be put in suspense account 99905. The problem is that this process was not taking place smoothly: The Simex computers would often crash, making it impossible for Barings to know what its correct situation was. This made activity in account 99905 complicated and messy. This activity was communicated to London each day, but on July 3, 1992, Gordon Bowser, head of futures and options settlement at the London office, decided that the settlement software could not cope with all the errors taking place in Singapore that might simply be due to crashes of Simex computers. He therefore asked Leeson to no longer provide information on minor errors. Leeson replied that he would create a new account to contain minor errors. He asked a secretary what her lucky number was. She said 8. The new account received number 88888 since Simex accounts had five numbers.

On August 18, disaster struck. A clerk took an order for a trade and thought it was for a sale of 20 Nikkei futures contracts when it was for a purchase. Unfortunately, the Nikkei increased sharply during the day. To rectify the mistake would cost £18,000. Leeson decided to hide this cost in account 88888 and hoped to make profits to cover it eventually. He would not have to report the balance of account 88888 until the end of the month. At the end of the month, however, because he was in charge of settlement, he could transfer money from customer accounts into account 88888 for a couple of days to reduce the balance of 88888, thereby burying the problem. Eventually, everything that went wrong got put in 88888. Much went wrong because Leeson was overly aggressive in trading to get business for the firm—essentially, he was giving money away to customers and financed the gifts out of 88888. By fall 1993, he had £5.5 million in hidden losses. He needed an inflow of cash to finance these losses since he would need to have a small end-of-month balance in the account. To solve his problem, Leeson had a brilliant solution. He started arbitrage trades between Osaka and Simex contracts. He realized that London thought that an arbitrage trade required twice the margin payment: Once in Osaka and once on Simex. London did not know that Simex encouraged arbitrage between the two markets by allowing a netting of margin. Hence, as the arbitrage grew, it generated huge inflows of cash from London. Only part of that cash was required for margin deposits. The rest could be parked in 88888.

Source: John Gapper and Nicholas Denton, "How Nick Leeson bought friends and favour," *Financial Times*, September 18, 1996, 8.

To prevent such a problem, firms implement procedures that make it harder to conceal transactions. A key procedure is that the person who does the trading is not the person who does the settlement. In this way the settlement and trading records have to agree. It then becomes harder for a trader to alter the trading record and disguise transactions because all his trades are settled by somebody else. At Barings, Leeson was in charge both of the trading and the back office.

An important difficulty with inventory taking is that new products are created all the time. What if a new exotic option becomes available that has never traded before? In a computerized inventory system, there may be no place for this exotic option until the system has been adapted. Hence, if a trader takes a position in that option before the system is ready, it could happen that the firm may not know about it. One way firms deal with this issue is to institute an approval process for new securities. A trader is then not allowed to take a position in a new security until that security has been incorporated in the firm's systems.

19.2.2.B. Valuation problems

It is easy to assign values to positions for financial instruments that are traded constantly on financial markets. All one has to do is find the price of the financial instrument on financial markets at the precise time that we want to value it. If a firm has a large position in IBM stock and the firm is marked to market at 4:00 P.M., all that is needed to value the position is to find the price of IBM stock at 4:00 P.M. It is harder when financial instruments are not frequently traded. A firm might have a large position in barrier options on the DM for which no financial data vendor provides prices. The firm has to estimate the value of these barrier options, which requires the use of a pricing model. Which model? Traders often use proprietary models to construct their trading strategies. Can the firm use these models? Not typically. When they do, this may create problems. As *Business Week* reports for the case of Enron, "Traders made unrealistic assumptions about future commodity prices so that their deals would look more profitable and their bonuses would be bigger." Traders are rewarded not for the quality of their pricing models but for the profits they make. They also rely on other information and it is perfectly possible for a trader to make large profits with a poor pricing model. Pricing also requires assumptions. In option pricing models, the assumptions about volatility are crucial. A trader's models may make assumptions about volatility that differ from the assumptions made by the risk manager. Traders might further be tempted to make assumptions that justify their intuition about profitable trades.

To value a portfolio for the purpose of risk management, a firm must use a pricing model that incorporates the same assumptions about volatility as the assumptions used to compute the VaR. Box 19.2, NatWest's £50 million loss, shows that differences in valuation between trader models and the models of risk managers can be far from trivial.

Differences in valuation also yield differences in delta. First, different pricing models yield different deltas. For example, one firm might compute European stock index option prices using Merton's formula for options on stock paying a constant dividend. Another firm might allow for jumps in index prices. Starting from the same stock index return volatility, the two firms would have different option prices and different option deltas. Option prices can differ for many other reasons. Firms might use different risk-free rates, or use prices of the underlying index computed at different points during the day.

The Bank of England has surveyed how financial institutions value derivatives. One survey asked 40 institutions to report valuations of various interest rate and

NatWest's £50 million loss   *Box 19.2*

At the beginning of March 1997, the British bank NatWest announced a £50 million loss from trading in options. A 30-year-old option trader, Mr. Kyriacos Papouis, was held responsible for the loss. Mr. Papouis immediately hired the lawyer used by Leeson of Barings. Yet, Mr. Papouis had not committed fraud and had not concealed anything from anybody.

Mr. Papouis was one of five European swaps and options traders in a 60 traders derivatives group. The options he was trading were traded over the counter. They were mostly caps and floors. To determine the price, he would use a pricing model, NatWest's pricing model. To implement the pricing model, he would input a volatility estimate. After having made a trade, the trade was checked by the bank's "middle office," which was composed of controllers who would make sure that the price was fair to the bank. Despite this safeguard, NatWest's investigators eventually concluded that Mr. Papouis overestimated the price of options for over a year. As a result, NatWest ended up with a portfolio that was erroneously valued.

How was it possible for these pricing mistakes to last for such a long period? Part of the problem was that the volatility estimates were out of line, but not so much that the trader could not justify them. Options that are out-of-the-money are particularly illiquid. To price them, one has to take into account the biases in the models used to price options. If models tend to underprice out-of-money options, it is common to adjust the volatility to get more accurate prices. A trader can therefore construct a plausible story to justify his option prices. There is no easy way for a risk manager to check the trader's story. The risk manager can try to get outside price estimates from brokers. In the absence of a liquid market and of a willingness of the risk manager to buy or sell at those prices, the prices obtained from brokers may not be more credible than those of the trader. Also, doing this can be complicated and time consuming.

When NatWest finally realized that there was a problem and revalued the portfolio, the loss was sizable. Yet, all that happened is that valuation is not enough of a science to eliminate the role of human beings and different human beings end up with different prices. A Swiss bank took a trader to court, claiming that he misvalued an options book by $60 million. The bank lost. A risk management specialist quoted in the newspaper article that reports the NatWest loss says: "There is a thin line between optimistic pricing, and a simple difference of opinion on what a price should be."

Source: John Gapper, "When the smile is wiped off," *The Financial Times*, March 8/March 9, 1997.

currency derivatives as of 4:15 P.M. on December 4, 1996, assuming a double-A counterparty. The results are striking. For plain vanilla derivatives, there was generally little disagreement. For a 10-month at the money sterling/deutschmark straddle, the percentage standard deviation of values was 2.7 percent. Yet, the percentage standard deviation of deltas was almost twice the percentage standard deviation of values. For double-barrier knock-out options on sterling/deutschmark (the option gets knocked out at each barrier), the volatility of values was an astonishing 66.1 percent. Similar results were obtained for the interest rate derivatives, namely, low dispersion of values for plain vanilla derivatives but much higher dispersion for more exotic instruments. It is not surprising, therefore, that when a firm decides to change its valuation model for some derivatives, the value of the book can change substantially. Financial institutions can fall in the trap of viewing models as black boxes and conclude that, because the computer says that this is the value, this must be the value. Models can fail, and valuation software is subject to bugs. There are even traders who call themselves "bug hunters," and attempt to trade with traders whose software they know to have bugs.

19.2.2.C. Assignment problems and VaR computation problems
Most firms have a great number of different financial positions. A firm that has positions in 50,000 different financial assets has to choose for each asset a comparable RiskMetrics™ asset or a comparable portfolio of such assets. With derivatives, the underlyings have to be matched to RiskMetrics™ assets.

Suppose two firms have the same portfolios and the same RiskMetrics™ inputs. Their VaRs could differ because of different valuation models for their derivatives. Their VaRs also could differ because of different assignments to RiskMetrics™ assets and different computation methods for the VaR. This raises the question as to whether problems with implementing RiskMetrics™ can lead to significantly different VaR estimates for firms with the same portfolios.

Marshall and Siegel (1997) asked vendors whose products make it possible to compute a VaR using RiskMetrics™ to obtain VaR estimates for several portfolios. They received responses from six vendors.

The simplest portfolio is a portfolio of forward exchange rate contracts. The standard deviation of the VaR estimates as a fraction of the median VaR produced by the vendors was an extremely low 1 percent. There were greater differences for portfolios of government bonds and swaps. The portfolio of government bonds had a median valuation from the vendors of $357 million with a median VaR of $3.8 million. The standard deviation of the VaRs was $652,762 or 17 percent of the median VaR. The standard deviation of VaRs of the portfolio of swaps was 21 percent of the median valuation. A foreign exchange option portfolio and interest rate option portfolio had VaR standard deviations relative to median valuations of 25 and 23 percent, respectively.

Marshall and Siegel also asked the vendors to produce the equivalent of a whole firm VaR by considering the VaR of a portfolio formed by adding up the more specialized portfolios. The whole firm VaR differences are quite large. The median VaR for the whole firm portfolio is $4,306,162. The VaR standard deviation as a fraction of the median VaR is 25 percent. The VaR standard deviation is an especially large 75 percent of the median VaR when the VaR of the nonlinear components of the portfolio is computed. It would be surprising if such large differences would be observed today for such an experiment because vendors of risk management products have acquired a lot more experience and bugs have been weeded out. Unfortunately, the study of Marshall and Siegel has not been replicated more recently. However, it is still the case that estimates of VaR can differ substantially when using different vendors.

19.3. Is it the right risk measure?

Choices of the implementer are significant in implementing RiskMetrics™ or any other approach to estimating risk. Managers must make decisions and inputs have to be procured. They can produce the wrong VaR because they have made the wrong decisions or obtained invalid inputs. If a firm cannot measure and value its portfolio with reasonable accuracy, its VaR will be of poor quality.

If a firm computes a 95 percent delta-VaR using RiskMetrics™ with no implementation errors, what could be wrong? Recognize that the firm assumes crucially that RiskMetrics™ provides the correct forecast of the variance-covariance matrix, that returns are normally distributed, and that the delta approach is appropriate over short intervals. In fact, the firm could be fooled because it has made the wrong assumptions in computing VaR and think it has little risk. Consider a firm using delta-VaR when its books have straddles. The delta of a straddle can be zero, leading the firm to believe that it has no risk. Yet the assumptions made ignore the fact that firm value can change by a large amount if there is a large price move or a jump in volatility. The problem the firm faces is that the delta-VaR model may be an inappropriate model because of the nature of the firm's positions. The VaR the firm computes might be perfectly appropriate if the firm had no derivatives, for example. Alternatively, a firm could compute the VaR of its securities marked to market correctly, but this measure would not be the right measure of risk for the firm because most of its assets are illiquid and not marked to market, so that the firm might face financial distress if it has a poor cash flow.

Several studies compare portfolio VaRs computed using different approaches. Hendricks (1996) focuses on plain vanilla foreign currency positions and finds that VaR estimates have a standard deviation around the mean of 10 percent to 15 percent, suggesting that differences of 30 percent between VaRs produced using different approaches would not be surprising. Beder (1995) investigates eight different methods of computing VaR for portfolios with derivatives. She finds that the highest VaR estimate can be 6 to 14 times greater than the lowest VaR estimate.

There are many reasons why a VaR estimate might not be very good. It is therefore necessary to audit how VaR is produced and how well it does. The same applies for CaR or any other risk measure. It also is necessary to understand what the strengths and weaknesses of the risk measures we use are. We provide some tools to monitor VaR estimates in section 19.3.1. In section 19.3.2, we explore the sensitivity of VaR estimates to assumptions about the distribution of returns. In section 19.3.3, we discuss other statistics that can be valuable to cope with the limitations of VaR and alternate risk measures.

19.3.1. VaR diagnostics

VaR is a statistical estimate. Like all statistical estimates, it is affected by sampling variation. Suppose that we estimate the VaR on a stock portfolio and that the return of the stock portfolio is i.i.d. If we estimate VaR using different periods to obtain the data, we will get different estimates. Consider the case where the return comes from a normal distribution and that the true dollar volatility of the portfolio is $100 million. For a normally distributed variable, the standard error of the volatility estimate is $\sigma(1/2T)^{0.5}$, where σ is the true volatility and T is the number of observations. Consider a firm that uses 1,000 days of returns to estimate a volatility. The true VaR is \$165 million. Using the formula for the standard error of the volatility estimate, we can construct a confidence interval and find that there is a 95 percent chance that the estimate the firm would obtain by using a period of 1,000 days as its sample would be below an upper bound of $1.65 \times (\$100M + 2 \times \$100M(1/2000)^{0.5})$, or \$172.379 million, and above a lower bound of \$157.621 million. We could therefore present our VaR estimate with a confidence interval. Note that if we had fewer observations, say one year, the interval would be wider with a lower bound of \$144.121 million and upper bound of \$185.871 million. So, with few observations, we cannot estimate VaR precisely. However, were we to know that the distribution is the normal distribution, then estimating the VaR from the historical standard deviation would be more efficient than using the historical method for VaR where we pick the 5th quantile of the historical distribution. Jorion (1995) shows that the standard error of the VaR historical method is larger than the standard error of the volatility-based estimate of VaR when we know the true distribution.

Unfortunately, we do not know the true distribution of the data. This suggests that we have to use ways to evaluate VaR estimates that do not rely on us assuming that we know this distribution. The VaR at 5 percent is the loss that has a 5 percent probability of being exceeded. The definition suggests a natural approach to check whether our estimates of VaR are unbiased estimates. For VaR at the x percent level, it should be the case that the percentage of exceedances (i.e., the percentage of times that we exceed VaR) should not be significantly different from x percent. The problem is that different samples will produce different results. If we have 100 daily VaR observations and compute the VaR at 5 percent, we might find eight exceedances or two. To know whether eight is too many, we need to know the distribution of exceedances and evaluate the probability of observing eight exceedances if the VaR estimates are unbiased. With an unbiased estimate, we should get 5 percent of the losses to exceed the VaR as the sample becomes large.

Let x be the decimal confidence level, so that for the VaR at 5 percent, x is 0.05. Let q be the decimal fraction of observations that exceed VaR. Each period, the VaR is either exceeded or it is not. If the true probability of exceedance is x, then the probability of observing ne exceedances out of N observations is given by the binomial distribution as:

Probability of *ne* exceedances out of N observations

if true probability of exceedance is *x*

$$x^{ne}(1 - x)^{N - ne} \tag{19.1}$$

Suppose we have N observations and ne exceedances. It has been shown that the quantity LR (likelihood ratio) follows a chi-squared distribution with one degree of freedom. This distribution is available on Excel under CHIDIST. The quantity LR is:

$$LR = 2\left[\ln\left(q^{ne}(1 - q)^{N - ne}\right) - \ln\left(x^{ne}(1 - x)^{N - ne}\right)\right] \tag{19.2}$$

Let's consider an example. Suppose that we compute the VaR at the 1 percent level. We have 250 daily observations and 5 exceedances. Consequently, LR is equal to:

$$\text{LR} = 2\left[\ln\left(0.02^5(1 - 0.02)^{250 - 5}\right) - \ln\left(0.01^5(1 - 0.01)^{250 - 5}\right)\right]$$

$$= 1.95681 \qquad\qquad (19.3)$$

Using Excel, we find that the probability of observing 1.95681 for a variable that follows the chi-squared distribution with one degree of freedom is 0.16. This means there is a probability of 0.16 that the exceedances come from a distribution where the probability of exceedance is 0.01. The conventional probability level required to reject the hypothesis that data are generated by a particular model is 0.05—we reject the hypothesis if the probability that the data is generated by the hypothesis is 0.05 or less. In this case, even though we have twice as many exceedances as expected, we cannot reject the hypothesis that the VaR is unbiased. In general, we can only reject the hypothesis that the VaR is unbiased when it is biased with either a large number of exceedances or a lot of data.

Panel A of Figure 19.2 shows the probability of observing a given number of exceedances out of 250 daily observations if the true probability of an exceedance is 0.01. We see that we can reject the hypothesis that the VaR is unbiased if we observe no exceedance or more than seven. In the range of one through six exceedances, we cannot reject the hypothesis that the VaR is unbiased with 250 observations.

In Panel B of Figure 19.2, we show the probability of observing 2 percent of exceedances if the true probability is 0.01. To reject the hypothesis that the VaR is unbiased if we get 2 percent of exceedances we need 491 observations, which is almost two years of data.

We can apply the test presented here to LTCM. If we estimate LTCM's VaR using the historical volatility and the normal distribution, it had at least five exceedances of its weekly VaR in 1998 before September 21. Using our test, we have $ne = 5$, $N = 38$, and $x = 0.05$. The LR is then 3.75, so there is a 0.052 probability that the true mean of the percentage of exceedances is 5 percent. Based on this statistic, the five exceedances that LTCM experienced would not have been sufficient to reject the hypothesis that the VaR estimates were unbiased.

This test for bias does not attempt to relate exceedances to information available when the VaR estimate is made. Suppose, however, that we find that the VaR is unbiased using this test, but that VaR exceedances are bunched together. They occur, for example, whenever volatilities are high. In this case, the VaR estimate would be biased conditional on the level of volatility. With high volatility, the VaR would be too low on average; it would be too high for low volatility. We could use this information to improve the VaR estimate. There are statistical tests that evaluate VaR conditionally.[4] If returns are independent, successive

---

4 See Christoffersen (1998) for such statistical tests.

Figure 19.2   Finding a bias in VaR estimates

Panel A gives the probability of observing five exceedances if the true probability of an exceedance is 0.01. Panel B gives the probability of observing 2 percent of exceedances if the true probability of an exceedance is 0.01 as a function of the number of observations.

Panel A

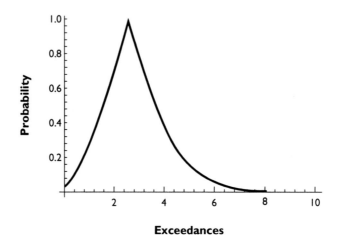

Panel B

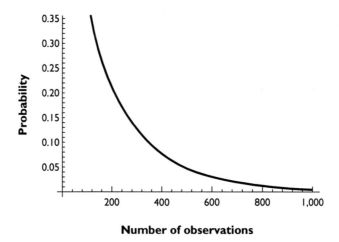

exceedances should be rare. Two exceedances in a row if VaR is computed correctly at the 5 percent level have a probability of occurring of 0.05×0.05, or 0.0025.

Such a test would have shown that the VaR estimate we used for LTCM based on historical volatility was not very good. The assumptions for VaR assume independent returns from one week to the next. Yet our VaR estimate for LTCM experienced five weekly exceedances in a row. The probability of observing five exceedances in a row with independent returns is 0.05^5, low enough to conclude that the distributional assumptions made to compute VaR were not correct.

19.3.2. Fat tails and the distribution of extreme returns

VaR could be biased because of implementation problems. If we miss assets in the inventory process, and these assets do not hedge the portfolio, we will understate VaR. VaR could be biased for a more fundamental reason if we are assuming the wrong distribution for the portfolio return.

Suppose that we assume returns to be normally distributed. We could have the wrong VaR because our estimates of the parameters of the distribution are poor. This could be because volatilities and expected returns change over time. We are using historical information accurately, but volatility has increased, and our VaR estimates are too low. With changing volatilities, our VaR estimates would be conditionally biased—too low when volatility has increased and too high when it has fallen. Changing correlations could lead to the same problems. Or, we simply have the wrong distribution because returns are not normal.

A good example of the inadequacy of the normal distribution as a representation of daily returns is the S&P 500 return on the day of the October 1987 crash. It was about 25 standard deviations away from the mean expected return. A move of 25 standard deviations from the mean has essentially a probability of zero with the normal distribution. Perhaps more importantly, moves of five standard deviations are not rare in financial markets (there were eight of them in the S&P 500 between 1986 and 1996). Yet, with the normal distribution, we would expect such a move every 10^{23} days, which means that we would expect such moves to almost never occur.[5]

A useful statistic for judging whether data comes from a normal distribution is the studentized range. Define x to be a random variable, x_i to be a realization of that random variable, and $Std(x)$ the standard deviation of the realizations in the sample. With this notation, the studentized range is:

$$SR = \frac{Max(x_i) - Min(x_i)}{Std(x)}$$

LTCM produced 54 monthly returns. The highest monthly return was 8.4 percent and the lowest was −83 percent. The standard deviation of monthly returns was 13 percent. The studentized range for LTCM is $(0.084 + 0.83)/0.13$, which is 7. If returns are normally distributed, Table 19.1 shows that there is a 95 percent chance that SR would be between 3.72 and 5.54 for 50 observations. We can therefore reject the hypothesis that the LTCM returns were normally distributed at the 95 percent confidence level (and at the 99.5 percent confidence level also).

Figure 19.3 provides some insights into the implication of fat tails for VaR estimates. It shows the left tail of the distributions of returns for the standardized normal distribution and for a distribution that exhibits fat tails, the Student's *t*

---

5 Duffie and Pan (1997) show the number of five standard deviations moves for the 1986 to 1996 period for a large number of financial assets. A statistic used to measure the fatness of the tails is called excess kurtosis. If x is a random variable, kurtosis is the expected value of $[x - E(x)]^4$. Kurtosis is equal to 3 for a normally distributed random variable. The excess kurtosis is the kurtosis minus 3.

Table 19.1   Fractiles SR(p, T) of the distribution of the studentized range in samples of size T from a normal population

Lower percentage Points (p)					Upper Percentage Points (p)					Size of Sample
0.005	0.01	0.025	0.050	0.10	0.90	0.95	0.975	0.99	0.995	T
					1.997	1.999	2.000	2.000	2.000	3
					2.409	2.429	2.439	2.445	2.447	4
					2.712	2.753	2.782	2.803	2.813	5
					2.949	3.012	3.056	3.095	3.115	6
					3.143	3.222	3.282	3.338	3.369	7
					3.308	3.399	3.471	3.543	3.585	8
					3.449	3.552	3.634	3.720	3.772	9
2.47	2.51	2.59	2.67	2.77	3.57	3.685	3.777	3.875	3.935	10
2.53	2.58	2.66	2.74	2.84	3.68	3.80	3.903	4.012	4.079	11
2.59	2.65	2.73	2.80	2.91	3.78	3.91	4.01	4.134	4.208	12
2.65	2.70	2.78	2.86	2.97	3.87	4.00	4.11	4.244	4.325	13
2.70	2.75	2.83	2.91	3.02	3.95	4.09	4.21	4.34	4.431	14
2.75	2.80	2.88	2.96	3.07	4.02	4.17	4.29	4.43	4.53	15
2.80	2.85	2.93	3.01	3.13	4.09	4.24	4.37	4.51	4.62	16
2.84	2.90	2.98	3.06	3.17	4.15	4.31	4.44	4.59	4.69	17
2.88	2.94	3.02	3.10	3.21	4.21	4.38	4.51	4.66	4.77	18
2.92	2.98	3.06	3.14	3.25	4.27	4.43	4.57	4.73	4.84	19
2.95	3.01	3.10	3.18	3.29	4.32	4.49	4.63	4.79	4.91	20
3.22	3.27	3.37	3.46	3.58	4.70	4.89	5.06	5.25	5.39	30
3.41	3.46	3.57	3.66	3.79	4.96	5.15	5.34	5.54	5.69	40
3.57	3.61	3.72	3.82	3.94	5.15	5.35	5.54	5.77	5.91	50
3.69	3.74	3.85	3.95	4.07	5.29	5.50	5.70	5.93	6.09	60
3.88	3.93	4.05	4.15	4.27	5.51	5.73	5.93	6.18	6.35	80
4.02	4.00	4.20	4.31	4.44	5.68	5.90	6.11	6.36	6.54	100
4.30	4.36	4.47	4.59	4.72	5.96	6.18	6.39	6.64	6.84	150
4.50	4.56	4.67	4.78	4.90	6.15	6.38	6.59	6.85	7.03	200
5.06	5.13	5.25	5.37	5.49	6.72	6.94	7.15	7.42	7.60	500
5.50	5.57	5.68	5.79	5.92	7.11	7.33	7.54	7.80	7.99	1000

Source: H. A. David, H. O. Hartley, and E. S. Pearson, "The distribution of the ratio, in a single normal sample, of range to standard deviation," *Biometrika*, 61 (1954): 491. Reprinted by permission.

distribution (which is available on Excel under TDIST). The two distributions are parameterized so that the variance is the same. For the normal distribution, we have a mean of zero and a standard deviation of 1.73. Student's *t* distribution is parameterized by the number of degrees of freedom. To obtain a standard deviation of 1.73, we need 3 degrees of freedom. As the number of degrees of freedom falls, Student's *t* distribution exhibits fatter tails. As the number of degrees

Student's *t* distribution and the normal distribution

Figure 19.3

The normal distribution has zero mean and a volatility of 1.73. The Student's *t* distribution has 3 degrees of freedom. Both distributions have the same variance. Panel A shows the density functions and Panel B shows the cumulative distribution functions.

Panel A

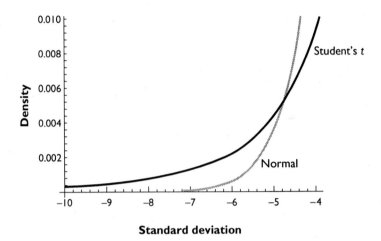

Panel B

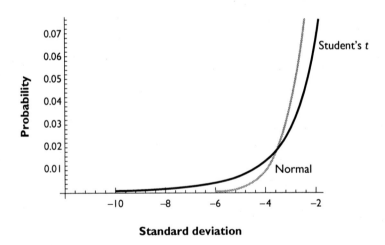

of freedom increases, Student's *t* distribution becomes closer and closer to the normal distribution.

In this example, a risk manager who estimates the standard deviation to obtain a VaR estimate assuming that the distribution is normal would not be able to distinguish between the two distributions. If the manager had a time series of returns, she could find out which distribution is better by looking at whether there are more large returns in absolute value than predicted by the normal distribution.

The probability of a loss exceeding a high threshold is much higher with the Student *t* distribution than with the normal distribution when both distributions have the same variance. The probability of a loss greater than 7 is 0.3 percent with Student's *t* distribution but 0.003 percent with the normal distribution. At the same time, for this parameterization, the 1 percent or the 5 percent VaRs are higher if the risk manager assumes the normal distribution. The 5 percent VaR is 2.85 with our assumption, but with Student's *t* distribution, the probability of a loss exceeding 2.85 is only 3.2 percent. The 5 percent VaR with Student's t distribution for our example would be 2.35. It follows from this example that fat tails make the VaR estimate too low for low probability (high confidence) levels and too high for high probability (low confidence) levels.

A risk manager could use Student's t distribution to compute the VaR. We first estimate the number of degrees of freedom, assuming that the mean is zero. Then we compute the quantile of the distribution corresponding to the probability level we have chosen.

It may well be that the distribution of non-extreme returns is described well by the normal distribution while the distribution of extreme returns is not. Much effort has been expended to understand the distribution of extreme returns for financial data. A well-developed branch of statistics called **extreme value theory** (EVT) shows that, as the sample becomes large and some other conditions are satisfied, the distribution of extreme returns satisfies the "generalized extreme-value distribution function" regardless of the distribution of the non-extreme returns.

In addition to a large sample, however, the use of EVT's generalized distribution for the extreme returns requires that the extreme returns are not predictable. This assumption is often reasonable, but there is also some evidence of clustering in extreme returns, especially for emerging markets. When such clustering occurs, the predictable part of extreme returns has first to be filtered out to apply EVT. Danielsson and de Vries (1998) have pioneered the use of EVT for estimates of VaR. They investigate daily extreme returns for seven stocks and the S&P 500 from 1990 to 1996. They find no consecutive days of lower tail events for the S&P 500. They also find that there is little correlation in extreme events for their stocks. They then advocate the use of EVT for the distribution of extreme events.

The EVT approach fits a function to the tail of the distribution so that the distribution of extreme returns is given by that function. This approach produces better VaR estimates for very high probability levels. In 500 random portfolios simulated over 1,000 days, Danielsson and de Vries find that the RiskMetrics™ approach does just fine at the 5 percent level. At the 1 percent level, the exceedances of the RiskMetrics™ approach are too high by about 60 percent. At the 0.01 percent level, the exceedances of the RiskMetrics™ approach are too high by a factor of twenty—instead of 0.01 percent of exceedances, 0.2 percent is found. This suggests that EVT can be useful at very high probability levels.

19.3.3. Alternative risk measures

By itself, the VaR estimate provides no information as to the size of the maximum loss or more generally the nature of the losses if the VaR is exceeded. Consider an institution that obtains a VaR estimate of $100 million at the 95 percent confidence level. There is a 5 percent probability that the firm will make a loss in excess of $100 million. The VaR estimate could just as well describe a situation where the firm has a 5 percent probability of losing $101 million or a 5 percent probability of losing up to $100 billion. The firm would act differently if the maximum loss is $101 million or $100 billion, and some have argued that we should not estimate VaR itself, but the maximum loss or the expected loss in excess of VaR. It generally makes little sense for a corporation to focus on the maximum loss or to try to estimate it. With normally distributed returns, the maximum loss is infinite if there is uncertainty.

The nature of the loss a firm incurs when it exceeds its VaR can have a dramatic impact on how likely the firm is to keep its credit rating. To see this, suppose that our firm with a VaR of $100 million can lose at most $101 million. It uses a daily VaR to monitor its risk. Say that the firm uses a 5 percent VaR. This means that over the course of a year it expects to exceed that VaR 12.5 times.

Breaching the VaR 12.5 times means that at the end of the year the firm will most likely have made a cumulative loss in excess of VaR of $12.5 million. In contrast, if the firm loses $100 billion whenever it breaches the VaR, however, it can expect a cumulative loss of $1.25 trillion in excess of VaR at the end of the year. The firm with the loss of $12.5 million does not have to worry much about exceeding VaR, while the other firm is likely to be destroyed the first or second time it happens.

Despite having the same VaR, the firm with the large loss is taking too much risk because it defaults with probability 1 during the year. To understand how VaR exceedances affect the firm over time, one has to know their distribution.

If the firm knows its distribution of returns, it can use that distribution to compute other risk measures besides VaR. Rather than computing the loss at some confidence interval, the firm might compute the expected loss outside the confidence interval. In other words, instead of asking "What is our maximum loss for a given confidence interval?" the firm might ask "What is our expected loss in the unlikely event of an extreme negative return?" With a parametric distribution, the firm can compute the expected loss conditional on the loss exceeding a threshold. In this case, the threshold is the VaR. This expected loss is called **expected tail loss** or **conditional VaR**. If the firm uses the historical approach, it does not have a parametric distribution, but it can still compute the expected loss if the loss exceeds VaR by averaging across outcomes.

Rather than computing the expected loss if VaR is exceeded, the firm can compute outcomes for various scenarios, whether historical or simulated. The firm might want to be in a situation where it can survive the occurrence of various historical events. An example is surviving a repeat of the stock market crash of 1987. Such an approach is called a stress test and was discussed in Chapter 13.

Another way a firm with a portfolio of assets can evaluate the risk it is exposed to is to simulate a path of prices and rates over a period of time and compute the value of the portfolio along that path. Instead of thinking of the scenario as the terminal point of this path, we can think of the scenario as the evolution of the portfolio along this path. Such an approach is difficult to implement because the portfolio will change over time. As prices and rates change, the traders will change their positions. To investigate the firm's risk in such a setting, it is necessary to take into account trading strategies. If this is not the case, we do not have a good estimate of the risk over the period. Focusing on how the portfolio evolves through time as prices and rates evolve makes it possible to have an estimate of the risk of the portfolio that takes into account trading strategies. Such an approach has been developed by the firm Algorithmic and is called Mark-to-Future.

Using additional risk measures can be important simply because people tend to game the risk measure that is used, which reduces its effectiveness. For instance, suppose a trader is told that he cannot exceed a 5 percent VaR of $10 million for his trading book. He may be tempted to construct trades with the following feature. His trades make a small profit 97 percent of the time but a large loss 3 percent of the time. The loss is not measured by VaR because its probability is too low. As more traders behave this way in a firm, the days that VaR is breached correspond to large losses. Risk managers have to always be on the lookout for ways to game their risk measures. Using alternate measures can help identify instances where people are gaming the system.

There is some evidence that gaming of the risk measurement system was going on at Enron. An article in *Business Week* reports that "Partnoy says people told him Enron deliberately reduced its trading portfolio's riskiness on the day each month when the value at risk was measured."[6] Apparently, traders at Enron had a "prudence" account that they would use to smooth out the profits from their trades.

19.3.4. Measuring operational risk

When a firm decides to make an investment, say buying a security or building a factory, there is risk involved. The security may lose value or the factory may turn out to be useless because its products cannot be sold. We have seen how such risks are quantified. Implementation risks create a different problem, which is that the firm's management might have decided to do something, but what is done is different because something went wrong in the implementation. For example, it could be that a directive was misunderstood, that a loan was made that should not have been made, that the factory was built differently from expected because of graft, that an employee took the money, and so on. This implementation risk creates an additional dimension of risk for the firm, which may be uncorrelated with the risks that we have discussed but can lead to large losses when the implementation failure is something like the error account of Mr. Leeson. Firms generally use the term operational risk to define all the possible implementation problems that might arise. To the extent that operational risk losses are uncorrelated with other returns, the firm can focus on them separately. The firm would want to know the distribution of its operational risk losses. In general, there are some types of operational risk losses that can be quantified. For example, the probability distribution of having tellers make counting mistakes can be easily established for a bank. However, the probability of having a large operational loss is harder to quantify because those losses tend to be rare. Because of the difficulty of estimating the distribution of medium and large operational losses, consulting firms have worked on establishing industry-wide databases, so that individual

---

6 Peter Coy and Stephanie Anderson Forest, "Enron: How good an energy trader?" *Business Week*, February 11, 2002.

firms can compute a distribution of operational losses from an industry-wide distribution.

19.4. The current regulatory environment

Partly because of the problems that some firms encountered when using derivatives, the 1990s saw a number of regulatory developments that affect the use of derivatives. The most important one is the introduction in the United States and the United Kingdom of new standards for the accounting treatment of derivatives. There are also disclosure standards for derivatives.

19.4.1. SFAS 133

In June 1998, the Financial Accounting Standards Board (FASB) adopted the Statement of Financial Accounting Standards 133 (SFAS 133) after much debate. Even the Chairman of the Federal Reserve Board was critical of the standard, and banks generally feared that it would affect derivatives usage adversely. The original plan was to apply SFAS 133 for fiscal years starting after June 15, 1999, but the starting date was postponed to fiscal years beginning after June 15, 2000. Even before June 15, 2000, the FASB promulgated a new statement, SFAS 138, which amends SFAS 133.

We focus here on the general principles of the statement and their implications.

1. **Derivatives instruments should be reported in financial statements.** A number of derivative contracts have no value when entered into. For example, neither a forward contract nor a swap have value at inception. From an accounting perspective, a position that has no value when entered into does not constitute an expense or revenue. We know, however, that over time forward contracts and swaps evolve so that they have positive value for one of the parties and a negative value for the other one. These changes in values should be reported in accounting statements.

2. **Fair value is the appropriate measure for the value of derivatives.** Fair value means a reasonable estimate of the derivative's market value at the time the financial statements are produced. Fair value is different from cost. For a derivative, fair value corresponds to the marked-to-market value of the derivative if that derivative were to be marked to market. With SFAS 133, derivatives that have value should be recognized in the firm's financial statements. Before SFAS 133, a firm would not have had to report on its balance sheet a swap position that had a negative marked-to-market value unless it had entered the swap position for trading purposes.

3. **Derivatives should be recognized in financial statements whether they are used for hedging purposes or for other purposes.** Derivatives are treated as assets and liabilities. The change in the value of a derivative must be recognized as a gain if positive and as a loss if negative. The gains and losses on derivatives cannot be deferred but have to be recognized immediately. This principle was the subject of considerable controversy because it implies that derivatives can generate volatility in the firm's

financial statements as their value changes. Before SFAS 133, this was not the case for forwards and swaps. Now, the values of forwards and swaps change with their marked-to-market values in quarterly statements.

4. **The treatment of the accounting gain or loss of a derivative depends on whether it qualifies as a hedge.** If a derivative does not qualify as a hedge, the change in fair value flows through the earnings statement. Therefore, changes in the value of forward contracts that do not qualify as hedges produce earnings volatility. For a derivative to qualify as a hedge, it must meet a test of hedging effectiveness. This standard has to be defined at inception of the hedge, and the methodology used to define effectiveness has to be consistent with the risk management strategy underlying the hedge. The standard distinguishes among three types of hedges: cash flow hedges, fair value hedges, and foreign currency hedges. The accounting treatment of each type of hedge differs:

A. **Cash flow hedges.** Firms have cash flows that are stochastic and wish to hedge them. A **cash flow hedge** reduces the variability of cash flows due to variable rates or prices. For example, a firm with floating rate debt that enters a swap to transform floating rate payments into fixed rate payments would be entering a cash flow hedge. If a firm has undertaken a cash flow hedge, it has to demonstrate that this hedge is "effective." If a cash flow hedge is effective, the derivative qualifies for hedge accounting treatment. The effectiveness of a hedge requires the hedge to meet a standard set by the company as to how the gains of the hedge offset the changes in cash flows being hedged. This standard has to be set at the time the derivative position is entered. If the standard is no longer met at some point during the life of the hedge, the firm loses the use of hedge accounting. The effective part of a hedge is the part of the gains and losses of the derivative that offset the changes in cash flows being hedged.

The gains and losses of the derivatives flow through "other comprehensive income" rather than earnings and hence do not affect earnings as long as the gains and losses of the hedged cash flows are not recognized. When the gains or losses on the hedged cash flows are realized, the gains and losses that went through "other comprehensive income" are used to offset the gains or losses on the hedged cash flows.

Suppose a firm has floating rate debt it hedges with a swap. Absent hedge accounting, any change in the value of a swap to hedge the floating interest rate payments would affect earnings. With hedge accounting, changes in the value of the swap that offset changes in interest rates to be paid later would not affect earnings now. A change in the derivative's fair value that does not offset a change in the hedged cash flows is recognized as earnings as it occurs.

B. **Fair value hedges.** Firms enter into transactions that create fixed cash flows. An example is a firm that issues fixed-rate debt or makes a fixed-price commitment to purchase an asset. The fair value of these transactions changes with interest rates, foreign exchange rates, commodity prices, or credit risk. Hedges that protect the fair value of fixed cash flows are called **fair value hedges**. If a hedge qualifies as a fair value hedge, the changes in the fair value of the hedge instrument are recognized in earnings and so are changes in the fair value of the fixed cash flows. As a result, if a firm has a completely effective fair value hedge, the impact on earnings of changes in the hedge exactly offset the impact on earnings of changes in the hedged fair value of the fixed cash flows. In this case, the derivative position entered into to create a fair value hedge does not create earnings volatility.

To qualify as a fair value hedge, a derivative must provide an effective hedge. This means that it is expected to provide a good offset for changes in the fair value of the fixed cash flow the firm is hedging. The methodology to assess effectiveness has to be documented at inception of the hedge and should be consistent with the risk management strategy pursued by the firm. With fair value hedging, the ineffective part of the hedge is recognized in earnings immediately.

C. **Foreign currency hedges.** A foreign currency hedge protects the fair value, the cash flows, or the net investments in foreign currency against exchange rate changes. An example is a forecasted purchase of equipment from a foreign country denominated in foreign currency. For foreign currency hedges, the firm can use one of three accounting models to hedge its foreign currency exposure: (1) the fair value hedge accounting model for firm commitments in foreign currency, (2) the cash flow hedge accounting model for forecasted commitments in foreign currency, and (3) hedging of the exposure of the net investment in a foreign operation. The effective portion of the hedge is reported in other comprehensive income, thereby not affecting earnings, but the ineffective portion of the hedge affects earnings directly.

SFAS 133 is complex and has a significant impact on the accounting treatment of derivatives. It implies that some hedges that make sense from an economic perspective may require what looks like an unfavorable accounting treatment. For example, consider a firm that has a yen exposure not because it exports to Japan but because its competitors are Japanese. The firm has no yen transactions on its books, but its shareholders might approve of management hedging its yen exposure. Such a hedge would not qualify for hedge accounting.

In general, if management is focused on economic value, the accounting details of how derivatives positions affect financial statements will not have an impact on decisions about the use of derivatives. The details could become an issue if the firm is struggling with tight covenants so that it would not want to take derivatives positions that might increase earnings uncertainty. Further, if management is using derivatives to smooth accounting earnings, accounting rules that determine how derivatives gains and losses affect earnings may constrain the firm's ability to do so.

One might suspect firms would be tempted to embed derivatives used f or hedging in other transactions to avoid dealing with the difficulties of derivatives accounting. For example, a firm could invest in commercial paper that has embedded options so that it provides a useful hedge for the firm even though the firm does not buy options directly. In principle, this cannot be done. SFAS 133 specifies that embedded derivatives have to be stripped from the underlying securities for accounting purposes.

19.4.2. Disclosure

Early on, there were no clear standards of disclosure for off-balance sheet derivatives such as swaps. The fact that swaps could be hidden undoubtedly made them attractive to some managers. This has changed over time. The FASB introduced first the SFAS 105 and then SFAS 119, since superseded by SFAS 133. These statements force firms to reveal more information about their derivatives positions. SFAS 105 required firms to provide information about their derivatives positions in footnotes and SFAS 119 went a step further, requiring firms to provide information about the fair value of their derivatives. SFAS 133 now requires firms to provide qualitative disclosures addressing the objectives and strategies for the uses of derivatives instruments. It also requires firms to provide an indication as to whether the hedging objectives are met. Finally, it forces firms to disclose specific information about other comprehensive income as we have described.

As firms were experiencing large losses on derivatives positions, regulators pushed firms to disclose more information about such positions. An unfortunate consequence is that firms must disclose the risks of derivatives separately rather than disclose the risks of exposures hedged with derivatives. As we have seen throughout this book, when derivatives are used for risk management, a firm often makes a loss when the exposure it hedges with derivatives experiences a gain. Making losses with derivatives is not a sign of poor management when the derivatives are part of an effective hedge, but regulators have pushed firms to disclose information about derivatives positions viewed as stand-alone positions rather than as hedges.

In the United States, the SEC amended various regulations in January 1997 to require firms to provide information about the market risks they are exposed to through derivatives. One way a firm can provide this information is to disclose a VaR estimate for its derivatives positions. Stress tests are an acceptable alternative approach. A final approach is a so-called tabular presentation that provides enough information so that investors can understand the derivatives positions of the firm and the cash flows associated with these derivatives.

19.5. Empirical evidence on risk management practice

We have seen important reasons for firms to manage risk. Generally, a firm wants to manage the risk of losses that impose costs on the firm in addition to the loss itself—deadweight costs. The benefits of managing the risks of such losses vary across firms. We would expect risk management to be especially valuable for firms for which financial distress is costly and firms with valuable investment opportunities that might be lost in the presence of financial distress.

There are two types of evidence on the use of risk management by firms. The first is survey evidence. The second is analysis of firm-specific data of derivatives usage and hedging. Research shows that firms that use derivatives have lower volatility and higher value.

19.5.1. The survey evidence

Most surveys focus on derivatives usage rather than risk management.

19.5.1.A. The Dolde survey

Dolde (1993) sent a questionnaire to all Fortune 500 companies in 1992. A total of 244 companies responded. Of these, 85 percent reported using swaps, forwards, futures, or options in managing financial risks. Users of risk management tools were much larger firms than nonusers. For example, the average market value of equity for users is $5.4 billion compared to the average market value of nonusers of $1.8 billion. Larger firms are less likely to hedge their foreign exchange and interest rate exposures intensively. Firms that hedge a greater fraction of their exposures than the median fraction of exposures hedged are about half the size of the firms that hedge less than the median fraction of exposures.

This evidence is paradoxical: Larger Fortune 500 firms are more likely to use derivatives, but smaller Fortune 500 firms that use derivatives hedge a greater fraction of their exposures. Could it be that the smaller firms that do not use derivatives are firms without exposures? The answer is no. They have large exposures. They might be unlikely to experience financial distress, so that they would not benefit from derivatives use. Alternatively, they may manage their risk in more expensive ways than with financial instruments.

The overwhelming evidence is that a firm's market views matter and affect its hedging decision. A firm may finance its business issuing long-term debt and be concerned about long-term interest rates. It could decide to completely insulate itself from changes in long-term interest rates, whatever its views about future interest rates. Or it could decide to hedge more when it expects rates to increase than when it expects them to decrease. The typical attitude of firms seems to be captured by the following quotation from a Fortune 500 manager: "Hedge 30% to 50% if we think the market will move our way, 100% if we think it will move against us" (Dolde, 1993, p. 40). Dolde (1993b) also finds that views matter less for smaller Fortune 500 firms than for larger firms. When they hold a view, smaller firms hedge more than larger firms.

19.5.1.B. The Wharton/Chase and the Wharton/CIBC survey

The Wharton/Chase survey questionnaire was sent to a random sample of 2,000 nonfinancial firms in November 1994. This sample includes firms that are much smaller than the smallest firms included in the Dolde sample. The authors of the survey received 530 useable responses. Only 183, or 34.5 percent, of the firms that responded use derivatives. When the authors split the firms according to size, they find that 65 percent of firms with market value above $250 million use derivatives, but only 13 percent of firms with market value below $50 million use them.

Firms in the survey use derivatives mostly to hedge firm commitments (75.4 percent of the responding firms using derivatives). The majority of these firms say they do so frequently. Further, 44.8 percent of the firms frequently use derivatives to hedge transactions anticipated within the next 12 months, but only 14.2 percent frequently hedge transactions anticipated beyond 12 months. Additionally, 60.7 percent claim that they never use derivatives to arbitrage markets, and 51.9 percent say that they never use them to hedge their balance sheet. About 66 percent state that they do not use derivatives to hedge economic or competitive exposures. Finally, 52.5 percent say that they never use them to reduce funding costs by taking a view.

The Wharton/CIBC survey questionnaire was sent out in October 1995 to the same sample plus the Fortune 500 firms that were not in the 1994 survey. Of the 350 responses, 142 firms, or 41 percent, reported using derivatives. Interestingly, when only firms that responded to the first survey are considered, their use of derivatives had increased from 35 to 39 percent.

The second survey then considers the type of derivatives users take positions in. Of the users, 76 percent use foreign currency derivative instruments and their most popular instrument is the forward contract. A total of 73 percent use interest rate derivatives with the preferred instrument the swap. Finally, 37 percent of the users use commodity derivative instruments, and their preferred instrument is futures contracts.

The second survey provides a more detailed picture of why and what firms hedge. Of the firms using derivatives, 49 percent identify the most important goal to be management of cash flow volatility; 42 percent identify accounting earnings volatility; 8 percent identify the volatility of the market value of the firm; and 1 percent identify the balance sheet volatility. In the case of foreign exchange exposures, firms focus mostly on contractual commitments and anticipated transactions. They seem to pay little attention to exposures that mature in more than one year. For example, 53 percent of firms that use derivatives hold only short-dated derivatives that mature within 180 days or before the end of the fiscal year.

There is again evidence in this survey that firms let their views affect their hedges. A majority of firms say that their view sometimes affects the timing of their hedges for interest rate hedges and foreign exchange hedges. Interestingly, 33 percent of the users say that they sometimes "actively take positions" based on an exchange rate view. Counterparty risk appears to be the most important concern about derivatives; 35 percent of the users use a VaR measure for their derivatives positions. Of 141 firms responding, 53 value their derivatives monthly, and 25 do so daily.

These surveys agree on several points: (1) Large firms are more likely to practice risk management with derivatives; (2) firms tend to hedge cash flow and accounting earnings rather than market value; (3) firms focus on short-term instruments; and (4) firms typically do not hedge systematically, but rather practice so-called selective hedging taking their views into account when assuming derivatives positions.

19.5.2. Studies relating derivatives usage to firm characteristics

A number of studies analyze firm-specific information about derivatives usage. These studies take two forms. Some studies focus on the responses to surveys of firms. Hence, they then can relate a firm's response to a survey question to firm characteristics. Other studies attempt to explain the cross-sectional variation in the exposure of firms. If firms hedge a risk completely, they have no exposure left in that risk. Hence, by measuring exposure, one can determine whether a firm hedges completely or not.

19.5.2.A. Survey answers and risk management theories Nance, Smith, and Smithson (1993) asked firms in the Fortune 500 and/or the S&P 500 whether they used derivatives in the fiscal year of 1986. Out of 535 firms, 169 answered; of these respondents, 104 firms used derivatives. The authors document that firms with derivatives have significantly more investment tax credits than those that do not and are more likely to have taxable income such that their tax rate increases with income. They find that firms using derivatives are significantly larger than the firms that do not use derivatives. This may be because there are economies of scale in risk management. Firms with derivatives have significantly higher R&D expenses as a fraction of firm value. Distress costs are likely to be more important for firms that have higher R&D expenditures because they face greater information asymmetries. Also, firms with more R&D expenditures are more likely to need substantial funds for investment.

Surprisingly perhaps, firms with derivatives and firms without derivatives do not significantly differ in leverage and interest coverage ratios. Dolde (1993b) also finds this result. Everything else equal, we would expect firms with higher leverage or a lower interest coverage ratio to be more subject to financial distress and hence to benefit more from risk management. In the Nance, Smith, and Smithson study, variables that measure the probability of financial distress do not seem to matter, however. It may be that firms with higher leverage or lower interest coverage have less cash flow volatility and lower costs of financial distress. In this case, it would be hard to make predictions about the use of derivatives by these firms because higher leverage would push them to use more derivatives while lower volatility and lower costs of financial distress would push them in the other direction. Firms with derivatives and those without do not differ in their market-to-book ratios in the Nance, Smith, and Smithson study.

Nance, Smith, and Smithson estimate many regressions using different combinations of explanatory variables. Few of these variables are found significant, but in general the probability a firm uses derivatives increases with firm value, the ratio of R&D to firm value, and investment tax credits.

19.5.2.B. The Geczy, Minton, and Schrand study More recent studies benefit from changes in reporting requirements that make it possible to learn about derivatives activity from the footnotes of the annual reports. Geczy, Minton, and Schrand (1995) study the publicly traded Fortune 500 firms for which data are available for the fiscal years 1990 and 1991. This leaves them with 411 companies. To obtain data on derivatives use, they use the accounting footnotes to annual reports and/or 10-K filings for fiscal year-end 1991.

For 1991, Geczy, Minton, and Schrand find that 230 of the 411 firms disclose some use of derivatives, or 56 percent of their sample. Interestingly, this percentage grows to 70 percent by 1993. They find that derivatives users have:

1. Lower liquidity than nonusers. The cash and cash-equivalents of nonuser firms exceed current liabilities by about 0.40 times. This compares to 0.22 times by user firms.

2. Better investment opportunities and a ratio of R&D to sales almost twice the ratio of nonusers.

3. Greater analyst coverage and percentage institutional ownership, but this may be due to size.

To disentangle the role of size from the role of the other variables, the authors estimate a regression model. Size does not seem to matter, but the variables listed continue to significantly affect whether a firm uses derivatives. If firms use derivatives for hedging purposes, one would view this evidence as consistent with the distress avoidance argument and with the argument that firms benefit from hedging to secure funds for investment programs.

19.5.2.C. The Tufano study   Tufano (1995) explores the determinants of hedging in the gold industry. Because gold firms explain very precisely how much they hedge, Tufano can compute the fraction of gold production over the next three years that is covered by risk management activities. His evidence is presented in Table 19.2. Again there is wide variation in risk management practices. Few firms hedge nothing, but no firm hedges everything. The median average degree of hedging in his sample is 22.9 percent, meaning that the typical firm hedges 22.9 percent of its three-year production.

Table 19.2	Risk management practices in the North American gold industry, 1990–1993

For each of the 48 firms and quarter in the sample, Tufano computes the fraction of the production of the following three calendar years that has been effectively sold short. He uses a pricing model to translate option positions into short positions.

Fraction of production effectively sold short	Percentage of firms in sample
Exactly 0	14.6%
0.1%–10%	14.6
10–20	14.6
20–30	14.6
30–40	25.0
40–50	2.1
50–60	4.2
60–70	4.2
70–80	4.2
80–90	2.1
90–100	0
Mean fraction of production effectively sold short	25.6%
Median	22.9%
Standard deviation	22.4%

Source: This table is constructed from Table II, page 1105, of Tufano (1996).

Why does hedging differ so much across firms? Tufano tries to explain the degree of hedging using multivariate regressions whose explanatory variables are firm characteristics that affect the benefit from hedging. As with the other studies discussed here, leverage does not seem to matter. Firms that explore more hedge less, which is rather surprising. Firms with more reserves also appear to hedge less. Finally, firms with more cash balances hedge less as well. None of these results are very strong.

The strongest results all have to do with ownership variables. Firms whose managers own more shares are firms that hedge more. This is consistent with the stakeholder argument discussed in Chapter 3, but it could also be consistent with entrenchment of management and maximization of private benefits. The private benefits of hedging for management are that it bears less risk. Depending on the costs of hedging, this might be expensive for shareholders. Evidence to this effect might be that in Tufano's sample firms with large nonmanagerial block ownership seem to hedge less. It therefore appears that large shareholders moderate management's desire to hedge.

Finally, management hedges less when it holds more options. This evidence shows that the hedging practices of firms depend crucially on the incentives of management. If managers own a lot of shares and these shares represent a large fraction of their wealth, it would not be surprising for managers to want to reduce the risk of their shares. If managers' compensation increases a lot with unusually good outcomes, they may be more willing to gamble to achieve such outcomes.

19.5.2.D. The Haushalter study Haushalter (1998) studies the oil and gas industry risk management from 1992 to 1994. Like Tufano, he tries to explain the hedge ratio of the industry. His study differs from other studies in that he looks at basis risk. Derivatives in the oil and gas industry are more effective at hedging oil and gas extracted in some locations than others. Haushalter finds that firms that extract in locations where hedging can be undertaken more effectively tend to hedge more. Unlike other researchers, Haushalter finds strong results showing that firms hedge more as their leverage increases.

19.5.2.E. The Venkatachalam study Venkatachalam (1996) studies SFAS 119 disclosures on the fair value of derivatives at commercial banks. SFAS 119 requires disclosure of fair value of derivatives for banks but, in contrast to the subsequent SFAS 133, it does not treat derivatives as assets and liabilities, so derivatives can remain off-balance sheet items. The sample consists of 99 bank holding companies that have assets in excess of $150 million at the end of 1994 and use off-balance sheet financial derivatives. The mean market value of equity for these banks is $2,779.63 million and the median is $1,277.04 million at the end of 1994. The mean (median) notional amount of derivatives used for risk management purposes is $12,643.80 million ($1,286.10 million), while the mean (median) notional amount of derivatives held for trading is $131,457.40 million ($93.39 million). The typical bank holds more derivatives for risk management than for trading purposes, judging by the notional amounts of the derivatives held, but some banks have extremely large trading positions in derivatives, which explains why the results using means are different from those using medians. Given our understanding of the determinants of the value of derivatives, it is not surprising that fair values are small compared to notional amounts. The mean (median) fair value of the derivatives held for risk management is –$93.81 million (–$11.43 million).

Venkatachalam investigates whether bank market values reflect the fair value of derivatives used for risk management. An increase in the fair value of these derivatives evidently has a positive impact on the market value of a bank, but controlling for the fair value of derivatives, an increase in the notional amount of derivatives outstanding has a significant negative impact on bank value.

SFAS 107 requires banks to provide information on the fair value of assets and liabilities when these fair values can be computed. This enables Venkatachalam to see to what extent banks hedge these fair values with derivatives. He finds a significant negative relation between fair value gains and losses of on-balance sheet items and fair value gains and losses of derivatives held for risk management. This is the relation we would expect to see if banks hedge these fair values with derivatives, but many banks in the sample do not appear to hedge fair values.

19.5.2.F. The Schrand and Unal study   Schrand and Unal (1998) explore the hedging behavior of savings and loans that have recently converted from the mutual form of ownership to the stock form. For savings and loans (S&Ls), a key exposure is exposure to interest rate changes. One measure of this exposure is the one-year gap studied in Chapter 9, which is the difference between assets whose interest rate changes within a year and liabilities whose interest rate changes within a year. As S&Ls convert from the mutual to the stock form of ownership, managers become able to acquire a stake in the firm, and compensation through options becomes possible. Schrand and Unal find that the one-year gap of the S&L depends crucially on the nature of management's compensation. The one-year gap is narrower if management mostly holds shares in the converted S&L. It is wider if management is compensated through options.

19.5.2.G. Summarizing the evidence   Smithson (1999) reviewed 15 studies examining the determinants of derivatives uses for non-financial firms. His study does not include Haushalter but we include it, thereby extending the summary to 16 studies. Among the main reasons we discussed for why risk management increases firm value are:

1. **Taxes.** The consensus evidence is that firms with more carry-forwards and more tax credits hedge more. Presumably, one reason is that for those firms the tax rate is more likely to change for values of net income that are probable. No study finds significant effects going in the opposite direction.

2. **Costs of financial distress.** All significant results are that firms hedge less when they have greater interest coverage. Most studies find that firms hedge more when they have greater leverage. There is a strong relation between R&D expenses and hedging; no study finds evidence of a negative relation between R&D and derivatives use. The evidence on market-to-book and hedging is more mixed, but the preponderance of the evidence is that firms with higher market-to-book ratios hedge more.

3. **Managerial incentives.** The evidence seems fairly consistent that firms whose managers hold more equity hedge more. The evidence on the relation between the use of options in compensation and hedging is conflicting.

19.5.3. Risk management, risk, and value

The more direct question is whether the use of derivatives affects firm risk and value. Guay (1999) looks at firms that start using derivatives. He constructs a sample of 254 firms that start using derivatives from one year to the next. Firms are found to experience a significant decrease in volatility as they start using derivatives. Firms using interest rate derivatives experience a decrease of 22 percent in the interest rate exposure of their common stock; firms using exchange rate derivatives experience a decrease of 11 percent in the foreign exchange exposure of their common stock. When he investigates why firms start hedging programs, Guay finds that larger firms, firms with higher leverage, firms with lower interest coverage, firms with higher market-to-book ratios, and firms with greater operating income volatility are all more likely to start a hedging program. He finds that the change in interest rate exposure over the previous three years plays a significant role in explaining why firms enter a hedging program. In another study that looks at the impact of derivatives use on exposures, Tufano (1998) finds hedging reduces the exposure of gold mining firms to gold prices.

Allayannis and Weston (2001) consider whether firms that use foreign exchange derivatives are worth more. They examine 720 large U.S. nonfinancial firms between 1990 and 1995. They estimate for these firms a valuation measure called Tobin's q, which is roughly the market value of the firm over the book value of the firm's assets. If a firm has a higher Tobin's q, it creates more value out of the assets it purchases. The mean Tobin's q of firms with foreign sales that use derivatives is 1.27; the mean Tobin's q for firms with foreign sales that do not use derivatives is 1.10. The difference between the two means is highly significant. This evidence indicates that firms that use foreign exchange derivatives are worth more.

The difficulty with simple comparisons of Tobin's q across firms that use derivatives and those that do not is that Tobin's q is influenced by many firm characteristics other than financial. For example, consider a firm with high R&D expenses, which are not capitalized. R&D expenses do create the economic equivalent of an asset for the firm. Since this asset is ignored in the computation of the denominator of Tobin's q but is capitalized by the market in the numerator of Tobin's q, firms with higher R&D expenses have a higher Tobin's q.

The next step in the analysis for Allayannis and Weston is to investigate whether the difference in Tobin's q between firms that use derivatives and firms that do not is due to differences in firm characteristics other than the difference in derivatives use. They use a regression whose independent variables are the various variables that affect Tobin's q. Firms that use derivatives and have foreign sales have a higher Tobin's q than firms that do not use derivatives. The premium for firms that use derivatives ranges from 3.6 to 5.3 percent. This evidence is consistent with the view that derivatives can be used to significantly increase firm value.

19.6. Summary

In this chapter, we reviewed recent developments in risk management and surveyed the evidence on the use of derivatives for risk management. The field of risk management changes all the time because markets change, firms change, and financial innovations take place. We saw that the difficulties of LTCM were largely due to changes in markets that were partly brought about by LTCM itself. Success begets imitation and imitation reduces profits and liquidity. Though LTCM was extremely good at the operational details of risk management, many things can go wrong when implementing a risk management strategy. We reviewed some of those things that can go wrong in the context of the implementation of a risk measurement system and assumed the system to be RiskMetrics™. We saw that the risk manager has to watch out for problems at every stage of the implementation of the system and discuss ways to address some of the problems. We reviewed recent developments in accounting for derivatives and in the disclosure requirements for derivatives. We then examined the existing empirical evidence on the use of derivatives for risk management. Many corporations use derivatives, and the number of those that do will keep increasing over time as their benefits become better understood. The empirical evidence shows that firms generally use derivatives for the reasons discussed in this book, but it is also clear that there is room for improvement in existing practices and that many firms consciously limit their use of derivatives—perhaps because they do not believe that they understand them as well as they should to make more use of them.

Key Concepts

cash flow hedge, 628
conditional VaR, 625
expected tail loss, 625
extreme value theory, 624

fair value hedges, 629
fat tails, 609
operational risk, 611

Review Questions

1. Why might VaR estimates have been downward biased in late August and September 1998?

2. What are the four key steps in implementing VaR with RiskMetrics™?

3. Can you give an example of implementation risk in estimating VaR with RiskMetrics™ for each of the four key steps?

4. What could you do to find out whether a 5 percent VaR exceeded 7 times over 100 days is an unbiased measure of the true VaR?

5. What do fat tails imply for a VaR estimate computed assuming that the normal distribution holds for returns?

6. How are scenarios used?

7. What is SFAS 133?

8. What are the implications of hedge accounting under SFAS 133?

9. How do size and R&D affect derivatives usage of firms?

10. What are the risk and value implications of derivative use at the firm level?

Questions and Exercises

1. Suppose that your firm's trading portfolio has 10 million shares of a stock and nothing else. The return of the stock is assumed to be normally distributed. You estimated the volatility of the stock return at 3 percent per day using closing prices on the NYSE. The marked-to-market position is based on the NYSE closing price. What is the daily marked-to-market loss that is not exceeded 95 percent of the days?

2. Your boss becomes concerned that he might be forced to liquidate the position if there is a large negative return and move into cash. He wants to know whether the liquidation value of the portfolio differs from the marked-to-market value of the position based on NYSE closing prices. On what would your answer depend?

3. Suppose that in answering question 2, you find that the liquidation value of the position will always be $1 per share lower than the marked-to-market value of the portfolio assuming the portfolio is not liquidated because of the price concession required to sell all of the portfolio. Your boss wants you to compute a risk measure that represents the one-day loss in the portfolio's liquidation value at the 95 percent confidence interval.

4. Suppose that instead you had found that the price at which the portfolio can be liquidated at the end of the trading day is 98 percent of the closing price. How would this change your answer to question 3?

5. Suppose that in December 1997, LTCM had brought you in as a consultant and asked you to backtest a 1 percent VaR computed assuming the normal distribution for the portfolio return. As can be seen from Figure 19.1, LTCM until then had not had a month with large losses. The data they gave you indicated that, over 32 months, the 1 percent VaR would never have been exceeded. Using the test presented in section 19.3, would you have concluded that the 1 percent VaR estimate computed assuming the normal distribution for the portfolio return was an unbiased VaR? If you concluded otherwise, what can you say about the nature of the bias?

6. Suppose that you hold a portfolio of traded securities. You assume that the return of the portfolio is normally distributed but you are concerned about fat tails. You have computed the monthly 5 percent VaR of the portfolio using the monthly volatility of 12 percent. A consultant concludes that the distribution of returns is normal except that there is a 0.1 percent probability of a loss corresponding to −50 percent in addition to the return from the normal distribution. The return of the portfolio is therefore the normally distributed return plus a return that takes value zero with probability 0.99 and −50 percent with probability 0.01. This return is uncorrelated with the normally distributed part of the return. When you estimated the VaR using 24 months of data, there were two returns corresponding to a

loss of 50 percent or higher in the dataset you used. Does this information tell you that your VaR estimate is biased? If yes, which way?

7. How could you use the information in question 6 to come up with an unbiased estimate of VaR?

8. You are working for a U.S. company. It is June and you just recommended that the company hedge the foreign currency risk of an anticipated euro-denominated sale that will take place in 18 months with a forward contract. The company has a December fiscal year end. Under which conditions will the hedge affect this year's earnings?

9. Suppose that you manage a hedge fund. You just lost $1 billion and are left with $4 billion. Before the loss, each dollar supported $20 of debt. The one-month 5 percent VaR was 20 percent. What is the impact of the loss on the VaR of the hedge fund?

10. Consider the hedge fund of question 9. Assume that it cannot raise outside funds. It wants to bring back the VaR to 20 percent. It owns both highly liquid securities and illiquid securities. The manager decides to do so quickly by selling the most liquid securities he owns, so that its sales have no market impact. What are the risks of this strategy? If the manager decided to sell illiquid securities, would he have to sell more securities? If yes, why? Would it be a mistake to do so?

Literature Note

Jorion (2000) provides an analysis of the difficulties of LTCM from a risk measurement perspective. Lowenstein (2000) presents the history of LTCM. Perold (1999) provides much data about LTCM. Stulz (2000) analyzes the risk management implications of the difficulties of LTCM. Diebold et al. (1999) discusses how to take into account the distribution of changes in liquidity in VaR estimates. The book published by KPMG and *Risk* Publications titled "VaR: Understanding and Applying Value at Risk" provides a compendium of articles published on VaR in *RISK Magazine*. The Bank of England survey is described in "Price check," by Howard Walwyn and Wayne Byres, *Risk*, November 1997, 18–24. Jorion (1995) shows some implications of the fact that sampling error affects VaR estimates. Kupiec (1995) provides the test discussed in section 19.3.1. Christopherson (1998) provides conditional tests for unbiasedness of VaR. Danielsson and de Vries (1998) and Longin (2000) are useful starting points for using extreme-value theory in computing VaR. Kiesel, Perraudin, and Taylor (2000) show how to deal with clustering when using EVT. Boudoukh, Richardson, and Whitelaw (1997) show how to measure the expected loss if VaR is exceeded. Pearson and Ju (1999) and Basak and Shapiro (2001) provide discussions of possible manipulation of VaR. The quotes in the chapter concerning Enron are from "Enron: How good an energy trader?" *Business Week*, February 11, 2002, 42–43.

A useful presentation of operational risk is Crouhy and Marks (1999). KPMG (1998) provides a detailed tutorial on SFAS 133. Deloitte and Touche provides useful updates and commentary on SFAS 133 through their "Heads-up" on their website.

Part 4

Conclusion

Epilogue

In this book, we have seen how to manage risk using derivatives and that risk management through derivatives creates wealth for shareholders. Throughout the book, we have talked about many problems firms encountered with derivatives. Often, observers are tempted to focus on such problems to argue that firms should not use derivatives. Such an attitude does not make sense. After all, if a firm's computer system crashes, would the firm stop using computers? Certainly not—that would put it behind its competitors. The same applies to derivatives. Nevertheless, successfully managing risk with derivatives requires knowledge and skills, and after learning the material in this book, you now have what it takes to succeed.

Those managers who got into trouble with derivatives also had knowledge and skills, so why did they run into difficulties where you will not? Why is it that they reduced the wealth of their firm's shareholders whereas you will increase the wealth of your firm's shareholders? The only way that you can succeed where they did not is if you remember the key lessons that were discussed throughout the book. Let's summarize these lessons:

1. **Quantify risk.** Throughout the book, we saw that you can measure risk. You can do so for the firm as a whole, for specific firm activities, and for the derivatives you use. We saw many examples of firms that measure risk and devoted considerable resources to doing so. We saw that investment banks measure risk at all levels of their organization—from individual traders and securities to the firm as a whole. We saw corporations that measure their cash flow at risk and firms that know how unexpected changes in exchange rates would affect cash flow and stock price. Without risk measurement, there cannot be risk management.

2. **Choose which risks to bear.** The key rule we emphasized is that a firm should bear the risks that it has a comparative advantage in bearing and that it should get rid of the other risks. Risks are expensive for corporations because of deadweight costs. An adverse outcome—for instance, a drop in the price of gold for a gold producer—can have additional effects on the firm besides reducing the income from gold sales. It can force the firm to cut back investment so that the firm loses valuable growth opportunities. This additional cost of the drop in the price of gold is a

deadweight cost. It can be avoided through risk management. When firms take the risk of incurring deadweight costs that they could eliminate by using derivatives judiciously, they let the money of their shareholders walk out the door.

3. **Choose cost-effective ways to eliminate risks that the corporation should not bear.** A corporation could eliminate all risk by simply selling its assets and investing the proceeds in a money market fund, but by doing so, the corporation would kill off all those assets that are worth more to the firm than to other firms or investors. Derivatives offer a cheap way to eliminate risks, but there are many different derivatives and it is important to choose the right ones. The decision of which derivative to use depends not only on the promised payoff of the derivative, but also on whether the derivative can be easily traded and on the ability of the corporation to measure the risk and value of the derivative.

Quantifying risks, deciding which risks to bear, and managing risks with derivatives go a long way towards creating shareholder wealth. However, it is important to perform these tasks well, and it is easy to fall into traps. The two most important traps are:

1. **Making money consistently does not mean there is no risk.** We saw a number of examples where a firm was making a lot of money from an activity and wanted to do more of that activity. Barings thought it was in great shape with Mr. Leeson because he was making so much money. LTCM was viewed as a money machine with little risk. Metallgesellschaft was acquiring market share at full speed. In all these cases, there was an insufficient understanding of how the money was made. Selling earthquake insurance makes a lot of money most of the time, but most of the money made gets wiped out when there is an earthquake. Markets are efficient enough that making money is hard. If it comes too easily, it often means that one is blindly taking risks. There is no good risk management without an understanding of why it makes economic sense for a firm to make the profits it is making.

2. **The world changes.** For any firm, the markets in which it operates change over time. The actions of the firm, as we saw in the case of LTCM, can change the markets. To manage risk, changes in markets have to be understood and anticipated to the extent possible. Having a risk management strategy that would have been optimal over the last five years is of no use. The risk management strategy has to be optimal over the period of implementation. Since new derivatives that can be used for risk management are introduced all the time, today's best risk management strategy has to make use of the most appropriate derivatives available.

With the help of the lessons from this book, you can design risk management strategies that respond to changes in a firm's situation and make use of the latest financial innovations. To design risk management strategies, you can now quantify risks, choose which ones the firm should bear, and choose the appropriate derivatives to manage these risks.

A

agency costs of managerial discretion costs caused by management's ability to pursue its own interests at the expense of the firm's shareholders.

American option option that can be exercised at maturity and before.

amortizing swap swap where the notional amount falls over time according to a well-defined schedule.

arbitrage pricing pricing an asset by relying on the condition that there be no arbitrage opportunity, i.e., no opportunity to make riskless profits.

arbitrage profits riskless profits that can be obtained without investing any of one's own money.

asset allocation specifies how wealth is allocated across types of securities or asset classes.

asset or nothing digital call option pays the underlying if its price exceeds the exercise price at maturity.

asset sensitive a bank where an increase in interest rates increases income from its assets more than it increases the payments it has to make on its liabilities over the near-term.

B

backwardation describes a situation where the price for future delivery is lower for delivery dates that are farther in the future.

bankruptcy costs costs incurred as a result of a bankruptcy filing.

barrier option an exotic derivative that can be exercised only if the price of the underlying during the life of the option satisfies some condition defined by a barrier.

basis the difference between the spot price and the futures price on a given date.

basis risk the risk due to random changes in the basis.

basket option an option to buy a basket or portfolio of foreign currencies at a given exercise price.

beta for a security, the covariance of the return of the security with the return of the market portfolio divided by the variance of the return of the market portfolio.

binomial distribution the probability distribution of a random variable that can take only one of two values for each realization. An example is the probability distribution of getting j black balls and $q - j$ red balls when drawing q balls with replacement from an urn that has black and red balls such that each ball has probability p of being a black ball.

binomial model option pricing model based on the assumption that the price of the underlying asset can reach only one of two values after one period has elapsed.

Black formula for the pricing of American calls $C^{Black}(S, K, T, t) = \text{Max}\{c(S - P_t(t')D, K, T, t), c(S, K, t', t)\}$, where $c(S - P_t(t')D, K, T, t)$ is the price of a European option on a stock with price S at t paying dividend D at t'. The option matures at T and has exercise price K. $P_t(t')$ is the price at t of a zero-coupon bond that pays one dollar at t'. $c(S, K, t', t)$ is the price of a European call option on the stock with price S, maturity at t' before the dividend is paid, and exercise price K. The option prices are given by the Black-Scholes formula.

Black formula for the pricing of options on futures $c(G, K, T, t) = P_t(T)GN(d) - P_t(T)KN(d-\sigma\sqrt{(T - t)})$, where $d = \ln(G/K) / \sigma\sqrt{(T - t)} + 0.5\sigma\sqrt{(T - t)}$. This is the price of a call option on the futures price G with exercise price K and maturity at T. σ is the volatility of the futures price. $P_t(T)$ is the price at t of a zero-coupon bond that pays one dollar at T. $N(d)$ is the cumulative normal distribution evaluated at d.

Black-Scholes formula provides prices of options on common stock as well as other financial assets when trading in the risk-free asset and in the underlying takes place continuously throughout the day and the price of the financial asset follows the lognormal distribution. For a European call at t on a stock with price S maturing at T and exercise price of K, the formula is $c(S, K, T, t) = SN(d) - P_t(T)KN(d - \sigma\sqrt{(T - t)})$, where $d = \ln(S/P_t(T)K)/\sigma\sqrt{(T - t)} + 0.5\sigma\sqrt{(T - t)}$ σ is the volatility of the futures price. $P_t(T)$ is the price at t of a zero-coupon bond that pays one dollar at T.

bond convexity an approximate measure of the curvature of the relation between bond price and yield, so that the greater the convexity measure, the more convex the relation between bond and yield is.

bond price tree shows how a bond price evolves when the interest rate has a binomial distribution.

C

call option the right to buy a fixed number of shares at a contractually specified price.

cap pays the difference between the floating rate payment and what the payment would be at a contracted fixed rate whenever this difference is positive during the life of the cap.

capital asset pricing model (CAPM) the expected return of a risky security is equal to the risk-free rate plus a risk premium given by the systematic risk of that security measured by its beta times the market's risk premium.

caplet a claim to a single cap payment.

capped options barrier options that trade at the Chicago Board Options Exchange.

cap rate a contracted fixed rate in a cap.

CaR impact of a project the change in a firm's cash flow at risk brought about by a project.

cash flow at risk (CaR) when CaR is estimated at the probability level p, it is the cash flow shortfall that has probability p of being exceeded.

cash flow beta the covariance of the cash flow of the division with the cash flow of the firm divided by the variance of the cash flow of the firm.

cash flow hedge reduces the variability of cash flows due to variable rates or prices.

cash-or-nothing digital option an option that pays a fixed amount of money if the underlying exceeds the exercise price upon exercise.

clearinghouse an institution set up by the exchange as a counterparty both to long and short traders.

collar the simultaneous purchase of a cap and sale of a floor.

competitive exposure the sensitivity of the firm's cash flow to a change in the risk factor resulting from changes in the firm's competitive position.

conditional VaR the expected loss conditional on the loss exceeding a threshold; see expected tail loss.

constant linear relation an assumption that the relation between futures price and cash position changes remains constant.

contango describes the situation where the price for future delivery is higher for delivery dates that are farther in the future.

contractual exposure exposure to a risk factor resulting from contractual commitments, both booked and unbooked.

contribution of a division to CaR the fraction of CaR that is due to division i is equal to the beta of the cash flow of division i with respect to firm cash flow.

contribution of a trader to VaR the fraction of VaR that is due to a trader's book is the portfolio share of his book times the beta of his return with respect to the portfolio return.

convenience yield the benefit one derives from holding a commodity physically.

cost of carry cost of financing a position in the underlying of a futures contract until maturity of the contract.

costs of financial distress costs firms incur because of a poor financial situation.

counterparty risks the risk that a counterparty fails to deliver the promised payoff, either because of being financially unable to do so or for other reasons.

covariance the expected value of the product of the deviations of two random variables from their mean.

credit default swap party A makes fixed payments to party B and party B provides to party A a put on debt issued by a third party, such as a firm or a country.

credit derivative a derivative whose payoff is a function of the credit of one or several firms.

credit event includes (1) failure to make a required payment, (2) restructuring that makes any creditor worse off, (3) invocation of cross-default clause, and (4) bankruptcy.

credit risk the risk that someone who owes money might fail to make promised payments.

credit spread the difference between the yield on risky debt and the yield on risk-free debt of same maturity.

CreditMetrics™ a risk model that provides the distribution of the value of a portfolio of debt claims, which leads to a VaR measure for the portfolio.

cross-hedge using a futures contract to hedge a cash position on a good that would not be deliverable with the futures contract.

cumulative distribution function specifies the probability that the realization of the random variable will be no greater than a certain value.

currency swap one party agrees to make interest payments in currency A at a fixed rate on a notional amount N and to pay that notional amount in currency A at maturity of the swap to a counterparty in exchange for receiving from it all interest rate payments in currency B on a notional amount N^* and receiving N^* in currency B at maturity.

D

deadweight costs indirect costs imposed on firms by financial losses in addition to the direct costs corresponding to the losses themselves.

debt overhang a situation where a firm has so much debt that it makes investment decisions that benefit shareholders but adversely affect its total value.

delta exposure of cash flow to a risk factor cash flow change for a unit change in the risk factor evaluated for an infinitesimal change in the risk factor.

delta-VaR VaR estimated by using the portfolio formula and estimating the return of options (and other derivatives with option-like feature) by the return of a portfolio in the underlying and the riskless asset, where the position of the portfolio in the underlying is obtained by using the options' delta.

digital options options with a fixed payoff if they are in the money.

diversifiable risk risk that disappears in a well-diversified portfolio.

diversification the extent to which invested funds are distributed across securities to lessen the dependence of the portfolio's return on the returns of individual securities.

dollar maturity gap the amount of assets that reprice as a result of a change in interest rates (i.e., change in interest payment) over a repricing interval minus the amount of liabilities that reprice over that interval.

down-and-in option has value at maturity only if the stock price falls below the barrier at some point before maturity.

down-and-out barrier option an option that loses its value if the price of the underlying falls below the barrier.

duration measures how the cash flows of a bond are spread over time; it is the weighted average time to receipt of cash flows, where the weight is the present value of the cash flow as a proportion of the bond value.

E

efficient frontier upward-sloping part of the curve graphing for each expected return the lowest volatility portfolio that produces that expected return.

European cash or nothing digital call option pays a fixed amount of cash if the price of the underlying exceeds the exercise price at maturity.

European option option that can be exercised only at maturity, not before.

exchange option an option that pays the difference between the price of stock A and the price of stock B.

exercise price a contractually specified price at which an option can be exercised.

exotic derivatives nonstandard derivatives whose payoffs cannot be created through a portfolio of plain vanilla derivatives.

expected return probability-weighted average of all possible returns.

expected tail loss the expected loss conditional on the loss exceeding a threshold; see conditional VaR.

expected value for a random variable, a probability-weighted average of all possible distinct outcomes of that variable.

exposure the sensitivity of cash flow to unexpected changes in a risk factor.

exposure of cash flow to risk factor change in cash flow per unit change in risk factor.

extreme value theory statistical theory that describes the behavior of extreme observations.

F

fair value hedges hedges that protect the fair value of fixed cash flows; the changes in the fair value of the hedge instrument are recognized in earnings and so are the changes in the fair value of the fixed cash flows.

fat tails a distribution where extreme returns have higher probabilities than with the normal distribution.

Fischer-Weil duration in computing the duration of a bond, the present values are computed using the term structure of zero-coupon bonds rather than the bond's yield.

floor a contract that promises for each payment period to pay the difference between the floor rate and the contractual interest rate times the principal.

floorlet a claim to one payment of a floor.

forward contract one party agrees to buy the underlying from another party at maturity of the contract and pay for it then a price agreed upon when the contract is originated with no cash changing hands before maturity.

forward rate agreement the buyer commits to pay the fixed contract rate on a given amount over a period of time, and the seller pays the reference rate on the same amount at maturity of the contract.

forward swap swap where the fixed rate payments are agreed upon today but the first payment period starts at some future date.

full-valuation Monte Carlo VaR VaR computation where the financial instruments in the portfolio are valued for each set of values of the risk factors generated by the simulation.

futures contract contract traded on an exchange enabling one party to buy for future delivery and another to sell for future delivery with gains and losses settled daily.

G

Greeks exposures of derivatives to the variables that determine their price.

H

hedge the use of financial instruments or of other tools to reduce exposure to a risk factor.

hedge ratio the size of the hedge for a one-unit exposure to a risk factor.

hedging costs costs of putting on a hedge; examples include transactions costs, monitoring costs, and design costs.

hedging irrelevance proposition hedging a risk does not increase firm value when the cost of bearing the risk is the same whether the risk is borne within the firm or outside the firm by the capital markets.

historical VaR generating possible prices by applying past returns to the current prices to obtain a generated distribution of portfolio values.

homemade hedging an investor hedges on his own account the exposures of the firm to risk factors using financial instruments.

I

i.i.d. denotes random variables that are identically independently distributed.

implied volatility the volatility that makes the model price for a derivative equal to its market price.

information asymmetry when one party to a deal knows more than the other.

initial margin the required initial collateral on a futures contract.

interest rate call option pays upon exercise the difference between the current interest rate and a contractual interest rate computed on a given amount of principal.

interest rate swap exchange of cash flows where one party makes fixed interest rate payments on a notional amount and the other party makes floating interest rate payments on the same notional amount.

intrinsic value the payoff if the option were exercised immediately; with stock price S, the intrinsic value of a call option with exercise price K is Max $(S - K, 0)$ while the intrinsic value of a put option is Max $(K - S, 0)$.

K

KMV model a model for the probability of default that uses the market value of the firm's equity in an extension of Merton's model for the pricing of risky debt.

knock-out provision specifies that a security will cease to exist if some price falls below the knock-out barrier.

L

levered swap swap in which the cash flows are those of a plain vanilla swap with additional borrowing.

liability sensitive a bank whose liabilities reprice faster than its assets.

LIBOR the rate at which a London bank can borrow in dollars from another London bank.

liquidity risk the risk that we might have to trade in an illiquid market to obtain a particular payoff.

lognormal distribution a distribution where the log of a random variable is normally distributed.

long a position in a security or derivative that benefits from an increase in the price of the security or derivative.

loss given default (LGD) a firm's expected loss if default occurs.

M

maintenance margin an amount that the balance in an account must be at least equal to before the start of trading each day.

margin call received if the account balance falls below the maintenance margin.

market impact impact of a trade on market prices..

market impact cost the additional cost resulting from the market impact of the trade on prices.

market portfolio the value-weighted portfolio of all outstanding financial assets.

market risk risk associated with changes in market prices or rates

marking the contract to market the gains and losses due to changes in the market price are paid by the parties every day as they accrue on future contracts that trade on organized exchanges.

Merton's model model for the pricing of risky debt that uses the Black-Scholes formula and sets the price of debt equal to the value of the firm minus the value of equity, where the value of equity is computed as the value of a call on the value of the firm.

model risk risk due to the use of an inappropriate model

modified duration duration with present values computed using the yield of the bond and divided by one plus the yield.

Monte Carlo analysis generates realizations of random variables from draws of these random variables from their assumed distribution.

moral hazard the risk resulting from the ability of one party to a contract to take unobserved actions that adversely affect the value of the contract for the other party.

multivariate normal changes model an estimation model based on the assumption that over any time interval of identical length, the futures price changes are independently identically normally distributed, that the cash position changes are independently identically normally distributed, and that there is a constant linear relation between the futures price changes and the cash position changes.

N

normal distribution the distribution that produces the familiar bell-shaped curve; the values that a random variable can take are symmetrically spread around its mean, so that we only need information about mean and variance to determine the characteristics of the distribution.

notional amount the quantity of the underlying used to determine the payoff of the derivative.

O

obligors those who have legal financial obligations to a firm.

open interest a measure of the liquidity of a futures market; derived from adding all the long positions or short positions.

operational risk for risk management, the risk that things go wrong in the implementation of a risk management measurement system and strategy or due to a mishap in its operations; more generally, the risk that something can go wrong in the implementation of the firm's strategy and in its operations.

optimal capital structure capital structure that maximizes firm values.

option delta the sensitivity or exposure of the option price with respect to the stock price.

option gamma the sensitivity or exposure of the option delta with respect to the stock price.

option premium the price at which an option can be bought.

option on the average an option where the underlying at exercise is the arithmetic average of a price over a period of time.

option vega the sensitivity or exposure of the option price with respect to the volatility.

option writer whoever sells an option at inception of the contract.

P

percentage maturity gap maturity gap expressed as a percentage of assets.

perfect financial markets markets that satisfy the assumption that the frictions that affect financial markets are unimportant.

perfect hedge eliminates all risk so that the hedged position, defined as the cash position plus the hedge, has no exposure to the risk factor.

plain vanilla derivatives conventional calls, puts, forwards, and futures contracts generally traded on exchanges or on liquid over-the-counter markets.

portfolio insurance guarantees an investor a pre-specified minimum amount of wealth at the end of the insurance period.

portfolio share the fraction of the portfolio invested in a security.

price limits limits exist on many futures price contracts. If the limit is hit, trading stops for some time.

price risk risk resulting from unexpected changes in prices.

probability density function is used to obtain the probability that a portfo-lio's value will fall within a range of values.

proportional volatility the volatility of the percentage change in a variable, not of the level of the variable.

put-call parity theorem the price of a European put is equal to the value of a portfolio long the call, long an investment in discount bonds for the present value of the exercise price of the call and the same maturity as the call, and short the underlying asset.

put option gives its holder the right to sell a fixed quantity of the underlying at the contractually agreed upon price.

Q

quantity risk risk associated with the actual exposure being different from the expected exposure.

quanto an option on a random number of units of foreign currency.

R

rating transition matrix gives the probability that a credit will migrate from one rating to another over one year.

recovery rate the amount received in the event of default as a fraction of the principal.

replicating portfolio a portfolio that replicates the payoff of a security without containing the security.

repo a transaction that involves a spot market sale of a security and the promise to repurchase the security at a later day at a given price.

return probability distribution quantifies the likelihood of various returns.

reverse repo a repo transaction viewed from the perspective of the dealer who receives the securities.

risk factor a variable, price, or quantity that impacts cash flow or return and can change unexpectedly for reasons beyond one's control; an identifiable source of risk.

risk-neutral probabilities the probabilities that, given the financial asset's payoffs, make its expected return equal to the risk-free rate, which is the expected return the asset would have if investors were risk neutral.

risk premium the expected return of a security or portfolio in excess of the risk-free rate.

rollover risk the risk that arises because the difference between the price of the contract we close and the price of the contract we open is random.

S

security market line the relation between expected return and beta that results from the capital asset pricing model.

settlement variation the daily gains and losses payment for a futures contract.

short a position in a security or derivative that benefits from a decrease in the price of the security or derivative.

short sale an investor borrows shares from a third party and then sells them.

spot interest rate model specifies how the interest rate for the shortest maturity evolves over time.

square root rule for volatility if a random variable is identically independently distributed with a volatility per period σ, the volatility of that random variable over N periods is σ times the square root of N.

stakeholders individuals and companies whose welfare depends on how well a firm is doing.

standard deviation square root of the variance.

standard normal distribution normal distribution for a random variable with a mean of zero and volatility of one.

static hedge a hedge position that is put in place at one time and is not changed until the maturity of the exposure.

static portfolio replicating strategy takes a position in a portfolio that yields the desired payoff and requires no trading after the portfolio is purchased.

stress test computations of the value of portfolios for specific values of risk factors.

structured Monte Carlo method uses Monte Carlo to generate returns on assets but then computes the return on derivatives using the delta approximation or the delta-gamma approximation.

swap rate the interest rate paid on the fixed interest rate leg of the swap.

swap spread the difference between the fixed rate paid on the swap and the fixed rate on a par default-free bond of the same maturity.

swaps exchanges of cash flows computed on a notional amount and corresponding to different underlyings.

swaption an option to enter into a swap with a specified fixed rate payment at maturity of the option.

systematic risk risk that cannot be eliminated through diversification.

T

tailing the hedge reducing the size of the hedge to reflect the fact that, because of the marking to market of futures contracts, one earns interest on the gains one makes on the futures position. The tailed hedge is the hedge one would put on absent marking to market multiplied by the present value of a dollar to be paid at maturity of the hedge.

tangency portfolio the portfolio that has the highest reward per unit of volatility, so that an investor cannot do better than investing in the risk-free asset and in that portfolio.

tax shield from debt tax savings due to tax deductibility of the interest expenses of debt.

total return swap requires one party to pay the total return on a reference asset or portfolio to a counterparty in exchange for the total return on another reference asset or portfolio so that the reference assets or portfolios have the same market value at inception of the swap.

transaction exposure exposure to a risk factor that results from contractual payments to be received and to be made.

U

up-and-in option converts into a plain vanilla option if and only if the barrier is exceeded once before maturity.

up-and-out put loses all its value if the price of the underlying exceeds a pre-specified barrier.

V

value at risk (VaR) the loss in value of the portfolio that has a specified probability of being exceeded over a certain period .

VaR impact of a project the change in VaR brought about by the project.

variance quantitative measure of how the realizations of a random variable are distributed around their expected value; expected value of squares of deviations from the mean.

volatility the square root of the variance; also called standard deviation.

vulnerable option an option with default risk.

Z

zero-coupon bonds bonds in which the interest payment comes in the form of capital appreciation of the bond, so that no coupon is paid.

A

Adler, Michael, and Bernard Dumas, "Exposure to currency risk: Definition and measurement," *Financial Management*, 1984, 13(2), 41–50.

Allayannis, G., and J. P. Weston, "The use of foreign currency derivatives and firm market value," *Review of Financial Studies*, 2001, 14(1, Spring), 243–276.

Allen, Franklin, and Douglas Gale, "Arbitrage, short sales, and financial innovation," *Econometrica*, 1991, 59(4), 1041–1068.

Allen, Franklin, and Douglas Gale, *Financial innovation and risk sharing*, Cambridge, MA: MIT Press, 1994.

Amin, Kaushik I., and Robert A. Jarrow, "Pricing options on risky assets in a stochastic interest rate economy," *Mathematical Finance*, 1992, 2(4), 217–237.

Amin, Kaushik I., and Andrew J. Morton, "Implied volatility functions and arbitrage-free term structure models," *Journal of Financial Economics*, 1994, 35(2), 141–180.

Anderson, Ronald W., and Jean-Pierre Danthine, "Cross hedging," *Journal of Political Economy*, 1981, 89(6), 1182–1196.

Anderson, Ronald W., and Jean-Pierre Danthine, "The time pattern of hedging and the volatility of futures prices," *Review of Economic Studies*, 1983, 50(161), 249–266.

Anderson, Ronald W., and Suresh Sundaresan, "Design and valuation of debt contracts," *Review of Financial Studies*, 1996, 9(1, Spring), 37–68.

Arak, Marcelle, Arturo Estrella, Laurie Goodman, and Andrew Silver, "Interest rate swaps: An alternative explanation," *Financial Management*, 1988, 17(2), 12–18.

Arditti, Fred, and John Curran, "Futures contract on the cards," *Risk*, November 1998, (Credit Risk Special Report), 30–32.

B

Bakshi, Gurdip, Charles Cao, and Zhiwu Chen, "Empirical performance of alternative option pricing models," *Journal of Finance*, December 1997, 52(5), 2003–2049.

Bainbridge, Rown, and Miles Kennedy, "BHP: A strategic view of risk," *Risk*, March 2001, S20–22.

Bailey, Warren, Edward Ng, and René M. Stulz, "Optimal hedging of stock portfolios against foreign exchange risk: Theory and application," *Global Finance Journal*, 1992, 3(2), 97–114.

Baillie, R. T., and R. J. Myers, "Bivariate garch estimation of the optimal commodity futures hedge," *Journal of Applied Econometrics*, 1991, 6(2), 109–124.

Basak, S., and A. Shapiro, "Value-at-risk-based risk management: Optimal policies and asset prices," *Review of Financial Studies*, June 2001, 14(2), 371–405.

Beder, Tanya Styblo, "VAR: Seductive but dangerous," *Financial Analyst Journal*, 1995, 51(5), 12–24.

Benninga, Simon, Rafael Eldor, and Itzhak Zilcha, "The optimal hedge ratio in unbiased futures markets," *Journal of Futures Markets*, 1984, 4(2), 155–159.

Bensman, Miriam, "Getting out fast and early in futures," *The Magazine of Commodities & Options*, August 1993, 22–23.

Berger, Philip G., and Eli Ofek, "Diversification's effect on firm value," *Journal of Financial Economics*, 1995, 37(1), 39–65.

Berkowitz, J., and J. O'Brien, "How accurate are value-at-risk models at commercial banks?" Discussion paper, 2001, Federal Reserve Board.

Bernstein, P., *Capital ideas: The improbable origins of modern Wall Street*, New York: Free Press, 1992.

Bessembinder, Hendrik, "Forward contracts and firm value: Investment incentive and contracting effects," *Journal of Financial and Quantitative Analysis*, 1991, 26(4), 519–532.

Bierwag, Gerald O., George G. Kaufman, and Alden Toevs, eds., "Innovations in bond portfolio management: Duration analysis and immunization," *Contemporary Studies in Economics and Financial Analysis*, 41, Greenwich, CT: JAI Press, 1983.

Black, F., and M. Scholes, "The valuation of options and corporate liabilities," *Journal of Political Economy*, 1973, 81, 637–654.

Black, Fischer, "The pricing of commodity contracts," *Journal of Financial Economics*, 1976, 3(1/2), 167–179.

Black, Fischer, "How we came up with the option formula," *Journal of Portfolio Management*, 1989, 15(2), 4–8.

Black, Fischer, and John C. Cox, "Valuing corporate securities: Some effects of bond indenture provisions," *Journal of Finance*, 1976, 31(2), 351–367.

Black, Fischer, Emanuel Derman, and William Toy, "A one-factor model of interest rates and its application to treasury bond options," *Financial Analyst Journal*, 1990, 46(1), 33–39.

Black, Fischer, and Piotr Karasinski, "Bond and option pricing when short rates are lognormal," *Financial Analyst Journal*, 1991, 47(4), 52–59.

Bock, David R., "Fixed-to-fixed currency swap: The origins of the World Bank swap programme," in Boris Antl, ed., *Swap finance*, 2, Euromoney Publications, 1986, 218–223.

Bollen, Nicolas, and Robert Whaley, "Simulating supply," *Risk*, September 1998, 143–147.

Bookstaber, Richard, and Joseph A. Langsam, "Portfolio insurance trading rules," *Journal of Futures Markets*, 1988, 8(1), 15–32.

Boudoukh, Jacob, Matthew Richardson, and Robert F. Whitelaw, "Investigation of a class of volatility estimators," *Journal of Derivatives*, 1997, 4(3, Spring), 63–71.

Boyle, Phelim P., and Sok Hoon Lau, "Bumping up against the barrier with binomial method," *Journal of Derivatives*, 1994, 1(4, Summer), 6–14.

Brealey, Richard, and Stewart Myers, *Principles of corporate finance*, New York: McGraw Hill, 2002.

Breeden, Douglas, and S. Viswanathan, "Why do firms hedge? An asymmetric information model," Working paper, Duke University, Durham, NC: 1998.

Brennan, Michael J. "A theory of price limits in futures markets," *Journal of Financial Economics*, 1986, 16(2), 213–233.

Brennan, Michael, and Alan Kraus, "Efficient financing under asymmetric information," *Journal of Finance*, 1987, 42(5), 1225–1243.

Brennan, Michael J., and Eduardo S. Schwartz, "A continuous time approach to the pricing of bonds," *Journal of Banking and Finance*, 1979, 3(2), 133–156.

Brenner, Robin J., Richard H. Harjes, and Kenneth F. Kroner, "Another look at models of the short-term interest rate," *Journal of Financial and Quantitative Analysis*, March 1996, 31(1), 85–108.

Brown, Gregory, and Donald H. Chew Jr., *Corporate risk: Strategies and management*, London, England: Risk Publications, 1999.

Buhler, Wolfgang, Marliese Uhrig-Homburg, Ulrich Walter, and Thomas Weber, "An empirical comparison of forward-rate and spot-rate models for valuing interest-rate options," *Journal of Finance*, February 1999, 54(1), 269–305.

C

Callinicos, Brent, "Trimming risk from Micro-soft's corporate tree," in Brown and Chew, eds., *Corporate risk: Strategies and management*, London, England: Risk Publications, 1999.

Canina, Linda, and Stephen Figlewski, "The information content of implied volatility," *Review of Financial Studies*, 1993, 6, 659–681.

Carr, Peter, Katrina Ellis, and Vishal Gupta, "Static hedging of exotic options," *Journal of Finance*, June 1998, 53, 1165–1190.

Cecchetti, Stephen G., Robert E. Cumby, and Stephen Figlewski, "Estimation of the optimal futures hedges," *Review of Economics and Statistics*, 1988, 70(4), 623–630.

Chan, K. C., G. Andrew Karolyi, Francis A. Longstaff, and Anthony B. Sanders, "An empirical comparison of alternative models of short-term interest rate," *Journal of Finance*, 1992, 47(3), 1209–1228.

Chancellor, Edward, *Devil take the hindmost—A history of financial speculation*, New York: Farrar Straus Giroux, 1999.

Christensen, B. J., and N. R. Prabhala, "The relation between implied and realized volatility," Unpublished working paper, Yale University, New Haven, CT, 1998.

Christoffersen, Peter F., "Evaluating interval forecasts," *International Economic Review*, November 1998, 39(4), 841–862.

Chung, Y. Peter, "A transactions data test of stock index futures market efficiency and index arbitrage profitability," *Journal of Finance*, 1991, 46(5), 1791–1810.

Clewclow, L., and C. Strickland, "Valuing energy options in a one factor model fitted to forward prices," Research paper, Quantitative Finance Research Group, University of Technology, Sydney, Australia, 1999.

Cooper, Ian A., and Antonio S. Mello. "The default risk of swaps," *Journal of Finance*, 1991, 46(2), 597–620.

Copeland, Tom, and Yash Joshi, "Why derivatives don't reduce FX risk," *The McKinsey Quarterly*, 1996, 1, 66–79.

Copeland, Tom, Tim Koller, and Jack Murrin, *Valuation: Measuring and managing the value of companies*, 2nd Edition, New York: Wiley, 1996.

Cornell, Bradford, and Marc R. Reinganum, "Forward and futures prices: Evidence from the foreign exchange markets," *Journal of Finance*, 1981, 36(5), 1035–1045.

Cox, J. C., and M. Rubinstein, *Options markets*, Englewood Cliffs, NJ: Prentice Hall, 1985.

Cox, John C., Jonathan E. Ingersoll, Jr., and Stephen A. Ross, "The relation between forward prices and futures prices," *Journal of Financial Economics*, 1981, 9(4), 321–346.

Cox, John C., Jonathan E. Ingersoll, Jr., and Stephen A. Ross, "A theory of the term structure of interest rates," *Econometrica*, 1985, 53(2), 385–408.

Cox, John C., and Stephen A. Ross, "The valuation of options for alternative stochastic processes," *Journal of Financial Economics*, 1976, 3(1/2), 145–166.

Cox, John C., Stephen A. Ross, and Mark Rubinstein, "Option pricing: A simplified approach," *Journal of Financial Economics*, 1979, 7(3), 229–264.

Crouhy, M., D. Galai, and R. Mark, "A comparative analysis of current credit risk models," *Journal of Banking and Finance*, 2000, 24, 59–117.

Culp, Christopher L., and Merton H. Miller, "Hedging a flow of commodity deliveries with futures: Lessons from metallgeselschaft," *Derivatives Quarterly*, 1994, 1(1, Fall), 7–15.

D

Danielsson, Jon, and Casper G. De Vries, "Tail index and quantile estimation with very high frequency data," *Journal of Empirical Finance*, June 1997, 4(2–3), 239–256.

Das, Sanjiv Ranjan, and Peter Tufano, "Pricing credit-sensitive debt when interest rates, credit ratings and credit spreads are stochastic," *Journal of Financial Engineering*, June 1996, 5(2), 161–198.

Das, Styajit, *Swaps and financial derivatives*, 2nd Edition, 1, London, England: IFR Books, 1994.

Delbaen, Freddy, Jean-Marc Eber, and David Heath, "Thinking coherently," *Risk*, 1997, 10 (11), 68–71.

DeMarzo, Peter M., and Darrell Duffie, "Corporate financial hedging with proprietary information," *Journal of Economic Theory*, 1991, 53(2), 261–286.

Deventer, Donald R., and Kenji Imai, *Financial risk analytics: A term structure model approach for banking, insurance and investment management*, Chicago, IL: Irwin, 1997.

Diamond, Douglas W., "Financial intermediation and delegated monitoring," *Review of Economic Studies*, 1984, 51(166), 393–414.

Diebold, Francis S., Jinyong Hahn, and Anthony S. Tay, "Multivariate density fore-cast evaluation and calibration in financial risk management: High-frequency returns on foreign exchange," *Review of Economics and Statistics*, November 1999, 81(4), 661–673.

Dolde, Walter, "The trajectory of corporate financial risk management," *Journal of Applied Corporate Finance*, 1993, 6(3), 33–41.

Drieesen, Joost, Pieter Klaassen, and Bertand Melenberg, "The performance of multi-factor term structure models for pricing and hedging caps and swaptions," Unpublished working paper, Tilburg University, Holland, 2000.

Duffee, Gregory R., "The relation between treasury yields and corporate bond yield spreads," *Journal of Finance*, December 1998, 53(6), 2225–2242.

Duffie, D., and K. J. Singleton, "Modeling term structures of defaultable bonds," *Review of Financial Studies*, 1999, 12(Special), 687–720.

Duffie, Darrell, "Debt management and interest rate risk," in W. Beaver, and G. Parker, eds., *Risk management: Challenges and solutions*, New York: McGraw-Hill, 1994.

Duffie, Darrell, *Futures markets*, Englewood Cliffs, NJ: Prentice Hall, 1989.

Duffie, Darrell, and Matthew O. Jackson, "Optimal innovation of futures contracts," *Review of Financial Studies*, 1989, 2(3), 275–296.

Duffie, Darrell, and Jun Pan, "An overview of value at risk," *Journal of Derivatives*, 1997, 4(3, Spring), 7–49.

Duffie, Darrell, and Kenneth J. Singleton, "An econometric model of the term structure of interest-rate swap yields," *Journal of Finance*, September 1997, 52(4), 1287–1321.

E

Eberhart, A. C., W. T. Moore, and R. L. Roenfeldt, "Security pricing and deviations from the absolute priority rule in bankruptcy proceedings," *Journal of Finance*, 1990, 1457–1470.

Edwards, Franklin R., and Michael S. Canter, "The collapse of metallgesellschaft: Unhedgeable risks, poor hedging strategy, or just bad luck?" *Journal of Futures Markets*, 1995, 15(3), 211–264.

Elton, Edwin J., Martin J. Gruber, *Stephen J. Brown, and William N. Goetzmann, Modern, portfolio theory and investment analysis*, New York: John Wiley and Sons, 2002.

Etzioni, Ethan S., "Rebalance disciplines for portfolio insurance," *Journal of Portfolio Management*, 1986 (Fall), 59–62.

F

Fabozzi, Frank, *Bond markets, analysis and strategies*, Englewood Cliffs, NY: Prentice-Hall, 1996.

Fama, Eugene F., "The behavior of stock market prices," *Journal of Business*, 1965, 38, 34–105.

Fama, Eugene F., and Kenneth French, "Permanent and temporary components of stock prices," *Journal of Political Economy*, 1988, 96, 246–273.

Fama, Eugene F., "Efficient capital markets: A review of theory and empirical work," *Journal of Finance*, 1970, 25, 383–417.

Fama, Eugene F., "Efficient capital markets: II," *Journal of Finance*, 1991, 46, 1575–1618.

Fazzari, Steven M., R. Glenn Hubbard, and Bruce C. Petersen, "Financing constraints and corporate investment," *Brookings Papers*, 1988, 19(1), 141–195.

Figlewski, Stephen, "Options arbitrage in imperfect markets," *Journal of Finance*, 1989, 44(5), 1289–1312.

Finnerty, John D., "An overview of corporate securities innovation," *Journal of Applied Corporate Finance*, 1992, 4 (Winter), 23–39.

Fisher, Lawrence, and Romand L. Weil, "Coping with the risk of interest-rate fluctuations: Returns to bondholders from naive and optimal strategies," *Journal of Business*, 1971, 44(4), 408–431.

French, Kenneth R., "A comparison of futures and forward prices," *Journal of Financial Economics*, 1983, 12(3), 311–342.

Froot, Kenneth A., David S. Scharfstein, and Jeremy C. Stein, "Risk management: Coordinating corporate investment and financing policies," *Journal of Finance*, 1993, 48(5), 1629–1658.

Froot, Kenneth A., and Jeremy C. Stein, "Risk management, capital budgeting, and capital structure policy for financial institutions: An integrated approach," *Journal of Financial Economics*, January 1998, 47(1), 55–82.

Froot, Kenneth A., and Richard H. Thaler, "Anomalies: Foreign exchange," *Journal of Economic Perspectives*, 1990, 4(3), 179–192.

G

Garman, Mark B., and Steven W. Kohlhagen, "Foreign currency option values," *Journal of International Money and Finance*, 1983, 2(3), 231–237.

Gentle, D., "Basket weaving," *Risk*, 1993, 6(6), 51–52.

Geske, Robert, "The valuation of corporate liabilities as compound options," *Journal of Financial and Quantitative Analysis*, 1977, 12(4), 541–552.

Geske, Robert, "The valuation of compound options," *Journal of Financial Economics*, 1979, 7(1), 63–82.

Geczy, Christopher, Bernadette A. Minton, and Catherine Schrand, "Why firms use currency derivatives," *Journal of Finance*, September 1997, 52(4), 1323–1354.

Giddy, Ian H., and Gunter Dufey, "Uses and abuses of currency options," *Journal of Applied Corporate Finance*, 1995, 8(3, Fall), 49–57.

Glasserman, Paul, and Mark Nathan Broadie, *Hedging with trees: Advances in pricing and risk managing derivatives*, London, England: Risk Books, 1998.

Goldstein, R. S., "The term structure of interest rates as a random field," *Review of Financial Studies*, April 2000, 13(2), 365–384.

Gordy, Michael B., "A comparative anatomy of credit risk models," *Journal of Banking and Finance*, 2000, 24(1–2), 119–149.

Grabbe, J. Orlin, "The pricing of call and put options on foreign exchange," *Journal of International Money and Finance*, 1983, 2(3), 239–253.

Graham, John R., and Daniel A. Rodgers, "Is corporate hedging consistent with value maximization? An empirical analysis," Unpublished working paper, Duke University, Durham, NC, 1999.

Graham, John R., and Clifford W. Smith, Jr., "Tax incentives to hedge," *Journal of Finance*, December 1999, 54(6), 2241–2262.

Green, Richard C., "Investment incentives, debt, and warrants," *Journal of Financial Economics*, 1984, 13(1), 115–136.

Griffin, J. M., and R. M. Stulz, "International competition and exchange rate shocks: A cross-country industry analysis of stock returns," *Review of Financial Studies*, March 2001, 14(1), 215–241.

Grinblatt, Mark, and Narasimhan Jegadeesh, "The relative price of eurodollar futures and forward contracts," *Journal of Finance*, September 1996, 51(4), 1499–1522.

Guay, Wayne R., "The impact of derivatives on firm risk: An empirical examination of new derivative users," *Journal of Accounting and Economics*, January 1999, 26(1–3), 319–351.

H

Haushalter, G. David, "Financing policy, basis risk, and corporate hedging: Evidence from oil and gas producers," *Journal of Finance*, February 2000, 55(1), 107–152.

Heath, David, Robert Jarrow, and Andrew Morton, "Bond pricing and the term structure of interest rates: A new methodology for contingent claims valuation," *Econometrica*, 1992, 60(1), 77–106.

Heath, David, Robert Jarrow, and Andrew Morton, "Bond pricing and the term structure of interest rates: A discrete time approximation," *Journal of Financial and Quantitative Analysis*, 1990, 25(4), 419–440.

Helwege, Jean, and Christopher M. Turner, "The slope of the credit yield for speculative-grade Issuers," *Journal of Finance*, October 1999, 54(5), 1869–1884.

Hendricks, Darryll, "Evaluation of value-at-risk model using historical data," *Federal Reserve Board of New York Economic Policy Review*, April 1996, 2(1), 39–69.

Hendricks, Darryll, and Beverly Hirtle, "Bank capital requirements for market risk: The internal models approach," *Federal Reserve Board of New York Economic Policy Review*, October 1997, 1–12.

Ho, Thomas S.Y., *Strategic fixed income investment*, Homewood, IL: Dow Jones Irwin, 1990.

Ho, Thomas S. Y., and Sang-Bin Lee, "Term structure movements and pricing interest rate contingent claims," *Journal of Finance*, 1986, 41(5), 1011–1030.

Hodrick, Robert, "The empirical evidence on the efficiency of forward and futures foreign exchange market," in Jacque Lesourne and Hugo Sonnenschein, eds., *Fundamentals of pure and applied economics*, 24, New York: Harwood Academic Publishers, 1987

Hubbard, R. Glenn, "Capital-market imperfections and investment," *Journal of Economic Literature*, March 1998, 36(1), 193–225.

Hughston, Lane, *Vasicek and beyond: Approaches to building and applying interest rate models*, London, England: Risk Publications, 1996.

Hull, John, and Alan White, "Pricing interest-rate-derivative securities," *Review of Financial Studies*, 1990, 3(4), 573–592.

I

Illmanen, Antti, "How well does duration measure interest rate risk?" *The Journal of Fixed Income*, 1992, 1(4), 43–51.

Ingersoll, Jonathan E., Jr., Jeffrey Skelton, and Roman L. Weil, "Duration forty years later," *Journal of Financial and Quantitative Analysis*, 1978, 13(4), 627–650.

J

Jarrow, Robert, *Over the rainbow developments in exotic options & complex swaps*, London, England: Risk Books, 1996.

Jarrow, Robert A., and George S. Oldfield, "Forward contracts and futures contracts," *Journal of Financial Economics*, 1981, 9(4), 373–382.

Jarrow, Robert A., and Stuart M. Turnbull, "Pricing derivatives on financial securities subject to credit risk," *Journal of Finance*, 1995, 50, 53–85.

Jarrow, R. A., D. Lando, and S. M. Turnbull, "A Markov model for the term structure of credit risk spreads," *Review of Financial Studies*, 1997, 10(2, Summer), 481–523.

Jarrow, Robert A., and Stuart M. Turnbull, "When swaps are dropped," *Risk*, May 1997, 70–75.

Jarrow, Robert A., and Stuart M. Turnbull, "The intersection of market and credit risk," *Journal of Banking and Finance*, 2000, 24, 271–299.

Johnson, Leland L., "The theory of hedging and speculation in commodity futures," *Review of Economic Studies*, 1960, 27(74), 139–151.

Johnson, Herb, and René Stulz, "The pricing of options with default risk,"

Journal of Finance, 1987, 42(2), 267–280.

Johnston, Elizabeth Tashjian, and John J. McConnell, "Requiem for a market: An analysis of the rise and fall of a financial futures contract," *Review of Financial Studies*, 1989, 2(1), 1–24.

Jones, E. Philip, "Option arbitrage and strategy with large price changes," *Journal of Financial Economics*, 1984, 13, 91–113.

Jones, E. Philip, Scott P. Mason, and Eric Rosenfeld, "Contingent claims analysis of corporate capital structures: An empirical investigation," *Journal of Finance*, 1984, 39(3), 611–625.

Jordan, Bradford, Stephen A. Ross, and Randolph Westerfield, *Essentials of corporate finance*, New York: McGraw-Hill Higher Education, 2002.

Jorion, Philippe, "The exchange-rate exposure of U.S. multinationals," *Journal of Business*, 1990, 63(3), 331–346.

Jorion, Philippe, "Predicting volatility in the foreign exchange market," *Journal of Finance*, 1995, 50(2), 507–528.

Jorion, Philippe, *Value at risk: The new benchmark for controlling market risk*, Chicago, IL: Irwin, 1997.

Jorion, Philippe, "Risk management lessons from long-term capital management," *European Financial Management*, September 2000, 6(3), 277–300.

Jorion, Philippe, *Financial risk manager handbook*, New York: Wiley, 2001.

K

Kairys, Joseph P., Jr., and Nicholas Valerio, III, "The market for equity options in the 1870s," *Journal of Finance*, September 1997, 52(4), 1707–1723.

Kane, Edward J., "Market incompleteness and divergences between forward and future interest rates," *Journal of Finance*, 1980, 35(2), 221–234.

Kawaller, Ira G., "Tailing futures hedges/tailing spreads," *Journal of Derivatives*, 1997, 5(2, Winter), 62–70.

Kim, In Joon, Krishna Ramaswamy, and Suresh Sundaresan, "Does default risk in coupons affect the valuation of corporate bonds?—A contingent claims model," *Financial Management*, 1993, 22, 117–131.

Kim, Yong Cheol, and René M. Stulz, "The eurobond market and corporate financial policy: A test of the clientele hypothesis," *Journal of Financial Economics*, 1988, 22(2), 189–206.

Koenigsberg, Mark, Janet L. Showers, and James Streit, "The term structure of volatility and bond option valuation," *Journal of Fixed Income*, 1991, 1, 19–36.

KPMG Peat Marwick LLP, *Derivatives and hedging handbook*, July 1998.

Krugman, Paul R., and Maurice Obstfeld, *International economics: Theory and policy*, Reading, MA: Addison-Wesley Publishing, 2000.

Kupiec, Paul H, "Techniques for verifying the accuracy of risk measurement models," *Journal of Derivatives*, 1995, 3(2, Winter), 73–84.

L

Lamont, Owen, "Cash flow and investment: Evidence from internal capital markets," *Journal of Finance*, March 1997, 52(1), 83–109.

Lang, Larry H. P., and René M. Stulz, "Tobin's q, corporate diversification, and firm performance," *Journal of Political Economy*, 1994, 102(6), 1248–1280.

Latane, Henry A., and Richard J. Rendleman, Jr., "Standard deviations of stock price ratios implied in option prices," *Journal of Finance*, 1976, 31(2), 369–381.

Leland, Hayne E., "Option pricing and replication with transactions costs," *Journal of Finance*, 1985, 40(5), 1283–1301.

Leland, Hayne E., "Corporate debt value, bond covenants, and optimal capital Structure," *Journal of Finance*, 1994, 49(4), 1213–1252.

Leland, Hayne E., "Presidential address: Agency costs, risk management, and capital structure," *Journal of Finance*, August 1998, 53(4), 1213–1243.

Lessard, Donald R., *International financial management: Theory and application*, New York: Wiley, 1979.

Levi, Maurice D., *International finance: The markets and financial management of mutinational business*, New York: McGraw-Hill, 1994.

Lewent, Judy, and John Kearney, "Identifying, measuring and hedging currency risk at Merck," in Brown and Chew, eds., *Corporate risk: Strategies and management*, London, England: Risk Publications, 1999.

Litterman, Robert, "Hot spots and hedges," *Journal of Portfolio Management*, 1997, 23(3, Special), 52–75.

Litterman, Robert, and Jose Scheinkman, "Common factors affecting bond re-turns," *Journal of Fixed Income*, 1991, 1(1), 54–61.

Litzenberger, Robert H., "Presidential address: Swaps: Plain and simple," *Journal of Finance*, 1992, 47(3), 831–850.

Lo, Andrew, and A. Craig MacKinlay, "Stock market prices do not follow random walks: Evidence from a simple specification test," *Review of Financial Studies*, 1988, 1, 41–66.

Logue, Dennis E., "When theory fails: Globalization as a response to the (hostile) market for foreign exchange," *Journal of Applied Corporate Finance*, 1995, 8(3, Fall), 39–48.

Longstaff, Francis A., Pedro Santa-Clara, and Eduardo S. Schwartz, "Throwing away a billion dollars: The cost of suboptimal exercise strategies in the swaptions market," *Journal of Financial Economics*, October 2001, 62(1), 39–66.

Longstaff, Francis A., and Eduardo S. Schwartz, "Interest rate volatility and the term structure: A two-factor general equilibrium model," *Journal of Finance*, 1992, 47(4), 1259–1282.

Longstaff, Francis A., and Eduardo S. Schwartz, "Implementation of the Longstaff-Schwartz interest rate model," *Journal of Fixed Income*, 1993, 3(2), 7–14.

Longstaff, Francis A., and Eduardo S. Schwartz, "A simple approach to valuing risky fixed and floating rate debt," *Journal of Finance*, 1995, 50(3), 789–819.

Lowenstein, Roger, *When genius failed: The risk and fall of Long-Term Capital Management*, New York, Random House, 2000.

M

Madan, Dilip B., and Haluk Unal, "Pricing the risks of default," *Review of Derivatives Research*, 1998, 2(2, 3), 121–160.

Makin, John H., "Portfolio theory and the problem of foreign exchange risk," *Journal of Finance*, 1978, 33(2), 517–534.

Markowitz, Harry, "Portfolio selection," *Journal of Finance*, 1952, 7, 77–91.

Marshall, Chris, and Michael Siegel, "Value at risk: Implementing a risk measurement standard," *Journal of Derivatives*," 1997, 4(3, Spring), 91–111.

Marston, Richard, "The effects of industry structure on economic exposure," *Journal of International Money and Finance*, April 2001, 20(2), 149–164.

Matten, Chris, *Managing bank capital: Capital allocation and performance measurement*, New York: Wiley, 1996.

Mayers, David, "Why firms issue convertible bonds: The matching of financial and real investment options," *Journal of Financial Economics*, January 1998, 47(1), 83–102.

Mayers, David, and Clifford W. Smith, Jr., "Corporate insurance and the underinvestment problem," *Journal of Risk and Insurance*, 1987, 54(1), 45–54.

McDonald, Robert, "The tax (dis)advantage of a firm issuing options on its own stock," Working paper, Northwestern University, Evanston, IL: February 2002.

Melamed, Leo, and Bob Tamarkin, *Escape to the futures*, New York: John Wiley & Sons, 1996.

Mello, A. S., and J. E. Parsons, "Hedging and liquidity," *Review of Financial Studies*, 2000, 13(1, Spring), 127–153.

Mello, Antonio S., and John E. Parsons, "Hedging with a flow of commodity deliveries with futures: Problems with a rolling stack," *Derivatives Quarterly*, 1995, 1(4, Summer), 16–19.

Mello, Antonio S., John E. Parsons, and Alexander J. Triantis, "An integrated model of multinational flexibility and financial hedging," *Journal of International Economics*, 1995, 39(1/2), 27–51.

Merton, Robert. C., "The theory of rational option pricing," *Bell Journal of Economics*, 1973, 4(1), 141–183.

Merton, Robert C., "On the pricing of corporate debt: The risk structure of interest rates," *Journal of Finance*, 1974, 29(2), 449–470.

Merton, Robert C., "Option pricing when underlaying stock returns are discontinuous," *Journal of Financial Economics*, 1976, 3(1/2), 12–144.

Merton, Robert C., "Financial innovation and economic performance," *Journal of Applied Corporate Finance*, 1992, 4 (Winter), 12–22.

Merton, Robert C., "Operation and regulation in financial intermediation: A functional perspective," in P. Englund, ed., *Operation and regulation of financial markets*, Stockholm: The Economic Council, 1993.

Merton, Robert C., and Andre F. Perold, "Theory of risk capital in financial firms," *Journal of Applied Corporate Finance*, 1993, 6(3), 16–32.

Meulbroek, Lisa, "A comparison of forward and future prices of an interest rate sensitive financial asset," *Journal of Finance*, 1992, 47(1), 381–396.

Miller, Merton H., "Financial innovation: Achievements and prospects," *Journal* of Applied Corporate Finance, 1992, 4 (Winter), 4–11.

Miller, Merton H., "Debt and taxes," Journal of Finance, 1977, 32(2), 261–275.

Minton, Bernadette A., "An empirical examination of basic valuation models for plain vanilla U.S. interest rate swaps," Journal of Financial Economics, May 1997, 44(2), 251–277.

Modigliani, Franco, and M. H. Miller, "The cost of capital, corporation finance and the theory of investment," American Economic Review, 1958, 48(3), 261–297.

Mood, Alexander M., Franklin A. Graybill, and Duane C. Boes, Introduction to the theory of statistics, New York: McGraw-Hill, 1974.

Myers, Stewart C., "Determinants of corporate borrowing," Journal of Financial Economics, 1977, 5(2), 147–175.

Myers, Stewart C., and Nicholas S. Majluf, "Corporate financing and investment decisions when firms have information that investors do not have," Journal of Financial Economics, 1984, 13(2), 187–221.

N

Nance, Deana R., Clifford W. Smith, Jr., and Charles W. Smithson, "On the determinants of corporate hedging," Journal of Finance, 1993, 48(1), 267–284.

Nelken, Israel, The handbook of exotic options: Instruments, analysis and applications, Chicago, IL: Irwin Professional Pub., 1996.

O

Opler, Tim, Lee Pinkowitz, René Stulz, and Rohan Williamson, "The determinants and implications of corporate cash holdings," Journal of Financial Economics, April 1999, 52(1), 3–46.

P

Perold, Andre F., and Evan C. Schulman, "The free lunch in currency hedging: Implications for investment policy and peformance standards," Financial Analyst Journal, 1988, 44(3), 45–52.

Pearson, Niel, and X. Ju, "Using value-at-risk to control risk taking: How wrong can you be?" Journal of Risk, 1999, 1(2), 5–36.

Peck, Anne E., "Hedging and income stability: Concepts, implications, and an example," American Journal of Agricultural Economics, 1975, 57(3), 410–419.

Perold, Andre F., Long-Term Capital Management, L.P. (A-D), Harvard Business School Press, November 1999.

Petersen, Mitchell A., and S. Ramu Thiagarajan, "Risk measurment and hedging: With and without derivatives," Financial Management, 2000, 29(4), 5–30.

Picoult, Evan, "Calculating value-at-risk with Monte Carlo simulation," in Risk Management for Financial Institutions, London, England: Risk Publications, 73–92.

Pirrong, Stephen Craig, "Metallgesellschaft: A prudent hedger ruined, or a wildcatter on NYMEX?" Journal of Futures Markets, August 1997, 17(5), 543–578.

Pritsker, Matt, "The hidden dangers of historical simulation," Working paper, Board of Governors of the Federal Reserve System, 2001.

Pritsker, Matthew, "Evaluating value at risk methodologies: Accuracy versus computational time," Journal of Financial Services Research, October/December 1997, 12(2/3), 201–242.

R

Ramaswamy, Krishna, and Suresh M. Sundaresan, "The valuation of floating-rate instruments: Theory and evidence," *Journal of Financial Economics*, 1986, 17(2), 251–272.

Rawnsley, Judith H., *Total risk: Nick Leeson and the fall of Barings Bank*, New York: Harper Collins Publisher, 1995.

Rhee, S. Ghon, and Rosita P. Chang, "Intra-day arbitrage opportunities in foreign exchange and eurocurrency markets," *Journal of Finance*, 1992, 47(1), 363–380.

Richard, Scott F., and M. Sundaresan, "A continuous time equilibrium model of forward prices and future prices in a multigood economy," *Journal of Financial Economics*, 1981, 9(4), 347–371.

Rolfo, Jacques, "Optimal hedging under price and quantity uncertainty: The case of a cocoa producer," *Journal of Political Economy*, 1980, 88(1), 100–116.

Ross, Michael, "Corporate hedging: What, why and how?" Working paper, University of California—Berkeley, 1997.

Ross, Stephen A., "Institutional markets, financial marketing, and financial innovation," *Journal of Finance*, July 1989, 44, 541–556.

Routledge, Bryan R., Duane J. Seppi, and Chester S. Spatt, "Equilibrium forward curves for commodities," *Journal of Finance*, June 2000, 55(3), 1297–1338.

Rubinstein, Mark, "Alternative paths to portfolio insurance," *Financial Analyst Journal*, 1985, 41(4), 42–52.

Rubinstein, Mark, "Presidential address: Implied binomial trees," *Journal of Finance*, 1994, 49(3), 771–818.

Rubinstein, Mark, and Eric Reiner, "Breaking down the barriers," *Risk*, September 1991, 4.

Rutledge, D. J. S., "A note on the variability of futures prices," *Review of Economics and Statistics*, 1976, 58(1), 118–120.

S

Saita, Francesco, "Allocation of risk capital in financial institutions," *Financial Management*, 1999, 28, 95–111.

Santa-Clara, P., and D. Sornette, "The dynamics of the forward interest rate curve with stochastic string shocks," *Review of Financial Studies*, March 2001, 14(1), 149–185.

Santomero, Anthony M., "Commercial bank risk management: An analysis of the process," Working paper, Wharton, 1995, 95–11.

Schrand, Catherine, and Haluk Unal, "Hedging and coordinated risk management: Evidence from thrift conversions," *Journal of Finance*, June 1998, 53(3), 979–1013.

Shapiro, Alan C., *Multinational financial management*, Boston: Allyn and Bacon, 1999.

Sharpe, William F., "Capital asset prices: A theory of market equilibrium under conditions of risk," *Journal of Finance*, 1964, 19, 425–442.

Shimko, David C., Naohiko Tejima, and Donald R. Van Deventer, "The pricing of risky debt when interest rates are stochastic," *Journal of Fixed Income*, 1993, 3(2), 58–66.

Siegel, Daniel, and Diane Siegel, *Futures markets*, Dryden Press, 1990.

Smith, C. W., C. W. Smithson, and L. M. Wakeman, "The evolving market for swaps," *Midland Corporate Finance Journal*, 1986, 3 (Winter), 20–36.

Smith, Clifford W., and René M. Stulz, "The determinants of firm's hedging policies," *Journal of Financial and Quantitative Analysis*, 1985, 20, 391–406.

Smith, Clifford W., Jr., "Investment banking and the capital acquisition process," *Journal of Financial Economics*, 1986, 15(1/2), 3–29.

Smith, Donald J., "Aggressive corporate finance: A close look at the Procter &

Gamble—Bankers Trust leveraged swap," *Journal of Derivatives*, 1997, 4, 67–79.

Smithson, Charles, "Measuring op risk," *Risk*, March 2000.

Stein, J. L., "The simultaneous determination of spot and futures prices," *American Economic Review*, 1961, 51(5), 1012–1025.

Stoll, Hans R., "The relationship between put and call option prices," *Journal of Finance*, 1969, 24(5), 801–824.

Stoughton, Neal M., and Josef Zechner, "IPO-mechanisms, monitoring and ownership structure," *Journal of Financial Economics*, July 1998, 49(1), 45–77.

Stulz, René M., "Optimal hedging policies," *Journal of Financial and Quantitative Analysis*, 1984, 19(2), 127–140.

Stulz, René M., "Managerial discretion and optimal financing policies," *Journal of Financial Economics*, 1990, 26(1), 3–28.

Stulz, René, "Rethinking risk management," *Journal of Applied Corporate Finance*, 1996 (Fall), 8–24.

Stulz, René, "Why risk management is not rocket science," *Financial Times*, June 27, 2000, Mastering Risk Series.

Stulz, René M., and Herb Johnson, "An analysis of secured debt," *Journal of Financial Economics*, 1985, 14(4), 501–522.

Stulz, René M., Walter Wasserfallen, and Thomas Stucki, "Stock index futures in switzerand: Pricing and hedging performance," *Review of Futures Markets*, 1990, 9(3), 576–592.

Stulz, René, and Rohan Williamson, "Identifying and quantifying exposures," in Robert Jameson, ed., *Financial Risk and the corporate treasury: New developments in strategy and control*," London, England: Risk Publications, 1997, 33–51.

Sun, Tong-Sheng, Suresh Sundaresan, and Ching Wang. "Interest rate swaps: An empirical investigation," *Journal of Financial Economics*, 1993, 34(1), 77–99.

Sundaresan, Suresh., "Futures prices on yields, forward prices, and implied forward prices from term structure," *Journal of Financial and Quantitative Analysis*, 1991, 26(3), 409–424.

T

Titman, Sheridan, "Interest rate swaps and corporate financing choices," *Journal of Finance*, 1992, 47(4), 1503–1516.

Tuckman, Bruce, *Fixed income securities: Tools for today's markets*, New York: J. Wiley, 1995.

Tufano, Peter, "Financial innovation and first-mover advantages," *Journal of Financial Economics*, 1989, 25, 213–240.

Tufano, Peter, "Who manages risk? An empirical examination of risk management practices in the gold mining industry," *Journal of Finance*, 1996, 51, 1097–1137.

Tufano, Peter, "Do fools rush in? Rewards to buying and selling the newest financial products," Working Paper, Harvard Business School, Boston, MA, 1996.

Tufano, Peter, "Agency costs of corporate risk management," *Financial Management*, 1998, (Spring), 67–77.

Tufano, Peter, "The determinants of stock price exposure: Financial engineering and the gold mining industry," *Journal of Finance*, June 1998, 53(3), 1015–1052

Turnbull, Stuart M., "Swaps: A zero sum game?" *Financial Management*, 1987, 16(1), 15–21.

V

Vasicek, O., "An equilibrium characterization of the term structure," *Journal of Financial Economics*, 1977, 5(2), 177–188.

Venkatachalam, Mohan, "Value-relevance of banks' derivatives disclosures," *Journal of Accounting and Economics*, August–December 1996, 22(1–3), 327–355.

Vorst, T., "Average options," in I. Nelken ed., *The handbook of exotic options*, Homewood, IL: Irwin, 1996.

W

Whaley, Robert, "Valuation of American call options on dividend paying stocks: Empirical tests," *Journal of Financial Economics*, 1982, 10, 29–58.

Weisbach, Michael S., "CEO turnover and the firm's investment decisions," *Journal of Financial Economics*, 1995, 37(2), 159–188.

Weiss, Lawrence A., "Bankruptcy resolution: Direct costs and violation of priority of claims," *Journal of Financial Economics*, 1990, 27(2), 285–314.

Williamson, Rohan, "Exchange rate exposure and competition: Evidence from the automotive industry," *Journal of Financial Economics*, March 2001, 59(3), 441–475.

Witt, Harvey J., Ted C. Schroeder, and Marvin L. Hayenga, "Comparison of analytical approaches for estimating hedge ratios for agricultural commodities," *Journal of Futures Markets*, 1987, 7(2), 135–146.

Z

Zaik, Edward, John Walter, Gabriela Kelling, and Christopher James, "RAROC at Bank of America: From theory to practice," *Journal of Applied Corporate Finance*, 1996, 9(2), 83–93.